THE COLLECTED WORKS OF
RALPH WALDO EMERSON

The Collected Works of Ralph Waldo Emerson

VOLUME IV

REPRESENTATIVE MEN:

SEVEN LECTURES

Historical Introduction and Notes by Wallace E. Williams

Text Established and Textual Introduction and Apparatus by Douglas Emory Wilson

The Belknap Press of Harvard University Press
Cambridge, Massachusetts, and London, England
1987

This book is printed on acid-free paper, and its binding materials have been chosen for strength and durability.

Library of Congress Cataloging in Publication Data

Emerson, Ralph Waldo, 1803–1882.
    Representative men.

    (The Collected works of Ralph Waldo Emerson ; v. 4)
    Bibliography: p.
    Includes index.
    Contents: Uses of great men—Plato, or the
philosopher—Swedenborg, or the mystic—[etc.]
    1. Biography. I. Williams, Wallace E. II. Wilson,
Douglas Emory. III. Title. IV. Series: Emerson,
Ralph Waldo, 1803–1882. Works. 1971 ; v. 4.

PS1600.F71   vol. 4   814'.3 s   86-31257
[PS1621]   [920'.02]
ISBN 0-674-13991-7 (alk. paper)

CENTER FOR
SCHOLARLY EDITIONS

AN APPROVED EDITION

MODERN LANGUAGE
ASSOCIATION OF AMERICA

Editorial expenses for the preparation of this volume have been supported
by grants from the National Endowment for the Humanities.

PREFACE

The Historical Introduction and the Informational Notes in this volume were written by Wallace E. Williams; the text was established and the Textual Introduction and Apparatus (including the Annex and Appendices) were prepared by Douglas Emory Wilson. Both editors worked closely together throughout, especially in checking the text and apparatus against the manuscript and previous editions, in preparing the Informational Notes, and in assembling the list of parallel passages. They received much valuable advice and checking of their work from Joseph Slater, the General Editor.

Many institutions and individuals have helped bring this volume to completion. The National Endowment for the Humanities, through the Center for Editions of American Authors, provided support for planning of the whole edition, and through a direct grant supported the work on this volume. William H. Bond, Carolyn Jakeman, Marte Shaw, and others of the staff of the Houghton Library of Harvard University were generous, as always, with learned and courteous assistance and with permissions to quote and reproduce. William H. Loos, Curator of Rare Books in the Buffalo and Erie County (New York) Public Library, was most helpful in allowing the editors access to the manuscript of *Representative Men* and in providing a microfilm of it, photographs of several of its pages, and permission to reproduce the latter. Professor Williams received valuable support from the staffs of the Indiana University Library, the Lilly Library of Indiana University, the Boston Public Library, and the Boston

Athenæum. Dean of Libraries Alta L. Millican of Jacksonville (Alabama) State University and members of the staff of the University Library gave similar assistance to Colonel Wilson, especially in interlibrary loan service. The Concord (Massachusetts) Free Public Library kindly permitted the reproduction of a portrait of Emerson in its possession. The Ralph Waldo Emerson Memorial Association gave permission to use Emerson materials in the Houghton Library.

For the Historical Introduction and Notes, we have drawn on the published work of others, and wish to acknowledge here our indebtedness to the following: Kenneth W. Cameron for his lists of Emerson's withdrawals of books from the Boston Athenæum, the Harvard College Library, and the Boston Library Society; Townsend Scudder III, William Charvat, and Eleanor Tilton for their listings of Emerson's lecture engagements; and Frank Davidson for helpful hints in his earlier annotations of "Napoleon." Our dependence on the work of the editors of *The Journals and Miscellaneous Notebooks of Ralph Waldo Emerson* is clear from the many references to those volumes throughout this book.

Both volume editors and the General Editor proofread the galleys and page proofs of the entire volume. Ann Louise McLaughlin of the Harvard University Press edited copy with diligence and accuracy and made useful suggestions for improvement. Richard L. Rust, for the Committee on Scholarly Editions of the Modern Language Association, read the text, Textual Introduction, and Apparatus, and provided valuable criticism and suggestions. We gratefully acknowledge help of various kinds from Don L. Cook, Charlyne Dodge, Charles R. Forker, Timothy Long, Joel Myerson, David J. Nordloh, Ralph H. Orth, Margaret Richards, Samuel N. Rosenberg, Anthony W. Shipps, Nancy Craig Simmons, Albert J. von Frank, and Barry Wood; and special thanks to James H. Justus, who has assisted us in many generous ways.

CONTENTS

ILLUSTRATIONS

(following page xl)

Portrait sketch of Emerson (in or about 1850) by Frederika Bremer, popular Swedish novelist (1801–1865), who visited the Emersons for several days in January 1850. (By permission of the Concord Free Public Library)

End-papers of Emerson's copy of the first printing of *Representative Men,* showing his pasted-in list of errors to be corrected. (By permission of the Houghton Library, Harvard University)

Pages 40–41 of the manuscript of "Swedenborg," containing corrections and revisions. (By permission of the Buffalo and Erie County Public Library)

Page 57 of the manuscript of "Swedenborg," containing alterations in almost every line. (By permission of the Buffalo and Erie County Public Library)

Historical Introduction
Statement of Editorial Principles
Textual Introduction

ABBREVIATIONS

BAL	Jacob Blanck. *Bibliography of American Literature.* New Haven, Yale University Press, 1959. III, 16–70.
CD	*The Century Dictionary and Cyclopedia.* Edited by William D. Whitney. 6 vols. New York, 1889.
CEC	*The Correspondence of Emerson and Carlyle.* Edited by Joseph Slater. New York, Columbia University Press, 1964.
CW (or *CWRWE*)	*The Collected Works of Ralph Waldo Emerson.* Edited by Alfred R. Ferguson, Joseph Slater, et al. 4 vols. to date. Cambridge, The Belknap Press of Harvard University Press, 1971– .
DAE	*A Dictionary of American English.* Edited by Sir William A. Craigie and James R. Hulbert. 4 vols. Chicago, University of Chicago Press, 1938–1944.
EL	*The Early Lectures of Ralph Waldo Emerson, 1833–1842.* Edited by Stephen E. Whicher et al. 3 vols. Cambridge, The Belknap Press of Harvard University Press, 1959–1972.
Furness	*Records of a Lifelong Friendship, 1807–1882: Ralph Waldo Emerson and William Henry Furness.* Edited by H. H. Furness. Boston and New York, Houghton Mifflin Company, 1910.
Houghton	The Houghton Library, Harvard University.
J	*The Journals of Ralph Waldo Emerson.* Edited by Edward Waldo Emerson and Waldo Emerson Forbes. 10 vols. Boston and New York, Houghton Mifflin Company, 1909–1914.
JMN	*The Journals and Miscellaneous Notebooks of Ralph Waldo Emerson.* Edited by William H. Gilman, Ralph H. Orth, et al. 16 vols. Cambridge, The Belknap Press of Harvard University Press, 1960–1982.
L	*The Letters of Ralph Waldo Emerson.* Edited by Ralph L. Rusk. 6 vols. New York, Columbia University Press, 1939.
Myerson	Joel Myerson. *Ralph Waldo Emerson /A Descriptive Bibliography.* Pittsburgh, University of Pittsburgh Press, 1982.
OED	*The Oxford English Dictionary.* Edited by James A. H. Murray et al. 13 vols. Oxford, Clarendon Press, 1933.
PP	Parallel Passages (in this volume).
RSS	Rejected Substantives and Spellings (in Textual Apparatus of this volume).
Rusk	Ralph L. Rusk. *The Life of Ralph Waldo Emerson.* New York, Charles Scribner's Sons, 1949.
W	*The Complete Works of Ralph Waldo Emerson.* Edited by Edward Waldo Emerson. Centenary Edition. 12 vols. Boston and New York, Houghton, Mifflin and Company, 1903–1904.
Webster	*An American Dictionary of the English Language.* Edited by Noah Webster. 2 vols. New York, 1828.
Worcester	*A Comprehensive Pronouncing and Explanatory Dictionary of the English Language.* Edited by Joseph E. Worcester. Boston, 1838.
WT	Manuscript transcript of *Representative Men* made in 1849 by Elizabeth Weir (no longer extant).

Historical Introduction

By 1844 ten years of lecturing had brought Emerson renown, some notoriety, and a modest living. *Nature* and two books of essays had laid the groundwork for his small but growing reputation as a writer of distinction. A few of his lectures had slipped into print in a pinch—five in *The Dial,* two in *Essays: Second Series*—and four addresses had been published in pamphlet form, but most lectures had been variously recast and enriched from his journals to form the essays, a genre Emerson thought of as different from lectures, which he considered freer in form, more eloquent, and grander in scope. *Representative Men: Seven Lectures* is a significant departure from his earlier work in being a published course of lectures, modified to some extent between their composition and first delivery in 1845–46 and publication in 1850, but essentially the course brought to eloquent polish. The book tells us much of Emerson's aspiration for eloquence from the lyceum desk and comes at the height of his powers. This new edition, based on printer's copy that doubtless incorporated many manuscript leaves from the lectures, has a freshness of the spoken word that was muted in *Essays: First Series* as well as a freedom and daring of the lecture hall; it marks a turn in Emerson's compositional method that would inform many of his later works. It is unique in that it is a polished course of lectures only minimally expanded as it was revised for publication. Its composition and revision reflect the habits of the mature lecturer, not quite yet the Sage of Concord and still best known among his contemporaries as the daring performer.

After the publication of *Essays: Second Series* in October 1844, Emerson was faced with a lecture season for which he was ill supplied; the new volume and *The Dial* had reduced his stock of lectures to a popular "Domestic Life" and a truncated series on New England. He had made no extended engagements for the season other than a series of four in late November before the Nantucket Athenaeum; for the rest he lectured in scattered appearances in Massachusetts and New Hampshire and in Providence. In August, knowing that he would be wholly engaged with his book for another two months, he had accepted an invitation to lecture at Newburyport, but declined the invitation of the prestigious Boston Mercantile Library Association, to which he had the previous season given "The Young American." When the second book of essays was published, it was natural that the confident man of the lyceum should provide himself, out of his reading, a new lecture on "Napoleon," a rival in popularity with "Domestic Life," and that he should use it in his scattered engagements even before it was finished and fitted into a new series suitable for Boston the next year. The composition of the series of lectures on Representative Men illustrates the way in which Emerson maturely developed out of his interests a polished statement that would serve him well. The pattern of preparation has the strength of organic growth.

Emerson wrote to his young friend Samuel Gray Ward on December 2, 1844, that he had "read Napoleon's memoirs lately & could not help grudging to Europe that grand executive faculty" (*L*, III, 268). Although the reference could be to any of several books, he most likely meant one of the first four volumes of *Memoirs of the History of France during the Reign of Napoleon, Dictated by the Emperor at Saint Helena . . .* , 7 vols. (London, 1822–1824). Certainly by January 1845 Emerson was reading with another purpose. He borrowed from the Boston Athenæum most of the memoirs, recollections, and histories that he used in his lecture on Napoleon and copied extracts from them into his journal V, which shows a correlation with the January withdrawals. Edward Emerson conjectured that the lecture on Napoleon "was in demand by the Lyceum Committees" in the winter of 1844-45 (*J*, VII, 3); at least the records of the Concord Lyceum show that on April 2 Emerson read "Bonaparte," and September 29, 1845, in making plans for a winter reading of the new series on Representative Men to the Lowell Mechanics' Association, he recalled that he had "already delivered in Lowell & to *you*" the "lecture on Napoleon though in an incomplete state. It was the first written, though it should be last in the course" (*L*, III, 305). If this was the engagement at the Lowell Lyceum on January 8, 1845, rather than a later one, the lecture must have been very incomplete, judging by the dates of Emerson's borrowings from the Boston Athenæum.

Although Emerson wrote and used an early version of the lecture on Napoleon in the early part of 1845, it is not likely that he had planned the series yet; as late as June 29 he described to his friend Thomas Carlyle a nebulous plan: "Meantime, I think to set a few heads before me as good texts for winter evening entertainments. I wrote a deal about Napoleon a few months ago, after reading a library of memoirs. Now I have Plato, Montaigne, & Swedenborg, and more in the clouds behind" (*CEC*, p. 379). Despite a certain ambiguity of expression, Emerson meant that he had only one of the lectures in hand. Other matters, the business of the letter (plans for a new Philadelphia edition of Carlyle's *Critical and Miscellaneous Essays,* for example), and the characteristic early summer life in Concord after the lecture season had ended took more of his time than would permit much thought on next year's lectures. His lightly mocking pastoral version leads to his major concern in the early summer: "I creep along the roads & fields of this town as I have done from year to year. When my garden is shamefully overgrown with weeds, I pull up some of them. I prune my apples & pears. I have a few friends who gild many hours of the year. I sometimes write verses. I tell you with some unwillingness, as knowing your distaste for such things, that I have received so many applications from readers & printers for a volume of poems, that I have seriously taken in hand the collection, transcription, or scription of such a volume & may do the enormity before New Years day" (*CEC*, p. 379). That he hoped to publish his poems by the end of the year is apparent from letters to John Chapman, the London publisher of *Essays: Second Series,* and to Evert Duyckinck, who represented Wiley & Putnam in soliciting material from Emerson. The hope lasted through the summer, and he declined "to take any leading part" in a new transatlantic journal he understood Chapman to have proposed, postponed a collection of miscellanies suggested by both Chapman and Duyckinck, and considered but rejected Wiley & Putnam's proposal that he select for them a multivolume new edition of Landor (*L,* III, 288, 296–297, 301–302)—all because he expected to finish the volume of poems.

Another specific commitment occupied Emerson's time. He had agreed to deliver an address at Middlebury College on July 22, 1845, and he duly gave thought to his subject, the responsibilities of the scholar or the clerisy, in the new journal W, which he began in March. That journal also reflects, as do a few pages at the front of journal V, which it succeeded, passages by and about Plato that ended up in *Representative Men.* To Sam Ward he wrote at the end of April: "I have been reading a little in Plato (in translation unhappily) with great comfort and refreshment" (*L,* III, 283). This casual interest becomes clear retrospectively from a letter he wrote to Charles King Newcomb on September 1, just as his plans for biographical lectures in Boston began to crystallize, refusing to lend a volume to his young friend: "I see the 'Taylor's Timaeus' this morning . . . I have entertained the project all summer, if no longer, of making a study for a Lecture of some dialogues of Plato, meaning if I dare some day or deep midnight to draw a profile of the Great Shade himself; and, as at some hours lately; this study seemed more possible, I have not been willing to diminish my apparatus by so much as a single book" (*L,* III, 300). Perhaps this interest in Plato continued through the summer, but the lecture, along with those on Swedenborg and Montaigne, remained with "others in the clouds behind."

As July 22 drew near, the reading of Plato and the preparation of poems must have ceased, and Emerson brought together an eloquent and substantial discourse which he read on that day before the Philomathesian Society of Middlebury College. He returned from Vermont—but probably not to work on either poems or winter lectures. In a letter to his new friend and future editor James Elliot Cabot on August 3, Emerson excused himself for not returning borrowed manuscripts and books (including *The Bhagavat Geeta,* which he carried with him to Middlebury) because of "the accident of some company," a common summer diversion from work, and because of finishing the house he was building across the road for his sister-in-law, Lucy Brown (*L,* III, 293–294). He might also have mentioned an appearance and "remarks" he had made two days before at the Waltham meeting to celebrate, as he had done the previous year in Concord with an address, the anniversary of West Indian emancipation. Apparently Emerson had too little time to make the revisions he had intended before repeating the Middlebury discourse at Wesleyan University on August 6 (*L,* III, 294, 299). From Middletown, Connecticut, he went to Staten Island to visit his brother William, saw Margaret Fuller in New York City, and returned by way of Albany and Lenox to visit Sam and Anna Ward (*L,* III, 294–296). A month had been lost when Emerson reached home on August 13 and found himself at once engaged in more rather than fewer literary projects.

Emerson wrote Evert Duyckinck on August 25 that he could not provide a new book for Wiley & Putnam, and on September 5 that he could not do the proposed edition of Landor for that publishing house, which might, however, be interested in his volume of poems. He was declining both projects because he had "undertaken to read a new course of lectures in Boston early in the season" (*L,* III, 296–297, 301). This abrupt decision was precipitated by a proposal that Emerson read lectures under the auspices of the Boston Lyceum. On August 26 he answered the corresponding secretary, Nathaniel W. Coffin, with tentative interest: "I hardly know what to say to your proposition respecting my lectures. I intend to read some lectures in town if I can get ready in time. For some reasons . . . it seems better for my lectures to be read independently of any society: but there are other accounts on which I should value the alliance of the Lyceum and the prospect of relief from the preliminary arrangements, the finance department, &c. is very attractive to me. My own plan was of a course of

six or at most eight lectures. I shall therefore willingly hear anything which the Lyceum has to say on the matter" (*L,* III, 298).

Ten days later, when Emerson accepted the offer, he announced that his course of six or seven lectures would have "a biographical basis" but could give no details; even the date was
uncertain, though in a postscript he added that he preferred "not
to begin before the middle or end of November" (*L,* III, 300),
doubtless thinking of his plans for the volume of poems that he
mentioned the same day in his letter to Duyckinck. But by mid-
October, even after serious negotiations with Wiley & Putnam
had begun, he wrote Duyckinck that his pledge to the Lyceum
would "not now permit attention to the Poems." Two weeks later
he wrote William that the poems still needed work: "as the Lectures could not stop, the poems must; and I have laid them aside
for two months" (*L,* III, 301, 307–308, 310).

By the beginning of October, Emerson could give William specific details of the Boston course: "seven lectures . . . beginning in
the beginning of December on 'Representative Men' consisting
with perhaps a Preliminary Discourse

> on Plato or the Philosopher
> Swedenborg or the Mystic
> Montaigne or the Skeptic
> Shakspeare or the Poet
> Napoleon or the Man of the World
> Goethe or the Writer

Perhaps I shall modify my list" (*L,* III, 305–306). That the course
was only now shaping up is evident in the greater tentativeness
about a lecture on Goethe just three days earlier, when Emerson
replied to the inquiry from the Lowell Mechanics' Association,
and in the fact that neither Goethe nor a preliminary lecture is
mentioned in a letter to Carlyle two weeks earlier (*CEC,* pp.
381–382). Although Emerson had vague plans at the end of June,
it was only after August 25, 1845, that he quickly pulled together
his inventory and planned his course to the point of engagement.

The journals and notebooks show something about the manner

in which Emerson could find and delineate his topic and about how it grew, seemingly without much conscious direction until it was needed. Journal V was used during the period May 1844 to March 1845, but it is not sequential as most of the other journals are, and it contains later material. In it are most of the passages from the "library of memoirs" Emerson read in December 1844 and January and February 1845, and from which he prepared his early lecture on Napoleon. A list of these and earlier journal passages, a gathering of material preparatory to outlining the early lecture on Napoleon, is in the working notebook Index Minor (*JMN*, XII, 531–532). Sometime in March 1845 journal W succeeded journal V; like most of the others, it seems to be generally sequential. An early entry in this new journal indicates that Emerson had in fact looked forward beyond his summer tasks: "I have found a subject, *On the use of great men* ... But, in the first place, there should be a chapter *on the distribution of the hand into fingers*, or on the great value of these individuals as counterweights, checks on each other" (*JMN*, IX, 188). Again under "Topics" Emerson listed "What is the use of great men?" and followed it by "On the misuse of men," three other quite unrelated topics, and "Swedenborg & Fourier" (*JMN*, IX, 219–220). Further on in journal W is a partial list of his topics at some later stage during the summer: "Plato philosopher, Swedenborg mystic, affirmer, Montaigne skeptic, Shakspeare poet, Napoleon practical will make my circle" (*JMN*, IX, 223). Journal W was succeeded by journal Y in September 1845, and Emerson by that time had committed himself to a course of lectures on "a biographical basis." In turning back to his indexes and journals he found good material unused. And he must have remembered that the unpublished discourse at Middlebury contained golden pages. In Index Minor, perhaps at this time, he added inside the front cover the notation of four new collections of journal material he now had in this workbook: "Great Men," "Philosopher," "Mystic," and "Writer." The first two of these seem to be generally material for Representative Men in planning stages, while the latter two are specifically collections for Swedenborg and Goethe (*JMN*, XII, 568–569, 571–572, 558–560, 539–540). There are throughout this much-used workbook lists of passages that make their way into the printed version of the series. We may conjecture that in late August and early September, as Emerson worked toward the specifics of his lecture series, he used empty pages of Index Minor while he reviewed his journals and their indexes, attempting to confirm his idea of a subject. As if to set the seal of definition in the workbook, Emerson made a list on its last page: "1 [blank] / 2 Plato / 3 Swedenborg / 4 Montaigne / 5 Shakspear Saadi / 6 Goethe / 7 Napoleon / 8 Fourier." This reflects the stage in planning at the end of August when he responded to the secretary of the Boston Lyceum—"a course of six or at most eight"—and the overall topic was best described only as having "a biographical basis."

At the end of September both a "Preliminary Discourse" and "Goethe" are conjectural in Emerson's plans, according to his letters, but the list sent to William on October 2 includes both; the course seems fixed, although, except for a preliminary version of "Napoleon," still unwritten. Journal Y contains many passages that went into the lectures on Plato, Swedenborg, Shakespeare, Montaigne, and some schematic outlines for classes of great men. It is the immediate context from September to December for most of the lectures on Representative Men.

One of Emerson's choices of subjects is not surprising: Napoleon was a figure of great interest not only to Emerson but also to the whole nineteenth century. The stir created in Boston by the Russian campaign and the later defeat of the Emperor must have made considerable impression on the youth, who in a "poetical Essay" in 1815 used Napoleon as the most recent victim in the ancient conflict between ambition and independence (Rusk, p. 35; *L*, VI, 330–332). Emerson's early view of Napoleon doubtless was formed by William Ellery Channing's influential two-part essay, "Remarks on the Life and Character of Napoleon Bonaparte," in *The Christian Examiner* (1827–28). This ostensible review of Sir Walter Scott's impressive three-volume *The Life of Napoleon Buonaparte, Emperor of the French* (1827), with a great show of liberal and moral judiciousness, effectively destroys any ambiguity about the character of Napoleon and rejects the conservative Scott's generous impartiality. The notes called "Tests" of character, which Emerson made about the time of his lectures on Biography in 1835, reflect this devastating criticism of Napoleon. He finds that "Napoleon had an Aim & a Bad one"; he "was no more a believer [in his ends] than a grocer who disposes his shop-window invitingly, quite French"; he "worked gloomily alone" and was "pitiful jealous"; he did not "have that intellect which sets in motion the intellect of others"; it is a pun to call him great, for his "greatness seems to be a quite numerical thing . . . He is great by armies, by kings, by physical power but by one generous sentiment never. . . . Of Napoleon the strength consisted of his renunciation of all Conscience. The devil helps him"; and it is uncertain whether he even thought of himself as open to "Supernal influence" (*EL,* I, 424). Although Emerson was casually taken by Carlyle's "doctrine 'that every great man, Napoleon himself, is an Idealist, a poet with different degrees of Utterance' " (*JMN,* IV, 363), Napoleon is generally alluded to in the early journals as military man, conqueror, man without moral principle. But there is a dramatic shift in Emerson's interest in Napoleon in 1838 only indirectly precipitated by Carlyle's *The French Revolution,* which Emerson reprinted in Boston for the author's benefit.

The French Revolution is strategically punctuated by glimpses of the dark-complexioned artillery officer whose destined emergence terminates the history of the Revolution. In 1837 this theme may well have attracted Emerson, but in his second reading, in early March 1838, he was dissatisfied not only with Carlyle's trifling and joking but also with artful history itself: "Philosophes must not write history for me. They know too much. . . . So is my subject exhausted & my end as an artist not furthered" (*JMN,* V, 372; *CEC,* p. 167; *JMN,* V, 459, 462). As if to refresh himself "as an artist," Emerson turned almost at once to reading artless memoirs of Napoleon and entering into journal C extensive extracts from Barry Edward O'Meara, *Napoleon in Exile: or, A Voice from St. Helena,* 2 vols. (Boston, 1823), and Count Emmanuel Augustin Dieudonné de Las Cases, *Mémorial de Sainte Hélène. Journal of the Private Life and Conversation of the Emperor Napoleon at Saint Helena,* 4 vols. (Boston, 1823). These earnest but relatively unsophisticated accounts inspire Emerson to his first recognition of an attractive Napoleon: "I like the man in O'Meara's picture. He is goodnatured as greatness always is & not pompous"; and: "Napoleon in [Las Cases] has an admirable candor which belongs to philosophy, rails at no enemy, puts every crime down to the ignorance of the agent, & stands ready to make a marshal of him one day." When he finds from the same source that Napoleon has "a fund of justice & a disposition open to attachment," Emerson again is pleased (*JMN*, V, 472, 482, 483–484). We can see him generating on the same pages ideas that contribute to the conception of the great man and the "inextinguishable dualism" implicit in the very assertion of unity—ideas that will be germane to *Representative Men*. These engagingly favorable memoirs emphasize the human side of the fallen Emperor.

Emerson's interest in Napoleon as a great man, derived from the reading of O'Meara and Las Cases in 1838, antedates Carlyle's treatment of Napoleon in *On Heroes, Hero-Worship and the Heroic in History*, but he may have seen the possibilities in 1841 when he read the new book. Emerson's Napoleon bears little relation to Carlyle's. One reason is that Carlyle deals with Cromwell and Napoleon together as king, the able man who has the right to seize power in the revolution. Having raised the issue of usurpation, Carlyle lavishes detail on the sincerity of Cromwell. By contrast Napoleon is the lesser man because he lies and is caught in falsehood and substitutes appearance for reality. Although Emerson, no admirer of Cromwell, might agree about the particular failures of Napoleon, he cannot have agreed with the comparison, which in effect denies the greatness of the Emperor on the spurious issue of kingship. Moreover, in his comparison Carlyle neglects Napoleon's destined calling, the magnificent expediency, which he takes care to elaborate for Cromwell; having juxtaposed Cromwell to the Parliamentary heroes who quibble about democratic ideology, he understandably neglects to make Napoleon a champion of the common man or attorney of the middle class. Thus, though one or two anecdotes are borrowed from common sources and though the mixed nature of Napoleon's greatness emerges in both lectures, Emerson's Napoleon is both greater and more fatally flawed than Carlyle's second-best approximation to the ideal king. He becomes a central example in the paradox of great men.

The topic certainly was not the exclusive property of Carlyle; and Emerson in December 1844, pressed for lecture material and remembering that O'Meara and Las Cases had earlier stocked his journals with a substantial body of anecdotes and partially developed speculation, turned apparently to a volume of Napoleon's own *Memoirs*. With refreshed inspiration he began in January and February a project that might best be called research, checking out from the Boston Athenæum at least one more volume of Napoleon's *Memoirs* (he quotes from the first four volumes); the very useful four volumes of Louis Antoine Fauvelet de Bourrienne, *Private Memoirs of Napoleon Bonaparte* ... (London, 1830); *Recollections of Caulincourt* ..., 2 vols. (London, 1838); Louis François Joseph de Bausset, *Private Memoirs of the Court of Napoleon* ... (Philadelphia, 1828); the first of two volumes of Francesco Antommarchi, *The Last Days of the Emperor Napoleon* (London, 1825); the anonymous *The Court and Camp of Buonaparte* (London, 1831); John Gibson Lockhart, *The History of Napoleon Buonaparte*, 2 vols. (London, 1829); *Memoirs of Joseph Fouché* (Boston and New York, 1825); Charles Maxime de Villemarest, *Life of Prince Talleyrand*, 4 vols. (London, 1834–1836); and the first volume at least of Georgette Ducrest, *Memoirs of the Empress Josephine* ..., 3 vols. (London, 1829). The detail of the mountain of translated memoirs taught Emerson more about Napoleon than he would know of any other great man in an external, biographical sense. Though most are below the level of successful intellectual, historical, or aesthetic synthesis, they have the refreshing excitement of anecdote rather than theory and offer the experience of actual human moral questions fleshed out from a number of points of view. Emerson was invited to judge and did so in a way that preserves the essential complexity and ambiguity of the moral question. If great man was a pun when applied to Napoleon, Emerson was keen on puns and ambiguities when from anecdotal memoirs he began to see the representative nature of the human paradox. The thesis of the course of lectures that would develop a year later is illustrated and determined in "Napoleon": The great man fills our sky, is representative of man, or is at least the man of the age, but as individual he is limited and falls short of universal man. "Napoleon" differs from the other lectures, not only because of the different nature of this man of the world but also because Emerson knew more of his biography. The pattern set here would determine for the book the richness of biographical and other detail and the dialectic implied in great men. The relation between the actual detail and the universal, generalized concept had become an important interest for Emerson by 1845.

It is not surprising that *Representative Men* is less closely related to Emerson's series of lectures on Biography, read in 1835, than to his more contemporaneous works. He had lost interest in those early lectures when he told John Chapman in 1846 that the two printed in *The North American Review* he had not looked at since and he was "not very eager to recall either . . . to notice." But if Chapman wished to reprint them in his selections from the *Review,* Emerson hoped he would do so without "my name" (*L,* III, 359). Emerson left the subject of biography for ten years and returned to it in the Representative Men lectures a far more mature lecturer in both rhetoric and subtlety of thought. Though interesting and popular, the early lectures on Biography reveal no Emersonian brilliance either in matter or method. His journals indicate that he went into that 1835 series convinced that the value of biography lay in "the perfect sympathy that exists between like minds," that we "participate" in the acts of Socrates, Saint Paul, Antoninus, Luther, and Milton "by our thorough understanding" of them (*JMN,* V, 11). Emerson's lost introduction to the series included among "the true views of biography" the theme that "Man and not particular men are the subject of endless interest," since we "hold these fellow minds as mirrors before ourselves to learn the deepest secret of our capacity" (*EL,* I, 165, 450). But this professed concern for the type of man is quickly lost in the exemplary emphasis of the lecture series. Michelangelo lived, Emerson suggests, to show his fellow men that the "worlds of grandeur and grace" are available to them only through the "severest discipline" of all faculties (*EL,* I, 116); Luther, "the simple sincere man," illustrates "the superiority of immaterial to material power" (*EL,* I, 141–143); we are all "fortified by the remembrance" of Milton's bravery, purity, temperance, toil, and devotion (*EL,* I, 163); the poor, unlearned George Fox serves Emerson as a reminder of what common men can do for themselves (*EL,* I, 186).

If in his use of these famous men as instructive models for their own and future ages the young lecturer seems to have worn his idea thin in rhetorical variations, it is perhaps because Plutarchian exemplary biography was not adequate to express the romantic vision of man that Emerson was progressively developing. During the next decade Emerson's interest in biography came more and more to be expressed in the ways in which great men show the "capacity" of all men, one of the themes of *Representative Men.* The shift in emphasis results from Emerson's further consideration of the relation between the actual and the real, a major concern developed independently of the specific question of men and Man.

Although after the 1835 lectures Emerson dropped specific biography as a subject, the question of genius and of great men recurred in his writings and developed in ways that mark a difference between his early treatment of great men and the strategies of *Representative Men.* In "The American Scholar" (1837) he used the figure of "One Man,—present to all particular men only partially, or through one faculty" and hence the notion "that you must take the whole society to find the whole man" (*CW,* I, 53). This central fable of the universal man frees Emerson from specific biography, yet allows him a standard of comparison, an ideal against which men may be measured. But a more advanced figure appears in "Literary Ethics" (1838), that of the great man as mediator, who "should occupy the whole space between God or pure mind, and the multitude of uneducated men." Having the "twofold merit" of practical application and inspiration, this figure "must draw from the infinite Reason, on one side; and he must penetrate into the heart and sense of the crowd, on the other.

From one, he must draw his strength; to the other, he must owe his aim. The one yokes him to the real; the other, to the apparent. At one pole is Reason; at the other, Common Sense" (*CW,* I, 113). In its original journal form (November 1836) this figure was illustrated by "Jesus, dwelling in mind with pure God, & dwelling in social position & hearty love with fishers and women," and by Shakespeare, "drawing direct from the soul at one end, & piercing into the play going populace at the other" (*JMN,* V, 249). Both the figure of the universal, undistributed man and the figure of the great man as mediator look ahead to *Representative Men:* they illustrate Emerson's growing proficiency in relating the particular to the abstract representation, even as they minimize the detail of exemplary moralism.

Little enough is added in *Essays: First Series* to Emerson's conception of great men. "Heroism" is a pale application offered as only one aspect; "Intellect" repeats forcefully the idea that the self-reliant mind will struggle with the doctrines of Swedenborg, Kant, Coleridge, Hegel, or Cousin until "the excess of influence" is withdrawn (*CW,* II, 302); and in his most striking variation on the theme of universals, "Circles," Emerson asserts that "every ultimate fact is only the first of a new series" and that, accordingly, "Men cease to interest us when we find their limitations" (*CW,* II, 181–182). The seeming discontinuity between this volume, published in March 1841, and the remarkable oration that Emerson delivered at Waterville College only six months later is largely accounted for by the facts that *Essays: First Series* incorporates large amounts of material from early lectures and journals going back to 1835 and that its final composition extended over a long period of time (see *CW,* II, xxiv–xxix).

The shift in Emerson's method is apparent in "The Method of Nature," the Waterville piece, in which the multiple perspectives by which we view the "always interesting topics of Man and Nature" provide the greater complexity in conception. If, on the one hand, we demand of men "a richness and universality we do not find," seeing something "indigent and tedious about them," the obverse is that there "is no attractiveness like that of a new man," since "A man, a personal ascendency is the only great phenomenon." When we inspect the biography of the great and the wise, we are apt to find that none, "compared with his promise or idea, will justify the cost of that enormous apparatus of means by which this spotted and defective person was at last procured." But against this deficiency Emerson shifts the angle and declares that "When nature has work to be done, she creates a genius to do it. Follow the great man, and you shall see what the world has at heart in these ages" (*CW,* I, 122, 126, 128). Such contrasts in point of view dominate his writing in the next several years, culminating in the basic method of *Representative Men.*

The dialectic underlying that volume is evident in the work immediately preceding it. Having dealt with the ideal in *Essays: First Series* (1841), Emerson was still in the process of relating it to the actual in *Essays: Second Series* (1844), as he tells us in "Experience," the method of which is anticipated in the "Introductory Lecture" to the new series on The Times, begun in December 1841. "And why not draw for these times a portrait gallery?" he asked himself in preparing the new course (*JMN,* VIII, 125-126; *CW,* I, 170). The portraits of representative abstractions—the reformer, the conservative, the transcendentalist, the poet—prefigure the types implied in the subtitles of the Representative Men lectures. Characteristically, Emerson found the truth and strength of each qualified by partiality. Only the poet stood apart from the other fragmentary types as "the benefactor of the world," "the representative man, in virtue of being the largest power to give and receive" (*EL,* III, 356). In "Prospects," Emerson concludes that in his consideration of "this and that hero," all of them "are hints and segments, no more" (*EL,* III, 380–381). His point, however, is finally that this partiality affirms us in the belief that the universal reality is important, and if we do not see it embodied, we yet have access to it within: "Our self-reliance it is reliance on this. Our sin it is condemnation of this majesty: our hope, our Future,—it is the irresistible asseveration of this Prophetic Heart" (*EL,* III, 382). What Emerson achieves by his dialectic method is a statement of our paradoxical relation to great men. If they are exemplary, they are so only partially and thus drive us back on the universal.

Emerson evolves his dialectic method out of the perceived inadequacy in the application of his most famous statement—"Trust thyself." Though "Experience" provides the rationale for his shift to a more complex understanding of the relation between the actual and the ideal, "Nominalist and Realist" addresses the question in a way that leads directly to *Representative Men*. The central point of this essay, which in 1843 or 1844 was indexed, collected, and drafted in the working notebook as "Representative" (*JMN*, XII, 520–521, 541, 576–577), turns on the conception of the universe as "but one thing, this old Two-Face, creator-creature, mind-matter, right-wrong, of which any proposition may be affirmed or denied" (*CW*, III, 144). If one view is that "General ideas are essences" that "round and ennoble the most partial and sordid way of living," another is that "it is not the intention of nature that we should live by general views" (*CW*, III, 136, 139). What we cannot come at by universals and abstractions we might come at by particulars, and the principal illustration Emerson uses is great men. "Great men or men of great gifts you shall easily find, but symmetrical men never" (*CW*, III, 134). But if heroes fail to satisfy our idea, there is another side to great men, one in accord with the method of nature, which is growth: "there is somewhat spheral and infinite in every man, especially in every genius, which, if you can come very near him, sports with all your limitations" (*CW*, III, 142). Emerson, who in his major transcendental phase had been primarily a Realist, to the exclusion generally of concrete biography, now proposes: "If we cannot make voluntary and conscious steps in the admirable science of universals, let us see the parts wisely, and infer the genius of nature from the best particulars with a becoming charity" (*CW*, III, 143). An immediate result would seem to be the lecture on "Napoleon, or the Man of the World."

In the Middlebury College oration, written just as the lecture course on Representative Men was about to take shape in his mind, Emerson demonstrates his shift to the Nominalists' camp as he enumerates "the godhead in distribution": "I delight in Euclid, who is geometry; in Plato, who is philosophy; in Swedenborg, who is symbolism; in Shakspeare, who is imagination and human life; ... in Napoleon, who carries a campaign of Europe in his head; in Humboldt, who can represent in their order and symmetry the vast and the minute of the system of nature." His praise goes to the individual who is so "ripened" that he "touches both the center and the circumference." No longer content with the single model of the undistributed universal man of, say, "The American Scholar," Emerson at Middlebury College now needs another one: "I love talents and accomplishments, the feet and hands of genius. ... I delight to see the godhead in distribution; to see men that can come at their ends" (Houghton bMS Am 1280.199 [9]). He incorporated two large chunks of this new address into "Montaigne" and "Goethe" (see PP).

Emerson's undertaking new biographical lectures is not so much a return to his early interest in biography as a development of ideas far beyond the 1835 lectures. Half of his mode in the 1840s is to turn to "the best particulars with a becoming charity," and the other half is to bring the parts into relation with "the admirable science of universals." The post-1841 Emerson found the means of doing this effectively in the portraits of types, and the next logical step would be to flesh out the types biographically. This does not suggest that Emerson is merely gleaning from his journals his favorite passages to reveal at last his major biographical interests, but all his representative men were familiar and important to him. There is a dynamic to the individuals in his pantheon and an unstatic, evolving, personal relationship that makes *Representative Men* a book of 1850 rather than 1836. If Fourier and Saadi were temporarily considered, they were rejected because the pantheon included only the oldest friends. It is Napoleon rather than Plato or Shakespeare who precipitates both thesis and structure, not only because the lecture on him was written first but also because the man of the world, the man of mundane power, is the pivot of interest to the lecturer emerging from the ephemeral mists of transcendentalism into the robust daylight of New York and London.

The immediate inspiration for a lecture on Plato seems to grow out of Emerson's casual reading in the spring of 1845, and in this it resembles the earlier lecture on Napoleon. There is renewed interest in Plato, as we have seen from Emerson's letter to Ward in April, and a hope to write about him, or at least his dialogues, expressed in the letter to Newcomb at the end of the summer. It is a commonplace to cite Plato as a major, lifelong source for Emerson. While it is true that the forces of Platonism are everywhere at work and Emerson can be called in a qualified sense a Platonist or Neoplatonist, rather remarkably his real interest in reading Plato is sporadic and not central until the 1840s. Although Emerson could read Greek, he confessed himself ignorant of the untranslated works of Plato while at Divinity School (*L*, I, 228) and remained so apparently the rest of his life. His library contains no Greek text of Plato, not surprising in his time even for the dedicated amateur. His sparse early knowledge of Plato is displayed in his Bowdoin Prize dissertation, "The Character of Socrates" (1820), as stilted, conventional, and about what one would learn in college. He had, perhaps by way of preparation, borrowed from the Boston Library Society in 1819 the English translation of André Dacier's French translation, *The Works of Plato Abridg'd*, 2 vols. (London, 1772), and continued to use it from time to time for several years. In 1826, 1827, and 1829 he borrowed from Harvard College the fourth volume of *The Works of Plato . . . Nine of the Dialogues* [Translated] *by the Late Floyer Sydenham, and the Remainder by Thomas Taylor*, 5 vols. (London, 1804), which he knew as the standard translation, but in 1828 he found it "not good," less intelligible than the vulgar Dacier, and "very Greek indeed" (*L*, I, 228). He nevertheless continued to borrow the volumes from the Boston Athenæum sporadically from 1830 to 1845, when late in the summer, as he began to write his Representative Men lectures, he bought a set from the library of Charles Lane, whose books and other property Emerson was managing after the English reformer left the failed Fruitlands experiment (Rusk, p. 309). That Emerson relied on the Taylor edition is significant in that, with its elaborate introductions, interpretations, and comprehensive glosses, Plato is thoroughly neoplatonized in the long tradition that included the ancient interpreters Proclus and Plotinus, whom Emerson also owned and read in Taylor's translations, and the more modern ones who were to influence Emerson as he moved into his transcendental phase.

Emerson's interest in Plato's works seems small through 1831, though in his journals he uses the name often, citing his works chiefly from other sources—Plutarch, Montaigne, Bacon, and Coleridge. Such sources and Taylor's text led Emerson in the middle 1830s to a natural association of Plato with the First Philosophy and greater emphasis on "the purple light of Plato which shines yet into all ages & is a test of the sublimest intellects" (*JMN*, IV, 380). He found that his "debt to Plato is a certain number of sentences" and that "the discerning man reads in his ... Plato only that least part, only the authentic utterances" (*JMN*, V, 140, 347). Emerson's concentration on reading the text of Plato began in earnest in the early 1840s; by 1842 he owned and was reading in Taylor's selected translation of *The Cratylus, Phaedo, Parmenides and Timaeus of Plato* (London, 1793), even as he continued borrowing the longer edition until he bought it. This new interest in reading Plato seems to have been sparked by his neighbors in Concord who, as a gift for his free lectures, gave him the thirteen-volume set of Victor Cousin's translation, *Oeuvres de Platon* (Paris, 1822–1840), a better and, if not uncolored, at least a differently interpreted edition. This he had and began reading in early 1840 (*L*, II, 207–208; *JMN*, VII, 334), and during the spring and summer that ended in the plans for his lectures on Representative Men, Emerson's journals give concentrated evidence of his reading not only in Taylor's translation, but with more satisfaction in Cousin's: "There was an ugly rumour went about from London to Boston & in other places a twelvemonth since, that Cousin was dished, & now I owe to him this magnificent 'Republic'; and how many scholars will thank him for a century to come for this translation!" (*JMN*, IX, 217). Thus, if Plato was an old and admired friend, Emerson's enthusiasm for him was at its peak in the spring and summer of 1845, mainly as a result of his renewed and larger reading of Plato's works as a literary diversion from his set tasks. "It is easy," he wrote among the new passages in journal W, "to read Plato, difficult to read his commentators" (*JMN*, IX, 216). But his dependence on translations and commentators would yet cost him anxious rewriting before his lectures were made into a book.

Emerson's choice of Emanuel Swedenborg as a representative man was not surprising in 1845, as it may seem nearly a century and a half later. The dedication that year, at the meeting of the General Convention of the Church of the New Jerusalem, of the capacious new Swedenborgian church in the shadow of Boston's State House was an event that marked the rapid growth of a sect that had much influence in the United States throughout the nineteenth century—an oddly disproportionate influence considering the small number of formal adherents (perhaps about a thousand by 1845). Emerson's lecture is timely, near the culmination of Swedenborgian intellectual influence as distinct from the growth of the New Church. By midcentury, particularly in England and America, Swedenborg's extensive writings were being newly edited and translated as a result of the gradual formalization of the sect. In its origins the movement had not thought of itself as an organized church, and for some, following Swedenborg's own views, that question was still open. In the nonsectarian nature of the early movement it had made its influence felt among Anglicans and Methodists—even among Quakers—as a newness in Christian religion.

By 1845 a challenge and an attraction were felt among liberal Unitarians, Fourierists, Mesmerists, and New England Transcendentalists. The formal organization of churches gave strong impetus to a renewed general interest in Swedenborg. There had been an excitement about Swedenborgianism in Boston and Cambridge from 1818, which naturally attracted the Harvard undergraduate Emerson. The first local Society was formally established by students and recent graduates slightly older than he, and among them were friends and acquaintances like Sampson and Caleb Reed, Samuel and Thomas Worcester, and Theophilus Parsons. Emerson was much impressed by Sampson Reed's oration on genius, delivered to his own graduating class of 1821, and by his *Observations on the Growth of the Mind* (1826); he ranked him, along with Swedenborg, among the significant manifestations of the times. Characteristically Emerson speaks warmly of Swedenborg and, as one would expect of a liberal Unitarian, finds that new directions in Christianity are good for the church. Emerson's early journals show little evidence of much firsthand knowledge of Swedenborg's writings, but his friends and the reading in their American periodical, *The New Jerusalem Magazine,* would tell him much. From abroad Coleridge, too, would have strengthened his interest.

It remained a detached interest, however, and once freed from the pulpit he remained wary of sectarian ties. In January 1835, bored by the Unitarians, he went one Sunday morning to the New Jerusalem Chapel and in the afternoon to Father Taylor's Seamen's Bethel. He saw thus "two living chapels," but the life of the Methodist's homely and powerful sermon overwhelmed, in Emerson's description, the Swedenborgian sermon, which was "severely simple & in method & manner had much the style of a problem in geometry wholly uncoloured & unimpassioned." There was, as he told Sampson Reed, little said in the Swedenborgian chapel that could not be said in a decorous Unitarian church (*JMN,* V, 4–5). During their engagement to be married Waldo and Lidian were falsely rumored by interested parties to be Swedenborgians (Rusk, pp. 215, 220), but that speculation reflects the currency of Swedenborgianism in their intellectual circles. It had its attractions: fashionable, speculatively intellectual, solidly virtuous, founded on love, and, unlike Fourierism, for example, affirming marriage as a central figure of community. Swedenborgians had been influential in the early antislavery movement in England; they emphasized good works and charity and were much taken by the current enthusiasm for homeopathic medicine, all interests of Emerson's second wife. Neither husband nor wife, however, could be drawn to the sect any more than they could remain with a doctrinaire Transcendentalism. Swedenborg, his insights, and his resulting sect in fact serve Emerson usefully to illustrate a dialectic in the mind. Contemplating three months beforehand his liberating gospel to the students at Dartmouth in July 1838, he wrote of "the *limiting* instinct ... in our constitution so that the moment the mind by one bold leap (an impulse from the Universal) has set itself free of the old church and of a thousand years of dogma & seen the light of moral nature, say *with Swedenborg,* on the instant the defining lockjaw shuts down his fetters & cramps all round us, & we must needs think in the genius & speak in the phraseology of Swedenborg, & the last slavery is worse than the first" (*JMN,* V, 481). Just as Unitarianism and Transcendentalism, which Emerson offers as his next illustration, Swedenborgianism is dogma, not light. And this useful perception, which continues into his 1845 lecture, is there turned into his central observation that great men are of limited utility. Allusions to Swedenborg become more frequent after 1835 in journals and lectures, culminating in the early 1840s. He figures significantly in the lecture on "The Poet," at the end of 1841, as an example of the "grand poet" who succeeded Dante, Shakespeare, and Milton, and as translator of nature in the 1844 essay on "The Poet" (*EL,* III, 361; *CW,* III, 20–21). Aside from this emphasis on the writer of strange prose poems, there is also a more direct handling of Swedenborg as great man in Emerson's fragmentary lecture on "Recent Literary and Spiritual Influences," operating from abroad—along with Coleridge, Wordsworth, and Carlyle. In a hastily assembled manuscript, first read in 1843 in Philadelphia for the series on New England, passages on Swedenborg are brought together, some perhaps from a version of "The Poet," to make a statement about his influence in New England. Thus Emerson had, before he undertook the new lecture in the Representative Men series, at least considered Swedenborg as material. Although the earlier use of him indicates no profound, comprehensive, or well considered assessment, the subject was there in a kind of trial run, and in referring to his "Swedenborgian Chapter" in a list of lecture topics for 1842–43 (*JMN,* VIII, 295), Emerson was aware that he had something to say on the Swedish mystic.

By 1845 Emerson may have had in his library the following translations of works by Swedenborg: *The Animal Kingdom,* trans. J. J. Garth Wilkinson, 2 vols. (London and Boston, 1843–44); *The Apocalypse Revealed,* 3 vols. (Boston, 1836); *The Delights of Wisdom Concerning Conjugial Love* (Boston, 1843); *The Doctrine of Life for the New Jerusalem* (Boston, 1831; another issue 1836); *The Doctrine of the*

New Jerusalem Concerning the Lord (Boston, 1833); *Of the New Jerusalem, and Its Heavenly Doctrine* (Boston, 1835); *On the Intercourse between the Soul and the Body* (Boston, 1828); *A Treatise Concerning Heaven and Its Wonders, and Also Concerning Hell* (London, 1823); and *The True Christian Religion* (Boston, 1843). Emerson made notes in half of these volumes and quoted from most of them in the published lecture. Evidence in journals W and Y suggests that he was first reading in Swedenborg's recently translated physiological work, *The Animal Kingdom,* in the summer and fall of 1845. This firsthand knowledge of the speculative scientist who incorporated and interpreted the encyclopedic science of his time may well have secured Swedenborg's place as a representative man in the lecture series. Aside from the currency of Swedenborg's religious impact, he was still being discovered as an intellectual giant of the eighteenth century, and an important revision of the lecture would yet incorporate others of his scientific works edited and translated after 1845.

The lectures on Napoleon, Plato, and Swedenborg result from Emerson's renewed interest in these familiar figures just before or as he planned the new course. This excitement is not so apparent for the other representative men, but they quickly fitted into the select list of old friends now relevant to Emerson's concerns in the 1840s. Emerson takes pleasure in recounting his long-standing familiarity with Montaigne and brings us up to date on the latest coincidences in his comfortable relation with the old Gascon. For years he had cited him with ease in his journals, lectures, and essays. Goethe and Shakespeare he had dealt with more formally. The two early lectures on Shakespeare in the 1836 series on English Literature remained unpublished. They are good examples of current bardolatry—sensitive readings that confirm Shakespeare as the unexcelled poet of human nature. The element that Emerson could add to his new lecture was the burgeoning biographical and theatrical information produced in the 1840s by antiquarians and scholars, giving him a lever—a dialectic of paradox already established in Napoleon and particularly in his pairing of the philosopher and the mystic. The ideal poet had hitherto been dealt with only ideally. Goethe had from the 1830s been important to Emerson. His reading was extensive both in translation and, from 1836 onward, in German. He had dealt with Goethe at some length in the *Dial* essay "Thoughts on Modern Literature" (1840), which had been put together from two lectures on "Literature" in The Present Age series (1839–40). Yet, as in the case of Shakespeare, the German man of many parts still could fit into the new scheme, though we have seen that Goethe was a late and uncertain choice. He could be fitted in, not because there was new biographical material pressing on Emerson in the summer of 1845, but because he had something new to say in his unpublished discourse for Middlebury College, written at the same time his ideas for a new lecture course were just taking shape. In this eloquent formulation of "the natural and permanent function of the scholar" (a more complex statement than the Phi Beta Kappa oration of 1837) he developed at length the need for the scholar as transcriber of nature, his apparent conflict with society, and the underlying identity of his speculation with the practical aims of his age. Goethe in the new course of lectures became the representative type of this scholar, and a large portion of the Middlebury address was incorporated into the lecture on him. Similarly, Montaigne serves as the illustrator of another new idea, foreshadowed in "Experience" but more explicitly stated in the Middlebury address, and a long section of the latter is the basis for the lecture on Montaigne: the passage developing the wise and prudent skepticism that falls back on the faith that man helps himself by larger generalizations than come to him in experience, in the illusions that seem to contradict the beneficent tendency that streams through nature.

New ideas such as this make Emerson in the 1840s a more interesting lecturer than before, a fact that shows in the structure of *Representative Men*. Each of the great men falls short of the Universal Man, the figure that touches the heavens with his head and treads the floor of the Pit, even though our perceptions of great men give us for a time this illusion. Representative men are not Universal Man, and they are shown to fail in accord with Emerson's new contrast between the sky of Law and the pismire of performance. These lectures characteristically turn to the failure of the great man in relation to the promise of what man aspires to do. "Uses of Great Men," the introductory lecture, makes this paradox explicit yet preserves the recurrent theme of aspiration, of larger generalization against the poor realization. This statement is more ambitious than Carlyle's theory expressed in his lectures published four years earlier as *On Heroes, Hero-Worship and the Heroic in History,* and it is incompatible with it. Except for Shakespeare, everyone's subject, and minimally Napoleon (Carlyle declined to deal with Goethe in his book), there is no overlap in the gallery of great men, but comparison between the two sets of lectures was inevitable. With only one allusion to Boswellism, Emerson in 1845 quietly and directly answers his friend, though not all his listeners recognized the answer.

With his topics fixed, at the end of the summer of 1845 Emerson had in hand an early version of one lecture; an address which had been too extensively reported in the press to be used as a new lecture, but which contained good material pertinent to both the man of letters and the skeptic; recent coverage of Plato and a wide acquaintance with and interest in all the figures he intended to treat; and most of all, a fresh, exciting idea that would give a peculiar meaning to lectures "on a biographical basis."

With deadlines fixed, the preparation of the course was by now routine for the experienced public lecturer: all other literary work—the poems, reprinting of his fugitive pieces, plans for publishers' enterprises—had to be set aside; domestic arrangements and social life were subject to lecture dates; extensive reading and journal writing turned on the given topics, which meant preparing indexes and outlines from old journals and, with more anxious awareness of the dates, writing up to individual deadlines. These are the habits of the preacher turned scholar and public lecturer. One matter had been taken care of: the mechanics of the stellar performance in Boston had been put into other hands. The sponsorship of the Boston Lyceum freed Emerson from the details of renting a hall, advertising, and printing tickets; by the fixed price per lecture, he knew his profit and accordingly decided on seven rather than six lectures.

Early in his preparation he was light-hearted and whimsical: "Are not Lectures a kind of Peter Parley's story of Uncle Plato, and of a puppetshow of Eleusinian Mysteries?" (*JMN*, IX, 282). But Emerson knew he was neither a purveyor of children's stories nor of transcendental hocus-pocus; and he continued hiving up useful excerpts from oriental books at hand, particularly from *The Vishńu Puráńa* and *The Practical Philosophy of the Muhammadan People . . . the Akhlāk-i-Jalāly*, his source for quotations and paraphrases from the Koran. He also addressed his announced topics more directly. We see evidence of his preparation from September to December in journals and letters. The large number of passages later incorporated into the lectures and the outlines and similar material for "Plato," "Swedenborg," "Montaigne," "Shakspeare," and "Uses of Great Men" indicate that during the fall of 1845 journal Y was Emerson's principal workbook for the unwritten portion of the course, succeeding the collections of material in Index Minor. The undated notes on Swedenborg in notebook Z (*JMN*, VI, 311–316) may be preparation for the new lecture, and part of a miscellaneous grouping of manuscript leaves survives as evidence that some of Emerson's preliminary work on "Goethe" was done outside notebooks and journals (Houghton bMS Am 1280.214 [108]). It is possible that the leaves from "Montaigne" and "Swedenborg" distributed in the Autograph Edition of Emerson's works were partially preliminary material, though they are more likely pages rejected in later revisions—perhaps in the case of "Swedenborg" the manuscript of the lecture, or rejected parts of it, which Edward Emerson alludes to and quotes from in his notes to the Centenary Edition.

Emerson felt that he needed two months for the preparation of his new lecture series, and with his busy life it was barely enough time. The family routine was punctuated by the complexities of arranging for a sojourn in Concord of the difficult Aunt Mary Moody Emerson (but not at her nephew's house), the wedding of Uncle Samuel Ripley's daughter, and a long visit by Caroline Sturgis, who noted the tedious days but social evenings (*L*, III, 302–303, 305; Rusk, p. 309). There was much correspondence through the fall months about lecture engagements for the season, doubtless spurred by the early announcement of the new course for the Boston Lyceum. In a stern letter, later made public in *The Liberator,* Emerson declined the invitation from the New Bedford Lyceum because it had voted to exclude Negroes. He wrote that he worked for popular education and that the Lyceum "should bribe and importune the humblest and most ignorant to come in, and exclude nobody, or, if any body, certainly the most cultivated" (*L,* III, 312). The tension of beginning the new series for Boston was exacerbated by a misunderstanding with Wiley & Putnam over their refusal to surrender Emerson's early presentation copy of Carlyle's new work, *Oliver Cromwell's Letters and Speeches,* until they had the first advantage in the American market—serious enough that Emerson inquired about legal action (*L,* III, 314–325, passim). This upsetting incident, which deprived Carlyle of his expected profit, nagged at Emerson throughout the Boston course, at the end of which he ended "the charms of wrath" by offering Wiley & Putnam the second edition of *The French Revolution* (*L,* III, 329–330).

Whatever the distractions, Emerson worked with a practical sureness that brought him to the Odeon with the first of his weekly lectures on the evening of Thursday, December 11, 1845. That he had all the rest of the lectures written out is unlikely. In acknowledging, nine days before the Boston course began, the receipt of nine volumes of the publications of the Shakespeare Society borrowed from H.W. Longfellow, Emerson indicated that he would like to keep the books five or six weeks, that is, nearly until the scheduled delivery of the lecture on Shakespeare (*L,* III, 313). Perhaps his working up to the deadlines accounts for the slight deviation in sequence from that projected at the beginning of October and retained in the book: a symmetry is broken by reading "Napoleon" as the fifth lecture and "Shakspeare," which may not have been finished in time, as the sixth. Even with some of his lectures incomplete, there would be nothing to make the experienced Emerson uneasy about his opening night. The day before, over Lidian's affected protests against his brashness, he wrote his old friend and financial adviser, Abel Adams, that he and Lidian would dine with him and his family before the lecture and return with them to spend the night (*L,* III, 315).

The Odeon, for the past ten years a lecture hall since its conversion from the Boston Theater, was on Federal Street and seated 1500, with standing room for many more. It was full, reported Longfellow, who had come to the opening lecture with the witty and magnetic Tom Appleton, adding a bit of literary and social fashion in the third row. They heard, according to Longfellow's diary: "Many striking and brilliant passages, but not so much as usual of that 'sweet rhetoricke' which usually flows from his lips; and many things to shock the sensitive ear and heart." Longfellow, who is a good reporter owing to his genuine liking for Emerson and his detachment from transcendental chic, may well have detected what distinguishes the Representative Men lectures from the earlier popular courses on Human Culture and Human Life, but the next week his attention shifted to the audience: "Heard Emerson's second lecture, on Plato. A theatre full. It is curious to see such an audience,—old men and young, bald heads and flowing transcendental locks, matrons and maidens, misanthropists and lovers,—listening to the reveries of the poet-philosopher." If Emerson's professed desire to educate in lyceums "the humblest and most ignorant" seems not quite fulfilled, neither had he sacrificed "the most cultivated" if we include Longfellow and his friends. Perhaps by his topic Emerson enticed the poet to walk from Cambridge to Boston on January 22, "in a fierce, cold wind, toward sunset," to hear the seventh and last lecture in the course, after taking tea with Charles Sumner "in a small café." Longfellow's comment on "Goethe" is just: "Very good, but not so pre-eminent as some of his discourses." More revealing of Emerson's stature is the hyperbolic compliment, "There is a great charm about him,—the Chrysostom and Sir Thomas Browne of the day." Far from being uneasy about his new lectures, Emerson surely recognized that he was being taken up, much solicited—that the taint of transcendental heresy no longer wholly accounted for his popularity. The shift was subtle in genteel Boston and Cambridge. There is a significance to one more Longfellow entry. When Emerson lectured in Cambridge on February 4, 1846, he declined Longfellow's generous invitation to stay the night with him, but accepted the invitation to tea (see *JMN*, IX, 257; *L*, III, 313). Longfellow wrote, on the same day that he noted he was "Putting to press a cheap edition" of his poems: "Emerson took tea with us; rather shy in his manner, but pleasant and friendly. We all drove down to hear him lecture, Lowell and [Appleton] being of the party. The lecture was on Napoleon. Very good and well spoken, and to the evident delight of the audience. We like Emerson,—his beautiful voice, deep thought, and mild melody of language" (*Life of Henry Wadsworth Longfellow,* ed. Samuel Longfellow, 2 vols. [Boston, 1886], II, 26–27, 30, 32).

Bronson Alcott, who had heard none of the new lectures yet, reported the end of the series to Charles Lane and, partly as a matter of faith and partly by reports, concluded that with these "Fine Heads of Representative Men" and "Carlyle's masterly Portraits, the Young World can scan its own Possibilities and kindle its Ambition." He noted that he had scarcely seen Emerson during the preparation of the lectures. Although Alcott seems to have missed the lecture on Plato read in Concord on December 31, he looked forward to the Concord course promised for later. Meanwhile Emerson was "much in demand at Lyceums in the neighboring towns" (*The Letters of A. Bronson Alcott,* ed. Richard L. Herrnstadt [Ames, Iowa, 1969], p. 125). Even before Emerson finished in Boston he began to read the series on a weekly basis before the Lowell Mechanics' Association, and on January 23 he read the first of six from it at Worcester. These, with the Boston series, brought him $635.50, but he also dipped into the course for other New England lyceums that requested only one or two lectures. By special request he repeated "Napoleon" for $30 before the fashionable Boston Mercantile Library Association, then as usual completed the season, without fee, with a continuation of the series at Concord from March 25 to April 29, including again "Napoleon" and ending with "Uses of Great Men."

Despite the success of the lectures on Representative Men, the Boston lecture on Swedenborg had stirred up trouble. Emerson had sent a complimentary ticket to his old, admired friend Sampson Reed, who was prominent in the New Church at Boston (*L,* III, 320–321), and presumably he attended. But also on that Christmas Day at the Odeon there was a more eagerly articulate critic in the audience. George Bush was an eminent biblical scholar from New York University who had recently converted to Swedenborgianism with much publicity and had become at once active in lecturing and publishing on behalf of the sect. His acquaintance with Emerson had been friendly, and his criticism is severely polemical but not personally hostile. He asked for and was given the opportunity to respond to Emerson in the Odeon on January 18, 1846, and in February he published a twenty-eight-page pamphlet, *Prof. Bush's Reply to Ralph Waldo Emerson on Swedenborg*. As Bush apologized, the reply had been made hastily and was based on a newspaper report of Emerson's lecture rather than on memory. He praises the eloquent style of the lecture and observes that people had been moved, even though old-fashioned piety must have been constantly shocked. He grants that the praise for Swedenborg's scientific works might well persuade people to accept the truth of his religious insight, but he objects to Emerson's calling Swedenborg a mystic (because of popular misconception of the meaning) and his "jesuitical tactics" in playing off the popular misunderstanding of the Last Judgment when he does not believe in it anyway. He commends Emerson for his perception that Swedenborg is the first to deal with the symbolic nature of the world "in a scientific way," but Bush easily changes the subject to "Spiritual Sense of the Word" and faults Emerson for his criticism of Swedenborg's narrow theological interpretation. Emerson's central failure, however, lies in his philosophy, "by which right becomes wrong and wrong right." The important thrust of the reply is that Bush is defending not just Swedenborgianism: it is plain that Emerson's lecture has a "bearing, rather open than latent, against *all* theology, as contradistinguished from a vague theosophy." Emerson posed a threat to all orthodoxy, not just the New Church, and this charge would be echoed when the lecture was published. A letter to the *Manufacturers and Farmers Journal & Providence and Pawtucket Advertiser* on March 5, 1846, after Emerson read the lecture on Swedenborg in Rhode Island, repeats Bush's strictures and recommends his *Reply*. But characteristic of the Swedenborgian response, it thanks Emerson for drawing attention to the "Swedish Seer."

Portrait sketch of Emerson (about 1850) by Frederika Bremer.

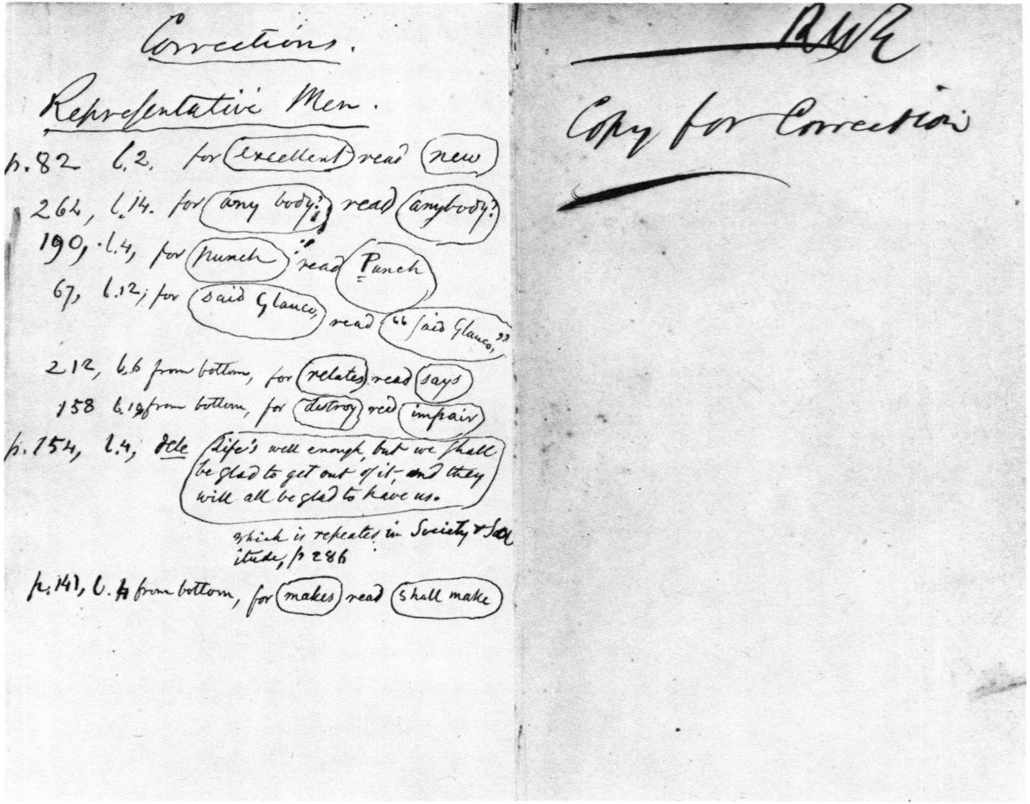
Corrections.

Representative Men.

p. 82 l. 2. for excellent read new

264, l. 14. for any body? read anybody?

190, l. 4, for punch read Punch

67, l. 12; for said Glauco, read "said Glauco,"

212, l. 6 from bottom, for relates read says

158 l. 13 from bottom, for destroy read impair

p. 154, l. 4, dele Life's well enough, but we shall be glad to get out of it, and they will all be glad to have us.

which is repeated in Society & Solitude, p 286

p. 141, l. 4 from bottom, for makes read shall make

RWE

Copy for Correction

Emerson's list of corrections to *Representative Men.*

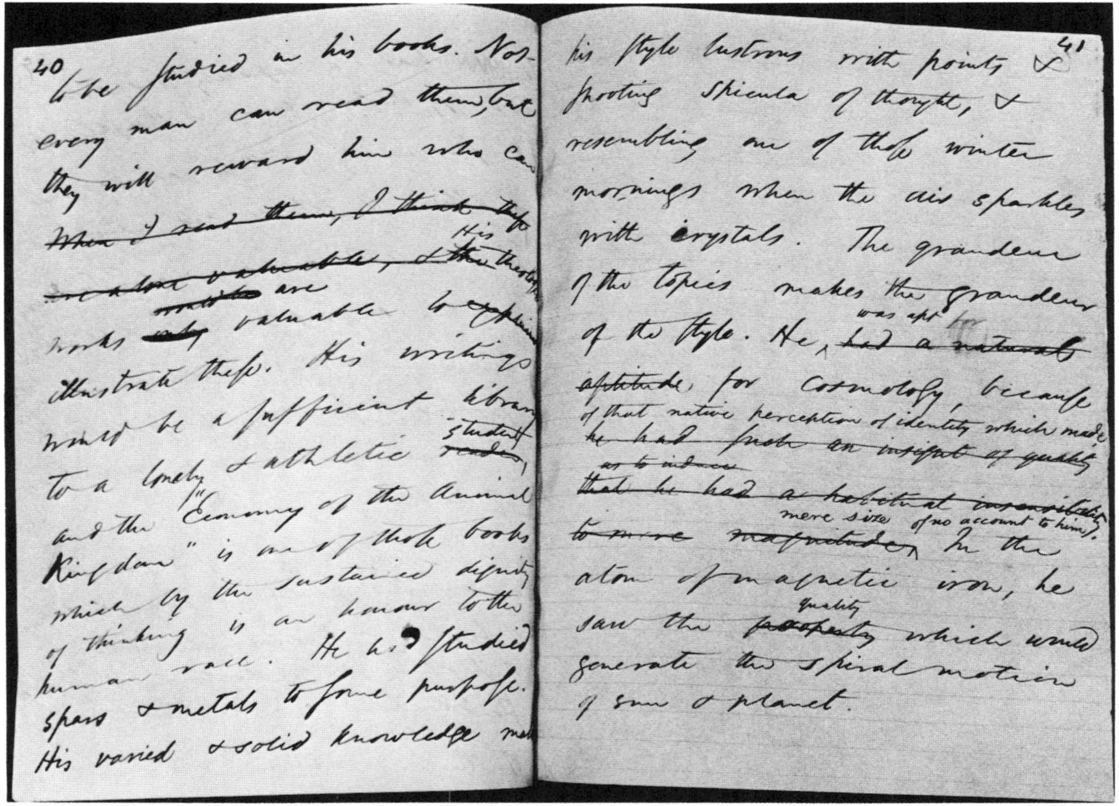
40
to be studied in his books. Not
every man can read them, but
they will reward him who can.
His theory
works are valuable to explain
illustrate these. His writings
would be a sufficient library
to a lonely & athletic student;
and the "Economy of the Animal
Kingdom" is one of those books
which by the sustained dignity
of thinking is an honour to the
human race. He had studied
spars & metals to some purpose.
His varied & solid knowledge ma

41
his style lustrous with points &
shooting spicula of thought, &
resembling one of those winter
mornings when the air sparkles
with crystals. The grandeur
of the topics makes the grandeur
of the style. He was apt for
for cosmology, because
of that native perception of identity which made
mere size of no account to him. In the
atom of magnetic iron, he
saw the quality which would
generate the spiral motion
of sun & planet.

Two manuscript pages of "Swedenborg." (See page 60.)

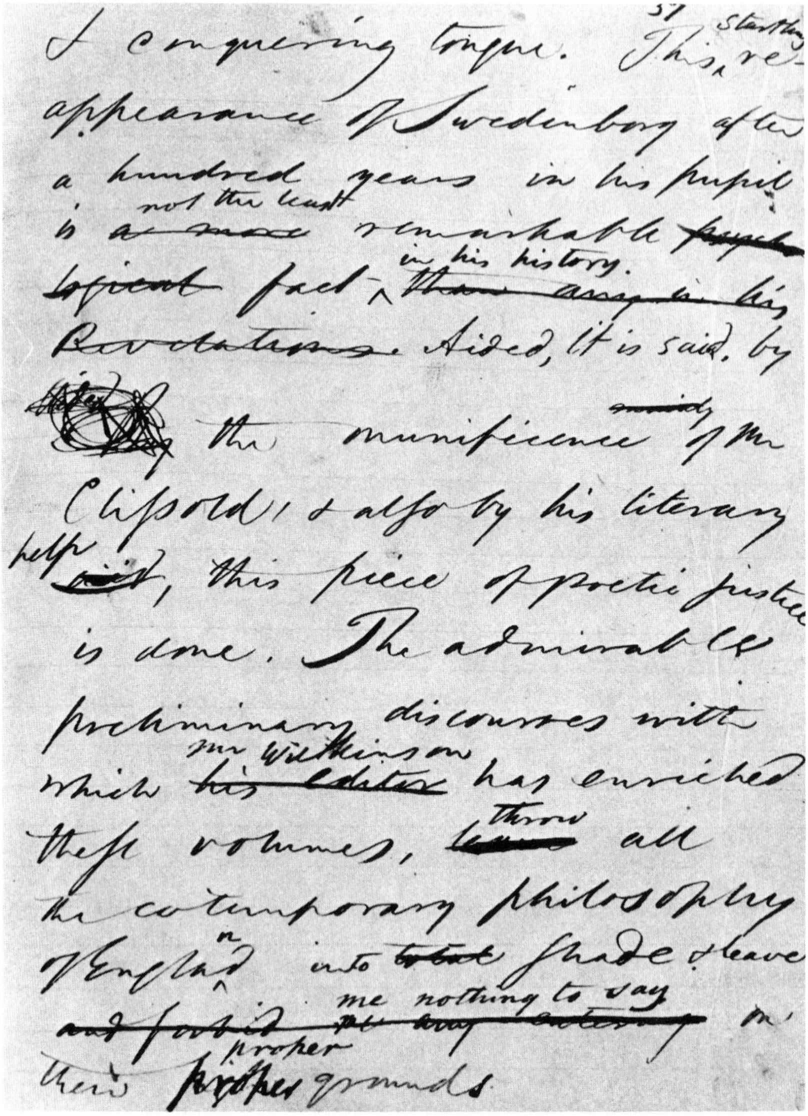

A much-revised manuscript page of "Swedenborg." (See page 63.)

Generally the lectures on Representative Men were praised. Rufus Griswold, in his revised, second edition of *The Prose Writers of America* in 1847, added to his flattering article on Emerson: "He has since [1844] delivered lectures on Swedenborg, Napoleon, New England and other subjects, which are regarded by some who have heard them as decidedly the finest of his works" (p. 440). Henry Thoreau, soon after he heard the new lectures in Concord, made a perceptive distinction in an essay on "Thomas Carlyle and His Works," to be published the next spring in *Graham's American Monthly Magazine:* "Carlyle, and our countryman Emerson ... are, to a certain extent, the complement of each other. ... The one has more sympathy with the heroes, or practical reformers, the other with the observers, or philosophers. Put these worthies together, and you will have a pretty fair representation of mankind; yet with one or more memorable exceptions." The exceptions are an implied criticism of both Emerson and Carlyle: "To say nothing of Christ, who yet awaits a just appreciation from literature, the peacefully practical hero, whom Columbus may represent, is obviously slighted; but above and after all, the Man of the Age, come to be called working-man, it is obvious that none yet speaks to his condition, for the speaker is not yet in his condition" (*Early Essays and Miscellanies,* ed. Joseph J. Moldenhauer et al. [Princeton, 1975], p. 251). Emerson had thought the first exception beyond his powers as he began planning the course (*JMN,* IX, 139), and he would do so again long afterward. He would also consider the omission of the last with some regret soon after *Representative Men* was published. But on the whole he was apparently pleased with his profitable new lecture course and, after other literary tasks, looked ahead to modest revision for publication.

The notebooks and journals do not indicate much work on *Representative Men* between April 1846 and October 1848. The manuscripts were serviceable enough either as separate lectures or as a flexible series. Judging by his practice with nearly contemporary lecture manuscripts that he did not publish but read a number of times, we may assume that errors in transcription, weak words and phrases, sentences awkward in the reading, and insufficient punctuation were mended as subsequent readings suggested—

perhaps even with an afterthought here and there. Such casual alterations may survive in some of the pages used as printer's copy for the American edition of the book, for Emerson generally took care that he not stumble in the reading or be forced to improvise for lack of clear manuscript. And doubtless these lectures showed the usual signs of composition under pressure: Emerson wrote to James Freeman Clarke, declining to lend the manuscript of "Montaigne" two days after its first reading, that "it is not fit for such eyes as yours at this present" (*L*, III, 323).

Even before he composed the series there was an implicit assumption that they could be published as a book. Duyckinck had assumed it, Emerson had quietly entertained the idea, and Carlyle, knowing his own method of lecturing from notes and then working up the material into a book, and having heard that the oral delivery had met with "renown enough," asked when the lectures would "get into print?" (*CEC*, p. 393). But Emerson's lectures were not notes, and in the spring of 1846 he felt that he had in hand a book if he could only find time to polish it. To W. H. Furness in Philadelphia, his friend from childhood, he wrote in May that he had no separable and substantial prose to contribute to *The Diadem;* but a whole book he had: "I am trying to put into printable condition my seven Lectures on Representative Men; but the topics were so large, & seem to require such spacious & solid reading, that what might pass to be spoken, does not promise to be fit to print in a hurry" (Furness, p. 53). This prospect seems not so gloomy, however, in an amusing letter he wrote nearly three weeks later to William Emerson, revealing his characteristic optimism about work in the dilatory late spring. Apparently his mother, Ruth Emerson, wanted the Representative Men manuscripts carried by Elizabeth Hoar to Staten Island for the edification of the extended family. Emerson wrote that he had protested to Madame Emerson that William was too busy "to read interminable Discourses on Representative Men or things ... *brochures* of this size and in MS, and still expecting correction & full interlinings ... But, dear Mother [he had argued], perhaps next winter, when I have written out these sketches, and better contented myself, who knows but I may carry them to N.Y. & entreat the whole Tabernacle to hear & urge William to go?—In vain; . . . so the most innocent looking one ["Goethe"] is sent . . . The rest of them lie in pile, and are, in a few days, it is to be hoped, to begin to receive their repairs—for printing, one day" (*L*, III, 333–334).

In the spring and summer of 1846 few repairs were done, probably, for he had already written John Chapman in London that he intended to have the still imperfect volume of poems ready for Christmas (*L*, III, 332). Aside from a Fourth of July address at Dedham to the Massachusetts Anti-Slavery Society, Emerson's literary work for the summer remained the poems, and the Representative Men lectures lay unrepaired. There is no indication that he had time to turn to the postponed manuscripts before he read five of them again in Bangor, Maine, in October. The publication of *Poems* at last left him free to lecture, but with diminished lyceum prospects. At the end of the year, thanking William Emerson for the children's Christmas gifts, he mentioned that he was polishing "Eloquence" for the Boston Mercantile Library, but remembered: "Other things new I have none, but much work of revision of the old before me, if I do as the booksellers solicit me." He also announced Alexander Ireland's proposal that he come to England to lecture and added promisingly, "I understand the Queenie, not Victoria but Lidian, to say that I must go!" (*L*, III, 366–367).

Emerson's first intimation to Carlyle, at the end of January 1847, of the possibility of the lecture tour of England evoked the recollection of his plans for Representative Men: "I should find my account in the strong inducement of a new audience to finish pieces which have lain waiting with little hope for months or years" (*CEC*, p. 413). Perhaps the still uncertain tour abroad spurred him to read some Swedenborg in March, as a casual allusion in a letter to Sam Ward indicates he had been doing (*L*, III, 387). But it is doubtful that the harried Emerson turned to much serious revision of his Representative Men manuscripts even in preparation for the English tour. He had a sense of near panic and disappointment that he could not fully supply himself against the undefined and uncertain extent of his engagements.

He must have looked upon the Representative Men lectures as his mainstay, but his plans for polishing the old lectures dwindled away as the spring passed. By April he found his days and weeks eaten up by the garden and a new orchard. He spent time as Charles Lane's agent in liquidating the now-defunct Fruitlands and worked at placing for publication Thoreau's *A Week on the Concord and Merrimack Rivers.* By the end of July, with the English trip a certainty, domestic matters had to be arranged: his mother was to go to Staten Island to stay with William Emerson's family for the year, Thoreau was to move in with the Concord Emersons to act as head of household, Lidian's sister Lucy Brown and her family were to become boarders to help defray expenses, money had to be borrowed, and William's usual assistance and consultation were essential. With his family away in August, Emerson had some time to prepare; as he wrote his new young friend Edward Bangs, the engagements in England "are of such a kind as to involve me in some reading & writing—more than is good—just now" (*L,* III, 410). Perhaps again part of the preparation was in connection with Swedenborg, as a letter in August to Margaret Fuller hints (*L,* III, 414). At least he must have remembered that the Swedenborg lecture needed attention, had been under attack, and was now significantly out of date because of new publications, translations of the scientific works, since 1845. But the summer passed with deadlines for seeing his revised edition of *Essays: First Series* through the press and urgent meetings with Theodore Parker, Cabot, and others about the projected *Massachusetts Quarterly Review,* in which Emerson was reluctantly becoming involved. Almost at the last minute Emerson wrote to his brother on September 24 with anxiety and disappointment: "this voyage of mine . . . would be much if I were ready for it: But I am not. All my life is a sort of College Examination. I shall never graduate. I have always some tormentors ahead. . . . I came to the preparation of lectures for England—which would have otherwise been a great pleasure—too late & am sadly fretted with miscellaneous parts" (*L,* III, 416–417). In October 1847, when Emerson transported to England the Representative Men manuscripts, they were doubtless in a form not much different from their original.

Even unrevised, the lectures on Representative Men served Emerson well in Great Britain, but as a course they did not carry him far. Beginning on November 2 and 3, Emerson read the course, omitting "Plato," on Tuesdays and Thursdays before the Manchester Athenaeum and on Wednesdays and Saturdays before the Liverpool Mechanics' Institution. The next week he began a third concurrent Monday-night series of four miscellaneous lectures, old and new, at the Manchester Mechanics' Institution. Keeping his rooms in Manchester, Emerson shuttled across the Midlands and the northern counties in December, January, and early February in an intricate pattern of engagements—one, two, three, or four lectures, ordinarily not on consecutive nights. He mixed popular old lectures like "Domestic Life" and miscellaneous rewritten or new lectures with "Napoleon," "Shakspeare," and, only once, "Uses of Great Men" from the Representative Men series. It was an embarrassment to Emerson that his lectures were so widely reported, and he had little time to pull others together. At Edinburgh, where he lectured four times in February to the distinguished Philosophical Institution, he was glad to have a brilliant new lecture on "Natural Aristocracy," but he ended his season by going out to Glasgow, Paisley, and Perth with combinations of "Eloquence," "Domestic Life," and "Napoleon."

There were dissenting voices. Besides the usual charge of obscurity, there was the equally old objection to unorthodoxy in religion and the threat to morals. "Swedenborg," given only in Manchester and Liverpool, caused trouble, not only among adherents of the New Church, as in New England, but also among the orthodox. Again the Swedenborgians, in their periodicals and from the pulpit, pointed out that the lecture was unfair in its criticism of their founder, was unchristian, and had shocking moral implications. But again they had mixed feelings, for it brought favorable notice to Swedenborg himself. Other Christians often joined them in denouncing Emerson's obvious denial of pure malignity and particularly his passage on the ascent of man's spirit even in jail and the brothel. Some serious effort was made by indignant citizens in Nottingham and Derby to prevent this dangerous man from speaking; in Scotland there was an organized journalistic campaign against his "pantheism"; one lone, patriotic Frenchman in England denounced Emerson's censures on Napoleon and the French people. Yet, on the whole, the balance tipped in Emerson's favor, with many warm expressions of praise and admiration in the newspapers and magazines for this bold and "elevating" Yankee and numerous special commendations for "Napoleon," "Shakspeare," and even "Montaigne."

It is uncertain why "Plato" was not read to any public audience in Great Britain. Emerson may have felt unease or dissatisfaction with it, as he had not at home. He may have suspected his audience was not right or even that he was not scholar enough. But as Emerson was not easily intimidated, he more likely held the lecture back for special occasions. The one occasion when he read it privately was special. On January 29, as a farewell to Manchester, he gave an all-night banquet in his rooms for about a dozen men who had in various ways been hospitable, receptive, or interesting to him. He wrote Lidian: "These are all men of merit & of various virtues & ingenuities" (*L,* IV, 15). One of them, Alexander Ireland, remembered: "His guests were principally young men—ardent, hopeful, enthusiastic moral and religious reformers, and independent thinkers, gathered together from Birmingham, Sheffield, Nottingham, Liverpool, Huddersfield, Newcastle and other towns" (*Ralph Waldo Emerson* [London, 1882], pp. 162–163). By more satiric accounts, there were poets and eccentrics among them. After dinner, urgently requested to do so, Emerson read them his lecure on Plato. A few remained for the breakfast that concluded the modern symposium. That Emerson thought well of this reserved lecture is evident from his urgent effort to have the manuscript sent to him from Manchester in time to read at the Edinburgh Philosophical Institution. He wrote Alexander Ireland, asking him to retrieve it from the bureau drawers in Emerson's rooms and send it quickly, for some friends had requested it as the final reading (Ireland, p. 200). It appears, however, that Emerson read "Eloquence" on February 19 instead.

A judiciously favorable but impressionistic report of Emerson's

Manchester series on Representative Men (based on three lectures and some hinted "meetings which may have occurred in private") appeared anonymously in *Howitt's Journal* for December 11, 1847. This popular liberal Christian publication, which had greeted Emerson warmly with favorable advance publicity, now honored him with a full-page likeness from an original sketch to accompany the review. The Manchester correspondent found the lectures rather difficult material for the appreciative audience. The delivery was subdued, says the correspondent, and sentences were often "connected only by some gossamer link of association with the subject in [Emerson's] mind." The lecture on Swedenborg "was like a golden mist around a setting sun,—you perceived nothing but splendid words, without anything definite, at first; but, by-and-bye, one object after another came clear out to the patient vision, invested with a glory from the medium through which they had passed; but that very medium made the whole obscure." After a beautiful beginning the lecture perplexingly "wandered far away into the mystical theories of Swedenborg." "Montaigne" was "a noble lecture. Though every sentence was (as before) loaded with meaning, I understood him throughout; although still the connexion between the separate parts was occasionally but very obscure." The lecture on Shakespeare was less to the correspondent's liking, but he perceived in it what he took to be the theme of Emerson's lectures on Representative Men: "that universal as Shakspere is, he was not satisfying to the reflective mind, whose object of thought was the discovery of the answer to the great problem of life, the purpose of this, our world." Throughout the tone is appreciative and generous and the large size of the audience is noted.

Emerson moved from Edinburgh to London at the end of February and took comfortable rooms in the house of John Chapman, his English publisher. Except for a brief visit to Oxford University, one to Stratford-on-Avon, a month's stay in revolutionary Paris in May, and a final excursion to Stonehenge with Carlyle, he remained there until his departure from Liverpool on July 15. The trip had not yet paid for itself, but there was the uncertain prospect of a fashionable, expensive series of lectures in

London, and Emerson polished "Natural Aristocracy" and wrote three new lectures he called "Natural History of Intellect." Most of his time was profitably spent in the social and intellectual brilliance of London, which received him with a gracious and generous curiosity and admiration.

Emerson and the London surgeon J. J. Garth Wilkinson, an editor and translator of Swedenborg's works and a leader in the New Church, now met and strengthened their respect for one another. Wilkinson had entertained Margaret Fuller and had become a friend of another of Emerson's Swedenborgian friends, Henry James, during his recent sojourn in England. Wilkinson had sent Emerson publications and had been one of the moderating voices in the furor Emerson caused among English Swedenborgians. Their friendship may have given Emerson some further insight into Swedenborg, but apparently no second thoughts about his major position. J. A. Heraud, another new acquaintance, was a thoughtful expounder of Swedenborgianism, but English intellectuals generally gave little insight or stimulation on either Swedenborg or Plato. Emerson recorded in March 1848 that the historian, "Mr. Hallam asked me at Lord Ashburton's, 'whether Swedenborg were all mad, or partly knave?' " He later remembered that Carlyle had read a new translation of Plato with displeasure—displeasure with Plato. As for Emerson's favorite English translator and interpreter of Plato, Emerson observed in London that Hallam "knew nothing of Thomas Taylor, nor did Milman, nor any Englishman"; he later moderated the absolutes and saw unconvincingly that it might reflect the literary wealth of England. The disturbing recollection may have been that, among the London intellectuals, "Plato is only read as a Greek book" (*JMN,* X, 260, 304, 512, 552).

Settling in at Chapman's gave Emerson an opportunity to discuss plans for publishing *Representative Men,* now nearly unusable as lectures. In 1846 Emerson had sent a separate manuscript of *Poems* to Chapman in order to get the advantage of the English market, and doubtless in London they now worked out the same plan for *Representative Men.* Chapman was more immediately useful to a seemingly diffident or reluctant Emerson. In late April, uncertain whether he would go to France or give lectures or both, Emerson wrote his wife: "It seems very doubtful whether I shall read lectures here even now. Chapman makes himself very busy about it, & a few people, and I shall, no doubt, have a good opportunity, but I am not ready, and it is a lottery business" (*L*, IV, 55). Nevertheless, he did read new lectures between June 6 and June 17 to a fashionable, even aristocratic, crowd at the Literary and Scientific Institution in Portman Square. With the overall title of "Mind and Manners of the Nineteenth Century," he read his three lectures on Natural History of Intellect, to which he added "Politics and Socialism" and "Poetry and Eloquence" (a refurbished older lecture) and his showpiece from Edinburgh, "Natural Aristocracy." By this audience Emerson perhaps redeemed himself in the eyes of Carlyle, who even graced the stage, and he doubtless gratified his London hosts, though not to the promised financial advantage.

A few days after the conclusion of his lectures at Portman Square, which apparently entailed much writing under pressure, the homesick Emerson wrote to Elizabeth Hoar, remembering that his pleasure was in his work: "I get ... many more good hours in a Concord week than in a London one. Then my *atelier* in all these years has gradually gathered a little sufficiency of tools & conveniences for me, & I have missed its apparatus continually in England; the rich Athenæum (Club) Library, yes, & the dismaying Library of the British Museum could not vie with mine in convenience And if my journeying has furnished me new materials, I only wanted my *atelier* the more" (*L*, IV, 88). Certainly the three popularly priced lectures he began two days later to a miscellaneous audience at Exeter Hall, sponsored by the Metropolitan Early Closing Association, required no preparation; the well-worn "Domestic Life" was sandwiched between the two favorites of the Representative Men series, "Napoleon" and "Shakspeare."

For Emerson the trip to England not only provided material for his wittiest book, *English Traits* (1856), and became a turning point in his popularity, but it also matured him, deprovincialized him, and brought him current with the intellectual tides of the mid-nineteenth century as his own study in Concord, the Boston Athenæum, and New York could not. He enjoyed his broadening social acquaintance and was quick to admire the cultural and intellectual brilliance of Edinburgh, London, and Paris, but he also assessed shrewdly the significance of British aristocracy and the strength and power of institutions. He was swept up in the excitement of the political crisis in England and the revolution in France. But these he judged from his own point of view. He gathered data, information, anecdotes, a record in his notebooks, and presented a colorful litany of social engagements and celebrities in his letters home to Lidian, mixing the account with his longing for the quiet sturdiness of Boston, Concord, and family. With the English notebooks and new lectures a more urbane Emerson brought home in July the old lectures on Representative Men, no longer useful on the podium and in need of revision, but now firmly destined for publication.

The new lectures—"Books," "The Superlative," "Natural Aristocracy," and three on "Natural History of Intellect"—Emerson revised for an American audience as an impressive series on Mind and Manners of the Nineteenth Century. Such old lectures as "Eloquence" and a refurbished "The Times," apparently pieced together in England from older material, could still be used selectively back home. And as a celebrated traveler he quickly evolved two lectures on England. With this stock he could manage an extensive and lucrative season from November 22, 1848, until May 2, 1849, including not only two lectures at the Boston Mercantile Library Association, but also a series of five at Boston's new Freeman Chapel. Furthermore, with little revision of the same stock of lectures, Emerson was able from December 12, 1849, to June 3, 1850, to lecture for a second season in scattered towns in New England, omitting Boston, Lowell, and Providence this year, and across the mountains for the first time to Cleveland and Cincinnati, the beginning of his career in the West. This strategy finally freed him in the summer and fall of 1849 to revise for publication the used-up course on Representative Men without the distraction of preparing new lectures.

1

Even before the earned free time of 1849, it is apparent that as early as October and November 1848 Emerson again found time to read in Plato, doubtless with the promised book publication in mind. In his journals he cited passages from the Taylor and the Cousin translations and entered a number of sentences from Thomas Stanley's *The History of Philosophy*. Because he could not accommodate James Freeman Clarke with a new lecture for the series at his new chapel, Clarke suggested that he read "Plato," perhaps knowing it was in process of revision; he furthermore offered Emerson the use of the chapel for the Mind and Manners series (*L*, IV, 119–121). A few days later, on November 8, Emerson borrowed from the Harvard College Library Friedrich Schleiermacher's *Introductions to the Dialogues of Plato*, Friedrich Ast's *Platon's Leben und Schriften*, and William Sewell's *An Introduction to the Dialogues of Plato*. We may suppose that the reading of "Plato" on December 4 is a revised version of the old lecture, but not yet its final form.

This early beginning of serious revision in late 1848 was interrupted inevitably by the new lecture season, postponing the important revisions for the book one last time. Even in May 1849, after the lecturing had ended, business and family matters claimed so much of his energy that Emerson was hard-pressed in turning to *Representative Men*. There were visitors—Aunt Mary, perhaps this time even in Emerson's house, Susan Emerson from Staten Island, and later William briefly—and Lidian was still "so feeble, this winter & spring," that Emerson engaged a housekeeper again. A pleasant diversion from work was the expanded social life offered in the formation of the Town and Country Club, a forerunner of the Saturday Club; at its meetings Emerson enjoyed the company of Ward, Cabot, Longfellow, Appleton, and others.

When he wrote his old friend Furness on December 16, 1848, Emerson may have recalled a similar but more sanguine letter in spring 1846, when he also could not spare prose for *The Diadem* because of the forthcoming book. Now *Representative Men* was more firmly promised than before; and with less enthusiasm than before about an early date, Emerson saw what problems were taking shape: "I hardly dare accept the opportunity you offer me of printing a chapter on Montaigne. All that I know, or, all that I know how to say, about him, is written in one of Seven Lectures, which, together, I call 'Representative Men'. . . I mean some day to print these together, whenever I shall have more adequately finished the resisting figures of Plato & Swedenborg" (Furness, p. 67). Yet there was one book promised ahead of it, though presumably without resisting figures. At the end of May 1849 he reported to William Emerson that he was "just reprinting" the long-planned *Nature, Addresses, and Lectures* and then would turn to *Representative Men* (*L*, IV, 149). But he was not to finish with it so readily; he felt the pressure of two literary projects as late as August 1, when the earlier collection was still a month away from publication: "Correcting MSS & proofs for printing, makes apparent the value of perspective as essential to good writing. Once we said genius was health; but now we say genius is Time" (*JMN*, XI, 139).

Emerson had not waited after all for the completion of his reprints before turning to the long-delayed lecture manuscripts. But as the expected leisure of summer approached, the serious problems defining themselves were met with an emerging sense of rashness and daring. He continued in his letter in May to William: when the volume of miscellanies is completed, "I hope to go to printing 'Representative Men,' if I dare. But who dare print, being unlearned, an account of Plato, or of Swedenborg, or, being uninspired, of Shakspeare? Yet there is no telling what we rowdy Americans, whose name is Dare, may do!" (*L*, IV, 149). There was still much work to do on "Plato" and "Swedenborg" and with bravado perhaps.

At the end of May and beginning of June, perhaps while waiting for his daughter Ellen to recover from mumps so that he could take her to Staten Island for a summer with William's family, Emerson began entries in journal TU reflecting his intended revisions of *Representative Men* (*JMN*, XI, 115ff.). On return from this trip, Emerson found he was chided for his absence by "four proof sheets [of *Nature, Addresses, and Lectures*] on my table & a do-little paddy in my garden, making it plain I should be at home" and continued with his interrupted plans, defining again his principal problems: "I have set myself a large stint of work in my library for this summer, and it will be good beyond hope if it should be well done: for, I suppose, I shall not dare to print on Swedenborg or Plato, unless I have additional lights, & who can look for them in three months?" (*L*, IV, 153).

The three months stretched into five, but Emerson's chief effort through the summer and fall of 1849 was the preparation of the Representative Men lectures for the press. Interruptions were minor. *Nature, Addresses, and Lectures* was published in September; at Worcester he was a speaker on August 3 to a large crowd gathered for the annual commemoration of emancipation in the British West Indies, but the address was brief, apparently extemporaneous, and must have distracted him from his work little if any. Lidian continued in poor health, and from time to time so did Ruth Emerson, whose two aging sisters paid an extended visit in the summer. It was a hot July, Emerson wrote, and he had to water his shrubs and small pear trees. The cholera became a national epidemic during the summer. There is a minimum of correspondence, but doubtless Emerson still found time to walk over Concord regularly with Ellery Channing, to socialize with the Town and Country group, and to write occasionally to Ellen in Staten Island. With no plans for new lectures in the next season, Emerson could work during the summer and fall with minimal interruption.

Emerson had agreed to meet deadlines in order to get the book on the market for the Christmas trade. On May 30 Phillips, Sampson & Co. wrote asking permission to announce as "in preparation" the new book "you had in view when talking with our Mr Phillips on the subject" (Houghton bMS Am 1280 [2534]). An agreement was drawn up and the announcement made. By August 18 Emerson, reluctant again to go to Staten Island to bring Ellen home, wrote of his schedule: "I hesitate to leave my writing table except on indispensable occasion before the end of October, as my 'Representative Men' must be ready for the printer about 20 Oct., which I interpret 1 November, & hardly dare certify for then" (*L*, IV, 157). The book was not finished on October 20, nor probably on November 1, though on October 10 Emerson still mentioned the latter as the expected date, suggesting that work was going well (*L*, IV, 167). On September 2 Alcott, visiting in Concord, recorded that after they returned from bathing at Walden, "Emerson reads to me the introductory paper to his book *Representative Men,* now nearly ready for the press, and we discuss Plato, Goethe, Swedenborg, and some others of his Representatives of the race" (*The Journals of A. Bronson Alcott,* ed. Odell Shepard, 2 vols. [Boston, 1938], I, 211–212). As late as October 28 Emerson acknowledged information he had asked for on the battle of Austerlitz from Edward Bangs, for which he could "hardly deny" himself "the ostentation of a note to enfol it in," but the footnote that in fact appeared in the text suggests that the information came too late (*L*, IV, 168, 169–170; see p. 135, below). Perhaps Emerson was already correcting proofs when he wrote on November 15, inviting George P. Bradford for a large Thanksgiving dinner: "I begin to see daylight through all the blottings of my book, which ought to be done, & Heaven to be thanked for, on the holiday" (*L*, IV, 170). And surely by November 29 there was festivity to mark the end, though a note from Phillips, Sampson & Co. on December 8 indicates that significant changes were still being made in proof: "Your proof and notes of today is at hand. We concur in opinion that 'Representative Men' *cannot* be published in time for 'Christmas.' Would therefore say, if 'important alterations' can be made by a little delay, that little had better be made;—and would not . . . in future make so much haste." A postscript announces the sending of "more proof today" (Houghton bMS Am 1280 [2535]). The "important alterations" remain an unidentified token of Emerson's care with the book that had taken five years to complete.

A few revisions were made to bring incidental contemporary allusions up to date, and as the manuscript that served as printer's copy for the Boston edition attests, there were stylistic improvements and corrections. Naturally enough, the introductory "Uses of Great Men" was, to judge by journal TU, revised or at least enriched in the fall of 1849. On the same evidence there was retouching of "Shakspeare" and "Montaigne," the latter in important passages; "Napoleon" and "Goethe" seem not to have been revised substantially. As Emerson had already indicated in letters, the resisting figures were Plato and Swedenborg, and revision of his lectures on them took, as he realized, intellectual daring. His difficulty, aside from not being a scholar of either in a strict sense, was that new material became available after he had written the lectures.

By late July 1849 Emerson had been reading "lately" the first volume of the new Bohn edition of Plato, translated by Henry Cary, and began to enter passages in his journal as he worked toward revision of "Plato" (*L*, IV, 155; *JMN*, XI, 135ff.). On August 18 the Boston bookseller James Munroe forwarded to him the second volume, translated by Henry Davis (Houghton bMS Am 1280 [2229]), and Emerson extended his work on Plato further, adding finally "Plato: New Readings" to address the matter directly, and continued his revisions of the original lecture. These new translations were enough to cause Emerson dissatisfaction or at least uneasiness about "Plato," though he abandoned neither Thomas Taylor nor, to judge by the newspaper account of his December 4, 1848, lecture, his own general conclusions about the philosopher. Cary, an Oxford scholar, initiated the new translations by declaring that the only previous complete edition in English, the one Emerson had used along with Cousin's French version, was inadequate: "Taylor's portion of the work is far from correct, and betrays an imperfect knowledge of Greek: that by Sydenham is much better, and evidently the work of a scholar, but in many instances, and these chiefly where difficulties present themselves, he obscures his author's meaning by too great amplification" ("Translator's Preface," I, vii). Based on solid Greek scholarship and with lucid, informative introductions and analyses that specifically undo the work of the Neoplatonists and present the texts as literary works, these first two volumes of the new standard translation were a popular challenge to the Plato Emerson had known. But, as we have seen, insecurity about the lecture on Plato antedates the publication of the Cary translation. Now, as Emerson pondered his own amateur abilities in late August or early September 1849, he was challenged by his erudite friend Theodore Parker. His answer, as he continued to rework "Plato," was characteristic: "Parker thinks, that, to know Plato, you must read Plato thoroughly, & his commentators &, I think, Parker would require a good drill in Greek history too. I have no objection to hear this urged on any but a Platonist. But when erudition is insisted on to Herbert or Henry More, I hear it as if to know the tree you should make me eat all the apples . . . and I believe fully, in spite of sneers, in interpreting the French Revolution by anecdotes, though not every diner out can do it" (*JMN*, XI, 149). If Emerson is not a Cambridge Platonist, he is, like Carlyle, a literary artist; he takes the promised name of "Dare," foreshadowed three months earlier in his letter to William, and finds himself still essentially committed to his earlier "Plato," even while incorporating passages from the new translation. "Plato: New Readings" is not New Views; it is acknowledgment of recent scholarship and an affirmation of Emerson's earlier conclusions.

The lecture on Swedenborg had been criticized as offensive to Swedenborgians, and ultimately to all Christians, and also, more particularly, for its interpretive errors about Swedenborg. If the lecture was to be made current, moreover, substantial volumes of Swedenborg's newly translated scientific work should be considered. The new publications had attracted a good bit of attention and in fact enlarged the aspect of Swedenborg that Emerson had been commended for noticing. In the summer and fall of 1845, while he was composing his lecture on Swedenborg, Emerson was reading the recently translated *The Animal Kingdom,* but he did not have in time for the first delivery the rest of Swedenborg's scientific works, which would make finally a considerable addition to the lecture. Such major works as *The Economy of the Animal Kingdom, Considered Anatomically, Physically, and Philosophically,* trans. Augustus Clissold, 2 vols. (London and Boston, 1845–1846) and *The Principia; Or, The First Principles of Natural Things, Being New Attempts toward a Philosophical Explanation of the Elementary World,* trans. Augustus Clissold, 2 vols. (London and Boston, 1845–1846) were sent as gifts to Emerson in December 1846 by Wilkinson on behalf of the London Swedenborg Association. The lecture on Swedenborg needed revision in preparation for the trip to England, and Emerson copied new material into his journals in 1847. But the principal revisions came in the fall of 1849, when he could turn to this still resisting figure, copying out more passages from his reading and drafting important paragraphs in his journals. He probably acquired Wilkinson's *Emanuel Swedenborg, a Biography* (Boston, 1849), a more authoritative source than those he had earlier at hand and a knowing treatment of Swedenborg's relevance in the modern world, as soon as it was published. The material Emerson incorporated in revision shifted his emphasis even more strongly than before toward the scientific Swedenborg, giving greater credit and authority to the Swedish mystic at the same time Emerson strengthened his own show of comprehensiveness in a difficult subject that had begun to exasperate him. In July he wrote: "I find what L[idian] read me this morning from 'Conjugial Love' to be in a Goody-Two-Shoes taste, the description of gold houses, & Sinbad Sailor fruit trees,—all tinsel and gingerbread." As revision came near its end, Emerson found Swedenborg "so painful that I should break with him forever but that I find him really scientific" (*JMN, XI,* 133, 179). Perhaps he was tiring of his subject. As in the case of "Plato," revision did not bring retraction. None of the offending passages, at least none of those noted in the attacks on the lecture, is missing from the printed book. He revised for completeness and authority. No Platonist, finally, and no Swedenborgian, Emerson remained daring, if not rowdy.

Representative Men missed the Christmas trade, but on January 1, 1850, *The Boston Daily Advertiser* announced that it was "received and for sale." Chapman's edition, printed from the transcription Emerson sent him, was published in London on or about the same day; a pirated edition appeared in London within the month; and this was followed by the Bohn edition, printed from revised sheets supplied by Phillips, Sampson & Co. As he habitually did, Emerson recorded in his journals complimentary copies, listing thirty-four to be given to family and friends. Longfellow's was inscribed and sent by a mutual friend on December 30, and the next day one was sent to William Emerson (Longfellow, *Life,* II, 154; *L,* IV, 174); others, like Elizabeth Hoar's, were dated December 1849. Emerson also recorded in his journal those to whom he asked Chapman to distribute copies: Carlyle, his brother John,

Wilkinson, and nine others; he noted that he "must add to the list by the next steamer" four he had forgotten, among them his friend Harriet Martineau (*JMN*, XI, 188–189).

Carlyle's response to *Representative Men,* seven months after its publication, praised it as "a most finished clear and perfect set of *Engravings in the line manner;* portraitures full of *likeness,* and abounding in instruction and materials for reflexion to me." But "Plato," the "most admired by many, did least for me: little save Socrates with his clogs and big ears remains alive with me from it." Although "Swedenborg" was "excellent in likeness," Carlyle found Emerson had failed to state the case: Swedenborg had "tumbled into Bedlam,—which is a terrible *miss,* if it were never so *near!*" Coming nearer to the divergence between Emerson's lectures and his own on heroes, Carlyle said, "In fact, I generally dissented a little about the *end* of all these Essays; which was notable, and not without instructive interest to me, as I had so lustily shouted 'Hear, hear!' all the way from the beginning up to that stage." Having just finished writing the bitter *Latter-Day Pamphlets,* Carlyle observed "what a deep cleft divides us, in our ways of practically looking at this world," but in a conciliatory offering he also saw "where the rock-strata, miles deep, unite again" (*CEC,* pp. 459–460).

Harriet Martineau's thanks came even later, and after two years she seemed not to remember the book distinctly. By contrast, Wilkinson's letter was prompt (February 8), specific, and extravagantly full, as Emerson must have expected from his thoughtful Swedenborgian friend. Having read the book "with delight a month ago," Wilkinson describes its high-flying effects on him: "It is for me full of vistas and views, a regular exhibition of the optics of the soul. You shew your men and things by new properties of light, hinting at all kinds of polarizations of these truths through which we see." The lecture on Swedenborg "will require some tough work at long arts and sciences" to reverse, but in the short run Wilkinson chides Emerson for dismissing the lower and unpleasant aspects of the spiritual world that Swedenborgianism incorporates. Even though there is no "finality in Swedenborg" and "the spiritual world is not absolute but fluxional or historical," his system cannot be disallowed merely because it is not comprehensive enough. Wilkinson concludes with humility about Emerson's allusion to him in *Representative Men,* which was the kind gesture in the original lectures that had initiated their correspondence four years earlier (Houghton bMS Am 1280 [3485]).

The new book was reviewed widely but not generously in Great Britain. A characteristic condescension is represented by *The Spectator* (January 12, 1850). First there is the common assertion that Emerson is a disciple of Carlyle, that this book is a rather weak derivative from *On Heroes, Hero-Worship and the Heroic in History,* and that the prose is but "a cultivated mannerism" compared to Carlyle's strong style. However, "As far as regards close and pointed expression, the present book may occasionally exhibit an improvement" over Emerson's earlier publications. "In other respects it makes no advance, if indeed it does not fall back. Paradox, which formerly was confined to particular ideas, now extends to whole sections of the book." But "Swedenborg," being the most informative, stands out as the best lecture despite being too laudatory. A week later *The Athenæum* faulted the oracular obscurity it found in the first three lectures and observed that "This unintelligibility is a thing to be seriously lamented in a writer who has a vein of pure and original thought underlying his verbal phantasies." After the lectures on Plato and Swedenborg the stylistic problem vanishes, apparently because Emerson is on top of his subjects. And the review is generous finally if admonitory: "The true ore is in this American:—its uses ought not to be lost to mankind through a fantastic and wayward fancy for wasting it in unsubstantial filagree work." A long lead article in *The British Quarterly Review* for May 1 was the heavy artillery. Aloof, kindly, and condescending, it took apart in learned, if witty, detail Emerson's scholarship lecture by lecture; for example, a long digressive show of the critic's own learning defended the truths of Christianity from Emerson's suggestion that Christianity is in Plato. Little is left to Emerson except his presumed good character and earnest intention.

Emerson's response to the English reviews centers on a repeated suggestion that *Representative Men* was a falling off. He was pained as he wrote: "The English journals snub my new book; as indeed they have all its foregoers. Only now they say, that this has less vigour & originality than the others. Where then was the degree of merit that entitled my books to their notice? They have never admitted the claims of either of them. The fate of my books is like the impression of my face. My acquaintances, as long back as I can remember, have always said, 'Seems to me you look a little thinner than when I saw you last'" (*JMN*, XI, 214–215). Nor could he have been especially pleased by the notice given his book by Émile Montégut, an early French admirer, welcoming the American to the company of Carlyle as a champion of individual greatness. Emerson's representative men lack true stature, however, in their easy grandeur, Montégut concluded, because Emerson's preference for the intellectual great man distinctly falls short of Carlyle's admiration for the more robust hero (*Revue des deux mondes*, August 15, 1850). Even so, the European response testified that Emerson's lecture tour, his celebrity, had not been without result: he was not ignored.

On this side of the Atlantic the positions had already been staked out and there were few surprises for Emerson. If sometimes his rhetoric was said to be murky and difficult, there were those who saw all too well his drift. In April 1850 *The Christian Review*, a Baptist quarterly, allowed that Emerson is a "man of unquestioned power, nay, of genius even," that "His style, . . . with some peculiarities and innovations in language, is uncommonly neat," and that *Representative Men*, a collection of lectures, contains "rather fewer positively objectionable statements of doctrine" than his other works because Emerson could not say face to face to an audience what he might say in an essay. These are concessions, however, and the article forcefully states conservative objections. Only Adam or Christ in a strict sense can be representative men; even so, Emerson has made weak choices—why not Aristotle or Bacon instead of Plato? Scott or Voltaire, instead of Goethe? Homer or Milton, instead of Shakespeare? "He quotes the Koran or the Vedas quite as often as the Bible, and with fully as much respect"; and Emerson is faulted for suggesting that the major religions are "cast in the same mould." Basically the recurrent theme of man's sufficiency without divine revelation is

Emerson's characteristic fallacy, but there are also minor revealing offenses: "Mr. Emerson can swear, too, it seems, in lectures delivered before polite audiences." Declining to quote, the review gives page numbers for any who "wish to study these pleasing amenities" (see pp. 16 and 88, below). Emerson has a "reprobate mind," and the review mocks him with his own words: "but forsooth, he belongs to that class of great men whose 'irregularities are not to be measured by village scales.'" Daniel March, a wittier Yale conservative, reviewed the book in *The New Englander* in May 1850 under the title "Popular Lectures," concluding that the lyceums ought to turn to practical truths rather than "the forced conceits of cloister criticism." He allows that "Napoleon," with the exception of a few "attempts at far-fetched theory, is quite as good as any thing" on the subject, but generally "the sketches have been drawn ... from a dim, uncertain, conception of an ideal character." The chief injury of the folly and wickedness in the book, like "bear-baiting, prize-fighting, and public executions," lies in its tendency to corrupt "the general morality, by familiarizing the minds of the many with things horrible and revolting." Emerson's daring originality is subtly dangerous, an argument that March warms to eloquently: "However sincere or unaffected Mr. Emerson may be in his ... own consciousness, he ... exhibit[s] himself ... [so] that his readers ... are fully justified in looking upon him only as a sort of intellectual Sam Patch, who makes it his profession to go about the world, leaping down precipices, plunging into abysses, in every deep seeking a still lower in which to expose himself for the sake of the applause and the pay ... And as the veritable Sam Patch has had an occasional imitator, so our oracular Sage, may sometimes secure a hearer who is simple-minded enough to suppose he is listening to the words of a prophet."

Among tasteful Unitarians in Boston, Emerson was no vulgar stuntman of the lyceum; they admired him and took him seriously as an important writer whose unorthodoxies they had come to tolerate if not accept. Cyrus Bartol in *The Christian Examiner* (March 1850) saw something of his daring stance when he observed that Emerson in "a sublime discontent ... takes the most adventurous positions, maintaining them by force, . . . by a defying statement and a soaring imagination." Bartol makes specific his moral and theological objection to this book but adds that the "mystic folds" would protect the public. Emerson's erroneous philosophy must be forgiven to some extent because of his character, integrity, and candor and in view of his brilliant prose, particularly in "Napoleon" and "Shakspeare." A month later Cornelius Conway Felton, in *The North American Review*, praised Emerson as "a great writer, and an honest and independent thinker, on the whole," but he is not, as "Some disciple" has written, a Phoebus Apollo. *Representative Men* has "the excellences and defects" of Emerson's other writings. Felton praises the style generally but finds passages which convey "no distinct sense" or are commonplaces "made to sound with the clangor of a braying trumpet," a stylistic influence of Carlyle, who is in every sense inferior to Emerson. Even allowing for the "vivid rhetoric," which is "perhaps due to the exigencies of the lecture form," there is a tone of exaggeration, particularly in the claims for Plato, whose "justice sanctioned perpetual bondage, and [whose] piety was not outraged by community of women, both of which were . . . ordainments of his ideal state." Felton concludes with Emerson's "striking peculiarity," again exhibited in this book—"his apparent indifference to positive religious belief, as shown by his manner of classing all beliefs together." Felton is shocked to think that "Mahomet and the Saviour are classed together as religious geniuses and reformers" or that "some . . . see nothing in the alliteration of 'Jesus or Judas' but a fine illustration of superiority to the prejudices of the world around them." Both of these Boston reviews are what Emerson had come to expect from the Unitarian establishment. They were written by friends who were making the best of the vagaries of his thought. They took his boldness seriously.

In the March issue of *The Massachusetts Quarterly Review* Theodore Parker had no problems with Emerson's religious or moral heresies. His comprehensive and generous review of Emerson's five volumes of prose and poetry is a substantial and important refutation of Emerson's critics—particularly those who argue his unorthodoxy, impiety, and threat to moral order. Parker criticizes his friend's want of logic, inconsistencies, excessive reliance on intuition, obscurity, exaggeration, and reckless and unlearned use of Oriental sources, but he concludes his retrospective by calling the graceful, Phoebus-like Emerson the best prose writer since Milton: "Reproached as an idler, he is active as the sun, and pours out his radiant truth on Lyceums at Chelmsford, at Waltham, at Lowell and all over the land." That Parker was not insensitive to the stylistic excellences of *Representative Men* is suggested by his generous use of passages from the new book for illustration. But Parker, still the ardent transcendentalist, has his preferences: "The last book . . . does not come up to the first Essays, neither in matter nor in manner. Yet we know not a man living and speaking English, that could have written one so good." He finds "Swedenborg" a "masterly appreciation" of a "great man" that "does not exaggerate" his merits; "Montaigne" he likes for similar reasons; "Shakspeare" and "Goethe" are "adequate and worthy of the theme." He is surprised that the lecture on Napoleon is silent on the Emperor's "legislative, organizing power," though "the other talents of Napoleon are sketched with a faithful hand." It is on "Plato" that the scholarly Parker turns pedant: "The lecture on Plato contains exaggerations not usual with Emerson; it fails to describe the man by genus or species. He gives you neither the principles nor the method of Plato, not even his conclusions. Nay, he does not give you the specimens to judge by. The article in the last classical dictionary, or the History of Philosophy for the French Normal Schools gives you a better account of the philosopher and the man." Emerson, who had known he could not satisfy Parker on Plato, may not have been prepared for this criticism, but he had been warned. Certainly he was pleased by his friend's general praise. Felton denied the Phoebus-like influence as an unwarranted piece of mythmaking, but Parker's hyperbole accorded with Emerson's own bold aspirations on the lecture circuit.

After the last days of correcting and revising proof, Emerson had expressed in his journals an understandable unsureness about the book: "Many after thoughts, as usual, with my printing, come just a little too late; & my new book seems to lose all value from their omission." He regretted that he had not stated Swedenborg's "most important defect, this namely, that he does not awaken ... the sentiment of piety." A more important omission was "the justice that should have been done to the unexpressed greatness of the common farmer & labourer" (*JMN*, XI, 192–193). A comment Emerson made three or four years later loses its force as criticism when read in its context: " 'Tis very costly, this thinking for the market in books or lectures: As soon as any one turns the conversation on my 'Representative men,' for instance, I am instantly sensible that there is nothing there for conversation, that the argument is all pinched & illiberal & popular." But this reflection on his most recent book, still selling well, is illustrative only, and Emerson quickly generalizes it into "Only what is private, & yours, & essential, should ever be printed or spoken. I will buy the suppressed part of the author's mind; you are welcome to all he published" (*JMN*, XIII, 141). The most telling second thought results from the popular excitement over Ernest Renan's *Vie de Jésus* (1863): "When I wrote 'Representative Men,' I felt that Jesus was the 'Rep. Man' whom I ought to sketch: but the task required great gifts,—steadiest insight & perfect temper; else, the consciousness of want of sympathy in the audience would make one petulant or sore, in spite of himself" (*JMN*, XV, 224). Nineteen years before, as he planned his lecture course on Representative Men, he had offered the same reason he should but could not write on "the world's chief saint" as representative man (*JMN*, IX, 139). This is not the book he wrote, however, and once in print Emerson contented himself with corrections and minor stylistic revisions of his most popular book to date.

Representative Men remained popular well into the twentieth century, partly because of its subject matter. But Emerson's turn from "the admirable science of universals" to "the best particulars," his bringing actual men into juxtaposition with the unrealizable Universal Man, has had its cost. "Uses of Great Men" had its place in the history of ideas; "Napoleon" and "Swedenborg" have been admired for their insights. But it is another quality in *Representative Men* that sustains its interest. In the planning stages, before the list of lecture topics had been finally fixed, Emerson wrote Carlyle on September 15, 1845: "I am to read to a society in Boston presently some lectures . . . if I dare, and much lecturing makes us incorrigibly rash. Perhaps before I end it, my list will be longer, and the measure of presumption overflowed" (*CEC*, pp. 381–382). In the revision of this first course of lectures he prepared for publication as a book, Emerson remembered his rashness and daring—the qualities of the lyceum desk, the eloquence of the lecture hall—and *Representative Men* preserves as no other of his books the freshness and freedom of the spoken word he aspired to. The book marks a new efficiency in his compositional methods as he began his long and successful career in the Midwest, lecturing almost each year for two decades to the edge of American cultural aspiration. His lectures henceforth were on this model, not the mines of his published essays but more the essays themselves—printable with revision. *Representative Men* displays Emerson at the height of his powers and freedom as a lecturer. If Emerson was pleased by Parker's likening him to Phoebus Apollo, pouring out "his radiant truths on Lyceums . . . all over the land," he might also have seen, deducting the scornful intention of a hostile reviewer, a fulfillment of his aspiration to eloquence in the comparison with the daredevil Sam Patch.

Statement of Editorial Principles

The intention of this edition is to provide for the first time critical texts of those works of Emerson which were originally published in his lifetime and under his supervision. The canon and order follow the physical arrangment which Emerson himself suggested in 1869 when he sent his first six volumes of prose to the printer as text for the first American edition of his collected prose. To this group have been added as volumes seven, eight, and nine respectively, *Society and Solitude, Letters and Social Aims,* and the *Poems,* in the positions assigned to them in all collected editions since they were first included in the Little Classic edition of 1876. One volume of the prose pieces published by Emerson but not collected in any permanent position by him replaces the three posthumous volumes of prose included in the Riverside and Centenary editions. The other material included in those posthumous volumes will be published in the separate edition of Emerson's later lectures, newly edited from the manuscripts used by James Elliot Cabot and Edward Emerson.

Adapting the theories of Sir Walter Greg to the particular problems of nineteenth-century American printed texts, the present edition is critical and unmodernized. It neither provides a reprint of any single earlier edition, nor limits itself to the authority of earlier editions.

The central editorial principles of this edition are that the copy-text is the text closest to the author's initial coherent intention and that determining his subsequent intention depends on the use of evidence from other relevant forms of the text according to conservative editorial principles. The rationale of copy-text assumes that in printed works each resetting is likely to introduce additional non-authorial corruption into the text, both in substantives and in accidentals.* The earliest feasible form, therefore, is normally chosen as copy-text. In cases where the manuscript or printer's proof has not survived, this edition chooses the first printed form as copy-text, except that magazine or newspaper publication of only part of an essay is not so used. When earlier forms, such as the printer's copy for *Representative Men,* have been chosen, the choice has been made on the argument that they better preserve Emerson's intention than the first published forms.

Each emendation of copy-text is carefully justified on the basis of error, as in obvious misprints, or on the basis of authorial intervention. In the case of variant accidentals there is generally no evidence on which to base emendation, and copy-text is usually followed, even though this means, in the case of printed copy-text, following much house styling. For substantive emendation clearer evidence is usually available, and this must be adduced to support the claims of authorial intervention and to exclude subsequent substantive variants which have no authority.

In practical terms there are three principal classes of evidence for emendation of copy-text: the author's handwritten corrections and revisions in extant texts; external authorial instructions concerning the text; and subsequent variants which correct, modify, add, or delete. The first and second classes apply to both substantives and accidentals. The third applies primarily to substantive emendation, and even so must be justified as authorial: known similar revision, context, kind of revision, and the like must be weighed as probabilities against non-authorial emendation (sophistication) or printer's error. All emendation, however, involves editorial judgment and responsibility; and these classes of evidence for emendation do not preclude the rare and judicious emendation of obvious and gross error or misprint overlooked by

---

* "Substantives" are the words themselves, the word-order, and any punctuation that affects the author's meaning or the essence of his expression; "accidentals" are matters of punctuation, spelling, word-division, capitalization and the like that affect mainly the formal presentation of the text.

the author and by printers, proofreaders, and editors in all relevant forms—on the assumption that the author did not intend such error, but with the proviso that the errors constitute impossibilities and not mere inelegancies or irregularities. In emendation, pre-copy-text forms and parallel passages from journals and lectures, as well as Emerson's established usage and preference, may cautiously be adduced as supporting evidence without diminishing the primary editorial responsibility.

In order to preserve a clear page, free of all subsidiary information except Emerson's own footnotes, the record of emendations and relevant variant readings is appended at the end of each volume in the textual apparatus. The list of Emendations in Copy-Text reports all changes made in copy-text, whether in accidentals or substantives, except for certain types of emendation made silently and explained in the prefatory remarks. A list of Rejected Substantives records those variants (including, in some cases, variants in spelling and word-division) which are not accepted into the present edition. Textual notes are introduced into those lists to justify editorial choices that require special explanation. Variants in the Riverside and Centenary editions are included in these lists even though those texts are not authoritative. Variants in British editions which are not authoritative are not normally included, although some are cited when they are of historical interest or when it is thought that they may throw some light on prepublication states of the text. Lists of line-end hyphenations (in the copy-text and in the present edition) are also included in the textual apparatus. Revisions in the manuscripts are recorded in those volumes where this is appropriate. Finally, the list of Parallel Passages from Emerson's other writings, although included primarily for other reasons, may also provide evidence for the solution of textual problems.

The Textual Introduction includes a history of the text, a bibliographic description of the work insofar as it bears on the establishment of copy-text, an explanation of any special editorial problems and practices relating to the particular volume, and the identification and location of those copies of the book actually used in the collation.

Textual Introduction

Like other volumes in *The Collected Works of Ralph Waldo Emerson*, this is a critical and unmodernized edition of its text. Unlike the first three, the fifth, and parts of the later volumes, it is based on manuscript rather than on a printed version: a manuscript entirely in Emerson's hand, complete (except for one paragraph to be discussed later), used as printer's copy for the first Boston edition of 1850, and now owned by the Buffalo and Erie County (New York) Public Library.[1] Its physical characteristics, including the signs that it was used in the printing office, and the author's alterations in it are described in Annex A and its appendixes. The present text corrects the manuscript's occasional errors and deficiencies in accidentals either from the 1850 or later editions, from Emerson's correction copy, or by editorial conjecture and incorporates from published editions all variants in sub-

1. When Phillips, Sampson and Company, the original publishers of *Representative Men*, went out of business in 1859, the manuscript was saved by Francis H. Underwood, a company employee and an acquaintance of Emerson's (later an editor on *The Atlantic Monthly*). His statement is now bound in the front of the manuscript: "This volume is made up of the Original Mss. sent to the press by the illustrious author. The handwriting is well known, and the autograph in the title page is a sufficient attestation. The Mss. were preserved by me, while in the employ of the publishers of the works of Emerson, Messrs Phillips, Sampson & Co. between 1853, & 1859. / Francis H. Underwood / Boston Dec. 7, 1873 —." There is no evidence whether Emerson was aware of this action. It was presumably Underwood who gave or sold the MS to James R. Osgood, from whose collection it was advertised for sale in March 1886 by William Evarts Benjamin, a New York dealer (for $500); and it was presumably bought from Benjamin by James Fraser Gluck, who gave it to the Buffalo Public Library in 1887.

stantives that are known or can reasonably be adjudged to be Emerson's own. Before the rationale for such changes in this volume can be made clear, it is necessary to describe the several versions of the text and their interrelations and to explain the reasons for selecting the manuscript as copy-text.

Versions of the text

The lectures and the manuscript. Emerson started writing the lectures which were to become *Representative Men* in 1845 (see Historical Introduction), and delivered them at various times from December 1845 until after his English visit of 1847–48. Many contemporary accounts and reminiscences of Emerson describe how he read his lectures from longhand scripts, sometimes rearranging the pages before he started (or even while he read), or combining parts of two or more lectures to make one. Evidently he wrote them in such a way that separate units of thought comprising one or more paragraphs occupied separate sheets (or groups of sheets) of paper, and sometimes he used a fresh sheet to begin a new unit of thought even if he had not completely filled the preceding sheet. Some of the extant manuscripts of his lectures, especially those before 1848, are written on double sheets of paper folded so as to make four-page folios, with additional single sheets occasionally inserted between or inside them (*EL,* I, xxiii).

No manuscripts of the Representative Men lectures, as such, are known to exist. However, it is possible that some leaves from them are incorporated into the extant manuscript of the book (referred to hereafter as "the Buffalo MS" or "the MS"). The MS was extensively revised on many pages before being sent to the printer; there is evidence that numerous pages (or groups of pages) were rearranged from their original order; and some pages on which there is little or no revision appear to be rewritten versions substituted for parts of an earlier draft, while other pages, though marked for complete deletion, remain in the MS. The numbering and renumbering of pages, together with a supplemental numbering system for four-page units (see the lists in Annex A), suggest that many pages, like those of the lecture manuscripts, are written on double sheets folded into four-page folios, while others are on single sheets inserted between or inside the double sheets. (This cannot be verified without removing the present binding, which the Buffalo Library is understandably unwilling to do.) This may indicate only that Emerson did most of his writing on such sheets, whether for lecturing or for publication. Further, a rather large number of paragraphs begin at the top of a recto page which (to judge from its numbering) is probably the first of a four-page group; and in many such cases the preceding verso page is partly or wholly blank. In one deleted passage (see entry for 25.18 in Appendix 2) Emerson says, "I have called these lectures biographical."[2] From these and similar indications it is likely that some parts of the MS, especially those with much revision or with renumbering of pages, may be fragments of the original lecture MSS.

In any case, the MS as we have it is quite clearly the one that Emerson submitted to his Boston publishers, Phillips, Sampson and Company, in late October or early November 1849 as printer's copy for the book which they hoped to publish in time for the Christmas trade. It thus represents the closest recoverable approximation to what at that time he intended to be published, although undoubtedly he would have wished his slips of the pen to be corrected and any missing punctuation marks to be supplied. To a considerable extent, and with a fairly high degree of accuracy in substantives (though not in accidentals), his wishes were carried out in the first American edition.

The Boston 1850 edition and its reprints. Emerson and his Boston publishers had set a target date of October 20, 1849, for delivery of the final copy; in a letter to his brother William on August 18, 1849, Emerson said he interpreted this as November 1, and in a letter to his London publisher John Chapman on October 10 he mentioned November 1 as the probable date (*L*, IV, 157, 167). He may have been a few days late, for on December 8 Phillips and

---

2. Since the sections of the book are called "Seven Lectures" on the title page of the first and later editions, this canceled sentence does not prove that the page was once part of a lecture manuscript, though it may have been.

Sampson, acknowledging receipt of corrected proofs, agreed that they would probably be unable to publish in time for Christmas as originally planned (*L,* IV, 171). Nevertheless presentation copies were ready late in December, and the volume was officially published on January 1, 1850, in an edition of 3500 copies, of which 68 went to the press for review and Emerson gave away 48.[3] Emerson retained ownership of the stereotype plates, for which (including the cost of typesetting) he paid $208.80. The book sold for a dollar a copy, on each of which Emerson received twenty cents. (The presentation copies cost him sixty-seven cents each, the wholesale price.) On July 1, 1850, he was paid royalties on 2201 copies sold, and on January 1, 1851, on another 931 copies. Further printings of 500 copies each from the same plates were issued by Phillips, Sampson and Company in 1852, 1854, 1855, 1856, and 1857, along with one of 250 copies on fine paper some time before 1857 (probably 1856).[4] Under the imprints of Emerson's later publishers, Ticknor & Fields and their successors (through Houghton, Mifflin & Company), additional printings continued to be issued to meet the demand, even after other editions were available; the latest one observed is dated 1882, by which time the original plates were badly worn.

The 3500 copies issued with an 1850 title page actually comprise two printings, which were probably run off at about the same time (*BAL* 5219; Myerson A22.1.a & b). The first has 290 pages, of which pages 285–286 are on an inserted leaf; it is on somewhat thinner paper than the second, has only one style of binding, and carries no advertising. The second has 288 pages (no inserted leaves) and three different styles of binding, and has publisher's advertisements on pages 287–288; one binding state also

3. For title page and description see Myerson, pp. 209–211. It is a twelvemo (in sixes). Subsequent printings bore the same title page except for the date and, after 1859, the publisher; but one printing was undated and carried the imprint: "BOSTON: | PHILLIPS, SAMPSON AND COMPANY. | NEW YORK: | JAMES C. DERBY." Evidence of plate wear shows that it was printed some time between 1852 and 1856.

4. Emerson's "Account Book 11 (Leger)," in the Houghton Library, Harvard University, pp. 23–25 (Houghton MS AM 1280 H.112j).

has advertisements on the endpapers. Machine-collation of five copies of the first printing and five copies of the second[5] revealed no variants that could be attributed to press-correction within or between printings except for a few repairs to damaged types and the correction of one error: namely, after "man" at the end of the last line on page 20 (9.31 in this edition), two copies of the first printing have a comma, which is incorrect, whereas the other three copies of this printing and all those of the second printing have the correct punctuation, a period.

The edition is on the whole a fairly accurate transcription of the substantives of the MS, especially considering the difficulties that must have been caused by Emerson's many revisions. There are a few errors in spelling and punctuation, but none that can be called pure "typos," such as bad spacing, turned letters, wrong font, and the like. There are over three thousand variations between MS and print, but the great majority are in accidentals, and most of these do not affect the meaning. Of the 139 variations in substantives, 24 are corrections of obvious slips of the pen (mainly repetitions or omissions of unimportant words), often caused by incomplete revision. The others are differences in the choice, form, or order of words, some of which affect meaning more than others. Some of these are almost certainly errors in typesetting that were not noticed in proofreading; others can with greater or less confidence be accepted as authorial proof-corrections.

The Weir transcript and Chapman's London edition. At some time while Emerson was preparing *Representative Men* for publication, he had a copy of it made by Elizabeth Weir, a professional copyist

---

5. Ten copies of the 1850 printings (nine in the Houghton Library, one from the *CWRWE* collection) were collated on the Lindstrand Comparator in the Houghton Library. The undated copy mentioned in note 3 and copies of the 1857 and 1881 printings, all in Widener Library (Harvard), were collated against a copy of the 1850 printing, some by machine and some by sight; and copies of the 1852, 1856, and 1876 printings (Heidelberg College Library, *CWRWE* collection, and Library of Congress, respectively) were sight-collated against a copy of the 1850 printing. Copies of the 1860, 1865, and 1871 printings (all Widener Library) were spot-checked but not collated.

who worked for him over a period of several years.[6] He may have intended to use this as printer's copy for his Boston publishers; if so, he changed his mind. During his visit to England in 1847–48 he had promised the British publication rights for his next book to his friend John Chapman. In August 1849, however, he learned that Phillips, Sampson and Company had without his knowledge made a similar arrangement with Henry G. Bohn. Emerson apologized to Chapman for being unable to keep his part of the bargain and said that he proposed to give "the MS" to Thomas Delf, a former employee of Chapman who had set up in business for himself, since it would no longer be of any use to Chapman (*L*, IV, 159–160).[7] Evidently Chapman persuaded Emerson that their agreement could still be carried out, for although he would not have the exclusive authorized English edition, he might at least have the first. On October 10 Emerson wrote that he would try to send Chapman part or all of the MS around the first of November, when he hoped to have his copy ready for Phillips, Sampson and Company (*L*, IV, 167). The MS he sent Chapman was almost certainly the Weir transcript (hereafter referred to as "WT"), since the Buffalo MS could not have been sent to both places at once. This action enabled Chapman to bring out his edition[8] on or close to January 1, 1850, the same day as the Boston edition and several weeks before Bohn's (*BAL*, III, 26).

6. Emerson's "Account Book 5" (Houghton MS AM 1280 H.112d, p. 55) records that on 1 January 1850 he paid Miss Weir $8.00 for copying *Representative Men*. If this was the only payment, her rate was a little over one cent a page; however, a month later he paid her $6.40 more for unspecified work (p. 63). For another job the following October she was paid by the day: $3.50 "for writing seven days at .50" (p. 106).

7. Emerson had known him as early as 1842, when Delf was working for publisher Wiley & Putnam in New York (*L*, III, 33, 41).

8. For title page and description see Myerson, pp. 215–217. Three copies were collated by sight (for substantive variants only) against 1850 Boston printing: one in the Houghton Library (Harvard), one in Lilly Library (Indiana), one in the University of Georgia Library. There were two issues, one designated The Catholic Series and the other undesignated; as far as can be determined without machine collation, they were printed from the same setting of type and have identical texts. In November 1850 Chapman paid

Although Chapman's edition is somewhat closer to the MS in accidentals than is the Boston edition, it is less so in substantives: it has almost three hundred substantive variants from the Boston edition, most of which are also variants from the MS. Probably many of these are the result of errors of copying in the WT, which, though no doubt a much cleaner (and perhaps more legible) copy than the Buffalo MS, was inevitably less accurate. Others may be due to errors by Chapman's printers in copying from the WT, and to the haste with which, in the race against Bohn, the book was being rushed into print. But still others resulted from the fact that Emerson continued to revise the Buffalo MS after the WT was made; numerous readings in Chapman agree with passages that Emerson changed or canceled before sending the MS to Phillips and Sampson. It is also likely (though this cannot be proved) that in glancing through the WT before sending it to Chapman, Emerson made a few changes in it which did not get into the Buffalo MS, but some of which he made again later while correcting proof. Although Chapman's edition has considerable interest and some value for textual analysis, it has no independent textual authority. No readings of the present edition are based on it except as confirmation of readings from other sources, and its readings are not cited in the Textual Apparatus except as supportive evidence.

The Bohn, Routledge, and Orr London editions. Little needs to be said about the other London editions of 1850 from a textual point of view. Bohn's edition was set from proof sent over by the Boston publishers.[9] Because it incorporates almost all the substantive changes from the MS, both correct and incorrect, made in the Boston edition, it must have been based on corrected proofs or revises (as Bohn claimed in his "Advertisment"). Thus, it provides no evidence of what was actually set in type by the Boston printers before Emerson corrected proof. It has about forty-five sub-

---

Emerson ten pounds ($50) for the manuscript (Emerson's "Account Book 5," p. 46).

9. For title page and description see Myerson, pp. 222–223. One copy was collated against Boston 1850 printing: University of Illinois Library.

stantive variations from the Boston edition, none of which agree with the MS. Most if not all of these are probably the result of compositorial errors made in the haste with which Bohn's men were working in the race against Chapman.

The edition published by Routledge in London between the other two is of no textual interest.[10] It has most of the substantive variants found in Chapman's text, plus a number of new ones of its own, but apparently none of those in Bohn's. It was obviously pirated from Chapman's edition. Curiously, neither Chapman nor Bohn but Routledge became the authorized English publisher of Emerson's next book, *English Traits.*

In 1851 a volume titled *Essays, Lectures and Orations,* a collection of all Emerson's prose works published previously in book form (except "New England Reformers" in *Essays, Second Series* and "The Young American" in *Nature, Addresses, and Lectures*) was issued by the London publisher William S. Orr.[11] Its text of *Representative Men* presumably was pirated from that of Bohn, as is shown by errors common (and exclusive) to the two editions.

Emerson's correction copy and the 1857 printing. The Houghton Library at Harvard has a copy of the first state of the 1850 printing (*AC 85.Em 345.849 rb(c)), on the front flyleaf of which is written, in Emerson's hand, "RWE / copy for Correction."; pasted inside the front cover is a sheet of paper headed *"Corrections. / Representative Men."* with a list of eight corrigenda. Seven of these, along with thirty-four others, are marked in the text itself, both within the lines where they occur and by proofreader's symbols in the margin alongside.[12] Four of those listed inside the front cover

10. One copy in Widener Library (Harvard) was examined and spot-checked but not fully collated. According to *BAL* (III, 26), it appeared less than three weeks after Chapman's; according to Myerson (pp. 219, 223), before Bohn's.

11. One copy in the Indiana University Library was examined and spot-checked but not fully collated.

12. In addition, the sentence "Each is selfdefended" at 16.35 is lined through in pencil, but without any deletion symbol in the margin or any other notation. The sentence is retained in this edition, since it is not clear that Emerson wished to delete it. The only correction listed inside the front cover

are also included in notes on the back endpapers. All the corrections appear to be in Emerson's handwriting. Of those in the text, some are in ink, some in pencil, and some in ink traced over pencil. The list in the front is in ink, the notes in the back in pencil. Eighteen of the forty-two revisions involve substantives. About one-third of the total restore the MS readings from errors in the 1850 edition; the rest are improvements in wording, word-division, punctuation, and minor accidentals.

Since Underwood's statement in the front of the MS (see note 1) makes it appear likely that the MS was never returned to Emerson, and since a number of errors in the 1850 edition are not noted in the correction copy, the author probably did not make a systematic check through the whole volume—much less collate it against the MS—but only marked those points that he noticed while browsing in it or that were pointed out to him by others. He may have made the entries at various times, for some of the corrections were adopted in the 1857 printing, some in the 1870 edition, one (perhaps by coincidence) in the posthumous Riverside edition, and several in no edition before the present one. I doubt whether this is the same copy of *Representative Men* that Emerson sent to Fields, Osgood & Company on July 26, 1869, as one of the "six volumes corrected for the press" (*L,* VI, 78); if it was, it was returned to him, for at least one correction must have been made after that date. In three places—the list in the front, the text itself, and a note in the back—he directed that a sentence at 88.1 (see Emendations) be deleted, and in each entry gave as his reason the fact that he had used it on page 286 of *Society and Solitude,* a book not published until 1870. I also doubt whether this copy was consulted during the preparation of the 1876, Riverside, or Centenary editions. On the assumption that all the corrections not adopted in 1857 and 1870 (or the later editions) were made after

---

that is not marked in the text is the insertion of quotation marks around "said Glauco" at 36.31. Emerson listed two typographical errors for correction in his "Index Major" (Houghton MS AM 1280 H.106), pp. 94–95: "satifaction" at 131.29, which is also noted in the correction copy, and "inportation" at 76.9, which is not.

the 1870 was printed, all of them (except the deletion mentioned in note 12) are accepted as emendations in the present edition.

The stereotype plates of the 1850 edition were corrected for the 1857 printing to incorporate thirteen of Emerson's corrigenda; and these were only such as could be made without changing more than a single line of type in any one place. All but three changes are substitutions, deletions, or additions of single letters or punctuation marks. Except for repair of damaged type in a few places, these are the only changes made in the 1857 printing, and no other changes, except those caused by wear or batter, have been found in any earlier or later printings from these plates.

The 1870 (1869) edition. In October 1869, but with the date 1870 on the title page, Fields, Osgood & Company (successors of Ticknor & Fields, who had become Emerson's publishers in 1859) brought out an edition of the prose works in two volumes, based on copies of earlier editions in which Emerson had made corrections. *Representative Men* occupies the first third of Volume Two.[13] This was the first new setting of type for the book in almost twenty years. It incorporated all but one of the changes made in 1857 (a faulty comma after "man" at 6.36 crept back in), and sixteen more of the corrigenda that Emerson had noted in his copy of the 1850 printing. Many other changes were made. Among accidentals, for example, "everything," "anything," and some similar compounds, generally written as one word in the MS but printed as two in 1850, are printed as one word here; and most words ending in "-ise" or "-ize", often spelled with "s" in 1850, are spelled here with "z." Emerson had made some of these

---

13. THE | PROSE WORKS | OF | RALPH WALDO EMERSON. | *NEW AND REVISED EDITION.* | IN TWO VOLUMES. | VOL. II. | [*Device*] | BOSTON: | FIELDS, OSGOOD, & CO. | 1870. It is a twelvemo of 491 pages, *Representative Men* being pp. 3–155 inclusive. Three copies of 1869 printing were collated against 1850 edition: Houghton Library (Harvard), Cincinnati Public Library, and Wilson collection. One copy of 1875 printing (*CWRWE* collection) and one copy of 1879 printing (Duke University Library) were machine-collated against 1850 edition, and Wilson and *CWRWE* collection copies were machine-collated against each other. A copy of the 1883 printing (*CWRWE* collection) was spot-checked.

changes in his correction copy, but not consistently; those in the 1870 edition may have been directed by him or may be the result of house style. As for substantives, not counting those marked in the correction copy, 1870 has thirty-two changes from 1850. Some are obvious errors, such as "beasts" for "leasts" at 64.27; some are corrections of errors, such as "axles" for "axes" at 63.23; others may be the author's revisions to improve style or clarify meaning, such as "no one else" for "no one" at 41.3. The majority, however, though they could be authorial changes, look more like compositors' errors or editors' sophistications. Emerson probably corrected proofs for this edition (see *L*, VI, 83, where "errata" may refer either to proofs or to previous editions used as printer's copy), though probably less carefully than he had done in 1850.

Printings from the electrotype plates of this edition continued to be issued as late as 1883 (a third volume, containing works first published after 1869, was added in 1879), but no variants have been found in them except those resulting from wear on the plates.

The 1876 edition. James R. Osgood and Company (successor to Fields, Osgood) brought out a collected edition of Emerson's works in nine small volumes in 1876, *Representative Men* being Volume IV.[14] It was known as the Little Classic edition, a general title that Osgood was using for similar editions of several of his popular authors. Although this edition is a new setting of type, it follows the 1870 *Prose Works* very closely in both substantives and accidentals, introducing only nine new substantive variants. Emerson saw the proofs of at least some volumes of this edition

---

14. For description, see Myerson, p. 225. This is bound as an octavo, but is signed as both octavo and twelvemo. The first printing was 1500 copies. Two copies of 1876 printing were collated against 1850 edition: Houghton Library (Harvard) and Library of Congress. One copy of 1878 printing was spot-checked: Houghton Library. One copy of 1879 printing was collated against 1850 edition: *CWRWE* collection. The same plates were used for the five-volume Fireside Edition of 1879 (for description, see Myerson, p. 547), in which *Representative Men* was the first half of Volume II. One copy was collated against 1850 edition: Widener Library (Harvard). One copy of 1882 printing was spot-checked: Widener Library.

(see *CW*, I, xxxvii), but because of his age and declining ability to concentrate, much of the work may well have been done by his daughter Ellen. Some of the new variants look more like editorial sophistications than authorial revisions: for instance, "Asia is" for "Asia are" at 31.5, and "beast are not" for "beast is not" at 70.31. For these reasons all these variants have been viewed with skepticism, and only a few have been adopted in the present edition.

The electrotype plates of 1876 were used not only for later printings in the same format but also for an edition of the collected works in five volumes, in which *Representative Men* shared Volume II with *Society and Solitude.* No variants have been found in any printings of either of these editions except those caused by the usual plate wear.

The Riverside and Centenary editions. Soon after Emerson's death James Elliot Cabot prepared a new collection of the works for Houghton, Mifflin and Company (successor to Osgood), the Riverside Edition of 1883–93 in twelve volumes, with *Representative Men* again as Volume IV.[15] Cabot seems to have used as his copytext the 1850 edition—probably a post-1857 printing of it, since he adopted most of the 1857 variants, even deleting the comma at 6.36 which had reappeared in 1870. He also adopted many (though by no means all) of the substantive variants in the 1870 and 1876 editions, probably using a copy of 1876 for reference. Besides these, some of which were almost certainly not by Emerson originally, the Riverside introduced thirty-four new substantive variants of its own, none of which have any textual authority. A few are printer's errors, such as "knowing not" for "not knowing" at 134.18; but most are Cabot's attempts to correct or improve Emerson's grammar or his Greek, or to clear up what seemed to him obscurities (see the RSS entry for 38.33). In accidentals he modernized spelling and punctuation, but generally

15. Eleven volumes were published in 1883–84; the twelfth, *Natural History of Intellect,* was added in 1893, having been first issued in the Little Classic Edition. In *Representative Men,* a few corrections were made in the plates between 1884 and 1886, only five of which are substantive. All these changes restored the readings of the MS and all early editions, and were followed in the Centenary Edition; the same is true of all but one of the thirteen variations in accidentals.

followed the 1850 edition in word-division and some other details; his punctuation, because it is so much lighter than that of all the earlier editions, is often closer to that of the MS than any of them. He does not seem to have been aware of Emerson's correction copy, for he used only those corrections that had already been adopted in 1857 and 1870, and one other (the quotation marks before and after "said Glauco" at 36.31), which he could easily have made independently.[16] Although the Riverside is not a critical edition by modern standards, it is carefully edited and has fewer errors than most late-nineteenth-century editions of earlier American authors.

The Centenary Edition of 1903–04, also in twelve volumes with *Representative Men* as Volume IV, was edited for Houghton, Mifflin by Emerson's son Edward. Although very valuable for its explanatory notes, it is of no interest textually, being a close copy of the Riverside. Apart from a few variants in accidentals, such as the correction of French accents at 5.10 and 92.30, it introduces only four new substantive variants, two of which are certainly printer's errors ("round" for "ground" at 151.15 and "mine" for "mind" at 153.13), as the other two probably are. This text has been the basis for almost all subsequent editions of and selections from Emerson's works, although in many important respects it is the furthest from what he actually wrote.[17]

16. In a letter called to my attention by Nancy Craig Simmons (Edward Emerson to Cabot, 5 June 1883, Houghton bMS Am 1280.226 [270]; and see Simmons, "Arranging the Sibylline Leaves: James Elliot Cabot's Work as Emerson's Literary Executor," *SAR* [1983], pp. 335–389, esp. p. 365), Edward Emerson wrote that he was sending Cabot a copy of the Little Classic edition of *Representative Men* which had authorial changes on pages 43 and 159. The only variation in the Riverside Edition volume in the parts of its text that correspond to those pages in the Little Classic volume, other than minor punctuation variants, is the change from "John of Meun" to "John of Meung" at 114.1. Since Emerson spelled this name both ways (see *JMN*, IX, 51, and *EL*, I, 284), the alteration may have been his. In the absence of certainty, however, I have retained the MS spelling in the present text.

17. The Signet Classics *Selected Writings of Ralph Waldo Emerson*, ed. William H. Gilman (New York: New American Library, 1965), uses the 1870 edition as copy-text for all the essay selections except the two not included in 1870. Only one is from *Representative Men.*

The relationships of the different versions of the text to one another are shown in the accompanying diagram. Solid lines are drawn around extant versions, dotted lines around those no longer extant. Dates within parentheses are those of reprints as distinct from new editions. Question marks indicate uncertainty as to which edition or printing was used as copy-text.

Choice of copy-text

For some authors a good case can be made, when a holograph manuscript exists, for using a printed edition—normally the first—as the copy-text for a critical edition. The argument, as presented by Philip Gaskell, is that "most authors . . . expect their spelling, capitalization, and punctuation to be corrected or supplied by the printer, . . . implicitly endorsing [the process] (with or without further amendment) when correcting proofs."[18] This is true, for example, of Byron, whose principal stop was the dash and who gave his friends and publishers carte blanche to punctuate his writings as they saw fit. It is not true of Mark Twain, who had been a printer himself, knew exactly how he wished his books printed, and, when told that a proofreader was "improving" his punctuation, ordered his publisher to have the man taken out and shot without time to say his prayers.[19] Emerson, it seems to me, was somewhere between those two extremes, and a little closer to Twain's end of the spectrum, though no doubt less violent.

He was generally a careful, if not always consistent, speller and punctuator. Sometimes when writing rapidly he neglected to put in all the commas, periods, and quotation marks; sometimes in revising the MS he failed to change all the capital letters and

18. *A New Introduction to Bibliography* (New York and Oxford: Oxford University Press, 1972), pp. 338–343; words quoted on p. 339. See also James Thorpe, *Principles of Textual Criticism* (San Marino, Calif.: The Huntington Library, 1972), pp. 164–170, 192–193, for a similar view.

19. Thorpe, *Principles*, pp. 145, 147; see also *Byron's Letters and Journals*, ed. Leslie A. Marchand (Cambridge, Mass.: Belknap Press of Harvard University Press, 1973–1982), passim, esp. letters to John Murray, Byron's publisher.

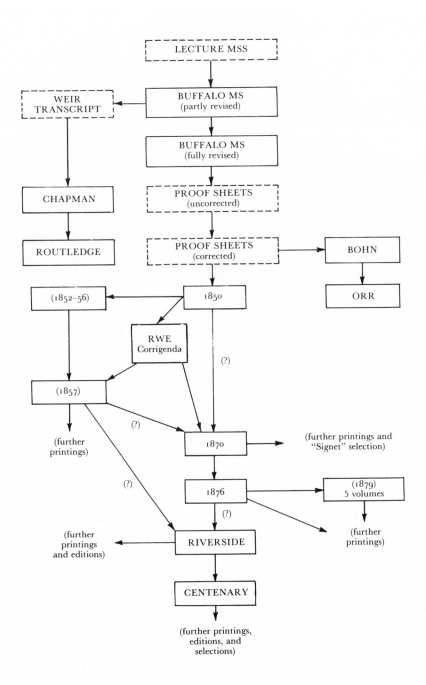

end-stops to fit the new sentence structure. Otherwise, however, the Buffalo MS needs very little correction in its accidentals. Emerson had a punctuation system which, though somewhat unorthodox, he understood and generally followed. William H. Gilman describes it thus: "use of a single comma between subject and verb, commas around restrictive as well as nonrestrictive clauses [I would modity this to read: a comma after but not before a restrictive relative clause], a comma between a verb and a noun clause introduced by *that,* and a comma after a coordinating conjunction, like *and,* or *for.* . . . Obviously they reflect Emerson's sense of the proper rhythm of his sentences, of the kinds of pauses and emphases he felt as he wrote, or as he read what he had written."[20] He also had a principle for deciding whether to use a colon or a semicolon, and sometimes changed from one to the other in revising the text. His spelling, word-division, and capitalization, though somewhat old-fashioned and not always consistent, are for the most part "correct" or at least acceptable by the standards of his time, as shown in contemporary dictionaries and in citations in the *OED;* like his punctuation, they reflect the way he used the language. As a modest man, Emerson may have thought that the professionals understood these matters better than he, and as a peaceful man he probably felt that his commas and semicolons were not worth fighting about so long as his meaning was clear. He may have accepted without protest the three thousand changes the printers made in his accidentals. The proofs are not available, so we have no way of knowing how many others he did not accept, or whether any of the three thousand were his own. But we cannot assume that he was indifferent to the matter: four-sevenths of the changes he marked in his correction copy were of accidentals—some to restore the correct MS reading, others to make the meaning clearer or to improve the rhythm of the sentence. He did the same thing in the correction copies of several of his other volumes.

20. *Selected Writings,* ed. Gilman, p. xxxiii. Gilman used 1870 as his copy-text because he thought it was closest to Emerson's final intentions in both substantives and accidentals. He does not mention the MS of this volume.

The style of punctuation favored by the publishers and/or printers of the 1850 edition is exceedingly fussy and heavy. They usually set off with commas prepositional and participial phrases, which Emerson did not normally do. Then to mark the stronger pauses they often changed Emerson's commas to semicolons or colons. They changed many of his semicolons to colons and vice versa, usually without any apparent reason. Although they deleted a few of Emerson's commas, the net result was to add a great many more than they subtracted. They kept most of the features mentioned by Gilman, but overlaid them with a system of their own. A single illustration will suffice to show the difference. At 39.18 Emerson wrote: "When an artificer in the fabrication of any work looks to that which always subsists according to *the Same* and employing a model of this kind expresses its idea and power in his work, it must follow that his production should be beautiful." The present edition inserts a comma after *"Same"* to improve clarity and to conform with Emerson's usual practice. But the 1850 edition printed the sentence thus, changing the rhythm and slowing down the tempo: "When an artificer, in the fabrication of any work, looks to that which always subsists according *to the same;* and, employing a model of this kind, expresses its idea and power in his work; it must follow, that his production should be beautiful."

In deciding in favor of using the MS as copy-text, we have listened to Emerson's own words in "Goethe" (162.25): "But, through every clause and part of speech of a right book, I meet the eyes of the most determined of men: his force and terror inundate every word: the commas and dashes are alive; so that the writing is athletic and nimble, can go far and live long." We believe that he would have preferred to stand on his own commas and dashes, which, though sometimes a little eccentric, are more alive than those of his printers.

Special editorial problems

Most of the problems encountered in editing this volume are covered by the Statement of Editorial Principles. Some particular applications of those principles in the circumstances surrounding the writing and publication of *Representative Men,* however, should be clarified. They are concerned chiefly with those accidentals of the MS that call for emendation in a critical edition; with the rationale for emendation (or nonemendation) of substantives where the variants cannot be shown by external evidence—such as that of Emerson's correction copy—to be authorial; and with unexplained cases of textual agreement between the 1850 Boston and Chapman editions against the MS.

Emending accidentals of the MS. Although the MS comes closer than any printed edition to Emerson's intentions, it does not always represent what his final intentions for a published version would have been, even at the moment he sent it to the publishers. Because he was working to meet a deadline, he probably did not give it the careful scrutiny it would have needed to make it suitable for exact reproduction as a printed text. He knew that the printers would automatically render his thousands of ampersands as "and" and would put periods at the ends of sentences if he had omitted them. These and a few other types of emendation are made silently in this edition and are listed in the prefatory section of the Textual Apparatus; in almost all such cases the reading of the 1850 edition is followed.

Other emendations are more debatable, and when made in this edition are always recorded in the Apparatus. Orthography, for example; when should we correct Emerson's spelling? Ordinarily we do so only when no eighteenth- or nineteenth-century authority can be found for the form he uses, or when it is contrary to his usual practice. For example, "achievments" (55.35) is emended to "achievements"; but "zodiack" (8.14), "instructer" (9.13), "ideot" (14.25), and "guaged" (35.9) are retained. Most words ending in "-ise" are regularized to "-ize" because Emerson changed one of them this way in his correction copy, and because it is sometimes hard to tell whether the MS has "s" or "z" in these words. (They were generally spelled with "z" in 1870.) Some foreign words are changed to conform with standard usage in their own language—capitals for German nouns, accents in French and Greek—since Emerson often made such corrections in his MS, and would presumably have done so in all cases if he had noticed the error.

In revising the MS Emerson sometimes failed to make all the changes necessary, especially in punctuation and capitalization; in such cases a period is followed by a small letter, or a comma by a capital, often with deleted matter between them. Sometimes a word that seems necessary for the meaning is deleted, no doubt accidentally, or a word at the end of a line (or page) is repeated at the beginning of the next. In these cases we always attempt to print what we think Emerson intended, which may or may not be the version in the 1850 edition, and record the emendation in the Apparatus.[21]

Emerson's handwriting in the MS is quite clear, and there is almost never any doubt about what letters are intended. However, with certain initial letters (especially "c," "o," "v," and "w," and sometimes "a," "e," "g," "m," "n," "p," and "s") it is hard to distinguish between Emerson's capital and lower-case forms. It can also be difficult to determine whether some compounds are intended as one word or two. Often the words (or elements of the word) are linked together or written closer together than other words in the same line; in other cases they are run together but spaced more widely; sometimes neighboring words obviously not intended to be printed as one word are linked in the same manner as the compounds. Editorial decisions in such cases are based on Emerson's customary usage elsewhere in this MS or in his journals, lectures, or letters of the same period, or on his probable intention as suggested by the context. The form adopted is often but not always that of the 1850 edition, except that hyphens are not inserted (as they often are in 1850) in compounds which do not have them in the MS. New paragraphs sometimes are, or appear to be, marked in the MS (by indentation, spacing between lines, or the sign ¶) but are not so divided in the 1850 edition; or the reverse situation occurs. Here editorial decisions are made on the basis of what seems to be the organization and structure of Emerson's ideas in the passage.

21. For the treatment of certain punctuation marks in deleted passages, see the prefatory section of Annex A, Appendix 2.

Adoption or rejection of substantive variants. The only substantive emendations about whose authority one can be certain are those which Emerson himself made in his correction copy. It is even possible that he changed his mind about some of these; nevertheless, with but one exception, all are adopted in this edition. Since no proofs of any edition of this book printed in Emerson's lifetime are known to exist, we cannot be sure which changes in those editions were his, though we can be reasonably sure of some. When "his book on mines" (57.1) in the MS becomes "his Dædalus Hyperboreus" in 1850, the chances are about one in a million that a compositor or copy-editor would have made such a change on his own. And when "ascribed to it" (133.24) in the MS and 1850 becomes "ascribed it to" in 1870, the resulting nonsense cannot be ascribed to Emerson. But between those extremes are many variants for which an editor must rely on logic, common sense, or intuition.

Some general principles can help in solving these problems.[22] One may be called the principle of similarity: the greater the similarity between the variants, the less likely that the change was made by the author. Indifferent variants like "hands" (5.1) in 1850 for MS "hand," or "meanness" (53.9) in 1870 for MS and 1850 "meannesses," are rejected because they are probably due to misreading of the copy-text. On the other hand, 1850's "excellent" (62.36) for MS "admirable" could hardly be a misreading and is accepted as very likely an authorial change. Some words that do not look at all alike in print may be quite similar in the handwriting of a particular author; thus, such variants in 1850 as "spread" for "opened" (26.18) and "freezing" for "sneering" (102.28) are rejected because they could easily be misreadings of Emerson's hand.

Another principle which an editor may use is that of unfamiliarity, or the more difficult reading. That is, if an unusual word in a manuscript or early edition is replaced by a more common one in a later version of the text, the change was more likely made by an editor or compositor than by the author; conversely, a change

22. For the identification of the principle of similarity, I am indebted to Charlyne Dodge, textual editor of the Harold Frederic Edition.

from a more common to a less common word or form is more likely to be the author's. 1850's "practical" (23.6) for MS "practick" and 1870's "established" (60.32) for MS and 1850 "stablished" are therefore rejected as probably not Emerson's.

The principle of eye-skip can be helpful in cases of omitted material, especially when one can see the printer's copy from which an edition was set, as is possible here. When several successive phrases or clauses begin or end with the same word, the compositor sometimes omits one of them; thus, "with customs," at 100.23, the fifth of a series of seven phrases beginning with "with" in the MS, is not in the 1850 edition. Similarly, when two lines in succession (or close together) begin or end with the same word, the compositor's eye may skip from one to the other. An interesting variation on this occurs at 71.12, where "his greatest and most perfect" in the MS is reduced to "his perfect" in 1850. This apparently happened because in the MS "his" is the last word on one page, the first half of the first line on the next page is deleted, "greatest and most" occupies the second half of that line, and "perfect" begins the second line. The compositor, seeing the deletion, skipped over the undeleted part of the first line as well.

The principle of improvement is difficult to apply, for changes that improve grammar, style, or clarity of meaning may be made either by the author or by an editor or compositor. At 14.25 the 1850 reading "not a mowing idiot" seems idiomatically preferable to the MS "not the mowing ideot"; but since the source passage in Emerson's journal has "the" (although with a slightly different wording), it is retained. On the other hand, "enlargements are purchased" (76.37) in 1870 as a change from "enlargements purchased" in the MS and 1850 is not needed for either grammar or clarity; however, it does improve the rhythm and style of the passage and therefore seems more likely to be Emerson's.

Agreements between the Boston and Chapman editions. Because there is only one agent of transmission (the Boston compositor[23]) between Emerson and the Phillips, Sampson and Company edition,

23. I refer to compositor in the singular, although there were several, because for any one reading only one compositor was involved. For their accuracy, see Annex A, Appendix 1. Nothing is known about the compositors who set Chapman's edition, or about Weir's accuracy.

but two (Weir and the London compositor) between him and Chapman's edition, the Boston edition has superior textual authority. In every case, therefore, where the Boston edition (hereafter referred to as "B") and the MS agree against Chapman's edition (referred to as "C"), the MS/B reading is retained.[24] Where the MS and C agree against B, however, the case is not so clear, for the B reading may be either an error or a change made by Emerson in proof; each such case must be decided on its merits. Examples are "excellences" (MS/C): "excellencies" (B) at 32.32, where the MS/C reading is retained, and "help" (MS/C): "skill" (B) at 63.12, where the B reading is adopted, both under the principle of similarity. There are no cases where all three versions have different readings, except in accidentals, such as "Kreeshna" (MS): "Krishna" (B): "Kreshna" (C) at 97.33, where the B reading is adopted because it is Emerson's usual spelling.[25]

Agreements between B and C against the MS are harder to explain than the other combinations. It is possible that after sending the original MS to Phillips, Sampson and Company, Emerson looked through the WT before mailing it to Chapman and made a few last-minute changes, some (or perhaps all) of which he also made when correcting the proofs of B. The fact that the majority of the B/C agreements occur in the last thirty pages of the book suggests that he may have sent the WT to Chapman in install-

24. This includes cases where C agrees with an uncorrected or now-deleted version in the MS, and B agrees with the corrected or final version. However, there are two cases in which C introduced changes that agree with those Emerson made later in his correction copy (and in the 1857 printing): "charlatanism" for "charlatan" at 50.13, and "which sees . . . and asks" for "who see . . . and ask" at 119.16. Both these improvements could have occurred independently to Emerson and Chapman. A more likely explanation is that these were both changes that Emerson made in the Weir transcript but not in his printer's copy or proofs of B, and that he made them again in his correction copy and in the 1857 printing, as well as in the 1870 *Prose Works*.

25. There are cases where three different versions of one sentence are found; on analysis these are seen to be combinations of two or more different two-versus-one agreements.

ments, and made these changes only in the final one.[26] A few cases may result from independent correction by both B and C (editor or compositor) of an obvious error in the MS. For example, at 34.6 "analytic" (MS) is replaced by "analysis" (B/C) because "analytic" is inconsistent in form with the other words in the context. Emerson's revision of the passage, though incomplete, showed what he intended; however, it did not make clear the order of words in the list, which is different in B and C because of ambiguous interlineation.[27] Likewise, some B/C agreements may be due to indtependent identical error by two agents of transmission: the B compositor and either Weir or the C compositor.

These hypotheses do not easily account for all the anomalous agreements. At 153.21 where the MS has "mesmerism, or phrenology," B has "mesmerism, or California," and C has "mesmerism, phrenology, or California"; the MS and C agree in retaining "phrenology," but B and C agree in adding "California." A similar case is at 165.30, where the MS has "that side," B has "that side; (namely, of Paris.)," and C has "that side (of Paris.)." Since none of these changes are likely to have been made by anyone but Emerson, the B readings, which presumably represent his latest thoughts, are adopted in this edition. Probably, in correcting the proofs of B, Emerson remembered that he had made changes in the Weir transcript at these points, but did not remember exactly what they were.

Another such problem is the omission from the MS of a whole paragraph (94.5–11) which appears in both B and C with only one slight variation (an error in C). Here the explanation is probably bibliographical. The missing paragraph could have been written on a single leaf of paper and inserted between pages 46 and 47 of the "Montaigne" section of the MS; it would probably

26. They are adopted in this edition and recorded under Emendations. A few cases occur earlier in the volume, and may perhaps be explained in the same way.

27. Weir must have been responsible for this incorrect word-order in C. But probably she did not change "analytic" to "analysis"; if she had noticed that "analytic" was an error, presumably she would have called it to Emerson's attention, and he would have corrected the MS.

have been numbered 46½ and (if the verso was used) 46⅔. On page 47 only one sentence is written; this has been deleted and re-written without change (except for the addition of a comma) at the bottom of page 46 in a smaller handwriting. The only apparent reason for the transfer is that Emerson wished this sentence (the last in its paragraph) to precede the new paragraph that he was adding. The paragraph was routinely copied by Weir (and thus got into C), and the original was sent to the printers of B along with the rest of the MS. Presumably after printing it somehow fell out and was lost.[28]

Decisions on such substantive points reduce themselves ultimately to the editor's judgment (or hunch) about what agency was the cause of each variation. Since these judgments may not always be correct, all relevant evidence is presented in the Textual Apparatus so that each reader may make his own decision.

28. Although there is only circumstantial evidence for this theory, it seems to be the only one that fits all the facts.

USES OF GREAT MEN

I

Uses of Great Men

It is natural to believe in great men. If the companions of our childhood should turn out to be heroes, and their condition regal, it would not surprise us. All mythology opens with demigods, and the circumstance is high and poetic, that is, their genius is paramount. In the legends of the Gautama, the first men ate the earth, and found it deliciously sweet.

Nature seems to exist for the excellent. The world is upheld by the veracity of good men. They make the earth wholesome. They who lived with them, found life glad and nutricious. Life is sweet and tolerable only in our belief in such society; and actually, or ideally, we manage to live with superiors. We call our children and our lands by their names, their names are wrought into the verbs of language, their works and effigies are in our houses, and every circumstance of the day recalls an anecdote of them.

The search after the great is the dream of youth, and the most serious occupation of manhood. We travel into foreign parts to find his works — if possible, to get a glimpse of him. But we are put off with fortune instead. You say, the English are practical, the Germans are hospitable, in Valencia, the climate is delicious; and in the hills of the Sacramento, there is gold for the gathering. Yes, but I do not travel to find comfortable, rich, and hospitable people, or clear sky, or ingots that cost too much. But if there were any magnet that would point to the countries and houses where are the persons who are intrinsically rich and powerful, — I would sell all, and buy it, and put myself on the road today.

The race goes with us on their credit. The knowledge that in the city is a man who invented the railroad, raises the credit of all the citizens. But enormous populations, if they be beggars, are disgusting, like moving cheese, like hills of ants, or of fleas, — the more, the worse.

Our religion is the love and cherishing of these patrons. The gods of fable are the shining moments of great men. We run all our vessels into one mould. Our colossal theologies of Judaism, Christism, Buddhism, Mahometism are the necessary and structural action of the human mind. The student of history is like a man going into a warehouse to buy cloths or carpets: he fancies he has a new article. If he go to the factory, he shall find that his new stuff still repeats the scrolls and rosettes which are found on the interior walls of the pyramids of Thebes. Our theism is the purification of the human mind. Man can paint or make or think nothing but man. He believes that the great material elements had their origin from his thought. And our philosophy finds one essence collected or distributed.

If now we proceed to enquire into the kinds of service we derive from others, let us be warned of the danger of modern studies and begin low enough. We must not contend against love, or deny the substantial existence of other people. I know not what would happen to us. We have social strengths. Our affection toward others creates a sort of vantage or purchase which nothing will supply. I can do that by another which I cannot do alone. I can say to you what I cannot first say to myself. Other men are lenses through which we read our own minds. Each man seeks those of different quality from his own, and such as are good of their kind; that is, he seeks other men, and *the otherest*. The stronger the nature, the more it is reactive. Let us have the quality pure. A little genius let us leave alone. A main difference betwixt men, is, whether they attend their own affair or not. Man is that noble endogenous plant, which grows, like the palm, from within outward. His own affair, though impossible to others, he can open with celerity and in sport. It is easy to sugar to be sweet, and to nitre to be salt. We take a great deal of pains to waylay and en-

trap that which of itself will fall into our hand. I count him a
great man who inhabits a higher sphere of thought, into which
other men rise with labor and difficulty: he has but to open his
eyes to see things in a true light and in large relations; whilst they
must make painful corrections, and keep a vigilant eye on many
sources of error. His service to us is of like sort. It costs a beautiful
person no exertion to paint her image on our eyes: Yet how splendid is that benefit! It costs no more for a wise soul to convey his
quality to other men. And every one can do his best thing easiest.
"Peu de moyens, beaucoup d'effet." He is great who is what he is from
nature, and who never reminds us of others.

But he must be related to us, and our life receive from him
some promise of explanation. I cannot tell what I would know,
but I have observed that there are persons who in their characters
and actions answer questions which I have not skill to put. One
man answers some question which none of his contemporaries
put, and is isolated. The past and passing religions and philosophies answer some other question. Certain men affect us as rich
possibilities, but helpless to themselves and to their times, — the
sport perhaps of some instinct that rules in the air; they do not
speak to our want. But the great are near; we know them at sight.
They satisfy expectation, and fall into place. What is good is effective, generative; makes for itself room, food, and allies. A sound
apple produces seed, — a hybrid does not. Is a man in his place,
he is constructive, fertile, magnetic, inundating armies with his
purpose, which is thus executed. The river makes its own shores,
and each legitimate idea makes its own channels and welcome;
harvests for food, institutions for expression, weapons to fight
with, and disciples to explain it. The true artist has the planet for
his pedestal: the adventurer after years of strife has nothing
broader than his own shoes.

Our common discourse respects two kinds of use or service from
superior men. Direct giving is agreeable to the early belief of men;
direct giving of material or metaphysical aid, as of health, eternal
youth, fine senses, arts of healing, magical power and prophecy.
The boy believes there is a teacher who can sell him wisdom.
Churches believe in imputed merit. But, in strictness, we are not

much cognisant of direct serving. Man is endogenous, and education is his unfolding. The aid we have from others is mechanical, compared with the discoveries of nature in us. What is thus learned is delightful in the doing, and the effect remains. Right ethics are central, and go from the soul outward. Gift is contrary to the law of the universe. Serving others is serving us. I must absolve me to myself. 'Mind thy affair,' says the Spirit: — 'Coxcomb! would you meddle with the skies, or with other people?' — Indirect service is left. Men have a pictorial or representative quality, and serve us in the intellect. Behmen and Swedenborg saw that things were representative. Men are also representative; first, of things, and, secondly, of ideas.

As plants convert the minerals into food for animals, so each man converts some raw material in nature to human use. The inventors of fire, electricity, magnetism, iron, lead, glass, linen, silk, cotton; the makers of tools; the inventor of decimal notation, the geometer, the engineer, the musician, severally make an easy way for all through unknown and impossible confusions. Each man is, by secret liking, connected with some district of nature whose agent and interpreter he is, as Linnæus, of plants; Huber, of bees; Fries of lichens; Van Mons of pears; Dalton of atomic forms; Euclid of lines; Newton of fluxions.

A man is a centre for nature, running out threads of relation through everything fluid and solid, material and elemental; the earth rolls, every clod and stone comes to the meridian. So every organ, function, acid, crystal, grain of dust, has its relation to the brain. It waits long, but its turn comes. Each plant has its parasite, and each created thing its lover and poet. Justice has already been done to steam, to iron, to wood, to coal, to loadstone, to iodine, to corn, and cotton; but how few materials are yet used by our arts! The mass of creatures and of qualities are still hid and expectant. It would seem as if each waited, like the enchanted princess in fairy tales, for a destined human deliverer. Each must be disenchanted, and walk forth to the day in human shape. In the history of discovery the ripe and latent truth seems to have fashioned a brain for itself. A magnet must be made man in some Gilbert, or Swedenborg, or Oersted, before the general mind can come to entertain its powers.

6

If we limit ourselves to the first advantages, — a sober grace adheres to the mineral and botanic kingdoms, which, in the highest moments, comes up as the charm of nature, — the glitter of the spar, the sureness of affinity, the veracity of angles. Light and darkness, heat and cold, hunger and food, sweet and sour, solid, liquid, and gas, circle us round in a wreath of pleasures, and, by their agreeable quarrel, beguile the day of life. The eye repeats every day the first eulogy on things: He saw that they were good. We know where to find them: and these performers are relished all the more after a little experience of the pretending races. We are entitled also to higher advantages. Something is wanting to science until it has been humanized. The table of logarithms is one thing, and its vital play in botany, music, optics, and architecture, another. There are advancements to numbers, anatomy, architecture, astronomy, little suspected at first, when, by union with intellect and will, they ascend into the life, and reappear in conversation, character and politics.

But this comes later. We speak now only of our acquaintance with them in their own sphere, and the way in which they seem to fascinate and draw to them some genius who occupies himself with one thing all his life long. The possibility of interpretation lies in the identity of the observer with the observed. Each material thing has its celestial side; has its translation through humanity into the spiritual and necessary sphere, where it plays a part as indestructible as any other. And to these their ends all things continually ascend. The gases gather to the solid firmament: the chemic lump arrives at the plant, and grows; arrives at the quadruped, and walks; arrives at the man, and thinks. But also the constituency determines the vote of the representative. He is not only representative but participant. Like can only be known by like. The reason why he knows about them, is that he is of them: he has just come out of nature, or from being a part of that thing. Animated chlorine knows of chlorine, and incarnate zinc of zinc. Their quality makes his career, and he can variously publish their virtues, because they compose him. Man made of the dust of the world does not forget his origin: and all that is yet inanimate will one day speak and reason. Unpublished nature will have its whole secret told. Shall we say that quartz mountains will pulverize into innumerable Werners, Von Buchs, and Beaumonts, and the laboratory of the atmosphere holds in solution I know not what Berzeliuses and Davys?

Thus we sit by the fire, and take hold on the poles of the earth. This *quasi* omnipresence supplies the imbecility of our condition. In one of those celestial days when heaven and earth meet and adorn each other, it seems a poverty that we can only spend it once. We wish for a thousand heads, a thousand bodies, that we might celebrate its immense beauty in many ways and places. Is this fancy? Well, in good faith, we are multiplied by our proxies. How easily we adopt their labours! Every ship that comes to America got its chart from Columbus. Every novel is a debtor to Homer. Every carpenter who shaves with a foreplane borrows the genius of a forgotten inventor. Life is girt all round with a zodiac of sciences, the contribution of men who have perished to add their point of light to our sky. Engineer, broker, jurist, physician, moralist, theologian, and every man, inasmuch as he has any science, is a definer and map-maker of the latitudes and longitudes of our condition. These road-makers on every hand enrich us. We must extend the area of life, and multiply our relations. We are as much gainers by finding a new property in the old earth, as by acquiring a new planet.

We are too passive in the reception of these material or semi-material aids. We must not be sacks and stomachs. To ascend one step; — we are better served through our sympathy. Activity is contagious. Looking where others look, and conversing with the same things, we catch the charm which lured them. Napoleon said, "You must not fight too often with one enemy or you will teach him all your art of war." Talk much with any man of vigorous mind, and we acquire very fast the habit of looking at things in the same light, and, on each occurrence, we anticipate his thought.

Men are helpful through the intellect and the affections. Other help I find a false appearance. If you affect to give me bread and fire, I perceive that I pay for it the full price, and at last it leaves me as it found me, neither better nor worse; but all mental and moral force is a positive good. It goes out from you, whether you will or not, and profits me whom you never thought of. I cannot even hear of personal vigour of any kind, great power of performance, without fresh resolution. We are emulous of all that man can do. Cecil's saying of Sir Walter Raleigh, "I know that he can toil terribly," is an electric touch. So are Clarendon's portraits, — of Hampden; "who was of an industry and vigilance not to be tired out or wearied by the most laborious, and of parts not to be imposed on by the most subtle and sharp, and of a personal courage equal to his best parts." — Of Falkland; — "who was so severe an adorer of truth, that he could as easily have given himself leave to steal, as to dissemble." We cannot read Plutarch without a tingling of the blood; and I accept the saying of the Chinese Mencius; "A sage is the instructer of a hundred ages. When the manners of Loo are heard of, the stupid become intelligent, and the wavering, determined."

This is the moral of biography; yet it is hard for departed men to touch the quick like our own companions, whose names may not last as long. What is he whom I never think of? whilst in every solitude are those who succour our genius, and stimulate us in wonderful manners. There is a power in love to divine another's destiny better than that other can, and by heroic encouragements hold him to his task. What has friendship so signal as its sublime attraction to whatever virtue is in us? We will never more think cheaply of ourselves or of life. We are piqued to some purpose, and the industry of the diggers on the railroad will not again shame us.

Under this head, too, falls that homage, very pure, as I think, which all ranks pay to the hero of the day, — from Coriolanus and Gracchus, down to Pitt, Lafayette, Wellington, Webster, Lamartine: Hear the shouts in the street! The people cannot see him enough. They delight in a man. Here is a head and a trunk! What a front; what eyes; Atlantean shoulders; and the whole carriage heroic, with equal inward force to guide the great machine! This pleasure of full expression to that which in their private experience is usually cramped and obstructed, runs also much higher, and is the secret of the reader's joy in literary genius. Nothing is kept back: there is fire enough to fuse the mountain of ore. Shak-

9

speare's principal merit may be conveyed in saying, that he of all men best understands the English language, and can say what he will. Yet these unchoked channels and floodgates of expression are only health or fortunate constitution. Shakspeare's name suggests other and purely intellectual benefits.

Senates and sovereigns have no compliment with their medals, swords, and armorial coats, like the addressing to a human being thoughts out of a certain height, and presupposing his intelligence. This honour, which is possible in personal intercourse scarcely twice in a lifetime, genius perpetually pays, contented if now and then in a century, the proffer is accepted. The indicators of the values of matter are degraded to a sort of cooks and confectioners on the appearance of the indicators of ideas. Genius is the naturalist or geographer of the supersensible regions, and draws their map; and, by acquainting us with new fields of activity, cools our affection for the old. These are at once accepted as the reality, of which the world we have conversed with is the show.

We go to the gymnasium and the swimming-school to see the power and beauty of the body: there is the like pleasure and a higher benefit from witnessing intellectual feats of all kinds, as feats of memory, of mathematical combination, great power of abstraction, the transmutings of the imagination, even versatility, and concentration, as these acts expose the invisible organs and members of the mind, which respond member for member to the parts of the body. For we thus enter a new gymnasium and learn to choose men by their truest marks, taught, with Plato, "to choose those who can without aid from the eyes, or any other sense, proceed to truth and to Being." Foremost among these activities are the summersaults, spells, and resurrections wrought by the imagination. When this wakes, a man seems to multiply ten times or a thousand times his force. It opens the delicious sense of indeterminate size, and inspires an audacious mental habit. We are as elastic as the gas of gunpowder, and a sentence in a book, or a word dropped in conversation, sets free our fancy, and instantly our heads are bathed with galaxies, and our feet tread the floor of the Pit. And this benefit is real, because we are entitled to these enlargements, and, once having passed the bounds, shall never again be quite the miserable pedants we were.

Uses of Great Men

The high functions of the intellect are so allied, that some imaginative power usually appears in all eminent minds: even in arithmeticians of the first class, but especially in meditative men of an intuitive habit of thought. This class serve us, so that they have the perception of identity and the perception of reaction. The eyes of Plato, Shakspeare, Swedenborg, Goethe, never shut on either of these laws. The perception of these laws is a kind of metre of the mind. Little minds are little through failure to see them.

Even these feasts have their surfeit. Our delight in Reason degenerates into idolatry of the herald. Especially when a mind of powerful method has instructed men, we find the examples of oppression. The dominion of Aristotle, the Ptolemaic astronomy, the credit of Luther; of Bacon; of Locke; in religion, the history of hierarchies, of saints, and the sects which have taken the name of each founder, are in point. Alas, every man is such a victim. The imbecility of men is always inviting the impudence of power. It is the delight of vulgar talent to dazzle and to blind the beholder. But true genius seeks to defend us from itself. True genius will not impoverish, but will liberate, and add new senses. If a wise man should appear in our village, he would create in those who conversed with him a new consciousness of wealth, by opening their eyes to unobserved advantages: he would establish a sense of immoveable equality, calm us with assurances that we could not be cheated; as every one would discern the checks and guaranties of condition. The rich would see their mistakes and poverty; the poor, their escapes and their resources.

But nature brings all this about in due time. Rotation is her remedy. The soul is impatient of masters, and eager for change. Housekeepers say of a domestic who has been valuable, "She had lived with me long enough." We are tendencies, or rather symptoms, and none of us complete. We touch and go, and sip the foam of many lives. Rotation is the law of nature. When Nature removes a great man, people explore the horizon for a successor; but none comes, and none will. His class is extinguished with him. In some other and quite different field, the next man will appear: not Jefferson, not Franklin, but now a great salesman; then a road-contractor; then a student of fishes; then a buffalo-hunting explorer; or a semi-savage Western general. Thus we make a stand against our rougher masters; but against the best there is a finer remedy. The power which they communicate is not theirs. When we are exalted by ideas, we do not owe this to Plato, but to the idea, to which also Plato was debtor.

I must not forget that we have a special debt to a single class. Life is a scale of degrees. Between rank and rank of our great men, are wide intervals. Mankind have, in all ages, attached themselves to a few persons, who, either by the quality of that idea they embodied, or by the largeness of their reception, were entitled to the position of leaders and lawgivers. These teach us the qualities of primary nature, admit us to the constitution of things. We swim, day by day, on a river of delusions, and are effectually amused with houses and towns in the air, of which the men about us are dupes. But life is a sincerity. In lucid intervals, we say, 'Let there be an entrance opened for me into realities; I have worn the fool's cap too long.' We will know the meaning of our economies and politics. Give us the cipher, and, if persons and things are scores of a celestial music, let us read off the strains. We have been cheated of our reason, — yet there have been sane men who enjoyed a rich and related existence. What they know, they know for us. With each new mind a new secret of nature transpires, nor can the bible be closed until the last great man is born. These men correct the delirium of the animal spirits, make us considerate, and engage us to new aims and powers. The veneration of mankind selects these for the highest place. Witness the multitude of statues, pictures, and memorials which recall their genius in every city, village, house, and ship.

> "Ever their phantoms arise before us,
> Our loftier brothers, but one in blood,
> At bed and table they lord it o'er us,
> With looks of beauty, and words of good."

How to illustrate the distinctive benefit of ideas, the service rendered by those who introduce moral truths into the general mind? — I am plagued in all my living with a perpetual tariff of prices. If I work in my garden, and prune an appletree, I am well enough entertained, and could continue indefinitely in the like occupation. But it comes to mind that a day is gone, and I have got this precious nothing done. I go to Boston or New York, and run up and down on my affairs; they are sped, but so is the day. I am vexed by the recollection of this price I have paid for a trifling advantage. I remember the *peau d'âne,* on which whoso sat, should have his desire, but a piece of the skin was gone for every wish. I go to a convention of philanthropists. Do what I can, I cannot keep my eyes off the clock. But if there should appear in the company some gentle soul who knows little of persons or parties, of Carolina or Cuba, but who announces a law that disposes these particulars, and so certifies me of the equity which checkmates every false player, bankrupts every selfseeker, and apprises me of my independence on any conditions of country, or time, or human body, that man liberates me; I forget the clock; I pass out of the sore relation to persons; I am healed of my hurts; I am made immortal by apprehending my possession of incorruptible goods. Here is great competition of rich and poor. We live in a market, where is only so much wheat, or wool, or land; and if I have so much more, every other must have so much less. I seem to have no good, without breach of good manners. Nobody is glad in the gladness of another, and our system is one of war, of an injurious superiority. Every child of the Saxon race is educated to wish to be first. It is our system: and a man comes to measure his greatness by the regrets, envies, and hatreds of his competitors. But in these new fields, there is room: here are no selfesteems, no exclusions.

I admire great men of all classes, those who stand for facts, and for thoughts; I like rough and smooth, "Scourges of God," and "Darlings of the human race;" I like the first Cæsar; and Charles V of Spain; and Charles XII of Sweden; Richard Plantagenet; and Bonaparte in France. I applaud a sufficient man, an officer equal to his office; captains, ministers, senators: I like a master standing firm on legs of iron; well born, rich, handsome, eloquent, loaded with advantages, drawing all men by fascination into tributaries and supporters of his power. Sword and staff, or talents sword-like or staff-like, carry on the work of the world. But I find him greater, when he can abolish himself and all heroes, by letting in this element of reason, irrespective of persons, this subtilizer, and irresistible upward force, into our thought, destroying individualism; — the power so great, that the potentate is nothing. Then he is a monarch who gives a constitution to his people; a pontiff, who preaches the equality of souls, and releases his servants from their barbarous homages; an emperor, who can spare his empire.

But I intended to specify with a little minuteness two or three points of service. Nature never spares the opium or nepenthe, but wherever she mars her creature with some deformity or defect, lays her poppies plentifully on the bruise, and the sufferer goes joyfully through life, ignorant of the ruin, and incapable of seeing it, though all the world point their finger at it every day. The worthless and offensive members of society, whose existence is a social pest, invariably think themselves the most ill used people alive, and never get over their astonishment at the ingratitude and selfishness of their contemporaries. Our globe discovers its hidden virtues not only in heroes and archangels, but in gossips and nurses. Is it not a rare contrivance that lodged the due inertia in every creature, the conserving resisting energy, the anger at being waked or changed? Altogether independent of the intellectual force in each, is the pride of opinion, the security that we are right. Not the feeblest grandame, not the mowing ideot, but uses what spark of perception and faculty is left, to chuckle and triumph in his or her opinion over the absurdities of all the rest. Difference from me is the measure of absurdity. Not one has a misgiving of being wrong. Was it not a bright thought that made things cohere with this bitumen, fastest of cements? But in the midst of this chuckle of selfgratulation, some figure goes by, which Thersites too can love and admire. This is he that should marshal us the way we were going. There is no end to his aid. Without Plato, we should almost lose our faith in the possibility of a reasonable book. We seem to want but one, but we want one. We love to associate with heroic persons, since our receptivity is unlimited, and, with the great, our thoughts and manners easily become great. We are all wise in capacity, though so few in energy. There needs but one wise man in a company, and all are wise, — so rapid is the contagion.

Great men are thus a collyrium to clear our eyes from egotism, and enable us to see other people and their works. But there are vices and follies incident to whole populations and ages. Men resemble their contemporaries, even more than their progenitors. It is observed in old couples, or in persons who have been housemates for a course of years, that they grow alike, and, if they should live long enough, we should not be able to know them apart. Nature abhors these complaisances, which threaten to melt the world into a lump, and hastens to break up such maudlin agglutinations. The like assimilation goes on between men of one town, of one sect, of one political party: and the ideas of the time are in the air, and infect all who breathe it. Viewed from any high point, this city of New York, yonder city of London, the western civilization would seem a bundle of insanities. We keep each other in countenance, and exasperate by emulation the frenzy of the time. The shield against the stingings of conscience, is, the universal practice, or our contemporaries. Again; it is very easy to be as wise and good as your companions. We learn of our contemporaries what they know, without effort, and almost through the pores of the skin. We catch it by sympathy, or, as a wife arrives at the intellectual and moral elevations of her husband. But we stop where they stop. Very hardly can we take another step. The great, or such as hold of nature, and transcend fashions, by their fidelity to universal ideas, are saviours from these federal errors, and defend us from our contemporaries. They are the exceptions which we want, where all grows alike. A foreign greatness is the antidote for cabalism.

Thus we feed on genius, and refresh ourselves from too much conversation with our mates, and exult in the depth of nature in that direction in which he leads us. What indemnification is one great man for populations of pigmies! Every mother wishes one son a genius, though all the rest should be mediocre. But a new danger appears in the excess of influence of the great man. His attractions warp us from our place. We have become underlings and intellectual suicides. Ah! yonder in the horizon is our help: other great men, new qualities, counterweights and checks on each other. We cloy of the honey of each peculiar greatness. Every hero becomes a bore at last. Perhaps Voltaire was not badhearted, yet he said of the good Jesus, even, "I pray you, let me never hear that man's name again." They cry up the virtues of George Washington. "Damn George Washington!" is the poor Jacobin's whole speech and confutation. But it is human nature's indispensable defence. The centripetence augments the centrifugence. We balance one man with his opposite, and the health of the state depends on the see-saw.

There is however a speedy limit to the use of heroes. Every genius is defended from approach by quantities of unavailableness. They are very attractive, and seem at a distance our own: but we are hindered on all sides from approach. The more we are drawn, the more we are repelled. There is something not solid in the good that is done for us. The best discovery the discoverer makes for himself. It has something unreal for his companion, until he too has substantiated it. It seems as if the Deity dressed each soul which he sends into nature in certain virtues and powers not communicable to other men, and, sending it to perform one more turn through the circle of beings, wrote *"Not Transferable,"* and *"Good for this trip only,"* on these garments of the soul. There is somewhat deceptive about the intercourse of minds. The boundaries are invisible, but they are never crossed. There is such goodwill to impart, and such goodwill to receive, that each threatens to become the other; but the law of individuality collects its secret strength; you are you, and I am I, and so we remain.

For nature wishes everything to remain itself, and, whilst every individual strives to grow and exclude, and to exclude and grow, to the extremities of the Universe, and to impose the law of its being on every other creature, nature steadily aims to protect each against every other. Each is selfdefended. Nothing is more marked than the power by which individuals are guarded from individuals, in a world where every benefactor becomes so easily a malefactor, only by continuation of his activity into places where it is not due: where children seem so much at the mercy of their foolish parents, and where almost all men are too social and interfering. We rightly speak of the guardian angels of children. How superior in their security from infusions of evil persons, from vulgarity, and second thought! They shed their own abundant beauty on the objects they behold. Therefore they are not at the mercy of such poor educators as we adults. If we huff and chide them, they soon come not to mind it, and get a selfreliance: and if we indulge them to folly, they learn the limitation elsewhere.

We need not fear excessive influence. A more generous trust is permitted. Serve the great. Stick at no humiliation. Grudge no office thou canst render. Be the limb of their body, the breath of their mouth. Compromise thy egotism: Who cares for that, so thou gain aught wider and nobler? Never mind the taunt of Boswellism: the devotion may easily be greater than the wretched pride which is guarding its own skirts. Be another: not thyself, but a Platonist; not a soul, but a Christian; not a naturalist, but a Cartesian; not a poet, but a Shakspearian. In vain. The wheels of tendency will not stop, nor will all the forces of inertia, fear, or of love itself, hold thee there. On, and forever onward! The microscope observes a monad or wheel-insect among the infusories circulating in water. Presently, a dot appears on the animal, which enlarges to a slit, and it becomes two perfect animals. The everproceeding detachment appears not less in all thought and in society. Children think they cannot live without their parents: But long before they are aware of it, the black dot has appeared, and the detachment taken place. Any accident will now reveal to them their independence.

But *great men:* the word is injurious. Is there caste? is there Fate? What becomes of the promise to Virtue? The thoughtful youth laments the superfœtation of nature. 'Generous and handsome,' he says, 'is your hero; but look at yonder poor paddy, whose country is his wheelbarrow: look at his whole nation of paddies.' Why are the masses, from the dawn of history down, food for knives

and powder? The idea dignifies a few leaders, who have sentiment, opinion, love, selfdevotion, and they make war and death
sacred; — but what for the wretches whom they hire and kill? —
The cheapness of man is every day's tragedy. It is as real a loss
that others should be low, as that we should be low: — for we
must have society.

Is it a reply to these suggestions, to say, society is a Pestalozzian
school: all are teachers and pupils in turn. We are equally served
by receiving and by imparting. Men who know the same things
are not long the best company for each other. But bring to each
an intelligent person of another experience, and it is as if you let
off water from a lake by cutting a lower basin. It seems a mechanical advantage, and great benefit it is to each speaker, as he can
now paint out his thought to himself. We pass very fast in our
personal moods from dignity to dependence. And if any appear
never to assume the chair, but always to stand and serve, it is because we do not see the company in a sufficiently long period for
the whole rotation of parts to come about. As to what we call the
masses, and common men; — there are no common men. All men
are at last of a size, and true art is only possible on the conviction
that every talent has its apotheosis somewhere. Fair play and an
open field! and freshest laurels to all who have won them! But
heaven reserves an equal scope for every creature. Each is uneasy
until he has produced his private ray unto the concave sphere,
and beheld his talent also in its last nobility and exaltation. The
heroes of the hour are relatively great; of a faster growth; or they
are such in whom, at the moment of success, a quality is ripe
which is then in request. Other days will demand other qualities.
Some rays escape the common observer, and want a finely
adapted eye. Ask the great man if there be none greater? His
companions are: and not the less great, but the more, that society
cannot see them. Nature never sends a great man into the planet,
without confiding the secret to another soul.

One gracious fact emerges from these studies, that there is true
ascension in our love. The reputations of the nineteenth century
will one day be quoted to prove its barbarism. The genius of humanity is the real subject whose biography is written in our

annals. We must infer much, and supply many chasms in the record. The history of the universe is symptomatic, and life is mnemonical. No man in all the procession of famous men is reason or illumination, or that essence we were looking for; but is an exhibition in some quarter of new possibilities. Could we one day complete the immense figure which these flagrant points compose! — The study of many individuals leads us to an elemental region wherein the individual is lost, or wherein all touch by their summits. Thought and feeling that break out there, cannot be impounded by any fence of personality. This is the key to the power of the greatest men, — their spirit diffuses itself. A new quality of mind travels by night and by day in concentric circles from its origin, and publishes itself by unknown methods; the union of all minds appears intimate; what gets admission to one, cannot be kept out of any other: the smallest acquisition of truth or of energy, in any quarter, is so much good to the commonwealth of souls. If the disparities of talent and position vanish, when the individuals are seen in the duration which is necessary to complete the career of each; even more swiftly the seeming injustice disappears, when we ascend to the central identity of all the individuals, and know that they are made of the substance which ordaineth and doeth.

The genius of humanity is the right point of view of history. The qualities abide; the men who exhibit them have now more, now less, and pass away; the qualities remain on another brow. No experience is more familiar. Once you saw phœnixes: they are gone: the world is not therefore disenchanted. The vessels on which you read sacred emblems, turn out to be common pottery, but the sense of the pictures is sacred, and you may still read them transferred to the walls of the world. For a time our teachers serve us personally, as metres or milestones of progress. Once they were angels of knowledge, and their figures touched the sky. Then we drew near, saw their means, culture, and limits; and they yielded their place to other geniuses. Happy, if a few names remain so high, that we have not been able to read them nearer, and age and comparison have not robbed them of a ray. But at last we shall cease to look in men for completeness, and shall content ourselves with their social and delegated quality. All that respects the individual is temporary and prospective, like the individual himself, who is ascending out of his limits into a catholic existence. We have never come at the true and best benefit of any genius, so long as we believe him an original force. In the moment when he ceases to help us as a cause, he begins to help us more as an effect. Then he appears as an exponent of a vaster mind and will. The opake self becomes transparent with the light of the First Cause.

Yet within the limits of human education and agency, we may say, great men exist that there may be greater men. The destiny of organized nature is amelioration, and who can tell its limits? It is for man to tame the chaos; on every side, whilst he lives, to scatter the seeds of science and of song, that climate, corn, animals, men, may be milder, and the germs of love and benefit may be multiplied.

PLATO, OR
THE PHILOSOPHER

II

Plato, or the Philosopher

Among secular books, Plato only is entitled to Omar's fanatical compliment to the Koran, when he said, "Burn the libraries; for their value is in this book." These sentences contain the culture of nations; these are the cornerstone of schools; these are the fountainhead of literatures. A discipline it is in logic; arithmetic; taste; symmetry; poetry; language; rhetoric; ontology; morals, or practick wisdom. There was never such range of speculation. Out of Plato come all things that are still written and debated among men of thought. Great havoc makes he among our originalities. We have reached the mountain from which all these drift boulders were detached. The Bible of the learned for twenty-two hundred years, every brisk young man who says in succession fine things to each reluctant generation, — Boethius, Rabelais, Erasmus, Bruno, Locke, Rousseau, Alfieri, Coleridge, — is some reader of Plato, translating into the vernacular wittily his good things. Even the men of grander proportion suffer some deduction from the misfortune (shall I say?) of coming after this exhausting generalizer; — St Augustine, Copernicus, Newton, Behmen, Swedenborg, Goethe, are likewise his debtors, and must say after him. For it is fair to credit the broadest generalizer with all the particulars deducible from his thesis.

Plato is philosophy, and philosophy Plato, at once the glory and the shame of mankind; since neither Saxon nor Roman have availed to add any idea to his categories. No wife, no children had he, and the thinkers of all civilized nations are his posterity, and are tinged with his mind. How many great men Nature is incessantly sending up out of night to be *his men*, Platonists! The Alexandrians, a constellation of genius; the Elizabethans, not less: Sir Thomas More, Henry More, John Hales, John Smith, Lord Bacon, Jeremy Taylor, Ralph Cudworth, Sydenham, Thomas Taylor; — Marcilius Ficinus, and Picus Mirandola. Calvinism is in his Phædo: Christianity is in it. Mahometanism draws all its philosophy, in its hand-book of morals, the Akhlak-y-Jalaly, from him. Mysticism finds in Plato all its texts. This citizen of a town in Greece is no villager nor patriot. An Englishman reads and says, 'how English!' a German, 'how Teutonic!' an Italian, 'how Roman and how Greek!' As they say that Helen of Argos had that universal beauty, that every body felt related to her, so Plato seems to a reader in New England an American genius. His broad humanity transcends all sectional lines.

This range of Plato instructs us what to think of the vexed question concerning his reputed works, what are genuine, what spurious. It is singular that wherever we find a man higher by a whole head than any of his contemporaries, it is sure to come into doubt, what are his real works. Thus Homer, Plato, Raffaelle, Shakspeare. For these men magnetize their contemporaries, so that their companions can do for them what they can never do for themselves, and the great man does thus live in several bodies, and write or paint or act, by many hands; and, after some time, it is not easy to say what is the authentic work of the master, and what is only of his school.

Plato, too, like every great man, consumed his own times. What is a great man, but one of great affinities, who takes up into himself all arts, sciences, all knowables, as his food? he can spare nothing; he can dispose of every thing. What is not good for virtue, is good for knowledge. Hence his contemporaries tax him with plagiarism. But the inventor only knows how to borrow: and society is glad to forget the innumerable laborers who ministered to this architect, and reserves all its gratitude for him. When we are praising Plato it seems we are praising quotations from Solon, and Sophron, and Philolaus. Be it so. Every book is a quotation; and every house is a quotation out of all forests, and mines, and stonequarries; and every man is a quotation from all his ancestors.

24

And this grasping inventor puts all nations under contribution.

Plato absorbed the learning of his times, — Philolaus, Timæus, Heraclitus, Parmenides, and what else: then his master Socrates; and, finding himself still capable of a larger synthesis, — beyond all example then or since, — he travelled into Italy, to gain what Pythagoras had for him; then into Egypt, and perhaps still farther east, to import the other element, which Europe wanted, into the European mind. This breadth entitles him to stand as the Representative of Philosophy. He says in the Republic, "Such a genius as philosophers must of necessity have, is wont but seldom in all its parts to meet in one man; but its different parts generally spring up in 'different persons." Every man who would do anything well, must come to it from a higher ground; a philosopher must be more than a philosopher. Plato is clothed with the powers of a poet; stands upon the highest place of the poet; and, (though I doubt he wanted the decisive gift of lyric expression,) mainly is not a poet, because he chose to use the poetic gift to an ulterior purpose.

Great geniuses have the shortest biographies. Their cousins can tell you nothing about them. They lived in their writing, and so their house- and street-life was trivial and commonplace. If you would know their tastes and complexions, the most admiring of their readers most resembles them. Plato, especially, has no external biography. If he had lover, wife, or children, we hear nothing of them. He ground them all into paint. As a good chimney burns its smoke, so a philosopher converts the value of all his fortunes into his intellectual performances.

He was born 430 A.C. about the time of the death of Pericles; was of patrician connection in his times and city; and is said to have had an early inclination for war: but in his twentieth year meeting with Socrates, was easily dissuaded from this pursuit, and remained for ten years his scholar, until the death of Socrates. He then went to Megara; accepted the invitations of Dion, and of Dionysius, to the court of Sicily; and went thither three times, though very capriciously treated. He travelled into Italy; then into Egypt, where he stayed a long time; some say, three, — some say, thirteen years. It is said, he went farther, into Babylonia; this

25

is uncertain. Returning to Athens, he gave lessons in the Academy to those whom his fame drew thither; — and died, as we have received it, in the act of writing, at eighty-one years.

But the biography of Plato is interior. We are to account for the supreme elevation of this man in the intellectual history of our race; how it happens that, in proportion to the culture of men, they become his scholars: that, as our Jewish Bible has implanted itself in the tabletalk and household life of every man and woman in the European and American nations, so the writings of Plato have preoccupied every school of learning, every lover of thought, every church, every poet, making it impossible to think on certain levels, except through him. He stands between the truth and every man's mind, and has almost impressed language and the primary forms of thought with his name and seal. I am struck in reading him with the extreme modernness of his style and spirit. Here is the germ of that Europe we know so well, in its long history of arts and arms: here are all its traits already discernible in the mind of Plato; — and in none before him. It has opened itself since into a hundred histories, but has added no new element. This perpetual modernness is the measure of merit in every work of art; since the author of it was not misled by anything shortlived or local, but abode by real and abiding traits. How Plato came thus to be Europe and philosophy, and almost literature, is the problem for us to solve.

This could not have happened without a sound, sincere, and catholic man, able to honour at the same time the ideal, or laws of the mind, and Fate, or the order of nature. The first period of a nation as of an individual, is the period of unconscious strength. Children cry, and scream, and stamp with fury, unable to express their desires. As soon as they can speak and tell their want and the reason of it, they become gentle. In adult life, whilst the perceptions are obtuse, men and women talk vehemently and superlatively, blunder and quarrel: their manners are full of desperation, their speech is full of oaths. As soon as with culture things have cleared up a little, and they see them no longer in lumps and masses, but accurately distributed, they desist from that weak vehemence, and explain their meaning in detail. If the tongue had not been framed for articulation, man would still be a beast in the forest. The same weakness and want on a higher plane, occurs daily in the education of ardent young men and women. "Ah! you don't understand me: I have never met with any one who comprehends me:" and they sigh and weep, write verses, and walk alone, — fault of power to express their precise meaning. In a month or two, through the favour of their good genius, they meet some one so related as to assist their volcanic estate, and, good communication being once established, they are thenceforward good citizens. — It is ever thus. The progress is to accuracy, to skill, to truth, from blind force.

There is a moment in the history of every nation, when, proceeding out of this brute youth, the perceptive powers reach their ripeness, and have not yet become microscopic, so that man, at that instant, extends across the entire scale, and, with his feet still planted on the immense forces of Night, converses by his eyes and brain with solar and stellar creation. That is the moment of adult health, the culmination of power.

Such is the history of Europe in all points, and such in philosophy. Its early records, almost perished, are of the immigrations from Asia, bringing with them the dreams of barbarians; a confusion of crude notions of morals and of natural philosophy, gradually subsiding, through the partial insight of single teachers. Before Pericles, came the seven wise masters, and we have the beginnings of geometry, metaphysics and ethics: Then the partialists, — deducing the origin of things from flux or water; or from air; or from fire; or from mind. All mix with these causes mythologic pictures. At last, comes Plato, the distributor, who needs no barbaric paint, or tattoo, or whooping, for he can define. He leaves with Asia the vast and superlative; he is the arrival of accuracy and intelligence. "He shall be as a god to me who can rightly divide and define."

This defining is philosophy. Philosophy is the account which the human mind gives to itself of the constitution of the world. Two cardinal facts lie forever at the base; the One; and the two. 1. Unity or Identity; and, 2. Variety. We unite all things by perceiving the law which pervades them, by perceiving the superficial differences, and the profound resemblances. But every mental act, — this very perception of identity or oneness, recognizes the difference of things. Oneness and Otherness. It is impossible to speak, or to think without embracing both.

The mind is urged to ask for one cause of many effects; then for the cause of that; and again the cause, diving still into the profound; self-assured that it shall arrive at an absolute and sufficient One, a One that shall be All. "In the midst of the sun is the light, in the midst of the light is truth, and in the midst of truth is the unperishable being," say the Vedas.

All philosophy of east and west has the same centripetence. Urged by an opposite necessity, the mind returns from the one, to that which is not one, but other or many; from cause to effect; and affirms the necessary existence of variety, the selfexistence of both, as each is involved in the other. These strictly-blended elements it is the problem of thought to separate and to reconcile. Their existence is mutually contradictory and exclusive; and each so fast slides into the other, that we can never say what is one, and what it is not. The Proteus is as nimble in the highest, as in the lowest grounds, — when we contemplate the one, the true, the good, as in the surfaces and extremities of matter.

In all nations, there are minds which incline to dwell in the conception of the fundamental Unity. The raptures of prayer and ecstasy of devotion lose all beings in one Being. This tendency finds its highest expression in the religious writings of the East, and chiefly in the Indian scriptures, in the Vedas, the Bhagavat Geeta, and the Vishnu Purana. Those writings contain little else than this idea, and they rise to pure and sublime strains in celebrating it.

The Same, the Same: friend and foe are of one stuff; the ploughman, the plough, and the furrow are of one stuff; and the stuff is such and so much that the variations of form are unimportant. "You are fit," (says the supreme Krishna to a sage,) "to apprehend that you are not distinct from me. That which I am, thou art, and that also is this world, with its gods, and heroes, and mankind. Men contemplate distinctions, because they are stupefied with ignorance." "The words *I* and *mine* constitute ignorance.

What is the great end of all, you shall now learn from me. It is soul, one in all bodies, pervading, uniform, perfect, preeminent over nature, exempt from birth, growth, and decay, omnipresent, made up of true knowledge, independent, unconnected with unrealities, with name, species, and the rest, in time past, present, and to come. The knowledge that this spirit, which is essentially one, is in one's own, and in all other bodies, is the wisdom of one who knows the unity of things. As one diffusive air passing through the perforations of a flute, is distinguished as the notes of a scale, so the nature of the great spirit is single, though its forms be manifold, arising from the consequences of acts. When the difference of the investing form, as that of god, or the rest, is destroyed, there is no distinction." — "The whole world is but a manifestation of Vishnu, who is identical with all things, and is to be regarded by the wise as not differing from, but as the same as, themselves. I neither am going nor coming, nor is my dwelling in any one place, nor art thou, thou, nor are others, others; nor am I, I." — As if he had said, — All is for the soul, and the soul is Vishnu, and animals and stars are transient paintings, and light is whitewash; and durations are deceptive; and form is imprisonment, and heaven itself a decoy. That which the soul seeks, is, resolution into being above form, out of Tartarus, and out of heaven, liberation from nature.

If speculation tends thus to a terrific unity, in which all things are absorbed, — action tends directly backwards to diversity. The first is the course or gravitation of mind; the second is the power of nature. Nature is the manifold. The unity absorbs and melts or reduces. Nature opens and creates. These two principles reappear and interpenetrate all things, all thought: the one, the many. One is being; the other, intellect: one is necessity; the other, freedom: one, rest; the other, motion: one, power; the other, distribution: one, strength; the other, pleasure: one, consciousness; the other, definition: one, genius; the other, talent: one, earnestness; the other, knowledge: one, possession; the other, trade: one, caste; the other, culture: one, king; the other, democracy: and, if we dare carry these generalizations a step higher, and name the last tendency of both, we might say, that the end of the one is escape from organization, pure science: and the end of the other is the highest instrumentality, or use of means, or, executive deity.

Each student adheres by temperament and by habit to the first or to the second or these gods of the mind. By religion, he tends to unity; by intellect, or by the senses, to the many. A too rapid unification, and an excessive appliance to parts and particulars, are the twin dangers of speculation.

To this partiality the history of nations corresponded. The country of unity, of immoveable institutions, the seat of a philosophy delighting in abstractions, of men faithful in doctrine and in practice to the idea of a deaf, unimplorable, immense Fate, is Asia; and it realizes this faith in the social institution of caste. On the other side, the genius of Europe is active and creative: it resists caste by culture: its philosophy was a discipline: it is a land of arts, inventions, trade, freedom. If the East loved infinity, the West delighted in boundaries.

European civility is the triumph of talent, the extension of system, the sharpened understanding, adaptive skill, delight in forms, delight in manipulation, in comprehensible results. Pericles, Athens, Greece, had been working in this element with the joy of genius not yet chilled by any foresight of the detriment of an excess. They saw before them no sinister political economy, no ominous Malthus, no Paris or London, no pitiless subdivision of classes, the doom of the pinmakers, the doom of the weavers, of dressers, of stockingers, of carders, of spinners, of colliers; no Ireland; no Indian caste, superinduced by the efforts of Europe to throw it off. The understanding was in its health and prime. Art was in its splendid novelty. They cut the Pentelican marble as if it were snow, and their perfect works in architecture and sculpture seemed things of course, not more difficult than the completion of a new ship at the Medford yards, or new mills at Lowell. These things are in course, and may be taken for granted; — the Roman legion, Byzantine legislation, English trade, the saloons of Versailles, the cafés of Paris, the steammill, steamboat, steamcoach, — may all be seen in perspective, — the townmeeting, the ballotbox, the newspaper and cheap press.

Meantime, Plato, in Egypt and in Eastern pilgrimages, imbibed the idea of one Deity, in which all things are absorbed. The unity of Asia and the detail of Europe, the infinitude of the Asiatic soul, and the defining, result-loving, machine-making, surface-seeking, operagoing Europe, Plato came to join, and, by contact, to enhance the energy of each. The excellence of Europe and Asia are in his brain. Metaphysics and natural philosophy expressed the genius of Europe; he substructs the religion of Asia as the base.

In short, a balanced soul was born, perceptive of the two elements. It is as easy to be great as to be small. The reason why we do not at once believe in admirable souls, is, because they are not in our experience. In actual life, they are so rare, as to be incredible; but, primarily, there is not only no presumption against them, but the strongest presumption in favour of their appearance. But whether voices were heard in the sky, or not; whether his mother or his father dreamed that the infant manchild was the son of Apollo; whether a swarm of bees settled on his lips, or not; a man who could see two sides of a thing was born. The wonderful synthesis so familiar in nature, the upper and the under side of the medal of Jove, the union of impossibilities which reappears in every object, its real and its ideal power, was now also transferred entire to the consciousness of a man.

The balanced soul came. If he loved abstract truth, he saved himself by propounding the most popular of all principles, the absolute good, which rules rulers, and judges the judge. If he made transcendental distinctions, he fortified himself by drawing all his illustrations from sources disdained by orators and polite conversers, from mares and puppies, from pitchers and soupladles, from cooks and criers, the shops of potters, horsedoctors, butchers, and fishmongers. He cannot forgive in himself a partiality, but is resolved that the two poles of thought shall appear in his statement. His argument and his sentence are selfpoised and spherical. The two poles appear, yes, and become two hands to grasp and appropriate their own.

Every great artist has been such by synthesis. Our strength is transitional, alternating, or, shall I say, a thread of two strands. The seashore, sea seen from shore, shore seen from sea, the taste of two metals in contact, and our enlarged powers at the approach and at the departure of a friend; the experience of poetic creativeness, which is not found in staying at home nor yet in travelling, but in transitions from one to the other, which must therefore be adroitly managed to present as much transitional surface as possible; this command of two elements must explain the power and the charm of Plato. Art expresses the one or the same by the different. Thought seeks to know unity in unity; poetry to show it by variety, that is, always by an object or symbol. Plato keeps the two vases, one of æther and one of pigment, at his side, and invariably uses both. Things added to things, as statistics, civil history, are inventories. Things used as language are inexhaustibly attractive. Plato turns incessantly the obverse and the reverse of the medal of Jove.

To take an example: The physical philosophers had sketched each his theory of the world, — the theory of atoms; of fire; of flux; of spirit; theories mechanical and chemical in their genius. Plato, a master of mathematics, studious of all natural laws and causes, feels these, as second causes, to be no theories of the world, but bare inventories and lists. To the study of nature, he, therefore, prefixes the dogma: — "Let us declare the cause which led the Supreme Ordainer to produce and compose the Universe. He was good, and he who is good has no kind of envy. Exempt from envy, he wished that all things should be as much as possible like himself. Whosoever, taught by wise men, shall admit this as the prime cause of the origin and foundation of the world, will be in the truth." "All things are for the sake of the Good, and it is the cause of everything beautiful." This dogma animates and impersonates his philosophy.

The synthesis which makes the character of his mind appears in all his talents. Where there is great compass of wit, we usually find excellences that combine easily in the living man, but in description appear incompatible. The mind of Plato is not to be exhibited by a Chinese catalogue, but is to be apprehended by an original mind in the exercise of its original power. In him the freest abandonment is united with the precision of a geometer. His daring imagination gives him the more solid grasp of facts; as the birds of highest flight have the strongest alar bones. His patrician polish, his intrinsic elegance, edged by an irony so subtle that it stings and paralyzes, adorn the soundest health and strength of frame. According to the old sentence, "if Jove should descend to the earth, he would speak in the style of Plato."

With this palatial air, there is for the direct aim of several of his works, and running through the tenour of them all, a certain earnestness, which mounts in the Republic, and in the Phædo, to piety. He has been charged with feigning sickness at the time of the death of Socrates. But the anecdotes that have come down from the times attest his manly interference before the people in his master's behalf, since even the savage cry of the assembly to Plato is preserved; and the indignation towards popular government, in many of his pieces, expresses a personal exasperation. He has a probity, a native reverence for justice and honour, a humanity which makes him tender for the superstitions of the people. Add to this, he believes that poetry, prophecy, and the high insight are from a wisdom of which man is not master; that the gods never philosophize; but by a celestial mania, these miracles are accomplished. Horsed on these winged steeds, he sweeps the dim regions, visits worlds which flesh cannot enter; he saw the souls in pain; he hears the doom of the Judge; he beholds the penal metempsychosis; the Fates, with the rock and shears; and hears the intoxicating hum of their spindle.

But his circumspection never forsook him. One would say, he had read the inscription on the gates of Busyrane, "Be bold;" and on the second gate, "Be bold, be bold, and evermore, be bold:" and then again had paused well at the third gate, "Be not too bold." His strength is like the momentum of a falling planet, and his discretion the return of its due and perfect curve, so excellent is his Greek love of boundary, and his skill in definition. In reading logarithms, one is not more secure, than in following Plato in his flights. Nothing can be colder than his head, when the lightnings of his imagination are playing in the sky. He has finished his thinking, before he brings it to the reader; and he abounds in the surprises of a literary master. He has that opulence which furnishes at every turn the precise weapon he needs. As the rich man wears no more garments, drives no more horses, sits in no more chambers, than the poor, but he has that one dress, or equipage, or instrument, which is fit for the hour and the need; so Plato in his plenty is never restricted, but has the fit word. There is indeed no weapon in all the armory of wit which he did not possess and use, epic, analysis, mania, intuition, music, satire and irony, down to the customary and polite. His illustrations are poetry, and his jests illustrations. Socrates' profession of obstetric art is good philosophy, and his finding that word 'cookery' and 'adulatory art' for rhetoric, in the Gorgias, does us a substantial service still. No orator can measure in effect with him who can give good nicknames.

What moderation and understatement and checking his thunder in mid volley! He has goodnaturedly furnished the courtier and citizen with all that can be said against the schools. "For philosophy is an elegant thing, if any one moderately meddles with it; but if he is conversant with it more than is becoming, it corrupts the man." He could well afford to be generous, he who from the sunlike centrality and reach of his vision had a faith without cloud. Such as his perception, was his speech; he plays with the doubt and makes the most of it: he paints and quibbles, and by and by comes a sentence that moves the sea and land. The admirable earnest comes not only at intervals in the perfect yes and no of the dialogue, but in bursts of light. "I, therefore, Callicles, am persuaded by these accounts, and consider how I may exhibit my soul before the judge in a healthy condition. Wherefore, disregarding the honours that most men value, and looking to the truth, I shall endeavour in reality to live as virtuously as I can, and, when I die, to die so. And I invite all other men to the utmost of my power, and you, too, I in turn invite to this contest, which, I affirm, surpasses all contests here."

He is a great average man, one who, to the best thinking adds a proportion and equality in his faculties, so that men see in him their own dreams and glimpses made available, and made to pass for what they are. A great commonsense is his warrant and qualification to be the world's interpreter. He has reason, as all the philosophic and poetic class have, but he has also what they have not, this strong solving sense to reconcile his poetry with the appearances of the world, and build a bridge from the streets of cities to the Atlantis. He omits never this graduation, but slopes his thought, however picturesque the precipice on one side, to an access from the plain. He never writes in ecstasy, or catches us up into poetic raptures.

Plato apprehended the cardinal facts. He could prostrate himself on the earth, and cover his eyes, whilst he adored that which cannot be numbered, or guaged, or known, or named; that of which everything can be affirmed and denied; that "which is entity and nonentity." He called it super-essential. He even stood ready, as in the Parmenides, to demonstrate that it was so; that this Being exceeded the limits of intellect. No man ever more fully acknowledged the Ineffable. Having paid his homage, as for the human race, to the Illimitable, he then stood erect, and for the human race, affirmed, — And yet things are knowable! That is, the Asia in his mind was first heartily honoured, — the ocean of love and power, before form, before will, before knowledge, the Same, the Good, the One, — and now, refreshed and empowered by this worship, the instinct of Europe, namely, Culture, returns, and he cries, *Yet things are knowable!* They are knowable, because, being from one, things correspond. There is a scale: and the correspondence of heaven to earth, of matter to mind, of the part to the whole, is our guide. As there is a science of stars, called astronomy; a science of quantities, called mathematics; a science of qualities, called chemistry; so there is a science of sciences, — I call it Dialectic, — which is the Intellect discriminating the false and the true. It rests on the observation of identity and diversity, for, to judge, is to unite to an object the notion which belongs to it. The sciences, even the best, mathematics and astronomy, are like sportsmen who seize whatever prey offers, even without being able to make any use of it. Dialectic must teach the use of them. "This is of that rank that no intellectual man will enter on any study for its own sake, but only with a view to advance himself in that one sole science which embraces all."

"The essence or peculiarity of man is to comprehend a whole; or, that which, in the diversity of sensations, can be comprised under a rational unity." "The soul which has never perceived the truth, cannot pass into the human form." I announce to men the Intellect. I announce the good of being interpenetrated by the mind that made nature; this benefit, namely; that it can understand nature, which it made and maketh. Nature is good, but Intellect is better; as the Lawgiver is before the lawreceiver. I give you joy, O sons of men! that truth is altogether wholesome; that we have hope to search out what might be the very self of everything. The misery of man is to be baulked of the sight of essence, and to be stuffed with conjectures: but the supreme good is reality, the supreme beauty is reality; and all virtue and all felicity depend on this science of the real: for, courage is nothing else than knowledge; the fairest fortune that can befal man is to be guided by his dæmon to that which is truly his own. This also is the essence of justice, to attend every one his own: nay, the notion of Virtue is not to be arrived at, except through direct contemplation of the divine Essence. Courage, then! for, "the persuasion that we must search that which we do not know, will render us beyond comparison better, braver, and more industrious, than if we thought it impossible to discover what we do not know, and useless to search for it." He secures a position not to be commanded, by his passion for reality; valuing philosophy only as it is the pleasure of conversing with real being.

Thus, full of the genius of Europe, he said *Culture*. He saw the institutions of Sparta, and recognized more genially, one would say, than any since, the hope of education. He delighted in every accomplishment, in every graceful and useful and truthful performance; above all in the splendours of genius and intellectual achievement. "The whole of life, O Socrates," said Glauco, "is with the wise the measure of hearing such discourses as these." What a price he sets on the feats of talent, on the powers of Pericles, of Isocrates, of Parmenides! What price above price on the talents themselves! He called the several faculties, gods, — in his beautiful personation. What value he gives to the art of gymnastics in education; what to geometry; what to music; what to astronomy, whose appeasing and medicinal power he celebrates! In the Timæus he indicates the highest employment of the eyes. "By us it is asserted, that God invented and bestowed sight on us for this purpose, that on surveying the circles of intelligence in the heavens, we might properly employ those of our own minds, which, though disturbed when compared with the others that are uniform, are still allied to their circulations; and that, having thus learned, and being naturally possessed of a correct reasoning faculty, we might by imitating the uniform revolutions of divinity set right our own wanderings and blunders." And in the Republic; "By each of these disciplines a certain organ of the soul is both purified and reanimated, which is blinded and buried by studies of another kind; an organ better worth saving than ten thousand eyes, since truth is perceived by this alone."

He said *Culture,* but he first admitted its basis, and gave immeasurably the first place to advantages of nature. His patrician tastes laid stress on the distinctions of birth. In the doctrine of the organic character and disposition is the origin of caste. "Such as were fit to govern, into their composition the informing Deity mingled gold; into the military, silver; iron and brass for husbandmen and artificers." The East confirms itself in all ages in this faith. The Koran is explicit on this point of caste. "Men have their metal as of gold and silver; those of you who were the worthy ones in the state of ignorance, will be the worthy ones in the state of faith, as soon as you embrace it." Plato was not less firm. "Of the five orders of things, only four can be taught to the generality of men." In the Republic, he insists on the temperaments of the youth, as first of the first.

A happier example of the stress laid on nature is in the dialogue with the young Theages, who wishes to receive lessons from Socrates. Socrates declares, that, if some have grown wise by associating with him, no thanks are due to him; but, simply, whilst they were with him, they grew wise, not because of him: he pretends not to know the way of it. "It is adverse to many, nor can those be benefited by associating with me, whom the Dæmon opposes, so that it is not possible for me to live with these. With many, however, he does not prevent me from conversing, who yet are not at

37

all benefited by associating with me. Such, O Theages, is the association with me; for if it pleases the God, you will make great and rapid proficiency; you will not, if he does not please. Judge whether it is not safer to be instructed by some one of those who have power over the benefit which they impart to men, than by me, who benefit or not, just as it may happen." As if he had said, 'I have no system. I cannot be answerable for you. You will be what you must. If there is love between us, inconceivably delicious and profitable will our intercourse be: if not, your time is lost, and you will only annoy me. I shall seem to you stupid, and the reputation I have, false. Quite above us, beyond the will of you or me, is this secret affinity or repulsion laid. All my good is magnetic, and I educate, not by lessons, but by going about my business.'

He said Culture, he said Nature, and he failed not to add, *There is also the Divine*. There is no thought in any mind, but it quickly tends to convert itself into a power, and organizes a huge instrumentality of means. Plato, lover of limits, loved the illimitable, saw the enlargement and nobility which come from Truth itself and Good itself, and attempted, as if on the part of the human intellect, once for all, to do it adequate homage; homage fit for the Immense Soul to receive, and yet homage becoming the Intellect to render. He said, then, 'Our faculties run out into infinity, and return to us thence: We can define but a little way: but here is a fact which will not be skipped, and which to shut our eyes upon is suicide. All things are in a scale, and, begin where we will, ascend and ascend. All things are symbolical; and what we call results are beginnings.'

A key to the method and completeness of Plato is his twice bisected line. After he has illustrated the relation between the absolute Good and True and the forms of the intelligible world, he says: — "Let there be a line cut in two unequal parts. Cut again each of these two parts, one representing the visible, the other the intelligible world, and these two new sections representing the bright part and the dark part of these worlds, you will have, for one of the sections of the visible world, — images, that is, both shadows and reflections; for the other section, the objects of these images, that is, plants, animals, and the works of art and nature. Then divide the intelligible world in like manner; the one section will be of opinions and hypotheses, and the other section, of truths." To these four sections, the four operations of the soul correspond: conjecture, faith, understanding, Reason. As every pool reflects the image of the sun, so every thought and thing restores us an image and creature of the Supreme Good. The universe is perforated by a million channels for his activity. All things mount and mount.

All his thought has this ascension; in Phædrus, teaching that Beauty is the most lovely of all things, exciting hilarity and shedding desire and confidence through the universe, wherever it enters, and it enters in some degree into all things: but that there is another, which is as much more beautiful than Beauty, as Beauty is than Chaos, namely, Wisdom, which our wonderful organ of sight cannot reach unto, but which, could it be seen, would ravish us with its perfect reality. He has the same regard to it as the source of excellence in works of art. "When an artificer in the fabrication of any work looks to that which always subsists according to *the Same,* and employing a model of this kind expresses its idea and power in his work, it must follow that his production should be beautiful. But when he beholds that which is born and dies, it will be far from beautiful." Thus ever: the Banquet is a teaching in the same spirit, familiar now to all the poetry, and to all the sermons of the world, that the love of the sexes is initial, and symbolizes at a distance the passion of the soul for that immense lake of beauty it exists to seek. This faith in the Divinity is never out of mind and constitutes the ground of all his dogmas. Body cannot teach wisdom, God only. In the same mind, he constantly affirms, that Virtue cannot be taught; that it is not a science, but an inspiration; that the greatest goods are produced to us through mania, and are assigned to us by a divine gift.

This leads me to that central figure which he has established in his academy as the organ through which every considered opinion shall be announced, and whose biography he has likewise so laboured that the historic facts are lost in the light of Plato's mind. Socrates and Plato are the double star which the most powerful instruments will not entirely separate. Socrates, again, in his traits and genius, is the best example of that synthesis which constitutes Plato's extraordinary power: Socrates, — a man of humble stem, but honest enough; of the commonest history, of a personal home-liness so remarkable as to be a cause of wit in others; — the rather that his broad good nature and exquisite taste for a joke, invited the sally, — which was sure to be paid. The players personated him on the stage, the potters copied his ugly face on their stone jugs. He was a cool fellow, adding to his humor a perfect temper, and a knowledge of his man, — be he who he might whom he talked with, — which laid the companion open to certain defeat in any debate, — and in debate he immoderately delighted. The young men are prodigiously fond of him, and invite him to their feasts, whither he goes for conversation: he can drink too; has the strongest head in Athens, and, after leaving the whole party under the table, goes away, as if nothing had happened, to begin new dialogues with somebody that is sober. In short, he was what our country people call *an old one.*

He affected a good many citizen-like tastes, was monstrously fond of Athens, hated trees, never willingly went beyond the walls, knew the old characters; valued the bores and philistines; thought everything in Athens a little better than anything in any other place. He was plain as a Quaker in habit and speech, af-fected low phrases, and illustrations from cocks and quails, soup-pans and sycamore-spoons, grooms and farriers, and unnameable offices; — especially if he talked with any superfine person. He had a Franklin-like wisdom. Thus, he showed one who was afraid to go on foot to Olympia, that it was no more than his daily walk within doors, if continuously extended, would easily reach.

Plain old uncle as he was, with his great ears, and immense talker, the rumor ran, that, on one or two occasions, in the war with Bœotia, he had shown a determination which had covered the retreat of a troop: and there was some story, that under cover of folly, he had in the city government, when one day he chanced to hold a seat there, evinced a courage in opposing singly the pop-ular voice, which had wellnigh ruined him. He is very poor, but then he is hardy as a soldier, and can live on a few olives: usually,

in the strictest sense, on bread and water, except when entertained by his friends. His necessary expenses were exceedingly
small, and no one else could live as he did. He wore no undergar-
ment; his upper garment was the same for summer and winter;
and he went barefooted; and it is said, that, to procure this pleasure which he loves, of talking at his ease all day with the most
elegant and cultivated young men, he will now and then return to
his shop, and carve statues good or bad, for sale. However that be,
it is certain, that he had grown to delight in nothing else than this
conversation, and that, under his hypocritical pretence of knowing nothing, he attacks and brings down all the fine speakers, all
the fine philosophers of Athens, whether natives or strangers from
Asia Minor and the Islands. Nobody can refuse to talk with him,
he is so honest and really curious to know: A man who was willingly confuted, if he did not speak the truth, and who willingly
confuted others asserting what was false; and not less pleased
when confuted, than when confuting: for he thought not any evil
happened to men, of such a magnitude as false opinion respecting
the just and unjust. A pitiless disputant — who knows nothing, — but the bounds of whose conquering intelligence no man
had ever reached; whose temper was imperturbable; whose
dreadful logic was always leisurely and sportive; so careless and
ignorant as to disarm the wariest, and draw them in the pleasantest manner, into horrible doubts and confusion. But he always
knew the way out; knew it, yet would not tell it. No escape: he
drives them to terrible choices by his dilemmas, and tosses the
Hippiases and Gorgiases with their grand reputations, as a boy
tosses his balls. The tyrannous realist! — Meno has discoursed a
thousand times at length on Virtue, before many companies, and
very well, as it appeared to him: but, at this moment, he cannot
even tell what it is, — this crampfish of a Socrates has so
bewitched him.

This hardheaded humourist, whose strange conceits, drollery,
and bonhommie diverted the young patricians, whilst the rumour
of his sayings and quibbles gets abroad every day, turns out in the
sequel, to have a probity as invincible as his logic; and to be either
insane, or, at least, under cover of this play, enthusiastic in his re-

ligion. When accused before the judges of subverting the popular creed, he affirms the immortality of the soul, the future reward and punishment; — and, refusing to recant, — in a caprice of the popular government, was condemned to die, and sent to the prison. Socrates entered the prison, and took away all ignominy from the place, which could not be a prison, whilst he was there. Crito bribed the jailer; but Socrates would not go out by treachery. "Whatever inconvenience ensue, nothing is to be preferred before justice. These things I hear like pipes and drums, whose sound makes me deaf to everything you say." The fame of this prison, the fame of the discourses there, and the drinking of the hemlock, are one of the most precious passages in the history of the world.

The rare coincidence in one ugly body, of the droll and the martyr, the keen street- and market-debater with the sweetest saint known to any history, at that time, had forcibly struck the mind of Plato, — so capacious of these contrasts; — and the figure of Socrates by a necessity placed itself in the foreground of the scene, as the fittest dispenser of the intellectual treasures he had to communicate. It was a rare fortune that this Æsop of the mob, and this robed scholar, should meet, to make each other immortal in their mutual faculty. The strange synthesis in the character of Socrates capped the synthesis in the mind of Plato. Moreover, by this means, he was able in the direct way and without envy to avail himself of the wit and weight of Socrates, to which unquestionably his own debt was great; and these derived again their principal advantage from the perfect art of Plato.

It remains to say that the defect of Plato in power, is only that which results inevitably from his quality. He is intellectual in his aim, and therefore in expression literary. Mounting into heaven, diving into the Pit, expounding the laws of the state, the passion of love, the remorse of crime, the hope of the parting soul, he is literary, and never otherwise. It is almost the sole deduction from the merit of Plato, that his writings have not, what is no doubt incident to this regnancy of intellect in his work, the vital authority which the screams of prophets and the sermons of unlettered Arabs and Jews possess. There is an interval, and, to cohesion, contact is necessary.

I know not what can be said in reply to this criticism, but that we have come to a fact in the nature of things: an oak is not an orange. The qualities of sugar remain with sugar, and those of salt with salt.

In the second place, he has not a system. The dearest defenders and disciples are at fault. He attempted a theory of the Universe. And his theory is not complete or selfevident. One man thinks he means this; and another, that; he has said one thing in one place, and the reverse of it in another place. He is charged with having failed to make the transition from ideas to matter. Here is the world sound as a nut, perfect, not the smallest piece of chaos left, never a stitch nor an end, not a mark of haste, or botching, or second thought; but the theory of the world is a thing of shreds and patches.

The longest wave is quickly lost in the sea. Plato would willingly have a Platonism, a known and accurate expression for the world, and it should be accurate. It shall be the world passed through the mind of Plato; — nothing less. Every atom shall have the Platonic tinge; every atom, every relation, or quality, you knew before, you shall know again, and find here, but now ordered; not nature, but art. And you shall feel that Alexander indeed overran, with men and horses, some countries of the planet; but countries and things of which countries are made, elements, planet itself, laws of planet and of men, have passed through this man as bread into his body, and become no longer bread, but body: so all this mammoth morsel has become Plato. He has clapped copyright on the world. This is the ambition of Individualism. But the mouthful proves too large. Boa Constrictor has good will to eat it, but he is foiled. He falls abroad in the attempt, and biting gets strangled: the bitten world holds the biter fast by his own teeth. There he perishes; Unconquered Nature lives on, and forgets him. So it fares with all: so must it fare with Plato. In view of eternal Nature, Plato turns out to be philosophical exercitations. He argues on this side, and on that. The acutest German, the lovingest disciple, could never tell what Platonism was: indeed admirable texts can be quoted on both sides of every great question from him.

These things we are forced to say, if we must consider the effort of Plato or any Philosopher to dispose of Nature, — which will not be disposed of. No power of genius has ever yet had the smallest success in explaining existence. The perfect enigma remains. But there is an injustice in assuming this ambition for Plato. Let us not seem to treat with flippancy his venerable name. Men, in proportion to their intellect, have admitted his transcendant claims. The way to honour him is to compare him, not with nature, but with other men. How many ages have gone by, and he remains unapproached! A chief structure of human wit, like Karnac, or the mediæval cathedrals, or the Etrurian remains, it requires all the breadth of human faculty to know it. I think it is trueliest seen, when seen with the most respect. His sense deepens, his merits multiply with study. When we say, here is a fine collection of fables; or, when we praise the style; or the common sense; or arithmetic; we speak as boys, and much of our impatient criticism of the Dialectic, I suspect, is no better. The criticism is like our impatience of miles, when we are in a hurry; but it is still best that a mile should have seventeen hundred and sixty yards. The greateyed Plato proportioned the lights and shades after the Genius of our life.

Plato: New Readings

The publication in Mr Bohn's serial "Library," of the new translations of Plato, which we esteem one of the chief benefits the cheap press has yielded, gives us an occasion to take hastily a few more notes of the elevation and bearings of this fixed star, or to add a bulletin like the journals of *Plato at the latest dates*.

Modern science by the extent of its generalization has learned to indemnify the student of man for the defects of individuals by tracing growth and ascent in races; and, by the simple expedient of lighting up the vast background, generates a feeling of complacency and hope. The human being has the saurian and the plant in his rear. His arts and sciences, the easy issue of his brain, look glorious when prospectively beheld from the distant brain of ox, crocodile, and fish. It seems as if Nature, in regarding the geologic night behind her, when, in five or six millenniums, she had turned out five or six men, as Homer, Phidias, Menu, and Columbus, was nowise discontented with the result. These samples attested the virtue of the tree. These were a clear amelioration of trilobite and saurus, and a good basis for further proceeding. With this artist time and space are cheap, and she is insensible to what you say of tedious preparation. She waited tranquilly the flowing periods of paleontology for the hour to be struck when man should arrive. Then periods must pass before the motion of the earth can be suspected; then before the map of the instincts and the cultivable powers can be drawn. But as of races, so the succession of individual men is fatal and beautiful, and Plato has the fortune in the history of mankind to mark an epoch.

Plato's fame does not stand on a syllogism, or on any master-pieces of the Socratic reasoning or on any thesis, as, for example, the immortality of the soul. He is more than an expert, or a schoolman, or a geometer or the prophet of a peculiar message. He represents the privilege of the intellect, the power, namely, of carrying up every fact to successive platforms, and so disclosing in every fact a germ of expansion. These expansions are in the essence of thought: The naturalist would never help us to them by any discoveries of the extent of the universe, but is as poor, when cataloguing the resolved nebula of Orion, as when measuring the angles of an acre. But the "Republic" of Plato, by these expansions, may be said to require, and so to anticipate, the astronomy of Laplace. The expansions are organic. The mind does not create what it perceives, any more than the eye creates the rose. In ascribing to Plato the merit of announcing them, we only say, here was a more complete man who could apply to nature the whole scale of the senses, the understanding, and the reason.

These expansions or extensions consist in continuing the spiritual sight where the horizon falls on our natural vision, and by this secondsight discovering the long lines of law which shoot in every direction. Everywhere he stands on a path which has no end, but runs continuously round the universe. Therefore, every word becomes an exponent of nature. Whatever he looks upon discloses a second sense, and ulterior senses. His perception of the generation of contraries, of death out of life, and life out of death, — that law by which in Nature, decomposition is recomposition, and putrefaction and cholera are only signals of a new creation: his discernment of the little in the large, and the large in the small, studying the state in the citizen, and the citizen in the state, and leaving it doubtful whether he exhibited the "Republic" as an allegory on the education of the private soul; his beautiful definitions, of ideas, of time, of form, of figure, of the line, sometimes hypothetically given, as his defining of Virtue, courage, justice, temperance; his love of the apologue, and his apologues themselves; the cave of Trophonius; the ring of Gyges; the charioteer and two horses; the golden, silver, brass, and iron temperaments; Theuth and Thamus; and the visions of Hades and the Fates, fables which have imprinted themselves in the human memory like the signs of the zodiack; his soliform eye and his boniform soul; his doctrine of assimilation; his doctrine of reminiscence; his clear vision of the laws of *return* or *reaction,* which secure instant justice throughout the universe, instanced everywhere but specially in the doctrine, "What comes from God to us returns from us to God," and in Socrates's belief that the laws below are sisters of the laws above.

More striking examples are his moral conclusions. Plato affirms the coincidence of science and virtue; for vice can never know itself and virtue; but virtue knows both itself and vice. The eye attested that justice was best, as long as it was profitable; Plato affirms that it is profitable throughout; that the profit is intrinsic, though the just conceal his justice from gods and men; that it is better to suffer injustice, than to do it; that the sinner ought to covet punishment; that the lie was more hurtful than homicide; and that ignorance, or the involuntary lie, was more calamitous than involuntary homicide; that the soul is unwillingly deprived of true opinions, and that no man sins willingly; that the order or proceeding of nature was from the mind to the body, and that though a sound body cannot restore an unsound mind, yet a good soul can by its virtue render the body the best possible. The intelligent have a right over the ignorant, namely, the right of instructing them. The right punishment of one out of tune is to make him play in tune; the fine which the good refusing to govern ought to pay, is, to be governed by a worse man; that his guards shall not handle gold and silver but shall be instructed that there is gold and silver in their souls, which will make men willing to give them everything which they need.

This secondsight explains the stress laid on geometry. He saw that the globe of earth was not more lawful and precise than was the supersensible; that a celestial geometry was in place there, as a logic of lines and angles here below; that the world was throughout mathematical; the proportions are constant of oxygen, azote, and lime; there is just so much water, and slate, and magnesia; not less are the proportions constant of the moral elements.

This eldest Goethe, hating varnish and falsehood, delighted in revealing the real at the base of the accidental; in discovering connexion, continuity, and representation, everywhere; hating insulation; and appears like the god of wealth among the cabins of vagabonds, opening power and capability in everything he touches. Ethical science was new and vacant, when Plato could write thus: — "Of all whose arguments are left to the men of the present time, no one has ever yet condemned injustice, or praised justice, otherwise than as respects the repute, honours, and emoluments arising therefrom; while, as respects either of them in itself, and subsisting by its own power in the soul of the possessor, and concealed both from gods and men, no one has yet sufficiently investigated either in poetry or prose-writing, — how, namely, that the one is the greatest of all the evils that the soul has within it, and justice the greatest good."

His definition of Ideas as what is simple, permanent, uniform, and selfexistent, forever discriminating them from the notions of the understanding, marks an era in the world. He was born to behold the selfevolving power of spirit, endless generator of new ends, a power which is the key at once to the centrality and the evanescence of things. Plato is so centred, that he can well spare all his dogmas. Thus the fact of knowledge and ideas reveals to him the fact of eternity; and the doctrine of Reminiscence he offers as the most probable particular explication. Call that fanciful, it matters not; the connection between our knowledge and the abyss of Being is still real, and the explication must be not less magnificent.

He has indicated every eminent point in speculation. He wrote on the scale of the mind itself, so that all things have symmetry in his tablet. He put in all the past, without weariness, and descended into detail with a courage like that he witnessed in nature. One would say, that his forerunners had mapped out each a farm or a district, or an island, in intellectual geography, but that Plato first drew the sphere. He domesticates the soul in nature;

man is the microcosm. All the circles of the visible heaven represent as many circles in the rational soul. There is no lawless particle and there is nothing casual in the action of the human mind. The names of things, too, are fatal, following the nature of things. All the gods of the Pantheon are by their names significant of a profound sense. The gods are the ideas. Pan is speech or manifestation; Saturn, the contemplative; Jove, the regal soul; and Mars, passion. Venus is proportion; Calliope, the soul of the world; Aglaia, intellectual illustration.

These thoughts in sparkles of light had appeared often to pious and to poetic souls, but this well-bred all-knowing Greek geometer comes with command, gathers them all up into rank and gradation, the Euclid of holiness, and marries the two parts of nature. Before all men, he saw the intellectual values of the moral sentiment. He describes his own ideal, when he paints in Timæus a god leading things from disorder into order. He kindled a fire so truly in the centre that we see the sphere illuminated, and can distinguish poles, equator, and lines of latitude, every arc and node: a theory so averaged, so modulated, that you would say, the winds of ages had swept through this rhythmic structure, and not that it was the brief extempore blotting of one shortlived scribe. Hence it has happened that a very wellmarked class of souls, namely, those who delight in giving a spiritual, that is, an ethico-intellectual expansion to every truth by exhibiting an ulterior end which is yet legitimate to it, are said to Platonize. Thus Michel Angelo is a Platonist in his sonnets. Shakspeare is a Platonist when he writes, "Nature is made better by no mean but nature makes that mean," or

> "He that can endure
> To follow with allegiance a fallen lord
> Does conquer him that did his master conquer,
> And earns a place in the story."

Hamlet is a pure Platonist, and 'tis only the magnitude of Shakspeare's proper genius that hinders him from being classed as the most eminent of this school. Swedenborg throughout his prose poem of "Conjugal Love" is a Platonist.

His subtlety commended him to men of thought. The secret of his popular success is the moral aim, which endeared him to mankind. "Intellect," he said, "is king of heaven and of earth," but, in Plato, intellect is always moral. His writings have also the sempiternal youth of poetry. For their argument, most of them might have been couched in sonnets: and poetry has never soared higher than in the Timæus and the Phædrus. As the poet, too, he is only contemplative. He did not, like Pythagoras, break himself with an institution. All his painting in the Republic must be esteemed mythical with intent to bring out, sometimes in violent colours, his thought. You cannot institute, without peril of charlatanism.

It was a high scheme, his absolute privilege for the best, (which to make emphatic, he expressed by community of women,) as the premium which he would set on grandeur. There shall be exempts of two kinds; first, those who by demerit have put themselves below protection, outlaws; and secondly those who by eminence of nature and desert, are out of the reach of your rewards; let such be free of the city and above the law. We confide them to themselves, let them do with us as they will. Let none presume to measure the irregularities of Michel Angelo and Socrates by village scales.

In his eighth book of the Republic, he throws a little mathematical dust in our eyes. I am sorry to see him, after such noble superiorities, permitting the lie to governors. Plato plays Providence a little with the baser sort, as people allow themselves with their dogs and cats.

SWEDENBORG, OR
THE MYSTIC

III

Swedenborg, or the Mystic

Among eminent persons, those who are most dear to men are not of the class which the economist calls producers; they have nothing in their hands; they have not cultivated corn, nor made bread: they have not led out a colony nor invented a loom. A higher class in the estimation and love of this city-building market-going race of mankind, are the Poets, who, from the intellectual kingdom, feed the thought and imagination with ideas and pictures which raise men out of the world of corn and money, and console them for the shortcomings of the day, and the meannesses of labour and traffic. Then also the philosopher has his value, who flatters the intellect of this labourer, by engaging him with subtleties which instruct him in new faculties. Others may build cities; he is to understand them, and keep them in awe.

But there is a class who lead us into another region, the world of morals or of will. What is singular about this region of thought, is, its claim. Wherever the sentiment of right comes in, it takes precedence of everything else. For other things, — I make poetry of them; but the moral sentiment makes poetry of me.

I have sometimes thought that he would render the greatest service to modern criticism, who shall draw the line of relation that subsists between Shakspeare and Swedenborg. The human mind stands ever in perplexity, demanding intellect, demanding sanctity, impatient equally of each without the other. The reconciler has not yet appeared. If we tire of the saints, Shakspeare is our city of refuge. Yet the instincts presently teach, that the problem of Essence must take precedence of all others, the questions of

Whence? and What? and Whither? and the solution of these must be in a life, and not in a book. A drama or poem is a proximate or oblique reply; but Moses, Menu, Jesus, work directly on this problem. The atmosphere of moral sentiment is a region of grandeur which reduces all material magnificence to toys, yet opens to every wretch that has reason, the doors of the universe. Almost with a fierce haste it lays its empire on the man. In the language of the Koran, "God said, the heaven and the earth and all that is between them, think ye that we created them in jest, and that ye shall not return to us?" It is the kingdom of the will, and by inspiring the will, which is the seat of personality, seems to convert the universe into a person.

> "The realms of being to no other bow,
> Not only all are thine, but all are Thou."

All men are commanded by the saint. The Koran makes a distinct class of those who are by nature good, and whose goodness has an influence on others, and pronounces this class to be the aim of creation: the other classes are admitted to the feast of being, only as following in the train of this. And the Persian Poet exclaims to a soul of this kind,

> "Go boldly forth, and feast on being's banquet;
> Thou art the called, — the rest admitted with thee."

The privilege of this caste is an access to the secrets and structure of nature, by some higher method than by experience. In common parlance, what one man is said to learn by experience, a man of extraordinary sagacity is said, without experience, to divine. The Arabians say, that Abul Khair the mystic, and Abu Ali Seena, the philosopher, conferred together, and, on parting, the philosopher said, "All that he sees, I know;" and the mystic said, "All that he knows, I see." If one should ask the reason of this intuition, the solution would lead us into that property which Plato denoted as Reminiscence, and which is implied by the Bramins in the tenet of Transmigration. The soul having been often born, or, as the Hindoos say, "travelling the path of existence through thousands of births," having beheld the things which are here, those which are in heaven, and those which are beneath, there is nothing of which she has not gained the knowledge: no wonder that she is able to recollect in regard to any one thing what formerly she knew. "For, all things in nature being linked and related, and the soul having heretofore known all, nothing hinders but that any man who has recalled to mind, or, according to the common phrase, has learned one thing only, should of himself recover all his ancient knowledge, and find out again all the rest, if he have but courage, and faint not in the midst of his researches. For inquiry and learning is reminiscence all." How much more, if he that inquires be a holy and godlike soul. For, by being assimilated to the original Soul, by whom, and after whom, all things subsist, the soul of man does then easily flow into all things, and all things flow into it; they mix; and he is present and sympathetic with their structure and law.

This path is difficult, secret, and beset with terror. The ancients called it *ecstasy* or absence, a getting out of their bodies to think. All religious history contains traces of the trance of saints; a beatitude, but without any sign of joy; earnest, solitary, even sad; "the flight," Plotinus called it, "of the alone to the alone." Μύεσις, the closing of the eyes, whence our word Mystic. The trances of Socrates, Plotinus, Porphyry, Behmen, Bunyan, Fox, Pascal, Guion, Swedenborg, will readily come to mind. But what as readily comes to mind is the accompaniment of disease. This beatitude comes in terror, and with shocks to the mind of the receiver. "It o'erinforms the tenement of clay," and drives the man mad, or gives a certain violent bias, which taints his judgment. In the chief examples of religious illumination, somewhat morbid has mingled, in spite of the unquestionable increase of mental power. Must the highest good drag after it a quality which neutralizes and discredits it?

> "Indeed it takes
> From our achievements when performed at height
> The pith and marrow of our attribute."

Shall we say that the economical mother disburses so much earth and so much fire, by weight and metre, to make a man, and will not add a pennyweight, though a nation is perishing for a leader? Therefore the men of God purchased their science by folly or pain. If you will have pure carbon, carbuncle, or diamond, to make the brain transparent, the trunk and organs shall be so much the grosser; instead of porcelain, they are potter's earth, clay, or mud.

In modern times, no such remarkable example of this introverted mind has occurred as in Emanuel Swedenborg, born in Stockholm, in 1688. This man, who appeared to his contemporaries a visionary and elixir of moonbeams, no doubt led the most real life of any man then in the world; and now when the royal and ducal Fredericks, Cristierns, and Brunswicks, of that day, have slid into oblivion, he begins to spread himself into the minds of thousands. As happens in great men, he seemed by the variety and amount of his powers to be a composition of several persons, like the giant fruits which are matured in gardens by the union of four or five single blossoms. His frame is on a larger scale, and possesses the advantages of size. As it is easier to see the reflection of the great sphere in large globes, though defaced by some crack or blemish, than in drops of water, so men of large calibre though with some eccentricity or madness, like Pascal or Newton, help us more than balanced mediocre minds.

His youth and training could not fail to be extraordinary. Such a boy could not whistle or dance, but goes grubbing into mines and mountains, prying into chemistry and optics, physiology, mathematics, and astronomy to find images fit for the measure of his versatile and capacious brain.

He was a scholar from a child, and was educated at Upsala. At the age of twenty-eight, he was made Assessor of the Board of Mines, by Charles XII. In 1716, he left home for four years, and visited the universities of England, Holland, France, and Germany. He performed a notable feat of engineering in 1718, at the siege of Fredericshall, by haling two galleys, five boats, and a sloop, some fourteen English miles overland, for the royal service. In 1721, he journeyed over Europe to examine mines and smelting works. He published, in 1716, his Dædalus Hyperboreus, and from this time for the next thirty years was employed in the composition and publication of his scientific works. With the like force he threw himself into theology. In 1743, when he was fifty-four years old, what is called his illumination began. All his metallurgy and transportation of ships overland was absorbed into this ecstasy. He ceased to publish any more scientific books, withdrew from his practical labours, and devoted himself to the writing and publication of his voluminous theological works, which were printed at his own expense, or at that of the Duke of Brunswick, or other prince, at Dresden, Leipsic, London, or Amsterdam. Later, he resigned his office of Assessor: the salary attached to this office continued to be paid to him during his life. His duties had brought him into intimate acquaintance with King Charles XII, by whom he was much consulted and honoured. The like favour was continued to him by his successor. At the Diet of 1751, Count Hopken says, the most solid memorials on Finance were from his pen. In Sweden, he appears to have attracted a marked regard. His rare science and practical skill and the added fame of second-sight and extraordinary religious knowledge and gifts drew to him queens, nobles, clergy, shipmasters, and people about the ports through which he was wont to pass in his many voyages. The clergy interfered a little with the importation and publication of his religious works; but he seems to have kept the friendship of men in power. He was never married. He had great modesty and gentleness of bearing. His habits were simple; he lived on bread, milk, and vegetables. He lived in a house situated in a large garden. He went several times to England, where he does not seem to have attracted any attention whatever from the learned or the eminent; and died, at London, 29 March, 1772, of apoplexy, in his eighty-fifth year. He is described when in London as a man of a quiet clerical habit, not averse to tea and coffee, and kind to children. He wore a sword when in full velvet dress, and whenever he walked out, carried a goldheaded cane. There is a common portrait of him in antique coat and wig, but the face has a wandering or vacant air.

The genius which was to penetrate the science of the age with a far more subtle science, to pass the bounds of space and time; venture into the dim spirit-realm, and attempt to establish a new religion in the world, begun its lessons in quarries and forges, in the smelting-pot and crucible, in shipyards and dissecting-rooms. No one man is perhaps able to judge of the merits of his works on so many subjects. One is glad to learn that his books on mines and metals are held in the highest esteem by those who understand these matters. It seems that he anticipated much science of the nineteenth century; anticipated in astronomy, the discovery of the seventh planet, but unhappily not also of the eighth: anticipated the views of modern astronomy in regard to the generation of earths by the sun: in magnetism, some important experiments and conclusions of later students; in chemistry, the atomic theory; in anatomy, the discoveries of Schlichting, Monro, and Wilson, and first demonstrated the office of the lungs. His excellent English editor magnanimously lays no stress on his discoveries, since he was too great to care to be original, and we are to judge by what he can spare, of what remains.

A colossal soul, he lies vast abroad on his times, uncomprehended by them, and requires a long focal distance to be seen: suggests, as Aristotle, Bacon, Selden, Humboldt, that a certain vastness of learning, a *quasi*-omnipresence of the human soul in nature is possible. His superb speculation as from a tower over nature and arts, without ever losing sight of the texture and sequence of things almost realizes his own picture, in the "Principia," of the original integrity of man. Over and above the merit of his particular discoveries, is the capital merit of his self-equality. A drop of water has the properties of the sea, but cannot exhibit a storm. There is beauty of a concert, as well as of a flute; strength of a host, as well as of a hero; and, in Swedenborg, those who are best acquainted with modern books, will most admire the merit of mass. One of the missouriums and mastodons of literature, he is not to be measured by whole colleges of ordinary scholars. His stalwart presence would flutter the gowns of an university. Our books are false by being fragmentary: their sentences are *bonmots,* and not parts of natural discourse; childish expressions of surprise or pleasure in nature; or, worse, owing a brief notoriety to their petulance or aversion from the order of nature, being some curiosity or oddity designedly not in harmony with nature, and purposely framed to excite surprise, as jugglers do by concealing their means. But Swedenborg is systematic and respective of the world in every sentence: all the means are orderly given; his faculties work with astronomic punctuality, and this admirable writing is pure from all pertness or egotism.

Swedenborg was born into an atmosphere of great ideas. 'Tis hard to say what was his own; yet his life was dignified by noblest pictures of the universe. The robust Aristotelian method with its breadth and adequateness, shaming our sterile and linear logic by its genial radiation, conversant with series and degree, with effects and ends, skilful to discriminate power from form, essence from accident, and opening by its terminology and definition high roads into nature, had trained a race of athletic philosophers. Harvey had shown the circulation of the blood: Gilbert had shown that the earth was a magnet: Descartes, taught by Gilbert's magnet with its vortex, spiral, and polarity, had filled Europe with the leading thought of vortical motion, as the secret of nature. Newton, in the year in which Swedenborg was born, published the "Principia," and established the Universal Gravity. Malpighi, following the high doctrines of Hippocrates, Leucippus, and Lucretius, had given emphasis to the dogma, that Nature works in leasts, "tota in minimis existit natura." Unrivalled dissectors, Swammerdam, Leeuwenhoek, Winslow, Eustachius, Heister, Vesalius, Boerhaave, had left little for scalpel or microscope to reveal in human or comparative anatomy: Linnæus, his contemporary, was affirming in his beautiful science, that "Nature is always like herself:" and, lastly, the nobility of method, the largest application of principles had been exhibited by Leibnitz and Christian Wolff, in Cosmology; whilst Locke and Grotius had drawn the moral argument. What was left for a genius of the largest calibre, but to go over their ground, and verify and unite? It is easy to see in these minds the origin of Swedenborg's studies, and the suggestion of his problems. He had a capacity to entertain and vivify these volumes of thought. Yet the proximity of these geniuses, one or other of whom had introduced

59

all his leading ideas, makes Swedenborg another example of the difficulty, even in a highly fertile genius, of proving originality, the first birth and annunciation of one of the laws of nature.

He named his favorite views, the doctrine of Forms, the doctrine of Series and Degrees, the doctrine of Influx, the doctrine of Correspondence. His statement of these doctrines deserves to be studied in his books. Not every man can read them, but they will reward him who can. His theologic works are valuable to illustrate these. His writings would be a sufficient library to a lonely and athletic student, and the "Economy of the Animal Kingdom" is one of those books which by the sustained dignity of thinking is an honour to the human race. He had studied spars and metals to some purpose. His varied and solid knowledge makes his style lustrous with points and shooting spicula of thought, and resembling one of those winter mornings when the air sparkles with crystals. The grandeur of the topics makes the grandeur of the style. He was apt for cosmology, because of that native perception of identity which made mere size of no account to him. In the atom of magnetic iron, he saw the quality which would generate the spiral motion of sun and planet. The thoughts in which he lived were, the universality of each law in nature; the Platonic doctrine of the scale or degrees; the version or conversion of each into other, and so the correspondence of all the parts; the fine secret that little explains large, and large little; the centrality of man in nature, and the connection that subsists throughout all things. He saw that the human body was strictly universal, or an instrument through which the soul feeds and is fed by the whole of matter: so that he held, in exact antagonism to the skeptics, that, "the wiser a man is, the more will he be a worshipper of the Deity." In short, he was a believer in the Identity-philosophy, which he held not idly, as the dreamers of Berlin or Boston, but which he experimented with and stablished through years of labor with the heart and strength of the rudest Viking that his rough Sweden ever sent to battle.

This theory dates from the oldest philosophers, and derives perhaps its best illustration from the newest. It is this; that nature iterates her means perpetually on successive planes. In the old aphorism, *Nature is always selfsimilar.* In the plant, the eye or germinative point opens to a leaf, then to another leaf, with a power of transforming the leaf into radicle, stamen, pistil, petal, bract, sepal, or seed. The whole art of the plant is still to repeat leaf on leaf without end, the more or less of heat, light, moisture, and food determining the form it shall assume. In the animal, nature makes a vertebra, or a spine of vertebræ, and helps herself still by a new spine, with a limited power of modifying its form, — spine on spine, to the end of the world. A poetic anatomist in our own day teaches that a snake, being a horizontal line, and man, being an erect line, constitute a right angle, and between the lines of this mystical quadrant all animated beings find their place, and he assumes the hair-worm, the spanworm, or the snake, as the type or prediction of the spine. Manifestly, at the end of the spine, nature puts out smaller spines, as arms; at the end of the arms, new spines as hands; at the other end, she repeats the process, as legs and feet. At the top of the column, she puts out another spine which doubles or loops itself over as a spanworm into a ball, and forms the skull, — with extremities again; the hands being now the upper jaw, the feet the lower jaw, the fingers and toes being represented this time by upper and lower teeth. This new spine is destined to high uses. It is a new man on the shoulders of the last. It can almost shed its trunk, and manage to live alone, according to the Platonic idea in the Timæus. Within it, on a higher plane, all that was done in the trunk, repeats itself. Nature recites her lesson once more in a higher mood. The mind is a finer body, and resumes its functions of feeding, digesting, absorbing, excluding, and generating, in a new and ethereal element. Here in the brain is all the process of alimentation repeated, in the acquiring, comparing, digesting, and assimilating of experience. Here again is the mystery of generation repeated. In the brain, are male and female faculties: here is marriage, here is fruit. And there is no limit to this ascending scale, but series on series. Everything at the end of one use is taken up into the next, each series punctually repeating every organ and process of the last. We are adapted to infinity. We are hard to please, and love nothing which ends: and in nature is no end, but everything, at the end of one use, is lifted into a superior, and the ascent of these things climbs into dæmonic and celestial natures. Creative force, like a musical composer, goes on unweariedly repeating a simple air or theme, now high, now low, in solo, in chorus, ten thousand times reverberated, till it fills earth and heaven with the chant.

Gravitation as explained by Newton is good, but grander, when we find chemistry only an extension of the law of masses into particles, and that the atomic theory shows the action of chemistry to be mechanical also. Metaphysics shows us a sort of gravitation operative also in the mental phenomena; and the terrible tabulation of the French statists brings every piece of whim and humour to be reducible also to exact numerical ratios. If one man in twenty thousand or in thirty thousand eats shoes, or marries his grandmother, then in every twenty thousand or thirty thousand is found one man who eats shoes or marries his grandmother. What we call gravitation, and fancy ultimate, is one fork of a mightier stream for which we have yet no name. Astronomy is excellent, but it must come up into life to have its full value, and not remain there in globes and spaces. The globule of blood gyrates around its own axis in the human veins, as the planet in the sky, and the circles of intellect relate to those of the heavens. Each law of nature has the like universality, eating, sleep or hybernation, rotation, generation, metamorphosis, vortical motion which is seen in eggs as in planets. These grand rhymes or returns in nature, — the dear best-known face startling us at every turn under a mask so unexpected that we think it the face of a stranger, and carrying up the semblance into divine forms, — delighted the prophetic eye of Swedenborg, and he must be reckoned a leader in that revolution, which, by giving to science an idea, has given to an aimless accumulation of experiments, guidance and form and a beating heart.

I own with some regret that his printed works amount to about fifty stout octavos, his scientific works being about half of the whole number: and it appears that a mass of manuscript still unedited remains in the Royal Library at Stockholm. The scientific works have just now been translated into English in an excellent edition.

Swedenborg printed these scientific books in the ten years from 1734 to 1744, and they remained from that time neglected, and now, after their century is complete, he has at last found a pupil in Mr Wilkinson, in London, a philosophic critic with a coequal vigour of understanding and imagination comparable only to Lord Bacon's, who has produced his master's buried books to the day, and transferred them with every advantage from their forgotten Latin into English, to go round the world in our commercial and conquering tongue. This startling reappearance of Swedenborg after a hundred years in his pupil is not the least remarkable fact in his history. Aided, it is said, by the munificence of Mr Clissold, and also by his literary skill, this piece of poetic justice is done. The admirable preliminary discourses with which Mr Wilkinson has enriched these volumes, throw all the cotemporary philosophy of England into shade and leave me nothing to say on their proper grounds.

The "Animal Kingdom" is a book of wonderful merits. It was written with the highest end, to put science and the soul, long estranged from each other, at one again. It was an anatomist's account of the human body in the highest style of poetry. Nothing can exceed the bold and brilliant treatment of a subject usually so dry and repulsive. He saw nature "wreathing through an everlasting spiral, with wheels that never dry, on axles that never creak," and sometimes sought "to uncover those secret recesses where nature is sitting at the fires in the depths of her laboratory;" whilst the picture comes recommended by the hard fidelity with which it is based on practical anatomy. It is remarkable that this sublime genius decides peremptorily for the analytic, against the synthetic method, and, in a book whose genius is a daring poetic synthesis, claims to confine himself to a rigid experience.

He knows, if he only, the flowing of nature, and how wise was that old answer of Amasis to him who bade him drink up the sea, — "Yes, willingly, if you will stop the rivers that flow in." Few knew as much about nature and her subtle manners, or expressed more subtly her goings. He thought as large a demand is made on our faith by nature as by miracles. He noted that in her proceeding from first principles through her several subordinations, there was no state through which she did not pass, as if her path lay through all things. "For as often as she betakes herself upward from visible phenomena, or, in other words, withdraws herself inward, she instantly, as it were, disappears, while no one knows what has become of her, or whither she is gone, so that it is necessary to take science as a guide in pursuing her steps." The pursuing the inquiry under the light of an end or final cause, gives wonderful animation, a sort of personality to the whole writing. This book announces his favourite dogmas. The ancient doctrine of Hippocrates that the brain is a gland, and of Leucippus that the atom may be known by the mass, or, in Plato, the macrocosm by the microcosm, and, in the verses of Lucretius,

> Ossa videlicet e pauxillis atque minutis
> Ossibus, sic et de pauxillis atque minutis
> Visceribus viscus gigni, sanguenque creari
> Sanguinis inter se multis coeuntibus guttis;
> Ex aurique putat micis consistere posse
> Aurum, et de terris terram concrescere parvis;
> Ignibus ex igneis, humorem humoribus esse.
>
> Lib. I. 835

> "The principle of all things entrails made
> Of smallest entrails; bone of smallest bone;
> Blood, of small sanguine drops reduced to one;
> Gold, of small grains; earth of small sands compacted;
> Small drops to water, sparks to fire contracted:"

and which Malpighi had summed in his maxim, that "Nature exists entire in leasts;" — is a favourite thought of Swedenborg. "It is a constant law of the organic body, that large, compound, or visible forms exist and subsist from smaller, simpler, and ultimately from invisible forms, which act similarly to the larger ones, but more perfectly, and more universally, and the least forms so perfectly and universally, as to involve an idea representative of their entire universe." The unities of each organ are so many little organs homogeneous with their compound; the unities of the tongue are little tongues, those of the stomach, little stomachs, those of the heart are little hearts. This fruitful idea furnishes a key to every secret. What was too small for the eye to detect was read by the aggregates; what was too large, by the units. There is no end to his application of the thought. "Hunger is an aggregate of very many little hungers or losses of blood by the little veins all over the body." It is a key to his theology also. "Man is a kind of very minute heaven corresponding to the world of spirits and to heaven. Every particular idea of man, and every affection, yea, every smallest part of his affection, is an image and effigy of him. A spirit may be known from only a single thought. God is the grand man."

The hardihood and thoroughness of his study of nature required a theory of forms also. "Forms ascend in order from the lowest to the highest. The lowest form is angular, or the terrestrial and corporeal. The second and next higher form is the circular, which is also called the perpetual-angular, because the circumference of a circle is a perpetual angle. The form above this, is the spiral, parent and measure of circular forms: its diameters are not rectilinear, but variously circular, and have a spherical surface for centre; therefore it is called the perpetual-circular. The form above this is the vortical, or perpetual-spiral: next, the perpetual-vortical, or celestial: last, the perpetual-celestial, or spiritual."

Was it strange that a genius so bold should take the last step also, conceive that he might attain the science of all sciences, to unlock the meaning of the world? In the first volume of the "Animal Kingdom," he broaches the subject in a remarkable note.

"In our doctrine of Representations and Correspondences, we shall treat of both these symbolical and typical resemblances and of the astonishing things which occur, I will not say, in the living body only, but throughout nature, and which correspond so entirely to supreme and spiritual things, that one would swear that the physical world was purely symbolical of the spiritual world; insomuch that if we choose to express any natural truth in physical and definite vocal terms, and to convert these terms only into the corresponding spiritual terms, we shall by this means elicit a spiritual truth, or theological dogma, in place of the physical truth or precept: although no mortal would have predicted that anything of the kind could possibly arise by bare literal transposition; inasmuch as the one precept considered separately from the other appears to have absolutely no relation to it. I intend hereafter to communicate a number of examples of such correspondences, together with a vocabulary containing the terms of spiritual things, as well as of the physical things for which they are to be substituted. This symbolism pervades the living body."

The fact thus explicitly stated is implied in all poetry, in allegory, in fable, in the use of emblems, and in the structure of language. Plato knew of it, as is evident from his twice bisected line in the sixth book of the Republic. Lord Bacon had found that truth and nature differed only as seal and print, and he instanced some physical propositions with their translation into a moral or political sense. Behmen, and all mystics imply this law in their dark riddle writing. The poets, in as far as they are poets, use it, but it is known to them, only as the magnet was known for ages, as a toy. Swedenborg first put the fact into a detached and scientific statement, because it was habitually present to him, and never not seen. It was involved as we explained already in the doctrine of identity and iteration, because the mental series exactly tallies with the material series. It required an insight that could rank things in order and series, or rather, it required such rightness of position, that the poles of the eye should coincide with the axis of the world. The earth had fed its mankind through five or six millenniums, and they had sciences, religions, philosophies, and yet had failed to see the correspondence of meaning between every part and every other part. And, down to this hour, literature has no book in which the symbolism of things is scientifically opened. One would say, that, as soon as men had the first hint that every sensible object, — animal, rock, river, air, — nay, space or time, subsists not for itself, nor finally to a material end, but as a picture-language, to tell another story of beings and duties, other science would be put by, and a science of such grand presage would absorb all faculties: that each man would ask of all objects what they mean: Why does the horizon hold me fast with my joy and grief in this centre? Why hear I the same sense from countless differing voices, and read one never quite expressed fact in endless picture-language? — Yet, whether it be that these things will not be intellectually learned, or, that many centuries must elaborate and compose so rare and opulent a soul, — there is no comet, rockstratum, fossil, fish, quadruped, spider, or fungus, that for itself does not interest more scholars and classifiers, than the meaning and upshot of the frame of things.

But Swedenborg was not content with the culinary use of the world. In his fifty-fourth year, these thoughts held him fast, and his profound mind admitted the perilous opinion, too frequent in religious history, that he was an abnormal person, to whom was granted the privilege of conversing with angels and spirits; and this ecstasy connected itself with just this office of explaining the moral import of the sensible world. To a right perception, at once broad and minute, of the order of nature, he added the comprehension of the moral laws in their widest social aspects; but whatever he saw, through some excessive determination to form in his constitution, he saw not abstractly, but in pictures, heard it in dialogues, constructed it in events. When he attempted to announce the law most sanely, he was forced to couch it in parable.

Modern psychology offers no similar example of a deranged balance. The principal powers continued to maintain a healthy action; and to a reader who can make due allowance in the report for the reporter's peculiarities, the results are still instructive, and a more striking testimony to the sublime laws he announced, than any that balanced dulness could afford. He attempts to give some account of the *modus* of the new state, affirming that "his presence in the spiritual world is attended with a certain separation, but only as to the intellectual part of his mind, not as to the will-part;" and he affirms that "he sees with the internal sight the things that are in another life, more clearly than he sees the things which are here in the world."

Having adopted the belief that certain books of the Old and New Testaments were exact allegories, or written in the angelic and ecstatic mode, he employed his remaining years in extricating from the literal the universal sense. He had borrowed from Plato, the fine fable of "a most ancient people, men better than we, and dwelling nigher to the gods," and Swedenborg added, that they used the earth symbolically; that these, when they saw terrestrial objects, did not think at all about them, but only about those which they signified. The correspondence between thoughts and things henceforward occupied him. "The very organic form resembles the end inscribed on it." A man is in general and in particular an organized justice or injustice, selfishness or gratitude. And the cause of this harmony he assigned in the Arcana; "The reason why all and single things in the heavens and on earth are representative, is because they exist from an influx of the Lord through heaven." This design of exhibiting such correspondences, which, if adequately executed, would be the poem of the world, in which all history and science would play an essential part, was narrowed and defeated by the exclusively theologic direction which his inquiries took. His perception of nature is not human and universal, but is mystical and Hebraic. He fastens each natural object to a theologic notion; a horse signifies carnal understanding; a tree, perception; the moon, faith; a cat means this; an ostrich, that; an artichoke, this other; and poorly tethers every symbol to a several ecclesiastic sense. The slippery Proteus is not so easily caught. In nature, each individual symbol plays innumerable parts, as each particle of matter circulates in turn through every system. The central identity enables any one symbol to express successively all the qualities and shades of real being. In the transmission of the heavenly waters, every hose fits every hydrant. Nature avenges herself speedily on the hard pedantry that would chain her waves. She is no literalist. Everything must be taken genially, and we must be at the top of our condition, to understand anything rightly.

His theological bias thus fatally narrowed his interpretation of nature, and the dictionary of symbols is yet to be written. But the interpreter whom mankind must still expect will find no predecessor who has approached so near to the true problem.

Swedenborg styles himself in the title page of his books, "Servant of the Lord Jesus Christ;" and by force of intellect, and in effect, he is the last Father in the Church, and is not likely to have a successor. No wonder that his depth of ethical wisdom should give him influence as a teacher. To the withered traditional church yielding dry catechisms, he let in nature again, and the worshipper escaping from the vestry of verbs and texts, is surprised to find himself a party to the whole of his religion: his religion thinks for him, and is of universal application: he turns it on every side, it fits every part of life, interprets and dignifies every circumstance. Instead of a religion which visited him diplomatically three of four times, when he was born, when he married, when he fell sick, and when he died, and for the rest never interfered with him, here was a teaching which accompanied him all day, accompanied him even into sleep and dreams; into his thinking, and showed him through what a long ancestry his thoughts descend; into society, and showed by what affinities he was girt to his equals and his counterparts; into natural objects, and showed their origin and meaning, what are friendly and what are hurtful: and opened the future world by indicating the continuity of the same laws. His disciples allege that their intellect is invigorated by the study of his books.

There is no such problem for criticism as his theological writings, their merits are so commanding, yet such grave deductions must be made. Their immense and sandy diffuseness is like the prairie or the desert, and their incongruities are like the last deliration. He is superfluously explanatory, and his feeling of the ignorance of men strangely exaggerated. Men take truths of this nature very fast. Yet, he abounds in assertions; he is a rich discoverer, and of things which most import us to know. His thought dwells in essential resemblances, like the resemblance of a house to the man who built it. He saw things in their law, in likeness of function, not of structure. There is an invariable method and order in his delivery of his truth, the habitual proceeding of the mind from inmost to outmost. What earnestness and weightiness, his eye never roving, without one swell of vanity, or one look to self, in any common form of literary pride! A theoretic or speculative man, but whom no practical man in the universe could affect to scorn. Plato is a gownsman: his garment, though of purple, and almost sky-woven, is an academic robe, and hinders action with its voluminous folds. But this mystic is awful to Cæsar. Lycurgus himself would bow.

The moral insight of Swedenborg, the correction of popular errors, the announcement of ethical laws, take him out of comparison with any other modern writer, and entitle him to a place vacant for some ages among the lawgivers of mankind. That slow but commanding influence which he has acquired, like that of other religious geniuses, must be excessive also, and have its tides, before it subsides into a permanent amount. Of course, what is real and universal cannot be confined to the circle of those who sympathize strictly with his genius, but will pass forth into the common stock of wise and just thinking. The world has a sure chemistry by which it extracts what is excellent in its children, and lets fall the infirmities and limitations of the grandest mind.

That metempsychosis which is familiar in the old mythology of the Greeks, collected in Ovid, and in the Indian Transmigration, and is there *objective,* or really takes place in bodies by alien will, — in Swedenborg's mind has a more philosophic character. It is subjective, or depends entirely upon the thought of the person. All things in the universe arrange themselves to each person anew, according to his ruling love. Man is such as his affection and thought are. Man is man by virtue of willing, not by virtue of knowing and understanding. As he is, so he sees. The marriages of the world are broken up. Interiors associate all in the spiritual world. Whatever the angels looked upon was to them celestial. Each Satan appears to himself a man; to those as bad as he, a comely man; to the purified, a heap of carrion. Nothing can resist states; everything gravitates: like will to like: what we call poetic justice takes effect on the spot. We have come into a world which is a living poem. Everything is as I am. Bird and beast is not bird and beast, but emanation and effluvia of the minds and wills of men there present. Every one makes his own house and state. The ghosts are tormented with the fear of death, and cannot remember that they have died. They who are in evil and falsehood, are afraid of all others. Such as have deprived themselves of charity, wander and flee: the societies which they approach, discover their quality and drive them away. The covetous seem to themselves to be abiding in cells where their money is deposited, and these to be infested with mice. They who place merit in good works, seem to themselves to cut wood. "I asked such if they were not wearied? They replied, that they have not yet done work enough to merit heaven."

He delivers golden sayings which express with singular beauty the ethical laws; as when he uttered that famed sentence that "in heaven the angels are advancing continually to the springtime of their youth, so that the oldest angel appears the youngest:" "The more angels the more room:" "The perfection of man is the love of use:" "Man in his greatest and most perfect form is heaven:" "What is from Him is Him:" "Ends always ascend as nature descends:" and the truly poetic account of the writing in the inmost heaven, which, as it consists of inflexions according to the form of heaven, can be read without instruction. He almost justifies his claim to preternatural vision by strange insights of the structure of the human body and mind. "It is never permitted to any one in heaven to stand behind another and look at the back of his head; for then the influx which is from the Lord is disturbed." The angels from the sound of the voice know a man's love, from the articulation of the sound his wisdom, and from the sense of the words his science.

In the "Conjugal Love," he has unfolded the science of marriage. Of this book, one would say, that, with the highest elements, it has failed of success. It came near to be the Hymn of Love, which Plato attempted in the "Banquet;" the Love which, Dante says, Casella sung among the angels in Paradise; and which, as rightly celebrated, in its genesis, fruition and effect, might well entrance the souls, as it would lay open the genesis of all institutions, customs, and manners. The book had been grand if the Hebraism had been omitted, and the law stated without Gothicism as ethics, and with that scope for ascension of state which the nature of things requires. It is a fine Platonic development of the science of marriage; teaching that sex is universal, and not local; virility in the male qualifying every organ, act, and thought; and the feminine in woman. Therefore, in the real or spiritual world, the nuptial union is not momentary, but incessant and total; and chastity not a local, but a universal virtue; unchastity being discovered as much in the trading or planting or speaking or philosophizing as in generation; and, that, though the virgins he saw, in heaven, were beautiful, the wives were incomparably more beautiful, and went on increasing in beauty evermore.

Yet Swedenborg after his mode pinned his theory to a temporary form. He exaggerates the circumstance of marriage, and, though he finds false marriages on earth, fancies a wiser choice in heaven. But of progressive souls, all loves and friendships are momentary. *Do you love me?* means, Do you see the same truth? If you do, we are happy with the same happiness: but presently one of us passes into the perception of new truth; we are divorced, and no tension in nature can hold us to each other. I know how delicious is this cup of love, — I existing for you, you existing for me; but it is a child's clinging to his toy, an attempt to eternize the fireside and nuptial chamber, to keep the picture-alphabet through which our first lessons are prettily conveyed. The Eden of God is bare and grand: like the outdoor landscape remembered from the evening fireside, it seems cold and desolate, whilst you cower over the coals, but once abroad again, we pity those who can forego the magnificence of nature for candlelight and cards. Perhaps, the true subject of the "Conjugal Love," is *Conversation*, whose laws are profoundly eliminated. It is false, if literally applied to marriage. For God is the bride or bridegroom of the soul. Heaven is not the pairing of two, but the communion of all souls. We meet and dwell an instant under the temple of one thought, and part as though we parted not, to join another thought in other fellowships of joy. So far from there being anything divine in the low and proprietary sense of *Do you love me*, it is only when you leave and lose me by casting yourself on a sentiment which is higher than both of us, that I draw near and find myself at your side; and I am repelled if you fix your eye on me, and demand love. In fact, in the spiritual world, we change sexes every moment. You love the worth in me, then I am your husband; but it is not me, but the worth, that fixes the love: and that worth is a drop of the ocean of worth that is beyond me. Meantime, I adore the greater worth in another, and so become his wife. He aspires to a higher worth in another spirit, and is wife or receiver of that influence.

Whether a self-inquisitorial habit that he grew into from jealousy of the sins to which men of thought are liable, he has acquired in disentangling and demonstrating that particular form of moral disease an acumen which no conscience can resist. I refer to his feeling of the profanation of thinking to what is good "from scientifics." "To reason about faith, is to doubt and deny." He was painfully alive to the difference between knowing and doing, and this sensibility is incessantly expressed. Philosophers are therefore vipers, cockatrices, asps, hemorrhoids, presters, and flying serpents; literary men are conjurors and charlatans.

But this topic suggests a sad afterthought, that here we find the seat of his own pain. Possibly Swedenborg paid the penalty of introverted faculties. Success or a fortunate genius seems to depend on a happy adjustment of heart and brain, on a due proportion hard to hit of moral and mental power, which perhaps obeys the law of those chemical ratios which make a proportion in volumes necessary to combination, as when gases will combine in certain fixed rates but not at any rate. It is hard to carry a full cup, and this man, profusely endowed in heart and mind, early fell into dangerous discord with himself. In his "Animal Kingdom" he surprised us by declaring that he loved analysis and not synthesis; and now, after his fiftieth year, he falls into jealousy of his intellect, and, though aware that truth is not solitary nor is goodness solitary, but both must ever mix and marry, he makes war on his mind, takes the part of the conscience against it, and on all occasions traduces and blasphemes it. The violence is instantly avenged. Beauty is disgraced, love is unlovely, when truth the half part of heaven is denied, as much as when a bitterness in men of talent leads to satire, and destroys the judgment. He is wise, but wise in his own despite. There is an air of infinite grief and the sound of wailing all over and through this lurid universe. A vampyre sits in the seat of the prophet and turns with gloomy appetite to the images of pain. Indeed, a bird does not more readily weave its nest, or a mole bore into the ground, than this seer of the souls substructs a new hell and pit, each more abominable than the last, round every new crew of offenders. He was let down through a column that seemed of brass, but it was formed of angelic spirits, that he might descend safely amongst the unhappy, and witness the vastation of souls; and heard there for a long continuance their lamentations; he saw their tormentors, who increase and strain pangs to infinity; he saw the hell of the jugglers, the hell of the assassins, the hell of the lascivious; the hell of robbers who kill and boil men; the infernal tun of the deceitful; the excrementitious hells; the hell of the revengeful, whose faces resembled a round broad cake, and their arms rotate like a wheel. Except Rabelais and Dean Swift, nobody ever had such science of filth and corruption.

These books should be used with caution. It is dangerous to sculpture these evanescing images of thought. True in transition, they become false, if fixed. It requires for his just apprehension almost a genius equal to his own. But when his visions become the stereotyped language of multitudes of persons of all degrees of age and capacity, they are perverted. The wise people of the Greek race were accustomed to lead the most intelligent and virtuous young men, as part of their education, through the Eleusinian Mysteries, wherein, with much pomp and graduation, the highest truths known to ancient wisdom were taught. An ardent and contemplative young man, at eighteen or twenty years, might read once these books of Swedenborg, these mysteries of love and conscience, and then throw them aside forever. Genius is ever haunted by similar dreams, when the hells and the heavens are opened to it. But these pictures are to be held as mystical, that is, as a quite arbitrary and accidental picture of the truth, not as the truth. Any other symbol would be as good: then this is safely seen.

Swedenborg's system of the world wants central spontaneity; it is dynamic not vital, and lacks power to generate life. There is no individual in it. The Universe is a gigantic crystal, all whose atoms and laminæ lie in uninterrupted order, and with unbroken unity, but cold and still. What seems an individual and a will, is none. There is an immense chain of intermediation extending from centre to extremes, which bereaves every agency of all freedom and character. The universe in his poem suffers under a magnetic sleep, and only reflects the mind of the magnetizer. Every thought comes into each mind by infusion from a society of spirits that surround it, and into these from a higher society, and so on. All his types mean the same few things. All his figures speak one speech. All his interlocutors Swedenborgize. Be they who they may, to this complexion must they come at last. This Charon ferries them all over in his boat, kings, counsellors, cavaliers, doctors, Sir Isaac Newton, Sir Hans Sloane, King George II, Mahomet, or whosoever, and all gather one grimness of hue and style. Only when Cicero comes by, our gentle seer sticks a little at saying he talked with Cicero, and with a touch of human relenting remarks, "one whom it was given me to believe was Cicero;" and when the *soi disant* Roman opens his mouth, Rome and eloquence have ebbed away, — it is plain theologic Swedenborg, like the rest. His heavens and hells are dull, fault of want of individualism. The thousandfold relation of men is not there. The interest that attaches in nature to each man, because he is right by his wrong, and wrong by his right, because he defies all dogmatizing and classification, so many allowances and contingences and futurities are to be taken into account, strong by his vices, often paralyzed by his virtues, — sinks into entire sympathy with his society. This want reacts to the centre of the system. Though the agency of "the Lord" is in every line referred to by name, it never becomes alive. There is no lustre in that eye which gazes from the centre, and which should vivify the immense dependency of beings.

The vice of Swedenborg's mind is its theologic determination. Nothing with him has the liberality of universal wisdom, but we are always in a church. That Hebrew muse which taught the lore of right and wrong to men had the same excess of influence for him it has had for the nations. The mode as well as the essence was sacred. Palestine is ever the more valuable as a chapter in universal history, and ever the less an available element in education. The genius of Swedenborg, largest of all modern souls in this department of thought, wasted itself in the endeavour to reanimate and conserve what had already arrived at its natural term and, in the great secular Providence, was retiring from its prominence, before western modes of thought and expression. Swedenborg and Behmen both failed by attaching themselves to the Christian symbol, instead of to the moral sentiment, which carries innumerable christianities, humanities, divinities in its bosom.

The excess of influence shows itself in the incongruous importation of a foreign rhetoric. 'What have I to do,' asks the impatient reader, 'with jasper and sardonyx, beryl and chalcedony; what with arks and passovers, ephahs and ephods; what with lepers and emerods, what with heave offerings and unleavened bread; chariots of fire, dragons crowned and horned, behemoth, or unicorn? Good for orientals, these are nothing to me. The more learning you bring to explain them, the more glaring the impertinence. The more coherent and elaborate the system, the less I like it. I say with the Spartan, "Why do you speak so much to the purpose of that which is nothing to the purpose?" My learning is such as God gave me in my birth and habit, in the delight and study of my eyes, and not of another man's. Of all absurdities, this of some foreigner proposing to take away my rhetoric, and substitute his own, and amuse me with pelican and stork, instead of thrush and robin, palmtrees and shittimwood instead of sassafrass and hickory, seems the most needless.'

Locke said, "God when he makes the prophet, does not unmake the man." Swedenborg's history points the remark. The parish disputes in the Swedish church between the friends and foes of Luther and Melancthon, concerning "faith alone" and "works alone," intrude themselves into his speculations upon the economy of the universe, and of the celestial societies. The Lutheran bishop's son, for whom the heavens are opened, so that he sees with eyes, and in the richest symbolic forms, the awful truth of things, and utters again in his books as under a heavenly mandate the indisputable secrets of moral nature, — with all these grandeurs resting upon him, remains the Lutheran bishop's son; his judgments are those of a Swedish polemic, and his vast enlargements are purchased by adamantine limitations. He carries his controversial memory with him in his visits to the souls. He is like Michel Angelo, who, in his frescoes, put the Cardinal who had offended him, to roast under a mountain of devils; or like Dante, who avenged in vindictive melodies all his private wrongs; or perhaps still more like Montaigne's parish priest, who, if a hailstorm passes over the village, thinks the Day of doom is come, and the cannibals already have got the pip. Swedenborg confounds us not less, with the pains of Melancthon and Luther and Wolfius, and his own books which he advertises among the angels.

Under the same theologic cramp, many of his dogmas are bound. His cardinal position in morals is, that evils should be shunned as sins. But he does not know what evil is, or what good is, who thinks any ground remains to be occupied, after saying, that evil is to be shunned as evil. I doubt not, he was led by the desire to insert the element of personality of Deity. But nothing is added. One man, you say, dreads erysipelas, — show him that this dread is evil; or one dreads hell; show him that *dread* is evil. He who loves goodness harbours angels, reveres reverence, and lives with God. The less we have to do with our sins, the better. No man can afford to waste his moments in compunctions. "That is active duty," say the Hindoos, "which is not for our bondage; that is knowledge, which is for our liberation: all other duty is good only unto weariness."

Another dogma growing out of this pernicious theologic limitation is this Inferno. Swedenborg has devils. Evil, according to old philosophy, is good in the making. That pure malignity can exist, is the extreme proposition of unbelief. It is not to be entertained by a rational agent: it is atheism: it is the last profanation. Euripides rightly said,

> "Goodness and being in the gods are one,
> He who imputes ill to them, makes them none."

To what a painful perversion had Gothic theology arrived that Swedenborg admitted no conversion for evil spirits! But the Divine effort is never relaxed; the carrion in the sun will convert itself to grass and flowers, and man, though in brothels, or jails, or on gibbets, is on his way to all that is good and true. Burns with the wild humour of his apostrophe to "poor old Nickie Ben," —

"O wad ye tak a thought and mend!"

has the advantage of the vindictive theologian. Everything is superficial and perishes, but love and truth only. The largest is always the truest sentiment, and we feel the more generous spirit of the Indian Vishnu, "I am the same to all mankind. There is not one who is worthy of my love or hatred. They who serve me with adoration — I am in them, and they in me. If one whose ways are altogether evil, serve me alone, he is as respectable as the just man; he is altogether well employed, he soon becometh of a virtuous spirit, and obtaineth eternal happiness."

For the anomalous pretension of Revelations of the other world, — only his probity and genius can entitle it to any serious regard. His revelations destroy their credit by running into detail. If a man say that the Holy Ghost has informed him that the Last Judgment, (or the last of the Judgments) took place in 1757; or, that the Dutch, in the other world, live in a heaven by themselves, and the English, in a heaven by themselves; I reply, that the Spirit which is holy is reserved, taciturn, and deals in laws. The rumours of ghosts and hobgoblins gossip and tell fortunes. The teachings of the high Spirit are abstemious, and, in regard to particulars, negative. Socrates's Genius did not advertise him to act or to find, but if he purposed to do somewhat not advantageous, it dissuaded him. "What God is," he said, "I know not; what he is not, I know." The Hindoos have denominated the Supreme Being, the "Internal Check." The illuminated Quakers explained their Light, not as somewhat which leads to any action, but it appears as an obstruction to anything unfit. But the right examples are private experiences, which are absolutely at one on this point. Strictly speaking, Swedenborg's revelation is a confounding of planes, — a capital offence in so learned a categorist. This is to carry the law of surface into the plane of substance, to carry individualism and its fopperies into the realm of essences and generals, which is dislocation and chaos.

The secret of heaven is kept from age to age. No imprudent, no sociable angel ever dropt an early syllable to answer the longings of saints, the fears of mortals. We should have listened on our knees to any favorite who by stricter obedience had brought his thoughts into parallelism with the celestial currents, and could hint to human ears the scenery and circumstance of the newly parted soul. But it is certain that it must tally with what is best in nature. It must not be inferior in tone to the already known works of the artist who sculptures the globes of the firmament, and writes the moral law. It must be fresher than rainbows, stabler than mountains, agreeing with flowers, with tides, and the rising and setting of autumnal stars. Melodious poets shall be hoarse as street ballads when once the penetrating keynote of nature and spirit is sounded, — the earth-beat, sea-beat, heart-beat, which makes the tune to which the sun rolls, and the globule of blood, and the sap of trees.

In this mood, we hear the rumour that the seer has arrived, and his tale is told. But there is no beauty, no heaven: for angels, goblins. The sad muse loves night and death and the pit. His Inferno is mesmeric. His spiritual world bears the same relation to the generosities and joys of truth, of which human souls have already made us cognisant, as a man's bad dreams bear to his ideal life. It is indeed very like, in its endless power of lurid pictures, to the phenomena of dreaming, which nightly turns many an honest gentleman, benevolent but dyspeptic, into a wretch skulking like a dog about the outer yards and kennels of creation. When he mounts into the heaven, I do not hear its language. A man should not tell me that he has walked among the angels; his proof is, that his eloquence shall make me one. Shall the archangels be less majestic and sweet than the figures that have actually walked the earth? These angels that Swedenborg paints give us no very high idea of their discipline and culture: they are all country-parsons. Their heaven is a *fête champêtre,* an evangelical picnic, or French distribution of prizes to virtuous peasants. Strange, scholastic, didactic, passionless, bloodless man, who denotes classes of souls as a botanist disposes of a carex, and visits doleful hells, as a stratum of chalk or hornblende! He has no sympathy. He goes up and down the world of men, a modern Rhadamanthus in goldheaded cane

79

and peruke, and with nonchalance, and the air of a referee, distributes souls. The warm many-weathered passionate-peopled world is to him a grammar of hieroglyphs or an emblematic free-masons' procession. How different is Jacob Behmen! *he* is tremulous with emotion, and listens awestruck with the gentlest humanity to the Teacher whose lessons he conveys, and when he asserts that, "in some sort, love is greater than God," his heart beats so high that the thumping against his leathern coat is audible across the centuries. 'Tis a great difference. Behmen is healthily and beautifully wise, notwithstanding the mystical narrowness and incommunicableness. Swedenborg is disagreeably wise, and with all his accumulated gifts paralyzes and repels.

It is the best sign of a great nature, that it opens a foreground, and like the breath of morning-landscapes invites us onward. Swedenborg is retrospective, nor can we divest him of his mattock and shroud. Some minds are forever restrained from descending into nature; others are forever prevented from ascending out of it. With a force of many men, he could never break the umbilical cord which held him to nature and he did not rise to the platform of pure genius.

It is remarkable that this man who by his perception of symbols saw the poetic construction of things and the primary relation of mind to matter, remained entirely devoid of the whole apparatus of poetic expression, which that perception creates. He knew the grammar and rudiments of the *Mother-Tongue*, — how could he not read off one strain into music? Was he like Saadi, who in his vision, designed to fill his lap with the celestial flowers as presents for his friends, but the fragrance of the roses so intoxicated him that the skirt dropped from his hands? or is reporting a breach of the manners of that heavenly society? or, was it, that he saw the vision intellectually and hence that chiding of the intellectual that pervades his books? Be it as it may, his books have no melody, no emotion, no humour, no relief to the dead prosaic level. In his profuse and accurate imagery is no pleasure, for there is no beauty. We wander forlorn in a lacklustre landscape. No bird ever sung in all these gardens of the dead. The entire want of poetry in so transcendant a mind betokens the disease, and like a hoarse voice in a beautiful person is a kind of warning. I think sometimes, he will not be read longer. His great name will turn a sentence. His books have become a monument. His laurel so largely mixed with cypress, a charnel breath so mingles with the temple-incense, that boys and maids will shun the spot.

Yet, in this immolation of genius and fame at the shrine of conscience, is a merit sublime beyond praise. He lived to purpose, he gave a verdict. He elected goodness as the clue to which the soul must cling in all this labyrinth of nature. Many opinions conflict as to the true centre. In the shipwreck, some cling to running-rigging, some to cask and barrel, some to spars, some to mast; the pilot chooses with science, — I plant myself here, all will sink before this, "he comes to land who sails with me." Do not rely on heavenly favour, or on compassion to folly, or on prudence, on common sense, the old usage and main chance of men. Nothing can keep you, not fate, nor health, nor admirable intellect, none can keep you but rectitude only, rectitude forever and ever! And with a tenacity that never swerved in all his studies, inventions, dreams, he adheres to this brave choice. I think of him as of some transmigrating votary of Indian legend, who says, though I be dog, or jackal, or pismire, in the last rudiments of nature, under what integument or ferocity, I cleave to right, as the sure ladder that leads up to man and to God.

Swedenborg has rendered a double service to mankind, which is now only beginning to be known. By the science of experiment and use, he made his first steps; he observed and published the laws of nature: and, ascending, by just degrees, from events to their summits and causes, he was fired with piety at the harmonies he felt, and abandoned himself to his joy and worship. This was his first service. If the glory was too bright for his eyes to bear, if he staggered under the trance of delight, the more excellent is the spectacle he saw, the realities of being which beam and blaze through him, and which no infirmities of the prophet are suffered to obscure; and he renders a second passive service to men not less than the first, — perhaps in the great circle of being and in the retributions of spiritual nature, not less glorious or less beautiful to himself.

MONTAIGNE, OR
THE SKEPTIC

IV

Montaigne, or the Skeptic

Every fact is related on one side to sensation, and, on the other, to morals. The game of thought is, on the appearance of one of these two sides, to find the other: given the upper, to find the under side. Nothing so thin, but has these two faces, and, when the observer has seen the obverse, he turns it over to see the reverse. Life is a pitching of this penny, — heads or tails. We never tire of the game, because there is still a slight shudder of astonishment at the exhibition of the other face, at the contrast of the two faces. A man is flushed with success, and bethinks himself what this good luck signifies. He drives his bargain in the street, but it occurs, that he also is bought and sold. He sees the beauty of a human face, and searches the cause of that beauty, which must be more beautiful. He builds his fortunes, maintains the laws, cherishes his children, but he asks himself, Why? and Whereto? This head and this tail are called in the language of philosophy, Infinite and Finite; Relative and Absolute; Apparent and Real; and many fine names beside.

Each man is born with a predisposition to one or the other of these sides of nature, and, it will easily happen that men will be found devoted to one or the other. One class has the perception of Difference, and is conversant with facts and surfaces; cities and persons; and the bringing certain things to pass; — the men of talent and action. Another class have the perception of Identity, and are men of faith and philosophy, men of genius.

Each of these riders drives too fast. Plotinus believes only in philosophers; Fénelon, in saints; Pindar and Byron, in poets. Read the haughty language in which Plato and the Platonists speak of all men who are not devoted to their own shining abstractions: Other men are rats and mice. The literary class is usually proud and exclusive. The correspondence of Pope and Swift describes mankind around them as monsters; and that of Goethe and Schiller, in our own time, is scarcely more kind.

It is easy to see how this arrogance comes. The genius is a genius by the first look he casts on any object. Is his eye creative? Does he not rest in angles and colours, but beholds the design; he will presently undervalue the actual object. In powerful moments, his thought has dissolved the works of art and nature into their causes, so that the works appear heavy and faulty. He has a conception of beauty, which the sculptor cannot embody. Picture, statue, temple, railroad, steamengine, existed first in an artist's mind, without flaw, mistake, or friction, which impair the executed models. So did the church, the state, college, court, social circle, and all the institutions. It is not strange that these men, remembering what they have seen and hoped of ideas, should affirm disdainfully the superiority of ideas. Having at some time seen that the happy soul will carry all the arts in power, they say, Why cumber ourselves with superfluous realizations? And, like dreaming beggars, they assume to speak and act as if these values were already substantiated.

On the other part, the men of toil and trade and luxury, the animal world, including the animal in the philosopher and poet also, — and the practical world, including the painful drudgeries which are never excused to philosopher or poet any more than to the rest, weigh heavily on the other side. The trade in our streets believes in no metaphysical causes, thinks nothing of the force which necessitated traders and a trading planet to exist; no, but sticks to cotton, sugar, wool, and salt. The ward-meetings on election-days are not softened by any misgiving of the value of these ballotings. Hot life is streaming in a single direction. To the men of this world, to the animal strength and spirits, to the men of practical power whilst immersed in it, the man of ideas appears out of his reason. They alone have reason.

Things always bring their own philosophy with them, that is, prudence. No man acquires property without acquiring with it a little arithmetic also. In England, the richest country that ever existed, property stands for more compared with personal ability, than in any other. After dinner, a man believes less, denies more: verities have lost some charm. After dinner, arithmetic is the only science: Ideas are disturbing, incendiary, follies of young men, repudiated by the solid portion of society: and a man comes to be valued by his athletic and animal qualities. Spence relates, that Mr Pope was with Sir Godfrey Kneller, one day, when his nephew, a Guinea trader, came in. "Nephew," said Sir Godfrey, "you have the honour of seeing the two greatest men in the world." — "I don't know how great men you may be," said the Guinea man, "but I don't like your looks. I have often bought a man much better than both of you, all muscles and bones, for ten guineas." Thus the men of the senses revenge themselves on the professors, and repay scorn for scorn. The first had leaped to conclusions not yet ripe, and say more than is true; the others make themselves merry with the philosopher, and weigh man by the pound. They believe that mustard bites the tongue, that pepper is hot, friction-matches are incendiary, revolvers to be avoided, and suspenders hold up pantaloons; that there is much sentiment in a chest of tea; and a man will be eloquent if you give him good wine. Are you tender and scrupulous, you must eat more mincepie. They hold that Luther had milk in him when he said,

> Wer nicht liebt Wein, Weib, und Gesang,
> Der bleibt ein Narr sein Leben lang,

and when he advised a young scholar perplexed with foreordination and free-will, to get well drunk. "The nerves," says Cabanis, "they are the man." My neighbor, a jolly farmer in the tavern bar-room, thinks that the use of money is sure and speedy spending. "For his part," he says, "he puts his down his neck, and gets the good of it."

The inconvenience of this way of thinking is that it runs into indifferentism, and then into disgust. Life is eating us up. We shall be fables presently. Keep cool: It will be all one a hundred years hence. Why should we fret and drudge? Our meat will taste tomorrow as it did yesterday, and we may at last have had enough of it. "Ah," said my languid gentleman at Oxford, "there's nothing new, or true, — and no matter."

With a little more bitterness the cynic moans, Our life is like an ass led to market by a bundle of hay being carried before him; he sees nothing but the bundle of hay. "There is so much trouble in coming into the world," said Lord Bolingbroke, "and so much more, as well as meanness, in going out of it, that 'tis hardly worth while to be here at all." I knew a philosopher of this kidney who was accustomed briefly to sum up his experience of human nature, in saying, "Mankind is a damned rascal." And the natural corollary is pretty sure to follow, 'The world lives by humbug, and so will I.'

The abstractionist and the materialist thus mutually exasperating each other, and the scoffer expressing the worst of materialism, there arises a third party to occupy the middle ground between these two, the skeptic, namely. He finds both wrong by being in extremes. He labours to plant his feet, to be the beam of the balance. He will not go beyond his card. He sees the onesidedness of these men of the street; he will not be a Gibeonite; he stands for the intellectual faculties, a cool head, and whatever serves to keep it cool: no unadvised industry, no unrewarded self-devotion, no loss of the brains in toil. Am I an ox or a dray? — You are both in extremes, he says. You who will have all solid, and a world of piglead, deceive yourselves grossly. You believe yourselves rooted and grounded on adamant, and yet if we uncover the last facts of our knowledge, you are spinning like bubbles in a river, you know not whither or whence, and you are bottomed and capped and wrapped in delusions.

Neither will he be betrayed to a book, and wrapped in a gown. The studious class are their own victims: they are thin and pale, their feet are cold, their heads are hot, the night is without sleep, the day a fear of interruption, pallor, squalor, hunger, and egotism. If you come near them, and see what conceits they entertain, — they are abstractionists, and spend their days and nights in dreaming some dream; in expecting the homage of society to some precious scheme built on a truth, but destitute of proportion in its presentment, of justness in its application, and of all energy of will in the schemer to embody and vitalize it.

But I see plainly, he says, that I cannot see. I know that human strength is not in extremes, but in avoiding extremes. I, at least, will shun the weakness of philosophizing beyond my depth. What is the use of pretending to powers we have not? What is the use of pretending to assurances we have not, respecting the other life? Why exaggerate the power of virtue? Why be an angel before your time? These strings wound up too high will snap. If there is a wish for immortality, and no evidence, why not say just that? If there are conflicting evidences, why not state them? If there is not ground for a candid thinker to make up his mind, yea or nay, — why not suspend the judgment? I weary of these dogmatizers. I tire of these hacks of routine, who deny the dogmas. I neither affirm nor deny. I stand here to try the case. I am here to consider, σκέπτειν, to consider how it is. I will try to keep the balance true. Of what use to take the chair, and glibly rattle off theories of society, religion, and nature, when I know that practical objections lie in the way insurmountable by me and by my mates? Why so talkative in public, when each of my neighbors can pin me to my seat by arguments I cannot refute? Why pretend that life is so simple a game, when we know how subtle and elusive the Proteus is? Why think to shut up all things in your narrow coop, when we know there are not one or two only, but ten, twenty, a thousand things, and unlike. Why fancy that you have all the truth in your keeping? There is much to say on all sides.

Who shall forbid a wise skepticism, seeing that there is no practical question on which anything more than an approximate solution can be had. Is not marriage an open question, when it is alleged, from the beginning of the world, that such as are in the institution wish to get out; and such as are out, wish to get in? And the reply of Socrates to him who asked whether he should choose a wife, still remains reasonable, "That, whether he should choose one or not, he would repent it." Is not the State a question? All society is divided in opinion on the subject of the State. Nobody loves it, great numbers dislike it, and suffer conscientious scruples to allegiance. And the only defence set up, is, the fear of doing worse in disorganizing. Is it otherwise with the Church? Or to put any of the questions which touch mankind nearest, Shall the young man aim at a leading part in law, in politics, in trade? It will not be pretended that a success in either of these kinds is quite coincident with what is best and inmost in his mind. Shall he, then, cutting the stays that hold him fast to the social state, put out to sea with no guidance but his genius? There is much to say on both sides. Remember the open question between the present order of "competition," and the friends of "attractive and associated Labour." The generous minds embrace the proposition of labour shared by all; it is the only honesty; nothing else is safe. It is from the poor man's hut alone, that strength and virtue come: and yet, on the other side, it is alleged, that labour impairs the form and breaks the spirit of man, and the labourers cry unanimously, 'We have no thoughts.' Culture, how indispensable! I cannot forgive you the want of accomplishments: and yet culture will instantly impair that chiefest beauty of spontaneousness. Excellent is culture for a savage; but once let him read in the book, and he is no longer able not to think of Plutarch's heroes. In short, since true fortitude of understanding consists "in not letting what we know be embarrassed by what we do not know," we ought to secure those advantages which we can command, and not risk them by clutching after the airy and unattainable. Come, no chimæras! Let us go abroad, let us mix in affairs, let us learn, and get, and have, and climb. "Men are a sort of moving plants, and, like trees, receive a great part of their nourishment from the air. If they keep too much at home, they pine." Let us have a robust manly life, let us know what we know for certain. What we have, let it be solid, and seasonable, and our own. A world in the hand is worth two in the bush. Let us have to do with real men and women, and not with skipping ghosts.

This, then, is the right ground of the skeptic, this of consideration, of selfcontaining, not at all of unbelief, not at all of universal denying, nor of universal doubting, doubting even that he doubts; least of all, of scoffing, and profligate jeering at all that is stable and good. These are no more his moods, than are those of religion and philosophy. He is the Considerer, the prudent, taking in sail, counting stock, husbanding his means, believing that a man has too many enemies, than that he can afford to be his own foe; that we cannot give ourselves too many advantages, in this unequal conflict, with powers so vast and unweariable ranged on one side, and this little conceited vulnerable popinjay that a man is, bobbing up and down into every danger, on the other. It is a position taken up for better defence, as of more safety, and one that can be maintained, and it is one of more opportunity and range; as, when we build a house, the rule is, to set it not too high nor too low, under the wind, but out of the dirt.

The philosophy we want is one of fluxions and mobility. The Spartan and Stoic schemes are too stark and stiff for our occasion. A theory of Saint John, and of nonresistance, seems, on the other hand, too thin and aerial. We want some coat woven of elastic steel, stout as the first, and limber as the second. We want a *ship,* in these billows we inhabit. An angular dogmatic house would be rent to chips and splinters, in this storm of many elements. No, it must be tight, and fit to the form of man, to live at all; as a shell must dictate the architecture of a house founded on the sea. The soul of man must be the type of our scheme, just as the body of man is the type after which a dwellinghouse is built. Adaptiveness is the peculiarity of human nature. We are golden averages, volitant stabilities, compensated or periodic errours, houses founded on the sea.

The wise skeptic wishes to have a near view of the best game, and the chief players, what is best in the planet, art and nature, places and events, but mainly men. Every thing that is excellent in mankind, a form of grace, an arm of iron, lips of persuasion, a brain of resources, every one skilful to play and win, he will see and judge.

The terms of admission to this spectacle, are, that he have a certain solid and intelligible way of living of his own, some method of answering the inevitable needs of human life; proof that he has played with skill and success: that he has evinced the temper, stoutness, and the range of qualities which, among his contemporaries and countrymen, entitle him to fellowship and trust. For, the secrets of life are not shown except to sympathy and likeness. Men do not confide themselves to boys, or coxcombs, or pedants, but to their peers. Some wise limitation, as the modern phrase is; some condition between the extremes, and having itself a positive quality, some stark and sufficient man, who is not salt or sugar, but sufficiently related to the world to do justice to Paris and London, and, at the same time, a vigorous and original thinker, whom cities cannot overawe, but who uses them, — is the fit person to occupy this ground of speculation. These qualities meet in the character of Montaigne. And yet, since the personal regard which I entertain for Montaigne may be unduly great, I will, under the shield of this prince of egotists, offer as an apology for electing him as the representative of Skepticism, a word or two to explain how my love began and grew for this admirable gossip.

A single odd volume of Cotton's translation of the Essays remained to me from my father's library, when a boy. It lay long neglected, until, after many years, when I was newly escaped from college, I read the book, and procured the remaining volumes. I remember the delight and wonder in which I lived with it. It seemed to me as if I had myself written the book in some former life, so sincerely it spoke to my thought and experience. It happened, when in Paris, in 1833, that, in the Cemetery of Père Lachaise, I came to a tomb of Auguste Collignon, who died in 1830, aged sixty-eight years, and who, said the monument, "lived to do right, and had formed himself to virtue on the Essays of Montaigne." Some years later, I became acquainted with an accomplished English poet, John Sterling, and, in prosecuting my correspondence, I found that, from a love of Montaigne, he had made a pilgrimage to his chateau, still standing near Castellan, in Périgord, and, after two hundred and fifty years, had copied from the walls of his library the inscriptions which Montaigne had written there. That Journal of Mr Sterling's, published in the (London) Westminster Review, Hazlitt has reprinted in the Prolegomena to his edition of the Essays. I heard with pleasure that one of the newly discovered autographs of William Shakspeare was in a copy of Florio's translation of Montaigne. It is the only book which we certainly know to have been in the poet's library.

And oddly enough, the duplicate copy of Florio which the British Museum purchased with a view of protecting the Shakspeare autograph, (as I was informed in the Museum,) turned out to have the autograph of Ben Jonson in the flyleaf. Leigh Hunt relates of Lord Byron, that Montaigne was the only great writer of past times whom he read with avowed satisfaction. Other coincidences not needful to be mentioned here, concurred to make this old Gascon still new and immortal for me.

In 1571, on the death of his father, Montaigne, then thirty-eight years old, retired from the practice of law at Bordeaux, and settled himself on his estate. Though he had been a man of pleasure, and sometimes a courtier, his studious habits now grew on him, and he loved the compass, staidness, and independence, of the country gentleman's life. He took up his economy in good earnest, and made his farms yield the most. Downright and plaindealing, and abhorring to be deceived or to deceive, he was esteemed in the country for his sense and probity. In the civil wars of the League, which converted every house into a fort, Montaigne kept his gates open, and his house without defence. All parties freely came and went, his courage and honour being universally esteemed. The neighboring lords and gentry brought jewels and papers to him for safe-keeping. Gibbon reckons in these bigoted times but two men of liberality in France, Henry IV and Montaigne.

Montaigne is the frankest and honestest of all writers. His French freedom runs into grossness, but he has anticipated all censure by the bounty of his own confessions. In his times, books were written to one sex only, and almost all were written in Latin; so that, in a humourist, a certain nakedness of statement was permitted, which our manners of a literature addressed equally to both sexes, do not allow. But, though a biblical plainness coupled with a most uncanonical levity, may shut his pages to many sensitive readers, yet the offence is superficial. He parades it: he makes the most of it: nobody can think or say worse of him, than he does. He pretends to most of the vices, and, if there be any virtue in him, he says, it got in by stealth. There is no man, in his opinion, who has not deserved hanging five or six times; and he pretends no exception in his own behalf. "Five or six as ridiculous stories," too, he says, "can be told of me, as of any man living." But, with all this really superfluous frankness, the opinion of an invincible probity grows into every reader's mind.

"When I the most strictly and religiously confess myself, I find that the best virtue I have has in it some tincture of vice; and I am afraid that Plato, in his purest virtue, (I, who am as sincere and perfect a lover of virtue of that stamp as any other whatever,) if he had listened, and laid his ear close to himself, would have heard some jarring sound of human mixture; but faint and remote, and only to be perceived by himself."

Here is an impatience and fastidiousness about colour or pretence of any kind. He has been in courts so long as to have conceived a furious disgust at appearances, he will indulge himself with a little cursing and swearing, he will talk with sailors and gipsies, use flash and streetballads: he has stayed in doors, till he is deadly sick; he will to the open air, though it rain bullets. He has seen too much of Gentlemen of the long robe, until he wishes for cannibals; and is so nervous by factitious life, that he thinks the more barbarous man is, the better he is. He likes his saddle. You may read theology and grammar and metaphysics elsewhere. Whatever you get here, shall smack of the earth and of real life, sweet or smart or stinging. He makes no hesitation to entertain you with the records of his disease; and his journey to Italy is quite full of that matter. He took and kept this position of equilibrium. Over his name, he drew an emblematic pair of scales, and wrote *Que sçais je?* under it. As I look at his effigy opposite the title page, I seem to hear him say, You may play Old Poz, if you will; you may rail and exaggerate. I stand here for truth, and will not, for all the states and churches and revenues and personal reputations of Europe, overstate the dry fact, as I see it; I will rather mumble and prose about what I certainly know; my house and barns; my father, my wife and my tenants; my old lean bald pate; my knives and forks; what meats I eat; and what drinks I prefer; and a hundred straws, just as ridiculous; than I will write with a fine crowquill a fine romance. I like gray days and autumn and winter weather. I am gray and autumnal myself, and think an undress, and old shoes that do not pinch my feet, and old friends who do not constrain me, and plain topics where I do not need to strain myself and pump my brains, the most suitable. Our condition as men is risky and ticklish enough. One cannot be sure of himself and his fortune an hour, but he may be whisked off into some pitiable or ridiculous plight. Why should I vapour and play the philosopher, instead of ballasting the best I can this dancing balloon. So, at least, I live within compass, keep myself ready for action, and can shoot the gulf, at last, with decency. If there be anything farcical in such a life, the blame is not mine: let it lie at Fate's and nature's door.

The Essays, therefore, are an entertaining soliloquy on every random topic that comes into his head, treating everything without ceremony, yet with masculine sense. There have been men with deeper insight, but, one would say, never a man with such abundance of thoughts. He is never dull, never insincere, and has the genius to make the reader care for all that he cares for.

The sincerity and marrow of the man reaches to his sentences. I know not anywhere the book that seems less written. It is the language of conversation transferred to a book. Cut these words, and they would bleed; they are vascular and alive. One has the same pleasure in it that we have in listening to the necessary speech of men about their work, when any unusual circumstance gives momentary importance to the dialogue. For blacksmiths and teamsters do not trip in their speech; it is a shower of bullets; it is Cambridge men who correct themselves, and begin again at every half sentence, and moreover will pun, and refine too much, and swerve from the matter to the expression. Montaigne talks with shrewdness, knows the world, and books, and himself, and uses the positive degree: never shrieks, or protests, or prays; no weakness, no convulsion, no superlative: does not wish to jump out of his skin, or play any antics, or annihilate space or time, but is stout and solid; tastes every moment of the day; likes pain, because it makes him feel himself, and realize things; as we pinch ourselves to know that we are awake. He keeps the plain; he rarely mounts or sinks; likes to feel solid ground, and the stones underneath. His writing has no enthusiasms, no aspiration; contented,

95

selfrespecting, and keeping the middle of the road. There is but one exception, — in his love for Socrates. In speaking of him, for once his cheek flushes, and his style rises to passion.

Montaigne died of a quinsy, at the age of sixty, in 1592. When he came to die, he caused the mass to be celebrated in his chamber. At the age of thirty-three, he had been married. "But," he says, "might I have had my own will, I would not have married Wisdom herself, if she would have had me: but 'tis to much purpose to evade it, the common custom and use of life will have it so. Most of my actions are guided by example, not choice." In the hour of death he gave the same weight to custom. *Que sçais je?* What do I know?

This book of Montaigne the world has endorsed, by translating it into all tongues, and printing seventy-five editions of it in Europe: and that, too, a circulation somewhat chosen, namely, among courtiers, soldiers, princes, men of the world, and men of wit and generosity.

Shall we say that Montaigne has spoken wisely, and given the right and permanent expression of the human mind on the conduct of life?

We are natural believers. Truth or the connection of cause and effect alone interests us. We are persuaded that a thread runs through all things: all worlds are strung on it as beads: and men and events and life come to us only because of that thread: they pass and repass only that we may know the direction and continuity of that line. A book or statement which goes to show that there is no line, but random and chaos; a calamity out of nothing, a prosperity and no account of it, a hero born from a fool, a fool from a hero, — dispirits us. Seen or unseen, we believe the tie exists. Talent makes counterfeit ties; Genius finds the real ones. We hearken to the man of science, because we anticipate the sequence in natural phenomena which he uncovers. We love whatever affirms, connects, preserves, and dislike what scatters or pulls down. One man appears whose nature is to all men's eyes conserving and constructive: His presence supposes a well-ordered society, agriculture, trade, large institutions, and empire. If these did not exist, they would begin to exist through his endeavours. Therefore he cheers and comforts men, who feel all this in him very readily. The non-conformist and the rebel say all manner of unanswerable things against the existing republic, but discover to our sense no plan of house or state of their own. Therefore, though the town and state and way of living which our counsellor contemplated, might be a very modest or musty prosperity, yet men rightly go for him, and reject the Reformer, so long as he comes only with axe and crowbar.

But though we are natural conservers and causationists, and reject a sour dumpish unbelief, the skeptical class which Montaigne represents, have reason, and every man, at some time, belongs to it. Every superior mind will pass through this domain of equilibration, — I should rather say, will know how to avail himself of the checks and balances in nature, as a natural weapon against the exaggeration and formalism of bigots and blockheads.

Skepticism is the attitude assumed by the student in relation to the particulars which society adores, but which he sees to be reverend only in their tendency and spirit. The ground occupied by the skeptic is the vestibule of the temple. Society does not like to have any breath of question blown on the existing order. But the interrogation of custom at all points is an inevitable stage in the growth of every superior mind, and is the evidence of its perception of the flowing power which remains itself in all changes.

The superior mind will find itself equally at odds with the evils of society, and with the projects that are offered to relieve them. The wise skeptic is a bad citizen; no conservative; he sees the selfishness of property and the drowsiness of institutions. But neither is he fit to work with any democratic party that ever was constituted; for parties wish every one committed, and he penetrates the popular patriotism. His politics are those of the "Soul's Errand" of Sir Walter Raleigh; or of Krishna, in the Bhagavat, "There is none who is worthy of my love or hatred;" whilst he sentences law, physic, divinity, commerce, and custom. He is a Reformer; yet he is no better member of the philanthropic association. It turns out that he is not the champion of the operative, the pauper, the prisoner, the slave. It stands in his mind, that our life in this world is not of quite so easy interpretation as churches and schoolbooks say. He does not wish to take ground against these benevolences, to play the part of devil's attorney, and blazon every doubt and sneer that darkens the sun for him. But he says, There are doubts.

I mean to use the occasion and celebrate the calendar-day of our Saint Michel de Montaigne, by counting and describing these doubts or negations. I wish to ferret them out of their holes, and sun them a little. We must do with them as the police do with old rogues, who are shown up to the public at the Marshal's office. They will never be so formidable, when once they have been identified and registered. But I mean honestly by them, that justice shall be done to their terrors. I shall not take Sunday objections, made up on purpose to be put down. I shall take the worst I can find, whether I can dispose of them, or they of me.

I do not press the skepticism of the materialist. I know, the quadruped opinion will not prevail. 'Tis of no importance what bats and oxen think. The first dangerous symptom I report is the levity of intellect, as if it were fatal to earnestness to know much. Knowledge is the knowing that we cannot know. The dull pray; the geniuses are light mockers. How respectable is earnestness on every platform! but intellect kills it. Nay, San Carlo, my subtle and admirable friend, one of the most penetrating of men, finds that all direct ascension, even of lofty piety, leads to this ghastly insight and sends back the votary orphaned. My astonishing San Carlo thought the lawgivers and saints infected. They found the ark empty, saw and would not tell; and tried to choke off their approaching followers, by saying, 'Action, action, my dear fellows, is for you!' Bad as was to me this detection by San Carlo, this frost in July, this blow from a bride, there was still a worse, namely, the cloy or satiety of the saints. In the mount of vision, ere they have yet risen from their knees, they say, We discover that this our homage and beatitude is partial and deformed. We must fly for relief to the suspected and reviled Intellect, to the Understanding, the Mephistopheles, to the gymnastics of talent.

This is Hobgoblin the first, and though it has been the subject of much elegy in our nineteenth century from Byron, Goethe, and other poets of less fame, not to mention many distinguished private observers, I confess, it is not very affecting to my imagination. For it seems to concern the shattering of babyhouses and crockery shops. What flutters the Church of Rome or of England or of Geneva or of Boston, may yet be very far from touching any principle of faith. I think that the intellect and moral sentiment are unanimous; and that though philosophy extirpates bugbears, yet it supplies the natural checks of vice, and polarity to the soul. I think that the wiser a man is, the more stupendous he finds the natural and moral economy, and lifts himself to a more absolute reliance.

There is the power of moods, each setting at nought all but its own tissue of facts and beliefs. There is the power of complexions — obviously modifying the dispositions and sentiments. The beliefs and unbeliefs appear to be structural, and, as soon as each man attains the poise and vivacity which allow the whole machinery to play, he will not need extreme examples, but will rapidly alternate all opinions in his own life. Our life is March weather, savage and serene in one hour. We go forth austere, dedicated, believing in the iron links of Destiny, and will not turn on our heel to save our life: but a book, or a bust, or only the sound of a name, shoots a spark through the nerves, and we suddenly believe in will; my finger-ring shall be the seal of Solomon; Fate is for imbeciles. All is possible to the resolved mind. Presently, a new experience gives a new turn to our thoughts; commonsense resumes its tyranny. We say, 'Well, the army, after all, is the gate to fame, manners, and poetry: and, look you, on the whole selfishness plants best, prunes best, makes the best commerce, and the best citizen.' Are the opinions of a man on right and wrong, on fate and causation, at the mercy of a broken sleep, or an indigestion? Is his belief in God and Duty no deeper than a stomach evidence? And what guaranty for the permanence of his opinions? I like not the French celerity, a new church and state once a week. This is the second negation; and I shall let it pass for what it will. As far as it asserts rotation of states of mind, I suppose it suggests its own remedy, namely, in the record of larger periods.

What is the mean of many states; of all the states? Does the general voice of ages affirm any principle, or is no community of sentiment discoverable in distant times and places? And when it shows the power of selfinterest, I accept that as part of the divine law and must reconcile it with aspiration the best I can.

The word Fate or Destiny expresses the sense of mankind in all ages that the laws of the world do not always befriend, but often hurt and crush us. Fate in the shape of *Kinde* or Nature, grows over us like grass. We paint Time with a scythe; Love and Fortune blind; and Destiny, deaf. We have too little power of resistance against this ferocity which champs us up. What front can we make against these unavoidable, victorious, maleficent forces? What can I do against the influence of *Race* in my history? What can I do against hereditary and constitutional habits, against scrofula, lymph, impotence? against climate, against barbarism, in my country? I can reason down or deny everything except this perpetual Belly: feed he must and will, and I cannot make him respectable.

But the main resistance which the affirmative impulse finds and one including all others is in the doctrine of the Illusionists. There is a painful rumour in circulation that we have been practised upon in all the principal performances of life, and free agency is the emptiest name. We have been sopped and drugged with the air, with food, with woman, with children, with customs, with sciences, with events; which leave us exactly where they found us. The mathematics, 'tis complained, leave the mind where they find it: so do all sciences, and so do all events and actions. I find a man who has passed through all the sciences the churl he was, and through all the offices, learned, civil, social, I can detect the child. We are not the less necessitated to dedicate life to them. In fact we may come to accept it as the fixed rule and theory of our state of education that God is a substance, and his method is illusion. The eastern sages owned the Goddess Yoganidra, the great illusory energy of Vishnu by whom as utter ignorance the whole world is beguiled.

Or, shall I state it thus? The astonishment of life, is, the absence of any appearance of reconciliation between the theory and practice of life. Reason, the prized reality, the Law, is apprehended now and then for a serene and profound moment amidst the hubbub of cares and works which have no direct bearing on it; — is then lost, for months or years, and again found, for an interval, to be lost again. If we compute it in time, we may, in fifty years, have half a dozen reasonable hours. But what are these cares and works the better? A method in the world we do not see, but this parallelism of great and little, which never react on each other, nor discover the smallest tendency to converge. Experiences, fortunes, governings, readings, writings, are nothing to the purpose; as when a man comes into the room, it does not appear whether he has been fed on yams or buffalo, — he has contrived to get so much bone and fibre as he wants, out of rice or out of snow. So vast is the disproportion between the sky of law and the pismire of performance under it, that, whether he is a man of worth or a sot, is not so great a matter as we say. Shall I add, as one juggle of this enchantment, the stunning non-intercourse law which makes co-operation impossible. The young spirit pants to enter society. But all the ways of culture and greatness lead to solitary imprisonment. He had been often balked. He did not expect a sympathy with his thought from the village, but he went with it to the chosen and intelligent, and found no entertainment for it, but mere misapprehension, distaste, and scoffing. Men are strangely mistimed and misapplied, and the excellence of each is an inflamed individualism which separates him more.

There are these and more than these diseases of thought, which our ordinary teachers do not attempt to remove. Now shall we, because a good nature inclines us to Virtue's side, say, There are no doubts, — and lie for the right? Is life to be led in a brave, or in a cowardly manner? and is not the satisfaction of the doubts essential to all manliness? Is the name of Virtue to be a barrier to that which is Virtue? Can you not believe that a man of earnest and burly habit may find small good in tea, essays, and catechism, and want a rougher instruction, want men, labour, trade, farming, war, hunger, plenty, love, hatred, doubt, and terror, to make things plain to him, and has he not a right to insist on being convinced in his own way? When he is convinced, he will be worth the pains.

Belief consists in accepting the affirmations of the soul; Unbelief, in denying them. Some minds are incapable of skepticism. The doubts they profess to entertain are rather a civility or accommodation to the common discourse of their company. They may well give themselves leave to speculate, for they are secure of a return. Once admitted to the heaven of thought, they see no relapse into night, but infinite invitation on the other side. Heaven is within heaven, and sky over sky, and they are encompassed with divinities. Others there are, to whom the heaven is brass, and it shuts down to the surface of the earth. It is a question of temperament, or of more or less immersion in nature. The last class must needs have a reflex or parasitic faith; not a sight of realities, but an instinctive reliance on the seers and believers of realities. The manners and thoughts of believers astonish them and convince them that these have seen something which is hid from themselves. But their sensual habit would fix the believer to his last position, whilst he as inevitably advances: and presently the unbeliever for love of belief burns the believer.

Great believers are always reckoned infidels, impracticable, fantastic, atheistic, and really men of no account. The spiritualist finds himself driven to express his faith by a series of skepticisms. Charitable souls come with their projects, and ask his cooperation. How can he hesitate? It is the rule of mere comity and courtesy, to agree where you can, and to turn your sentence with something auspicious and not sneering and sinister. But he is forced to say, 'O these things will be as they must be; what can you do? These particular griefs and crimes are the foliage and fruit of such trees as we see growing. It is vain to complain of the leaf or the berry: cut it off, it will bear another just as bad. You must begin your cure lower down.' The generosities of the day prove an intractable element for him. The people's questions are not his; their methods are not his; and against all the dictates of good nature, he is driven to say, he has no pleasure in them.

Even the doctrines dear to the hope of man, of the divine Providence, and of the immortality of the Soul, his neighbours cannot put the statement so, that he shall affirm it. But he denies out of more faith, and not less. He denies out of honesty. He had rather stand charged with the imbecility of skepticism, than with untruth. I believe, he says, in the moral design of the universe; it exists hospitably for the weal of souls; but your dogmas seem to me caricatures. Why should I make believe them? — Will any say this is cold and infidel? The wise and magnanimous will not say so. They will exult in his farsighted goodwill, that can abandon to the adversary all the ground of tradition and common belief, without losing a jot of strength. It sees to the end of all transgression. George Fox saw that there was "an ocean of darkness and death but withal an infinite ocean of light and love which flowed over that of darkness."

The final solution in which Skepticism is lost, is, in the moral sentiment, which never forfeits its supremacy. All moods may be safely tried, and their weight allowed to all objections: the moral sentiment as easily outweighs them all, as any one. This is the drop which balances the sea. I play with the miscellany of facts and take those superficial views which we call Skepticism but I know that they will presently appear to me in that order which makes Skepticism impossible. A man of thought must feel the thought that is parent of the universe: that the masses of nature do undulate and flow.

This faith avails to the whole emergency of life and objects. The world is saturated with deity and with law. He is content with just and unjust, with sots and fools, with the triumph of folly and fraud. He can behold with serenity, the yawning gulf between the ambition of man and his power of performance, between the demand and supply of power which makes the tragedy of all souls.

Charles Fourier announced that "the attractions of man are proportioned to his destinies;" in other words, that every desire predicts its own satisfaction. Yet all experience exhibits the reverse of this; the incompetency of power is the universal grief of young and ardent minds. They accuse the divine Providence of a certain parsimony. It has shown the heaven and earth to every

103

child, and filled him with a desire for the whole; a desire raging, infinite, a hunger as of space to be filled with planets; a cry of famine as of devils for souls. Then for the satisfaction; — to each man is administered a single drop, a bead of dew of vital power, *per day,* — a cup as large as space, and one drop of the water of life in it. Each man woke in the morning with an appetite that could eat the solar system like a cake; a spirit for action and passion without bounds; he could lay his hand on the morningstar; he could try conclusions with gravitation or chemistry; but on the first motion to prove his strength, hands, feet, senses, gave way, and would not serve him. He was an emperor deserted by his states, and left to whistle by himself or thrust into a mob of emperors all whistling: and still the sirens sung, "The attractions are proportioned to the destinies." In every house, in the heart of each maiden and of each boy, in the soul of the soaring saint, this chasm is found, — between the largest promise of ideal power, and the shabby experience.

The expansive nature of truth comes to our succour, elastic, not to be surrounded. Man helps himself by larger generalizations. The lesson of life is practically to generalize, to believe what the years and the centuries say against the hours; to resist the usurpation of particulars; to penetrate to their catholic sense. Things seem to say one thing, and say the reverse. The appearance is immoral; the result is moral. Things seem to tend downward, to justify despondency, to promote rogues, to defeat the just; and by knaves, as by martyrs, the just cause is carried forward. Although knaves win in every political struggle, although society seems to be delivered over from the hands of one set of criminals into the hands of another set of criminals, as fast as the government is changed, and the march of civilization is a train of felonies, yet, general ends are somehow answered. We see now, events forced on, which seem to retard or retrograde the civility of ages. But the world spirit is a good swimmer, and storms and waves cannot drown him. He snaps his finger at laws: and so, throughout history, heaven seems to affect low and poor means. (The needles are nothing; the magnetism is all.) Through the years and the centuries, through evil agents, through toys and atoms, a great and beneficent tendency irresistibly streams.

Let a man learn to look for the permanent in the mutable and fleeting; let him learn to bear the disappearance of things he was wont to reverence, without losing his reverence; let him learn that he is here not to work, but to be worked upon, and, that, though abyss open under abyss, and opinion displace opinion, all are at last contained in the eternal Cause.

"If my bark sink, 'tis to another sea."

SHAKSPEARE, OR
THE POET

V

Shakspeare, or the Poet

Great men are more distinguished by range and extent, than by originality. If we require the originality which consists in weaving like a spider their web from their own bowels, in finding clay, and making bricks, and building the house, no great men are original. Nor does valuable originality consist in unlikeness to other men. The hero is in the press of knights, and the thick of events, and, seeing what men want, and sharing their desire, he adds the needful length of sight and of arm to come at the desired point. The greatest genius is the most indebted man. A poet is no rattle-brain saying what comes uppermost, and, because he says everything, saying, at last, something good; but a heart in unison with his time and country. There is nothing whimsical and fantastic in his production, but sweet and sad earnest, freighted with the weightiest convictions and pointed with the most determined aim which any man or class knows of in his times.

The genius of our life is jealous of individuals, and will not have any individual great, except through the general. There is no choice to genius. A great man does not wake up on some fine morning, and say, I am full of life, I will go to sea, and find an Antarctic continent: today, I will square the circle: I will ransack botany, and find a new food for man: I have a new architecture in my mind: I foresee a new mechanic power: no; but he finds himself in the river of the thoughts and events, forced onward by the ideas and necessities of his contemporaries. He stands where all the eyes of men look one way, and their hands all point in the direction in which he should go. The Church has reared him amidst rites and pomps, and he carries out the advice which her music gave him, and builds a cathedral needed by her chants and processions. He finds a war raging; it educates him by trumpet in barracks, and he betters the instruction. He finds two counties groping to bring coal, or flour, or fish, from the place of production to the place of consumption, and he hits on a railroad. Every master has found his materials collected, and his power lay in his sympathy with his people, and in his love of the materials he wrought in. What an economy of power! and what a compensation for the shortness of life! All is done to his hand. The world has brought him thus far on his way. The human race has gone out before him, sunk the hills, filled the hollows, and bridged the rivers. Men, nations, poets, artisans, women, all have worked for him, and he enters into their labours. Choose any other thing, out of the line of tendency, out of the national feeling and history, and he would have all to do for himself: his powers would be expended in the first preparations. Great genial power, one would almost say, consists in not being original at all; in being altogether receptive; in letting the world do all, and suffering the spirit of the hour to pass unobstructed through the mind.

Shakspeare's youth fell in a time when the English people were importunate for dramatic entertainments. The court took offence easily at political allusions, and attempted to suppress them. The Puritans, a growing and energetic party, and the religious within the Anglican Church would suppress them. But the people wanted them. Innyards, houses without roofs, or extemporaneous enclosures at country fairs, were the ready theatres of strolling players. The people had tasted this new joy, and, as we could not hope to suppress newspapers now, no, not by the strongest party, neither then, could king, prelate, or puritan, alone or united, suppress an organ, which was ballad, epic, newspaper, caucus, lecture, Punch, and library, at the same time. Probably king, prelate, and puritan, all found their own account in it. It had become by all causes a national interest, — by no means conspicuous, so that some great scholar would have thought of treating it in an English history, — but not a whit less considerable because it was cheap, and of no account, like a baker's shop. The best proof of its vitality is the crowd of writers which suddenly broke into this field; Kyd, Marlow, Greene, Jonson, Chapman, Dekker, Webster, Heywood, Middleton, Peele, Ford, Massinger, Beaumont, and Fletcher.

The secure possession by the stage of the public mind is of the first importance to the poet who works for it. He loses no time in idle experiments. Here is audience and expectation prepared. In the case of Shakspeare, there is much more. At the time when he left Stratford, and went up to London, a great body of stage plays of all dates and writers existed in manuscript, and were in turn produced on the boards. Here is the Tale of Troy, which the audience will bear hearing some part of, every week: the Death of Julius Cæsar, and other stories out of Plutarch, which they never tire of: a shelf full of English history, from the Chronicles of Brut and Arthur, down to the royal Henries, which men hear eagerly: and a string of doleful tragedies, merry Italian tales, and Spanish voyages, which all the London prentices know. All the mass has been treated with more or less skill by every playwright, and the prompter has the soiled and tattered manuscripts. It is now no longer possible to say who wrote them first. They have been the property of the Theatre so long, and so many rising geniuses have enlarged or altered them, inserting a speech, or a whole scene, or adding a song, that no man can any longer claim copyright in this work of numbers. Happily, no man wishes to. They are not yet desired in that way. We have few readers, many spectators and hearers. They had best lie where they are.

Shakspeare, in common with his comrades, esteemed the mass of old plays waste stock, in which any experiment could be freely tried. Had the *prestige* which hedges about a modern tragedy existed, nothing could have been done. The rude warm blood of the living England circulated in the play, as in street ballads, and gave body which he wanted to his airy and majestic fancy. The poet needs a ground in popular tradition on which he may work, and which, again, may restrain his art within the due temperance. It holds him to the people, supplies a foundation for his edifice, and in furnishing so much work done to his hand, leaves him at leisure, and in full strength for the audacities of his imagination.

In short, the poet owes to his legend, what Sculpture owed to the temple. Sculpture in Egypt, and in Greece, grew up in subordination to architecture. It was the ornament of the temple wall: at first, a rude relief carved on pediments, then the relief became bolder, and a head or arm was projected from the wall, the groups being still arranged with reference to the building, which serves also as a frame to hold the figures, and when, at last, the greatest freedom of style and treatment was reached, the prevailing genius of architecture still enforced a certain calmness and continence in the statue. As soon as the statue was begun for itself, and with no reference to the temple or palace, the art began to decline: freak, extravagance, and exhibition, took the place of the old temperance. This balance-wheel which the sculptor found in architecture, the perilous irritability of poetic talent found in the accumulated dramatic materials to which the people were already wonted, and which had a certain excellence, which no single genius, however extraordinary, could hope to create.

In point of fact it appears that Shakspeare did owe debts in all directions, and was able to use whatever he found; and the amount of indebtedness may be inferred from Malone's laborious computations in regard to the second and third parts of Henry VI, in which, "out of 6043 lines, 1771 were written by some author preceding Shakspeare; 2373 by him on the foundation laid by his predecessors, and 1899 were entirely his own." And the proceeding investigation hardly leaves a single drama of his absolute invention. Malone's sentence is an important piece of external history. In Henry VIII, I think I see plainly the cropping out of the original rock on which his own finer stratum was laid. The first play was written by a superior thoughtful man, with a vicious ear. I can mark his lines, and know well their cadence. See Wolsey's soliloquy and the following scene with Cromwell, where, instead of the metre of Shakspeare, whose secret is, that the thought constructs the tune, so that reading for the sense will best bring out the rhythm, here the lines are constructed on a given tune, and the verse has even a trace of pulpit eloquence. But the play contains through all its length unmistakeable traits of Shakspeare's hand, and some passages, as the account of the Coronation, are like autographs. What is odd, the compliment to Queen Elizabeth is in the bad rhythm.

Shakspeare knew that tradition supplies a better fable than any invention can. If he lost any credit of design, he augmented his resources, and, at that day, our petulant demand for originality was not so much pressed. There was no literature for the million. The universal reading, the cheap press, were unknown. A great poet who appears in illiterate times, absorbs into his sphere all the light which is anywhere radiating. Every intellectual jewel, every flower of sentiment, it is his fine office to bring to his people; and he comes to value his memory, equally with his invention. He is therefore little solicitous whence his thoughts have been derived, whether through translation, whether through tradition, whether by travel in distant countries, whether by inspiration: from whatever source, they are equally welcome to his uncritical audience. Nay, he borrows very near home. Other men say wise things as well as he; only they say a good many foolish things, and do not know when they have spoken wisely. He knows the sparkle of the true stone, and puts it in high place, wherever he finds it.

Such is the happy position of Homer, perhaps; of Chaucer, of Saadi. They felt that all wit was their wit. And they are librarians and historiographers as well as poets. Each romancer was heir and dispenser of all the hundred tales of the world, —

> "Presenting Thebes' and Pelops' line,
> And the tale of Troy divine."

The influence of Chaucer is conspicuous in all our early literature: and, more recently, not only Pope and Dryden have been beholden to him, but in the whole society of English writers a large unacknowledged debt is easily traced. One is charmed with the opulence which feeds so many pensioners. But Chaucer is a huge borrower. Chaucer, it seems, drew continually through Lydgate and Caxton, from Guido di Colonna, whose Latin romance of the Trojan War was in turn a compilation from Dares Phrygius, Ovid, and Statius. Then Petrarch, Boccaccio, and the Provençal poets are his benefactors: the Romaunt of the Rose is only judicious translation from William of Lorris and John of Meun: Troilus and Creseide, from Lollius of Urbino: The Cock and the Fox, from the *Lais* of Marie: The House of Fame, from the French or Italian: and poor Gower he uses, as if he were only a brickkiln or stonequarry, out of which to build his house. He steals by this apology, that what he takes has no worth where he finds it, and the greatest where he leaves it. It has come to be practically a sort of rule in literature, that a man having once shown himself capable of original writing, is entitled thenceforth to steal from the writings of others at discretion. Thought is the property of him who can entertain it; and of him who can adequately place it. A certain aukwardness marks the use of borrowed thoughts; but as soon as we have learned what to do with them, they become our own.

Thus all originality is relative. Every thinker is retrospective. The learned member of the legislature at Westminster or at Washington, speaks and votes for thousands. Show us the constituency, and the now invisible channels by which the senator is made aware of their wishes, the crowd of practical and knowing men, who, by correspondence or conversation, are feeding him with evidence, anecdotes, and estimates, and it will bereave his fine attitude and resistance of something of their impressiveness. As Sir Robert Peel and Mr Webster vote, so Locke and Rousseau think for thousands; and so there were fountains all around Homer, Menu, Saadi, or Milton, from which they drew; friends, lovers, books, traditions, proverbs, — all perished, — which, if seen, would go to reduce the wonder. Did the bard speak with authority? did he feel himself overmatched by any companion? The appeal is to the consciousness of the writer. Is there at last in his breast a Delphi whereof to ask concerning any thought or thing, whether it be verily so, yea or nay? and to have answer, and to rely on that? All the debts which such a man could contract to other wit, would never disturb his consciousness of originality: for the ministrations of books and of other minds are a whiff of smoke to that most private reality with which he has conversed.

It is easy to see that what is best written or done by genius in the world was no man's work, but came by wide social labour, when a thousand wrought like one, sharing the same impulse. Our English Bible is a wonderful specimen of the strength and music of the English language. But it was not made by one man or at one time; but centuries and churches brought it to perfection. There never was a time when there was not some translation existing. The Liturgy, admired for its energy and pathos, is an anthology of the piety of ages and nations, a translation of the prayers and forms of the Catholic Church, — these selected, too, in long periods, from the prayers and meditations of every saint and sacred writer, all over the world. Grotius makes the like remark in respect to the Lord's Prayer, that the single clauses of which it is composed, were already in use, in the time of Christ, in the Rabbinical forms. He picked out the grains of gold. The nervous language of the Common Law, the impressive forms of our courts, and the precision and substantial truth of the legal distinctions, are the contribution of all the sharpsighted strong-minded men who have lived in the countries where these laws govern. The translation of Plutarch gets its excellence by being translation on translation. There never was a time when there was none. All the truly idiomatic and national phrases are kept, and all others successively picked out and thrown away. Something like the same process had gone on long before with the originals of these books. The world takes liberties with world-books. Vedas, Æsop's Fables, Pilpay, Arabian Nights, Cid, Iliad, Robin Hood, Scottish Minstrelsy, are not the work of single men. In the composition of such works, the time thinks, the market thinks, the mason, the carpenter, the merchant, the farmer, the fop, all think for us. Every book supplies its time with one good word; every municipal law, every trade, every folly of the day; and the generic catholic genius, who is not afraid or ashamed to owe his originality to the originality of all, stands with the next age as the recorder and embodiment of his own.

We have to thank the researches of antiquaries and the Shakspeare Society, for ascertaining the steps of the English Drama, from the Mysteries celebrated in churches and by churchmen, and the final detachment from the church, and the completion of secular plays, from Ferrex and Porrex, and Gammer Gurton's Needle, down to the possession of the stage by the very pieces which Shakspeare altered, remodelled, and finally made his own. Elated with success, and piqued by the growing interest of the problem, they have left no bookstall unsearched, no chest in a garret unopened, no file of old yellow accounts to decompose in damp and worms, so keen was the hope to discover whether the boy Shakspeare poached or not, whether he held horses at the theatre door, whether he kept school, and why he left in his will only his second best bed to Ann Hathaway his wife.

There is somewhat touching in the madness with which the passing age mischooses the object on which all candles shine, and all eyes are turned; the care with which it registers every trifle touching Queen Elizabeth and King James and the Essexes, Leicesters, Burleighs, and Buckinghams, and lets pass without a single valuable note the founder of another dynasty, which alone will cause the Tudor dynasty to be remembered, — the man who carries the Saxon race in him by the inspiration which feeds him, and on whose thoughts the foremost people of the world are now for some ages to be nourished, and minds to receive this, and not another bias. A popular player, nobody suspected he was the poet of the human race: and the secret was kept as faithfully from poets and intellectual men, as from courtiers and frivolous people. Bacon, who took the inventory of the human understanding for his times, never mentioned his name. Ben Jonson, though we have strained his few words of regard and panegyric, had no suspicion of the elastic fame whose first vibrations he was attempting. He, no doubt, thought the praise he has conceded to him generous, and esteemed himself, out of all question, the better poet of the two.

If it need wit to know wit, according to the proverb, Shakspeare's time should be capable of recognizing it. Sir Henry Wotton was born four years after Shakspeare, and died twenty-three years after him, and I find among his correspondents and acquaintances, the following persons: Theodore Beza, Isaac Casaubon, Sir Philip Sidney, Earl of Essex, Lord Bacon, Sir Walter Raleigh, John Milton, Sir Henry Vane, Isaak Walton, Dr Donne, Abraham Cowley, Bellarmine, Charles Cotton, John Pym, John Hales, Kepler, Vieta, Albericus Gentilis, Paul Sarpi, Arminius; with all of whom exists some token of his having communicated, without enumerating many others whom doubtless he saw, — Shakspeare, Spenser, Jonson, Beaumont, Massinger, two Herberts, Marlow, Chapman, and the rest. Since the constellation of great men who appeared in Greece, in the time of Pericles, there was never any such society; — yet their genius failed them to find out the best head in the universe. Our poet's mask was impenetrable. You cannot see the mountain near. It took a century to make it suspected; and not until two centuries had passed, after his death, did any criticism which we think adequate begin to appear. It was not possible to write the history of Shakspeare till now; for he is the father of German literature: it was on the introduction of Shakspeare into German, by Lessing, and the translation of his works by Wieland and Schlegel, that the rapid burst of German literature was most intimately connected. It was not until the nineteenth century, whose speculative genius is a sort of living Hamlet, that the tragedy of Hamlet could find such wondering readers. Now, literature, philosophy, and thought are Shakspearized. His mind is the horizon beyond which at present we do not see. Our ears are educated to music by his rhythm. Coleridge and Goethe are the only critics who have expressed our convictions with any adequate fidelity; but there is in all cultivated minds a silent appreciation of his superlative power and beauty, which, like Christianity, qualifies the period.

The Shakspeare Society have inquired in all directions, advertised the missing facts, offered money for any information that will lead to proof; — and with what result? Beside some important illustration of the history of the English stage to which I adverted, they have gleaned a few facts touching the property and dealings in regard to property of the Poet. It appears that from year to year he owned a larger share in the Blackfriars Theatre: its wardrobe and other appurtenances were his; that he bought an estate in his native village with his earnings as writer and shareholder; that he lived in the best house in Stratford; was intrusted by his neighbours with their commissions in London, as of borrowing money, and the like; that he was a veritable farmer. About the time when he was writing Macbeth, he sues Philip Rogers, in the borough-court of Stratford, for thirty-five shillings, tenpence, for corn delivered to him at different times; and, in all respects, appears as a good husband, with no reputation for eccentricity or excess. He was a goodnatured sort of man, an actor and shareholder in the theatre, not in any striking manner distinguished from other actors and managers. I admit the importance of this information. It was well worth the pains that have been taken to procure it.

But whatever scraps of information concerning his condition these researches may have rescued, they can shed no light upon that infinite invention which is the concealed magnet of his attraction for us. We are very clumsy writers of history. We tell the chronicle of parentage, birth, birthplace, schooling, schoolmates, earning of money, marriage, publication of books, celebrity, death, and when we have come to an end of this gossip, no ray of relation appears between it and the goddess-born; and it seems as if, had we dipped at random into the "Modern Plutarch," and read any other life there, it would have fitted the poems as well. It is the essence of poetry to spring like the rainbow daughter of Wonder from the invisible, to abolish the past, and refuse all history. Malone, Warburton, Dyce, and Collier have wasted their oil. The famed theatres Covent Garden, Drury Lane, the Park, and Tremont, have vainly assisted. Betterton, Garrick, Kemble, Kean, and Macready dedicate their lives to this genius; him they crown, elucidate, obey, and express. The Genius knows them not. The recitation begins; one golden word leaps out immortal from all this painted pedantry, and sweetly torments us with invitations to its own inaccessible homes. I remember I went once to see the Hamlet of a famed performer, the pride of the English stage, and all I then heard and all I now remember of the tragedian, was that in which the tragedian had no part, simply Hamlet's question to the ghost, —

> "What may this mean,
> That thou, dead corse, again in complete steel
> Revisit'st thus the glimpses of the moon?"

That imagination which dilates the closet he writes in to the world's dimension, crowds it with agents in rank and order, as quickly reduces the big reality to be the glimpses of the moon. These tricks of his magic spoil for us the illusions of the green room. Can any biography shed light on the localities into which the Midsummer Night's Dream admits me? Did Shakspeare confide to any notary or parish Recorder, sacristan, or surrogate in Stratford, the genesis of that delicate creation? The forest of Arden, the nimble air of Scone Castle, the moonlight of Portia's villa, "the antres vast and desarts idle" of Othello's captivity, — where is the third cousin or grandnephew, the chancellor's file of accounts, or private letter, that has kept one word of those transcendant secrets? In fine, in this drama, as in all great works of art, — in the Cyclopæan architecture of Egypt and India; in the Phidian sculpture; the Gothic minsters; the Italian painting; the Ballads of Spain and Scotland; — the Genius draws up the ladder after him, when the creative age goes up to heaven, and gives way to a new, which sees the works, and asks in vain for a history.

Shakspeare is the only biographer of Shakspeare, and even he can tell nothing except to the Shakspeare in us, that is, to our most apprehensive and sympathetic hour. He cannot step from off his tripod, and give us anecdotes of his inspirations. Read the antique documents extricated, analyzed, and compared, by the assiduous Dyce and Collier; and now read one of those skiey sentences, — aerolites, — which seem to have fallen out of heaven, and which, not your experience, but the man within the breast has accepted as words of fate, and tell me if they match: if the former account in any manner for the latter, or which gives the most historical insight into the man.

Hence, though our external history is so meagre, yet with Shakspeare for biographer, instead of Aubrey and Rowe, we have really the information which is material, that which describes character and fortune, that which, if we were about to meet the man and deal with him, would most import us to know. We have his recorded convictions on those questions which knock for answer at every heart, on life and death, on love, on wealth, and poverty, on the prizes of life, and the ways whereby we come at them, on the characters of men, and the influences occult and open which affect their fortunes, and on those mysterious and de-

moniacal powers which defy our science, and which yet interweave their malice and their gift in our brightest hours. Who ever
read the volume of the "Sonnets," without finding that the Poet
had there revealed, under masks that are no masks to the intelligent, the lore of friendship and of love; the confusion of sentiments in the most susceptible, and, at the same time, the most
intellectual of men? What trait of his private mind has he hidden
in his dramas? One can discern in his ample pictures of the gentleman and the king, what forms and humanities pleased him; his
delight in troops of friends, in large hospitality, in cheerful giving.
Let Timon, let Warwick, let Antonio the merchant, answer for his
great heart. So far from Shakspeare's being the least known, he is
the one person in all modern history known to us. What point of
morals, of manners, of economy, of philosophy, of religion, of
taste, of the conduct of life, has he not settled? What mystery has
he not signified his knowledge of? What office or function or district of man's work has he not remembered? What king has he not
taught state, as Talma taught Napoleon? What maiden has not
found him finer than her delicacy? What lover has he not out-
loved? What sage has he not outseen? What gentleman has he not
instructed in the rudeness of his behaviour?

Some able and appreciating critics think no criticism on Shakspeare valuable that does not rest purely on the dramatic merit;
that he is falsely judged as poet and philosopher. I think as highly
as these critics of his dramatic merit, but still think it secondary.
He was a full man who liked to talk; a brain exhaling thoughts
and images which seeking vent, found the drama next at hand.
Had he been less, we should have had to consider how well he
filled his place, how good a dramatist he was, and he is the best in
the world. But it turns out, that what he has to say is of that
weight, as to withdraw some attention from the vehicle; and he is
like some saint whose history is to be rendered into all languages,
into verse and prose, into songs and pictures, and cut up into
proverbs, so that the occasion which gave the saint's meaning the
form of a conversation or of a prayer or of a code of laws is immaterial, compared with the universality of its application. So it
fares with the wise Shakspeare and his book of life. He wrote the

airs for all our modern music. He wrote the text of modern life; the text of manners: he drew the man of England and Europe; the father of the man in America: he drew the man, and described the day, and what is done in it: he read the hearts of men and women, their probity, and their second thought and wiles; the wiles of innocence, and the transitions by which virtues and vices slide into their contraries: he could divide the mother's part from the father's part in the face of the child, or draw the fine demarcations of freedom and of fate: he knew the laws of repression, which make the police of nature: and all the sweets and all the terrors of human lot lay in his mind as truly but as softly as the landscape lies on the eye. And the importance of this wisdom of life sinks the form, as of Drama or Epic, out of notice. 'Tis like making a question concerning the paper on which a king's message is written.

Shakspeare is as much out of the category of eminent authors, as he is out of the crowd. He is inconceivably wise, the others conceivably. A good reader can in a sort nestle into Plato's brain, and think from thence, but not into Shakspeare's. We are still out of doors. For executive faculty, for creation, Shakspeare is unique. No man can imagine it better. He was the farthest reach of subtlety compatible with an individual self, — the subtlest of authors, and only just within the possibility of authorship. With this wisdom of life, is the equal endowment of imaginative and of lyric power. He clothed the creatures of his legend with form and sentiments, as if they were people who had lived under his roof, and few real men have left such distinct characters as these fictions. And they spoke in language as sweet as it was fit. Yet his talents never seduced him into an ostentation, nor did he harp on one string. An omnipresent humanity coordinates all his faculties. Give a man of talents a story to tell, and his partiality will presently appear. He has certain observations, opinions, topics, which have some accidental prominence, and which he disposes all to exhibit. He crams this part, and starves that other part, consulting not the fitness of the thing, but his fitness and strength. But Shakspeare has no peculiarity, no importunate topic, but all is duly given; no veins, no curiosities; no cowpainter, no birdfancier, no mannerist is he: he has no discoverable egotism: the great he tells greatly, the small subordinately. He is wise without emphasis or assertion; he is strong as nature is strong, who lifts the land into mountain slopes without effort, and by the same rule as she floats a bubble in the air, and likes as well to do the one as the other. This makes that equality of power in farce, tragedy, narrative, and lovesongs; a merit so incessant, that each reader is incredulous of the perception of other readers.

This power of expression, or of transferring the inmost truth of things into music and verse, makes him the type of the poet, and has added a new problem to metaphysics. This is that which throws him into natural history as a main production of the globe, and as announcing new eras and ameliorations. Things were mirrored in his poetry without loss or blur; he could paint the fine with precision, the great with compass; the tragic and the comic indifferently, and without any distortion or favour. He carried his powerful execution into minute details to a hair point; finishes an eyelash or a dimple as firmly as he draws a mountain; and yet these, like nature's, will bear the scrutiny of the solar microscope. In short, he is the chief example to prove that more or less of production, more or fewer pictures is a thing indifferent. He had the power to make one picture. Daguerre learned how to let one flower etch its image on his plate of iodine; and then proceeds at leisure to etch a million. There are always objects; but there was never representation. Here is perfect representation, at last, and now let the world of figures sit for their portraits. No recipe can be given for the making of a Shakspeare; but the possibility of the translation of things into song, is demonstrated.

His lyric power lies in the genius of the piece. The sonnets, though their excellence is lost in the splendour of the dramas, are as inimitable as they: and it is not a merit of lines, but a total merit of the piece; like the tone of voice of some incomparable person, so is this a speech of poetic beings, and any clause as unproducible now, as a whole poem. Though the speeches in the plays, and single lines have a beauty which tempts the ear to pause on them for their euphuism, yet the sentence is so loaded with meaning, and so linked with its foregoers and followers, that the logician is satisfied. His means are as admirable as his ends;

every subordinate invention by which he helps himself to connect some irreconcileable opposites, is a poem too. He is not reduced to dismount and walk, because his horses are running off with him in some distant direction: he always rides.

The finest poetry was first experience: but the thought has suffered a transformation since it was an experience. Cultivated men often attain a good degree of skill in writing verses, but it is easy to read through their poems their personal history: any one acquainted with parties, can name every figure: this is Andrew, and that is Rachel. The sense thus remains prosaic. It is a caterpillar with wings, and not yet a butterfly. In the poet's mind, the fact has gone quite over into the new element of thought, and has lost all that is exuvial. This generosity abides with Shakspeare. We say, from the truth and closeness of his pictures, that he knows the lesson by heart. Yet there is not a trace of egotism.

One more royal trait properly belongs to the Poet, I mean his cheerfulness, without which no man can be a poet, for beauty is his aim. He loves virtue, not for its obligation, but for its grace: he delights in the world, in man, in woman, for the lovely light which sparkles from them. Beauty, the spirit of joy and hilarity, he sheds over the universe. Epicurus says that poetry hath such charms that a lover might forsake his mistress to partake of them. And the true bards have been noted for their firm and cheerful temper. Homer lies in sunshine, Chaucer is glad and erect; and Saadi says, "it was rumoured abroad that I was penitent, but what had I to do with repentance?" Not less sovereign and cheerful, — much more sovereign and cheerful is the tone of Shakspeare. His name suggests joy and emancipation to the heart of men. If he should appear in any company of human souls, who would not march in his troop? He touches nothing that does not borrow health and longevity from his festal style.

And now how stands the account of man with this bard and benefactor, when in solitude, shutting our ears to the reverberations of his fame, we seek to strike the balance? Solitude has austere lessons, it can teach us to spare both heroes and poets; and it weighs Shakspeare also, and finds him to share the halfness and imperfection of humanity.

Shakspeare, Homer, Dante, Chaucer, saw the splendour of meaning that plays over the visible world; knew that a tree had another use than for apples, and corn another than for meal, and the ball of the earth than for tillage and roads: that these things bore a second and finer harvest to the mind, being emblems of its thoughts, and conveying in all their natural history a certain mute commentary on human life. Shakspeare employed them as colours to compose his picture. He rested in their beauty; and never took the step which seemed inevitable to such genius, namely, to explore the virtue which resides in these symbols, and imparts this power, — What is that which they themselves say? He converted the elements which waited on his command, into entertainments. He was master of the revels to mankind. Is it not as if one should have, through majestic powers of science, the comets given into his hand or the planets and their moons, and should draw them from their orbits to glare with the municipal fireworks on a holiday night, and advertise in all towns *very superior pyrotechny this evening?* Are the agents of nature and the power to understand them, worth no more than a street serenade or the breath of a cigar? One remembers again the trumpet text in the Koran, — "The Heavens and the earth and all that is between them, think ye we have created them in jest?" As long as the question is of talent and mental power, the world of men has not his equal to show. But when the question is to life, and its materials, and its auxiliaries, how does he profit me? What does it signify? It is but a Twelfth night, or Midsummer's night's dream, or a Winter evening's tale: What signifies another picture more or less? The Egyptian verdict of the Shakspeare Societies comes to mind, that he was a jovial actor and manager. I cannot marry this fact to his verse: Other admirable men have led lives in some sort of keeping with their thought, but this man in wide contrast. Had he been less, had he reached only the common measure of great authors, of Bacon, Milton, Tasso, Cervantes, we might leave the fact in the twilight of human fate; but that this man of men, he who gave to the science of mind a new and larger subject than had ever existed, and planted the standard of humanity some furlongs forward into Chaos, — that he should not be wise for himself, — it must even go into the world's history, that the best poet led an obscure and profane life, using his genius for the public amusement.

Well, other men, priest and prophet, Israelite, German, and Swede, beheld the same objects: they also saw through them that which was contained. And to what purpose? The beauty straightway vanished, they read commandments, all-excluding mountainous duty; an obligation, a sadness, as of piled mountains fell on them, and life became ghastly, joyless, a pilgrim's progress, a probation, beleaguered round with doleful histories of Adam's fall and curse, behind us; with Doomsdays and purgatorial and penal fires before us; and the heart of the seer and the heart of the listener sunk in them.

It must be conceded that these are halfviews of halfmen. The world still wants its poet-priest, a reconciler who shall not trifle, with Shakspeare the player, nor shall grope in graves, with Swedenborg the mourner, but who shall see, speak, and act, with equal inspiration. For knowledge will brighten the sunshine; right is more beautiful than private affection, and love is compatible with universal wisdom.

NAPOLEON, OR
THE MAN OF THE WORLD

VI

Napoleon, or the Man of the World

Among the eminent persons of the nineteenth century, Bonaparte is far the best known, and the most powerful, and owes his predominance to the fidelity with which he expresses the tone of thought and belief, the aims of the masses of active and cultivated men. It is Swedenborg's theory that every organ is made up of homogeneous particles, or, as it is sometimes expressed, every whole is made of similars; that is, the lungs are composed of infinitely small lungs, the liver of infinitely small livers, the kidney of little kidneys, &c. Following this analogy, if any man is found to carry with him the power and affections of vast numbers, if Napoleon is France, if Napoleon is Europe, it is because the people whom he sways are little Napoleons.

In our society, there is a standing antagonism between the conservative and the democratic classes; between those who have made their fortunes, and the young and the poor who have fortunes to make; between the interests of dead labour, that is, the labour of hands long ago still in the grave, which labour is now entombed in money stocks, or in land and buildings owned by idle capitalists, — and the interests of living labour, which seeks to possess itself of land, and buildings, and money stocks. The first class is timid, selfish, illiberal, hating innovation, and continually losing numbers by death. The second class is selfish also, encroaching, bold, self-relying, always outnumbering the other, and recruiting its numbers every hour by births. It desires to keep open every avenue to the competition of all, and to multiply avenues; — the class of business-men in America, in England, in

France, and throughout Europe; the class of industry and skill. Napoleon is its representative. The instinct of active, brave, able men throughout the middle class everywhere, has pointed out Napoleon as the incarnate Democrat. He had their virtues and their vices; above all, he had their spirit or aim. That tendency is material, pointing at a sensual success, and employing the richest and most various means to that end; conversant with mechanical powers, highly intellectual, widely and accurately learned and skilful, but subordinating all intellectual and spiritual forces into means to a material success. To be the rich man, is the end. "God has granted," says the Koran, "to every people a prophet in its own tongue." Paris and London and New York, the spirit of commerce, of money, and material power, were also to have their prophet, and Bonaparte was qualified and sent.

Every one of the million readers of anecdotes, or memoirs, or lives of Napoleon, delights in the page, because he studies in it his own history. Napoleon is thoroughly modern, and, at the highest point of his fortunes, has the very spirit of the newspapers. He is no saint, — to use his own word, "no capuchin," and he is no hero, in the high sense. The man in the street finds in him the qualities and powers of other men in the street. He finds him, like himself, by birth a citizen, who, by very intelligible merits, arrived at such a commanding position, that he could indulge all those tastes which the common man possesses, but is obliged to conceal and deny; good society, good books, fast travelling, dress, dinners, servants without number, personal weight, the execution of his ideas, the standing in the attitude of a benefactor to all persons about him, the refined enjoyments of pictures, statues, music, palaces, and conventional honours, — precisely what is agreeable to the heart of every man in the nineteenth century, this powerful man possessed.

It is true that a man of Napoleon's truth of adaptation to the mind of the masses around him, becomes not merely representative, but actually a monopolizer and usurper of other minds. Thus Mirabeau plagiarized every good thought, every good word that was spoken in France. Dumont relates that he sat in the gallery of the Convention, and heard Mirabeau make a speech. It struck Dumont that he could fit it with a peroration, which he wrote in pencil immediately, and showed to Lord Elgin, who sat by him. Lord Elgin approved it, and Dumont in the evening showed it to Mirabeau. Mirabeau read it, pronounced it admirable, and declared he would incorporate it into his harangue tomorrow to the Assembly. "It is impossible," said Dumont, "as, unfortunately, I have shown it to Lord Elgin." — "If you have shown it to Lord Elgin, and to fifty persons beside, I shall still speak it tomorrow;" and he did speak it with much effect, at the next day's session. For Mirabeau, with his overpowering personality, felt that these things, which his presence inspired, were as much his own, as if he had said them, and that his adoption of them gave them their weight. Much more absolute and centralizing was the successor to Mirabeau's popularity, and to much more than his predominance in France. Indeed a man of Napoleon's stamp almost ceases to have a private speech and opinion. He is so largely receptive, and is so placed, that he comes to be a bureau for all the intelligence, wit, and power, of the age and country. He gains the battles; he makes the code; he makes the system of weights and measures; he levels the Alps; he builds the road. All distinguished engineers, savans, statists, report to him: so likewise do all good heads in every kind: he adopts the best measures, sets his stamp on them, — and not these alone, but on every happy and memorable expression. Every sentence spoken by Napoleon, and every line of his writing, deserves reading, as it is the sense of France.

Bonaparte was the idol of common men, because he had in transcendent degree the qualities and powers of common men. There is a certain satisfaction in coming down to the lowest ground of politics, for we get rid of cant and hypocrisy. Bonaparte wrought, in common with that great class he represented, for power and wealth, — but Bonaparte specially without any scruple as to the means. All the sentiments which embarrass men's pursuit of these objects, he set aside. The sentiments were for women and children. Fontanes, in 1804, expressed Napoleon's own sense, when, in behalf of the Senate he addressed him, "Sire, the desire of perfection is the worst disease that ever afflicted the human mind." The advocates of liberty and of progress, are "ideologists;" — a word of contempt often in his mouth; — "Necker is an ideologist:" "Lafayette is an ideologist."

An Italian proverb, too well known, declares that, "if you would succeed, you must not be too good." It is an advantage, within certain limits, to have renounced the dominion of the sentiments of piety, gratitude, and generosity; since, what was an impassable bar to us, and still is to others, becomes a convenient weapon for our purposes; just as the river which was a formidable barrier, winter transforms into the smoothest of roads.

Napoleon renounced, once for all, sentiments and affections, and would help himself with his hands and his head. With him is no miracle, and no magic. He is a worker in brass, in iron, in wood, in earth, in roads, in buildings, in money, and in troops, and a very consistent and wise master workman. He is never weak and literary, but acts with the solidity and the precision of natural agents. He has not lost his native sense and sympathy with things. Men give way before such a man, as before natural events. To be sure, there are men enough who are immersed in things, as farmers, smiths, sailors, and mechanics generally, and we know how real and solid such men appear in the presence of scholars and grammarians: but these men ordinarily lack the power of arrangement, and are like hands without a head. But Bonaparte superadded to this mineral and animal force, insight and generalization, so that men saw in him combined the natural and the intellectual power, as if the sea and land had taken flesh and begun to cipher. Therefore the land and sea seem to presuppose him. He came unto his own, and they received him. This ciphering operative knows what he is working with, and what is the product. He knew the properties of gold and iron, of wheels and ships, of troops and diplomatists, and required that each should do after its kind.

The art of war was the game in which he exerted his arithmetic. It consisted, according to him, in having always more forces than the enemy, on the point where the enemy is attacked, or where he attacks: — and his whole talent is strained by endless manœuvre and evolution, to march always on the enemy at an angle, and destroy his forces in detail. It is obvious that a very small force skilfully and rapidly manœuvring, so as always to bring two men against one at the point of engagement, will be an overmatch for a much larger body of men.

The times, his constitution, and his early circumstances combined to develop this pattern democrat. He had the virtues of his class, and the conditions for their activity. That common sense, which no sooner respects any end, than it finds the means to effect it; the delight in the use of means, in the choice, simplification, and combining of means; the directness and thoroughness of his work; the prudence with which all was seen, and the energy with which all was done, make him the natural organ and head of what I may almost call from its extent the *modern* party.

Nature must have far the greatest share in every success, and so in his. Such a man was wanted, and such a man was born; a man of stone and iron, capable of sitting on horseback sixteen or seventeen hours, of going many days together without rest or food, except by snatches, and with the speed and spring of a tiger in action: a man not embarrassed by any scruples; compact, instant, selfish, prudent, and of a perception which did not suffer itself to be baulked or misled by any pretences of others, or any superstition or any heat or haste of his own. "My hand of iron," he said, "was not at the extremity of my arm; it was immediately connected with my head." He respected the power of nature and fortune, and ascribed to it his superiority, instead of valuing himself, like inferior men, on his opinionativeness, and waging war with nature. His favorite rhetoric lay in allusions to his star; and he pleased himself as well as the people, when he styled himself the "Child of Destiny." "They charge me," he said, "with the commission of great crimes: — Men of my stamp do not commit crimes. Nothing has been more simple than my elevation: 'tis in vain to ascribe it to intrigue or crime: it was owing to the peculiarity of the times, and to my reputation of having fought well against the enemies of my country. I have always marched with the opinion of great masses, and with events. Of what use then would crimes be to me?" Again he said, speaking of his son; "My son cannot replace me; I could not replace myself. I am the creature of circumstances."

He had a directness of action never before combined with so

much comprehension. He is a realist, terrific to all talkers and confused truth-obscuring persons. He sees where the matter hinges, throws himself on the precise point of resistance, and slights all other considerations. He is strong in the right manner, namely, by insight. He never blundered into victory, but won his battles in his head, before he won them on the field. His principal means are in himself. He asks counsel of no other. In 1796, he writes to the Directory: "I have conducted the campaign without consulting any one. I should have done no good, if I had been under the necessity of conforming to the notions of another person. I have gained some advantages over superior forces, and when totally destitute of everything, because, in the persuasion that your confidence was reposed in me, my actions were as prompt as my thoughts."

History is full, down to this day, of the imbecility of kings and governors. They are a class of persons much to be pitied, for they know not what they should do. The weavers strike for bread, and the king and his ministers, not knowing what to do, meet them with bayonets. But Napoleon understood his business. Here was a man who, in each moment and emergency, knew what to do next. It is an immense comfort and refreshment to the spirits, not only of kings, but of citizens. Few men have any next; they live from hand to mouth, without plan, and are ever at the end of their line, and, after each action, wait for an impulse from abroad. Napoleon had been the first man of the world, if his ends had been purely public. As he is, he inspires confidence and vigor by the extraordinary unity of his action. He is firm, sure, self-denying, self-postponing, sacrificing everything to his aim, — money, troops, generals, and his own safety also, to his aim; not misled, like common adventurers, by the splendour of his own means. "Incidents ought not to govern policy," he said, "but policy incidents." "To be hurried away by every event, is to have no political system at all." His victories were only so many doors, and he never for a moment lost sight of his way onward, in the dazzle and uproar of the present circumstance. He knew what to do, and he flew to his mark. He would shorten a straight line to come at his object. Horrible anecdotes may, no doubt, be collected from his history, of the price at which he bought his successes; but he must not therefore be set down as cruel, but only as one who knew no impediment to his will; not bloodthirsty, not cruel, — but wo to what thing or person stood in his way! Not bloodthirsty, but not sparing of blood, — and pitiless. He saw only the object: the obstacle must give way. "Sire, General Clarke cannot combine with General Junot, for the dreadful fire of the Austrian battery." — "Let him carry the battery." — "Sire, every regiment that approaches the heavy artillery is sacrificed: Sire, what orders?" — "Forward, forward!" Seruzier, a colonel of artillery, gives in his *Military Memoirs* the following sketch of a scene after the battle of Austerlitz. "At the moment in which the Russian army was making its retreat painfully but in good order on the ice of the lake, the Emperor Napoleon came riding at full speed towards the artillery. 'You are losing time,' he cried, 'fire upon those masses. They must be engulfed; fire upon the ice!' The order remained unexecuted for ten minutes. In vain, several officers and myself were placed on the slope of a hill to produce the effect: their balls and mine rolled upon the ice, without breaking it up. Seeing that, I tried a simple method of elevating light howitzers. The almost perpendicular fall of the heavy projectiles produced the desired effect. My method was immediately followed by the adjoining batteries, and in less than no time we buried" some* "thousands of Russians and Austrians under the waters of the lake."

In the plenitude of his resources, every obstacle seemed to vanish. "There shall be no Alps," he said, and he built his perfect roads, climbing by graded galleries their steepest precipices, until Italy was as open to Paris as any town in France. He laid his bones to, and wrought for his crown. Having decided what was to be done, he did that, with might and main. He put out all his strength. He risked everything, and spared nothing, neither ammunition, nor money, nor troops, nor generals, nor himself.

We like to see every thing do its office after its kind, whether it be a milch-cow or a rattlesnake; and, if fighting be the best mode of adjusting national differences, (as large majorities of men seem

---

*As I quote at second hand, and cannot procure Seruzier, I dare not adopt the high figure I find.

to agree,) certainly Bonaparte was right in making it thorough. "The grand principle of war," he said, "was, that an army ought always to be ready by day and by night, and at all hours, to make all the resistance it is capable of making." He never economized his ammunition, but on a hostile position rained a torrent of iron, — shells, balls, grapeshot, — to annihilate all defence. On any point of resistance, he concentrated squadron on squadron in overwhelming numbers, until it was swept out of existence. To a regiment of horse chasseurs at Lobenstein, two days before the battle of Jena, Napoleon said, "My lads, you must not fear death; when soldiers brave death, they drive him into the enemy's ranks." In the fury of assault, he no more spared himself. He went to the edge of his possibility. It is plain that in Italy he did what he could, and all that he could. He came several times within an inch of ruin, and his own person was all but lost. He was flung into the marsh at Arcola. The Austrians were between him and his troops, in the *mêlée,* and he was brought off with desperate efforts. At Lonato, and at other places, he was on the point of being taken prisoner. He fought sixty battles. He had never enough. Each victory was a new weapon. "My power would fall, were I not to support it by new achievements. Conquest has made me what I am, and conquest must maintain me." He felt, with every wise man, that as much life is needed for conservation, as for creation. We are always in peril, always in a bad plight, just on the edge of destruction, and only to be saved by invention and courage.

This vigour was guarded and tempered by the coldest prudence and punctuality. A thunderbolt in the attack, he was found invulnerable in his intrenchments. His very attack was never the inspiration of courage, but the result of calculation. His idea of the best defence consists in being still the attacking party. "My ambition," he says, "was great, but was of a cold nature." In one of his conversations with Las Cases, he remarked, "As to moral courage, I have rarely met with the two-o'clock-in-the-morning kind; I mean unprepared courage, that which is necessary on an unexpected occasion, and which, in spite of the most unforeseen events, leaves full freedom of judgment and decision:" and he did not hesitate to declare that he was himself eminently endowed with this "two-o'clock-in-the-morning courage, and that he had met with few persons equal to himself in this particular."

Everything depended on the nicety of his combinations, and the stars were not more punctual than his arithmetic. His personal attention descended to the smallest particulars. "At Montebello, I ordered Kellermann to attack with eight hundred horse, and with these he separated the six thousand Hungarian grenadiers before the very eyes of the Austrian cavalry. This cavalry was half a league off, and required a quarter of an hour to arrive on the field of action, and I have observed that it is always these quarters of an hour that decide the fate of a battle." "Before he fought a battle, Bonaparte thought little about what he should do in case of success, but a great deal about what he should do, in case of a reverse of fortune." The same prudence and good sense mark all his behaviour. His instructions to his secretary at the Tuileries are worth remembering. — "During the night, enter my chamber as seldom as possible. Do not awake me when you have any good news to communicate, with that there is no hurry. But when you bring bad news, rouse me instantly, for then there is not a moment to be lost." It was a whimsical economy of the same kind, which dictated his practice, when general in Italy, in regard to his burdensome correspondence. He directed Bourrienne to leave all letters unopened for three weeks, and then observed with satisfaction how large a part of the correspondence had thus disposed of itself, and no longer required an answer. His achievement of business was immense, and enlarges the known powers of man. There have been many working kings, from Ulysses to William of Orange, but none who accomplished a tithe of this man's performance.

To these gifts of nature, Napoleon added the advantage of having been born to a private and humble fortune. In his later days, he had the weakness of wishing to add to his crowns and badges the prescription of aristocracy; but he knew his debt to his austere education, and made no secret of his contempt for the born kings, and for "the hereditary asses," as he coarsely styled the Bourbons. He said, that, "in their exile they had learned nothing, and forgot nothing." Bonaparte had passed through all the degrees of military service, but also was citizen before he was emperor, and so has the key to citizenship. His remarks and estimates discover the information and justness of measurement of the middle class. Those who had to deal with him, found that he was not to be imposed upon, but could cipher as well as another man. This appears in all parts of his Memoirs dictated at St Helena. When the expenses of the Empress, of his household, of his palaces, had accumulated great debts, Napoleon examined the bills of the creditors himself, detected overcharges and errors, and reduced the claims by considerable sums.

His grand weapon, namely, the millions whom he directed, he owed to the representative character which clothed him. He interests us as he stands for France and for Europe, and he exists as captain and king, only as far as the Revolution, or the interest of the industrious masses, found an organ and a leader in him. In the social interests, he knew the meaning and value of labour, and threw himself naturally on that side. I like an incident mentioned by one of his biographers at St Helena. "When walking with Mrs Balcombe, some servants carrying heavy boxes passed by on the road, and Mrs Balcombe desired them, in rather an angry tone, to keep back. Napoleon interfered, saying, 'Respect the burden, Madam.' " In the time of the empire, he directed attention to the improvement and embellishment of the markets of the Capital. "The marketplace," he said, "is the Louvre of the common people." The principal works that have survived him, are his magnificent roads. He filled the troops with his spirit, and a sort of freedom and companionship grew up between him and them, which the forms of his court never permitted between the officers and himself. They performed under his eye that which no others could do. The best document of his relation to his troops, (and of the perfect understanding between them,) is the order of the day on the morning of the battle of Austerlitz, in which Napoleon promises the troops that he will keep his person out of reach of fire. This declaration, which is the reverse of that ordinarily made by generals and sovereigns on the eve of a battle, sufficiently explains the devotion of the army to their leader.

But though there is in particulars this identity between Napoleon and the mass of the people, his real strength lay in their conviction that he was their representative, in his genius and aims, not only when he courted, but when he controuled and even when he decimated them by his conscriptions. He knew, as well as any jacobin in France, how to philosophize on liberty and equality, and, when allusion was made to the precious blood of centuries, which was spilled by the killing of the Duc d'Enghien, he suggested, "Neither is my blood ditch-water." The people felt that no longer the throne was occupied, and the land sucked of all its nourishment by a small class of legitimates secluded from all community with the children of the soil, and holding the ideas and superstitions of a long-forgotten state of society. Instead of that vampire, a man of themselves held in the Tuileries knowledge and ideas like their own, opening, of course, to them and their children all places of power and trust. The day of sleepy, selfish policy, ever narrowing the means and opportunities of young men, was ended, and a day of expansion and demand was come. A market for all the powers and productions of man was opened; brilliant prizes glittered in the eyes of youth and talent. The old, ironbound, feudal France, was changed into a young Ohio or New York; and those who smarted under the immediate rigours of the new monarch, pardoned them as the necessary severities of the military system which had driven out the oppressor. And even when the majority of the people had begun to ask whether they had really gained anything, under the exhausting levies of men and money of the new master, — the whole talent of the country, in every rank and kindred, took his part, and defended him as its natural patron. In 1814, when advised to rely on the higher classes, Napoleon said to those around him, "Gentlemen, in the situation in which I stand, my only nobility is the rabble of the Faubourgs."

Napoleon met this natural expectation. The necessity of his position required a hospitality to every sort of talent, and its appointment to trusts; and his feeling went along with this policy. Like every superior person, he undoubtedly felt a desire for men and compeers, and a wish to measure his power with other masters, and an impatience of fools and underlings. In Italy, he sought for men, and found none. "Good God!" he said, "how rare men are! There are eighteen millions in Italy, and I have with difficulty found two, Dandolo and Melzi." In later years, with larger experience his respect for mankind was not increased. In a moment of bitterness, he said to one of his oldest friends, "Men deserve the contempt with which they inspire me. I have only to put some gold lace on the coat of my virtuous republicans, and they immediately become just what I wish them." This impatience at levity was however an oblique tribute of respect to those able persons who commanded his regard, not only when he found them friends and coadjutors, but also when they resisted his will. He could not confound Fox and Pitt, Carnot, Lafayette, and Bernadotte, with the danglers of his court; and, in spite of the detraction which his systematic egotism dictated towards the great captains who conquered with and for him, ample acknowledgments are made by him to Lannes, Duroc, Kleber, Dessaix, Masséna, Murat, Ney, and Augereau. If he felt himself their patron, and the founder of their fortunes, as when he said, "I made my generals out of mud," he could not hide his satisfaction in receiving from them a seconding and support commensurate with the grandeur of his enterprise. In the Russian campaign, he was so much impressed by the courage and resources of Marshal Ney, that he said, "I have two hundred millions in my coffers, and I would give them all for Ney." The characters which he has drawn of several of his Marshals, are discriminating, and, though they did not content the insatiable vanity of French officers, are, no doubt, substantially just. And, in fact, every species of merit was sought and advanced under his government. "I know," he said, "the depth or draught of water of every one of my generals." — Natural power was sure to be well received at his court. Seventeen men in his time were raised from common soldiers to the rank of king, marshal, duke, or general; and the crosses of his Legion of Honour were given to personal valour, and not to family connexion. "When soldiers have been baptized in the fire of a battlefield, they have all one rank in my eyes."

When a natural king becomes a titular king, every body is

pleased and satisfied. The Revolution entitled the strong populace of the Faubourg St Antoine, and every horseboy and powder monkey in the army to look on Napoleon, as flesh of his flesh, and the creature of *his* party; but there is something in the success of grand talent, which enlists an universal sympathy. For, in the prevalence of sense and spirit over stupidity and malversation, all reasonable men have an interest, and, as intellectual beings, we feel the air purified by the electric shock, when material force is overthrown by intellectual energies. As soon as we are removed out of the reach of local and accidental partialities, man feels that Napoleon fights for him; these are honest victories; this strong steamengine does our work. Whatever appeals to the imagination, by transcending the ordinary limits of human ability, wonderfully encourages and liberates us. This capacious head, revolving and sovereignly disposing trains of affairs, and animating such multitudes of agents; this eye, which looked through Europe; this prompt invention; this inexhaustible resource; what events, what romantic pictures! what strange situations! when spying the Alps by a sunset in the Sicilian sea; drawing up his army for battle, in sight of the Pyramids, and saying to his troops, "From the tops of those Pyramids, forty centuries look down on you:" fording the Red Sea; wading in the Gulf by the Isthmus of Suez; "On the shore of Ptolemais, gigantic projects agitated him." "Had Acre fallen, I should have changed the face of the world." His army, on the night of the battle of Austerlitz, which was the anniversary of his inauguration as Emperor, presented him with a bouquet of forty standards taken in the fight. Perhaps, it is a little puerile, the pleasure he took in making these contrasts glaring; as when he pleased himself with making kings wait in his antechambers, at Tilsit, at Paris, and at Erfurt.

We cannot in the universal imbecility, indecision, and indolence of men, sufficiently congratulate ourselves on this strong and ready actor, who took Occasion by the beard, and showed us how much may be accomplished by the mere force of such virtues as all men possess in less degrees; namely, by punctuality, by personal attention, by courage, and thoroughness. "The Austrians," he said, "do not know the value of time." I should cite him in his earlier years as a model of prudence. His power does not consist in any wild or extravagant force, in any enthusiasm like Mahomet's; or singular power of persuasion; but in the exercise of common-sense on each emergency, instead of abiding by rules and customs. The lesson he teaches is that which vigour always teaches, that there is always room for it. To what heaps of cowardly doubts, is not that man's life an answer! When he appeared, it was the belief of all military men, that there could be nothing new in war; as it is the belief of men today, that nothing new can be undertaken in politics, or in church, or in letters, or in trade, or in farming, or in our social manners and customs; and as it is, at all times, the be-lief of society, that the world is used up. But Bonaparte knew bet-ter than society, and, moreover, knew that he knew better. I think, all men know better than they do; know that the institutions we so volubly commend, are go-carts and baubles, but they dare not trust their presentiments. Bonaparte relied on his own sense, and did not care a bean for other people's. The world treated his nov-elties just as it treats every body's novelties, made infinite objec-tion; mustered all the impediments; but he snapped his finger at their objections. "What creates great difficulty," he remarks, "in the profession of the land-commander is the necessity of feeding so many men and animals. If he allows himself to be guided by the Commissaries, he will never stir, and all his expeditions will fail." An example of his commonsense is what he says of the pas-sage of the Alps in winter, which all writers, one repeating after the other, had described as impracticable. "The winter," says Na-poleon, "is not the most unfavorable season for the passage of lofty mountains. The snow is then firm, the weather settled, and there is nothing to fear from avalanches, the real and only danger to be apprehended in the Alps; on those high mountains, there are often very fine days in December, of a dry cold, with extreme calmness in the air." Read his account, too, of the way in which battles are gained. — "In all battles, a moment occurs, when the bravest troops, after having made the greatest efforts, feel inclined to run. That terror proceeds from a want of confidence in their own courage, and it only requires a slight opportunity, a pretence, to restore confidence to them. The art is to give rise to the opportunity, and to invent the pretence. At Arcole, I won the battle with twenty-five horsemen. I seized that moment of lassitude, gave every man a trumpet and gained the day with this handful. You see that two armies are two bodies which meet, and endeavour to frighten each other; a moment of panic occurs, and that moment must be turned to advantage. When a man has been present in many actions, he distinguishes that moment without difficulty: it is as easy as casting up an addition."

This deputy of the nineteenth century added to his gifts a capacity for speculation on general topics. He delighted in running through the range of practical, of literary, and of abstract questions. His opinion is always original and to the purpose. On the voyage to Egypt, he liked after dinner to fix on three or four persons to support a proposition, and as many to oppose it. He gave a subject, and the discussions turned on questions of religion, the different kinds of government, and the art of war. One day, he asked, whether the planets were inhabited? on another, what was the age of the world? then he proposed to consider the probability of the destruction of the globe either by water or by fire: at another time, the truth or fallacy of presentiments, and the interpretation of dreams. He was very fond of talking of religion. In 1806, he conversed with Fournier, bishop of Montpellier, on matters of theology. There were two points on which they could not agree, viz. that of Hell, and that of salvation out of the pale of the Church. The Emperor told Josephine that he disputed like a devil on these two points, on which the bishop was inexorable. To the philosophes he readily yielded all that was proved against religion as the work of men and time, but he would not hear of materialism. One fine night on deck, amid a clatter of materialism, Bonaparte pointed to the stars, and said, "You may talk as long as you please, gentlemen, but who made all that?" He delighted in the conversation of men of science, particularly of Monge and Berthollet; but the men of letters he slighted; "they were manufacturers of phrases." Of medicine, too, he was fond of talking, and with those of its practitioners whom he most esteemed, with Corvisart, at Paris, and with Antommarchi, at St Helena. "Believe me," he said to the last, "we had better leave off all these remedies: life is a fortress which neither you nor I know anything about. Why throw obstacles in the way of its defence? Its own means are superior to all the apparatus of your laboratories. Corvisart candidly agreed with me, that all your filthy mixtures are good for nothing. Medicine is a collection of uncertain prescriptions, the results of which, taken collectively, are more fatal than useful to mankind. Water, air, and cleanliness are the chief articles in my pharmacopeia."

His memoirs, dictated to Count Montholon and General Gourgaud, at St Helena, have great value, after all the deduction that, it seems, is to be made from them, on account of his known disingenuousness. He has the good nature of strength and conscious superiority. I admire his simple clear narrative of his battles; — good as Cæsar's: his goodnatured and sufficiently respectful account of Marshal Wurmser and his other antagonists, and his own equality as a writer to his varying subject. The most agreeable portion is the Campaign in Egypt.

He had hours of thought and wisdom. In intervals of leisure, either in the camp or the palace, Napoleon appears as a man of genius, directing on abstract questions the native appetite for truth, and the impatience of words he was wont to show in war. He could enjoy every play of invention, a romance, a bon mot, as well as a stratagem or a campaign. He delighted to fascinate Josephine and her ladies, in a dim lighted apartment, by the terrors of a fiction, to which his voice and dramatic power lent every addition.

I call Napoleon the agent or attorney of the Middle Class of modern society; of the throng who fill the markets, shops, counting-houses, manufactories, ships, of the modern world, aiming to be rich. He was the agitator, the destroyer of prescription, the internal improver, the liberal, the radical, the inventor of means, the opener of doors and markets, the subverter of monopoly and abuse. Of course, the rich and aristocratic did not like him. England the centre of capital, and Rome and Austria, centres of tradition and genealogy, opposed him. The consternation of the dull and conservative classes, the terror of the foolish old men and old women of the Roman Conclave, who in their despair took hold of anything, and would cling to red hot iron; the vain attempts of statists to amuse and deceive him, of the emperor of Austria to bribe him; and the instinct of the young, ardent, and active men, everywhere, which pointed him out as the Giant of the Middle Class, make this history bright and commanding. He had the virtues of the masses of his constituents: he had also their vices. I am sorry that the brilliant picture has its reverse. But that is the fatal quality which we discover in our pursuit of wealth, that it is treacherous, and is bought by the breaking or weakening of the sentiments; and it is inevitable that we should find the same fact in the history of this champion, who proposed to himself simply a brilliant career, without any stipulation or scruple concerning the means.

Bonaparte was singularly destitute of generous sentiments. The highest placed individual in the most cultivated age and population of the world, he has not the merit of common truth and honesty. He is unjust to his generals, egotistic, and monopolizing; meanly stealing the credit of their great actions from Kellermann, from Bernadotte; intriguing to involve his faithful Junot in hopeless bankruptcy, in order to drive him to a distance from Paris, because the familiarity of his manners offends the new pride of his throne. He is a boundless liar. The official paper, his "Moniteurs," and all his bulletins are proverbs for saying what he wished to be believed; and, worse, he sat in his premature old age, in his lonely island, coldly falsifying facts and dates and characters, and giving to history a theatrical éclat. Like all Frenchmen, he has a passion for stage-effect. Every action that breathes of generosity, is poisoned by this calculation. His star, his love of glory, his doctrine of the immortality of the soul, are all French. "I must dazzle and astonish. If I were to give the liberty of the press, my power could not last three days." To make a great noise, is his favorite design. "A great reputation is a great noise: the more there is made, the farther off it is heard. Laws, institutions, monuments, nations, all fall; but the noise continues, and resounds in after ages." His doctrine of immortality is simply fame. His theory of influence is not flattering. "There are two levers for moving men, interest and fear. Love is a silly infatuation, depend upon it. Friendship is but a name. I love nobody. I do not even love my brothers; perhaps Joseph, a little, from habit, and because he is my elder; and Duroc, I love him too; but why? because his character pleases me; he is stern and resolute, and, I believe, the fellow never shed a tear. For my part, I know very well, that I have no true friends. As long as I continue to be what I am, I may have as many pretended friends as I please. Leave sensibility to women: But men should be firm in heart and in purpose, or they should have nothing to do with war and government." He was thoroughly unscrupulous. He would steal, slander, assassinate, drown, and poison, as his interest dictated. He had no generosity, but mere vulgar hatred: he was intensely selfish; he was perfidious: he cheated at cards: he was a prodigious gossip; and opened letters; and delighted in his infamous police; and rubbed his hands with joy, when he had intercepted some morsel of intelligence concerning the men and women about him, boasting that "he knew everything;" and interfered with the cutting the dresses of the women; and listened after the hurrahs and the compliments of the street, incognito. His manners were coarse: He treated women with low familiarity. He had the habit of pulling their ears, and pinching their cheeks, when he was in good humour, and of pulling the ears and whiskers of men, and of striking, and horseplay with them, to his last days. It does not appear that he listened at keyholes, or, at least, that he was caught at it. In short, when you have penetrated through all the circles of power and splendour, you were not dealing with a gentleman at last, but with an impostor and a rogue: and he fully deserved the epithet of *Jupiter Scapin,* or a sort of Scamp Jupiter.

In describing the two parties into which modern society divides itself, the Democrat and the Conservative, I said, Bonaparte represents the Democrat, or the party of men of business, against the stationary or Conservative party. I omitted then to say, what is material to the statement, namely, that these two parties differ, only as young and old. The democrat is a young conservative: the conservative is an old democrat. The aristocrat is the democrat ripe, and gone to seed; because both parties stand on the one ground of the supreme value of property, which one endeavours to get, and the other to keep. Bonaparte may be said to represent the whole history of this party, its youth and its age; yes, and with poetic justice, its fate, in his own. The counter-revolution, the counterparty, still waits for its organ and representative in a lover, and a man of truly public and universal aims.

Here was an experiment under the most favorable conditions, of the powers of intellect without conscience. Never was such a leader, so endowed and so weaponed; never leader found such aids and followers. And what was the result of this vast talent and power, of these immense armies, burned cities, squandered treasures, immolated millions of men, of this demoralized Europe? It came to no result. All passed away, like the smoke of his artillery, and left no trace. He left France smaller, poorer, feebler than he found it, and the whole contest for freedom was to be begun again. The attempt was in principle suicidal. France served him with life and limb and estate as long as it could identify its interest with him: but when men saw, that, after victory was another war; after the destruction of armies, new conscriptions; and they who had toiled so desperately, were never nearer to the reward; they could not spend what they had earned; nor repose on their downbeds, nor strut in their chateaux, — they deserted him. Men found that his absorbing egotism was deadly to all other men. It resembled the torpedo, which inflicts a succession of shocks on any one who takes hold of it, producing spasms, which contract the muscles of the hand, so that the man cannot open his fingers, and the animal inflicts new and more violent shocks, until he paralyzes and kills his victim. So this exorbitant egotist narrowed, impoverished, and absorbed the power and existence of those who served him; and the universal cry of France and of Europe, in 1814, was, "Enough of him;" "*assez de Bonaparte.*"

It was not Bonaparte's fault. He did all that in him lay, to live and thrive without moral principle. It was the nature of things, the eternal law of man and of the world, which baulked and ruined him; and the result, in a million experiments, will be the same. Every experiment, by multitudes or by individuals, that has a sensual and selfish aim, will fail. The pacific Fourier will be as inefficient as the pernicious Napoleon. As long as our civilization is essentially one of property, of fences, of exclusiveness, it will be mocked by delusions. Our riches will leave us sick, there will be bitterness in our laughter, and our wine will burn our mouth. Only that good profits, which we can taste with all doors open, and which serves all men.

GOETHE, OR THE WRITER

VII

Goethe, or the Writer

I find a provision in the constitution of the world for the writer or secretary, who is to report the doings of the miraculous spirit of life that everywhere throbs and works. His office is a reception of the facts into the mind, and then a selection of the eminent and characteristic experiences.

Nature will be reported. All things are engaged in writing their history. The planet, the pebble, goes attended by its shadow. The rolling rock leaves its scratches on the mountain; the river its channel in the soil; the animal its bones in the stratum; the fern and leaf its modest epitaph in the coal. The falling drop makes its sculpture in the sand or the stone. Not a foot steps into the snow, or along the ground, but prints in characters more or less lasting a map of its march. Every act of the man inscribes itself in the memories of his fellows, and in his own manners and face. The air is full of sounds, the sky of tokens, the ground is all memoranda and signatures, and every object covered over with hints, which speak to the intelligent.

In nature, this self-registration is incessant, and the narrative is the print of the seal. It neither exceeds nor comes short of the fact. But nature strives upward and in man the report is something more than print of the seal. It is a new and finer form of the original. The record is alive, as that which it recorded is alive. In man, the memory is a kind of lookingglass, which, having received the images of surrounding objects, is touched with life, and disposes them in a new order. The facts which transpired do not lie in it inert, but some subside, and others shine, so that soon we have a

new picture composed of the eminent experiences. The man coop-
erates. He loves to communicate, and that which is for him to say,
lies as a load on his heart, until it is delivered. But, besides the
universal joy of conversation, some men are born with exalted
powers for this second creation. Men are born to write. The gardener saves every slip and seed and peachstone: his vocation is to
be a planter of plants. Not less does the writer attend his affair.
Whatever he beholds or experiences, comes to him as a model,
and sits for its picture. He counts it all nonsense that they say,
that some things are undescribable. He believes that all that can
be thought can be written, first or last; and he would report the
Holy Ghost, or attempt it. Nothing so broad, so subtle, or so dear,
but comes therefore commended to his pen, and he will write. In
his eyes, a man is the faculty of reporting, and the universe is the
possibility of being reported. In conversation, in calamity, he
finds new materials; as our German poet said, "Some God gave
me the power to paint what I suffer." He draws his rents from
rage and pain. By acting rashly, he buys the power of talking
wisely. Vexations and a tempest of passion only fill his sail; as the
good Luther writes, "When I am angry, I can pray well, and
preach well:" and, if we knew the genesis of fine strokes of eloquence, they might recall the complaisance of Sultan Amurath,
who struck off some Persian heads, that his physician Vesalius
might see the spasms in the muscles of the neck. His failures are
the preparation of his victories. A new thought or a crisis of passion apprises him that all that he has yet learned and written, is
exoteric, — is not the fact, but some rumour of the fact. What
then? Does he throw away the pen? no; he begins again to describe in the new light which has shined on him, — if by some
means he may yet save some true word. Nature conspires. Whatever can be thought can be spoken, and still rises for utterance,
though to rude and stammering organs. If they cannot compass it,
it waits and works, until at last it moulds them to its perfect will,
and is articulated.

This striving after imitative expression, which one meets everywhere, is significant of the aim of nature, but is mere stenography.
There are higher degrees, and nature has more splendid endow-
ments for those whom she elects to a superior office; for the class of

scholars or writers, namely, who see connexion, where the multitude see fragments, and who are impelled to exhibit the facts in ideal order, and so to supply the axis on which the frame of things turns. Nature has dearly at heart the formation of the speculative man, or scholar. It is an end never lost sight of, and is prepared in the original casting of things. He is no permissive or accidental appearance, but an organic agent in nature, one of the estates of the realm, provided and prepared from of old and from everlasting, in the knitting and contexture of things. Presentiments, impulses, cheer him. There is a certain heat in the breast which attends the perception of a primary truth, which is the shining of the spiritual sun down into the shaft of the mine. Every thought which dawns on the mind, in the moment of its emergence announces its own rank, — whether it is some whimsy, or whether it is a power.

If he have his incitements, there is, on the other side, invitation and need enough of his gift. Society has, at all times, the same want, namely, of one sane man with adequate powers of expression to hold up each object of monomania in its right relations. The ambitious and mercenary bring their last new mumbojumbo, whether tariff, Texas, railroad, Romanism, mesmerism, or California; and by detaching the object from its relations, easily succeed in making it seen in a glare, and a multitude go mad about it, and they are not to be reproved or cured by the opposite multitude who are kept from this particular insanity by an equal frenzy on another crotchet. But let one man have the comprehensive eye that can replace this isolated prodigy in its right neighborhood and bearings, the illusion vanishes, and the returning reason of the community thanks the reason of the monitor.

The scholar is the man of the ages, but he must also wish with other men to stand well with his contemporaries. But there is a certain ridicule among superficial people, thrown on the scholars or clerisy, which is of no import, unless the scholar heed it. In this country, the emphasis of conversation and of public opinion commends the practical man, and the solid portion of the community is named with significant respect in every circle. Our people are of Bonaparte's opinion concerning ideologists. Ideas are subversive of social order and comfort, and, at last make a fool of the possessor. It is believed, the ordering a cargo of goods from New York to Smyrna, or the running up and down to procure a company of subscribers to set agoing five or ten thousand spindles, or the negociations of a caucus, and the practising on the prejudices and facility of country-people to secure their votes in November, is practical and commendable.

If I were to compare action of a much higher strain with a life of contemplation, I should not venture to pronounce with much confidence in favor of the former. Mankind have such a deep stake in inward illumination, that there is much to be said by the hermit or monk in defence of his life of thought and prayer. A certain partiality, a headiness, and loss of balance, is the tax which all action must pay. Act, if you like, but you do it at your peril. Men's actions are too strong for them. Show me a man who has acted, and who has not been the victim and slave of his action: What they have done, commits and enforces them to do the same again. The first act, which was to be an experiment, becomes a sacrament. The fiery reformer embodies his aspiration in some rite or covenant, and he and his friends cleave to the form, and lose the aspiration. The Quaker has established Quakerism, the Shaker has established his monastery and his dance, and, although each prates of spirit, there is no spirit, but repetition, which is anti-spiritual. But where are his new things of today? In actions of enthusiasm, this drawback appears: but in those lower activities, which have no higher aim than to make us more comfortable and more cowardly, in actions of cunning, actions that steal and lie, actions that divorce the speculative from the practical faculty, and put a ban on reason and sentiment, there is nothing else but drawback and negation. The Hindoos write in their sacred books, "Children only and not the learned speak of the speculative and the practical faculties as two. They are but one, for both obtain the selfsame end, and the place which is gained by the followers of the one, is gained by the followers of the other. That man seeth, who seeth that the speculative and the practical doctrines are one." For great action must draw on the spiritual nature. The measure of action is, the sentiment from which it proceeds. The greatest action may easily be one of the most private circumstance.

This disparagement will not come from the leaders, but from inferior persons. The robust gentlemen who stand at the head of the practical class share the ideas of the time, and have too much sympathy with the speculative class. It is not from men excellent in any kind, that disparagement of any other is to be looked for. With such, Talleyrand's question is ever the main one, not, Is he rich? is he committed? is he wellmeaning? has he this or that faculty? is he of the movement? is he of the establishment? — but, *Is he anybody?* Does he stand for something? He must be good of his kind. That is all that Talleyrand, all that Statestreet, all that the commonsense of mankind asks. Be real and admirable, not as we know, but as you know. Able men do not care in what kind a man is able, so only that he is able. A master likes a master, and does not stipulate whether it be orator, artist, craftsman, or captain.

Society has really no graver interest than the wellbeing of the literary class. And it is not to be denied that men are cordial in their recognition and welcome of intellectual accomplishments. Still the writer does not stand with us on any commanding ground. I think this to be his own fault. A pound passes for a pound. There have been times when he was a sacred person: he wrote bibles; the first hymns; the codes; the epics, tragic songs, Sibylline verses, Chaldean oracles, Laconian sentences, inscribed on temple walls. Every word was true, and woke the nations to new life. He wrote without levity, and without choice. Every word was carved before his eyes into the earth and the sky, and the sun and stars were only letters of the same purport, and of no more necessity. But how can he be honoured when he does not honour himself, when he loses himself in the crowd; when he is no longer the lawgiver, but the sycophant, ducking to the giddy opinion of a reckless public; when he must sustain with shameless advocacy some bad government, or must bark all the year round in opposition; or write conventional criticism; or profligate novels; or, at any rate, write without thought and without recurrence by day and by night to the sources of inspiration?

Some reply to these questions may be furnished by looking over the list of men of literary genius in our age. Among these, no more instructive name occurs than that of Goethe, to represent the powers and duties of the scholar or writer.

I described Bonaparte as a representative of the popular external life and aims of the nineteeth century. Its other half, its poet is Goethe, a man quite domesticated in the century, breathing its air, enjoying its fruits, impossible at any earlier time, and taking away by his colossal parts the reproach of weakness, which, but for him, would lie on the intellectual works of the period. He appears at a time, when a general culture has spread itself, and has smoothed down all sharp individual traits; when, in the absence of heroic characters, a social comfort and cooperation have come in. There is no poet, but scores of poetic writers: no Columbus, but hundreds of post captains with transit-telescope, barometer, and concentrated soup and pemmican: no Demosthenes, no Chatham, but any number of clever parliamentary and forensic debaters; — no prophet or saint, but colleges of divinity; no learned man, but learned societies, a cheap press, readingrooms, and bookclubs, without number. There was never such a miscellany of facts. The world extends itself like American trade. We conceive Greek or Roman life, life in the Middle Ages, to be a simple and comprehensible affair; but modern life to respect a multitude of things which is distracting.

Goethe was the philosopher of this multiplicity, hundred-handed, Argus-eyed, able and happy to cope with this rolling miscellany of facts and sciences, and, by his own versatility, to dispose of them with ease; a manly mind unembarrassed by the variety of coats of convention with which life had got encrusted, easily able by his subtlety to pierce these, and to draw his strength from nature with which he lived in full communion. What is strange, too, he lived in a small town, in a petty state, in a defeated state, and in a time when Germany played no such leading part in the world's affairs as to swell the bosom of her sons with any metropolitan pride, such as might have cheered a French, or English, or once a Roman or Attic genius. Yet there is no trace of provincial limitation in his muse. He is not a debtor to his position, but was born with a free and controlling genius.

The Helena, or the second part of Faust, is a philosophy of literature set in poetry; the work of one who found himself the master of histories, mythologies, philosophies, sciences, and national literatures in the encyclopædical manner in which modern erudition with its international intercourse of the whole earth's population, researches into Indian, Etruscan, and all Cyclopean arts, geology, chemistry, astronomy; and every one of these kingdoms assuming a certain aerial and poetic character, by reason of the multitude. One looks at a king with reverence; but if one should chance to be at a congress of kings, the eye would take liberties with the peculiarities of each. These are not wild miraculous songs, but elaborate forms, to which the poet has confided the results of eighty years of observation. This reflective and critical wisdom makes the poem more truly the flower of this time. It dates itself. Still he is a poet, poet of a prouder laurel than any contemporary, and under this plague of microscopes (for he seems to see out of every pore of his skin) strikes the harp with a hero's strength and grace.

The wonder of the book is its superior intelligence. In the menstruum of this man's wit, the past and the present ages and their religions, politics, and modes of thinking are dissolved into archetypes and ideas. What new mythologies sail through his head! The Greeks said, that Alexander went as far as Chaos; Goethe went, only the other day, as far; and one step farther he hazarded, and brought himself safe back.

There is a heart-cheering freedom in his speculation. The immense horizon which journeys with us lends its majesty to trifles, and to matters of convenience and necessity, as to solemn and festal performances. He was the soul of his century. If that was learned, and had become by population, compact organization, and drill of parts, one great Exploring Expedition, accumulating a glut of facts and fruits too fast for any hitherto existing savans to classify, this man's mind had ample chambers for the distribution of all. He had a power to unite the detached atoms again by their own law. He has clothed our modern existence with poetry. Amid littleness and detail, he detected the Genius of life, the old cunning Proteus, nestling close beside us, and showed that the dulness and prose we ascribe to the age was only another of his masks:

"His very flight is presence in disguise:"

that he had put off a gay uniform for a fatigue dress, and was not a whit less vivacious or rich in Liverpool, or the Hague, than once in Rome or Antioch. He sought him in public squares and main streets, in boulevards and hotels; and, in the solidest kingdom of routine and the senses, he showed the lurking dæmonic power; that, in actions of routine a thread of mythology and fable spins itself: and this, by tracing the pedigree of every usage and practice, every institution, utensil and means, home to its origin in the structure of man. He had an extreme impatience of conjecture and of rhetoric. "I have guesses enough of my own; if a man write a book, let him set down only what he knows." He writes in the plainest and lowest tone, omitting a great deal more than he writes, and putting ever a thing for a word. He has explained the distinction between the antique and the modern spirit and art. He has defined Art, its scope and laws. He has said the best things about nature that ever were said. He treats nature as the old philosophers, as the seven wise masters did, and, with whatever loss of French tabulation and dissection, poetry and humanity remain to us; and they have some doctoral skill. Eyes are better, on the whole, than telescopes or microscopes. He has contributed a key to many parts of nature, through the rare turn for unity and simplicity in his mind. Thus Goethe suggested the leading idea of modern Botany, that a leaf or the eye of a leaf is the unit of botany, and that every part of the plant is only a transformed leaf to meet a new condition; and, by varying the conditions, a leaf may be converted into any other organ, and any other organ into a leaf. In like manner, in osteology, he assumed that one vertebra of the spine might be considered the unit of the skeleton: the head was only the uppermost vertebra transformed. "The plant goes from knot to knot, closing, at last, with the flower and the seed. So the tapeworm, the caterpillar, goes from knot to knot, and closes with the head. Man and the higher animals are built up through

the vertebræ, the powers being concentrated in the head." In optics, again, he rejected the artificial theory of seven colours, and
considered that every colour was the mixture of light and darkness in new proportions. It is really of very little consequence what
topic he writes upon. He sees at every pore, and has a certain
gravitation towards truth. He will realize what you say. He hates
to be trifled with, and to be made to say over again some old
wife's fable that has had possession of men's faith these thousand
years. He may as well see if it is true as another. He sifts it. I am
here, he would say, to be the measure and judge of these things:
Why should I take them on trust? And, therefore, what he says of
religion, of passion, of marriage, of manners, of property, of paper
money, of periods of belief, of omens, of luck, or whatever else, refuses to be forgotten.

Take the most remarkable example that could occur of this tendency to realize or verify every term in popular use. The Devil
had played an important part in mythology in all times. Goethe
would have no word that does not cover a thing. The same measure will still serve: — "I have never heard of any crime which I
might not have committed." — So he flies at the throat of this
imp. He shall be real, he shall be modern, he shall be European,
he shall dress like a gentleman, and accept the manners, and walk
in the streets, and be well initiated in the life of Vienna, and of
Heidelberg, in 1820, — or he shall not exist. Accordingly, he
stripped him of mythologic gear, of horns, cloven foot, harpoon
tail, brimstone, and bluefire, and, instead of looking in books and
pictures, looked for him in his own mind, in every shade of cold-
ness, selfishness and unbelief that in crowds, or in solitude darkens
over the human thought, and found that the portrait gained reality and terror by everything he added and by everything he took
away. He found that the essence of this hobgoblin, which had
hovered in shadow about the habitations of men ever since there
were men, was, pure intellect applied, as always there is a tendency, to the service of the senses: and he flung into literature, in
his Mephistopheles, the first organic figure that has been added
for some ages, and which will remain as long as the Prometheus.

I have no design to enter into any analysis of his numerous

works. They consist of translations, criticism, dramas, lyric and every other description of poems, literary journals, and portraits of distinguished men. Yet I cannot omit to specify the Wilhelm Meister.

Wilhelm Meister is a novel in every sense, the first of its kind, called by its admirers the only delineation of modern society, as if other novels, those of Scott, for example, dealt with costume and condition, this with the spirit of life. It is a book over which some veil is still drawn. It is read by very intelligent persons with wonder and delight. It is preferred by some such to Hamlet, as a work of genius. I suppose, no book of this century can compare with it in its delicious sweetness, so new, so provoking to the mind, gratifying it with so many and so solid thoughts, just insights into life and manners and characters; so many good hints for the conduct of life, so many unexpected glimpses into a higher sphere, and never a trace of rhetoric or dulness. A very provoking book to the curiosity of young men of genius, but a very unsatisfactory one. Lovers of light reading, those who look in it for the entertainment they find in a romance, are disappointed. On the other hand, those who begin it with the higher hope to read in it a worthy history of genius, and the just award of the laurel to its toils and denials, have also reason to complain. We had an English romance here not long ago, professing to embody the hope of a new age, and to unfold the political hope of the party called 'Young England,' in which the only reward of virtue is a seat in Parliament, and a peerage. Goethe's romance has a conclusion as lame and immoral. George Sand, in Consuelo and its continuation, — has sketched a truer and more dignified picture. In the progress of the story, the characters of the hero and heroine expand at a rate that shivers the porcelain chess table of aristocratic conventions; they quit the society and habits of their rank, they lose their wealth, they become the servants of great ideas, and of the most generous social ends, until, at last, the hero who is the centre and fountain of an association for the rendering of the noblest benefits to the human race, no longer answers to his own titled name; it sounds foreign and remote in his ear. "I am only man," he says, "I breathe and work for man," and this in poverty and extreme sacrifices. Goethe's hero, on the contrary, has so many weaknesses and impurities, and keeps such bad company, that the sober English public, when the book was translated, were disgusted. And yet it is so crammed with wisdom, with knowledge of the world, and with knowledge of laws, the persons so truly and subtly drawn, and with such few strokes, and not a word too much, the book remains ever so new and unexhausted, that we must even let it go its way, and be willing to get what good from it we can, assured that it has only begun its office, and has millions of readers yet to serve.

The argument is the passage of a democrat to the aristocracy, using both words in their best sense. And this passage is not made in any mean or creeping way, but through the hall door. Nature and character assist, and the rank is made real by sense and probity in the nobles. No generous youth can escape this charm of reality in the book, so that it is highly stimulating to intellect and courage.

The ardent and holy Novalis characterized the book as "thoroughly prosaic and modern, the Romantic is completely levelled in it, so is the poetry of nature, the Wonderful. The book treats only of the ordinary affairs of men: it is a poeticized civic and domestic story. The wonderful in it is expressly treated as fiction and enthusiastic dreaming:" — and yet, — what is also characteristic, Novalis soon returned to this book, and it remained his favorite reading to the end of his life.

What distinguishes Goethe for French and English readers is a property which he shares with his nation, a habitual reference to interior truth. In England and in America, there is a respect for talent, and, if it is exerted in support of any ascertained or intelligible interest or party, or in regular opposition to any, the public is satisfied. In France, there is even a greater delight in intellectual brilliancy, for its own sake. And, in all these countries, men of talent write from talent. It is enough if the understanding is occupied, the taste propitiated, — so many columns, so many hours, filled in a lively and creditable way. The German intellect wants the French spriteliness, the fine practical understanding of the English, and the American adventure; but it has a certain probity which never rests in a superficial performance, but asks steadily, *to what end?* A German public asks for a controlling sincerity. Here is activity of thought, but what is it for? What does the man mean? Whence? whence all these thoughts?

Talent alone cannot make a writer. There must be a man behind the book; a personality which by birth and quality is pledged to the doctrines there set forth, and which exists to see and state things so, and not otherwise: holding things because they are things. If he cannot rightly express himself today, the same things subsist, and will open themselves tomorrow. There lies the burden on his mind, — the burden of truth to be declared, — more or less understood, and it constitutes his business and calling in the world, to see those facts through, and to make them known. What signifies that he trips and stammers, that his voice is harsh or hissing, that his method or his tropes are inadequate? That message will find method and imagery, articulation and melody. Though he were dumb, it would speak. If not, — if there be no such God's word in the man, — what care we how adroit, how fluent, how brilliant he is?

It makes a great difference to the force of any sentence, whether there be a man behind it, or no. In the learned journal, in the influential newspaper, I discern no form, only some irresponsible shadow, oftener, some monied corporation, or some dangler, who hopes in the mask and robes of his paragraph, to pass for somebody. But, through every clause and part of speech of a right book, I meet the eyes of the most determined of men: his force and terror inundate every word: the commas and dashes are alive; so that the writing is athletic and nimble, can go far and live long.

In England and America, one may be an adept in the writings of a Greek or Latin poet, without any poetic taste or fire. That a man has spent years on Plato and Proclus, does not afford a presumption that he holds heroic opinions, or undervalues the fashions of his town. But the German nation have the most ridiculous good faith on these subjects; the student, out of the lecture-room, still broods on the lessons; and the professor cannot divest himself of the fancy that the truths of philosophy have some application to Berlin and Munich. This earnestness enables them to outsee men of much more talent. Hence almost all the valuable distinctions which are current in higher conversation, have been derived to us from Germany. But, whilst men distinguished for wit and learning, in England and France, adopt their study and their side with a certain levity, and are not understood to be very deeply engaged from grounds of character to the topic or the part they espouse, Goethe, the head and body of the German nation, does not speak from talent, but the truth shines through: he is very wise, though his talent often veils his wisdom. However excellent his sentence is, he has somewhat better in view. It awakens my curiosity. He has the formidable independence which converse with truth gives; — hear you, or forbear, his fact abides; and your interest in the writer is not confined to his story, and he dismissed from memory when he has performed his task creditably, as a baker when he has left his loaf, but his work is the least part of him. The old Eternal Genius, who built the world, has confided himself more to this man than to any other. I dare not say that Goethe ascended to the highest grounds from which genius has spoken. He has not worshipped the highest unity; he is incapable of a selfsurrender to the moral sentiment. There are nobler strains in poetry than any he has sounded. There are writers poorer in talent, whose tone is purer, and more touches the heart. Goethe can never be dear to men. His is not even the devotion to pure truth; but to truth for the sake of culture. He has no aims less large than the conquest of universal nature, of universal truth to be his portion: a man not to be bribed, nor deceived, nor overawed; of a stoical selfcommand and selfdenial, and having one test for all men, *What can you teach me?* All possessions are valued by him for that only; rank, privileges, health, time, being itself.

He is the type of culture, the amateur of all arts and sciences and events; artistic, but not artist; spiritual, but not spiritualist. There is nothing he had not right to know; there is no weapon in the armoury of universal genius he did not take into his hand, but with peremptory heed that he should not be for a moment prejudiced by his instruments. He lays a ray of light under every fact, and between himself and his dearest property. From him nothing was hid, nothing withholden. The lurking dæmons sat to him; and the Saint who saw the dæmons; and the metaphysical elements took form. "Piety itself," he says, "is no aim, but only a means, whereby through purest inward peace we may attain to highest culture." And his penetration of every secret of the Fine Arts will make Goethe still more statuesque. His affections help him like women employed by Cicero to worm out the secret of conspirators. Enmities he has none. Enemy of him you may be, if so you shall teach him aught which your goodwill cannot, — were it only what experience will accrue from your ruin. Enemy and welcome, but enemy on high terms. He cannot hate anybody; his time is worth too much. Temperamental antagonisms may be suffered, but like feuds of emperors who fight dignifiedly across kingdoms.

His autobiography under the title of "Poetry and Truth out of my Life" is the expression of this idea now familiar to the world through the German mind, but a novelty to England Old and New when that book appeared, that a man exists for Culture; not for what he can accomplish, but for what can be accomplished in him. The reaction of things on the man is the only noteworthy result. An intellectual man can see himself as a third person, therefore his faults and delusions interest him equally with his successes. Though he wishes to prosper in affairs, he wishes more to know the history and destiny of man; whilst the clouds of egotists drifting about him are only interested in a low success.

This idea reigns in the *Dichtung und Wahrheit,* and directs the selection of the incidents; and nowise the external importance of events, the rank of the personages, or the bulk of incomes. Of course, the book affords slender materials for what would be reckoned with us a "Life of Goethe;" few dates; no correspondence; no details of offices or employments; no light on his marriage; and a period of ten years that should be the most active in his life, after his settlement at Weimar, is sunk in silence. Meantime, certain love-affairs, that came to nothing, as people say, have the strangest importance. He crowds us with details: certain whimsical opinions, cosmogonies, and religions of his own invention, and, especially his relations to remarkable minds, and to critical epochs of thought, these he magnifies. His "Daily and Yearly

Journal," his "Italian Travels," his "Campaign in France," and the historical part of his "Theory of Colours," have the same interest. In the last, he rapidly notices Kepler, Roger Bacon, Galileo, Newton, Voltaire, &c. And the charm of this portion of the book consists in the simplest statement of the relation betwixt these grandees of European scientific history and himself; the mere drawing of the lines from Goethe to Kepler, from Goethe to Bacon, from Goethe to Newton. The drawing of the line is for the time and person a solution of the formidable problem, and gives pleasure when Iphigenia and Faust do not, without any cost of invention comparable to that of Iphigenia and Faust.

This lawgiver of art is not an artist. Was it that he knew too much, that his sight was microscopic, and interfered with the just perspective, the seeing of the whole? He is fragmentary; a writer of occasional poems, and of an encyclopædia of sentences. When he sits down to write a drama or a tale, he collects and sorts his observations from a hundred sides, and combines them into the body as fitly as he can. A great deal refuses to incorporate: this he adds loosely, as letters of the parties, leaves from their journals, or the like. A great deal still is left that will not find any place. This the bookbinder alone can give any cohesion to: and hence notwithstanding the looseness of many of his works, we have volumes of detached paragraphs, aphorisms, *Xenien*, &c.

I suppose the worldly tone of his tales grew out of the calculations of self culture. It was the infirmity of an admirable scholar who loved the world out of gratitude; who knew where libraries, galleries, architecture, laboratories, savans, and leisure were to be had, and who did not quite trust the compensations of poverty and nakedness. Socrates loved Athens; Montaigne Paris; and Madame de Staël said, she was only vulnerable on that side; (namely, of Paris.) It has its favorable aspect. All the geniuses are usually so ill assorted and sickly, that one is ever wishing them somewhere else. We seldom see anybody who is not uneasy or afraid to live. There is a slight blush of shame on the cheek of good men and aspiring men, and a spice of caricature. But this man was entirely at home and happy in his century and the world. None was so fit to live, or more heartily enjoyed the game. In this aim of Culture, which is the genius of his works, is their power. The idea of absolute eternal truth without reference to my own enlargement by it, is higher. The surrender to the torrent of poetic inspiration is higher; but, compared with any motives on which books are written in England and America, this is very truth, and has the power to inspire which belongs to truth. Thus has he brought back to a book some of its ancient might and dignity.

Goethe, coming into an overcivilized time and country, when original talent was oppressed under the load of books and mechanical auxiliaries and the distracting variety of claims, taught men how to dispose of this mountainous miscellany, and make it subservient. I join Napoleon with him as being both representatives of the impatience and reaction of nature against the *morgue* of conventions, — two stern realists, who, with their scholars, have severally set the axe at the root of the tree of cant and seeming, for this time, and for all time. This cheerful labourer, with no external popularity or provocation, drawing his motive and his plan from his own breast, tasked himself with stints for a giant, and without relaxation or rest, except by alternating his pursuits, worked on for eighty years with the steadiness of his first zeal.

It is the last lesson of modern science that the highest simplicity of structure is produced not by few elements, but by the highest complexity. Man is the most composite of all creatures: the wheel-insect, *volvox globator* is at the other extreme. We shall learn to draw rents and revenues from the immense patrimony of the old and the recent ages. Goethe teaches courage, and the equivalence of all times; that the disadvantages of any epoch exist only to the fainthearted. Genius hovers with his sunshine and music close by the darkest and deafest eras. No mortgage, no attainder, will hold on men or hours. The world is young: the former great men call to us affectionately. We too must write Bibles, to unite again the heavenly and the earthly world. The secret of genius is to suffer no fiction to exist for us; to realize all that we know; in the high refinement of modern life, in arts, in sciences, in books, in men, to exact good faith, reality, and a purpose; and first, last, midst, and without end, to honour every truth by use.

NOTES

TEXTUAL APPARATUS

ANNEXES

INDEX

NOTES

The informational notes that follow are keyed to the pages and lines of this text. The words introducing each note are normally those that begin and end the passage being annotated; sometimes, when that passage is long and complex, other words or phrases are included.

These notes are intended not just to guide scholars to Emerson's sources and to clarify obscurities but also to restore something of the context which existed for the reader in Emerson's time. Because, for example, few late-twentieth-century readers are steeped in Scripture, the notes include what once would have been unnecessary citations of chapter and verse. Because most readers are likely to ignore the instructions "See" and "Cf." and so not hear the words echoing in Emerson's mind, the notes often both cite and quote Scripture. Many once-famous lines of poetry are similarly treated, as is much of Shakespeare. Other kinds of contextual information—historical, biographical, geographical—are copiously supplied in the belief that understanding Emerson requires knowing what he knew.

Because Emerson relied heavily on translations and derivative sources, certain editions he used have been noted and cited; but where no textual problem is involved, major writers, ancient and modern, are cited by specific book, chapter, and paragraph or in standard editions. Unless otherwise noted, translations of Greek and Latin quotations are from the Loeb Classical Library and are reprinted by permission of Harvard University Press and the Loeb Classical Library. Biblical quotations are from the King James Version. Shakespeare citations are to *The Riverside Shakespeare* (Boston, Houghton Mifflin, 1974).

3.5 LEGENDS OF THE GAUTAMA ... DELICIOUSLY SWEET. Siddhartha Gautama (or Gotama), the Buddha, was the founder of Buddhism about the end of the sixth century B.C. The legend referred to here is in his twenty-seventh dialogue, sections 12–13, as recorded in the *Dīghanikāya*, III, 85–86, and is retold in the *Visuddhimagga,* ch. XIII, both Pali texts. Emerson may have known the legend from "Abridgment of the History of the Chalias, by Adrian Ragia Paksé, a Chief of that Cast" appended to an article by Mr. Joinville, "On the Religions and Manners of the People of Ceylon," *Asiatic Researches* (London ed.), 7 (1803), 438–443, a set of transactions he used otherwise, and he wrote a version of it in *JMN,* IX, 288–289.

3.7 THE WORLD IS . . . GOOD MEN. A slightly different version of this sentence is the epigraph for Emerson's journal Y, begun in September 1845 just as he was planning the lecture course on Representative Men. As the editors of *JMN* point out (IX, 258n.), it is a condensation and paraphrase of a passage in *The Vishńu Puráńa, a System of Hindu Mythology and Tradition,* trans. H. H. Wilson (London, 1840), p. 312: "The earth is upheld by the veracity of those who have subdued their passions, and, following righteous practices, are never contaminated by desire, covetousness, and wrath" (bk. III, ch. xii). Emerson borrowed this ancient Sanskrit classic from his new friend James Elliot Cabot, took it on his trip to Middlebury College, where he lectured in July 1845, read it "with wonder in the mountains" of Vermont, lent it "to a hungry soul" at the end of August, and copied many passages into his journal before returning it (*L,* III, 293, 299).

3.20 IN THE HILLS . . . FOR THE GATHERING. Gold was discovered near Coloma, California, on the south fork of the American River in January 1848. By the following winter a large migration had started to the newly acquired state—the gold rush of 1849—particularly prospecting in the foothills of the Sierra Nevada along the tributaries of the Sacramento and San Joaquin rivers. Emerson noted the excitement at the end of the summer of 1848: in addition to the railroad as the "sure topic for conversation . . . we have one more rival topic, California gold" (*JMN,* X, 353).

5.10 "PEU DE MOYENS, BEAUCOUP D'EFFET." In *JMN,* XI, 61, Emerson identified this quotation as from George Sand's novel *Le Compagnon du Tour de France* (Paris, 1843), p. 208 (ch. 18), the edition he owned. It was first published in 1840. This aesthetic insight in the novel is applied to architectural detail; in Francis George Shaw's translation, *The Journeyman Joiner; or, The Companion of the Tour of France* (New York, 1847), it is phrased "small means, great effect."

6.10 BEHMEN For the German mystic Jakob Boehme (or Behmen), see notes to 55.21 and 80.7.

6.20 LINNÆUS, OF PLANTS . . . NEWTON OF FLUXIONS. Carolus Linnaeus (1707–1778) or Karl von Linné was a Swedish botanist who set out the fundamental principles of modern binomial botanical classification. The Swiss naturalist François Huber (1750–1831) did extensive investigations of the habits and life cycle of the honeybee. Elias Magnus Fries (1794–1878) was a Swedish botanist who made the modern classification of fungi and lichens. Jean Baptiste van Mons (1765–1842), a Belgian chemist and horticulturist, was famous for developing better varieties of fruit trees, particularly pears, and published *Arbres fruitières; leur culture . . . et leur propagation par la graine; ou Pomonomie Belge, expérimentale et raisonnée . . .*, 2 vols. (Louvain, 1835–1836). John Dalton (1766–1844), an English chemist and physicist, revived and adapted to modern science the ancient atomic theory. The *Elements* of the Greek mathematician Euclid (fl. 300 B.C.) is the foundation of geometry. Essential to his major discoveries set forth in *Principia* and *Opticks,* the celebrated English mathematician and physicist Sir Isaac Newton (1642–1727) developed the calculus, formerly called the method of fluxions.

6.36 A MAGNET MUST . . . OR OERSTED, Hans Christian Oersted (1777–1851), Danish physicist and chemist, founded the study of electromagnetism by establishing the relation between electrical current and magnetism. The earlier contributions of William Gilbert and Emanuel Swedenborg are commented on by Emerson at pp. 59 and 58 (see also note to 59.16).

7.8 THE FIRST EULOGY . . . WERE GOOD. This eulogy is a close paraphrase of God's repeated observation on the various stages of His creation in the first chapter of Genesis.

8.1 INNUMERABLE WERNERS, . . . AND DAVYS? Abraham Gottlob Werner (1750–1817) was a noted German mineralogist and geologist who developed a theory that all rocks were deposits of a primeval ocean (Neptunism). His student, Baron Christian Leopold Von Buch (1774–1853), came to reject this theory, advancing much knowledge about volcanic processes (Vulcanism) in the formation of rock and land masses. The French geologist Jean Baptiste Armand Louis Léonce Elie de Beaumont (1798–1874) was most famous for his theory of the formation of mountain ranges. Jöns Jakob Berzelius (1779–1848), a Swedish chemist, whose major contributions were the determination of atomic and molecular weights, development of chemical symbolism, and isolation of many elements for the first time, took oxygen as the basis of reference for atomic weight; and among the many celebrated interests in chemistry of Sir Humphrey Davy (1778–1829) were his experiments with the medicinal virtues of various gases, including nitrous oxide, or laughing gas.

8.27 NAPOLEON SAID, "YOU . . . ART OF WAR." The earliest occurrence of a passage similar to this in *JMN*, IX, 252, suggests that it may not be an authentic quotation. *Stevenson's Book of Quotations* cites this lecture as the source of the attribution to Napoleon.

9.4 CECIL'S SAYING . . . CLARENDON'S PORTRAITS . . . TO DISSEMBLE." Emerson may have derived his first quotation from "Sir Walter Ra-

leigh," *The Edinburgh Review*, 71 (April 1840), 55 (American ed.): "An incidental remark by [Sir Robert] Cecil, contained in a private letter, has apprised us
of [Raleigh's] possession of a power scarcely less enviable than original genius
itself; and to which the extent of his acquisitions, so surprising in a man of
such active pursuits, was no doubt ascribable. 'He can toil terribly,' were the
words of the Secretary; and the intimation, though brief, furnishes us a valuable addition to our knowledge of his character." The letter from the secretary
of Queen Elizabeth I describes the demeanor of the famous adventurer, courtier, and poet Sir Walter Raleigh (1554?-1618), at the time of his
first arrest (1592). It was first published in the appendix to one of the books
under review: Mrs. A. T. Thomson [Katherine Byerley Thomson], *Memoirs of
the Life of Sir Walter Ralegh . . .* (London, 1830), p. 482. With slight adaptation
the characterizations of John Hampden (1594-1643) and Lucius Cary
(1610?-1643), second Viscount Falkland, both admired parliamentary leaders
during the reign of Charles I, are taken from Edward Hyde, first Earl of
Clarendon, *The History of the Rebellion and Civil Wars in England*, bk. VII, para.
84, and bk. IV, para. 123. Emerson owned a six-volume edition published in
Boston in 1827.

9.12 SAYING OF THE CHINESE MENCIUS . . . WAVERING, DETERMINED." As
indicated in *JMN*, IX, 8, the quotation is a paraphrase of *The Chinese Classical
Work Commonly Called The Four Books*, trans. David Collie (Malacca, 1828),
"Hea Mung," p. 130, which Emerson acquired in 1843. Mencius or Meng-tse
(371?-288? B.C.) was a Chinese Confucian philosopher whose work constitutes
one of the four books of *The Chinese Classics*. In that part, *The Works of Mencius*,
the original of Emerson's quotation is bk. VII, pt. ii, ch. 15. In the manuscript
of this lecture (see Annex A, Appendix 2), Emerson further modified his
source by substituting "Loo" for "Pih E," perhaps for better sound or for the
purpose of fictional generalization.

9.28 CORIOLANUS AND GRACCHUS, . . . PITT, LAFAYETTE, WELLINGTON,
WEBSTER, LAMARTINE. Gnaeus Marcius Coriolanus, an aloof Roman military hero, when his great popularity ebbed away, led his former enemies vic-
toriously against Rome (491? B.C.); but when he nobly spared the city, his new
followers killed him. Tiberius Sempronius Gracchus (163-133 B.C.) and his
brother Caius Sempronius Gracchus (154-121 B.C.) were popular radical social reformers in Rome; both were killed in riots, and their reforms were
quickly undone. William Pitt (1759-1806), an English statesman of great ora-
torical and political skill, dominated the House of Commons as prime minister (1784-1801, 1804-1806) and led popular opinion during the years of the
French Revolution and the wars against Napoleon. Marie Joseph Paul Yves
Roch Gilbert du Motier, Marquis de Lafayette (1757-1834), a French general
and politician, achieved his first fame by serving heroically in the American
Revolution. In the French Revolution his political leadership was dissipated
by his moderation and particularly by his firing into a popular crowd in 1791.

He fled the Revolution for a time and his political influence was felt again only after the Restoration. Arthur Wellesley, first Duke of Wellington (1769-1852), had great honors lavished on him for his success in the Peninsular War and the Waterloo campaign defeating Napoleon. In politics he was not so successful: as prime minister (1828-1830) he lost the support of his Tory party and at his fall there was mob violence against him. The American statesman, orator, and lawyer Daniel Webster (1782-1852) was in 1845 returned to the U.S. Senate from Massachusetts after a first term as secretary of state and he continued to distinguish himself as leading advocate of national unity. His presidential aspirations were already hampered by rising sectionalism and his opposition to the annexation of Texas. He was soon to lose anti-slavery support by his eloquence in defending, for the sake of the Union, the Compromise of 1850. Alphonse Marie Louis de Lamartine (1790-1869), French romantic poet, novelist, and statesman, represented popular liberal idealism somewhat aloof from the tumultous politics of the day. After the February Revolution of 1848 he was briefly head of the provisional government, but he alienated all except the most moderate revolutionaries and was among the candidates who lost the presidential election to Louis Napoleon Bonaparte in December 1848.

10.26 "TO CHOOSE THOSE ... TO BEING." This is paraphrased from Plato's *Republic*, bk. VII, ch. 16 (537 D) and refers to the selection of those capable of studying the dialectic, a choice to be made at age thirty in the training of the rulers of the state.

10.35 TREAD THE FLOOR OF THE PIT. In *JMN*, V, 370, Emerson wrote: " 'It is an expression of Pindar, that we tread the dark bottom of hell with necessities as hard as iron,' " giving his immediate source as *Plutarch's Morals ... Translated from the Greek, By Several Hands*, 5 vols. (London, 1718), I, 288. The passage, in the essay "Consolation to Apollonius," is drawn from Pindar, *Fragment* 207. This seventeenth-century translation of Plutarch's *Moralia*, which Emerson regularly cited, remains in his library in a broken and faultily bound set. See *JMN*, VII, 78, n. 218.

11.13 THE DOMINION OF ARISTOTLE ... OF LOCKE; Aristotle's philosophy, revived as medieval scholasticism, and his astronomy, elaborated by Ptolemy, fell at long last before the scientific and philosophical revolutions of the sixteenth and seventeenth centuries. Similarly the inductive method proposed by Sir Francis Bacon, the liberating religious reformation of Martin Luther, and the philosophical empiricism and the psychology of John Locke were by the end of the eighteenth century found to be dominating encumbrances from the past.

12.29 "EVER THEIR PHANTOMS ... WORDS OF GOOD." This is quoted with slight adaptation and variation from John Sterling's poem about Greek sculpture, "Dædalus," as Edward Waldo Emerson points out in *W*, IV, 306. Emerson had a copy of Sterling's *Poems* (London, 1839) in his library, a gift from this young friend, who died in 1844. See Emerson's further reference to Sterling at 92.26–34 and the note.

13.7 PEAU D'ÂNE . . . EVERY WISH.   Honoré de Balzac's philosophical novel *La Peau de chagrin* (Paris, 1831) turns on a talismanic wild ass's skin that shrinks as its owner is granted his every wish; when the skin so disappears, life is ended. Emerson apparently alludes to this novel, which was in 1843 published in translation in Boston under the peculiar title *Luck and Leather. A Parisian Romance*.

13.30 "SCOURGES OF GOD," . . . RICHARD PLANTAGENET;   Like Julius Caesar and Napoleon Bonaparte, the Holy Roman Emperor Charles V (1500–1558, who was also King Charles I of Spain), Charles XII (1682–1718), King of Sweden, and Richard I (1157–1199), King of England, were military leaders on a grand scale. Christopher Marlowe referred to his world conqueror as "the Scourge of God" (*Tamburlaine*, pt. II, V, iii, 248). As Emerson noted in *JMN*, VI, 209, the Roman Emperor Titus (39–81), who after a military career turned to a benevolent and constructive rule, was eulogized as "Deliciae humani generis" (Suetonius, *The Lives of the Caesars*, bk. VIII, "The Deified Titus," i).

14.32 THERSITES   As represented in the *Iliad* and in Shakespeare's *Troilus and Cressida*, Thersites is the ugliest and most scurrilous of the Greeks at Troy. He reviles the leaders and shows no respect for even the most heroic.

15.8 MEN RESEMBLE . . . THEIR PROGENITORS.   This sentence is among the many passages Emerson copied into his journal Y, probably in the fall of 1845 during the planning and composition of his lectures on Representative Men, from *Practical Philosophy of the Muhammadan People, Exhibited in Its Professed Connexion with the European, so far as to Render Either an Introduction to the Other; Being a Translation of the Akhlāk-i-Jalāly, the Most Esteemed Ethical Work of Middle Asia, from the Persian of Fakīr Jāny Muhammad Asāad . . .*, trans. W. F. Thompson (London, 1839). The compilation, which draws parallels between Islamic and Platonic thought, is from the fifteenth century and is ascribed to Jalāl al-Dīn Muhammad ibn As'ad al-Dawānī. Emerson's sentence is taken from p. 381, as noted in *JMN*, IX, 286, and like many passages that interested Emerson, is attributed in the original to other sources: "We are told in holy writ. . . ."

16.6 PERHAPS VOLTAIRE . . . NAME AGAIN."   Here perhaps Emerson echoes Thomas Carlyle's letter to him on November 3, 1844: "I daresay you are a little bored occasionally with 'Jesus' &c, as I confess I myself am . . . and an impatient person may exclaim with Voltaire, in serious moments: '*Au nom de Dieu, ne me parlez plus de cet homme-là!* I have had enough of him; — I tell you I am alive too!'" (*CEC*, p. 371). If this is an authentic quotation from the French writer François Marie Arouet de Voltaire (1694–1778), who as a deist notoriously attacked the divinity of Jesus, it has not been located. In 1843 Emerson wrote in his journal: "Name a friend once too often & you feel that a wrong is done to the friend & to ourselves. Yet you name the good Jesus until I hate the sound of him" (*JMN*, VIII, 337).

17.15 BOSWELLISM: In the last paragraph of his review-essay "Milton," Thomas Babington Macaulay apparently coined the word, which carries a negative import: "We are not much in the habit of idolizing either the living or the dead. And we think that there is no more certain indication of a weak and ill-regulated intellect than that propensity which, for want of a better name, we will venture to christen *Boswellism*" (*The Edinburgh Review*, 42 [August 1825], 346). Six years later, in his attack on John Wilson Croker's new edition of James Boswell's *The Life of Samuel Johnson* . . . , 5 vols. (London, 1831), Macaulay reiterated at length the old charges against Boswell's character, his meanness, and his attachment to great men, and raised the paradox of the smallest of men writing the greatest of biographies (*The Edinburgh Review*, 54 [September 1831], 16–20). Thomas Carlyle then joined issue in his two-part review of the same edition — "Biography" and "Boswell's Life of Johnson" — in *Fraser's Magazine*, 5 (April and May 1832), 253–260, 379–413. Particularly in the second part Carlyle defends Boswell and finds him "A cheering proof . . . that Loyalty, Discipleship, all that was ever meant by *Hero-worship*, lives perennially in the human bosom . . . James Boswell we can regard as a practical witness (or real *martyr*) to this high, everlasting truth" (p. 384). More immediately in Emerson's mind perhaps was Carlyle's lecture "The Hero as Man of Letters: Johnson, Rousseau, Burns" (May 1840), printed in *On Heroes, Hero-Worship and the Heroic in History* (London, 1841). Carlyle gives a paragraph to "poor Bozzy": "The foolish conceited Scotch Laird, the most conceited man of his time, approaching in such awestruck attitude the great dusty irascible Pedagogue in his mean garret there: it is genuine reverence for Excellence; a *worship* for Heroes, at a time when neither Heroes nor worship were surmised to exist" (pp. 296–297).

17.18 A CARTESIAN;   The celebrated French philosopher and scientist René Descartes (1596–1650) undertook to replace scholastic and Aristotelian philosophy by a method of mathematical certainty in metaphysical demonstration and emphasized the distinction between mind and matter, ascribing a reality to both dependent on the Creator. The influence of Cartesianism was important in the work of Nicolas Malebranche, Baruch Spinoza, and some of the rationalists, continuing into the eighteenth century.

17.21 THE MICROSCOPE OBSERVES . . . PERFECT ANIMALS. The wheel-insects (or wheel-animalcules as Emerson calls them in *JMN*, IX, 300) are the chief class, rotifera, of the phylum Trochelminthes. The microscopic rotifera are named for their rotary organs used in swimming, and some of them propagate by division as Emerson describes here. He apparently uses the word "monad" in its biological sense of any minute simple organism and "infusories" to mean Infusoria, either as one of its historically shifting biological classifications or in the general sense of microscopic animal life. For another use of the wheel-insect, see 166.22–23 and the note.

18.7 PESTALOZZIAN SCHOOL: . . . BY IMPARTING. The Swiss Johann Heinrich Pestalozzi (1746–1827) was celebrated for his experiments and theories of education. From Edward Biber, *Henry Pestalozzi and His Plan of Education* (London, 1831), p. 58, which Emerson withdrew from the Boston Athenæum in 1832 and 1836, he learned a "valuable fact" of Pestalozzi's experimental school: "that mutual teaching . . . where the tutors quitted their chair at the end of an hour to go and become with their scholars a class to receive instruction of another teacher each being in turn teacher & pupil" (*JMN*, V, 408).

19.26 PHŒNIXES: The Phenix or Phoenix is a fabulous Oriental bird of great beauty, which after living five or six centuries builds a funeral pyre upon which it expires, fanning the flames with its wings, only to be born again in fresh beauty from the ashes.

23.1 AMONG SECULAR BOOKS . . . IN THIS BOOK." The well-known but probably false anecdote of the order of Omar (ca. 581–644), the second caliph, to his general who in 640 captured Alexandria, anciently famed for its books, was probably fresh in Emerson's mind from his recent reading in *Memoirs of the History of France during the Reign of Napoleon, Dictated by the Emperor at Saint Helena* . . . , 7 vols. (London, 1823–1824). In the chapter "Religion of Egypt" Napoleon writes: "It is a prejudice widely spread and yet contradicted by history, that Mahomet was an enemy to the sciences and arts, and to literature. The caliph Omar's expression, when he caused the library of Alexandria to be burnt, has often been quoted: If this library contains what is in the Koran, it is useless; if it contains any thing else, it is dangerous" (II, 263). For Emerson's use of this work, see note to 144.8. Edward Waldo Emerson observes in his annotation, "The less usual use of 'secular,' as applied to books, in its strict classic sense, to mean *that live through the ages,* is characteristic" (*W*, IV, 311–312). Emerson used the word similarly in *CW*, II, 180, and III, 48. It first came into the present text in the 1876 edition (see Emendations in Copy-Text).

23.13 BOETHIUS, RABELAIS . . . HIS DEBTORS, The Roman philosopher and statesman Boethius (or Boetius or Boece; ca. 475–525) was one of the last ancient Neoplatonists. His *De consolatione philosophiae* and his commentaries on Aristotle were of great influence on the thought of the Middle Ages. The remainder of this succession of men who left a mark on their generation are, as Emerson implies, touched by Platonism, though less obviously: François Rabelais (ca. 1490–1533), a French humanist and physician, is famous for his books of *Gargantua* and *Pantagruel;* Desiderius Erasmus (1466?–1536), Dutch humanist and editor of the classics, the Church Fathers, and the New Testament, is best known for *The Praise of Folly;* the philosophical work of the Italian Giordano Bruno (1548–1600) is speculatively Platonic in revising the scholasticism of his time; the French writer and social thinker Jean Jacques Rousseau (1712–1778) made a great impact on succeeding generations; Vittorio, Conte Alfieri (1749–1803) was an Italian patriot and tragic poet; and Samuel Taylor Coleridge (1772–1834), the English romantic poet and philosophical prose writer, exerted a profound influence on Emerson's generation. The "men of grander proportion" are similarly "debtors" to Plato in varying degrees. Saint Augustine (354–430), Bishop of Hippo, was a Platonist before his conversion to Christianity; his *Confessions* and *City of God* are deeply colored by Platonic thought. Nicholas Copernicus (1473–1543), the Polish astronomer, created a scientific and theological revolution by positing a heliocentric universe to replace the Ptolemaic system. For the numerous parallels between Swedenborg and Plato see the next lecture, but little is made of the Platonism of Goethe in "Goethe, or the Writer." For Behmen, see note to 55.21; for Newton and Locke, see note to 59.16.

24.1 THE ALEXANDRIANS . . . PICUS MIRANDOLA. Alexandria, founded in Egypt by Alexander the Great, became in the third century B.C. the great center of learning. Emerson's constellation of Alexandrian Platonists apparently refers to a long succession of Neoplatonists connected prominently with that city, from the third century A.D. to the sixth century, even while their center moved to Rome, Athens, and elsewhere. The greatest of these was Plotinus (205–270), who before going to Rome studied in Alexandria with the Neoplatonist Ammonius Saccas, also the teacher of the Christian Origen (ca. 185–ca. 254). Hypatia (d. 415), a learned Alexandrian Neoplatonist, had as her student the Christian Neoplatonist Synesius (370–413), a noted orator and poet; Proclus (411–485), the great systematizer of Neoplatonic thought, also studied at Alexandria before going to Athens, and his fellow student Ammonius Hermiae remained in Alexandria to carry on the tradition. Even into the sixth century the Alexandrian line of Neoplatonists continued with Olympiodorus, the commentator on Plato. Only one Elizabethan is actually named by Emerson in his catalogue, but it is safe to assume that he alludes in a general way to the pervasive Platonism he saw in that age when he wrote in the chapter "Literature" in *English Traits:* "But Britain had many disciples of Plato . . . Hooker, Bacon, Sidney . . . Donne, Spenser, Chapman," and he continued there to show in what sense Sir Francis Bacon was a Platonist: "in the struc-

Notes

ture of his mind, [he] held of the analogists, of the idealists, or (as we popularly say, naming from the best example) Platonists" (*W*, V, 238–241). Sir Thomas More (1478–1535), an English statesman executed for treason, was also an important humanist, and his *Utopia* (1516) reflects Plato's *Republic.* Henry More (1614–1687), John Smith (1618–1652), and Ralph Cudworth (1617–1688) were English philosophers, members of a group called the Cambridge Platonists, who in response to the materialism of Thomas Hobbes, revived Platonic and Neoplatonic ideas. Cudworth's *The True Intellectual System of the Universe* (1678) was a book Emerson quoted from extensively. John Hales (1584–1656), English scholar and clergyman, was an advocate of moderate religious toleration, and in his posthumous *Golden Remains of the Ever Memorable Mr. John Hales* his humanism and Platonism are preserved. Jeremy Taylor (1613–1667) was an eminent and eloquent Anglican bishop whose theological and devotional works became classics. Floyer Sydenham (1710–1787) translated nine dialogues of Plato into English, and Thomas Taylor (1758–1835), a less scholarly translator but an enthusiastic Neoplatonist, continued Sydenham's work to make the first complete English translation of Plato. It was flawed in the view of nineteenth-century classical scholars by amplification and interpretation from the work of Plotinus and Proclus, which, along with other ancient Neoplatonists, Taylor also translated. Marsilio Ficino (1433–1499), an Italian philosopher, was the preeminent Platonist of his time. Translating into Latin the works of Plato and Plotinus, founding an academy in Florence, and interpreting Plato from a Neoplatonic point of view, he exerted a great influence on Renaissance humanism. His associate in the academy was Giovanni, Conte Pico della Mirandola (1463–1494), another important Italian humanist and advocate of Neoplatonism, whose major work undertook the reconciliation of Christianity and Platonic thought, bringing him into conflict with the Church.

24.6 MAHOMETANISM DRAWS . . . AKHLAK-Y-JALALY, FROM HIM. For *Practical Philosophy of the Muhammadan People . . . the Akhlāk-i-Jalāly,* see note to 15.8. The compilation itself draws heavily on Plato's works in making its commentary on Islamic thought. The translator, W. F. Thompson, says in his "Prolegomena": "From a comparison of the present work with the authorities it professes to consult, it appears that Muhammedan philosophy is neither more nor less than Grecian philosophy in an Eastern garb; a twin offspring of that common parent from which the sciences of Europe are proud to acknowledge their derivation" (p. xxv).

24.11 HELEN OF ARGOS Better known as Helen of Troy.

24.34 SOLON, AND SOPHRON, AND PHILOLAUS. Solon (ca. 639–ca. 559 B.C.), the great Athenian statesman and economic and social reformer, effected a set of laws that were the basis of classical Athenian democracy. Sophron of Syracuse (fl. ca. 430 B.C.) wrote prose dialogues depicting scenes of the common life of Sicilian Greeks. His writings are said to have been introduced to Athens by Plato, who admired them and found in them an inspiration for his own dialogues. For Philolaus, see note to 25.2.

25.2 PLATO ABSORBED THE . . . THE EUROPEAN MIND.   Philolaus (b. ca. 470 B.C.) and Timaeus (who may be a fictitious figure) were Pythagoreans from Graecia Major in southern Italy. The latter is the chief speaker in Plato's *Timaeus,* and a paraphrase of it was once attributed to him, though the work is now dated as probably from the first century A.D. There is an early, though rejected, legend that Plato's *Timaeus* was plagiarized from a lost work of Philolaus. Heraclitus (fl. ca. 500 B.C.), a famous Greek philosopher, developed the idea of a Logos, or divine law, in the constant flux of the universe. This is fire or wisdom that transcends man's knowledge. His contribution to Plato is an emphasis on finding through discourse the law not only in nature but especially in the depths of the soul. Parmenides (fl. fifth century B.C.), the Greek philosopher who figures in Plato's dialogue named for him, importantly distinguished between the real and the nominal and contributed to the definition of philosophical method. As his language here and at 25.35–26.1, where he expands the information, suggests, Emerson was aware that the travels of Plato were under scholarly attack. See note to 25.28.

25.9 "SUCH A GENIUS . . . DIFFERENT PERSONS."   *Republic,* 503 B (bk. VI, ch. 15).

25.25 HE GROUND THEM ALL INTO PAINT.   This echoes a popular whimsical poem by Emerson's late friend, the celebrated American painter, Washington Allston (1779–1843). "The Paint-King" was collected in 1813 and again posthumously in *Lectures on Art and Poems* in 1850. "Into paint will I grind thee, my bride!" the Paint-King threatens the deceived and abducted fair Ellen, and after pickling her in oil he proceeds to do so in order to make a portrait of his beloved queen of the fairies, Geraldine. But he fails for want of black pigment to finish the pupils of her eyes (a mouse has stolen Ellen's), and the scornful Geraldine hurls him into "the chasm profound" and calls Ellen forth from the painting. See *CW,* III, 141n.

25.28 HE WAS BORN 430 A.C. . . . AT EIGHTY-ONE YEARS.   The biographical information given here is not so widely divergent from mid-nineteenth-century scholarship as from later cautious data. The date for Plato's birth most widely accepted by scholars in the 1840s is 429 B.C., now modified to a conjectural 427 B.C. (see RSS). The stay in the Greek city of Megara, generally believed to be a self-imposed exile during which Plato studied with Euclid, is still thought to be authentic, as are the trips to Syracuse to the turbulent courts of Dionysius I (ca. 430–367) and Dionysius II (fl. 368–344), where Dion (409?–354), brother-in-law of the first tyrant and uncle of the second, sponsored the humane influence of Plato. Cicero (*The Republic,* I, x, 16) says that

Plato went to Egypt for thirteen years and to Italy and Sicily to study Pythagorean doctrines, though nineteenth-century scholars, while generally entertaining the possibility of those limited travels, pointed out that he need not
have traveled for that purpose. The extensions of the travels to Babylonia and
even Persia to study Hebrew religion and the doctrines of the Magi, scholars
of the 1840s rejected as attempts of early Christian writers to explain the connection of Platonism with Christianity. Most recent scholars accept the trip to
Italy (Graecia Minor), though not for the study of Pythagoras, but look upon
the Egyptian sojourn skeptically and reject the travels further east. Emerson's
cautious language shows his desire to keep at least the suggestion of an Eastern connection. Cicero, *De Senectute,* V, 13, is the source of the tradition about
Plato's death, but this, other biographical information, the travels, and philosophical influences on Plato are conveniently compiled in a work Emerson
borrowed from the Boston Athenæum in 1834 but apparently acquired for his
own library and began quoting from in October 1848: Thomas Stanley, *The
History of Philosophy* . . . (London, 1701), which is bound with Thomas Stanley,
The History of the Chaldaick Philosophy . . . (London, 1701). In *The History of Philosophy*, see particularly pt. V, "Plato," chs. II–V, IX, and XII.

27.24 BEFORE PERICLES, . . . FROM MIND.   Under the great statesman Pericles (ca. 495–429 B.C.) the Athenian empire flourished as an intellectual, cultural, and commercial center. The seven wise masters of Greece were
outstanding leaders and political philosphers of the late seventh and early
sixth centuries B.C., whose maxims and sayings were held in high esteem. The
list varies from author to author, but Emerson's list in *EL*, I, 358, is conventional: Bias, Chilon, Cleobulus, Periander, Pittacus, Solon, and Thales.
Among these Thales is said to be the introducer of geometry to the Greeks and
a metaphysician in that he held that all things originate in and return to
water, which is thus divine and eternal. By "partialists" Emerson seems to
mean the same as the "physical philosphers" mentioned at 32.15–17.

27.31 "HE SHALL BE . . . AND DEFINE."   Attributed to Plato by Emerson in
JMN, V, 79, this passage from *Phaedrus*, 266 B, probably is his own translation
of *Novum Organum*, bk. II, aph. xxvii (in the edition Emerson owned, *The Works
of Francis Bacon . . . ,* 10 vols. [London, 1824], VIII, 127): "non male dixit Plato,
Quod habendus sit tanquam pro Deo, qui definire et dividere bene sciat."

28.8 "IN THE MIDST OF THE SUN . . . THE VEDAS.   Henry Thomas Colebrooke, in an article "On the Religious Ceremonies of the Hindus, and of the
Brahmens Especially" in *Asiatic Researches* (London ed.), 5 (1799), 353, wrote:
"Thus, the venerable commentator says, 'In the midst of the sun stands the
moon, in the midst of the moon is fire, in the midst of light is truth, in the
midst of truth is the unperishable being.'" Emerson copied a condensation of
this into *JMN*, IX, 292, most likely from the reprint in Colebrooke's *Miscellaneous Essays*, 2 vols. (London, 1837), with an uncertainty about its ascription re-

solved only in the manuscript of this lecture, when Emerson decided that "the venerable commentator" should be incorporated into the Vedas and not understood to be a much later interpreter as implied by "Vedanta," his first ascription (see Annex A, Appendix 2). This uncertainty in ascription results from the unclear nature of his immediate source and from the fact that in this period he did not have available whole texts of the Vedas. Although the word generally means the original sacred lore of the ancient Hindus written down in the period from 1500 to 500 B.C., its specific meaning, Emerson knew from his sources, refers to the four *Samhitas:* the *Rig-Veda,* the *Sama-Veda,* the *Yajur-Veda,* and the *Atharva-Veda.* Emerson noted under "Vedas," in *JMN,* VIII, 559, two principal sources for selections from these earliest writings: "Extracts from the Vedas" in *The Works of Sir William Jones,* 6 vols. (London, 1799), VI, 415–430, and Colebrooke, "On the Védas, or Sacred Writings of the Hindus," *Asiatic Researches* (London ed.), 8 (1808), 377–497. Aside from offering extracts and describing the Vedas (in order "to convey some notion of" them because they "are too voluminous for a complete translation of the whole: and what they contain, would hardly reward labour of the reader; much less, that of the translator"), Colebrooke speculates on their composition: despite the alleged divine origin of the Vedas the true writers and compilers are many and worked at different times over a long period of time (pp. 497, 488–489).

28.19 PROTEUS   In Greek mythology Proteus is the old man of the sea, who, to avoid foretelling the future, changes himself into various shapes. Once caught and held, he reverts to his own shape and prophesies truly. He is described as nestling among the seals in *Odyssey,* bk. I, lines 384–570. See 68.20, 89.23, and 157.37.

28.26 THE INDIAN SCRIPTURES, IN THE VEDAS, THE BHAGAVAT GEETA, AND THE VISHNU PURANA.   For Emerson's use of translations of these Sanskrit writings see notes to 28.8, 78.8, and 3.7.

28.33 "YOU ARE FIT," ... AM I, I." —   What appear here as three quotations Emerson made up of five widely scattered passages, only slightly modified, from *The Vishńu Puráńa,* pp. 596, 659, 253, 132, and 225. The first quotation is from bk. V, ch. xxxiii; the first sentence of the second quotation is from bk. VI, ch. vii, and the remainder from bk. II, ch. xiv; the last quotation consists of two sentences from bk. I, ch. xvii, and bk. II, ch. xv, respectively. In *JMN,* IX, 319–321, these are among a collection of extracts from *The Vishńu Puráńa,* identified by Emerson and the editors. Vishnu (or Narayana) is one of the greatest of the Hindu gods, considered often the supreme deity; Krishna (also spelled Kreeshna), a hero who became the most popular and humanlike god of the Hindus, is the eighth incarnation of Vishnu.

30.22 SINISTER POLITICAL ECONOMY ... THROW IT OFF.   The English economist Thomas Robert Malthus (1766–1834), in *An Essay on the Principle of Pop-*

ulation as It Affects the Future Improvement of Society (1798), predicted that, as "population increases in a geometrical, food in an arithmetical ratio," a gloomy future of misery and want lay ahead. Emerson's knowledge of the urban, industrial, and social injustice of his time was reinforced by his second visit to Europe and by the great famines of Ireland, including one in 1846–1848. There was a growing recognition that India's problems, including its religiously based caste system, had only been exacerbated by British imperialism.

31.15 WHETHER HIS MOTHER . . . LIPS, OR NOT; Stanley, *The History of Philosophy,* pt. V, "Plato," chs. I, II, compiles these and other legends of the divinity of Plato. The bees are said to have made a honeycomb in the mouth of the infant, signifying his future mellifluousness.

32.21 "LET US DECLARE . . . OF EVERYTHING BEAUTIFUL." The first of these passages is from *Timaeus,* 29 E-30 A, and is, as *JMN,* IX, 280, notes, Emerson's translation from *Oeuvres de Platon,* trans. Victor Cousin, 13 vols. (Paris, 1822–1840), XII, 119. The Cousin translation was given to Emerson in 1839 by people who appreciated his free lectures to the Concord Lyceum. The second passage, immediately following in the journal, is identified as from *The Six Books of Proclus . . . on the Theology of Plato . . . ,* trans. Thomas Taylor, 2 vols. (London, 1816), I, 125, a book in Emerson's library. For earlier and later occurrences of the second passage see PP.

33.4 ACCORDING TO THE OLD SENTENCE . . . STYLE OF PLATO." In *JMN,* IX, 185, Emerson, drawing from Thomas Taylor's "General Introduction" to *The Works of Plato,* trans. Floyer Sydenham and Thomas Taylor, 5 vols. (London, 1804), I, ci, attributed a similar statement to "Ammianus," but he paraphrased the "old sentence" more closely as early as 1824, in a "Letter to Plato" (*JMN,* II, 246). Emerson borrowed volumes of this first complete English translation of Plato's works from the Harvard College Library and the Boston Athenæum until 1845, when he acquired his own set from the library of Charles Lane. Although it incorporates nine dialogues translated by Sydenham, it is mostly the work of Taylor, who translated the rest, compiled the extensive commentaries, interpreted passages, and published it. (See note to 24.1.)

33.11 HIS MANLY INTERFERENCE . . . IS PRESERVED; Stanley, *The History of Philosophy,* pt. III, "Socrates," ch. X, and pt. V, "Plato," ch. III, recounts the attempted speech of Plato at the trial of Socrates, and the "savage cry": "*Plato* went up into the Oratours Chair, intending to plead in his defence, and began thus; *Though I* (Athenians) *am the youngest of those who come up into this place.* But all the Senate crying out *of those who go down,* he was thereupon constrained to do so" (translated from Diogenes Laertius, *Lives and Opinions of Eminent Philosophers,* bk. II, ch. V [II, 44]).

33.20 HE SWEEPS THE DIM . . . THEIR SPINDLE. Emerson apparently refers here to the powerful fable that concludes the *Republic:* the tale of Er, a warrior returned from the land of the dead after twelve days (614 A–621 D).

33.26 THE INSCRIPTION ON . . . NOT TOO BOLD." See Britomart's entry into the house of Busyrane in Edmund Spenser's *The Faerie Queene,* bk. III, canto XI, stanzas l-liv; identified by Emerson in *JMN,* IX, 294–295.

34.8 SOCRATES' PROFESSION . . . SERVICE STILL. See *Theaetetus,* 148 E–151 E; *Gorgias,* 464 B–466 A; and *JMN,* X, 113.

34.15 "FOR PHILOSOPHY . . . THE MAN." In the manuscript Emerson identified this quotation as from Taylor's *The Works of Plato,* IV, 400 (see Annex A, Appendix 2).

34.24 "I, THEREFORE, CALLICLES . . . ALL CONTESTS HERE." *Gorgias,* 526 D–E; identified by Emerson in *JMN,* XI, 136, and in this manuscript, as from the Cary translation, p. 231 (see Annex A, Appendix 2). For the translations of Henry Cary and Henry Davis, see note to 45.1.

35.3 THE ATLANTIS. In the *Timaeus* Plato refers to the mythic island, seat of a great rival empire defeated nine thousand years earlier by the ancient Athenians, and now by cataclysm sunk into the Atlantic Ocean. In the fragmentary *Critias,* which was to have outlined its constitution, the original condition of Atlantis and its people is described as the ideal state in a land of plenty, existing in virtuous harmony.

36.1 "THE ESSENCE . . . THE HUMAN FORM." See *Phaedrus,* 249 B–C; *JMN,* X, 487.

36.31 "THE WHOLE OF . . . DISCOURSES AS THESE." *Republic,* 450 B (bk. V, ch. 2). In *JMN,* X, 476, Emerson gives Taylor's edition as his source. The name of Plato's brother, one of the interlocutors in *Republic,* is usually translated Glaucon.

36.34 ISOCRATES, The great teacher of Athenian orators, Isocrates (436–338 B.C.) was the pupil of Socrates, who is represented as predicting for him a brilliant future in *Phaedrus,* 278 E–279.

37.2 "BY US IT . . . BY THIS ALONE." *Timaeus,* 47 B–C (Davis translation with slight modification; see note to 45.1); *Republic,* 527 D–E.

37.17 IN THE DOCTRINE . . . EMBRACE IT." The idea for this passage, the matter of the origin of caste in "The East" as well as in Plato and the Koran, is taken from *Practical Philosophy of the Muhammadan People . . . the Akhlāk-i-*

Jalāly, p. 37, which in a footnote draws these parallels, quotes and translates the first quotation, slightly condensed here, and correctly identifies it as Plato, *Republic*, bk. III, ch. 21 (415 A). The footnote comments on the quotation from the Koran, which is given in the text. *JMN*, IX, 285 and 287, identify Emerson's immediate source of these two quotations, and *JMN*, X, 481, corrects Emerson's misidentification of the passage from Plato as *Timaeus*. See Annex A, Appendix 2, 37.23, where a canceled passage includes another quotation from *Practical Philosophy of the Muhammadan People . . . the Akhlāk-i-Jalāly*, p. 391.

37.25. "OF THE FIVE . . . THE FIRST." For the five, see canceled footnote in the manuscript. The insistence on the temperaments of the youth selected for training as guardians is in the *Republic*, bk. IV, chs. 15–16 (374 E–376 C).

37.31 SOCRATES DECLARES, THAT . . . IT MAY HAPPEN." *Theages*, 129 E–130 E, somewhat rearranged and with condensation of the quotation.

38.32 "LET THERE BE . . . UNDERSTANDING, REASON." Adapted from *Republic*, 509 D–510 C, 511 D–E (bk. VI, ch. 20, 21; probably Taylor's translation). See 66.11–12.

39.18 "WHEN AN ARTIFICER . . . FAR FROM BEAUTIFUL." *Timaeus*, 28 A–B, modified from Taylor's translation, which is identified in *JMN*, X, 481, but in this manuscript identified as from Cousin's French (XII, 116).

39.24 BANQUET. Better known as *Symposium*.

39.29 BODY CANNOT TEACH WISDOM, GOD ONLY. *Phaedo*, 65 A–67 C, is the source of the dogma, as Emerson indicates in *JMN*, X, 477.

40.7 THE PLAYERS PERSONATED . . . STONE JUGS. The phrasing of this sentence reveals its source in Stanley, *The History of Philosophy*, pt. III, "Socrates," ch. VIII, which in turn cites Aelian, *Varia historia*, II, 13. The comedy referred to here is Aristophanes, *The Clouds*, of which Stanley gives a translated version as a supplement to his treatment of Socrates.

40.27 THUS, HE SHOWED . . . EASILY REACH. The phrasing here indicates that Emerson took this sentence from Stanley, *The History of Philosophy*, pt. III, "Socrates," ch. V, sect. 2, which in turn translates Xenophon, *Memorabilia*, III, xiii, 5.

40.31 ON ONE OR TWO OCCASIONS, . . . RUINED HIM. Stanley, *The History of Philosophy*, pt. III, "Socrates," chs. VII–[VIII], tells the story of Socrates' heroic actions in the retreat from Delium in Boeotia and the story of how Socrates, as temporary presiding officer of the legislative body, risked condemnation himself by refusing to sign an unjust popular condemnation of naval commanders, pretending he could not write and furthermore did not know the form of the decree.

41.2 HIS NECESSARY EXPENSES . . . FOR SALE.   These details are drawn from Stanley, *The History of Philosophy*, pt. III, "Socrates," ch. II.

41.26 TOSSES THE HIPPIASES . . . BEWITCHED HIM.   Hippias of Elis and Gorgias of Leontine in Sicily were eminent rhetoricians and sophists who were separately confuted in several of Socrates' dialogues, *Lesser Hippias, Greater Hippias, Parmenides, Gorgias,* for example, and often mentioned, as in *Apology,* 19 E, as well-known and famous teachers in contrast to the obscure Socrates. The sentence about Meno is a paraphrase of *Meno,* 80 A–B, where the disciple of Gorgias protests that he is helpless against the subtle argument of Socrates. The crampfish is the electric ray or torpedo (family Torpedinidae), and it generates an electric current used in hunting and defense that is strong enough to stun humans, if not so fatally and dramatically as Emerson suggests at 147.24–28, where he calls it the torpedo. The ancient Greeks are said to have used it in the treatment of mental illness for shock therapy. But here Meno's charge is that Socrates' bewitching argument has numbed, as a crampfish might, his tongue and soul so that he cannot answer a question he has easily answered earlier in the dialogue and often before.

42.5 SOCRATES ENTERED THE PRISON . . . EVERYTHING YOU SAY."   The first sentence of the passage is taken from Stanley, *The History of Philosophy*, pt. III, "Socrates," ch. XI, who in turn is translating from Seneca, *De Consolatione ad Helviam,* XIII, 4. The quotation is a paraphrase of *Crito,* 54 D and closely echoes that given by Stanley.

44.9 KARNAC, . . . ETRURIAN REMAINS,   Karnak, a village along the Nile in central Egypt, is the site of part of the ancient city of Thebes. Among its many and massive ruins is the Great Temple of Amon. In Emerson's time the archaeology of the ancient Etrurian or Etruscan civilization had not discriminated definitively the Greek and later Roman components of its remains, but the sculpture in bronze and clay, the fresco work, and the naturalistic portraiture gave evidence of a highly developed civilization that reached its peak in the sixth century B.C., rivaling its neighbor Rome, before being finally swallowed up by the beginning of the first century B.C.

45.1 THE PUBLICATION IN MR BOHN'S . . . HAS YIELDED,   In 1846 the London bookseller and publisher Henry George Bohn began the cheap publication of quality books in a series or library — at first The Standard Library, translations of continental literature, followed by The Scientific, The Antiquarian, and, in 1848, The Classical Library, with others to follow. Emerson

commented on this enterprise with enthusiasm in 1849: "The cheap press &
the universal reading, which have come in together, have caused a great many
translations to be made from the Greek, the German, the Italian, & the
French. Bohn's Library now furnishes me with a new & portable Plato, as it
had already done with new Goethes. And John Carlyle translates Dante. To
me the command is loud to use the time by reading these books. And I should
as soon think of foregoing the railroad & the telegraph, as to neglect these.
With these belong the Mediaeval Chronicles . . . in Bohn" (*JMN*, XI, 137).
The Classical Library began with new translations of Plato, and Emerson was
in 1848 naturally eager to acquire them and in fact used the first two volumes
in revising his lecture on Plato and adding "New Readings" as addendum
(see Historical Introduction). The complete set of Plato remains in Emerson's
library: *The Works of Plato. A New and Literal Version Chiefly from the Text of Stall-
baum . . .* , 6 vols. (London, 1848–1854). The two volumes available to Emerson
in the final preparation of *Representative Men* contain *Apology of Socrates, Crito,
Phaedo, Gorgias, Protagoras, Phaedrus, Theaetetus, Euthyphron,* and *Lysis,* translated
by Henry Cary (vol. I), and *Republic, Timaeus,* and *Critias,* translated by Henry
Davis (vol. II).

45.15 PHIDIAS, MENU,   Phidias or Pheidius (ca. 500–ca. 432 B.C.) was the
greatest of Greek sculptors, whose works, highly praised by the ancients, are
now lost or survive only in copies of works ascribed to him. He was said to be a
close associate and adviser of Pericles, and the ancient Greeks particularly valued him for the moral significance of his colossal statues of the gods in bronze,
gold, and ivory. Sometimes he has been thought to be responsible for the
sculptures of the Parthenon, but the connection is tenuous. Manu (or Menu)
is the semi-legendary lawgiver in Hindu tradition, and to him are ascribed the
laws or institutes (compiled between 200 B.C. and A.D. 200) that Emerson
knew in the translation of Sir William Jones, *Institutes of Hindu Law; or, Ordi-
nances of Menu . . .* , published in *The Works of Sir William Jones,* 6 vols. (London,
1799), III, 53–466, a volume Emerson borrowed from the Boston Athenæum
in July 1840 and from which he transcribed extensive extracts in *JMN*, VI,
392–397. As he makes clear in the headnote to the selections published in *The
Dial,* 3 (January 1843), 331, he knew Jones's view that the code of Manu is
one of the oldest extant compositions — believed by Hindus to have been
written by the son or grandson of Brahma — though it may have undergone
successive abridgments. Emerson follows Jones's spelling, Menu, perhaps because he accepted Jones's derivation of it from the Sanskrit root for "to understand," signifying "intelligent"; Manu is the more common spelling.

46.13 WHEN CATALOGUING . . . OF LAPLACE.   Pierre Simon, Marquis de Laplace (1749–1827), French mathematician and astronomer, was noted, among
his other major contributions, for advancing the nebular theory of the origin
of the solar system. Emerson contrasts this great speculation with the mere

discovery over the years, with stronger and stronger telescopes, of the innumerable stars in the great nebula in the constellation Orion.

46.29 HIS PERCEPTION . . . NEW CREATION: This law is developed as an argument for the immortality of the soul in *Phaedo,* 70–72, but the present passage, including the illustration of cholera, is a close paraphrase of a passage that Emerson attributed to his half-uncle's wife, Sarah Alden Ripley, a woman of great learning (*JMN,* XI, 173, indexed in notebook OP Gulistan, p. 73).

47.2 HIS APOLOGUES THEMSELVES, THE CAVE . . . FATES, FABLES   Trophonius, an underground, oracular Boeotian god who turns up in various Greek writings, has nothing to do with Plato's fable of the cave in *Republic,* 514 A–517 A (bk. VII, chs. 1–2). That Emerson means this famous fable of the cave is apparent from his indexing the passage in the back of his copy of Davis' translation (the second volume of the Bohn edition). The only mention of Trophonius in writings attributed to Plato is *Axiochus,* 367 C, a spurious attribution. Among the other apologues and fables, the ring of Gyges, the metallic temperaments (see 37.17–21 and note), and the visions of Hades and the Fates are in *Republic,* 359 C (bk. II, ch. 3), 414 B–415 D (bk. III, ch. 21), and 614 B–621 D (bk. X, ch. 13–16). The fables of the charioteer and the two horses and of Theuth and Thamus are in *Phaedrus,* 253 C–254 E, and 274 D–275 B.

47.7 HIS SOLIFORM EYE AND HIS BONIFORM SOUL;   Emerson here refers to *Republic,* 508 E–509 A (bk. VI, ch. 19), which he thus indexed in his copy of *The Works of Plato,* 6 vols. (London, 1848–1854), II (1849), but instead of Davis' translation, he draws for his phrasing on the paraphrase of Ralph Cudworth in *The True Intellectual System of the Universe,* 4 vols. (London, 1820), I, 421–422, which he also similarly indexed in the back of his copy: "That though knowledge and truth be both of them excellent things, yet he that shall conclude the chief good to be something which transcends them both, will not be mistaken. For as light, and sight, or the seeing faculty, may both of them rightly be said to be soliform things, or of kin to the sun, but neither of them to be the sun itself; so knowledge and truth may likewise both of them be said to be boniform things, and of kin to the chief good, but neither of them to be that chief good itself; but this is still to be looked upon as a thing more august and honorable." Edward Waldo Emerson notes (*W,* IV, 320) that Oliver Wendell Holmes had detected that these "two quaint adjectives" are "from the mint of Cudworth" (*Ralph Waldo Emerson* [Boston, 1885], p. 200).

47.11 "WHAT COMES FROM GOD . . . THE LAWS ABOVE.   See Stanley's translation of Pico della Mirandola's "Platonick Discourse," pt. II, sec. XII, cited in the note to 49.4. The belief here credited to Socrates was a favorite saying of Emerson's.

47.19 IT IS BETTER . . . TO COVET PUNISHMENT;   The first clause is argued in *Gorgias*, 474 C–475 E; the second, as Emerson indicated in *JMN*, XI, 135, he found in Cary's translation of *Gorgias*, 480 C–D.

47.21 THAT THE LIE . . . INVOLUNTARY HOMICIDE;   These two clauses Emerson probably elaborated from *Republic*, 451 A (bk. V, ch. 2); the second he translated from that passage in Cousin's *Oeuvres de Platon*, IX, 254, in *JMN*, IX, 215.

47.23 THAT THE SOUL . . . SINS WILLINGLY;   The first clause is a version of *Republic*, 413 A (bk. III, ch. 19); an early source (given in *JMN*, VI, 95) may be Sir James Mackintosh, *A General View of the Progress of Ethical Philosophy, Chiefly During the Seventeenth and Eighteenth Centuries* (Philadelphia, 1832), p. 136. See *CW*, III, 233–234, note to 159.32. The idea is indexed and marked by Emerson in Davis' translation, *The Works of Plato*, II, 63 (*Republic*, bk. II, ch. 20), and on p. 62 of that translation may be the source for Emerson's second clause.

47.24 THAT THE ORDER . . . BEST POSSIBLE.   *Republic*, 403 D (bk. III, ch. 13, probably from the Davis translation, *The Works of Plato*, II, 83–84).

47.30 THE FINE WHICH . . . WORSE MAN;   The source for this paraphrase is identified in *JMN*, IX, 184, and X, 475, as *Republic*, 347 C (bk. I, ch. 19; Taylor's *The Works of Plato*, I, 125).

47.31 THAT HIS GUARDS . . . THEY NEED.   The source of this paraphrase, identified by Emerson in *JMN*, IX, 184, and X, 475, is *Republic*, 416 D–417 A (bk. III, ch. 22; Taylor's *The Works of Plato*, I, 258).

48.11 "OF ALL WHOSE . . . THE GREATEST GOOD."   *Republic*, 366 E (bk. II, ch. 9; Davis translation).

48.26 THUS THE FACT . . . PARTICULAR EXPLICATION.   Socrates set forth this argument for the immortality of the soul in the *Phaedo*. Emerson indexed as "Reminiscence" and marked in the Cary translation this passage: " 'And indeed,' said Cebes, interrupting him, 'according to that doctrine, Socrates, which you are frequently in the habit of advancing, if it is true, that our learning is nothing else than reminiscence . . . it is surely necessary that we must at some former time have learned what we now remember. But this is impossible, unless our soul existed somewhere before it came into this human form; so that from hence also the soul appears to be something immortal' " (*Phaedo*, 72 E–73 A).

49.4 THE NAMES OF THINGS . . . INTELLECTUAL ILLUSTRATION. The first sentence here is drawn from *Cratylus,* 390 D–E. The meaning of the name of Pan is taken from *Cratylus,* 408 D. The phrasings of the meanings of Jove, Mars, Venus, the Muse Calliope, and the Grace Aglaia are taken from a translation of "A Platonick Discourse . . . by John Picus Earl of Mirandula, In Explication of a Sonnet by Hieronimo Benivieni," pt. I, secs. VII–X, pt. II, sec. XII, which is printed as an appendix to Stanley, *The History of Philosophy,* pt. V, "Plato." Pico della Mirandola cites, as his source for Jove, Plato's *Philebus,* 30 C–D.

49.15 PAINTS IN TIMÆUS . . . DISORDER INTO ORDER. *Timaeus,* 30 A, continuing 32.21–27 above.

49.27 "NATURE IS MADE . . . IN THE STORY." *The Winter's Tale,* IV, iv, 89–90, and *Antony and Cleopatra,* III, xiii, 43–46.

50.1 SWEDENBORG THROUGHOUT HIS . . . IS A PLATONIST. See 71.24–73.3.

50.25 IN HIS EIGHTH BOOK . . . DOGS AND CATS. Book VIII of the *Republic,* in a brilliant display of Socrates' abilities, describes the four actual kinds of government as distinguished from the ideal republic and their degeneration through a cycle into the last, tyranny, because of the weaknesses of their corresponding human types. As a preliminary, Socrates digresses on the beginnings of the cause of degeneration: "To that which is divinely generated, there is a period which is comprehended by the perfect number; whereas, to that generated by man, there is one, in which the augmentations," and there follows in the Davis translation and all others a mathematical explanation of the "fatal number" that has baffled ancient and modern commentators, as Davis points out in a note and in an appendix (*The Works of Plato,* II, 235–236, 430–431). The passage, 546 A–D (bk. VIII, ch. 3), was ingeniously annotated by Cousin in his translation, but Emerson's view expressed here is pretty much to the point in regard to the main argument in the *Republic.* As a matter of civic survival, Socrates would "permit the lie to governors" in his ideal republic: "The rulers of the city may, if anybody, fitly lie on account of enemies or citizens for the benefit of the state; no others may have anything to do with it" (389 B–C; bk. III, ch. 3); "it seems likely that our rulers will have to make considerable use of falsehood and deception for the benefit of their subjects" (459 D; bk. V, ch. 8). Emerson's sentence is more colorfully generalized to all Platonists at 85.26–86.3.

54.8 "GOD SAID, THE HEAVEN . . . RETURN TO US?" This is a conflation and modification of a passage Emerson copied into *JMN,* IX, 284, from *Practical Philosophy of the Muhammadan People . . . the Akhlāk-i-Jalāly,* p. 12: "God saith, *The heavens, the earth, and all that is between them, we created not in sport;* — and again he saith, *Then think ye we have created ye in jest, and that ye are not to return to us?*" At *JMN*, IX, 263, he separated the two verses and identified them as from the Koran. That his modification of the second "ye" to "them" is intentional is evident in the context here and at 124.23–24, a further abbreviation of the passage, and seems consistent with the context of his immediate source but not with the widely separated passages in the Koran (xxiii, 115, and xxi, 16, repeated at xliv, 38).

54.13 "THE REALMS OF BEING . . . ALL ARE THOU." *Practical Philosophy of the Muhammadan People . . . the Akhlāk-i-Jalāly*, p. 114, whose translator does not identify the lines. Emerson's identification in *JMN*, XII, 558, *"Persian,"* refers to his source generally.

54.15 THE KORAN MAKES . . . ADMITTED WITH THEE." Neither in *JMN*, IX, 286, nor in Emerson's source (*Practical Philosophy of the Muhammadan People . . . the Akhlāk-i-Jalāly*, p. 391) is the classification attributed to the Koran. The lines of verse are not identified by the translator of the Persian book, and Emerson's attribution refers to his source generally.

54.27 THE ARABIANS SAY . . . KNOWS, I SEE." *Practical Philosophy of the Muhammadan People . . . the Akhlāk-i-Jalāly*, p. 25, though not attributed to the Arabians. See *JMN*, IX, 284. Abu Said ibn Abi al-Khair (967–1049), a Sufi dervish, was an innovator in mystical Persian poetry. Abu Ali al-Husain ibn Abdallah ibn Seena (980–1037) is also known as Avicenna, the famous medieval Islamic philosopher and physician.

54.33 THE SOUL HAVING BEEN . . . REMINISCENCE ALL." Within this paraphrase and quotation from Plato, *Meno*, 81 C–D (Taylor's edition), Emerson has introduced as the second participial phrase a slightly modified passage from *The Vishńu Puráńa*, p. 650 (bk. VI, ch. vii). See *JMN*, IX, 264, 290, 317, for versions of the Indian passage.

55.21 "THE FLIGHT," PLOTINUS . . . GUION, SWEDENBORG, The Plotinian phrase comes from a work Emerson owned, *Select Works of Plotinus . . .* , trans. Thomas Taylor (London, 1817), p. 506 (Ennead VI, bk. 9, para. xi): "This, therefore, is the life of the Gods, and of divine and happy men, a liberation from all terrene concerns, a life unaccompanied with human pleasures, and a flight of the alone to the alone." See PP for use of the passage in Greek and English. *OED* and standard etymological dictionaries ascribe the origin of "mystic" to μύστης, one initiated, from μυέιν, to be closed. See Emendations in Copy-Text for note on rejected forms. The trances or raptures of Socrates, the unions of Plotinus (205–270), the great Neoplatonist, and his editor and biographer, Porphyry (ca. 232–304), the visions or aurora of the German mystic, Jakob Boehme (or Behmen; 1575–1624), the mystical convulsions of George Fox (1624–1691), the founder of the Society of Friends (or Quakers), and the visions, illuminations, and mystical trances of Swedenborg are distinguished in "Religion," *EL,* II, 90–92, and "The Over-Soul," *CW,* II, 167; some indication of Emerson's sources is given there in notes. John Bunyan (1628–1688), best known for *The Pilgrim's Progress,* can be found to have had a number of mystical experiences if *Grace Abounding to the Chief of Sinners* is read as literal autobiography. Emerson had this work, bound with the falsely attributed *The World to Come; or, Visions of Heaven and Hell* (London, 1827), in his library. Blaise Pascal (1623–1662), the French mathematician and religious writer, became in his last years a reclusive ascetic, to whom a number of mystical experiences were attributed, and his posthumous *Pensées* (1670) had been authentically re-edited from manuscript in 1844 with considerable publicity. Jeanne Marie Bouvier de La Motte-Guyon (or Guion; 1648–1717) was a celebrated French Quietist for whom union with God was achieved by meditation which resulted in loss of understanding, affections, and will in God. Emerson had in his library her *Opuscules Spirituels* (Cologne, 1712) and Thomas C. Upham, *Life and Religious Opinions and Experience of Madame de La Mothe Guyon,* 2 vols. (New York, 1847).

55.27 "It o'erinforms the tenement of clay," Adapted from Dryden, *Absalom and Achitophel* [Part I], line 158.

55.34 "Indeed it takes . . . of our attribute." *Hamlet,* I, iv, 20–22; more accurately quoted in *JMN,* VII, 136 ("though" for "when").

56.14 Royal and ducal Fredericks, Cristierns, and Brunswicks, During Swedenborg's lifetime Frederick I and Adolphus Frederick, kings of Sweden, Christian (or Kristiern) V, Frederick IV, Christian VI, Frederick V, and Christian VII, kings of Denmark and Norway, and Frederick Augustus I and Frederick Augustus II, electors of Saxony and kings of Poland, were weak and ineffective, though often contentious and warlike. Among prominent but now obscure dukes and princes are Christian Albrecht and Christian August of Holstein-Gottorp, Frederick Adolf of Östergottland, Frederick IV of Hesse-Kassel, and Frederick Louis, Prince of Wales, nominal leader of opposition to his father, George II. The dukes of Brunswick-Wolfenbüttel in this period, Rudolf August, Anthony Ulrich, Augustus William, Louis Rudolph (Swedenborg's patron; see note to 57.10), and Charles, and the dukes of Brunswick-Bevern, Ferdinand Albert I and Ferdinand Albert II, were important in dynastic marriages and often in warfare. The Brunswick-Lüneburg line became electors of Hanover and, with the accession of George I, kings of England. The royal Fredericks of Prussia have not entirely slid into oblivion. All these dukes and kings were important in the political, dynastic, and military chaos of northern Europe, especially in the decline of Sweden after the assassination of Charles XII in 1718, and Swedenborg sustained personal contacts with a number of them.

56.32 IN 1716, HE ... SIEGE OF FREDERICSHALL, The newly graduated Swedenborg's five-year trip abroad to visit various universities occurred in 1710–1715 (James John Garth Wilkinson, *Emanuel Swedenborg: A Biography* [Boston, 1849], pp. 7–8). It was the first of many to. England and various places on the continent, but the only one fitting Emerson's description. Most of the biographical information accords with Wilkinson's book, which is in Emerson's library, and with his unsigned article on Swedenborg in *The Penny Cyclopædia for the Society for the Diffusion of Useful Knowledge* (London, 1842). Though he planned the daring military feat, Swedenborg was not actually present at the siege in which Charles XII lost his life (Wilkinson, *Emanuel Swedenborg,* p. 17). The Norwegian city, now Halden, was more commonly called Frederikshald.

57.1 DÆDALUS HYPERBOREUS, At his own expense Swedenborg published this first Swedish scientific journal in Stockholm and Uppsala in six irregular numbers from 1716 to 1718. It contained mainly reports of the mathematical and mechanical projects of Swedenborg and his mentor, the celebrated engineer and inventor Christopher Polhem (1661–1751). The journal helped bring Swedenborg into the favor of Charles XII.

57.10 DUKE OF BRUNSWICK ... OR AMSTERDAM. Although Swedenborg published his theological works in relatively uncensored Amsterdam and London, none was published during his lifetime in Leipzig or Dresden, according to the evidence of James Hyde, *A Bibliography of the Works of Emanuel Swedenborg* (London, 1906). He had published various scientific books before 1743 in all four of the cities and elsewhere. Emerson may have had in mind Wilkinson's information in *The Penny Cyclopædia* that Louis Rudolph, Duke of Brunswick from 1731 to 1735, defrayed the cost of the publication in 1734 in Dresden and Leipzig of the three folios, *Opera Philosophica et Mineralia.* Swedenborg dedicated the first to this patron; the second to William, Landgrave of Hesse-Kassel; and the third to Frederick I, King of Sweden. Wilkinson notes that he published also in Dresden and Leipzig in 1734 another scientific work, *Prodromus Philosophiæ Ratiocinantis de Infinito, et Causa Finali Creationis: deque Mechanismo Operationis Animæ et Corporis.*

57.16 AT THE DIET OF 1751 ... FROM HIS PEN. Wilkinson in *The Penny Cyclopædia* attributes the remark to the prime minister, Swedenborg's friend Count Anders Johan von Höpken (1712–1789), in reference to one memorial to the Diet of 1761. Swedenborg addressed three memorials to that session of the Riksdag concerning foreign exchange and a return to metallic currency. One was translated and published in London and Boston in 1842 and in New York in 1847 as *Memorial Respecting Finance, Presented by Swedenborg to the Diet of 1761.* Wilkinson, *Emanuel Swedenborg,* p. 130, quotes Höpken: "the most solid memorials, and the best penned, at the diet of 1761, on matters of finance, were presented by Swedenborg." Emerson errs in the date.

57.22 THE CLERGY INTERFERED . . . RELIGIOUS WORKS; Swedenborg could not publish his religious works in Sweden, and his religious influence there was minimal during his lifetime. From 1768–1770 there was a period of controversy during which he was under attack, and two of his adherents, both prominent clergymen, were charged with heresy. Swedenborg's response was spirited, and through the influence of his friends in the church, government, and the royal family the whole affair was dropped.

57.34 THERE IS A COMMON PORTRAIT . . . VACANT AIR. Of the books remaining in Emerson's library two translated works by Swedenborg have copperplate engravings of him that fit this description: *A Treatise Concerning Heaven and Its Wonders, and Also Concerning Hell: Being a Relation of Things Heard and Seen. From the Latin . . . Originally Published at London . . . 1758* (London, 1823) and *The True Christian Religion, Containing the Universal Theology of the New Church, Foretold by the Lord in Daniel vii. 13, 14, and in Revelation xxi. 1, 2 . . . from the Original Latin Edition, Printed at Amsterdam, in . . . 1771* (Boston, 1843). Both portraits are derived from a copperplate print published in 1782 which was attested as a likeness by an acquaintance. That print was in turn most likely derived from an oil copy by a Mr. Way from an anonymous oil portrait which hung in Swedenborg's bedroom. The two paintings are in the possession respectively of the London Swedenborg Society and the Academy of the New Church, Bryn Athyn, Pa. See James Hyde, *A Bibliography of the Works of Emanuel Swedenborg.*

58.9 ANTICIPATED IN ASTRONOMY . . . TO BE ORIGINAL, Emerson appears to be indebted here to his English friend John A. Heraud, who in a series called "Foreign Aid to Self-Intelligence, Designed for an Historical Introduction to the Study of Ontological Science, Preparatory to a Critique of Pure Being," devoted chapter four to Swedenborg in *The Monthly Magazine,* 3rd series, 5 (May 1841), 441–472. Commenting on *De Cultu et Amore Dei* (London, 1745), the first part of which concerns the origin of the earth, Heraud says: "Here, in explaining the principle of creation, [Swedenborg] declares that seven planets were created at the same time from the sun of our solar system, thus anticipating Dr. Herschel's discovery of the seventh planet" (p. 449). The seventh planet, Uranus, was discovered by Sir William Herschel in 1781, nine years after Swedenborg's death; the eighth, Neptune, was discovered in 1846 by J. C. Galle after the predictions of J. C. Adams and U. J. Leverrier. In August 1846 Emerson remarks on the mathematical discovery of Neptune (*JMN,* IX, 450). Writing of *On the Planets in Our Solar System* (*De Telluribus in Mundo Nostro Solari* [London, 1758]), a book in which Swedenborg visits the spirits of planets other than the earth and speaks of innumerable systems with many earths, Wilkinson, the English editor mentioned here and at 63.4–14 (see note to 62.33), observes: "It is remarkable as showing the limits of spiritual seership, that Swedenborg speaks of Saturn [the sixth] as the last planet of our system; his privilege of vision not enabling him to anticipate the place of

Herschel" (*Emanuel Swedenborg,* p. 119). Heraud, in the article cited above, discusses *The Economy of the Animal Kingdom* (first published in 1740), which contains Swedenborg's studies of the blood and brain, and comments that Swedenborg's disciples make claims for him "from the fact of [his] having . . . anticipated the discovery of Daniel Schlichting, concerning the constant and gentle motion which after birth the brain undergoes correspondingly with respiration . . . and another discovery of Dr. Wilson, concerning the vacuum which takes place when the blood is expelled from the contracted cavities . . . On these discoveries, however, it is clear that Swedenborg set no value, since he esteemed the sciences and mechanical arts as the ministers of wisdom only, and not the end" (p. 448). Jan Daniel Schlichting (b. 1703), a Dutch embryologist, published *Embryulcia Nova Detecta* in 1747, and Alexander Wilson (1718–1792), a Scottish philosophical writer and physician, published *An Inquiry into the Moving Powers Employed in the Circulation of the Blood* in 1774. Given the context, Emerson doubtless refers here to Alexander Monro (1733–1817), a Scottish anatomist who published *De Venis Lymphaticis Valvulosis* (1757) and *Microscopical Inquiries into the Nerves and Brain* (1780), although Monro's father (1697–1767) and son (1773–1859), both named Alexander, were also, like him, professors of anatomy in the University of Edinburgh.

58.21 SELDEN, HUMBOLDT, John Selden (1584–1654), English jurist, legal antiquarian, scholar, and orientalist, famous in his time for his comprehensive learning, is now best remembered for his *Table-Talk* (1689). Alexander von Humboldt (1769–1859), the eminent German naturalist and traveler, undertook in *Kosmos,* 5 vols. (1845–1862), a synthesis of scientific knowledge comparable to Aristotle's and Bacon's.

58.25 HIS OWN PICTURE, IN THE "PRINCIPIA," . . . INTEGRITY OF MAN. In *The Principia; or, The First Principles of Natural Things, Being New Attempts toward a Philosophical Explanation of the Elementary World,* trans. Augustus Clissold, 2 vols. (London and Boston, 1845–1846), pt. I, ch. I, sec. 4, a work in Emerson's library, Swedenborg contrasts man as first created with man in "the perverted and imperfect state . . . into which we are born at this day": Man "in his state of integrity and complete perfection . . . in whom all the parts were co-ordinated to receive the motions of all the elements, and to convey them successively . . . through a contiguous medium, to the extremely subtle active principle, must be deemed the most perfect and the first of all men, being one in whom the connections of ends and means was continuous . . . Such a man would be capable of taking his station as it were in the centre; and surveying from thence the whole circumference of his system at a single glance, he would be able to understand things actually before him, as well as other things in detail, both in regard to those that had occurred, and those likely to happen."

59.16 HARVEY HAD SHOWN . . . DRAWN THE MORAL ARGUMENT. This catalogue accurately reflects the context of Swedenborg's scientific work, and he
cites most of the writers in his studies. William Harvey (1578–1657) was an
English physician and anatomist who discovered by dissection the mechanics
of the circulation of blood; William Gilbert (1544–1603), also an English physician, published a rigorously experimental study of magnetism, *De Magnete,
Magnetisque Corporibus, et de Magno Magnete Tellure* (1600); René Descartes
(1596–1650) was a French philosopher whose *Principia Philosophiae* (1644) set
forth a mechanical and mathematical explanation of the universe by magnitude, figure, and motion which was with controversy replaced by Sir Isaac
Newton's (1642–1727) gravitational theory argued in *Philosophiae Naturalis
Principia Mathematica* (1687). Marcello Malpighi (1628–1694) was an Italian
physiologist who in 1661 completed the circulatory system of Harvey by discovering the capillary channels, thus emphasizing "the dogma, that Nature
works in leasts," which connects him with the Greek physician Hippocrates
(b. 460 B.C.), the father of medicine, who based his practice on minute observation and dealt with the body as a whole organism, with Leucippus (fifth
century B.C.), a Greek philosopher who, according to Aristotle, originated the
atomic theory of the universe, and with Titus Lucretius Carus (94?–55 B.C.),
author of *De Rerum Natura*, which set forth the atomic theory of Epicurus in
hexameters (see 64.9–27). Jan Swammerdam (1637–1680), a Dutch naturalist
and anatomist, studied circulation of the blood by means of injections and
described the metamorphosis of insects; Anthony van Leeuwenhoek
(1632–1723), another Dutch naturalist and anatomist, improved the microscope and thereby expanded Malpighi's work to the discovery of red corpus-
cles and also disproved by minute examination the idea of spontaneous
generation of small insects; Jacob Winslow (1669–1760) was a Danish descriptive anatomist, and Bartolomeo Eustachi (1524?–1574), an Italian who
studied in detail many parts of the body, published descriptive plates in 1552;
the German Lorenz Heister (1683–1758) published a famous standard text on
surgery in 1718; Andreas Vesalius (1514–1564), a Flemish anatomist and one
of the first to dissect human bodies, developed a standard anatomical nomen-
clature and published in 1543 *De Humani Corporis Fabria* with excellent illustrations; Hermann Boerhaave (1668–1738), a Dutch physician, whose lectures
Swedenborg may have attended (Wilkinson, *Emanuel Swedenborg*, p. 42), made
the University of Leiden into a famous center for medical instruction. Carolus
Linnaeus (Carl von Linné, 1707–1778) was a Swedish botanist who first established the principles for defining genera and species. Gottfried Wilhelm
von Leibnitz (1646–1716), influential German philosopher and mathemati-
cian, published *Essais de theodicée sur la bonté de dieu, la liberté de l'homme, et l'origin
du mal* (1710) and *La Monadologie* (1714), but it was his disciple Christian von
Wolff (1679–1754) who adapted and systematized the Leibnitzian ideas into a
comprehensive, rational cosmology which prevailed until the Kantian revolution. In the conclusion to *Principia Rerum Naturalium* (1734) Swedenborg ac-

knowledged the parallels with Wolff's *Philosophia Prima sive Ontologia* (1730) and *Cosmologia Generalis* (1731), though he pointed out that he had completed his work before seeing Wolff's. John Locke's (1632–1704) *An Essay Concerning Human Understanding* (1690) importantly argues that moral truth can be demonstrated as well as mathematical truth, and the famous work of the Dutch scholar Hugo Grotius (1583–1645), *De Juri Belli et Pacis* (1625) argues that a universal law of nature, based in human nature and independent of religion or the church for its validity, governs the laws of nations and people. The maxim "tota in minimis existit natura" is repeated in English at 64.27 and attributed to Malpighi, as the Latin is in *JMN*, IX, 410, and XI, 17. In *W*, VII, 176: " 'T is the very principle of science that Nature shows herself best in leasts; it was the maxim of Aristotle and Lucretius; and, in modern times, of Swedenborg and of Hahnemann." Another version of "Nature is always like herself" is called an "old aphorism" at 61.1; both are translations of "Natura sibi semper est similis," attributed to Linnaeus in *JMN*, XII, 555, 566. Edward Waldo Emerson, however, attributes this expression to Malpighi (*W*, IV, 326). Both maxims are central to Swedenborg's method, as shown in *The Principia*, pt. I, ch. IX, sec. 8, and pt. III, ch. I.

60.10 THE "ECONOMY OF THE ANIMAL KINGDOM"   See note to 62.33.

60.28 "THE WISER A MAN . . . OF THE DEITY."   *The Principia*, pt. I, ch. I, sec. 4.

61.1 NATURE IS ALWAYS SELFSIMILAR.   See 59.29 and note for 59.16.

61.1 IN THE PLANT . . . OF THE WORLD.   This is a summary of Goethe's discoveries in comparative morphology as expressed, for example, in *Versuch, die Metamorphose der Pflanzen zu erklären* (1790) and *Zur Morphologie* (1820). The last volume of the edition Emerson owned, Goethe's *Werke*, 55 vols. (Stuttgart and Tübingen, 1828–1833), contains selections from the botanical and osteological studies, but the ideas are also scattered elsewhere: in *Italiänische Reise* (vols. 27–29) and *Tag- und Jahres-Hefte als Ergänzung meiner sonstigen Bekenntnisse* (vols. 31–32), for example. In March 1849 Emerson borrowed from Harvard College Library *Oeuvres d'Histoire Naturelle de Goethe*, trans. Charles Frédéric Martins (Paris, 1837), which includes selections in French translation from Goethe's work on comparative anatomy and botany. See 158.25–159.1.

61.9 A POETIC ANATOMIST . . . TRUNK, REPEATS ITSELF.   For the various journal materials which go into this passage, see PP. It apparently is Emerson's version of the comprehensive system of anatomical classification and morphology set forth by Lorenz Oken (1779–1851), an eminent but controversial German naturalist. The basic thesis, similar to Goethe's, was published in 1807 as *Über die Bedeutung der Schädelknochen* and elaborated, for example, in

Lehrbuch der Naturphilosophie (1809–1811), the third edition of which was translated as *Elements of Physiophilosophy* (London, 1847). Emerson's library contains John Bernhard Stallo's *General Principles of the Philosophy of Nature: with an Outline of . . . Oken's System of Nature* (Boston, 1848). Emerson's passages "skull, — with extremities . . . and lower teeth" and "Within it, on . . . trunk, repeats itself" echo both *Elements of Physiophilosophy,* p. 408, and Stallo, p. 292. The commonplace idea in the passage "a snake, being a horizontal line . . . find their place," Emerson may have remembered from a similar passage he copied in 1835 into *JMN,* V, 67, from the manuscript of Elizabeth Peabody's translation of J. G. E. Oegger, *The True Messiah; or, The Old and New Testaments, Examined According to the Principles of the Language of Nature* (Boston, 1842), p. 15, which is in Emerson's library. In Plato's *Timaeus,* man is constructed so that the immortal part of his soul is housed in his head and rules by reason the body. It is uncomfortable in the body and gladly escapes at death (cf. *Timaeus,* 44 D–E, 69 C–D, 73 D–E, 81 E).

62.11 FRENCH STATISTS . . . WHO EATS SHOES OR MARRIES HIS GRAND-MOTHER.   In May 1849 Emerson wrote in his journal: "One must study Quetelet to know the limits of freedom. In 20,000, population, just so many men will marry their grandmothers" (*JMN,* XI, 91). A few months earlier he had copied four passages from Lambert Adolphe Jacques Quételet (1796–1874), *A Treatise on Man and the Development of His Faculties,* trans. Dr. R. Knox (Edinburgh, 1842) (*JMN,* XI, 67–68). Emerson's parody goes beyond the controversial Belgian statist or statistician, who was the leader in developing the idea that social and physical conditions more than individual will were significant in the physical, intellectual, moral, and criminal characteristics of man, for Quételet also dealt statistically with "the average man" (see 34.32). Aside from *Sur l'homme et le développement de ses facultés, ou Essai de physique sociale,* 2 vols. (Paris, 1835), the work cited above, Quételet also published *Lettres . . . sur la théorie des probabilités, appliquée aux sciences morales et politiques* (Brussels, 1846; trans. London, 1849) and *Du système social et des lois qui le réglissent* (Paris, 1848), all of which were widely reviewed.

62.33 HIS SCIENTIFIC WORKS . . . ENRICHED THESE VOLUMES,   About 1845 the Swedenborg Association joined with the larger Swedenborg Society, both in London, in the project of publishing in a standard edition the scientific works of Swedenborg from manuscript in the royal Academy of Sciences, Stockholm, and the Swedenborg Society published a number of translations of the scientific works before the publication of *Representative Men.* In the period of Swedenborg's great scientific production here referred to by Emerson, he published at Dresden and Leipzig in 1734 two related works referred to as his Philosophical and Mineralogical works: *Principia Rerum Naturalium sive Novorum Tentaminum Phænomena Mundi Elementaris Philosophice Explicandi* and *Regnum sive Minerale . . .* (2 vols.). In the same year and place he also published

Prodromus Philosophiæ Ratiocinantis de Infinito, et Causa Finali Creationis: Deque Mechanismo Operationis Animæ et Corporis. His anatomical work was first published in *Œconomia Regni Animalis in Transactiones Divisa . . . Anatomice, Physice, et Philosophice Perlustrata,* 2 vols. (London and Amsterdam, 1740–1741), and continued in a separate work with a similar title, *Regnum Animale, Anatomice, Physice, et Philosophice Perlustratum,* 3 vols. (The Hague and London, 1744–1745). These scientific works were translated in the 1840s as *The Principia; or, The First Principles of Natural Things, Being New Attempts toward a Philosophical Explanation of the Elementary World,* trans. Augustus Clissold, 2 vols. (London and Boston, 1845–1846), which contained also brief excerpts from the two companion volumes on minerals; *Outlines of a Philosophical Argument on the Infinite, and the Final Cause of Creation; and on the Intercourse between the Soul and the Body,* trans. James John Garth Wilkinson (London and Boston, 1847); *The Economy of the Animal Kingdom, Considered Anatomically, Physically, and Philosophically,* trans. Augustus Clissold [and partly by Wilkinson], 2 vols. (London and Boston, 1845–1846); and *The Animal Kingdom, Considered Anatomically, Physically, and Philosophically,* trans. James John Garth Wilkinson, 2 vols. (London and Boston, 1843–1844). Except for *Outlines . . . on the Infinite,* Emerson's library contains these translations. Some of the shorter unpublished scientific work of Swedenborg had been edited from manuscript by Wilkinson in two other volumes Emerson owned: *Opuscula quædam Argumenti Philosophici* (London, 1846) and *Œconomia Regni Animalis . . .* [additional manuscripts] (London, 1847), and Emerson probably knew that Wilkinson's *Posthumous Tracts, Now First Translated from the Latin of Emanuel Swedenborg* (London and Boston, 1847) contained some scientific work from the period 1734–1744.

James John Garth Wilkinson (1812–1899) was an English surgeon, apothecary, and homeopathic doctor best remembered for his editing, translating, and elucidation of Swedenborgian texts. He was also an early biographer of Swedenborg (see note to 56.32). As a leading member of the Swedenborg Society he was especially concerned with the publication of a complete and uniform edition of Swedenborg's works. Emerson and Wilkinson exchanged books in 1846, and their acquaintance through mutual friends grew into friendship during Emerson's visit to London in 1848. Emerson's generous remarks here and at 58.15–16 evoked an acknowledgment from Wilkinson in a letter commenting on Emerson's treatment of Swedenborg (see Historical Introduction). Augustus Clissold (1797?–1882) left the ministry of the Church of England and turned to his two translations of Swedenborg's scientific works. He was active in organizing the idea of a uniform edition and generous in his contribution to publication and in other gifts to the Swedenborg Society.

63.17 THE "ANIMAL KINGDOM" See note to 62.33.

63.32 ANSWER OF AMASIS . . . THAT FLOW IN." Amasis II (d. 525 B.C.), king of Egypt, was engaged in a combat of wisdom with the king of Ethiopia, who challenged him to drink up the ocean. Amasis sent for advice to Bias, the semi-legendary wise man of Greece, who gave him this reply to deliver to his rival. The story is told in Plutarch's *Moralia*, 151 B–D. The phrasing suggests that Emerson remembered it from "The Banquet of the Seven Wise Men" in the edition he owned of *Plutarch's Morals*, II, 11, but it also occurs in Stanley, *The History of Philosophy*, pt. I, "Bias," sec. 1. See *JMN*, XI, 91.

63.35 HE THOUGHT AS LARGE . . . HER STEPS." See *JMN*, X, 27. The source of the quotation has not been found.

64.9 THE ANCIENT DOCTRINE . . . ENTIRE IN LEASTS;" The doctrine that the brain is a gland is in Περὶ ἀδενων, "On the Glands," which is generally believed not to be by Hippocrates but by one of his followers. For the doctrines of Leucippus see Aristotle, *De Generatione et Corruptione*, bk. I, sec. 1, 2, 8, *De Anima*, bk. I, ch. II, and Stanley, *The History of Philosophy*, pt. XI, "Leucippus," and "Democritus," ch. IX. For Plato's doctrine of macrocosm and microcosm see 35.21–24. The translation of Lucretius, *De Rerum Natura*, lib. I, 835–841 (which states the principle of Anaxagoras) Emerson borrowed from Stanley, pt. II, "Anaxagoras," ch. I, sec. 1, as he notes in *JMN*, XI, 17–18. The maxim of Malpighi occurs also at 59.24 (see note to 59.16).

64.28 "IT IS A CONSTANT . . . OVER THE BODY." With some paraphrase and extension mixed with quotation, Emerson derived this passage from Swedenborg, *The Animal Kingdom*, trans. Wilkinson, I, 129–130 (pt. I, ch. IV, sec. 100–101). A further extension is made at 129.5–12.

65.8 "MAN IS A KIND . . . THE GRAND MAN." The quotation seems to be made up of paraphrases of several of Swedenborg's central ideas. The first sentence echoes part of *Heavenly Arcana*, Genesis, ch. xxx, n. 4041; for the second sentence, see especially ibid., ch. xxvii, n. 3628, and ch. xxxi, nn. 4219, 4222–4233; the fourth refers to an important idea explicit in ibid., ch. xxxi, n. 4219: "it is to be observed that the universal heaven is the GRAND MAN, and that heaven is named the GRAND MAN, because it corresponds to the Lord's Divine Human; for the Lord is the only Man, and so much as an angel and spirit, or a man on the earth, has from Him, so far they also are men." Emerson noted in *JMN*, VI, 314, "That, GOD IS A MAN. Angelic Wisd. Part I Sect. 72," summarizing the argument elaborated in *Angelic Wisdom Concerning the Divine Love and the Divine Wisdom. Translated from the Latin . . . Originally Published at Amsterdam, 1763*, pt. I, nn. 11ff., where, however, the concept "grand man" is not used. Emerson's library contains the translation published in Boston, New York, and Cincinnati in 1847, though he may have cited an earlier source. His annotation, incidentally, suggests that he may not have been familiar with *Angelic Wisdom Concerning the Divine Providence* (*Sapientia Angelica de Divina Providentia* [Amsterdam, 1764]), which is not now in his library and which he seems not to have used for this lecture, though translations were available. *Heavenly Arcana,* Swedenborg's massive commentary on Genesis and Exodus, interspersed with revelations seen in the spiritual world, is not in Emerson's library, though he alludes to it and quotes from it, perhaps from secondary sources or excerpts. It was published in London, 1749–1756, in thirteen installments as *Arcana Cælestia.* Among the translations available to Emerson was *Heavenly Arcana, Which Are in the Sacred Scriptures or Word of the Lord, Laid Open. Together with Wonderful Things Which Were Seen in the World of Spirits and in the Heaven of Angels . . .* , 12 vols. (Boston, 1837–1847).

65.14 "FORMS ASCEND IN ORDER . . . PERPETUAL-CELESTIAL, OR SPIR-ITUAL." This condensation of an explanatory footnote in Swedenborg, *The Animal Kingdom,* trans. Wilkinson, pt. I, ch. iv, sec. 97, states "the doctrine of Forms," mentioned above, 60.4, as the next quotation illustrates "the doctrine of Correspondence."

65.28 "IN OUR DOCTRINE . . . THE LIVING BODY." Swedenborg, *The Animal Kingdom,* trans. Wilkinson, pt. I, ch. xiv, sec. 293, n. (u), with "resemblances" (65.29) for Swedenborg's "representations."

66.11 PLATO KNEW OF IT . . . DARK RIDDLE WRITING. For Plato and the twice-bisected line, see 38.29–39.5. For the allusion to Bacon and the simile of the seal and its waxen imprint, Emerson probably had in mind: "certain it is that *Veritas* and *Bonitas* differ but as the seal and print; for Truth prints Goodness" (*Of the Advancement of Learning,* bk. I, ch. viii, para. 2, repeated in Latin in *De Dignitate et Augmentis Scientiarum,* lib. I, para. 86). For the analogies of physical truth with moral and political truth, see *Of the Advancement of Learning,* bk. II, ch. v, para. 2–3. In *JMN,* VIII, 161, Emerson attributed the following to Auguste Theodore Hilaire, baron Barchou de Penhoën, *Histoire de la Philosophie Allemande depuis Leibnitz jusqu'à Hegel,* 2 vols. (Paris, 1836), I, 123 (a work in his own library): "According to Boehmen the world was nothing else than the relievo the print of a seal of an invisible world concealed in his own bosom."

67.27 "HIS PRESENCE IN . . . THE WORLD." The first quotation, with "my" for "his," is quoted from an unnamed work in Wilkinson, *Emanuel Swedenborg,* p. 206. The second is a paraphrase of *A Treatise Concerning Heaven and . . . Hell,* ch. XV, n. 126.

67.36 HE HAD BORROWED . . . WHICH THEY SIGNIFIED. The quotation is from Plato, *Philebus,* 16 C; the addition of Swedenborg is a close paraphrase of what he learned from talking with the spirits of "the most ancient church," called "Man or Adam," and their immediate descendants in *Heavenly Arcana,* Genesis, ch. x, n. 1122. That Swedenborg means to identify his "most ancient church" with the fables of the classical writers is made explicit in ibid., Exodus, ch. xiii, n. 8118, and in the eloquent conclusion to his scientific work, *The Principia*, "The Paradise formed upon Our Earth, and the First Man" (pt. III, ch. xii). See note to 58.25.

68.5 "THE VERY ORGANIC . . . ON IT ."   This is a paraphrase of *Heavenly Arcana*, Genesis, ch. xxxi, n. 4223.

68.8 "THE REASON WHY . . . LORD THROUGH HEAVEN."   Swedenborg, *Heavenly Arcana*, Genesis, ch. xv, n. 1807.

70.2 LYCURGUS   The character of the legendary lawgiver of Sparta is rigid and stern simplicity, a calmness of spirit, and tireless industry in establishing the strong state. He was called by the Pythian priestess rather god than man.

70.16 THAT METEMPSYCHOSIS WHICH . . . THE INDIAN TRANSMIGRATION,   The idea of metempsychosis or transmigration of souls through a succession of human lives and other forms was familiar to Emerson not only from Pythagorean, Platonic, and Neoplatonic sources, but also from his reading in Hindu literature. The famous *Metamorphoses* by the Latin poet Publius Ovidius Naso (43 B.C. – ca. A.D. 17), a poetic collection of such myths and fables as Apollo's transformation of Daphne into a laurel tree or Venus' of Adonis into the anemone, is of course not an exposition of this doctrine.

70.21 ALL THINGS IN . . . TO MERIT HEAVEN."   Of this catalogue of illustrations of Swedenborg's emphasis on interiors, one's inner thought or state as his real being, only the second sentence is identified by Emerson in his journals (*JMN*, VI, 314), but many of the others are drawn from Swedenborg's writings as quotation, paraphrase, or extension. The first three sentences are derived from *A Treatise Concerning Heaven and . . . Hell*, ch. XLIX–L, nn. 477–490, ch. XXXIX, n. 358, and ch. XLIX, n. 474. *Conjugial Love*, n. 45, explains that after death married couples meet and at first resume their relationship, but that after a while they either remain together or not depending on their understanding of their relationship. If they do not remain together, they are given proper spouses. "Interiors associate all in the spiritual world" means that after death what spirits are "interiorly," rather than, as in life, "exteriorly," determines what other spirits they associate with. The sentence is taken from *The Apocalypse Revealed*, ch. II, n. 153, para. 10, as is the sentence about the appearance of the damned spirits (para. 11; both identified editorially in *JMN*, V, 116). The fear of death by the "ghosts" Emerson probably derived from the statement that those spirits utterly destitute of charity fear even death at the hands of other evil spirits, though death is not possible (*Heavenly Arcana*, Genesis, ch. iv, n. 391). For the temporary failure to recognize death because the inward man and his senses, desires, and thoughts continue,

Notes

see, for example, *A Treatise Concerning Heaven and . . . Hell,* ch. XLVIII, n. 461, and *The Apocalypse Revealed,* ch. II, n. 153. The passages on those in evil and falsehood and without charity, the covetous, and those who place merit in good works, that is, who believe salvation is by works alone, are drawn from *Heavenly Arcana,* Genesis, ch. iv, n. 391, ch. viii, n. 938, and ch. ix, n. 1110 (repeated at ch. xxxviii, n. 4943). The canceled next sentence in the manuscript (see Annex A, Appendix 2) adds an associated detail from ibid., Exodus, ch. xviii, n. 8740, where the spirits who place merit in good works are inhabitants of Jupiter and do not know a doctrine of faith. See note to 71.24 for the translation that Emerson owned of *Conjugial Love,* which was first published by Swedenborg in Amsterdam in 1768 as *Delitiæ Sapientiæ de Amore Conjugiali; Post quas Sequuntur Voluptates Insaniæ de Amore Scortatorio.* Swedenborg published in Amsterdam in 1766 *Apocalypsis Revelata.* The translation that Emerson annotated was given to Lidian Emerson by her Swedenborgian friend Sarah Searle and remains in his library: *The Apocalypse Revealed; Wherein Are Disclosed the Arcana There Foretold, Which Have Hitherto Remained Concealed,* 3 vols. (Boston, 1836).

71.7 HE DELIVERS GOLDEN . . . WORDS HIS SCIENCE. Some of the "golden sayings" are considerably adapted, but as Emerson read in the Swedenborgian literature over a number of years, he knew that there were competing translations, and he handled many quotations freely — perhaps from memory. The "famed sentence" is probably expanded from *Conjugial Love,* n. 44, but other possible sources are *Heavenly Arcana,* Genesis, ch. vi, n. 553, or *A Treatise Concerning Heaven and . . . Hell,* ch. XLII, n. 414. The next quotation is probably derived from ibid., ch. IX, n. 71 (see *JMN,* VIII, 320, and PP). "The perfection of man is the love of use" is from *Conjugial Love,* n. 183 (see *JMN,* IX, 171); Swedenborg's meaning of "use" is clarified in *Conjugial Love,* n. 266: "What is use but actual love of the neighbor, and what holds the heavens together but this love?" The quotation about man as heaven is taken from *A Treatise Concerning Heaven and . . . Hell,* ch. VIII, n. 60 (for further elaboration of the idea, see 65.8–12 and note). For "What is from Him is Him," see ibid., ch. XLIX, n. 481. The next sentence has not been found in Swedenborg's writings, but "the truly poetic account of the writing in the inmost heaven" occurs in ibid., ch. XXIX, nn. 260–261. The quotation about influx is from ibid., ch. XVI, n. 144, and the remainder of the paragraph from *Angelic Wisdom Concerning the Divine Love and the Divine Wisdom,* pt. III, n. 280. These two are identified by Emerson in *JMN,* VI, 314–315.

71.24 "CONJUGAL LOVE," Emerson owned *The Delights of Wisdom Concerning Conjugial Love: after Which Follow the Pleasures of Insanity Concerning Scortatory Love* (Boston, 1843). Emerson's spelling, though not prevailing, was commonly used even among Swedenborgians. The first partial English translation of *Amor Conjugialis,* issued by *The New Jerusalem Magazine,* used "conjugal," and Wilkinson, *Emanuel Swedenborg,* uses "conjugal" throughout. See Annex A, Appendix 2, 57.11, for Emerson's only use of "conjugial" in the manuscript — a canceled list.

71.26 HYMN OF LOVE ... ANGELS IN PARADISE; In *Purgatorio*, II, 76–117, Dante encounters the spirit of Casella, a musician who was his friend. After three attempts to embrace, the insubstantial spirit says, "Così com' io t'amai / nel mortal corpo, così t'amo sciolta" (As I loved you in my mortal body, I love you without it), whereupon Dante, moved by remembrance of the love songs Casella used to sing to him, asks him to sing again, and he sings, so sweetly that it entrances the fellow spirits around them, "Amor che ne la mente mi ragiona" (Love which converses with me in my mind), one of Dante's own canzoni, which he interpreted allegorically in *Convivio*, III, as a hymn to philosophy, expressing a love of the soul or reason for the unattainable perfect beauty of the beloved. This expression of a high conception of love thus resembles Plato's in *Symposium* (or *Banquet*), while Swedenborg's attempt fell short. Emerson had translated *Vita Nuova* in 1843 and was thus conversant with Dante's platonic interpretation of love, and he comments on Casella's song in *JMN*, VII, 86.

72.24 CONVERSATION, WHOSE LAWS ARE PROFOUNDLY ELIMINATED. Emerson here uses "conversation" in the now obsolete sense of "living in society," "having dealings with others," "living together intimately," "consociation"; the limited sense of conversation as talk or discourse with others is in fact taken up early and briefly in *Conjugial Love* (n. 5) as one of the conceptions of the joys of heaven which is only accessory, and those who think it the definitive joy tire of it after three days. Emerson uses the now obsolete meaning of "eliminated": "made known," "divulged" (see RSS).

73.8 PROFANATION OF THINKING ... DOUBT AND DENY." *Heavenly Arcana*, Genesis, ch. iii, nn. 229–233: "the rational [principle] of man suffered itself to be deceived ... so as to believe nothing but what it could see and feel ... At this day ... the evil is much greater than in former times, because men can now confirm the incredulity of the senses by scientifics, unknown to the ancients ... To explore the mysteries of faith by scientifics is as impossible as *for a camel to pass through the eye of a needle* ... those who consult the senses and science respecting what is to be believed, not only precipitate themselves in doubt, but also in denial." "Scientifics" is a translator's coinage for Swedenborg's "scientifica," which means, apparently, matters of knowledge derived from the senses and apprehended simply as external facts, without application or use (see ibid., ch. i, n. 27, and ch. xii, n. 1486). The recent fourth American revised edition uses the phrase "memory-knowledges."

73.11 PHILOSOPHERS ARE THEREFORE ... AND FLYING SERPENTS; Emerson conflated two passages from *Heavenly Arcana*, Genesis, ch. iii: one calls "those who form their opinions on heavenly subjects from sensual, scientific, and philosophical considerations ... not only *deaf serpents,* but also ... *flying serpents"* (n. 196), and the other enumerates and interprets these varieties of serpents or evils which derive from "scientifics" (n. 251). The cockatrice is a fabulous flying serpent whose glance causes death; the hemorrhoid, one whose bite causes unstanchable bleeding; the prester, a fiery one whose bite causes death by swelling and thirst.

74.4 HE WAS LET ... LIKE A WHEEL. Vastations, or purification through removal of evil attributes, occur in the spiritual world for a longer or shorter period of preparation for heaven. Some souls have nothing left after vastation and thus go to appropriate hells. Emerson here lists a sampling of the many hells seen by Swedenborg. "He was let ... their lamentations" is a close paraphrase of *Heavenly Arcana,* Genesis, ch. vii, n. 699, and the description of the tormentors is from ibid., n. 695. The hell of the jugglers (sorcerers in modern translation), prelates who deceitfully teach a doctrine of faith alone for salvation but also teach a doctrine of works as a means of securing obedience to the magistracy, is a fantasy that appears to be a place of worship, but is a house of clefts and chinks, containing a horrid beastly image, and standing on a bog, beneath which is a stone hiding the Word (*The Apocalypse Revealed,* ch. xxi, n. 926; cf. ibid., ch. x, n. 484, and *The True Christian Religion,* ch. vi, sec. ix, n. 390). The hells of the assassins are described in *Heavenly Arcana,* Genesis, ch. vii, n. 816, ch. viii, n. 829, ch. ix, n. 947, and ch. ix, n. 956, respectively. A large portion of the spirits in the hell for the sordidly avaricious are Jews, and the better sort of these are preyed upon by roving robbers (other Jews) who threaten to kill and boil them (ibid., ch. viii, nn. 940–941). In the excrementitious hells are those who delight both in cruelty and adulteries, those who deceptively commit adultery, and those who have made pleasure their end (ibid., nn. 824, 827, 943).

75.5 THE UNIVERSE IN ... OF THE MAGNETIZER. Animal magnetism, or mesmerism, was an early form of treatment of illness by hypnotism developed by Friedrich Anton Mesmer (1734–1815), a German physician. There were many controversial and fraudulent practitioners who succeeded him. Heraud, p. 452, made a similar suggestion in 1841: Swedenborg's "theological system could stand without any support of [spiritual intercourse]; and to what would it amount if the phenomena could be proved to have been Mesmeric? Would we accept a new dispensation on such testimony?" Wilkinson, in *Emanuel Swedenborg* (1849), apparently remembering the phrase from Emerson's lecture, wrote: "It has been reproached to Swedenborg by the first essayist of the day, that he represents the universe in a 'magnetic sleep,' which is true enough, because nothing else would give the hint of both life and death" (p. 74). For a repetition of Emerson's idea, see 79.19–20.

75.11 TO THIS COMPLEXION ... AT LAST. This clause is adapted from the last line of David Garrick's "Epitaph on James Quin[n]": "To this complexion thou must come at last," which in turn echoes Hamlet's wry observation on mortality as he contemplates the skull of Yorick: "let her paint an inch thick, to this favor she must come" (*Hamlet*, V, i, 193-194).

75.13 SIR ISAAC NEWTON ... LIKE THE REST. Those whom Swedenborg meets in the spiritual world are in various states of vastation and are beginning to apprehend spiritually. Swedenborg overheard Newton talking with angels who objected to his idea of a vacuum as being nothing, and the famous physicist readily assents, as he knows that Divine Being fills all things (*Angelic Wisdom Concerning the Divine Love and the Divine Wisdom*, pt. I, n. 82). Newton's successor as president of the Royal Society, Sir Hans Sloane (1660-1753), a naturalist and George II's physician, Swedenborg overheard in the spiritual world conversing with the third president of the Royal Society about the mediacy of nature in its generative operation from God. A beautiful bird appeared, which Sloane examined, knowing it was a spiritual rather than a natural production, and was at once convinced that nature contributes nothing and that what flows into the natural world is wholly owing to spiritual causes (ibid., pt. IV, n. 344; identified by Emerson in *JMN*, X, 27; see Annex A, Appendix 2, 71.6, for part of this relation canceled in manuscript). In *The Apocalypse Revealed* Swedenborg recounts how in the spiritual world he had heard George II discourse with six hundred English clergy who had ascended to a superior heaven to talk with him (ch. VI, n. 341) and how again, when Swedenborg and his tracts had been rejected by some English bishops in the spiritual world, King George, hearing this from heaven, descended to chastise his bishops (ch. XVI, n. 716). In the spiritual world the real Mohammed is not among his followers because of his desire to rule as a god. Swedenborg was present and heard him when he was momentarily raised up among them to discourage their sedition by his unspiritual appearance (*The True Christian Religion*, n. 830). The remarks on Swedenborg's encounter with Cicero are based, as Emerson noted in *JMN*, VIII, 225, on *A Treatise Concerning Heaven and ... Hell*, ch. XXXVI, n. 322. Cicero, with whom Swedenborg converses about wisdom, is delighted and deeply moved when passages from the prophets are read to him and knows something of the Christian dispensation, which he observes is the only salvation for man.

76.11 JASPER AND SARDONYX ... BEHEMOTH, OR UNICORN? The "foreign rhetoric" catalogued here and at 76.23-24 is from the Bible, mainly the Old Testament and The Revelation; Swedenborg offends mostly, as one would expect, in his exegetical works.

76.18 SPARTAN, "WHY DO ... NOTHING TO THE PURPOSE?" Edward Waldo Emerson points out that this is "One of the examples of Laconic speech given by Plutarch in the *Life of Lycurgus*" (*W*, IV, 332). Emerson's phrasing of the apothegm of King Leonidas (d. 480 B.C.) in Plutarch's *Lives*, "Lycurgus," para. xx, is a close adaptation of the translation by John and William Langhorne, which he owned.

76.26 LOCKE SAID, "GOD . . . UNMAKE THE MAN." John Locke, *An Essay Concerning Human Understanding*, bk. IV, ch. XIX, para. 14.

76.27 THE PARISH DISPUTES . . . AMONG THE ANGELS. Martin Luther (1483–1546) and Philip Melanchthon (1497–1560), leaders of the German Reformation, held strongly the position that salvation is effected by faith alone, and that doctrine prevailed in Reformed and Lutheran churches, such as the Swedish church, in which Swedenborg's father, Jesper Swedenborg, rose to a bishopric. A central doctrine in Swedenborg's writings is that the separation of faith and works is a false and pernicious distinction; "that faith without charity [works] is not faith, and charity without faith is not charity, and neither faith nor charity has any life in it but from the Lord"; and that the Protestant churches err grievously in teaching a doctrine of salvation by faith alone (*The True Christian Religion*, ch. VI, nn. 355–360). Swedenborg describes the anguish of both Luther and Melanchthon in the spiritual world, the former well on his way to purification through rejection of his false doctrine, the latter suffering more because he persists in the doctrine of faith alone (ibid., "Supplement," nn. 796–797). Swedenborg does not provide a named example of the suffering spirits who hold a doctrine of works alone, though he has generalized accounts (see, for example, 71.3–6 and note to 74.4). Emerson seems to supply this want by his allusion to Wolfius, that is, Christian von Wolff (see note to 59.16); but likely candidate as the Rationalist is, Swedenborg finds his spirit holding onto the skirt of Leibnitz in a painfully confused and futile dispute with the disciples of Aristotle and of Descartes over the merits of physical influx, spiritual influx, and preestablished harmony (ibid., ch. XI, n. 696). For examples of Swedenborg's advertisements of his own books to the angels, see ibid., "Supplement," nn. 846–848, and, above, note to 75.13. The allusion to Michelangelo reflects a famous anecdote of the painter's revenge on Pope Paul III's master of ceremonies, Messer Biagio da Cesena, who criticized the nudity in the unfinished Last Judgment (see Giorgio Vasari, *Le Vite de' più eccellenti Pittori, Scultori e Architetti*, 14 vols. [Florence, 1855], XII, 220). Dante's vengeance is widely displayed in *Inferno*. For the allusion to Montaigne's parish priest, see Montaigne's *Essays*, "Of the Education of Children," bk. I, ch. 26 (25, in Emerson's edition). The pip is a highly contagious and fatal disease of poultry. In the French original and in translation, both the pip and cannibals are used figuratively. Emerson's spelling of Melanchthon's name was common in the eighteenth and nineteenth centuries.

77.12 HIS CARDINAL POSITION . . . SHUNNED AS SINS. This orthodox Christian doctrine is especially elaborated in *The Doctrine of Life for the New Jerusalem, from the Commandments of the Decalogue* (*Doctrina Vitæ* . . . [Amsterdam, 1763]). The conclusion of the work is explicit: to shun evils merely as evils, because they are injurious to public welfare or against the laws of humane nature, for example, is the act of a natural moral man, who inwardly is not the same as a spiritual man and is therefore lifeless. Evils, such as those in the second table of the Decalogue, should, as a first step to regeneration, be shunned *because* they are sins (see especially ch. XIV, nn. 108–114). Emerson's library contains two copies of the translated work: Boston, 1831 and 1836.

77.21 "THAT IS ACTIVE . . . ONLY UNTO WEARINESS." The passage is identified by Emerson in *JMN*, IX, 319, as from *The Vishńu Puráńa*, p. 139 (bk. I, ch. xix).

77.29 EURIPIDES RIGHTLY SAID . . . MAKES THEM NONE." The couplet is slightly modified from the translation given in Plutarch's *Morals*, 5 vols. (London, 1718), II, 54, Emerson's source as noted in *JMN*, VIII, 183.

77.34 SWEDENBORG ADMITTED . . . EVIL SPIRITS! In this manuscript Emerson canceled his source for this statement: "See Arcana Vol I p 408 note" (Genesis, ch. ix, n. 967).

78.3 "POOR OLD . . . THOUGHT AND MEND!" Burns, "Address to the Deil," st. xxi, modified slightly for clarity.

78.8 INDIAN VISHNU, "I . . . OBTAINETH ETERNAL HAPPINESS." Krishna (not Vishnu) speaks these words in *The Bhăgvăt-Gēētā, or Dialogues of Krĕĕshnă and Arjŏŏn*, trans. Charles Wilkins (London, 1785), pp. 81–82 (ch. IX, 29–31). Emerson ordered the book from John Chapman in May 1845 and had received it by the end of September, when he returned James Elliot Cabot's copy, which he had borrowed in May or June (*L*, III, 288, 290, 299, 303).

78.17 IF A MAN SAY . . . ENGLISH, IN A HEAVEN BY THEMSELVES; Swedenborg's revelations of arcana are based throughout on direct experience in the spiritual world. He wrote in *The Last Judgment*, first published in 1758: "It was granted to me to see from beginning to end how the last judgment was accomplished, . . . to see all these things with my own eyes, in order that I might be able to testify of them. This last judgment was commenced in the beginning of the year 1757, and was fully accomplished at the end of that year" (sec. 45). This information is repeated elsewhere — for example, in the "Author's Preface" to *The Apocalypse Revealed*. This judgment, which occurred in the spiritual world, is the one foretold in The Revelation of Saint John and marks the end of the first Christian church, just as the flood had ended the most ancient church and as others had been judged successively, for a total of four judgments, making way for the church of the New Jerusalem (see *The Coronis, or Appendix to the True Christian Religion*). All nations, denominations, and religions dwell with their kind in the spiritual world and are arranged in relation to the light at the center. The Dutch and the English Swedenborg found in favored positions — the better sort of English at the very center of the Christian spirits (*The True Christian Religion,* "Supplement," nn. 800–812).

78.24 SOCRATES'S GENIUS DID . . . TO ANYTHING UNFIT. Socrates' account of his attendant spirit, his genius or daemon, is in Plato, *Apology,* 31 C–D and 40 A–C, and *Theages,* 128 D–129 D. The quotation attributed to Socrates in the second sentence Emerson found in Stanley, *The History of Philosophy,* pt. III, "Socrates," ch. V, sec. 1. In *JMN,* IX, 291, Emerson identified his Hindu source as Henry Thomas Colebrooke, *Miscellaneous Essays,* 2 vols. (London, 1837), I, 341; Colebrooke's essay "On the Philosophy of the Hindus: Part IV. On the Vedanta" quotes from a dialogue of Yájnyawalcya and Uddálaca. The idea attributed to the "illuminated Quakers" Emerson probably derived from his recollection of the views of Mary Rotch, a liberal and controversial member of the New Bedford Society of Friends; he recorded her account at some length in *JMN,* IV, 263–264.

79.19 HIS INFERNO IS MESMERIC. See note to 75.5.

79.38 RHADAMANTHUS Famous for justice while living, Rhadamanthus, son of Zeus and Europa, became after death one of the judges of Hades.

80.7 "IN SOME SORT, LOVE IS GREATER THAN GOD," Emerson's adaptation of the paradox in Boehme's *The Way to Christ,* bk. VI, para. 26–27, is misleading. This dialogue between teacher and student, "Of the Supersensual Life," immediately proceeds to explain that "the greatness of love is greater" in that where God does not dwell, love enters — as, for example, when Christ broke the bonds of hell or as when one is in anguish and God is not within. In 1844 or 1845 Emerson wrote: "I read a little in Behmen. . . . I have never had good luck with Behmen before today. And now I see that his excellence is in his comprehensiveness, not like Plato in his precision. His propositions are vague, inadequate, & straining. It is his aim that is great. He will know not one thing, but all things" (*JMN,* IX, 106). *The Works of Jacob Behmen,* 4 vols. (London, 1764–1781), is in Emerson's library.

80.26 WAS HE LIKE SAADI . . . FROM HIS HANDS? Saadi or Sa'di (1184–1291), a Persian Sufi poet whom Emerson much admired, tells this anecdote of another in "The Mocaddamah; or, Introduction" to his book of prose and poetry, *The Gulistan, or Flower-Garden, of Shaikh Sadī of Shīraz...*, trans. James Ross (London, 1823): "A good and pious man reclined his head on the bosom of contemplation, and was immersed in the ocean of reverie. At the instant when he awaked from this vision, one of his friends by way of pleasantry said, What rare gift have you brought us from that garden where you have been recreating? He replied, I fancied to myself and said, when I can reach the rose-bower I will fill my lap with the flowers, and bring them as a present to my friends; but when I got there the fragrance of the roses so intoxicated me that the skirt dropped from my hands." Emerson wrote Thoreau on October 25, 1843, as news, that he had had in his possession this translation ("The Emerson-Thoreau Correspondence," ed. F. B. Sanborn, *The Atlantic Monthly*, 69 [May 1892], 596). In November 1846 he also borrowed it from Harvard College Library.

81.13 "HE COMES TO LAND WHO SAILS WITH ME."   Edward Waldo Emerson pertinently notes: "From a poem by Nathaniel P. Willis called 'Lines on Leaving Europe,' in which he thus expresses his assurance of his safe return across the ocean because of his waiting mother's love and faith" (*W*, IV, 334). This popular poem, published in a shorter version called " 'Homeward Bound' " as early as 1840, also makes the point that the mother should make room in her heart for the bride Willis was bringing home from England. Perhaps from faulty memory Emerson substituted "land" for "shore."

85.26 READ THE HAUGHTY ... RATS AND MICE.   See 50.25-29.

87.8 SPENCE RELATES ... TEN GUINEAS."   In *JMN*, XII, 61, Emerson quoted and identified this anecdote from Joseph Spence, *Anecdotes, Observations, and Characters, of Books and Men. Collected from the Conversation of Mr. Pope, and Other Eminent Persons of His Time*, ed. Samuel Weller Singer (London, 1820), pp. 368-369. He borrowed this edition from the Boston Athenæum in 1830 and 1838. Sir Godfrey Kneller (1646-1723) was a German-born painter residing in England, a friend of the poet Alexander Pope. According to the editor of a recent edition of Spence, the "Guinea trader," or slave trader, was probably a nephew of Pope rather than Kneller, but the error is in Emerson's source.

87.24 LUTHER HAD MILK IN HIM ... GET WELL DRUNK.   Luther's advice to the perplexed young scholar is adapted from a remark Emerson recorded in *JMN*, X, 107, saying he got it from an unidentified "Mr Blecker," who apparently attributed it to one of Luther's letters. The allusion is to a letter Luther wrote to Jerome Weller (1499-1572), a student of theology who tutored his children and who suffered periods of depression. Luther, away from home, wrote to Weller that he must overcome the devil's temptations to despair: sometimes, he advises, it is good to drink a little more, be merry, or even commit some sin in defiance and contempt of the devil (Luther to Jerome

Weller, July 1530, *Briefwechsel*, 13 vols. [Weimar, 1930–1968], V, 518–520). On the same journal page as this allusion to Luther, Emerson noted a "well-known proverb of his remaining, which kicks the pail over" and later added that it is recorded at *JMN*, XI, 116, there identified as "Luther's famed verse." The couplet, which may be translated "Who does not love wine, women, song, / Remains a fool his whole life long," is in Luther's room at Wartburg Castle and is traditionally attributed to him.

87.28 "THE NERVES," SAYS CABANIS ... THE MAN." In *JMN*, VI, 367, Emerson ascribed a French version of this statement to the noted French physiologist and philosopher Pierre Jean George Cabanis (1757–1808). In his major work, *Rapports du physique et du morale de l'homme* (Paris, 1802), he argues that sensitivity, proceeding from the nervous system, is the foundation of consciousness, reducing the soul to a faculty. He was widely criticized as a materialist and sensationalist. However, his posthumously published *Lettre sur les causes premières* (Paris, 1824), included in a new edition of *Rapports* in 1844, reveals him as a vitalist arguing that life is something added to the organism. Emerson's quotation may be a paraphrase of the materialist and sensationalist monism of this widely criticized actor in the French Revolution.

87.29 MY NEIGHBOR ... GOOD OF IT." Emerson identified his neighbor, to whom a version of this anecdote is attributed in *JMN*, XI, 46, as "J. H.," conjectured by the editors to be John Hosmer.

88.3 "AH," SAID ... GENTLEMAN AT OXFORD ... NO MATTER." In *JMN*, X, 246, Emerson attributed this attitude to "the country gentleman," but it is placed among notes he took in connection with his visit to Oxford University in the spring of 1848.

88.5 OUR LIFE IS LIKE ... THE BUNDLE OF HAY. This simile Emerson attributed to "The wise Queen of Sheba" in *JMN*, IX, 201, meaning his second wife, Lidian Emerson, as the editors point out there.

88.7 "THERE IS SO MUCH TROUBLE ... BE HERE AT ALL." A few days before the death of Alexander Pope these sentiments were uttered by his friend, the Tory political leader, Henry St. John (1678–1751), first Viscount Bolingbroke. Emerson took the passage from Joseph Spence's *Anecdotes ...*, p. 320, as he indicated in quoting it in *JMN*, VI, 328.

88.12 "MANKIND IS A DAMNED RASCAL." The philosopher uttering these words was, according to Emerson's attribution in *JMN*, IX, 30, John L. Tuttle of Concord — a "next neighbor," Edward Waldo Emerson says (*W*, IV, 339).

88.21 A GIBEONITE; During the conquest of Canaan by Joshua, the inhabitants of Gibeon, fearing the same destruction that befell Jericho and Ai, sent to Joshua ambassadors who pretended to be from a distant land and deceptively entered into a league with Israel. This alliance was honored, but the punishment of the Gibeonites was that they were condemned to be forever hewers of wood and drawers of water for the altar of the Lord, that is, to remain forever bondmen and servants (Joshua 9).

88.31 NEITHER WILL HE . . . IN A GOWN.   The sentence echoes George Herbert's "Affliction (I)," lines 37–40: "Whereas my birth and spirit rather took / The way that takes the town; / Thou didst betray me to a lingring book, / And wrap me in a gown." These lines are also quoted in Izaak Walton's "The Life of Mr. George Herbert."

89.33 AND THE REPLY OF SOCRATES . . . REPENT IT."   In *JMN*, XII, 535, Emerson attributed this sentiment to Socrates "ap. Stobaeus." A possible source is Montaigne's "Upon Some Verses of Virgil" in *Essays*, bk. III, ch. 5. In the new edition by Hazlitt (mentioned at 92.33–34) Montaigne's source is identified as Diogenes Laertius, *Lives and Opinions of Eminent Philosophers*, II, 33 ("Socrates"). Another possible source for the paraphrase is Stanley, *The History of Philosophy*, pt. III, "Socrates," ch. V, sec. 4.

90.10 "ATTRACTIVE AND ASSOCIATED LABOUR."   While associationism or communitarianism as a solution to social and economic problems was advanced by a number of reformers (see "New England Reformers," *CW*, III, 155–156), "the friends of 'attractive . . . Labour' " makes Emerson's reference specifically directed toward the followers of Charles Fourier (see note to 103.32), for whom the theory and application of the doctrine of "Attractive Industry" were central, as Emerson points out in "Fourier and the Socialists," *The Dial*, 3 (July 1842), where he uses the phrase in quotation marks and defines its practical application: "By concert, and the allowing each laborer to choose his own work, it becomes pleasure" (p. 87).

90.21 "IN NOT LETTING . . . DO NOT KNOW,"   The quotation marks around this phrase do not appear in the manuscript but were added, presumably by Emerson, in the first edition (see Emendations in Copy-Text). A source has not been found.

90.26 "MEN ARE A SORT . . . THEY PINE."   Emerson condensed, and in the second sentence paraphrased, this passage from *JMN*, XII, 61, where he identified its source as Joseph Spence's *Anecdotes* . . . , p. 248.

92.15 A SINGLE ODD VOLUME . . . REMAINING VOLUMES.   Emerson's library contains Montaigne's *Essays*, trans. Charles Cotton (1630–1687) — vols. I and III in the second edition (London, 1693) and vol. II in the third edition (London, 1700). This is the set he marked, annotated, and quoted from. In *JMN*,

VIII, 376, he remembered that he read Montaigne in this translation in Roxbury in 1825.

92.22 WHEN IN PARIS . . . ESSAYS OF MONTAIGNE." Emerson, in translating, freely adapts the inscription as he copied it into his notebook, where it reads: "Ici repose Auguste Charles Collignon. . . . Il aima et chercha à faire du bien, et mena une vie douce et heureuse en suivant, autant qu'il put, la morale et les lecons des essais de Montaigne, et des Fables de la Fontaine" (*JMN*, IV, 408–409).

92.26 SOME YEARS LATER . . . STERLING . . . HAZLITT . . . EDITION OF THE ESSAYS. Emerson never met John Sterling, the promising young friend of Thomas Carlyle, but their correspondence, from 1839 until Sterling's early death in 1844, shows a growing intimacy and mutual regard. Emerson attempted unsuccessfully to have Sterling's works published in America. Sterling's account of his visit to Montaigne's chateau and tower is "a slovenly kind of appendage" to his essay on Montaigne, which was ostensibly a review of three books: Sir Frederick Madden, *Observations on an Autograph of Shakspere, and the Orthography of His Name* (London, 1838), *De la Servitude Voluntaire, ou le Contr'un, par Estienne de la Boëtie (1548), avec les Notes de M. Coste, et une Préface de F. de la Mennais* (Paris, 1835), and *Essais de Michel de Montaigne, avec des Notes de tous les Commentateurs* (Paris, 1834). Sterling's essay appeared originally in *The London and Westminster Review*, 29 (August 1838), 321–352, and was collected posthumously in *Essays and Tales*, ed. Julius Charles Hare, 2 vols. (London, 1848), I, 129–187, a work Emerson had in his library. The concluding excerpt from Sterling's journal included this passage: "The books indeed are gone; but the many small rafters of the roof [of Montaigne's study] are inscribed on their lower faces with mottoes and pithy sentences, which recall, as by a living voice, the favourite studies and thoughts of Montaigne. Such are these few hastily transcribed in a note-book." And there follow nine Greek and Latin inscriptions, three of them from Ecclesiastes. As Emerson points out, the account of the visit is included in the extensive front-matter of *The Complete Works of Michael de Montaigne; Comprising; the Essays (Translated by Cotton); the Letters; the Journey into Germany and Italy; Now First Translated; A Life, by the Editor; . . . the Critical Opinions of Eminent Authors on Montaigne . . .* (London, 1842). The editor, William Hazlitt (1811–1893), was the son of the well-known essayist. Of this new edition Emerson, on October 25, 1843, wrote to Henry Thoreau, then living on Staten Island: "In Concord no events. We have had the new Hazlitt's Montaigne, which contained the Journey into Italy, — new to me, — and the narrative of the death of the renowned friend Etienne de la Boëtie" ("The Emerson-Thoreau Correspondence," ed. F. B. Sanborn, *The Atlantic Monthly*, 69 [May 1892], 596).

92.34 I HEARD WITH PLEASURE . . . IN THE FLYLEAF. Emerson would have read of Shakespeare's autograph (which is in a copy of John Florio's English translation of Montaigne's *Essays,* published in 1603) in John Sterling's 1838 essay described in the note to 92.26. Sterling begins his article with a notice of the discovery announced in the pamphlet by Sir Frederick Madden. When Emerson visited the British Museum in 1848, he saw the autograph and learned from the keeper of books, Thomas Watts, about the duplicate copy with the signature of Ben Jonson (*JMN,* X, 295). The authenticity of Shakespeare's autograph has been both challenged and defended.

93.4 LEIGH HUNT RELATES . . . AVOWED SATISFACTION. Leigh Hunt in *Lord Byron and Some of His Contemporaries* (London, 1828), p. 46, wrote of Lord Byron's literary tastes: "The only great writer of past times, whom he read with avowed satisfaction, was Montaigne, as the reader may see by an article in the 'New Monthly Magazine.' In the same article may be seen the reasons why, and the passages that he marked in that author." Hunt refers to his own article, "Passages Marked in Montaigne's Essays by Lord Byron," *The New Monthly Magazine,* 19 (January and March 1827), 26–32, 240–245. Emerson's immediate source may have been the collection of critical opinions of eminent authors printed in the introductory material in Hazlitt's 1842 edition of Montaigne.

93.17 IN THE CIVIL WARS OF THE LEAGUE, Continuing the series of religious wars between Protestants and Catholics that disrupted France from 1562, a national league of Catholics, sometimes called the Holy League, was formed in 1576, variously allied with Henry III, the Papacy, and Spain. A bitter series of civil wars ensued until the final victory of their opponent Henry IV (Henry of Navarre) in 1594.

93.22 GIBBON RECKONS . . . HENRY IV AND MONTAIGNE. The English historian, Edward Gibbon (1737–1794), among his "Hints" for possible investigation of the "Difference of the civil wars in France and England," noted: "The effect of civil wars on the minds of men. A general ferment of fanaticism, discord, and faction. Two singular exceptions. Montaigne in his retirement. Henry IV. on the throne. He loved and trusted mankind. — How different from Charles II.!" This memorandum was included in *The Miscellaneous Works of Edward Gibbon, Esq. with Memoirs of His Life and Writings, Composed by Himself: Illustrated from His Letters, with Occasional Notes . . . A New Edition, with Considerable Additions,* ed. John, Lord Sheffield, 5 vols. (London, 1814), V, 537–538. Emerson's edition of *The Miscellaneous Works* (London, 1837), based on the first edition, did not contain this note, and he may have remembered it from the collection of critical opinions of eminent authors printed in the introductory material of Hazlitt's 1842 edition of Montaigne.

93.35 IF THERE BE . . . BY STEALTH. In *JMN,* V, 285, Emerson attributed a similar sentiment to Montaigne's *Essays,* "Vol. 2 p. 497," meaning in Emerson's own edition of the Cotton translation, bk. II, ch. 17 ("Of Presumption").

In that essay, on the page indicated, Montaigne says: "I think it very hard, that any other should have a meaner Opinion of himself; nay, that any other should have a meaner Opinion of me, than I have of my self. I look upon my self as one of the common sort, saving in this, that I have no better Opinion of my self; guilty of the meanest and most popular Defects, but not disown'd or excus'd, and do not value my self upon any other Account, than because I know my own Value. If there be any Glory in the Case, 'tis superficially infus'd into me by the treachery of my Complexion, and has no Body that my judgment can discern."

94.1 "FIVE OR SIX . . . MAN LIVING." This is paraphrased from Montaigne's *Essays*, bk. III, ch. 3, "Of Three Commerces."

94.5 "WHEN I THE MOST . . . BY HIMSELF." Emerson identified this passage in *JMN*, III, 315, and *JMN*, VI, 319, as from Montaigne's *Essays*, II, 557, in his edition — that is, bk. II, ch. 20, "That we Taste nothing pure."

94.26 HE DREW AN EMBLEMATIC . . . UNDER IT. In his "Apology for Raimonde de Sebonde" (bk. II, ch. 12) Montaigne says that the Pyrrhonian philosophers, the skeptics, are limited by language: that when they say "I doubt" or "I know not," they are caught by the throat and made to confess that at least they know they doubt. Thus they resort to specious comparisons to shelter themselves and pretend that statement is not an affirmation. He continues, making his own famous phrase: "This Fancy will be more certainly understood by Interrogation: *What do I know?* (as I bear it in the Emblem of a Balance)." This motto with a stylized pair of scales became his device, which he wore and emblazoned on various walls.

94.28 OLD POZ, Emerson's allusion here is to an instructive comic play for children, "Old Poz, the Mimic," in Maria Edgeworth's *The Parent's Assistant, or, Stories for Children,* first published in 1795 or 1796 and widely reprinted. As his name suggests, Justice Poz is comically certain in his opinions on all subjects.

96.6 "BUT, HE SAYS . . . NOT CHOICE." The passage is taken from Montaigne's *Essays*, bk. III, ch. 5, "Upon Some Verses of Virgil."

96.11 QUE SÇAIS JE? WHAT DO I KNOW? See 94.27 and note to 94.26.

97.32 HIS POLITICS ARE . . . LOVE OR HATRED;" Raleigh's famous poem is now more commonly known as "The Lie." In it the soul is charged with the errand of giving the lie to worldly powers, institutions, virtues, and qualities, an impolitic task that deserves "no lesse then stabbing," but the soul is told "no stab thy soule can kill." For the quotation from Krishna, see 78.8 and note.

98.23 SAN CARLO, Edward Waldo Emerson identified the "valued friend here alluded to" as Charles King Newcomb (1820–1894) and described him as "of a sensitive and beautiful character, a mystic, but with the Hamlet temperament to such an extent that he was paralyzed for all action by the tenderness of his conscience and the power with which all sides of a question presented themselves to him in turn" (*W*, IV, 342). Emerson published in *The Dial*, 3 (July 1842), 112–123, Newcomb's sketch "The Two Dolons."

100.8 KINDE OR NATURE, In *JMN*, XI, 118, Emerson made a distinction between the two words: *"Kinde* was the old English, which however only filled half the range of our fine Latin word, with its delicate future tense, *Natura, About to be born."*

100.33 THE GODDESS YOGANIDRA ... IS BEGUILED. The phrasing here is in a passage copied into *JMN*, IX, 322, which Emerson identifies as from *The Vishńu Puráńa ...*, p. 498 (bk. V, ch. I).

103.12 GEORGE FOX SAW ... THAT OF DARKNESS." This famous perception is recorded in *The Journal of George Fox*, ch. I, but the wording here indicates that Emerson's source was the paraphrase in William Sewell, *The History of the Rise, Increase, and Progress of the Christian People Called Quakers*, 3rd ed., 2 vols. (Philadelphia, 1823), I, 44, a work in Emerson's library.

103.32 CHARLES FOURIER ... TO HIS DESTINIES;" The doctrines and proposals of the French social reformer Charles Fourier (1772–1837) were widely discussed and promoted in the 1840s, and among those interested were some of Emerson's friends. Several communities in the United States were based on Fourier's principles; Brook Farm in 1845 reorganized as a Fourieristic phalanx and soon became the center for dissemination of propaganda through the publication of *The Harbinger*. Fourier based his detailed plan for radical reformation of society on an esoteric theory of a harmonic universe, and his axiom, "Les Attractions sont proportionelles aux Destinées," which was inscribed on his tomb in the cemetery of Montmartre, was the focus of hostile controversy. Fourier shared with other utopian reformers the premise that the evils of social institutions had warped the essential goodness of human nature, but he uniquely founded his reforms on the inborn passions or attractions — physical, moral, social, and spiritual — of human nature rather than on repression of them, and he argued the harmony between those God-given passions and the destiny of mankind. He developed this point, the law "des Attractions proportionelles aux destinées," in *Théorie de L'Unité Universelle* (originally published as *Traité de L'Association Domestique-Agricole ou Attraction Industrielle*) in *Œuvres Complètes de Ch. Fourier*, 6 vols. (Paris, 1841–1848), III, 304–346. Emerson's translation at 104.13–14, his French version at *JMN*, IX, 116, and his listing of all three axioms on the tomb at *JMN*, XI, 246, suggest he had the sentence at second-hand — perhaps from Parke Godwin, *A Popular View of the Doctrines of Charles Fourier* (New York, 1844), p. 25 — but the controversial axiom was available to him from many sources.

105.7 "IF MY BARK ... ANOTHER SEA." This is the last line of "A Poet's Hope," written by Emerson's friend William Ellery Channing (1817–1901), namesake and nephew of the distinguished Unitarian minister. This, his best-known poem, was an improvisation; challenged by Anna Barker Ward, Channing went to another room and quickly wrote its seventy-eight lines. It was published in *Poems* (Boston, 1843), where the line is printed as: "If my bark sinks, 't is to another sea."

110.17 GENIAL   Emerson uses the word here in its now obsolete meaning of inborn, native, belonging to one's nature or genius.

110.22 THE COURT ... CHURCH WOULD SUPPRESS THEM.   As early as 1559 Elizabeth I attempted to provide controls for dramatic production by authorizing mayors of towns and justices of the peace in the counties to examine stage plays and suppress those that criticized the established religious and political order. Abuses of authority occurred in London, inspired by the Puritans, who opposed stage productions for different reasons (general immorality, Sunday performances, boys playing women). The Mayor and Corporation of London attempted to suppress plays completely, even beyond London where they had no jurisdiction, because they thought plays interfered with business. Elizabeth checked these abuses in two ways: in 1581 she appointed Edmund Tilney as Master of the Revels, with jurisdiction throughout England and power formerly dispersed among the mayors and justices of the peace; and in 1583 she formed her own dramatic company, called the Queen's Men, which soon eclipsed the other companies, but was later overshadowed by the Admiral's and Lord Chamberlain's companies. Continuing support for drama by the monarchy is indicated by the growing number of performances sponsored for the entertainment of the Court: Elizabeth held about 90 performances between 1590 and 1603; in a similar period, 1603–1616, James I lavishly permitted 299. The complete suppression of public stage plays dates from an act of the Puritan Parliament on September 2, 1642.

110.32 PUNCH,   Emerson here probably refers to the English publication *Punch,* famous for its light humor and cartoons, founded in 1841, rather than to the popular Punch-and-Judy show.

111.1 THE CROWD OF WRITERS ... AND FLETCHER.   These are the most prominent of the playwrights who wrote at about the same time as Shakespeare. Of those named, Kyd, Peele, Greene, and Chapman were older than Shakespeare, though Chapman's career as a playwright began later; Marlowe (as his name is usually spelled) was the same age; and the others were younger.

111.11 THE TALE OF TROY . . . ROYAL HENRIES, Plays on many of the subjects Emerson mentions are known to have been written, though most of them (for example, those on Brut) have not survived. Emerson may also have had in mind some of the prose and verse chronicles, written at various times since the early twelfth century, on British legend and history: Wace's *Roman de Brut* (1155), for instance, or the Arthurian romances of Chrétien de Troyes. Brut (or Brutus), the great-grandson of Aeneas, was supposed to have settled Britain — which was named for him — with a band of Trojan followers in about the tenth century B.C. Arthur was believed to have ruled most of Britain in the sixth century A.D. Both of these heroes were dealt with at length in *The History of the Kings of Britain* (1136) by Geoffrey of Monmouth and later writers. The centuries of English history between the first of the "royal Henries" (1100–1135) and the eighth (1509–1547) were covered in such chronicles as those of Raphael Holinshed and Edward Hall, which Shakespeare knew and used; but there were few plays dealing with that period before Shakespeare began writing his, probably around 1591 or even earlier.

111.20 THEY HAVE BEEN . . . WORK OF NUMBERS. Emerson's account of pre-Shakespearean playwriting and revision may be correct in part, but is probably not as generally true as he believed. Of the very few surviving manuscripts of plays written before 1642, almost none shows signs of the kind of revision described here; one that does is *Sir Thomas More*, which Shakespeare (along with several others) is thought to have had a hand in. From the diary and other papers of Philip Henslowe, the theater manager and money-lender, we know that "additions" were occasionally made to established plays like *The Spanish Tragedy* and *Doctor Faustus;* internal evidence of the plays themselves (in different editions) confirms this. Emerson's view of the process was probably influenced by theories of eighteenth-century scholars such as Edmond Malone. But their concept of "continuous copy," which was held (in a somewhat different form) by the twentieth-century editor John Dover Wilson, has been almost completely discredited by the work of such recent scholars as E. K. Chambers, W. W. Greg, and Peter Alexander.

112.2 SCULPTURE IN EGYPT . . . IN THE STATUE. As an example of Greek sculpture that would seem to confirm the account Emerson gives here, he may have been thinking of the so-called Elgin Marbles from the frieze of the Parthenon, copies of which he saw at Benjamin Rogers' house in London (*L*, III, 426; *JMN*, X, 523).

112.19 THE AMOUNT OF . . . THE BAD RHYTHM. Emerson in this paragraph refers to two major problems concerning the authorship of plays attributed to Shakespeare: the nature of the *Henry VI* trilogy, and the authorship of *Henry VIII*. On the first he takes a position that is no longer generally held, but on the second he is one of the first to state what is now the majority view. On the authorship of the second and third parts of *Henry VI*, the leading theory for many years was that of Edmond Malone (1741–1812), an Irish scholar who believed that *The First Part of the Contention betwixt . . . York and Lancaster* (1594) and *The True Tragedie of Richard Duke of York* (1595) were source plays by other men which Shakespeare rewrote as the second and third parts of *Henry VI*, respectively. Emerson may have known that Charles Knight in "An Essay on the Three Parts of King Henry VI., and King Richard III.," included in *The Pictorial Edition of the Works of Shakspere*, 8 vols. (London, 1839–1842), II, xi ff, argued that *The . . . Contention* and *The True Tragedie* were early versions by Shakespeare himself. This was not the prevailing view, however. James Orchard Halliwell edited these two early plays as *The First Sketches of the Second and Third Parts of King Henry the Sixth* (London, 1843) and in his Introduction rejected Knight's position and argued that these plays were only partially revised by Shakespeare, not original works by him. Thus, Halliwell, in a work that Emerson probably had in his possession during the composition of his lecture (see note to 115.33), accepted, along with other eminent contemporary Shakespearean scholars like John Payne Collier, Malone's argument that the second and third parts of *Henry VI* were Shakespeare's revisions of the work of one or more early playwrights. Unlike Collier and others, Halliwell also agreed with Malone's outright rejection of the first part as not Shakespearean at all. In 1929 Peter Alexander proposed the theory that *The . . . Contention* and *The True Tragedie* were "bad quartos" (that is, memorial reconstructions) of the versions more accurately printed in the Folio of 1623; this is the theory most generally held today. In preparing his 1846 lecture Emerson apparently took his paraphrase of Malone from Isaac D'Israeli's essay on "Shakespeare" in *Amenities of Literature, Consisting of Sketches and Characters of English Literature*, 3 vols. (London, 1841), III, 44; Emerson had borrowed the volume from the Boston Athenæum from September 16, 1845, to January 28, 1846. He recorded the passage, including D'Israeli's error in one of the figures, in notes for the lecture outline at *JMN*, XII, 551. It is also apparent there and in the manuscript for *Representative Men* that Emerson at first misunderstood D'Israeli (and hence Malone) to be referring to all the historical plays rather than to the second and third parts of *Henry VI* only. Shortly before his book went to press in 1849, however, Emerson correctly identified (in *JMN*, XI, 174) the source for "the Malone sentence in my 'Shakspeare' " as Malone's "A Dissertation on the Three Parts of King Henry VI" in *The Plays and Poems of William Shakespeare*, 21 vols. (London, 1821), XVIII, 572. It may have been from this late entry or from Malone directly that Emerson made both corrections in printer's copy (see Annex A, Appendix 2 for 112.19 and marginal computations at 112.17). The sentence immediately following the paraphrase of Malone, much altered in manuscript, is also taken from D'Israeli's essay (III, 46), as indicated in *JMN*, IX, 253.

On the authorship of *Henry VIII* Emerson is much closer to twentieth-century opinion, although his suggestion that Shakespeare was here revising another man's work has been replaced by the theory that the play was a collaborative work by Shakespeare and John Fletcher. The history of the controversy over this problem is excellently summarized in the "Annotated Bibliography" (by Ephim Fogel) in *Evidence for Authorship: Essays on Problems of Attribution,* ed. David V. Erdman and Ephim G. Fogel (Ithaca, N.Y., 1966), pp. 457–478. Peculiarities of style, and especially of meter, throughout the play were first set forth in a note by Richard Roderick (d. 1756) in his "Remarks on Shakespear," posthumously published in the sixth edition (1758) of Thomas Edwards' *Canons of Criticism.* Other critics, beginning with Samuel Johnson in his edition of 1765, suspected that the prologue and epilogue were by another writer, probably Ben Jonson; Richard Farmer (1773) and Edmond Malone (1778) found signs of interpolation or revision by another hand in the body of the play. James Boswell, Jr. (1821), pointed out similarities in versification to that of John Fletcher; and the anonymous editor of Shakespeare's *Works* (London, 1843) thought that two scenes — Wolsey's farewells to his greatness and to Cromwell (III, ii) and Queen Katherine's description of Wolsey (IV, ii) — were added by a "reverent disciple" after Shakespeare's death. Fogel next discusses Emerson's "Shakspeare" lecture of 1846 (which became part of *Representative Men*), but fails to mention that Emerson had made very similar remarks in his second "Shakspear" lecture of December 1835 (*EL*, I, 309), where he pointed out that a large proportion of lines in *Henry VIII* have feminine endings and cited three passages from the play which are quite unlike Shakespeare's verse, but like that of "Beaumont and Fletcher or Massinger." He did not then suggest, however, as he does here, that Shakespeare was revising a play written by another. Fogel notes that Emerson gave the 1846 lecture several times in England (once in London) in 1847–48, and *Representative Men* was published there in 1850. Thus, his ideas on this question may have been known to James Spedding, whose letters "Who wrote Shakspere's Henry VIII?" were printed in *The Gentleman's Magazine* for August and October 1850, first proposing in print the theory of collaboration between Shakespeare and Fletcher. Spedding credited the suggestion of Fletcher as the co-author to Alfred Tennyson, whom Emerson had met during his 1847–48 visit, and with whom he may conceivably have discussed the problem. Some recent scholars and critics believe that Shakespeare was the sole author of the play, but they are in the minority. Others think that Shakespeare and Fletcher collaborated in *The Two Noble Kinsmen* and the lost play *Cardenio,* and that the passages in *Henry VIII* noted by Emerson as un-Shakespearean, along with some others listed by Spedding, were probably written by Fletcher.

113.3 SHAKSPEARE KNEW . . . INVENTION CAN. This saying, which seems to have been a favorite of Emerson's (see PP), he took from Madame de Staël's *Influence of Literature upon Society* (1813), I, 105.

113.22 EACH ROMANCER WAS HEIR . . . TROY DIVINE." Emerson's quotation from Milton's "Il Penseroso" (lines 99–100) applies more accurately to the major topics of Greek tragedy than to those of romance in general, as the context makes clear: "Som time let Gorgeous Tragedy / In scepter'd Pall com sweeping by, / Presenting *Thebs,* or *Pelops* line, / Or the tale of *Troy* divine." Pelops, the son of Tantalus, became king of Pisa (in Elis, the northwestern Peloponnesus, not in Italy) and sired a line of descendants whose lives and deaths provided subjects for many ancient (and some modern) tragedies: notably (in the first generation) the brother-enemies Atreus and Thyestes; (in the second) Agamemnon of Mycenae and Menelaus of Sparta, sons of Atreus, and Aegisthus, son of Thyestes; and (in the third) Orestes, Electra, and Iphigeneia, children of Agamemnon and Clytemnaestra, and Hermione, daughter of Menelaus and Helen. The principal extant Greek plays relating to them are the *Oresteia* trilogy of Aeschylus, *Electra* by Sophocles, and *Electra, Iphigeneia in Aulis,* and *Orestes* (and several others) by Euripides. "Thebes" refers to the almost equally ill-starred descendants of Cadmus, particularly his daughter Agave and her son Pentheus (the *Bacchae* of Euripides), and his great-grandson Laius and the latter's son Oedipus and his family, dealt with by Sophocles in *Oedipus Tyrannos, Oedipus at Colonus,* and *Antigone,* by Aeschylus in *The Seven Against Thebes,* and by Euripides in *The Phoenician Women.* The tale of Troy was of course the subject of several Greek epics and tragedies. Material from all three of these topics was also used in Latin epic and tragedy, as well as in medieval romance.

113.30 BUT CHAUCER IS . . . WHERE HE LEAVES IT. Many of the statements in this passage are either misleading or incorrect. Chaucer could not have drawn material "through Lydgate and Caxton," who came after him. Most of his material on the Trojan war comes from the *Filostrato* of Boccaccio, which Emerson does not mention. Boccaccio had developed the story of Troilus and Criseyde from the "Guido" whom Emerson names; but Guido's "Latin romance" was mainly a translation from the French of Benoît de Sainte-More, who had taken his materials from Dares (and Dictys Cretensis), with additions from Ovid and Virgil—not from Statius, as Emerson thought. No direct indebtedness to Provençal poetry can be traced in Chaucer; and "The Cock and the Fox" ("The Nun's Priest's Tale") is not thought by modern Chaucer scholars to have any connection with the fable *Dou Coc et dou Werpil* by Marie de France. No specific source is known for *The House of Fame,* though it does have French and Italian analogues, and was certainly influenced by Dante. The "Lollius of Urbino" whom Chaucer named as his principal source for the Troilus and Criseyde story (without assigning him to Urbino or any other place) never existed, though Chaucer apparently thought that he was an ancient authority on the Trojan war (see *The House of Fame,* line 1468, and *Troilus and Criseyde,* I, 394)—probably on the basis of a misunderstanding of a line in Horace (*Epistles,* I, ii, 1); see F. N. Robinson's discussion in his edition of *The Works of Geoffrey Chaucer,* 2nd ed. (Boston, Houghton Mifflin, 1957), p. 812. Chaucer did borrow a tale or two from Gower, but this was less than he took from several other writers. Emerson had made most, though not all, of these same errors in his "Chaucer" lecture in the 1835 English Literature series (*EL*, I, 283–284). B. J. Whiting, in "Emerson, Chaucer, and Thomas Warton," *American Literature*, 17 (1945), 75–78, has shown that Emerson got most of his misinformation from Thomas Warton's *History of English Poetry*, 4 vols. (London, 1824), I, 128–131, which he had taken out of the Boston Athenæum from July 22 to December 10, 1835, while preparing the earlier lecture series. Apart from these inaccuracies, Emerson's main point, that Chaucer was "a huge borrower," is sound. But not all of his sources were by any means of "no worth where he finds [them]"—Dante, Petrarch, and Boccaccio, to name only three—and he often expressed high regard for them, as well as for Gower.

114.23 SIR ROBERT PEEL   Sir Robert Peel (1788–1850) was prime minister of England in 1833–1834 and 1841–1846.

114.30 DELPHI   Delphi is prominent in Greek mythology and literature as a place where, through an intermediary priestess, one could obtain inspired wisdom or prophecy from the gods.

115.2 OUR ENGLISH BIBLE ... TRANSLATION EXISTING.   Not strictly accurate; translations from the Hebrew Old Testament and the Greek New Testament did not appear for some time after the original texts were written, and there was no English translation (except for short selections) before Wycliff's in the late fourteenth century. But there was a series of translations between Wycliff's and the Authorized (King James) version of 1611, each depending to some extent on one or more of its predecessors.

115.6 THE LITURGY,   Edward Waldo Emerson comments that his father "had tender associations with the Book of Common Prayer. His mother had been brought up in the Episcopal communion, and the prayer-book of her youth was always by her" (*W*, IV, 351). That Emerson here refers to the Anglican liturgy is supported by the source for the passage in *JMN*, X, 35.

115.10 GROTIUS MAKES ... RABBINICAL FORMS.   The ultimate source for this paraphrase of Grotius' comment on Matthew 6: 9-15 is his *Annotationes in Libros Evangeliorum* ... (1641); see *Opera Omnia Theologica* ..., 4 vols. (Basel, 1732), II, 78. Emerson referred to the comment as early as 1832 in *JMN*, III, 328, and perhaps knew it from his training for the ministry.

115.18 THE TRANSLATION ... WAS NONE.   Sir Thomas North's translation in 1579 of Plutarch's *Lives*, used by Shakespeare as a source for several plays, was made not from the Greek original but from the French of Jacques Amyot's translation in 1559. Again, "There never was a time when there was none" is an exaggeration.

115.23 THE WORLD ... SINGLE MEN.   Pilpay or Bidpai is the supposed author of a collection of animal fables, apologues, and proverbs that circulated
in the Middle Ages in various Persian, Arabic, and European versions and adaptations and appeared in the eighteenth century in English as *Instructive and
Entertaining Fables of Pilpay, an Ancient Indian Philosopher.* Another English version, from the Arabic, was published as *Kalila and Dimna, or The Fables of Bidpai,* trans. Wyndham Knatchbull (Oxford, 1819). Emerson owned *The
Hĕĕtōpădēs of Vĕĕshnoͦ-Sărmā, in a Series of Connected Fables, Interspersed with Moral,
Prudential, and Political Maxims ...,* trans. Sir Charles Wilkins (Bath, 1787),
and on the basis of its preface he wrote when he extracted maxims and aphorisms for *The Dial,* 3 (July 1842), 82: "The following sentences are taken from
Charles Wilkins' translation of the Heetopades or Amicable Instructions of
Veeshnoo Sarma, according to Sir William Jones, the most beautiful, if not
the most ancient collection of apologues in the world, the original source of
the book, which passes in the modern languages of Europe and America,
under the false name of Pilpay." The complexities of the source and transmission of the fables attributed to Bidpai are greater than Jones, Wilkins, or
Emerson supposed, but, like Aesop's fables and *The Thousand and One Nights,*
they illustrate Emerson's point, borne out in later scholarship. In the same
number of *The Dial* Emerson reviewed the first American edition of J. G.
Lockhart's *Ancient Spanish Ballads* (New York, 1842), noting with approval the
addition of a long review essay reprinted from *The Edinburgh Review,* "On the
Origin, Antiquity, Character, and Influence of the Ancient Ballads of Spain"
and an analysis of *The Cid.* Admiring this publishing enterprise, he called for a
reprint of Robert Southey's *Chronicle of the Cid,* a call duly heard by a Lowell
publisher in 1846, who sent Emerson a copy. From these sources he would
know the complexities of the body of legend, folklore, literature, the *Poema del
Cid,* the two chronicles, and the hundreds of ballads, evolving between the
twelfth and sixteenth centuries from the legend of Spain's greatest hero, Ro-
drigo Díaz de Bivar, called El Cid and El Campeador (ca. 1040–1099). In the
review of Lockhart's book he wrote: "The Iliad, the Nibelungen, the Cid, the
Robin Hood Ballads, Frithiof's Saga ... are five admirable collections of early
popular poetry of so many nations; and ... they possess strong mutual resemblances, chiefly apparent in the spirit which they communicate to the reader,
of health, vigor, cheerfulness, and good hope" (p. 128). In 1839 Emerson had
observed that the present age "has groped in all nations where was any literature for the early poetry, not only dramatic, but for the popular sort, the ballads, the songs, for the Nibelungen Lied and Hans Sachs in Germany, for the
Cid in Spain, for the ruder verse of the interior nations of Europe, and in
England for the ballads of Scotland and Robinhood" (*EL,* III, 210). Emerson
would of course know the German criticism that attributed the *Iliad* and the
Odyssey not to Homer but to a process of folk compilation, and he knew that
the Vedas were the work of centuries of compilation and accretion (see note to
28.8).

115.33 THE RESEARCHES ... MADE HIS OWN. The Shakespeare Society of London, founded in 1840, published from 1841 through 1845 twenty-nine volumes edited by John Payne Collier, James Orchard Halliwell, and others of papers, theatrical records, memoirs, and plays of the pre-Shakespearean and Shakespearean periods. By the end of 1849 the Society had published thirteen more volumes. Late in November 1845, while Emerson was preparing the Representative Men lectures, he borrowed from Longfellow nine of the Shakespeare Society volumes—the ones Longfellow thought most useful—and "made at least some progress into their contents" (*L*, III, 313). Collier, the director of the Society, who had not yet been accused of forging some of his documents, was well known for *The History of English Dramatic Poetry to the Time of Shakespeare; and Annals of the Stage to the Restoration* (London, 1831), 3 vols., and his edition of *The Works of William Shakespeare* (London, 1842–1844), 8 vols. To the latter he prefixed a "History of the English Drama and Stage to the Time of Shakespeare" and a "Life of William Shakespeare," which (while introducing some material no longer accepted) exhibit the kind of antiquarian zeal and success that Emerson describes in this paragraph. Emerson refers to the earliest English formal tragedy, *Gorboduc* (1561 or 1562) by Thomas Sackville (1536–1608) and Thomas Norton (1532–1584), sometimes known as "Ferrex and Porrex" after the principal characters; and *Gammer Gurton's Needle*, one of the first English formal comedies (as opposed to "interludes," which often had comic themes and characters), written between 1552 and 1563 by "Mr. S., Master of Art," probably William Stevenson, a Fellow of Christ's College at Cambridge University, where it was first performed. As for "the very pieces which Shakspeare altered ... and finally made his own," few of them are extant. *The Taming of a Shrew* and *The Troublesome Reign of King John* may be two of these, but some scholars think they are "bad quartos" (memorial reconstructions) of Shakespeare's *Taming of the Shrew* and *King John*. He also used plot material or characters from Whetstone's *Promos and Cassandra* (in *Measure for Measure*) and the anonymous *Famous Victories of Henry V* and *King Leir*, but in these cases other sources were more important, and he did much more than alter and remodel them—he completely rewrote them. A few others, including *Hamlet*, were probably based on plays now lost. But for the majority of his plays Shakespeare found his chief sources in nondramatic writings: Holinshed's *Chronicles*, Plutarch's *Lives* (North's translation), and various prose and verse romances (see Kenneth Muir, *The Sources of Shakespeare's Plays* [New Haven, 1978]). Sources for some of his plays have never been identified. Emerson, however, was echoing the view held by most Shakespearean scholars of his time.

116.23 BEN JONSON ... REGARD AND PANEGYRIC, Jonson's formal tributes are two poems in Shakespeare's First Folio (1623): "To the Reader" and the eloquent "To the Memory of My Beloved, the Author Mr. William Shakespeare: and What He Hath Left Us." Emerson had earlier noted (*EL*, I, 306) the "frugal encomium" in Jonson's critical summary of Shakespeare as a writer in *Timber: or, Discoveries,* lines 647–668: "There was ever more in him to be praysed, then to be pardoned."

116.30 SIR HENRY WOTTON . . . AND THE REST. The source for this passage is Emerson's eighth lecture in the 1835–36 series on English Literature, "Ben Jonson, Herrick, Herbert, Wotton," where he writes with fuller detail: "Sir Henry Wotton was born in 1568 and was a kinsman and correspondent of Lord Bacon. Pursuing his studies at Oxford he became the friend of Albericus Gentilis, then Professor of Civil Law, and of his fellow student Dr. Donne. In his travels into Switzerland and Italy he became acquainted with Arminius, at Leyden, Theodore Beza, and at Geneva he lodged with Isaac Casaubon. At Venice he lived on terms of intimacy with Father Paul the historian of the Council of Trent. He visited Kepler at Lintz, and gave him Lord Bacon's Novum Organon, and Vieta at Venice and Robert Bellarmine at Rome. The Earl of Essex, Bacon's benefactor and Shakspear's friend, made Wotton his secretary and W[otton] accompanied him in a voyage to [the] Spanish main. He was the friend of the ever memorable John Hales, and Cowley, of Sir Walter Raleigh, and Sir Philip Sidney. He was in habits of intercourse with John Pym the patriot, and Sir Henry Vane. Isaac Walton the Angler was his friend and biographer, and Milton had a short acquaintance with him, presented his Comus, and received from him a letter of advice on setting forth on his travels. He was employed by Elizabeth and by King James abroad and finally made Provost of Eton College at home. Beside this wonderful circle of friends . . . his acquaintance with Spenser, with Shakspear, and Ben Jonson may be fairly presumed, though we have no record of the fact" (*EL,* I, 353–354). Charles Cotton, a friend of Wotton and translator of Montaigne, is not included in the early passage, but he with all the rest may be readily gleaned from Izaak Walton, *The Lives of Donne, Wotton, Hooker, Herbert, and Sanderson,* 2 vols. (Boston, 1832) and from Sir Henry Wotton, *Reliquiae Wotton-ianae* (London, 1685), both of which Emerson owned and read. Among those not previously identified or not obvious are Theodore Beza (1519–1605), a French theologian who was a close associate of Calvin; Isaac Casaubon (1559–1614), a Genevan by birth, but later a theologian and classical scholar in England; Robert Devereux (1567–1601), second Earl of Essex, an English soldier and courtier, who was executed for his rebellion against Queen Elizabeth I; Sir Henry Vane (1613–1662), an English Puritan statesman and Governor of Massachusetts (1636–1637), executed for treason; Abraham Cowley (1618–1667), English metaphysical poet; Robert Bellarmine (1542–1621), an Italian Jesuit theologian, polemicist, and churchman, a principal leader in the Catholic Reformation, who in 1930 was canonized and made a Doctor of the Church the next year; John Pym (1583?–1643), Puritan Parliamentary leader; François Vieta (or Viète; 1540–1603), a French mathematician, founder of algebra, and distinguished lawyer and courtier; Alberto Gentili (1552–1608),

Italian-born legal scholar, a Protestant refugee to England, whose important work laid the foundation for international law; Paolo Sarpi (1552–1623), Venetian statesman and theologian, a champion of the right of states against ecclesiastical authority. The "two Herberts," in the context of the list of writers, almost certainly refers to Edward Herbert (1583–1648), first Baron Herbert of Cherbury, English philosopher, poet, and diplomat, and his now more widely known brother, George Herbert (1593–1633), the metaphysical poet.

117.11 IT WAS ON . . . ADEQUATE FIDELITY;   The influence of Shakespeare on German literature is an idea Emerson stated more than once (see PP). The editors of *JMN*, VII, 116, suggest that he may have drawn the idea for this passage from Carlyle's "State of German Literature," *The Edinburgh Review*, 46 (October 1827). The influential German philosopher and dramatist Gotthold Ephraim Lessing (1729–1781) argued effectively in his critical writings against French drama as a model and introduced into Germany an admiration for Shakespeare's plays and English literature generally. His contemporary Christoph Martin Wieland (1733–1813) also contributed to the flowering of German literature in the late eighteenth century and translated twenty-two of Shakespeare's plays. Perhaps the most important contribution to Shakespeare's influence in Germany, however, was the translated edition begun in 1797 by the poet and scholar August Wilhelm von Schlegel (1767–1845) and completed by others. Goethe's lifelong interest in Shakespeare and his extensive formal and informal criticism Emerson knew from his reading of Goethe. Similarly the Shakespearean criticism of Coleridge, still regarded as important, Emerson knew from *Biographia Literaria*, *The Friend*, *The Literary Remains*, *Specimens of the Table Talk*, and other works in his library. Coleridge's *Notes and Lectures upon Shakespeare*, published the year *Representative Men* was completed, is largely a reprint.

117.29 IT APPEARS THAT . . . APPURTENANCES WERE HIS;   Unlike the rest of the paragraph on the biographical findings of the Shakespeare Society, this passage is based on a forgery John Payne Collier first included in *New Facts Regarding the Life of Shakespeare* (London, 1835) and later incorporated into his work for the Society (see note to 115.33). The Blackfriars was an indoor theater used by the King's Men from 1609, even as they continued to use the Globe. The proprietors of both theaters were James Burbage and his sons; Shakespeare and other principal members of the acting company shared in the profits.

118.15 THE "MODERN PLUTARCH,"   Emerson may have had in mind Francis Wraugham's *The British Plutarch, Containing the Lives of the Most Eminent Divines, Patriots, Statesmen, Warriors, Philosophers, Poets, and Artists of Great Britain and Ireland, from the Accession of Henry VIII to the Present Time*, new ed. (London, 1816), 6 vols.

118.17 THE RAINBOW DAUGHTER OF WONDER   Iris (Rainbow) is described as the daughter of Thaumas (Wonder or Miracle) in Hesiod's *Theogony*, lines 265–269, 780. In the *Iliad* she is repeatedly the swift-footed messenger of the other gods.

118.19 WARBURTON, DYCE . . . THIS GENIUS;   Bishop William Warburton (1698–1779), English polemicist and critic, published an eight-volume edition of Shakespeare in 1747. Alexander Dyce (1798–1869), a Scottish clergyman-scholar, editor of Elizabethan and Jacobean dramatists, had attained eminence as a Shakespearean in the 1840s, particularly as a severe critic of Collier's edition of Shakespeare. His own edition was not published until 1857. Covent Garden and Drury Lane were famous London theaters; Covent Garden, in bankruptcy by 1822, reopened in 1847 as the Royal Italian Opera House. The Park and the Tremont were Boston theaters. Thomas Betterton (ca. 1635–1710), preeminent actor of the Restoration, as manager of Drury Lane and other theaters, produced adaptations of and acted in many of Shakespeare's plays. He also made a journey to Warwickshire to collect information on Shakespeare. David Garrick (1717–1779), the greatest actor of the eighteenth century, was best known for his creation of Shakespearean tragic heroes. He was manager of Drury Lane from 1747 until 1776. Among the well-known actors and actresses of the Kemble family (some also managers of Covent Garden and Drury Lane), Emerson most likely refers to John Philip Kemble (1757–1823), a famous Shakespearean tragedian, or his younger brother, Charles Kemble (1775–1854), who was highly successful in his American tour of 1832–34, accompanied by his even more celebrated daughter Frances Anne Kemble (1809–1893). Because Fanny Kemble, who had settled in America, resumed her career in 1848–49 with a successful series of dramatic readings in Boston and elsewhere, it is possible that Emerson may allude here to her. Emerson may refer to either Edmund Kean (ca. 1787–1833) or his son Charles John Kean (1811–1868), both leading Shakespearean tragedians in the nineteenth-century English theater who toured the United States. William Charles Macready (1793–1873), manager of Covent Garden and later of Drury Lane, was the principal rival to Edmund Kean as a Shakespearean tragedian. Emerson met him in 1843 (see note to 118.24). On Macready's last tour of the United States, in 1849, his intense rivalry with the American actor Edwin Forrest sparked the Astor Place riot in which several people were killed.

118.24 THE RECITATION BEGINS . . . OTHELLO'S CAPTIVITY,— The green-room in older theaters was the room adjacent to the stage where actors and actresses awaited their cues to come on stage; here Emerson uses it in a transferred sense to refer to the actors' art in contrast to the poetry of the play. He offers as examples of this poetic magic, not only the creation of the fairy woods near Athens in *A Midsummer Night's Dream*, the Forest of Arden in *As You Like*

It, and Portia's villa in *The Merchant of Venice,* but deft, incidental allusions resembling "the glimpses of the moon" (*Hamlet,* I, iv, 53): Inverness castle (not Scone, the Scottish royal palace), whose "air / Nimbly and sweetly recommends itself / Unto our gentle senses" (*Macbeth,* I, vi, 1–3), and the striking images of Othello's reference to his travels after his redemption from captivity, "antres vast and desarts idle" (I, iii, 140). The "famed performer" is William Charles Macready, whom Emerson called upon in Boston and saw in *Hamlet* at the National Theatre on November 15, 1843 (*L,* III, 223). Edward Waldo Emerson (*W,* IV, 354–355) quotes from an article by Edwin P. Whipple ("Some Recollections of Ralph Waldo Emerson," *Harper's New Monthly Magazine,* 65 [September 1882], 576–587) that recalls this anecdote in its prelecture form. A few days after the Macready performance the young Whipple accompanied Emerson driving home after a lecture; they discussed the acting of Shakespeare's plays, and Emerson confessed his inability to appreciate Shakespearean acting because he was always "carried away by the poet.... [Then] actor, theatre, all vanished in view of the solving and dissolving imagination, which could reduce this big globe and all it inherits into mere 'glimpses of the moon.'" Emerson glanced as he drove along, according to Whipple, at "the same moon which must have given birth to Shakspeare's thought." Whipple later heard Emerson deliver the lecture on "Shakspeare" and quotes in his article part of this passage from his recollection or notes, adding from "the printed lecture" a favorite sentence ("The recitation begins ... inaccessible homes"), which presumably was not in the lecture when Whipple heard it delivered.

119.29 AUBREY AND ROWE, John Aubrey (1626–1697), an English antiquarian, collected anecdotes about Shakespeare. In a later generation Nicholas Rowe, a poet and dramatist, was Shakespeare's first important editor, with major editions in 1709 and 1714. He was also Shakespeare's first biographer, relying heavily on legends from sources like Thomas Betterton, the actor.

120.8 HIS AMPLE PICTURES ... GREAT HEART. Warwick could be either Richard Beauchamp, who appears in the second part of *Henry IV, Henry V,* and the first part of *Henry VI,* or his son-in-law Richard Neville, "the King-Maker," who figures in the last two parts of *Henry VI* and who is noted particularly for his generous hospitality by Emerson in *English Traits* (*W,* V, 176). This would seem to align him with the protagonist of *Timon of Athens,* at least in the opening scenes, and with the good-hearted Antonio of *The Merchant of Venice.* Shakespeare's "delight in troops of friends" echoes *Macbeth,* V, iii, 25.

120.18 AS TALMA TAUGHT NAPOLEON? François Joseph Talma (1763–1826), the great tragedian of the French theater during the Revolution, was an admired and intimate friend of Napoleon, who took him to Erfurt in 1808 to perform before the royalty gathered for the treaty and again in 1813 to Dresden.

120.22 SOME ABLE AND APPRECIATING ... ITS APPLICATION. In the late summer of 1849, before completing *Representative Men* for the press, Emerson wrote this passage in his journal TU; there, however, it began: "My Edinburgh critic of Shakspeare &, it seems, Gervinus also, think no criticism valuable" (*JMN*, XI, 150). Georg Gottfried Gervinus (1805–1871), a German literary and political historian, had just begun to publish *Shakespeare*, 4 vols. (1849–1850; translated as *Shakespeare Commentaries* in 1862), which illustrates, play by play, the moral unity of the dramatic structure. If Emerson, as the journal passage suggests, was uncertain about Gervinus as a critic who insisted on "dramatic merit," there was no doubt about "My Edinburgh critic." Pretty much scorning the books at hand, the reviewer forcefully condemns the modern German philosophical criticism of Shakespeare (not mentioning Gervinus) and the poetic, that is, Coleridgean, English practice. He finds there is some hopeful sign that the contemporary French critics are turning to dramatic criticism, which he distinguishes from theatrical criticism ("Shakspeare's Critics: English and Foreign," *The Edinburgh Review*, 90 [July 1849], 21–41). The article is impressive, and it challenges Emerson's central position, which he takes pains to defend in this paragraph.

122.18 SOLAR MICROSCOPE. A microscope that projects its enlarged image by means of sunlight.

122.21 DAGUERRE LEARNED ... ETCH A MILLION. The French pioneer of photography, Louis Jacques Mandé Daguerre (1789–1851), published in 1839 his process of making the daguerreotype on a silver plate coated with silver iodide. Almost simultaneous developments, primarily by Fox Talbot, resulted in a different method of photography that allowed reproduction of prints, as the daguerreotype did not.

123.21 EPICURUS SAYS ... PARTAKE OF THEM. According to the entry in Emerson's journal (*JMN*, VI, 341) on which this sentence is based, "Epicurus tells us from Xenophon, that, Poetry had such charms of pleasure in it, as were sufficient even to make a lover forget he was in love to partake of them. *Plutarch's Morals.* Vol II p. 40." It is true that Xenophon said something like this—but not about poetry; nor was it Epicurus who quoted him. In *Cynegeticus*, a treatise on hunting, Xenophon, discussing the hunting of the hare, wrote: "So charming is the sight that to see a hare tracked, found, pursued and caught is enough to make any man forget his heart's desire" (ch. V, sec. 33). Plutarch, in his essay "That it is not possible to live pleasurably according to the Doctrine of *Epicurus*," adapted this figure from Xenophon and applied it to poetry, saying of the poets that "they seem to do what was once said by

Xenophon, to make a Man even to forget the Joys of Love, so powerful and overcoming is the Pleasures they bring us" (*Plutarch's Morals*, trans. by Several Hands, 5 vols. [London, 1718—the edition that Emerson owned], II, 171); he went on to point out that Epicurus (341-270 B.C.) and his philosophical school had no place in their concept of pleasure for such higher pleasures as that of poetry. In another essay in the *Morals*, "How a Young Man ought to Hear . . . Poems," Plutarch again referred to Epicurus' indifference to poetry. The translator of that essay, in a particularly pedantic and turgid footnote from which Emerson was quoting in his journal entry, wrote: "in the same Treatise [on the doctrine of Epicurus] he [Plutarch] acquaints us, that *Epicurus* had the same Opinion concerning *Poetry*, so that, though he [Plutarch] tells us from *Xenophon*, that *Poetry had such charms of Pleasure in it, as were sufficient even to make a Lover forget he was in Love to partake of them;* yet he adds, *That the* Epicureans *neither did partake of that Pleasure,* . . . nor would" (*Morals*, trans. Several Hands, II, 39-40). Emerson evidently mistook the second "he" to refer to Epicurus rather than Plutarch and wrongly attributed the saying to the former.

123.25 SAADI SAYS . . . WITH REPENTANCE?" This quotation is condensed from *JMN*, IX, 37-38, where it is identified as from *The Gulistan, or Flower-Garden, of Shaikh Sadī of Shīraz* . . . , trans. James Ross (London, 1823), p. 36.

124.23 "THE HEAVENS . . . IN JEST?" See 54.8-10 and note.

124.28 IT IS BUT . . . EVENING'S TALE: Emerson deliberately varies the usual forms of the titles of these plays (by not capitalizing all the nouns, by adding " 's" to "Midsummer," and by inserting "evening's" in "Winter's Tale") to show that he is using them in a transferred sense.

124.35 TASSO, CERVANTES, Torquato Tasso (1544-1595), Italian poet, author of the epic *Gerusalemme Liberata;* Miguel de Cervantes Saavedra (1547-1616), Spanish writer, author of *Don Quixote.*

129.5 IT IS SWEDENBORG'S THEORY . . . LITTLE KIDNEYS, &C. See 64.28-65.7 and note.

130.10 "GOD HAS GRANTED," . . . ITS OWN TONGUE." In *JMN*, VI, 292, Emerson indicated that his source for the quotation was Goethe, *Werke*, XLVI, 262, a review of Carlyle's *German Romance*, vol. 4. See the Koran, sura X, verse 47.

130.19 "NO CAPUCHIN," The phrase is quoted from Louis Antoine Fauvelet de Bourrienne, *Private Memoirs of Napoleon Bonaparte, During the Periods of the Directory, the Consulate, and the Empire*, 4 vols. (London, 1830), I, 188-189.

Emerson borrowed all four volumes from the Boston Athenæum in January 1845, and these vivid memoirs by Napoleon's private secretary, who broke with him in 1802, are one of his major sources in this lecture. Later editions are considerably expanded from other sources in an attempt to correct Bourrienne and supplement his lack of military detail, but Emerson used only this translation based on the first edition.

130.35 MIRABEAU PLAGIARIZED . . . NEXT DAY'S SESSION.   Honoré Gabriel Riquetti, comte de Mirabeau (1749–1791), popular political leader in the early stages of the French Revolution, was noted for his fiery eloquence in the States-General and the Constituent Assembly. Emerson improved somewhat upon the retort in this anecdote, which served another purpose in the account by Mirabeau's speech-writer, Pierre Etienne Louis Dumont (1759–1829), in *Recollections of Mirabeau, and of the Two First Legislative Assemblies of France* (London, 1832), pp. 63–67. Emerson copied other passages, but not this one, into *JMN*, IX, 137–138, from either this edition of the translation or the Philadelphia, 1833, edition. The British diplomat Thomas Bruce, seventh Earl of Elgin (1766–1841), later arranged to have the Elgin Marbles brought to England from Greece.

131.20 HE LEVELS THE ALPS: See 135.26–28 and note. The phrasing may derive from Francesco Antommarchi, *The Last Days of the Emperor Napoleon*, 2 vols. (London, 1825), I, 349, which lists as one of Napoleon's achievements "The Alps levelled!" Emerson borrowed this volume from the Boston Athenæum at the beginning of January 1845.

131.21 SAVANS, STATISTS,   The obsolete French spelling for savants, men of learning or science, was commonly used in nineteenth-century English. It is uncertain whether Emerson here uses "statists" to mean statisticians (as at 62.11) or in the older sense of statesmen or politicians (as at 145.1).

131.35 FONTANES . . . HUMAN MIND."   Louis de Fontanes was president of the legislative body under the Consulate in the spring months of 1804, during which the maneuvers to declare the First Consul hereditary Emperor were enacted. First the tribunate proposed the elevation of Napoleon; then the senate confirmed; and finally, as the legislative body was not in session, Fontanes secured the support of those members in Paris and carried to Napoleon an address on behalf of the legislative body expressing its approval of the measure of the tribunate and the senate. Emerson indicated in *JMN*, V, 242, where his account is precise in its details, that his source was a review of A. C. Thibaudeau's *Mémoirs sur le consulat . . .* and *Le Consulat et l'empire . . .* in *The Foreign Quarterly Review*, XVII (July 1836), 359.

132.1 THE ADVOCATES OF LIBERTY . . . "LAFAYETTE IS AN IDEOLOGIST."   Bourrienne writes: "The word *idéologue* was often in Bonaparte's mouth; and in using it he endeavoured to throw ridicule on those men whom he fancied to have a tendency towards the doctrine of indefinite perfectibility. He esteemed them for their morality, yet he looked upon them as dreamers, seeking for the type of a universal constitution, and considering the character of man in the abstract only" (II, 90). Passing through Geneva in 1800, Napoleon met Jacques Necker (1732–1804), French financier and statesman under both the monarchy and the republic and father of Madame de Staël. Disappointed with the man, Napoleon told Bourrienne, "M. Necker . . . said nothing remarkable. He is an ideologist. A banker. It is impossible that such a man can have any but narrow views" (II, 167). Lafayette (see note to 9.28), in addition to his military role in the American Revolution, was important politically in France as a moderate revolutionary leader. He was named counsellor by Napoleon but resisted Napoleon's rise to imperial power. In recounting the opposition to declaring Napoleon consul for life in 1802, Bourrienne says that Napoleon, "with the view to disparaging the real friends of constitutional liberty, always called them *idéologues,* or terrorists," and then goes on to detail Napoleon's difficult relations with Lafayette and to quote Lafayette's letter of opposition to the vote without strong guarantees of political liberty (II, 321–327; see also note to 140.12). But Emerson, before he read Bourrienne, wrote in *JMN,* VIII, 88, "Napoleon hated Lafayette & the ideologists" and again, on page 105, "Bonaparte did not like ideologists," probably inferring the connection from his earlier readng of the review cited in note to 131.35, which several times uses the word "ideologists" to describe the opponents to the consulship-for-life, without naming Lafayette in particular.

132.4 AN ITALIAN PROVERB . . . TOO GOOD."   Emerson alludes to this saying as early as 1823, but he calls it a "Spanish adage" (*JMN,* II, 130).

132.33 THE ART OF WAR . . . FORCES IN DETAIL.   The first clause of the second sentence Emerson attributed in *JMN,* IX, 155, to Bourrienne, III, 296. Much earlier, in *JMN,* VI, 33, 229, he had attributed the idea, "the leading maxim of Buonaparte," to Count Philippe Paul de Ségur, whose differently phrased version appears in *History of the Expedition to Russia, Undertaken by the Emperor Napoleon, in the Year 1812,* 2 vols. (London, 1825), II, 8–9. Emerson also may have remembered that Sir Walter Scott emphasized this Napoleonic strategy in *The Life of Napoleon Buonaparte,* 3 vols. (Philadelphia, 1827), I, 302–303; III, 359. This was the edition Emerson owned, and Scott's words may be echoed in the later phrase "destroy his forces in detail." But the immediate source of this maxim of strategy is Bourrienne. There is, however, no convincing source known for Emerson's attribution to Napoleon of marching "always on the enemy at an angle" as a maneuver. Frank Davidson, in his edition of *Napoleon; or, The Man of the World* (Bloomington, Ind., 1947), p. 38, understood Emerson to mean "moving troops at an angle" and interpreted that apparently as marching in echelon, citing *The Confidential Correspondence of Napoleon Bonaparte with His Brother Joseph, Sometime King of Spain,* 2 vols. (New

York, 1856), I, 168, 169, 174, 177, and John Gibson Lockhart, *The History of Napoleon Buonaparte,* 2 vols., The Family Library, nos. 1 and 2 (London, 1829), II, 100. These citations are in the first instance advice by Napoleon that his brother maintain his troops in echelon and in the second instance, cited from a work that Emerson borrowed from the Boston Athenæum in January 1845, the account of an unsuccessful tactical move by Napoleon at the Battle of Asperne in 1809. An echelon is a formation of units of troops whereby each unit is somewhat to the right or left of the unit to its rear, forming a steplike front. A more probable meaning to marching "always on the enemy at an angle" would be the maneuver of attack in oblique order, whereby an attacking general masses increasing strength against one wing of an enemy, while secondary forces keep the remainder of the line under pressure in order to prevent the moving of reserves to the key sector. This ancient strategy, important in the warfare of Frederick the Great, became a significant part of late Napoleonic strategic battle. Emerson's phrasing, however, is ambiguous and may mean the same as his unambiguous journal entry of 1844 or 1845 in which his contextual concern is oratory not military tactics: "Napoleon's famous tactics of marching on the angle of an army, & so always presenting a superiority of numbers, is the orator's secret also" (*JMN,* IX, 122–123). This phrasing he retained in "Eloquence" (*W,* VII, 84), and it suggests that Emerson really has no source in fact for this imputed Napoleonic maneuver.

133.21 "MY HAND OF IRON," . . . WITH MY HEAD." The quotation is identified in *JMN,* V, 508, as from Count Emmanuel Augustin Dieudonné de Las Cases, *Mémorial de Sainte Hélène. Journal of the Private Life and Conversations of the Emperor Napoleon at Saint Helena,* 4 vols. (Boston, 1823), IV, vii, 123, a translation Emerson quoted from extensively in 1838. While he found in the conversations of Napoleon and Las Cases, his companion and informal secretary during the first year of exile at Saint Helena, "much rhodomontade . . . much about glory & principles that is not glory & that are not principles," he also found that "Napoleon in Las Cases has an admirable candor which belongs to philosophy, rails at no enemy, puts every crime down to the ignorance of the agent, & stands ready to make a marshal of him one day" (*JMN,* V, 311, 482).

133.26 HIS FAVORITE RHETORIC . . . CREATURE OF CIRCUMSTANCES." The point Emerson makes here is derived from a pastiche of his reading. The first clause, for example, may echo a passage in a work he borrowed from the Boston Athenæum in January 1845, Armand Augustin Louis Caulaincourt, *Recollections of Caulincourt, Duke of Vicenza,* 2 vols. (London, 1838), I, 22–23: "When the Emperor was informed [at the Battle of Dresden] of [the traitor] Moreau's death [just as he entered the enemy camp], he hastily turned to the Duke de Vicenza, and whispered in his ear—'My star! Caulincourt! My fortunate star!' . . . The words which he whispered in the ear of his friend were characteristic of his feelings—'My star! Caulincourt!' " The rest of the sentence may reflect a passage in another work Emerson borrowed from the Boston Athenæum in January 1845, Joseph Fouché, *The Memoirs of Joseph Fouché, Duke of Otranto* (Boston, 1825), p. 215: After the imperial victories in the Prussian campaign of 1806, France "prided herself upon having been saluted with the name of the great nation by her emperor, who had triumphed over the genius and the work of Frederic; and Napoleon believed himself the son of Destiny, called to break every sceptre." The sentences on Napoleon's elevation by marching with great masses and with events rather than by the commission of great crimes is a mixture of close paraphrase and quotation that Emerson recorded in *JMN*, V, 472, 474, drawn from Barry Edward O'Meara, *Napoleon in Exile; or, A Voice from St. Helena*, 2 vols. (Boston, 1823), I, 297–298. Emerson alluded in his journals and notebooks five times to Napoleon's belief that, as a "child of circumstances," he was irreplaceable, but he never identified the source. Emerson probably remembered a passage from a work he owned and read, Victor Cousin, *Introduction to the Philosophy of History*, trans. Henning Gotfried Linberg (Boston, 1832), p. 305: "A soldier who had seated himself upon a throne was once told: Sire, the education of your son should be watched over with great attention, he must be educated so that he may replace you. Replace me! answered he, I could not replace myself; I am the child of circumstances." In April 1838 Emerson read with approval the anecdotes, opinions, and reflections of Napoleon published by O'Meara, his surgeon at Saint Helena. Among the extracts Emerson copied into his journal, he wrote, "I like the man in O'Meara's picture. He is goodnatured as greatness always is & not pompous" (*JMN*, V, 472).

134.7 IN 1796, HE . . . AS MY THOUGHTS." Emerson noted in *JMN*, IX, 143, that Napoleon's letter is printed in *Memoirs of the History of France during the Reign of Napoleon, Dictated by the Emperor at Saint Helena . . .*, 7 vols. (London, 1823-1824), IV, 472–474. For more information on this work and Emerson's use of it see note to 144.8.

134.30 "INCIDENTS OUGHT NOT . . . SYSTEM AT ALL." Both quotations are drawn from *Memoirs of the History of France . . .*, IV, 277, 281 (*JMN*, IX, 116, 142). The first is called "his usual adage," and the second is Napoleon's response to the hasty plans of the Directory to go to war with Austria over insults to French representatives.

134.36 HE WOULD SHORTEN A STRAIGHT LINE The figure, jotted down in *JMN*, IX, 145, is drawn from Bourrienne, II, 467, where it is applied to Napoleon's dislike of literature as being time-consuming.

135.6 "SIRE, GENERAL CLARKE . . . GENERAL JUNOT . . . FORWARD, FORWARD!" Henri Jacques Guillaume Clarke (1765-1818), Duke of Feltre, was educated as a soldier and joined Napoleon in Italy, where he served in various capacities until 1799, when he became a councillor of state and subsequently served in administrative positions. High in the favor of Napoleon, though never of great ability, he became war minister. Andoche Junot (1771–1813), Duke of Abrantès, served with heroic distinction in Napoleon's early campaigns in Italy and Egypt. Rewarded with various administrative posts for his services, he was brash, arrogant, and sometimes an embarrassment, but he was a courageous soldier at Austerlitz, in Portugal, Spain, and Russia. No source has been found for the dialogue here quoted; the use of the word "Sire" indicates that if based on fact the incident reported would have occurred after 1804, when, as emperor, Napoleon was first so addressed.

135.10 SERUZIER, A COLONEL . . . WATERS OF THE LAKE." Emerson's secondhand source was his young friend Edward Bangs, a lawyer with a literary turn, to whom he apparently wrote in late October 1849, asking information about this anecdote. Bangs's reply, now in Columbia University Library, Emerson received with gratitude: "I am heartily obliged," he wrote, "by your efficient attention to my request. I am indeed quite proud of so much learning suddenly mustered to aid, & can hardly deny myself the ostentation of a note to unfold it in. The authorities will amply vouch for all I want of the anecdote" (*L*, IV, 168–170). But in quoting "at second hand" from Théodore Jean Joseph, baron Séruzier, *Mémoirs militaires du B[aron] Séruzier, colonel d'artillerie légère . . . mis en ordre et rédigés par son ami, M. Le Mière de Corvey . . .* (Paris, 1823), pp. 28–29, Emerson still had difficulties with the number of Russians and Austrians killed on the ice, as his manuscript revisions and footnote indicate. He did not adopt Séruzier's "quinze mille" nor Lockhart's "nearly 20,000" (I, 298) nor other figures he might have known, all of which were exaggerations. The Battle of Austerlitz, twelve miles south of Brünn in Moravia, was Napoleon's most brilliant military victory. On December 2, 1805, he decisively defeated the Austrian and Russian armies under Emperor Francis II and Czar Alexander I, destroying the third coalition against him and forcing the Treaty of Pressburg. The battle is sometimes called the Battle of the Three Emperors.

135.26 "THERE SHALL BE NO ALPS," . . . ANY TOWN IN FRANCE. This quotation and its context were probably derived from Bourrienne, II, 134, which reads: "In the great work of bridges and highways, Bonaparte's chief object was to remove the obstacles and barriers which nature had raised up as the limits of old France. . . . Thus in Savoy, a road, smooth as a garden-walk, superseded the dangerous risings and fallings of the wood of Bramant; thus was the passage of Mount Cenis a pleasant promenade at almost every season of the year; thus did the Simplon bow his head, and Bonaparte might have said, 'There are now no Alps,' with more reason than Louis XVI. said, 'There are now no Pyrenees.' " In the edition cited here, the one Emerson used, there is a misprint, and other editions correctly attribute the saying to Louis XIV, who is reputed to have made the statement on the ascension to the Spanish throne by his grandson, the Duke d'Anjou. It would be pleasant to think that the penciled correction in the copy Emerson borrowed from the Boston Athenæum is his.

135.31 HE RISKED EVERYTHING, AND SPARED NOTHING, The phrasing, which Emerson used in *JMN*, IX, 158, is from Bourrienne, II, 27.

136.2 "THE GRAND PRINCIPLE ... CAPABLE OF MAKING." The quotation, modified from "an axiom" to "the grand principle," is drawn from *Memoirs of the History of France* . . . , IV, 321. See *JMN*, IX, 142.

136.8 TO A REGIMENT ... THE ENEMY'S RANKS." The passage is part of an anecdote Emerson recorded more fully in *JMN*, V, 508, where it is identified as taken from Las Cases, IV, vii, 121–122. The regiment, consisting of "many raw troops," was moved to an enthusiasm presaging its "memorable victory" in part of the Battle of Jena, where on October 14, 1806, Napoleon decisively defeated the Prussians.

136.13 IT IS PLAIN THAT IN ITALY ... ARCOLA ... LONATO ... TAKEN PRIS-ONER. Napoleon made his great military reputation against the Austrians in his brilliant Italian campaign of 1796–97. The incidents Emerson refers to were available to him from a number of sources, and neither in this passage nor its draft in *JMN*, IX, 144, can a specific source be identified. Lockhart's version of the incident at the three-day Battle of Arcola in November 1796, where Napoleon personally and heroically led one of the several charges into the town over one of the three narrow dikes across marshy terrain, is memorably detailed: "Buonaparte, perceiving the necessity of carrying the point . . . now threw himself on the bridge, and seizing a standard, urged his grenadiers once more to the charge. The fire was tremendous; once more the French gave way. Napoleon himself, lost in the tumult, was borne backwards, forced over the dyke, and had nearly been smothered in the morass, while some of the advancing Austrians were already between him and his baffled column. His imminent danger was observed: the soldiers caught the alarm, and rushing forwards, with the cry 'Save the general,' overthrew the Germans with irresistible violence, plucked Napoleon from the bog, and carried the bridge. This was the first battle of Arcola" (I, 69–70). Similar accounts of the incident Emerson would have known in Napoleon's *Memoirs of the History of France*, III, 361–363, and Scott, I, 349–350; a different version is recounted by O'Meara, II, 161. Emerson might also have remembered Lockhart's account of Napoleon's ingenious narrow escape immediately after the strategic victory at Lonato in August 1796: "One of the many defeated divisions of the [Austrian] army, wandering about in some anxiety . . . came suddenly on Lonato, the scene of the late battle, at a moment when Napoleon was there with only his staff and guards about him. He knew not that any considerable body of Austrians remained together in the neighbourhood; and but for the presence of mind must have been their prisoner . . . The [Austrian] officer sent to demand the surrender of the town was brought blindfolded, as is the custom, to his headquarters; Buonaparte, by a secret sign, caused his whole staff to draw up around him, and when the bandage was removed from the messenger's eyes, saluted him thus: 'What means this insolence? Do you beard the French general in the middle of his army?' The German recognized the person of Napoleon, and retreated stammering and blushing. He assured his commander that Lonato was occupied by the French in numbers that made resistance impossible; 4000 men laid down their arms; and then discovered that, if they had used them, nothing could have prevented Napoleon from being their prize" (I, 57–58). Scott's account is even more detailed (I, 339). Las Cases, I, ii, 1–3, 7–8, 39–40, 66–69, and Scott, I, 327–328, relate incidents of other personal risk to Napoleon in the same campaign.

136.19 HE FOUGHT SIXTY BATTLES.   Emerson first wrote down this information in *JMN*, V, 475, during the time he was reading Las Cases, where the observation is made: "Napoleon, during his military career, fought sixty battles; Caesar fought but fifty" (IV, vii, 119). On the same page of his journal Emerson recorded excerpts from O'Meara, I, 298, but overlooked or rejected the attribution there to Napoleon: "I have fought fifty pitched battles, almost all of which I have gained." Bourrienne, "Introduction," I, x, speaks of Napoleon's "sixty victories."

136.20 "MY POWER WOULD FALL . . . MAINTAIN ME."   Emerson took the quotation from Bourrienne, II, 25, as he indicated in *JMN*, IX, 160.

136.28 PUNCTUALITY.   Here Emerson uses the word in its somewhat archaic sense of exactness, minuteness, or preciseness. See also "punctual" at 137.5.

136.31 "MY AMBITION," HE SAYS, . . . COLD NATURE."   Quoted with slight modification from O'Meara, I, 298.

136.32 IN ONE OF HIS CONVERSATIONS . . . IN THIS PARTICULAR."   Las Cases, I, ii, 10.

137.6 "AT MONTEBELLO . . . OF A BATTLE."   The engagement at Montebello, in the Po Valley, occurred on June 9, 1800, four days before the great victory of Marengo, where François Etienne de Kellermann (1770–1835) also distinguished himself. See note to 145.16. The slightly condensed quotation, as Emerson indicated in *JMN*, IX, 153, is taken from Antommarchi, I, 167.

137.12 "BEFORE HE FOUGHT . . . REQUIRED AN ANSWER.   All three illustrations of Napoleon's "prudence and good sense" are drawn from the account of his private secretary: Bourrienne, II, 27, 22; I, 73. The two quotations are so identified by Emerson in *JMN,* IX, 158, 154. From the paraphrased third illustration Emerson deleted Bourrienne's exception of letters "by extraordinary courier."

137.28 WILLIAM OF ORANGE, Emerson probably refers to William I, Prince of Orange (1533–1584), often called William the Silent. That this great leader in the struggle against Spain for the independence of the Netherlands qualifies as "working king" is made clear by Emerson's use of the phrase elsewhere: in *JMN,* VIII, 370, he is "oftener off the throne . . . than on it," and in "The Young American," *CW,* I, 238, "Mr. Johnson, *Working king,*" "has a talent for righting wrong, for administering difficult affairs" and other talents, but no crown. See also the entry for this line in Annex A, Appendix 2, where other "working kings" are listed in the manuscript—the complete list also appearing in Chapman's London edition.

137.35 HIS CONTEMPT . . . FORGOT NOTHING." Emerson's paraphrases of his source, O'Meara, are more accurate in *JMN,* V, 472, 473, than here. O'Meara, recording the conversation of August 27, 1816, wrote that Napoleon ridiculed the now-returned aristocracy of the prerevolutionary days: " 'These old emigrants hate, and are jealous of all who are not hereditary asses like themselves.' I asked him if the king of Prussia was a man of talent. 'Who,' said he, 'the king of Prussia?' He burst into a fit of laughter. 'He a man of talent! The greatest blockhead on earth . . . (A blockhead, who has neither talents nor information.) A Don Quixote in appearance. I know him well. He cannot hold a conversation for five minutes . . .' He then conversed . . . about the Bourbons. 'They want,' said he, 'to introduce the old system of nobility into the army . . . to confine it entirely to the old nobility, . . . to emigres like that old blockhead Montchenu. When you have seen Montchenu, you have seen all the old nobility of France before the revolution. Such were all the race, and such they have returned, ignorant, vain, and arrogant as they left it. *Ils n'ont rien appris, ils n'ont rien oublié.* (They have learned nothing, they have forgotten nothing.)' " (I, 88). The last saying, however, Napoleon later applied to the Bourbons, but not in the context from which Emerson quoted it in *JMN,* V, 473 (O'Meara, II, 118). Though Emerson and O'Meara may not have known it, the observation, applied either to the Bourbons or their courtiers, had currency as early as the 1790s.

138.5 THOSE WHO HAD TO DEAL . . . CONSIDERABLE SUMS. Examples of Napoleon's personal intervention in checking public accounts for error and graft are reported in Las Cases, I, ii, 132–133. Bourrienne reports his own role in examining the inflated debts of Josephine at the insistence of the First Consul and remarks on her continued extravagance as Empress (II, 122ff).

138.19 "WHEN WALKING WITH MRS BALCOMBE . . . BURDEN, MADAM.' "
Emerson identified the source of the anecdote in *JMN,* V, 485, as Las Cases, I,

i, 160–161. Jane Balcombe was the wife of William Balcombe, the principal merchant at Saint Helena. Emerson's source, which he follows in his journal passage, uses the word "slaves" instead of "servants," accurately translating the French.

138.23 IN THE TIME . . . THE COMMON PEOPLE." With only slight modification both sentences are quoted from Las Cases, IV, vii, 120, as Emerson indicated in *JMN*, V, 474. Napoleon, by his conquests, vastly expanded the art collections of the Louvre, since the sixteenth century the principal royal gallery in Paris. It was opened to the public in 1793.

138.31 THE BEST DOCUMENT . . . TO THEIR LEADER. This passage is derived from Scott, who describes the celebration of the soldiers, "an extempore illumination" made with bunches of lighted hay on poles, when Napoleon's incognito presence was discovered among them in the night before the great victory at Austerlitz on December 2, 1805, which would be the first anniversary of his coronation as emperor. Napoleon's promise to his soldiers, made during this pre-battle celebration, he confirmed in the morning with a proclamation (II, 79). The passage also reflects in some of its detail Lockhart's account (I, 297). See 141.24–27 and note.

139.5 HE KNEW, AS WELL AS ANY JACOBIN . . . BLOOD DITCH-WATER." Louis Antoine Henri de Bourbon Condé, Duc d'Enghien (1772–1804) was an extremely well-connected young leader of the *émigrés*, refugees from the French Revolution. Until the peace of 1801, he had been distinguished in the military opposition to the Revolution. In 1804 he was erroneously thought to be involved in a conspiracy against the First Consul, was secretly arrested in Baden, and brought to France for trial. The charges were changed to having borne arms against France in the last war and conspiracy in the new coalition, and he was irregularly tried and shot, becoming a celebrated international cause because of his royal blood. There ensued much dispute over Napoleon's intentions and direct responsibility, which he did little to clarify. Bourrienne devoted three chapters to the controversy and its consequences—fatal, according to the former secretary. Las Cases, whom Emerson is summarizing here, reports that Napoleon at Saint Helena had two ways of arguing the case. Privately he admitted that he might have been severe in the case of the young martyr, but that "all the forms required by law had been regularly observed and strictly attended to." Among strangers, Las Cases continues, Napoleon argued that he "had the right of nature, of legitimate self-defence," for the Duke and his party and family "had constantly but one object in view, that of taking away my life. . . . Blood for blood; such is the natural, inevitable, and infallible law of retaliation: woe to him who provokes it!" Presumably it is this argument that Emerson likens to the radical arguments of the Jacobins, the extremists of the Revolution, and Emerson's direct quotation (all he recorded in *JMN*, V, 503) is his polishing of the most memorable and telling clause in the long harangue reported by Las Cases (IV, vii, 131–136; quotation from p. 133).

139.14 THE TUILERIES   This sixteenth-century royal palace, the principal residence in Paris of Napoleon, had been little used by the kings until the revolutionaries forced Louis XVI and his family to live there—in Paris, rather than at Versailles. It was burned during the violence of 1871.

139.29 IN 1814, WHEN ADVISED . . . OF THE FAUBOURGS."   Bourrienne, the source Emerson cited in *JMN*, IX, 157, gives both the context and a further twist to this sentence: In January 1814, during the invasion of France, the hard-pressed Napoleon was advised to seek the aid of the Jacobins. "For a moment," Bourrienne continues, "he was inclined to adopt this advice. He rode on horseback through the [working-class] suburbs of Saint-Antoine and Saint-Marceau, courted the populace, affectionately replied to their acclamations, and he thought he saw the possibility of turning to account the attachment which the people evinced for him. On his return to the palace some prudent persons ventured to represent to him, that instead of courting this absurd sort of popularity it would be more advisable to rely on the nobility, and the higher classes of society:—'Gentlemen,' replied he, 'you may say what you please, but in the situation in which I stand, my only nobility is the rabble of the faubourgs, and I know of no rabble but the nobility whom I have created.' This was a strange compliment to all ranks, for it was only saying that they were all rabble together" (IV, 256).

140.1 IN ITALY, HE . . . DANDOLO AND MELZI."   In *JMN*, IX, 145, Emerson identified his source for the passage, including "he sought for men, and found none," as Bourrienne, I, 72. Vincenzo Dandolo (1758–1819), a Venetian chemist and patriot, and Francesco Melzi d'Eril (1753–1816), a Milanese politician, joined Napoleon in 1797 in the effort to rid northern Italy of Austrian rule. Both were instrumental in the Cisalpine Republic. Dandolo, made a count by Napoleon and rewarded with the Legion of Honor, later distinguished himself by constructive agricultural reforms while governing Dalmatia under Napoleon; Melzi became chancellor of the Napoleonic Kingdom of Italy and was created Duke of Lodi.

140.6 TO ONE OF HIS OLDEST FRIENDS . . . WHAT I WISH THEM."   In *JMN*, IX, 145, Emerson identified this comment as taken from Bourrienne, II, 334. It is addressed to Bourrienne, his private secretary, who had been his friend from their childhood days at the military school in Brienne.

140.12 HE COULD NOT CONFOUND FOX . . . NEY, AND AUGEREAU.   The last grouping of names represents Napoleon's outstanding military commanders. Jean Lannes (1769–1809), Duke of Montebello and marshal of France, was one of Napoleon's ablest generals in the Italian and Egyptian campaigns, distinguished himself at Montebello, Austerlitz, Jena, and elsewhere, and was killed at the battle of Essling (see note to 145.16). Geraud Christophe Michel Duroc (1772–1813), Duke of Friouli, after the Italian campaign of 1796–97, where he distinguished himself, was Napoleon's aide-de-camp, responsible for his personal safety, and showed many acts of heroism in this capacity. Jean Baptiste Kléber (1753–1800), having served in the Austrian army, joined the Revolution and became one of the most effective generals, putting down the royalist uprising in the Vendée, before joining Napoleon as an effective leader in the campaign in Egypt (1798), where as Napoleon's successor he was assassinated by a Turk. Joseph Marie, Count Dessaix (1764–1834), served Napoleon from the Italian campaign to the Hundred Days, distinguishing himself particularly at the battle of Wagram and suffering wounds twice in the Russian campaign. Andrea Masséna (1758–1817), Duke of Rivoli and Prince of Essling, though he slipped from favor after 1810, was an able, intelligent, and heroic marshal in battle. Joachim Murat (1767–1815), marshal of France and, from 1808, King of Naples, was a brilliant commander of cavalry in Egypt, in the Russian campaign, and at Leipzig. Michel Ney (1769–1815), marshal of France, Duke of Elchingen, and Prince of Moskowa, made a brilliant rise in the Revolutionary armies, seized Elchingen, conquered the Tyrol, and was decisive in the battle of Friedland; he is best known for his rear-guard defense in the retreat from Moscow and his role in supporting Napoleon at Waterloo after having at first joined the Restoration. Pierre François Charles Augereau (1757–1816), marshal of France and Duke of Castiglione, was something of a soldier of fortune before joining the Revolutionary army, where he rose rapidly; under Napoleon in Italy, at Millesimo, Lodi, and Castiglione, and later at Jena he did heroic service even though sometimes in disgrace. As Emerson points out and as their imperial titles suggest, these military leaders were honored for their very real abilities, even in some instances military genius, by Napoleon, despite various periods of disgrace and in some instances defection at the fall of their Emperor. Bourrienne's record of Napoleon's judgments and the characterizations in Napoleon's *Memoirs of the History of France* repeatedly show a generosity on behalf of true ability. Napoleon also extended respect to his able opponents, those named in the first list. Although Charles James Fox (1749–1806), the brilliant British orator and liberal statesman, is known for his opposition to coercion of the American colonies and was a friend of the French Revolution and opponent of the repressive internal policies of the British government in the wars it waged against the Directory and Napoleon, he supported the wars of the third coalition against Napoleon even after he became foreign secretary briefly in 1806. This reformist and liberal champion, even when he met Napoleon in Paris, was not impressed by the betrayer of the Revolution. Napoleon characteristically remarked to Bourrienne, "Mr. Fox is truly a great man, and pleases me much" (II, 334). William Pitt (see note to 9.28), Fox's great and equally capable rival, as prime minister effected many reforms, but in the crises with France he suppressed the right of habeas corpus and instituted other measures to silence his radical opposition. His first and second coalitions (1793 and 1798) against France were ineffective except for naval victories. He was recalled to office (1804) in the crisis of an expected invasion of England and formed with greater dedication a third coalition of nations against Napoleon, but he died after hearing of the victory at Austerlitz, which took Austria out of the coalition and caused Russia to withdraw its armies. Lazare Nicholas Marguerite Carnot (1753–1823), a military engineer before the Revolution, became prominent militarily and politically by organizing and leading the army; he was called "the organizer of victory." He was one of the conservative members of the Directory overthrown by a coup in 1797, but he came out of retirement to be minister of war in 1799 and 1800 under the Consulate. As a sincere republican, he opposed Napoleon's seizure of power and was pensioned by the Emperor in 1809 to return to his old expertise of writing on the theory of fortifications. In 1814 he came to Napoleon's support as a general and as military governor of Antwerp and stuck with him in the Hundred Days. Napoleon's political and ideological mistrust of Lafayette (see note to 132.1) was tempered by respect. Lafayette refused Napoleon's offer of a seat in the Senate, Bourrienne reports, but "he continued nevertheless to see the Consul, and to be with him on terms of reciprocal esteem" (II, 324–325). After Lafayette's opposition to the consulship for life, Napoleon "was by no means pleased with M. de La Fayette's scruples," Bourrienne tells us, yet he quotes Napoleon as saying, he "labours under a political monomania; he does not understand me. I am sorry for it, as he is an honest man" (II, 327). For Bernadotte, see note to 145.16.

140.19 "I MADE . . . OF MUD," Continuing the conversation quoted in the note to 137.35, O'Meara reports Napoleon's indignation against the restoration of the old aristocracy: "It is of such as them that the Bourbons want to make generals. I made most of mine de la boue (of clay.)" (I, 88). In April 1838 Emerson did not transcribe O'Meara's parenthetical translation, leaving himself free later on to put more colorful words in Napoleon's mouth.

140.22 IN THE RUSSIAN CAMPAIGN . . . ALL FOR NEY:" For Michel Ney, whom Napoleon called "the bravest of the brave," the brilliant defender of the rear guard in the disastrous retreat from Moscow in 1812, see note to 140.12. The quotation, and with slight modification the whole sentence, Emerson took from Las Cases, IV, vii, 123, as noted in *JMN*, V, 508, and VII, 11.

140.29 "I KNOW," . . . MY GENERALS." Emerson's source for the quotation is identified in *JMN*, V, 475, as Las Cases, I, ii, 11, where Napoleon completes his figure thus: "Some . . . will sink to the waist, some to the chin, others over the head; but the number of the latter is very small, I assure you."

140.31 SEVENTEEN MEN . . . OR GENERAL; It is difficult to understand Emerson here and to reconcile the facts with his statement. If the sentence means as presumably it does from the context, that these men were elevated from common soldiers by Napoleon's agency or while he was in power, most of the nearly thirty marshals Napoleon created had already been officers during the Revolutionary wars—mostly generals before they became associated with Napoleon. As emperor he lavished imperial dukedoms on his marshals and ministers, and he made kings of three of his brothers and his brother-in-law, Marshal Murat, in addition to bestowing the title King of Rome on his infant son. Yet, the tenor of Emerson's overall point from 140.14 to the end of the paragraph is sound and well grounded in his sources, and by including "generals" in this list of elevations from the common ranks, he may have some unknown source for this statement. Davidson, p. 51, quotes Lockhart, I, 276, as a possibility: "Seventeen generals . . . were named Marshals of the Empire." Aside from the fact that Lockhart lists eighteen in parentheses, an error not easily noted by the casual reader, it should be added that Lockhart is specifically referring to Napoleon's initial appointments to that rank in May 1804.

140.33 THE CROSSES OF HIS LEGION OF HONOUR   Against Senatorial opposition to the creation of any orders or distinctions, Napoleon established in 1802 the Legion of Honor as a recognition of civil or military merit. Citizens over twenty-five years of age were eligible without regard to birth, rank, or religion. An oath to support the principles of liberty and equality was required, and a stipend was attached to the order. Originally the decoration was the Napoleonic cross and a ribbon.

140.35 "WHEN SOLDIERS . . . IN MY EYES."   As noted in *JMN*, V, 486, the source for this statement by Napoleon is Las Cases, II, iii, 147, where the translation reads "christened" rather than "baptized."

141.2 FAUBOURG ST ANTOINE,   An industrial, working-class suburb incorporated into Paris before the French Revolution.

141.2 POWDER MONKEY   Primarily a naval term for the boy who brings the gunpowder to the guns from its storage room; a powder-boy.

141.18 WHEN SPYING THE ALPS . . . THE PYRAMIDS, . . . OF THE WORLD."
The "romantic pictures" and "strange situations" listed here are drawn from Bourrienne, I, 221, 289–290, 291–292, 325 (as indicated in *JMN*, IX, 152) and represent dramatic highlights of Napoleon's expedition to Egypt and Syria in 1798–99 as seen by Bourrienne, who accompanied him. Bourrienne, however, was not present at the Battle of the Pyramids, a decisive victory over the Mameluke rulers of Egypt, and Emerson added Napoleon's celebrated words from his *Memoirs of the History of France*, II, 246 (see *JMN*, IX, 140). Napoleon and Bourrienne waded one day through the shallows at the head of the Red Sea and then, returning to camp that night, crossed with some difficulty dur-

ing a higher tide. This was at the outset of the expedition into Syria, which ended at the unsuccessful sixty-one-day seige of Acre, anciently called Ptolemaïs, on the coast of Palestine. While the Turks and a small band of English sailors surprisingly resisted, Bourrienne frequently walked by the shore with Napoleon, who often spoke of how "The fate of the east lay in that small town" and projected the conquest of the Ottoman Empire and more. Bourrienne's point is that the last quotation, which he repeats from the fallen Emperor's reminiscences at Saint Helena, represents the stated ambition of 1799.

141.24 HIS ARMY, ON THE NIGHT . . . IN THE FIGHT.   The promise of this appropriate token was made the night before the battle in the celebration mentioned in the note to 138.31. See Scott, II, 79, 81.

141.28 AS WHEN HE PLEASED . . . AT ERFURT.   Bourrienne alludes to Frederick William III (1770–1840), King of Prussia, as one who "was doomed to wait for [Napoleon] in his antechamber at Tilsit" (II, 48). This seems to have been literally true at his first interview with Napoleon after the negotiations at Tilsit in July 1807 that had resulted in a disadvantageous peace between France and a badly defeated Prussia and an alliance between France and Russia (Las Cases, II, iv, 96). At least figuratively the king was again waiting in the antechamber when Napoleon and Alexander I, Emperor of Russia, met at Erfurt in October 1808, to reaffirm their alliance. Fouché notes that Napoleon as a "show of power" summoned to his court his client kings in December 1809 and required them to attend a "Te Deum" in Notre Dame in commemoration of his victories and of the anniversary of his coronation (p. 242).

141.36 "THE AUSTRIANS," . . . VALUE OF TIME."   Quoted from Napoleon's *Memoirs of the History of France*, IV, 324, as Emerson indicated in *JMN*, IX, 142.

142.20 "WHAT CREATES GREAT . . . WILL FAIL."   A source for this passage has not been located. The similar passages in *JMN*, IX, 180, 192, suggest the quotation may not be direct. Perhaps Emerson remembered Napoleon's remarks to Las Cases about the difficulties of provisioning troops in modern warfare (IV, vii, 97–98). Napoleon's campaigns necessarily depended for their success on living off the land, but Count Maximilian Yorck von Wartenburg observed, "It is altogether wrong to picture Napoleon as always pushing forward without any thought of his commissariat; he always kept his eye on it, only it never obscured the clearness of his military insight, nor did he permit it to interfere with the course and directions of his operations, and with respect to it as a rule, he always adhered to the phrase: 'In the conduct of our armies we must be guided by the principle that war must support war' " (*Napoleon as General*, 2 vols. [London, 1902], I, 27).

142.26 "THE WINTER," . . . IN THE AIR."   As *JMN*, IX, 144, notes, this quotation is taken from Napoleon's *Memoirs of the History of France*, II, 65.

142.33 "IN ALL BATTLES, . . . AN ADDITION." As Emerson indicated in *JMN,* IX, 139–140, the source of this passage is Antommarchi, I, 168–170, but it is considerably condensed and somewhat altered. Napoleon actually is reported to have said that with only twenty-five guides left, he sent them against "the flank of the enemy, with three trumpets sounding the charge." Napoleon's victory over the Austrians at Arcole or Arcola (November 15, 16, 17, 1796) in his Italian campaign was heroic, as indicated in the note to 136.13. Emerson uses either the variant Italian or French spelling, as do his sources.

143.12 ON THE VOYAGE TO EGYPT . . . FOURNIER . . . MY PHARMACO-PEIA." This passage illustrating Napoleon's speculative conversation is arranged topically, and its components are drawn from a number of sources. The first three sentences are, with slight abridgment and modification, from Bourrienne, I, 221–222 (as Emerson indicated in *JMN,* IX, 155). The transition, "He was very fond of talking of religion," and the nocturnal refutation of the materialists, also "on deck" during the voyage to Egypt, are taken, as he noted in *JMN,* IX, 154, from Bourrienne, II, 38, but the anecdote intruding between them—that of the argument with Bishop Fournier—is from Louis François Joseph, Baron de Bausset, *Private Memoirs of the Court of Napoleon and of Some Publick Events of the Imperial Reign, from 1805 to the First of May 1814 . . .* (Philadelphia, 1828), p. 74, which Emerson borrowed from the Boston Athenæum January 16 to February 11, 1845. The sentence contrasting Napoleon's delight in men of science and his slighting of men of letters Emerson put together from Bourrienne, II, 37 and 465. The quotation addressed to Antommarchi, Emerson identified in *JMN,* IX, 138–139, as from Antommarchi, I, 180–181, 182. In preparation for his military expedition to Egypt in 1798, Napoleon asked two distinguished French scientists, whom he had met in Italy, to select a scientific committee of learned men to accompany them and him to Egypt and the Near East. Gaspard Monge (1746–1818), a geometer and principal founder of l'Ecole Polytechnique, and his inseparable friend, Claude Louis Berthollet (1748–1822), an equally famous chemist, along with their scientific committee, afforded Napoleon intellectual diversion on the voyage aboard *l'Orient* and afterward; so did the admiral commanding the fleet, François Paul Brueys (1753–1798), soon to be killed in the battle of the Nile, with whom Napoleon often talked about naval maneuvers (Bourrienne, I, 219–220). Bourrienne, who accompanied Napoleon, says that Monge, "endowed with an ardent imagination, without exactly possessing religious principles, had a kind of predisposition for religious ideas which harmonized with the notions of Bonaparte," while "Berthollet was, with his cold imagination, constantly devoted to analysis and abstractions, inclined towards materialism, an opinion with which the General was always much dissatisfied" (I, 219). As for Napoleon's other speculative interlocutors, Marie Nicholas Fournier (1760–1834) was chaplain and almoner to the Emperor and his household and was in 1806 made Bishop of Montpellier. Jean Nicolas, Baron Corvisart

(1755-1821), a distinguished French physician and anatomist, became in 1799 official doctor for Napoleon and Josephine. Francesco Antommarchi (1789-1838), a Corsican by birth and admirer of Napoleon, was an anatomist in Italy when he was called on in 1819 to attend Napoleon as physician at Saint Helena.

144.8 HIS MEMOIRS, DICTATED ... CAMPAIGN IN EGYPT. Emerson here refers to *Memoirs of the History of France during the Reign of Napoleon, Dictated by the Emperor at Saint Helena to the Generals Who Shared His Captivity; and Published from the Original Manuscripts Corrected by Himself,* 7 vols. (London, 1823-1824), a work also published in French in London and Paris in the same years. Volumes 5-7 have the additional title *Historical Miscellanies,* volumes 1-3. In this lecture and in his journal V (1844-1845) Emerson quotes only from the first four volumes. The four-volume set is in Harvard College Library, and the seven volumes are in the Boston Athenæum, from which he borrowed at least one volume on January 8, 1845, though a month earlier he wrote that he had "read Napoleon's memoirs lately" (*L,* III, 268). The "Advertisement of the Editors" explains the method of composition: Napoleon "seldom wrote himself ... When he wished to write an account of any event, he caused the generals who surrounded him to investigate the subject; and when all the materials were collected, he dictated to them extempore. Napoleon revised the manuscript, correcting it with his own hand: he often dictated it anew; and still more frequently recommenced a whole page in the margin. ... Like Cæsar and Frederic, Napoleon writes in the third person; he was not very solicitous about his style" (I, iv,v). The first two volumes were dictated to Baron Gaspard Gourgaud (1783-1852) and the remaining volumes to Count (later Marquis) Charles Tristran Montholon (1782-1853), both generals who had distinguished themselves and accompanied Napoleon to Saint Helena as his closest confidants. The work has great authority and even a modesty implied in the French title: *Mémoirs pour servir à l'histoire de France sous Napoléon.* ... But it is also informed by the circumstances of its composition—Napoleon was in exile reviewing his career—and Bourrienne faults its accuracy and interpretation insofar as it conflicts with his own fragmentary but strongly interpretive account. Emerson's allusions in this passage to its contents come from the first four volumes. Napoleon's first large command in northern Italy against Austria in 1796-97 pitted him against an array of formidable experienced commanders: Joseph, Baron von Alvintzi (or Alvinci) (1735-1810), Jean Pierre Beaulieu (1725-1819), and Dagobert Siegmund, Count von Wurmser (1724-1797), all veterans of the Seven Years War who had been recently successful against the French Revolutionary army on other fronts but were defeated successively by the young Napoleon. In the narrative of battles and particularly in the summary tenth chapter of volume 4, "Observations on the Military Operations of the Campaigns of 1796 and 1797 in Italy," Napoleon treats them with respect, even bestowing on the first two their subsequent rank of field marshal. Archduke Charles of Austria (1771–1847), fresh from victories on the Rhine, at last took command and showed masterly skill, according to Napoleon, but it was too late to make a comeback, and a peace was negotiated. Napoleon's account of his campaign in Egypt (1798–99) displays "equality as a writer to his varying subject" by covering, in addition to land battles, the naval Battle of the Nile, the geography and demography of Egypt, and its religion, customs, sciences, and arts.

144.22 HE DELIGHTED TO FASCINATE . . . EVERY ADDITION. Bourrienne, III, 237–260, gives an example of Napoleon's fondness of extempore narration in the apartments of the Empress before her ladies in waiting. The terrifying tale of "Guilio" is presented, punctuated with Napoleon's dramatic actions and at least one shriek by the ladies as the imperial narrator pretends to draw a dagger, as recorded by one of the ladies and given to Bourrienne. "Led away by the subject," she says, "he paced the saloon with hasty strides; the intonations of his voice varied according to the characters of the personages he brought on the scene; he seemed to multiply himself, in order to play the different parts, and no person needed to feign the terror, which he really inspired, and which he loved to see depicted in the countenances of those who surrounded him." Bourrienne adds that he had frequently heard Napoleon relate such stories, always "in a dimly-lighted apartment" and recalls "the varied tones of his voice, his action, his look and the gestures with which he accompanied those improvisations."

144.35 FOOLISH OLD MEN AND WOMEN OF THE ROMAN CONCLAVE . . . BRIBE HIM; That Emerson refers to the Papal court rather than a more extended Roman Catholic opposition is probable from the language of his sources. O'Meara quotes Napoleon as saying, "After the treaty . . . [of] Tolentino with that imbecile and fraudulent court of old women at Rome" (II, 246); and Scott in describing the frantic preparations of the College of Cardinals and Pope Pius VI to resist Napoleon's march on the Papal States in January and February 1797, a futile resistance that cost the Papacy dearly in territory at the treaty of Tolentino, remarks: "the Pope was compared . . . to a man who, in the act of falling, would grasp for support at a hook of red-hot iron" (I, 365). Napoleon's relations with the Church remained difficult despite the Concordat of 1801, which reestablished the Church in France. Even after seizing Rome and the Papal States (1808–09), Napoleon found he could control Pius VII only by removing him from the influence of the Papal Court and holding him prisoner in France. Emerson here uses the word "statists" in the now archaic sense of statesmen or politicians, but he uses "statist" in the newer sense of statistician at 62.11 and possibly at 131.21. In April 1797, at the end of Napoleon's first Italian campaign, Austria began negotiations that resulted in the Peace of Leoben. Napoleon's *Memoirs of the History of France* says that Emperor Francis II (1768–1835), through one of his plenipotentiaries, "offered Napoleon to procure him, on the conclusion of peace, a sovereignty of 250,000 souls in Germany, for himself and his family, in order to place him beyond the reach of republican ingratitude" (IV, 103). Napoleon was at the time of this offer commanding general of the armies in Italy for the Directory.

145.16 HE IS UNJUST . . . OF HIS THRONE. Bourrienne says it is notorious that Napoleon often misattributed credit for the success of a battle (II, 315). He also tells of Napoleon's alleged failure to acknowledge properly the bold and crucial nature of General François Etienne de Kellermann's celebrated charge of cavalry at the decisive Battle of Marengo on June 14, 1800, and attributes the motive to Napoleon's self-aggrandizement: "He did not choose that a result so decisive be attributed to any other cause than the combinations of his genius." Although Bourrienne did not actually hear it said, it was widely known that Kellermann bitterly remarked to the First Consul, "I have placed the crown on your head" (II, 176-178). Emerson may also refer to Bourrienne's account of a quarrel between Bernadotte and Napoleon over credit in the Battle of Wagram, July 5-6, 1809. Bernadotte brashly issued an order of the day seeming to claim the victory for his Saxon troops, but Napoleon issued another order of the day firmly contradicting Bernadotte's claims and relieved him of command. From Bourrienne's account, friendly to Bernadotte, who confided the incident to him, it appears incorrectly that Napoleon was in the wrong (IV, 91-93). Jean Baptiste Bernadotte (1763-1844), a gifted soldier and diplomat, was a potential rival to Napoleon in French politics. He had opposed the overthrow of the Directory and held himself somewhat aloof from Napoleon thereafter, yet continued under the Consulate and the Empire to hold important diplomatic and military positions and to receive high honors—Marshal of France, Prince of Ponte Corvo. In 1810 he was elected crown prince of Sweden and, as effective ruler, he acted in the interest of Sweden, soon allying himself against Napoleon. He became Charles XIV of Sweden and Norway in 1818. In the third specific illustration of Napoleon's injustice to his generals, Emerson may have remembered an anecdote offered by Bourrienne that may or may not be true, but Emerson apparently confused two of Napoleon's generals, both equally characterized as faithful. Andoche Junot (1771-1813), Duke of Abrantès, was extravagant and prodigal, a poor administrator, but a brave soldier. His friendship with Napoleon, for whom he suffered serious wounds as a substitute in a duel in Egypt, endured despite various periods of disfavor and even despite his marriage to Laure Permon, whom Napoleon teasingly called his *petite peste*, a vivacious if not entirely trustworthy memoirist whom Emerson read. Junot was in 1807 sent to command the invasion of Portugal, allegedly because of his embarrassing romantic entanglement with Napoleon's sister Pauline. He died a suicide in 1813, apparently insane, partly as a result of multiple injuries he had acquired as a faithful and heroic soldier. But Bourrienne's anecdote, imperfectly remembered by Emerson, involves Jean Lannes (1769-1809), Duke of Montebello, one of Napoleon's ablest and most trusted marshals. He also was in Egypt with Napoleon and managed the difficult retreat from Syria. He was celebrated for his heroism and skill at Montebello, Marengo, Austerlitz, Jena, and Aspern-Essling, where he was mortally wounded and where Napoleon, who saw him carried off the battlefield, emotionally expressed his long-time affection for him. Bourrienne's story is intended to illustrate the vanity and intrigues of Napoleon and his whimsical habit of turning his generals into diplomats. "The appointment of Lannes [in 1801] to the court of Lisbon," says Bourrienne, "originated from causes which . . . serve . . . to point out . . . the means he disdained not to resort to, if he wished to banish his most faithful friends, when their presence was no longer agreeable to him." Lannes, an unceremonious and blunt old comrade, failed to take the hint when Napoleon ceased to address him in the second-person singular and thus offended by his familiarity the new decorum of the First Consul, who determined to send him away. Always careless with money, Lannes was persuaded by Napoleon to furnish extravagantly an appropriate *hôtel* on the assurance that Napoleon would give him the money. Napoleon then told him to advance himself the money to cover his expenditure (400,000 francs) from the Guards' funds. "Within twenty-four hours" after Lannes had informally obtained the money, Bourrienne says, Napoleon ordered an audit, forcing Lannes to borrow elsewhere, and conveniently denied the authorization. At the violent confrontation of old comrades, a duel was only narrowly avoided by the intervention of Junot, and Napoleon sent Lannes off to Portugal to enrich himself by graft and to spare the First Consul indecorous familiarity (II, 365–366). If Bourrienne's striking tale is true, he gives no account of the quick restoration to favor of the too familiar comrade, but that may be because Bourrienne himself soon fell out of favor and resigned as private secretary.

145.21 THE OFFICIAL PAPER, HIS "MONITEURS," . . . THEATRICAL ÉCLAT. *The Gazette Nationale; ou, Le Moniteur Universel,* a daily newspaper, was founded in Paris, May 5, 1789, and became the official organ of the state December 28, 1799, dropping the first half of its title December 30, 1810. Its title changed again later, but it remained the official French newspaper until December 31, 1868. In it were carried the official bulletins, which Bourrienne repeatedly discredits, reflecting proverbial recognition of Napoleon's propaganda. Bourienne writes: "The historian of these times ought to put no faith in the bulletins, dispatches, notes, proclamations . . . For my part, I believe that the proverb, 'As great a liar as a bulletin,' has as much truth in it as the axiom, two and two make four" (II, 314). Later he writes: Napoleon's "bulletins, which were destined to impose on the people of the interior of France and foreign countries, too fully justified the proverb,—'To lie like a bulletin' " (IV, 58–59). When once Bourrienne objected to having to write such bulletins, he reports that Napoleon observed that he was thus filling "the world with admiration" and would "inspire historians and poets" (I, 342). For Napoleon's own attempt at composing a history during his six years at Saint Helena, *Memoirs of the History of France,* see 144.8–16 and note. He knew also that his admiring companions at Saint Helena—Las Cases, O'Meara, and Antommarchi—recorded his conversations, which were often directed toward shaping history. For their books, see notes to 133.21, 133.26, and 131.20.

145.29 "I MUST DAZZLE . . . WAR AND GOVERNMENT." This passage of quotation, paraphrase, adaptation, and comment is mostly, though not entirely, derived from Bourrienne. As much of it is not recorded in Emerson's journals and notebooks, it suggests that he worked partly from notes now lost or from his sources directly but with considerable editorial freedom and with some reliance upon memory. The first sentence of the first quotation is taken from Bourrienne, II, 26, but the first-person pronoun has been substituted for "A newly born government." The second sentence of the synthetic quotation may be a recollection of Bourrienne, II, 289, where the secretary characterizes Napoleon as "at all times, the declared enemy of the liberty of the press, and, therefore, he ruled the journals with a hand of iron. I have often heard him say," Bourrienne continues, " 'Were I to loosen the reins, I should not continue three months in power.' " The second quotation, one of Napoleon's "favorite ideas," is quoted accurately from Bourrienne, II, 25. Emerson's statement of Napoleon's "doctrine of immortality" echoes such passages from Bourrienne as, Napoleon "often observed to me, that with him the opinion of posterity was the real immortality of the soul" (I, xvii) and "The perpetuity of a name in the memory of man was to him the immortality of the soul" (II, 38–39). What Emerson made into the final and longest quotation is made up of three separate items: the first sentence is quoted from Bourrienne, II, 28; the second (as Emerson indicated in *JMN,* IX, 153) from Caulaincourt, I, 135; and the remainder from Bourrienne, II, 28–29. Joseph Bonaparte (1768–1844) was made King of Naples in 1806 and, after little success there, became King of Spain in 1808. In 1813 he lost the military struggle to retain that throne. Despite having more thrust upon him than he was capable of managing, his relations with Napoleon were more amiable than those of the other three brothers. For Napoleon's principal aide-de-camp, Duroc, see note to 140.12.

146.27 JUPITER SCAPIN, As Edward Emerson pointed out, the "title . . . appears to have been applied to Napoleon by Abbé de Pradt" (*W,* IV, 365). Dominique Dufour de Pradt (1759–1837), Archbishop of Mechlin, was a prolific and opportunistic writer on various subjects who, in and out of Napoleon's favor, served sometimes as a diplomat. Napoleon characterized the Abbé in one of his turnings of loyalty: "De Pradt mérite qu'on lui donne le nom d'une fille de joie qui prête son corps à toute le monde pour l'argent" (deserves to be called a woman of pleasure who offers herself to all comers). In the vituperative preface to his post-Restoration *Histoire de L'Ambassade dans le Grand Duché de Varsovie* (Paris, 1815), pp. xiii–xiv, de Pradt wrote: Napoleon "présente une espèce de *Jupiter-Scapin* qui n'avait pas encore paru sur la scène du monde" (is a kind of Jupiter-Scapin never before seen on the world stage). Scapin is the valet, a knave and trickster, in Molière's comedy *Les Fourberies de Scapin*. Emerson perhaps remembered de Pradt's epithet from his 1838 readings in Las Cases, who quoted it in recounting Napoleon's reaction to an extract from the Abbé's book in an English periodical (I, ii, 26).

147.24 TORPEDO,   For the crampfish or torpedo, see note to 41.26.

147.37 THE PACIFIC FOURIER   American Fourierism particularly associated itself with the peace movement, and this whole harmonious scheme implied peaceful means of reform. In the context here it should be pointed out that Fourier built his utopian plans on private ownership of property. For the "sensual and selfish aim," see also note to 103.32.

152.16 AS OUR GERMAN POET . . . WHAT I SUFFER."   The quotation is the epigraph to Goethe's "Elegie," the second poem in his "Trilogie der Leidenschaft," in the third volume of the edition of Goethe's *Werke* that Emerson owned: "Und wenn der Mensch in seiner Qual verstummt, / Gab mir ein Gott zu sagen was ich leide" (And if humanity in its torment is dumb, some god gave me the power to tell what I suffer). A slightly different version is in Goethe's *Torquato Tasso*, V, v, lines 3433–3434 (*Werke*, IX).

152.20 "WHEN I AM . . . PREACH WELL:"   This may be a paraphrase of item number CCCXIX in William Hazlitt's new translation of *The Table Talk; or, Familiar Discourse of Martin Luther* (London, 1848). The translator is the editor of Montaigne named at 92.33—the son of William Hazlitt the essayist.

152.22 THE COMPLAISANCE OF SULTAN AMURATH . . . VESALIUS . . . MUSCLES OF THE NECK.   Emerson's first journal version of this anecdote (*JMN*, VI, 14) tells it of two other people: "Mahomet II they say cut off a slave's head to show the painter Belline the action of certain muscles." In *JMN*, VII, 311, he took from Robert Burton's *The Anatomy of Melancholy*, 2 vols. (London, 1804), I, 22, a volume in his library, the statement that "To discern the arteries better, Vesalius the anatomist, they say, was wont to cut up men alive." Andreas Vesalius (1514–1564), a Belgian, was one of the first to dissect the human body to study anatomy, was condemned by the Inquisition for doing so, and made a pilgrimage to the Holy Land as penance; but there is no evidence that he ever visited the court of any Ottoman sultan, and he died before the reign of Amurath (Murad) III (1574–1595). The Venetian painter Gentile Bellini (1429?–1507), however, did visit the court of Mahomet II (sultan 1451–1481), so the anecdote was probably told of him before it was transferred to Vesalius; or Emerson may simply have blended the two versions in his memory.

153.34 CLERISY, Emerson knew the recent use of the word to mean learned men as a body, including poets, philosophers, and scholars (no longer merely the clergy), from Coleridge, who introduced it in books Emerson used. See his own use of the word in "Manners": "The artist, the scholar, and, in general, the clerisy, wins its way" (*CW*, III, 84).

153.38 BONAPARTE'S OPINION CONCERNING IDEOLOGISTS. See 132.1–3 and note.

154.21 THE QUAKER ... THE SHAKER ... ANTI-SPIRITUAL. The Society of Friends, or Quakers, was founded in 1647 by George Fox and other enthusiasts opposed to formalism and the corruptions of organized religion, relying chiefly on an immediate, personal spiritual guidance and revelation. They were persecuted in England and America at first, but grew to a respectability that Emerson knew particularly in his Plymouth connections and in Philadelphia. Emerson lectured on George Fox in 1835, perceiving him as a truly inspired religious leader radically threatening the forms of orthodoxy. Although even Fox worked toward a degree of church organization from 1666 onward, meeting strong opposition from other adherents, the movement preserved a high degree of individual and antinomian emphasis, particularly until the radical movement led by Elias Hicks divided the American Quakers in the early nineteenth century. The reaction of the main body of Quakers was a move toward more conventional Christian organization, evangelism, and social work, while still preserving the essentials of Quakerism, an accommodation Emerson here notes. Emerson was also interested in the Shakers, a burgeoning movement he disapproved of, and he visited them at nearby Harvard, Massachusetts, with Hawthorne in September 1842 (*JMN*, VIII, 273–276). Also called The United Society of Believers in Christ's Second Appearing, and the Millennial Church, the Shakers were at first closely associated with the English "Shaking Quakers," a sect that trembled when in a state of enthusiasm, and were separated from them by Ann Lee (1736–1784), "Mother Ann," who was spiritually led to bring her followers to America in 1774. Under the leadership of her successors, by the beginning of the nineteenth century Shaker communities, which multiplied in New England, New York, and the Midwest, had established a rigid communalism emphasizing sexual purity (by discouraging marriage and by separating the sexes in dormitories) and a separation from the world. Their origin among the Shaking Quakers was preserved in their dances, representing the power of possession by the Holy Ghost. From 1837 there were spiritual manifestations given to the individual members, such as Mother Ann had had—visions, messages from Mother Ann, transportations to foreign cities, speaking in tongues—but these were withdrawn from them in 1847, leaving, as Emerson suggests, the "monastery" and the dance. The sect decreased rapidly at the end of the nineteenth century, owing largely to its rule of chastity, and is now gone, superseded by a trust that preserves its spiritual heritage and the remaining communities.

155.31 "CHILDREN ONLY ... ARE ONE." Emerson identified his source for this passage in *JMN*, IX, 231, as *The Bhăgvăt-Gēētā* ..., trans. Charles Wilkins, p. 57 (ch. V, 4–5).

155.8 TALLEYRAND'S QUESTION ... IS HE ANYBODY? The last question, what Talleyrand asked of one who sought a position for a friend, is identified in *JMN*, IX, 117, 177, as from Charles Maxime Catherinet de Villemarest, *Life of Prince Talleyrand*, 4 vols. (London, 1834–1836), IV, 202–203, a work Emerson borrowed from the Boston Athenæum in January and February 1845.

155.12 STATESTREET, State Street was the center of financial, legal, and mercantile interests in Boston.

155.24 SIBYLLINE VERSES ... TEMPLE WALLS. The famous Sibylline books or leaves, written in Greek hexameters, were sold by the Cumaean sibyl (one of the ten inspired classical prophetesses) to Tarquin the Proud, king of Rome, after she had in the bargaining process destroyed six of the nine books. These were used by a special college of curators in Rome to divine the necessary course of national action or expiation in dire emergencies. They were accidentally burned in the fire that destroyed the Temple of Jupiter on the Capitol in 83 B.C., but a new collection was made from many places and later edited to purify it from spurious oracles. That too was destroyed near the end of the fifth century A.D. Yet a few of these Sibylline verses were preserved otherwise, and there was also a literature of imitation, generally called the Sibylline oracles, apocalyptic Greek hexameters written by Hellenized Jews and Christians from about the middle of the second century B.C. to the second or third century A.D. Emerson uses the term "Chaldean oracles" for the oracles of Zoroaster and the Theurgists, following the practice of Thomas Taylor, his source for the selections made for *The Dial* as "Ethnical Scriptures" in April 1844. Thomas Taylor published his translations of the largely spurious but traditional sayings in three parts in *The Classical Journal* (London), vols. 16 and 17, nos. 32–34 (1817–1818), as "Collections of Chaldean Oracles." By "Laconian sentences" Emerson is unlikely to mean "Laconic Apophthegms," an essay he knew in Plutarch's *Morals*, for these were not inscribed on temple walls. He perhaps means laconian in the sense of laconic or concise speech, reputedly characteristic of the ancient Laconians, also called Lacedemonians or Spartans. If so, he probably means such inscriptions at temples connected with oracles as "Know thyself" and "Nothing too much," offered by Plutarch as examples of brevity in oracular sentences that have "set afoot amongst the Philosophers" "many Questions" and "a Multitude of Discourses" ("Of the

Word Eî, Engraven over the Gate of Apollo's Temple at Delphi," *Morals*, IV, 462). It is less likely that Emerson intended the phrase "Laconian sentences" as an appositive to "Chaldean oracles."

156.14 HUNDREDS OF POST CAPTAINS . . . NO CHATHAM, Emerson rhetorically exaggerates the number of post captains (those holding the rank of captain in the British Navy as distinct from those of whatever rank who were called captains because they commanded ships) engaged in exploration, but they were numerous, and the greatest celebrity of the period came to those who explored the polar regions. Emerson's interest is indicated by his borrowing from the Boston Athenæum in 1830 Captain Sir William Edward Parry's *Journal of a Second Voyage for the Discovery of a Northwest Passage from the Atlantic to the Pacific . . . 1821-22-23 . . .* (London, 1824) and *Journal of a Third Voyage . . . 1824-25* (London or Philadelphia, 1826); and in 1836 he borrowed Captain Sir John Ross's *Narrative of a Second Voyage in Search of a North-West Passage, and of a Residence in the Arctic Regions during the Years 1829, 1830, 1831, 1832, 1833 . . . Including the Reports of James Clark Ross . . . and the Discovery of the Northern Magnetic Pole* (London or Philadelphia, 1835). Perhaps the most celebrated contemporary post captain was Sir James Clark Ross (1800-1862), who in 1847 published *A Voyage of Discovery and Research in the Southern and Antarctic Regions, during the Years 1839-43* (London, 1847). The greatest publicity of polar explorations by captains of the Royal Navy is precisely contemporary with *Representative Men*. Sir John Franklin (1786-1847) began his ill-fated last trip to the Arctic in May 1845, and after more than a year of highly publicized agitation, delay, and preparation, Sir James Clark Ross was sent out to find him in May 1848, returning unsuccessful in November 1849; but already new plans were under way to send out Sir John Ross, who finally sailed in May 1850. That year others were on the search, but the fact that Franklin had died in 1847 and his expedition had come to disaster was not known for certain until 1857. Provisioning these modern expeditions was a matter of great concern, and most accounts list as preventives against scurvy, the plague of sailors from ancient times, such items as tinned, concentrated soup and pemmican — dried meat pounded and mixed with fat, an indigenous staple Captain Franklin had discovered on an earlier land exploration of the Arctic. Emerson also read in these accounts long lists of navigational instruments, and by "transit-telescope" he meant a telescope to take transits, or passages, of the fixed stars or the moon over the meridian. Such instruments, with various names, and accurate chronometers (developed in the late eighteenth century) made accurate determination of longitude from the Greenwich meridian possible and hence precise navigation and map-making. William Pitt (1708-1778), first Earl of Chatham, was a popular and powerful British statesman and orator, called the great commoner. He had a lifelong admiration for the greatest orator of the Athenian democracy, Demosthenes (384-322 B.C.).

156.25 ARGUS-EYED, A hero in Greek mythology who had eyes all over his body, making him all-seeing, Panoptes or Argus originally denoted the starry heavens. On his death the eyes were transferred to the tail of the peacock.

157.23 ALEXANDER WENT AS FAR AS CHAOS; Emerson may have recalled a poetic maxim in Sa'di's *The Gulistan, or Flower-Garden,* trans. James Ross: "Thou hast heard that Alexander got as far as chaos; but after all this toil, he drank not the water of immortality" (ch. VIII, "Of the Duties of Society," no. LXXVII).

158.3 "HIS VERY FLIGHT . . . IN DISGUISE:" As indicated in *JMN,* IX, 286, this line of verse is taken from *Practical Philosophy of the Muhammadan People . . . the Akhlāk-i-Jalāly,* p. 364.

158.32 "THE PLANT GOES . . . IN THE HEAD." The passage is quoted from Margaret Fuller's translation of Johann Peter Eckermann, *Conversations with Goethe in the Last Years of His Life* (Boston, 1839), p. 276 (February 13, 1829), a book in Emerson's library.

160.22 WE HAD AN ENGLISH ROMANCE . . . 'YOUNG ENGLAND,' . . . AND A PEERAGE. Both *Coningsby* (1844) and *Sybil* (1845) by Benjamin Disraeli (1804–1881), later prime minister and Earl of Beaconsfield, deal with the "Young England" movement, a group of younger Tory politicians, including Disraeli himself, who tried in the 1840s to make common cause with the working classes against the middle class. Of the two novels, Emerson's summary of the conclusion applies more closely to *Coningsby.*

160.27 GEORGE SAND, IN CONSUELO . . . EXTREME SACRIFICES. On January 31, 1844, Emerson wrote: "I have lately read George Sand's Consuelo, of which the first volume pleased me mightily, the other much less, and yet the whole book shows an extraordinary spirit. The writer apprehends the force of simplicity of behaviour, and enjoys, how greatly, the meeting of two strong natures" (*A Correspondence between John Sterling and Ralph Waldo Emerson* [Boston, 1897], p. 82). This refers to the popular novel of George Sand (Amandine Aurore Lucie Dupin, baronne Dudevant, 1804–1876), *Consuelo,* first published in book form in Paris, 1842–1843 (8 vols.). But Emerson's point in this lecture is derived from the continuation, *La Comtesse de Rudolstadt,* 5 vols. (Paris, 1844), in which a great reversal of plot and theme occurs, and his paraphrase is drawn from the post-epilogue "Lettre de Philon," at the end of this sequel. Emerson's library contains the revised and corrected edition (2 vols., Paris, 1845).

161.18 THE ARDENT AND HOLY NOVALIS . . . END OF HIS LIFE. Emerson seems to have acquired this information from *Characteristics of Goethe; from the*

German of Falk, von Muller, &c . . . , translated by Sarah Austin, 3 vols. (London, 1833), which was in his library. Footnote 18 (signed "Trans.") on I, 307–319, on a passage (I, 315) by Adolph Heller discussing Novalis' criticism of *Wilhelm Meister,* quotes statements by Novalis cited by Heller (but not used in the main text), which Emerson copies here with a few omissions but little other change. Neither Heller's account nor Austin's note, however, contains anything to support Emerson's final remark about Novalis' "favorite reading"— or, as Emerson expressed it in an unpublished manuscript note (Houghton bMS Am 1280.201 [108]), "Novalis hated but hugged it," which he ascribed to "Austin Vol. 1, 315." Novalis was the pen name of Friedrich Leopold von Hardenberg (1772–1801), German romantic poet and novelist.

164.3 "PIETY ITSELF," . . . HIGHEST CULTURE." This is Emerson's translation of contemplation 80 at the end of bk. II of Goethe's *Wilhelm Meisters Wanderjahre* (not included in Carlyle's translation).

164.7 LIKE WOMEN EMPLOYED . . . SECRET OF CONSPIRATORS. Emerson here may allude to the prominent role of the courtesan Fulvia, who seductively gathers information for Cicero from the plotters against Rome in Ben Jonson's *Catiline.*

165.23 XENIEN, Goethe and his friend Friedrich von Schiller published a series of epigrams, or *Xenien,* in 1796, castigating their contemporaries.

165.29 SOCRATES LOVED ATHENS; . . . OF PARIS). For Socrates, see 40.19– 23. Montaigne expresses his love of Paris in "Of Vanity," *Essays,* bk. III, ch. 9. The French writer Baronne Anne Louise Germaine Necker de Staël-Holstein (1766–1817) was exiled from Paris by Napoleon during the last ten years of his rule.

166.22 THE WHEEL-INSECT, VOLVOX GLOBATOR The volvox globator (or perglobator) is a spherical fresh-water organism that rolls over in the water— also called rolling alga. For the wheel-insect, see note to 17.21. If Emerson meant to equate the two minute and simple organisms, he might have recalled that Antony van Leeuwenhoek first discovered and named the class rotifera, to which the wheel-insect belongs, and also discovered and described the reproduction of the volvox globator, which resembles the division of the wheel-insect as Emerson describes it at 17.21–24.

TEXTUAL APPARATUS

The following textual information is provided: (1) a record of all changes made from the copy-text, whether substantive or accidental, except for certain silent emendations specified below; (2) a record of all variants in substantives or in spelling found in certain previous editions but not accepted in this edition; (3) a record of possible compounds divided at the ends of lines in copy-text and in this edition; and (4) a record, in a separate annex, of all revisions made by Emerson in the manuscript. The first two sections constitute the historical collation; and textual notes are inserted in both sections, where needed, after the entry involved. Thus any discussion of the basis for emendation of the copy-text or rejection of a variant occurs at the point where the decision is stated; and the subsequent history of any reading is made clear at once, since rejected variants are recorded in the emendation entry if an emendation is involved. The manuscript and the editions collated are described in the Textual Introduction, and the manuscript also in Annex A. The abbreviations (sigla) that follow represent the forms of the text that were collated.

MS   The holograph manuscript of *Representative Men.*

50   *Representative Men.* Boston: Phillips, Sampson & Company, 1850 [issued 1849].

RWE   Copy of 50 with holograph corrections (and corrigenda list) by R. W. Emerson. The Houghton Library, Harvard University.

Chap   *Representative Men.* London: John Chapman, 1850.

Bohn   *Representative Men.* London: Henry G. Bohn, 1850.

57   *Representative Men.* Boston: Phillips, Sampson & Company, 1857 (from same stereotype plates as 50, but with some corrections).

70   *The Prose Works of Ralph Waldo Emerson.* 2 vols. Boston: Fields, Osgood, & Co., 1870 [issued 1869]. (*Representative Men* occupies pp. 3–155 of vol. II.)

76   *Representative Men.* Boston: James R. Osgood and Company, 1876. (Little Classic Edition.)

R   *Representative Men.* Boston: Houghton, Mifflin and Company, 1884. (Vol. IV of the Riverside Edition.)

C   *Representative Men.* Boston and New York: Houghton, Mifflin and Company, 1903. (Vol. IV of the Centenary Edition.)

ed.   The present edition.

Some corrections were made in the original plates of the 1850 edition for the 1857 printing; subsequent printings from those plates (the latest one seen is dated 1882) carry the 1857 readings, but no other changes, except for evidence of wear and damage to the plates resulting in broken or lost letters and punctuation marks (and occasional repair of such damage). No changes have been found (except for possible repair of type damage) in the plates of any other edition before 1883, within or between printings. The Riverside and Centenary editions, although published after Emerson's death and without textual authority, have been fully collated, and their variant substantive readings are recorded, because they are the texts most familiar to modern readers. On the other hand, although the editions published in London in 1850 by John Chapman and H. G. Bohn have been collated (for substantives only), their readings are not recorded unless they are of special interest.

In the Emendations and Rejected Substantives and Spellings sections the symbol [¶] is used to indicate a new paragraph, [no ¶] to indicate the lack of paragraph division. "White line" means a one-line space between paragraphs. A solidus / marks the end of a line and // indicates the end of a page in either the manuscript or a printed edition; a word hyphenated at the end of a line is shown as, for example, "every-/thing." For other symbols which apply only to manuscript readings, see Appendix 2 to Annex A. An asterisk prefixed to an entry in the Emendations or Rejected Substantives and Spellings sections indicates that additional information in Appendix 2 may explain anomalous combinations of punctuation and capitalization in the copy-text or uncertainties regarding emendation or rejection of variants.

Emendations in the copy-text. The copy-text (the manuscript as finally revised by Emerson) can be re-created in all its essentials, since all changes from it in this edition are recorded except the following types of silent emendations:

The ampersand, which Emerson used for "and" in the vast majority of cases, is regularly expanded to "and," except in the abbreviation "&c." In some cases it is unclear whether the "&" begins a new sentence and should be printed as "And"; these are decided by editorial judgment and are not recorded as emendations.

Missing periods at the ends of what are clearly declarative sentences, when followed by a new sentence beginning with a capital letter, are silently supplied. On the other hand, all changes from lower-case to capital letters at the beginning of a sentence, or vice versa at a point originally (but no longer) the beginning of a sentence, are recorded as emendations. These changes usually, but not always, adopt the reading of the 1850 edition.

Emerson's occasional failure to hyphenate a word divided at the end of a line is not recorded unless there is doubt whether he intended it as one word or two.

Words printed with ligatured "æ" or "œ" in the 1850 edition are so printed in this edition, whether or not the ligature is indicated in the manuscript. Emerson sometimes wrote such words without a ligature and then rewrote them above the line with a ligature mark as a sign to the printer.

Emerson's occasional placing of a punctuation mark outside instead of inside closing quotation marks (usually as the result of crowding at the end of a line) is silently emended to conform with his normal practice.

The apostrophe is silently supplied before the contraction " 'tis"; the manuscript almost invariably omits it, and all editions print it.

In the manuscript as it is now bound, some letters (and possibly punctuation marks) at the ends of lines on verso pages, and, very rarely, in the left margins of recto pages, cannot be seen because of the binding. In such cases, missing parts of words are silently supplied from the 1850 edition; punctuation marks are likewise supplied if they are needed for clarity and are consistent with Emerson's normal usage.

Most emendations read as follows: at the left margin are the page and line numbers of this edition, then the reading adopted (the lemma) in place of the manuscript reading, followed by a right-hand square bracket. After the bracket appears the siglum (from the list above) for the edition in which the adopted reading was first printed, or other source of authority. (If the authority is Emerson's own correction and the change was made in a previous edition, the entry is, for example, "RWE, 70"; if this change has not been adopted previously, the entry is "RWE, ed." If a change is made on the authority of the present editors alone, "ed." is used.) This is followed by a semicolon, and the original (MS) reading. For clarity, the lemma and the copy-text reading include the word preceding and the word following the variant word or punctuation mark, except for variants in spelling, word-division, accents, and italics. Unless otherwise indicated, all American editions (through the Centenary) later than the one in which the lemma originated carry the lemma reading, except in such accidentals as punctuation and capitalization; in those classes there are so many variations between editions that a full listing would swell the apparatus to unmanageable size. Later printings from the plates of the 1850 edition, however, do not carry the corrected readings except where the siglum "57" is given for the lemma. Examples of entries using this format are as follows:

11.18 ˙to blind the] 70; to bind the
90.18 instantly impair that] RWE, 70; instantly destroy that

A different format is used if *not* all the editions later than the one responsible for the emendation carry the same reading. After the bracket appear the sigla for all the editions (and other authority, if any) which do carry the lemma reading; then a semicolon; after the original reading appear the sigla for the manuscript and any editions agreeing with it; if still other readings are found, they are shown after the original reading (separated from it by a semicolon, and separated from each other by semicolons if there are more than one), each followed by the sigla for the editions carrying it. (The siglum "57" is not used unless the 1857 and later printings from the 1850 plates differ from the first printing.) A dash between two sigla indicates a series of two or more editions in chronological order; "70–C" stands for 70, 76, R, and C, but "70, C" stands for those two editions only. British editions, if recorded, are shown separately, or discussed in a note. For example:

17.19 Shakspearian] 76; Shaksperian MS–50, R–C; Shakespearian 70
24.20 magnetize] 70–76; magnetise MS–50, R–C

Further explanation of each emendation is given, if needed, in a textual note following the entry.

Rejected Substantives and Spellings. All substantive variants and changes in spelling (including word-division and accents) appearing in the American editions from 1850 through the Centenary but not adopted in this edition (except those recorded with emendations) are listed here. Spelling variants, though not generally significant for meaning, are included in order to call attention to spelling as a feature of Emerson's style. However, other variants in accidentals, such as punctuation and capitalization, are not recorded unless they change meaning, syntax, or emphasis, or unless they involve changes directed by Emerson himself. A record of all variations in accidentals in the editions collated has been made and is retained by the editors.

Problems arising from the fact that the copy-text for this volume is a manuscript led us to decide to use a somewhat different format for this section of the apparatus from that used in some previous volumes of this edition, as well as from that used in the Emendations. After the page and line number of this edition, the lemma is followed by a right-hand square bracket, but without a siglum. The bracket is followed by the rejected variant (or variants) with the siglum or sigla for the edition(s) carrying that reading. All editions whose sigla do not appear agree with the lemma; if two or more editions carry a rejected reading, their sigla are cited as "70–R," "50, R–C," or the like, as explained in Emendations. Examples are as follows:

8.14   zodiack] zodiac 50–C [i.e., all editions, 50 through C]
25.12   anything] any thing 50 [i.e., 50 only]

Two or more rejected variants are given in chronological order of their first appearance.

3.15   great is] great men is 70–76; great man is R–C

The reason for the rejection of a specific variant in cases where such rejection might be considered debatable is explained in a textual note following the entry.

Word-Division. Two lists are appended to record line-end division of possible compounds. The first shows the forms adopted in this edition for such words that are (or may have been, or perhaps should have been) hyphenated at the line-end in copy-text. This task is made more difficult than usual by certain characteristics of the manuscript: the fact that some ends of lines (and perhaps some hyphens) cannot be seen because of the binding; and Emerson's inconsistencies in the use of the hyphen and in the formation of compounds. In a few cases, the same compound appears in different forms ("everything" and "every thing"; *"quasi* omnipresence" and *"quasi*-omnipresence"). In others, compounds with a common element are formed in different ways ("selfreliance" and "self-relying"; "wellmarked" and "well-managed"). In determining the form to be printed in this edition, evidence from Emerson's other writings (especially those in manuscript, such as the letters and journals) is used as much as possible. But the problem is complicated by Emerson's frequent failure to use hyphens in dividing words at the ends of lines, even those that are obviously meant to be printed solid: for example, "acquaint / ance"; "Shaks / peare"; and "individ / ualism." Thus, when possible compounds like "every / thing" and "every / body" are divided at line-end without a hyphen, the decision on how to print them is based on the fact that when they occur within the line in the MS, "everything" is almost always one word (about twenty times as often as "every thing"), whereas "every body" is always two words. Others such as "in / doors," which occur only once, must be decided on some other basis.

In contrast to other volumes in this edition for which copy-text is a printed edition (and in which only those possible compounds hyphenated at line-end are listed), this volume includes in the list that follows all possible compounds divided at line-end in the MS, either with or without a hyphen, and prints them in the form adopted in the present text. Each is followed by a superscript symbol showing how it is divided in the MS: ° for no hyphen, [1] for single hyphen (-), [2] for double hyphen (-), and [#] when the hyphen (if there is one) is lost in the binding. Because word-division in the 1850 edition of this book differs so markedly from that of the MS, the evidence of printed editions is used cautiously and has less weight than that of Emerson's manuscript writings.

The second list records the copy-text forms of possible compounds hyphenated at line-end in this edition. Words coincidentally divided at line-end both in this edition and in the MS are given in the form that would have been adopted had they fallen within the line here and are marked with a dagger (†). In these cases reference to the first list will show whether the MS division was with no hyphen, a double or single hyphen, or a possible hyphen lost in the binding.

I. *CW* forms of possible compounds which were divided at line-end in the copy-text:

3.3	demigods[1]	14.1	staff-like[1]
3.16	manhood[2]	28.14	selfexistence[1]
8.18	map-maker[1]	32.25	Whosoever[1] (Whoso-/)
12.25	mankind[2]	40.17	somebody[1]

40.27	Franklin-like[2]		101.19	non-intercourse[1]
42.10	everything[0]		112.13	balance-wheel[1]
48.9	everything[0]		115.16	sharpsighted[1]
48.17	prose-writing[1]		116.10	mischooses[1]
48.23	selfevolving[2]		116.31	twenty-three[0]
49.11	well-bred[2]		118.2	goodnatured[1]
58.2	spirit-realm[2]		119.7	moonlight[1]
63.9	reappearance[1]		125.8	†straightway[1]
65.17	perpetual-angular[2]		131.10	overpowering[0]
65.23	perpetual-celestial[2]		132.24	superadded[1]
67.2	picture-language[1]		135.31	everything[0]
68.32	mankind[2]		137.2	two-o'clock[0]
71.18	any one[0]		139.13	long-forgotten[2]
72.29	†fellowships[#]		141.9	overthrown[0]
80.2	passionate-peopled[2]		142.18	every body's[0]
81.4	†temple-incense[1]		142.21	land-commander[2]
81.10	†running-rigging[1]		144.13	goodnatured[1]
86.31	election-days[1]		151.18	self-registration[2]
87.20	friction-matches[2]		154.6	country-people[2]
89.29	anything[0]		154.25	drawback[1]
90.6	coincident[1]		156.14	post captains[0]
94.16	in doors[0]		162.34	lecture-room[1]
101.16	disproportion[2]		166.23	wheel-insect[2]

II. Copy-text forms of possible compounds that are hyphenated at line-end in *CW:*

8.23	semi-material		80.3	freemasons'
15.10	housemates		81.4	†temple-incense
17.14	ever-proceeding		81.10	†running-rigging
19.16	commonwealth		87.23	mince-pie
30.34	steamcoach		88.1	tomorrow
31.3	surfaceseeking		88.23	selfdevotion
34.11	nicknames		93.9	thirty-eight
40.24	soup-pans		101.4	hubbub
49.23	ethico-intellectual		101.19	cooperation
57.19	secondsight		101.25	mistimed
63.22	everlasting		109.9	rattlebrain
65.22	perpetual-vortical		115.16	strongminded
67.29	will-part		117.32	shareholder
72.6	evermore		118.2	shareholder
72.29	†fellowships		120.1	interweave

120.19	outloved	140.35	battle-field
125.8	†straightway	142.3	commonsense
131.5	tomorrow	156.24	hundredhanded
134.27	self-postponing		

This list does not include words, such as "everything," which Emerson sometimes wrote as one word and sometimes as two, but which he never hyphenated within the line.

I. USES OF GREAT MEN

Emendations in Copy-Text

1.   USES OF GREAT MEN] ed.; [no half-title in MS]; USES OF GREAT MEN. 50

    This edition regularizes the chapter headings on half-title pages and first pages of chapters, which are inconsistent in the MS but generally consistent in 50. For convenience, all titles in both the MS and 50 are listed here instead of in separate notes where they occur:

3.   Uses of Great Men MS; I. / USES OF GREAT MEN. 50

21.   II. / Plato, / or / The Philosopher. MS; PLATO; / OR, / THE PHILOSOPHER. 50

23.   [no heading in MS]; II. / PLATO; OR, THE PHILOSOPHER. 50

45.   [no half-title in either version] PLATO. / NEW READINGS. MS; PLATO: NEW READINGS. 50

51.   III. / Swedenborg; / or / The Mystic. MS; SWEDENBORG; / OR, / THE MYSTIC. 50

53.   Swedenborg [in upper left corner] MS; III. / SWEDENBORG; OR, THE MYSTIC. 50

83.   [no half-title in MS]; MONTAIGNE; / OR, / THE SKEPTIC. 50

85.   *The Skeptic.* MS; IV. / MONTAIGNE; OR, THE SKEPTIC. 50

107.   [no half-title in MS]; SHAKSPEARE / OR, / THE POET. 50 [semicolon after "SHAKSPEARE" may be broken off in type.]

109.   Shakspeare [in upper left corner] MS; V. / SHAKSPEARE; OR, THE POET. 50

127.   [no half-title in MS]; NAPOLEON; / OR, / THE MAN OF THE WORLD. 50

129.   VI / Napoleon, / or / The man of the world. MS; VI. / NAPOLEON; OR, THE MAN OF THE WORLD. 50

149.   [no half-title in MS]; GOETHE: / OR, / THE WRITER. 50
         [colon after "GOETHE" may be damaged semicolon.]

151.   GOETHE; OR THE WRITER. MS; VII. / GOETHE; OR,
         THE WRITER. 50

The wording and punctuation of chapter titles in the Table of Contents are generally consistent with the forms shown above for both the MS and 50, except that in the MS "Contents" the full title "Montaigne, or the Skeptic" is used instead of only "The Skeptic" as in the text. The forms used in this edition are closer to those of the MS than to those of 50.

5.10   *effet*] C; *effèt*

This edition normally corrects Emerson's misspellings and errors in accentuation and capitalization of foreign words.

6.24   elemental; the] ed.; elemental; The

The 1850 edition changed the semicolon to a period and kept the capital "T"; this edition adopts the opposite solution, as what Emerson probably intended. He frequently capitalized the first word after a colon (e.g., 5.7), but seldom after a semicolon. It is possible that in some of these cases he changed a period to a semicolon or colon, but neglected to reduce the capital to lower case.

7.10   races. [no ¶] We] 50; races. // [¶] We

A new paragraph does not seem to be needed here, and Emerson may have made the change in correcting proof. The MS page ending with "races" seems to have been rewritten.

8.15   sciences, the] 50; sciences the
*8.23   of these] 50; of These
*8.24   aids. We] 50; aids. we
9.23   us? We] 50; us. We

Emerson was not consistent in his punctuation of rhetorical questions, but a question mark seems to be needed here.

9.36   reader's] 50; readers
11.18   to blind the] 70; to bind the

An obvious improvement in meaning; it is not marked in Emerson's correction copy, but was probably changed by him in revising or proofreading for the 1870 edition.

11.26   condition. The] 50; condition, a new celestial geometry. The
         (Chap as in MS)

Because of its position on the MS page, the phrase is not likely to have been accidentally omitted by the compositor; presumably Emerson deleted it in proof. It is not in the source passage (*JMN*, IX, 258–259); but cf. 47.37.

13.7   *peau d'âne*] R-C; *Peau d'Ane* MS; *peau d'ane* 50–76
13.16   clock; I . . . persons; I . . . hurts; I] RWE, 70–76; clock. I . . . persons. I . . . hurts. I MS–50, R-C

14.3 subtilizer] 70; subtiliser
  Emerson wrote this word with an "s" here, but in some others ending in "ise" or "ize" (and their derivatives) it is not always clear which letter he used. In his correction copy he changed "Swedenborgise" to "Swedenborgize" at 75.10; and he seems to have preferred "z" in most words of this type (see the Emendations note for "recognize" at 9.10 in *CW*, II, 269), though not in certain others such as "advertise," "enterprise," and "cognisant." In general, words which were changed to the "z" spelling in 50 or 70 are similarly emended here; but see the Rejected Substantives and Spellings (RSS) notes at 6.1 and 79.22.

*14.6 Then he] 50; Then He
14.14 changed? Altogether] 50; changed. Altogether
*15.3 energy. There] 50; energy. there
*15.15 assimilation goes] 50; assimilation, goes
  Emerson deleted a parenthetical phrase in the MS between these two words, but failed to delete the comma before it.

15.19 civilization] 50; civilisation
17.6 thought! They] 50; thought! they
  Emerson was not consistent in capitalization after an exclamation point, but a capital letter seems preferable here, since a complete sentence follows.

17.19 Shakspearian] 76; Shaksperian MS–50, R–C; Shakespearian 70
  Emerson spelled the name and its derivatives in various ways at different periods of his life; see the Rejected Substantives notes in *CW*, I, 294 (for 61.36), and *CW*, II, 275 (for 5.6). Elsewhere in this MS, however, he always omits the first "e" and includes the second "a"; this form is adopted here for consistency. See also the RSS note for 9.37 below.

*18.15 dependence. And] 50; dependence, And
*18.22 them! But] 50; them! but

Rejected Substantives and Spellings

3.9 nutricious] nutritious 50–C
  Although Worcester's Dictionary does not authorize the MS spelling, the *OED* shows it as an alternate (but rare) form in the eighteenth and nineteenth centuries.

3.15 great is] great men is 70–76; great man is R–C
  The singular pronoun in the next sentence seems to rule against "men" as an authorial revision; "man" is better, but is a posthumous emendation by Cabot.

3.25 today] to-day 50–C
4.18 enquire] inquire 50–C

4.22   toward] towards 50–C
5.1   our hand. I] our hands. I 50–C
         The change from singular to plural seems unnecessary; it
         probably was a compositor's error.
5.14   observed that there] observed there 50–C
5.14   characters] character 50–C
6.1   cognisant] cognizant 50–C
         This word is consistently spelled with an "s" throughout the
         MS, and is an exception to Emerson's general preference for "z"
         in words of this type; see the Emendation note for 14.3.
6.24   everything] every thing 50, R–C
         Most compounds of "every" and "any" are usually written
         solid as one word in the MS, but are regularly printed as two
         words in 1850 and as one word in 1870. Because Emerson
         marked some of them in his correction copy of 1850 to change to
         one word, it is assumed that he generally preferred this form;
         however, in a few cases where the two-word form is used in the
         MS (and where the context suggests that two words may be
         preferable), the MS version is retained. See also the RSS note to
         24.12.
8.11   labours] labors 50–C
         Emerson spells the great majority of this class of words with
         the British "our" ending in this MS, as well as in some journals
         and letters of this period. But there are exceptions — e.g.,
         "labor" at 5.3. The copy-text spelling is followed in all cases in
         this edition. For convenience, all MS "our" spellings (all of
         which are changed to "or" in 1850 and later editions) are re-
         corded in the following list instead of in separate notes (unless
         entered for another reason) where they occur:
         9.2 vigour, 9.19 succour, 10.9 honour, 15.29 saviours, 26.26
         honour, 27.7 and 31.14 favour, 33.7 tenour, 34.27 honours, 34.28
         endeavour, 35.17 honoured, 36.30 splendours, 39.35 laboured,
         41.33 humourist, 41.34 rumour, 48.13 honours, 50.13 colours,
         53.10 labour, 53.11 labourer, 57.8 labours, 57.15 honoured,
         57.15 favour, 60.12 honour, 62.11 humour, 63.5 vigour, 64.9 and
         64.27 favourite, 76.2 endeavour, 77.19 harbours, 78.3 humour,
         78.21 rumours, 79.17 rumour, 81.14 favour, 86.9 colours, 87.11
         honour, 88.19 labours, 90.11–15 Labour . . . labour . . . labour
         . . . labourers, 91.24 errours, 93.20 honour, 93.29 humourist, 95.6
         vapour, 97.2 endeavours, 100.21 rumour, 101.36 labour, 103.1
         neighbours, 104.18 succour, 110.14 labours, 114.38 labour,
         117.34 neighbours, 120.21 behaviour, 122.15 favour, 122.29
         splendour, 123.25 rumoured, 124.3 splendour, 124.10 colours,
         129.16–19 labour (4 times), 130.29 honours, 134.30 splendour,

136.27 vigour, 137.16 behaviour, 138.17 labour, 139.23 rigours, 140.34 Honour, 140.34 valour, 142.5 vigour, 143.4 endeavour, 146.25 splendour, 147.1 endeavours, 152.27 rumour, 155.29 honoured ... honour, 159.2-3 colours ... colour, 163.34 armoury, 165.2 Colours, 166.15 labourer, 166.35 honour.

8.13   foreplane] fore-/plane R; fore-plane C

8.14   zodiack] zodiac 50–C

The MS spelling is not authorized by Webster (1828) or Worcester, but is cited in the *OED* for this period.

8.15   contribution] contributions 50–C

9.13   instructer] instructor 70–C

9.37   Shakspeare's] Shakespeare's 70

The MS is consistent in the spelling of this name throughout except at 17.19 (see the Emendation note to that line), and all editions except 1870 follow it. Further instances of this variant in 1870 are not recorded here.

11.8   metre] meter 76

11.23   immoveable] immovable 50–C

12.11   lawgivers] law-givers 50, R–C

12.32   good." / [no¶] How] good." / [¶] How 50–C

13.1   appletree] apple-tree 50–C

13.14   selfseeker] self-seeker 50–C

Although Emerson often hyphenated compounds of "self" in his journals (see the Emendation note to *The American Scholar*, 62.26 in *CW*, I, 292), he often did not; and in this MS he usually wrote them solid as one word.

13.27   selfesteems] self-esteems 50–C

13.30   Scourges of] Scourgers of 70

13.35   well born] well-/born 50; well-born 70–C

In the MS it is not clear whether this is one word or two.

14.17   ill used] ill-used 50–C

See the preceding note on 13.35.

14.25   not the mowing ideot] not a mowing idiot 50–C (Chap as in MS)

The source passage (*JMN*, IX, 265–266) has "the dimmest sighted ideot." The 1850 "a" seems a bit more idiomatic than the MS "the," but not enough so to make one feel confident that the change was made by the author. Worcester and Webster do not authorize the MS (and journal) "ideot," but the *OED* cites it as an alternate spelling as late as the nineteenth century.

14.31   selfgratulation] self-gratulation 50–C

14.32   marshal] marshall R

15.11   alike] like R–C

15.21   is, the universal] is, universal 76

15.31	alike] like R–C
15.36	pigmies] pygmies 70–76
16.6	badhearted] bad-hearted 50–C
16.27	goodwill ... goodwill] good will ... good will 50, R–C; good-will ... good-will 70–76
16.31	everything] every thing 50, R–C
16.35	Each is selfdefended.] [This sentence is lined through in pencil in Emerson's correction copy, but this is the only such mark in the text for which there is no deletion sign in the margin. Presumably Emerson decided not to delete it, and it is retained here.]
16.35	selfdefended] self-defended 50–C
17.9	selfreliance] self-reliance 50–C
18.2	selfdevotion] self-devotion 50–C
*18.25	exaltation. [no¶] The] exaltation. [¶] The 50–C
	Changes in the MS indicate that Emerson may have intended a new paragraph here, but changed his mind.
19.31	metres] meters 76
20.8	opake] opaque 50–C
	The MS spelling is authorized by Webster and Worcester, and Emerson used it elsewhere; e.g., in a deleted passage in another part of this MS, and in *Nature* at 43.31 (see note in *CW*, I, 291).

II. PLATO

Emendations in Copy-Text

23.1	among secular books] 76; among books
	This qualification of the original sweeping generalization was presumably made, or at least approved, by Emerson.
23.11	twenty-two hundred] 50; 2200
23.18	Augustine, Copernicus] 50; Augustine / Copernicus
23.20	generalizer] 50; generaliser
24.20	magnetize] 70–76; magnetise MS–50, R–C
*25.18	purpose. [¶] Great] 50; purpose. [¶] great
26.3	eighty-one] 50; eightyone
26.19	into a hundred] 50; into a / a hundred
*27.30	superlative; he] 50; superlative // he
28.2	recognizes] 50; recognises
28.20	good, as] ed.; good, — as
	The MS has dashes after "grounds" (line 20) and "good" (same line); the 1850 edition deletes the first and keeps the sec-

ond. But the balance of ideas is shown more clearly by keeping the first and deleting the second.

28.31   stuff; the] 50; stuff / the
28.33   sage,) "to] 50; sage,) to
28.37   *I* and *mine*] 50; I and mine [no ital.]
         In the source passage (*JMN*, IX, 321) quotation marks are used around "I" and "mine."
30.1   organization] 50; organisation
30.28   in its splendid] 50; in it splendid
         An obvious slip of the pen.
31.3   defining, result-loving] 50; defining result-loving
31.7   Europe; he] 50; Europe. he
*31.10   is as easy] 50; is as // as easy
*32.9   is, always] 50; is always
32.11   history, are] 50; history / are
33.3   paralyzes] 70; paralyses
33.10   Socrates. But] 50; Socrates; But
33.19   philosophize] 70; philosophise
33.24   spindle. [¶] But] 50; spindle. Poetry has never attempted heights beyond the Timaeus // [¶] But
         The omitted sentence is repeated (with modifications) at 50.8–9 in the printed text, and was probably deleted here by Emerson in correcting proofs. It is also omitted in Chapman's edition, and so may have been deleted from the Weir Transcript (see Textual Introduction).
33.26   Be bold] 50; Be Bold
*33.29   bold." His] 50; bold." his
*34.6   analysis, mania] 50; analytic mania
         The list as originally written was "epic, analytic [no comma] / musical, and intuitive," four adjectives. In revising the MS, Emerson neglected to change the second adjective to a noun like the others (but probably did so in correcting proofs). Chapman also changed "analytic" to "analysis," probably independently, but arranged the words in a different order as the result of Weir's interpretation of the MS interlineations.
34.14   volley! He] 50; volley / He
34.32   He is a] 50; He a
         An obvious slip of the pen.
*35.23   *knowable!* They] 50; *knowable!* they
*35.35   it. Dialectic] 50; it. dialectic
36.9   that truth] 50; that, truth
*36.28   education. He] 50; education. he
36.31   achievement] 50; achievment
         The MS spelling is fairly common in Emerson's journals and

letters, but it is not authorized by Webster or Worcester or recorded by the *OED*.

36.31   Socrates," said Glauco, "is] RWE (substantially), R–C; Socrates, said Glauco is MS; Socrates, said Glauco, is 50–76

Emerson originally had quotation marks here in the MS, but for some reason deleted them. He made the correction in the list pasted in the front of his correction copy (but with the quotation marks reversed, "said Glauco") but did not mark it in the text. The Riverside edition was the first to make the emendation, probably independently.

36.36   gymnastics] RWE, ed.; gymastic MS; gymnastic 50–C
*37.16   nature. His] 50; nature. his
37.21   artificers." The] 50; artificers. The
*37.23   silver; those] ed.; silver, // those

Emerson used a semicolon at the corresponding point in an earlier version of this passage (see Appendix 2); the 1850 edition uses a period and capital "T."

38.1   Such, O] 50; Such O
38.6   said, 'I . . . business.' [¶] He] 50; said; I . . . business. [¶] He
*38.15   add, *There*] ed.; add *There*

The 1850 edition inserts the comma, but uses single quotation marks instead of italics for the quoted sentence.

38.28   beginnings.' [¶] A 50; beginnings. // [¶] A
*38.32   says: — "Let] 50; says "Let
39.20   to *the Same,* and] ed.; to *the Same* and

The 1850 edition italicizes "to" and uses a semicolon after *"same"* (not capitalized); this is misleading, and was probably done by the compositor rather than the author.

39.28   the ground of] RWE, 70; the limitation of
40.28   that it] 50; that, it
41.3   one else could] 70–76; one could MS–50, R–C

This looks more like an author's than a compositor's correction; but it was not adopted by the Riverside and Centenary editors, who generally followed the substantives (though not the accidentals) of the first edition.

*42.2   affirms the immortality] 50; affirms the / the immortality
42.10   everything] 70–76; every / thing MS; every thing 50, R–C

Because "everything" is almost always written solid as one word elsewhere in the MS, it probably would have been here except for the line-end division, where Emerson frequently omitted the hyphen. It is solid in the source passage (*JMN*, X, 483).

42.34   not, what] ed.; not // what

The words "what . . . work," were inserted at the top of the

MS page after the rest of the sentence had been written. The 1850 edition has a comma and dash after "not" as well as after "work"; some punctuation is needed for clarity, but commas are adequate in both places.

43.21 art. And] 50; art: And

The MS punctuation makes the sentence quite long and rambling, with two somewhat different ideas. Emerson may have divided it while correcting proofs.

43.32 all: so] 50; all. so

*44.12 respect. His] 50; respect. his

44.18 seventeen hundred and sixty] 50; 1760

Rejected Substantives and Spellings

23.4 cornerstone] corner-stone 50–C

23.4 fountainhead] fountain-head 50–C

23.6 practick] practical 50–C (Chap as in 1850)

The MS word could be misread as "practicle," which the compositor may have taken for a misspelling. The source passage (*JMN,* IX, 245) has "practical," but Emerson's changing to the obsolescent form in the MS seems to indicate a preference for it. For "practick," cf. *JMN,* IV, 110, 314; VIII, 505, n. 59.

23.10 boulders] bowlders 76

24.12 every body] everybody 70–76

In contrast to "everything" and "everywhere," which Emerson usually wrote solid, he usually wrote "every body" and "every one" as two words.

24.29 every thing] everything 70–76

Although "everything" is usually one word in this MS (cf. RSS notes to 6.24 and 24.12), here it is clearly two, and a somewhat different meaning from its usual one seems intended.

24.37 stonequarries) stone quarries 50–70, R–C; stone-quarries 76

25.12 anything] any thing 50

25.20 writing] writings 50–C

25.21 house- and street-life] house and street life 50–C

25.28 born 430] born 427 R–C

The date 427 is probably more nearly correct for Plato's birth, but the correction is posthumous.

26.8 tabletalk] table-talk 50–C

26.18 has opened itself] has spread itself 50–C

Although this may be an author's revision in proof, it is more likely a compositor's misreading, for the word in Emerson's writing could easily be mistaken for "spread." Moreover, in the

context, "opened" seems the stronger as well as the more unusual word.

26.21   anything] any thing 50, R–C

26.21   shortlived] short-lived 50–C

26.29   cry, and scream] cry, scream 50–C

The source passage (*JMN*, IX, 324–325) has "cry and
scream."

27.24   teachers. [no ¶] Before] teachers. [¶] Before 50–C

The word "teachers" is the last on one MS page, "Before" the
first word on the next. A different compositor took over at "Before" and evidently set a new paragraph from force of habit,
since compositors' stints usually began at paragraph divisions.

28.10   unperishable] imperishable 50–C

The source passage (*JMN*, IX, 292) also reads "unperishable";
in Emerson's writing "un" could easily be misread as "im."

28.14   selfexistence] self-existence 50–C

In the MS the word is divided and hyphenated after "self" at
the end of a line; but as most "self" compounds are written solid
elsewhere in the MS (see note on 13.14), it is assumed that this
one would have been if occurring within the line. Note also
"selfexistent" at 48.21.

28.15   strictly-blended] strictly blended 70–76

28.24   all beings] all being 50–C (Chap as in 1850)

This would make sense either way, but with slightly different
meanings. Copy-text is followed to be on the safe side, even
though the change may be Emerson's.

29.2   preeminent] preëminent 50, R–C; pre-eminent 70–76

30.9   immoveable] immovable 50–C

30.19   manipulation] manifestation 50–C (Chap as in MS)

Probably "manifestation" is a misreading of the MS. Both
words make sense in the context: "manifestation" fits better with
"comprehensible results," but "manipulation" better with
"skill" and "forms." It is also noted that "manifestation" had
appeared at 29.14, and the compositor's memory of it may have
influenced his reading here.

30.24   pinmakers] pin-makers 50–C

30.34   steammill . . . steamcoach] steam-mill . . . steam-coach 50–C

30.35   townmeeting . . . ballotbox] town-meeting . . . ballot-box 50–C

31.3   surfaceseeking, operagoing] surface-seeking, opera-going 50–C

31.5   Asia are in] Asia is in 76

The 1876 change is an improvement grammatically; but
Emerson was not always precise about agreement of subject and
verb when a plural phrase came between them.

31.16   manchild] man-child 50–C

31.28	soupladles . . . horsedoctors] soup-ladles . . . horse-doctors 50–C
31.32	selfpoised] self-poised 50–C
31.37	seashore] sea-shore 50–C
32.10	æther] ether 76
32.28	everything] every thing 50, R–C
32.32	excellences] excellencies 50–C

A similar variation occurs in "Art" (*Essays: First Series;* see *CW*, II, 217.15): "extravagancies" in 1841, corrected in 1847 to "extravagances."

33.15	honour, a] honor, and a 50–C
34.2	but he has] but has 50–C
34.14	goodnaturedly] good-naturedly 50–C
34.16	moderately] modestly 50–C

Probably a misreading of the MS.

34.35	commonsense] common sense 50–70; common-sense 76–C
35.9	guaged] gauged 70–C

Although "gauged" is the spelling preferred by Worcester and other contemporary dictionaries, Emerson's spelling is accepted here because the *OED* records it as a fairly common alternate form in the eighteenth and nineteenth centuries.

35.10	everything] every thing 50, R–C
36.8	Lawgiver] law-/giver 50, R; law-giver 70–76, C
36.8	lawreceiver] law-receiver 50–C
36.10	everything] every thing 50
36.11	baulked] balked 70–76
36.15	befal] befall 50–C
36.16	dæmon] demon 70–76

This word and its derivatives are spelled with "e" instead of "æ" throughout the 1870 edition and usually (though not quite always) in the 1876. Further examples of this variant will not be recorded.

38.33	two parts . . . and these . . . sections representing . . . of these . . . worlds, you] two main parts . . . and let these . . . sections represent . . . of each of these . . . worlds. You R–C

This series of changes results from Cabot's attempt to clarify the passage, which is clear in the MS but had been muddied by an intrusive (and misleading) comma after "sections" (line 34) in 1850 and later editions.

39.18	artificer in] artificer, he says, in R–C

Cabot for some reason deleted the quotation marks around this passage and inserted "he says," perhaps to show that it was not an exact quotation.

39.23	beautiful." [no ¶] Thus] beautiful." [¶] Thus 50–C
40.6	good nature] good-nature 70–76

40.18   country people] country-/people 50; country-people 70–C

40.22   everything] every thing 50, R–C

40.22   anything] any thing 50

40.25   unnameable] unnamable C

40.30   ears, and immense] ears, — an immense 50–C

        Because "and" is written in the MS as "&," it is not a slip of the pen for "an"; the change could be Emerson's, but is more likely a compositor's error.

40.36   wellnigh] well-nigh 50, R–C

        As pointed out in the Emendation note to *The American Scholar*, 58.1 (*CW*, I, 292), Emerson had spelled this first as two words without hyphen, but accepted the change in the second edition to the solid form (which was preferred by Worcester but not Webster). He may also have directed the correction to that form here in the 1870 edition.

41.3   undergarment] under garment 50–C

41.5   this pleasure] the pleasure 50–C

41.18   such a magnitude] such magnitude 70–76

41.31   crampfish] cramp-fish 50–C

41.33   hardheaded] hard-headed 50–C

42.15   street- and market-debater] street and market debater 50–C

43.7   selfevident] self-evident 50–C

44.1   or any] or of any 50–C

44.6   transcendant] transcendent 70–C

        Although Emerson spelled "transcendental" and "Transcendentalism" in the preferred way (with the second "e"), he quite often spelled "transcendant" with an "a" as here in the MS. The *OED* records this as an alternate spelling. See Rejected Variant note to "The Method of Nature," 135.34 (*CW*, I, 302).

44.7   to honour him] to know him 50–C (Chap as in 50)

        The fact that Chapman agrees here with the 1850 edition may indicate that this was Emerson's change. However, the word as written in the MS could easily be misread as "know"; for a similar error by the first editors of Emerson's journals in transcribing "honours" as "knows," see *JMN*, I, xxix. In the context, "honour" seems the stronger and better word.

44.12   trueliest] truliest 76

        The MS spelling is not authorized by Webster or Worcester, but was accepted by the printers of all editions except 1876. Cf. "truelier" in the 1841 edition of "History" (*Essays: First Series*) in *CW*, II, 23.5, which probably represents a MS spelling, but was changed to "trulier," probably by the printer, in 1847.

44.19   greateyed] great-eyed 50–C

PLATO: NEW READINGS

Emendations in Copy-Text

45.1	new] RWE, ed.; excellent
*46.9	intellect, the] 50; intellect the
46.31	recomposition, and] 50; recomposition and
	The comma is needed for clarity.
46.36	soul; his] 50; soul. // his
*47.8	assimilation; his] 50; assimilation, his
	There may be a semicolon (now hidden by the binding) after the deleted matter which followed and was in apposition with "Doctrine of assimilation."
47.12	God," and] 50; God." &
47.18	intrinsic, though] 50; intrinsic; though
	The semicolon obscures the syntax and meaning.
47.32	instructed that ... in their] 50; instructed y^t ... in y^r
48.9	everything] 70 (every-/thing), 76–C; every / thing MS; every thing 50
	See the Emendation note to 42.10.
48.11	thus: — "Of] 50; thus; "of
*48.11	are left to] 50; are left // left to
48.27	him the fact] 50; him the / the fact
48.37	nature; man] 70–76; nature / man MS; nature: man 50, R–C
	Although Emerson's uses of the colon and semicolon were at times almost interchangeable, here a semicolon seems more in accord with his usual practice.
49.19	node: a theory] 50; node. a theory
*49.25	Platonize] 70; Platonise
49.26(2)	Platonist] 50; platonist
	Elsewhere always spelled with a capital "P."
49.27	writes, "Nature] 50; writes "Nature
	Emerson generally has some punctuation before a direct quotation.
49.28	mean," or] 50; mean." or
49.29	"He] 50; "he
	Emerson usually capitalized the first word of a direct quotation, though not always.
*50.2	is a Platonist] 50; is Platonist
	Emerson first wrote "is Plato," then changed "Plato" to "Platonist" but did not insert an article; probably he added it in proof, since he normally used "Platonist" as a noun.
50.13	of charlatanism. [¶] It] RWE, 57; of charlatan. [¶] It
	The 1850 edition, which here followed the MS, had its plates

corrected in several places for the 1857 printing. Chapman
made the same correction independently.

Rejected Substantives and Spellings

45.16   nowise] no wise 50, R–C
*46.22   reason. [¶] These] reason. [no ¶] These 50–C
46.25   secondsight] second sight 50–C
47.7   zodiack] zodiac 50–C
47.10   everywhere] every where 50
47.25   and that though] and, though 50–C
47.34   everything] every thing 50, R–C
47.35   secondsight] second sight 50–C
48.7   connexion] connection 50–C

Emerson generally preferred the spelling with "x," which is
listed by Webster (without approval) and authorized by
Worcester, but also spelled it "connection" in this MS, e.g., at
48.29.

48.17   prose-writing] prose writing 50–C
48.17   that the one is] that injustice is R–C

A stylistic sophistication, presumably by Cabot.

48.21   selfexistent] self-existent 50–C
48.23   selfevolving] self-evolving 50–C

The MS divides and hyphenates the word at the end of a line;
in view of "selfexistent" two lines above, and of other compounds of "self" throughout the book, presumably it would
have been written solid if within the line.

49.21   shortlived] short-lived 50–C
49.22   wellmarked] well-marked 50–C

It is not certain whether this is one word or two in the MS,
but no hyphen is used.

49.24   expansion] expression 50–C (Chap as in MS)

Either word makes sense in the context; but since "expansions" of thought were discussed in a previous paragraph (see
46.11), "expression" is probably a compositor's error.

49.25   Michel] Michael R–C
*49.33   'tis only the magnitude of] 'tis the magnitude only of 50–C
(Chap as in MS)

The compositor misread Emerson's marking for interlineation
in the MS.

50.7   argument, most] arguments, most 50–C (Chap as in MS)

The compositor misunderstood Emerson's meaning here, as is
shown by the incorrect comma after "them," three words further along, in the 1850 and later editions.

50.23   Michel] Michael R–C

III. SWEDENBORG

Emendations in Copy-Text

53.2   not of the] 50; not of / of the
53.8   pictures which] 50; pictures. // which
*54.16   class of] 50; class / Of
54.27   Abul Khair] ed.; Abul Khain
         The name is spelled "Abulkhair" in the source passage (*JMN*, IX, 284), and this is .nore nearly correct (see the Informational note) than the spelling Emerson used in the MS.
54.29(2)   said, "All] 50; said, "all
         Note the capital "A" at the beginning of the preceding quotation.
55.6   knew. "For] 50; knew. For
55.22   Μύεσις] ed.; Μυεσις MS–76; Μίησις R–C
         Because the *OED* and standard etymological dictionaries do not give either of these forms as the origin of "mystic" (deriving it rather from μύστης, one initiated, from μύειν, to close), the MS spelling is retained, but with accent added where it would normally go.
55.35   achievements] 50; achievments
56.31   twenty-eight] 50; twentyeight
57.1   Dædalus Hyperboreus] 50; book on mines (Chap as in MS)
57.4   fifty-four] 50; fiftyfour [above "54," not deleted]
57.22   through] 50; thro'
57.31   eighty-fifth] 50; 85th
59.26   left little for] 76; left nothing for MS–70, R–C
         A revision (presumably by Emerson) similar to that at 23.1.
60.33   Viking] 50; viking
         The "v" in the MS may be either capital or lower case.
61.6   food determining] 70; food, determining
61.14   spine. Manifestly, at] 50; spine. At
61.20   feet the] 50; feet, the
         The change is needed for clarity of meaning.
62.22   universality, eating] ed.; universality, / Eating (semicolon in 50)
62.36   an excellent edition] 50; an admirable edition (Chap as in MS)
         Perhaps changed in proof to avoid repetition with "admirable" in 63.13.
*63.12   literary skill, this] 50; literary help, this (Chap as in MS)
         "Aided . . . by his . . . help" would have been as tautological as the original "Aided . . . by his . . . aid"; it was probably changed by Emerson in proof.

63.18   soul, long] 50; soul long
63.23   on axles that] 70; on axes that
         Almost certainly "axes" was a slip of the pen.
*64.2   things. "For] ed.; things." "For
         In 1850 and all later editions, quotation marks appear around
         the sentence "He noted . . . all things." In changing from a di-
         rect to an indirect quotation in the MS, Emerson deleted the
         first words of the sentence (and thus, in effect, the quotation
         marks preceding them, though they are not actually lined
         through), but not the quotation marks at the end. It is believed
         that the punctuation of the present edition better reflects his in-
         tention.
64.12   by the microcosm] 50; by microcosm
         Another slip of the pen.
64.30   larger ones, but] 50; larger forms, but
         Probably Emerson changed this in proof to avoid the ex-
         cessive repetition of "forms" in the sentence.
66.17   known for] 50; known, for
         The comma slightly confuses the meaning of the sentence; but
         the 1850 edition, while correcting this fault, created more con-
         fusion by moving the comma earlier in the line from after
         "them" to after "only."
*66.25   world. [no ¶] The] 50; world: // [¶?] The
         The paragraph indentation in the MS is not certain; and the
         development of the idea does not seem to call for a new para-
         graph at this point.
67.9   fifty-fourth] 50; fiftyfourth
67.17   form in] R; form, in
         Deletion of the comma clarifies the fact that "form" is a noun,
         not the infinitive of a verb.
69.6   religion: his . . . application: he] RWE, 70–76; religion. His . . .
         application. He MS–50, R–C
69.16   counterparts; into] 50; counterparts, into
         The comma destroys the balance of the parallel phrases, sepa-
         rated elsewhere in the sentence by semicolons.
*70.7   mankind. That] 50; mankind that
70.23   Man is man by] 50; Man is man, by
70.24   knowing and understanding] 50; knowing & // and under-
         standing
70.29   states; everything] ed.; states; Everything (colon in 50)
71.4   wood. "I . . . heaven." [¶] He] 50; wood. I . . . heaven. [¶] He
         The quotation marks indicate that it is Swedenborg, not
         Emerson, who is speaking.
71.5   wearied? They] 50; wearied? they
*71.13   Him:" "Ends] 50; Him:" Ends

71.21 love, from ... wisdom, and] ed.; love from ... wisdom and

Some punctuation is needed; the 1850 edition uses semicolons at these points, and commas after "angels," "voice," "sound," and "words" — a heavier punctuation than Emerson generally uses in this manuscript.

*71.31 had been grand if] 50; had been grand // grand if

71.34 Platonic] 50; platonic

72.4 generation; and] 50; generation. and

*72.30 anything] 70–76; any ↑thing↓ MS; any thing 50, R–C

In the MS, "thing" is inserted above the line (with a caret below); the phrase was originally "any divine meaning." But "anything" is generally written as one word elsewhere.

*73.12 therefore vipers] 50; therefore Vipers

73.12 cockatrices, asps] 50; cockatrices / asps

*73.17 proportion hard to hit of] ed.; proportion / hard to hit // hard to hit / of

The 1850 edition eliminates the repetition, but inserts commas after "proportion" and "hit."

73.23 "Animal Kingdom"] ed. (after Chap); "animal kingdom"

The 1850 and later editions capitalize both words but drop the quotation marks, which Emerson generally used with book titles.

*73.25 falls into] 50; falls to ↑into↓

*74.14 filth and corruption] 50; ↑filth &↓ & corruption

75.6 magnetizer] 50; magnetiser

75.10 Swedenborgize] RWE, 70; Swedenborgise

75.18 *soi disant*] 50; *soidisant*

75.23 dogmatizing] 70; dogmatising

75.25 paralyzed] 70; paralysed

76.2 thought, wasted] 50; thought wasted

*76.10 do,' asks ... reader, 'with] 50; do' asks ... reader 'with

*76.12 arks and ... ephahs and] 50; arks, and ... ephahs, and

The commas in each case originally belonged to a series of three items; in reducing each series to two Emerson neglected to delete the commas, but he probably did so when correcting proof in order to make these two pairs of items balance with the two preceding and two following pairs.

76.13 lepers and] 50; lepers, and

No comma is needed in a series of two items; Emerson may have started this as another series of three and changed his mind.

76.19 purpose?" My] 50; purpose." My

*76.25 needless.' [¶] Locke] 50; needless. // [¶] Locke

The imaginary quotation originally continued for six more lines in the MS.

*76.28	in the] 50; ↑in↓ of the
76.35	nature, — with] 50; nature with

Some punctuation is needed here; and though the dash is not strictly necessary, it helps emphasize the contrast.

76.37	enlargements are purchased] 70–76; enlargements purchased MS–50, R–C

Emerson first wrote "enlargements seem purchased" and then deleted "seem" without substituting another word. He probably inserted "are" in 1870 as a stylistic improvement, since it is not needed for grammar or clarity.

77.5	wrongs; or] 50; wrongs. or
77.19	goodness harbours] ed.; goodness, harbours

The comma at the end of the restrictive relative clause confuses the syntax and meaning of the sentence, but it is in the source passage (*JMN*, XI, 177) and is retained in all previous editions.

77.34	spirits! But] 50; spirits. But
78.8	Vishnu, "I] ed.; Vishnu "I

The 1850 edition adds a dash to the comma.

*79.14	heart-beat, which makes the] 50; heart-beat, the

In the deleted passage following "heart-beat" in the MS, the word "make" is only partly deleted, and Emerson's intention is not clear. He probably clarified it while correcting proof.

*79.24	gentleman, benevolent] 50; gentleman benevolent
79.28	shall make me] RWE, ed.; makes me
80.3	freemasons'] ed.; freemason's

The word is at the end of the line in the MS, with almost no room for the apostrophe after the "s"; it is directly above the "s," and may have been intended to follow it.

80.4	Behmen! *he*] 50; Behmen! he
*80.11	wise, and with] 50; wise, and / and with
80.12	paralyzes] 50; paralyses
80.26	music? Was] 50; music. Was
80.29	hands? or] 50; hands. or
80.35	bird ever] 50; bird every

An obvious slip of the pen.

Rejected Substantives and Spellings

53.9	shortcomings] short-comings 50–70, R–C
53.9	meannesses] meanness 70–76
53.13	awe. [¶] But] awe. [no ¶] But 50–C
53.17	everything] every thing 50, R–C
53.20	who shall draw] who should draw R–C
54.1	Whence? and What] Whence? What 50–C

54.22	thee." [¶] The] thee." [no ¶] The 50–C
54.23	this caste is] this class is 70–76
55.13	he that inquires] he who inquires 76
55.19	*ecstasy*] *ecstacy* 50
55.24	Guion] Guyon R–C
55.28	o'erinforms] o'er-informs 70–76
56.2	metre] meter 76–C
56.14	Fredericks] Frederics 50–C
56.14	Cristierns] Christians R–C
56.27	chemistry and optics] chemistry, optics 70–76
56.29	brain. [¶] He] brain. [no ¶] He 50–C
56.35	Fredericshall] Frederickshald R–C
56.35	haling] hauling 50–C (Chap as in 1850)

Worcester and Webster give "hale" as a synonym for "haul," but it was less commonly used in that sense; it may have been either misread or "corrected" by both the Boston printer and either Weir or the London printer.

56.37	smelting works] smelting-works 70–76
57.19	secondsight] second sight 50–C
57.30	London, 29 March, 1772] London, March 29, 1772 50–C
57.34	goldheaded] gold-headed 50–C
58.3	begun] began 50–C

At several places in the MS, Emerson spelled the preterit of verbs of this class with "u" instead of the more usual "a"; these were all changed to "a" in the 1850 edition.

58.4	shipyards] ship-yards 50–C
58.21	Selden] Seldon 70
58.22	learning, a *quasi*-omnipresence] learning, or *quasi* omnipresence 50–C

The source passage (*JMN*, VII, 116) has "learning, an omnipresence." The "a" in the MS could be misread as "or."

58.25	in the "Principia] in his "Principia 70–76
58.34	of an university] of a university 70–76
59.8	'Tis] It is R–C

The MS lacks the apostrophe (see the introductory matter to the textual apparatus for silent emendations).

59.25	Leeuwenhoek] Leuwenhoek R–C
60.14	spicula] spiculæ R–C

The spelling "spicula" is correct as a Latin plural, but evidently Cabot (or someone else involved in the Riverside edition) mistook it for the Late Latin singular and thought it needed a plural in "æ." Cf. *CW*, III, 260 (n. to 104.31).

60.28	skeptics] sceptics 70–76

"Skeptic" and its derivatives are spelled with "c" instead of "k" throughout the 1870 and the 1876 editions, including the chapter title and running headline of Chapter IV. Further instances of this variant will not be recorded.

60.32 stablished] established 70–C

61.1 *selfsimilar*] *self-similar* 50–C

61.13 spanworm] span-worm 50–C

61.33 Everything] Every thing 50, R–C

61.37 everything] every thing 50, R–C

62.22 hybernation] hibernation 70–76

63.6 has produced his] has restored his 76–C

The 1876 and later editions have substituted a word that would perhaps be the more usual one in the context, but it seems more like an editorial than an authorial revision.

63.14 cotemporary] contemporary 70–C

Elsewhere in this MS Emerson uses the form with "con-"; but since he frequently used the form without "n" (see Rejected Variant note to *Nature*, 20.34, *CW*, I, 289, and others in that volume), copy-text is followed here.

64.27 in leasts] in beasts 70–76

An obvious typographical error; cf. 59.24.

65.25 also, conceive] also, should conceive R–C

65.36 corresponding spiritual] corresponding and spiritual 50–C

66.2 anything] any thing 50, R–C

66.11 knew of it] knew it 76–C

66.16 riddle writing] riddle-writing 50–C

66.32 space or time] space and time 50–C (Chap as in 1850)

Close examination of the MS shows that "&" was written first and then "or" over it; but it may have looked the other way round to both Weir and the Boston compositor.

67.5 rockstratum] rock-/stratum 50; rock-stratum 70–C

67.18 abstractly] abstractedly 70–76 (Bohn as in 70–76)

67.29 will-part] will part 50–C

68.27 Everything] Every thing 50, R–C

68.29 anything] any thing 50, R–C

68.34 title page] title-page 50–C

It is not clear whether the MS form is one word or two.

69.24 desart] desert 50–C

70.29 everything] every thing 50, R–C

70.31 Everything] Every thing 50, R–C

70.31 beast is not] beast are not 76

Probably an editorial "correction" of the grammar.

71.9 springtime] spring-time 50, R–C

*71.12 his greatest and most perfect] his perfect 50–C (Chap as in MS)

The omitted words were probably skipped by the compositor

because they occupied the second half of the first line on the MS page, the first half of that line being deleted.

71.28   sung] sang 50–C

72.23   candlelight] candle-light 50, R–C

72.25   profoundly eliminated. It] profoundly set forth. It R–C

Evidently Cabot thought that the use of "eliminated" in this somewhat archaic sense would not be understood by late-nineteenth-century readers.

73.34   vampyre] vampire 70–76

74.2   of the souls] of souls 70–76

74.28   forever] for ever 50, R–C

75.7   infusion] influence 50–C

Since "infusion" is the less common word and "influence" is somewhat similar in sound and appearance, the latter is probably a compositor's error.

75.14   whosoever] whomsoever R–C

75.21   thousandfold] thousand-fold 50–C

75.27   reacts] re-acts 76

76.9   importation] inportation 50

76.13   heave offerings] heave-offerings 50–C

76.14   behemoth, or unicorn] behemoth and unicorn 50–C (Chap as in MS)

The MS agrees with the wording of the source passage (*JMN*, VIII, 233).

76.24   palmtrees] palm-/trees 50, R; palm-trees 70–76, C

76.24   shittimwood] shittim-wood 50–C

77.3   Michel] Michael R–C

77.3   frescoes] frescos 70–76

77.6   hailstorm] hail-storm 50–C

77.26   is this Inferno] is his Inferno R–C

77.26   old philosophy, is] old philosophers, is 50–C

78.3   "poor old] poor "auld R–C

78.5   Everything] Every thing 50, R–C

78.24   Socrates's] Socrates' 70–76

78.24   not advertise him] not advise him 50–C

Emerson frequently used "advertise" in the older sense of "advise" or "give notice to."

78.30   anything] any thing 50, R–C

79.2   dropt] dropped 70–76

79.13   keynote] key-note 50–C

79.22   cognisant] cognizant 70–C

79.32   country-parsons] country parsons 50–C

79.38   goldheaded] gold-headed 50–C

80.14   morning-landscapes] morning landscapes 50–C

80.16	forever . . . forever] for ever . . . for ever 50, R–C
80.36	sung] sang 50–C
80.37	transcendant] transcendent 50–C
81.4	charnel breath] charnel-breath 50–C

The compound may possibly be written solid as one word in the MS, but is clearly two words in a canceled version of the same passage (see entry in Appendix 2 for 80.20).

81.4	temple-incense] temple incense 50–C
81.8	clue] clew 70–76
81.10	running-rigging] running rigging 50–C
81.15	common sense] common-sense 76
81.17	forever] for ever 50–C

IV. MONTAIGNE

Emendations in Copy-Text

85.10	street, but] ed.; street. but

The 1850 edition uses a semicolon.

85.26	Fénelon] ed.; Fenelon
86.14	artist's] 50; artists
87.19	pound. [no ¶] They] 70; pound. // [¶?] They

As in numerous cases where a sentence begins at the top of a MS page, it is uncertain whether a new paragraph is intended; but none seems needed here. The 1850 edition does not have a new paragraph, but inserts a dash (at the end of the line) after "pound." The spacing of words in this and the following line suggests that a new paragraph was set but was changed in proof, the dash being inserted to help fill up space. Chapman has neither a new paragraph nor a dash at this point.

87.25	Wein, Weib . . . Gesang . . . Narr . . . Leben] 50; wein, weib . . . gesang . . . narr . . . leben
88.1	hence. Why] RWE, ed.; hence. Life's well enough, but we shall be glad to get out of it, and they will all be glad to have us. Why

Emerson marked this sentence in his correction copy for deletion, probably some time after he had made corrections for the 1870 *Prose Works*; for he gave as his reason for deletion the fact that he had used it on page 286 of *Society and Solitude*, which was not published until after the *Prose Works*. (He mentioned this at three different places in the correction copy.) See *W*, VII, 320, and *JMN*, IX, 428.

88.25	You who will] RWE, ed.; You that will
88.26	deceive yourselves grossly] 50; deceive yourself grossly

Emerson probably changed this to agree with "yourselves" in the next sentence. Chapman also has "yourselves," perhaps by independent editorial emendation.

89.6 philosophizing 50; philosophising

89.14 dogmatizers 50; dogmatisers

89.17 σκέπτειν] ed.; sκεππειν [with incorrect form of sigma] MS; σκεππειν 50–76; σκοπεῖν R–C

Riverside edition's form is a possible one, but not the same verb that Emerson evidently had in mind. σκέπτεσθαι would be more nearly correct as the infinitive of the verb from which "skeptic" is derived.

89.29 anything] 70–76; any / thing MS; any thing 50, R–C

89.32 in? And] 50; in. And

Emerson's punctuation in this paragraph is not consistent in the MS: the first two questions end in periods, the other four in question marks. But the first is a general comment, while the next three are queries about specific institutions — marriage, state, and church. Emerson may have changed this period to a question mark in proof to show the parallel structure of these three questions.

90.18 instantly impair that] RWE, 70; instantly destroy that

90.21 consists "in . . . know," we] 50; consists in . . . know, we

The compositor would have no reason to insert quotation marks here unless Emerson had added them in proof.

90.35 doubts; least] 50; doubts, least

The semicolon is needed for clarity.

*90.36 stable and] 50; stable, and

91.3 own foe; that] 76–C; own. that MS; own; that 50–70

91.13 and Stoic] 50; and stoic

91.19 shell must dictate the] RWE, 70; shell is the

*91.23 are golden] 50; are Golden

91.27 art and] 50; art, and

92.22 Père Lachaise] R; Pere le Chaise MS–50; Père la Chaise 70–76

92.24 sixty-eight] 50; 68

92.30 Périgord] C; Perigord

92.30 two hundred and fifty] 50; 250

93.3 have the autograph of] 50; have the autograph // the autograph of

93.9 thirty-eight] 50; 38

93.23 Henry IV and] ed.; Henry IV. and

Emerson does not usually write a period after the Roman numeral following the name of a monarch (though the 1850 edition regularly prints one); here and at 112.21 he does.

93.28 Latin; so] 50; Latin. so

94.4   mind. [¶] "When I . . . by himself." [¶] Here is] 50; mind. // [¶] Here is

        The possible reasons why this paragraph is not in the MS (but is in the 1850 and Chapman editions) are discussed in the Textual Introduction.

94.17   though] 50; tho'
94.27   *sçais*] 50; *scais*
*95.13 head, treating] ed.; head. treating

        The 1850 edition uses a semicolon, which seems too heavy.

95.16   thoughts. He] ed.; thoughts. / he
*95.25 bullets; it] ed.; bullets; It
96.6   thirty-three] 50; thirtythree
96.6   "But," he] 50; "But, he
96.11   *Que sçais je?*] 50; Que scais je?

        Emerson used italics for the same phrase at 94.27.

96.14   seventy-five] 50; seventyfive
97.27   relieve] 50; releive
*97.29 neither is he fit] 50; neither he is fit

        "But he is fit" was written first, and "neither" inserted later without the needed inversion of word order.

97.33   Krishna] 50; Kreeshna (Kreshna Chap)

        Emerson's usual spelling was "Krishna" (cf. 28.33, and *JMN*, XI, 144), and it is likely that he made this change in proof.

97.33   Bhagavat, "There] 50; Bhagavat. / "There
98.1   stands in his mind, that our] 50; stands thus in his mind: Our (Chap as in 50 except for lack of comma)

        The agreement of 1850 and Chapman against the MS is puzzling, but it is considered to indicate that Emerson probably made the change while correcting proofs; perhaps he changed this passage (with some others) in the WT after the MS had gone to press and remembered to make the same corrections in the proofs. (See the Textual Introduction.)

98.7   calendar-day] 50; calender-day

        Emerson spells this word "calender" also in the deleted version of the passage on the preceding page; but the *OED* shows that this spelling had long been obsolete by this time.

98.23   Nay, San Carlo, my] 50; Nay San Carlo my
98.25   ascension, even . . . piety, leads] 50; ascension even . . . piety leads
*98.28 saw and would not tell; and] 50; saw and would not tell, // and would not tell; and
99.6   Boston, may yet be very] 50; Boston, is yet very

        Chapman's edition agrees with the MS. The qualification of an originally positive statement seems more likely the author's change than a compositor's.

*99.9   vice, and] 50; vice and

         The original sentence made it clear that "checks of" does not govern "polarity"; in revising, a comma was needed to show this, but was not supplied in the MS.

99.12   reliance. [¶] There] 50; reliance [¶] 2. There

         The numbers "3" and "4" (there is no corresponding "1") later in the MS were deleted.

*99.25   Presently, a new] 50; Presently, A new

*99.32   Duty no] 50; Duty, no

*100.1   states? Does] 50; states; Does

100.8   *Kinde*] 50; Kinde

100.13   history? What] 50; history. What

*100.17   Belly: feed] 50; Belly. feed

*100.21   that we] 50; that We

100.29   offices, learned, civil, social, I can] ed. (after Chap); offices learned civil social I can MS; offices, learned, civil, and social, can 50–C

         Chapman added the commas, as in the 1850 edition, but agreed with the MS in wording. The 1850 variants seem more like compositor's than author's changes.

100.33   Yoganidra, the] 50; Yoganidra the

         The comma is correct if "owned" means "recognized" and if "energy" is in apposition to "Yoganidra"; it is incorrect if the sentence means "The eastern sages accepted Yoganidra as (or, recognized her to be) the great illusory energy." There are no commas in this sentence in the MS, though the 1850 edition has four; there are in fact only two commas on the whole MS page (cf. 100.29), and Emerson may have forgotten to go back and put them in where needed. The source passage (*JMN*, IX, 322) has the comma but lacks "The eastern sages owned"; thus, it does not solve the problem of punctuation of the passage.

*101.26   misapplied, and] ed.; misapplied and

*102.15   faith; not] 50; faith. not

102.30   do? These] 50; do?' These

         The quotation ends, not here, but at line 33 below.

102.33   down.' The] 50 down." The

         The quotation began with a single quotation mark (line 29).

103.12   was "an] R; was an

         The MS has quotation marks after "darkness" (line 14), but none to show where the quotation begins. The 1850 edition begins it with "that" (line 12), but the placement in the Riverside edition seems more logical. In the source passage (*EL*, I, 171) no quotation marks are used around the passage.

103.29   performance, between] 50; performance // between

*104.19   generalizations. The] 50; generalizations, The

85.7   of the game] of this game 50–C (Chap as in MS)

The source passage (*JMN*, VIII, 82) reads "this game," and Emerson first wrote "this" in the MS but changed it to "the.") The compositor may have thought that the change was made the other way around.

86.9   design; he] design, — he 50–76; design? he R–C

Emerson's punctuation here, though somewhat eccentric, conveys his meaning better than the printers' versions.

86.14   steamengine] steam-engine 50–C

86.31   ward-meetings ... election-days] ward meetings ... election days 50–C

In the MS, "election-days" is divided and hyphenated at the end of a line.

86.35   whilst] while 70–76

87.13   a man much] a much 70–76

87.19   tongue, that pepper] tongue, and pepper 70–76

87.20   friction-matches are incendiary, revolvers to] friction-matches incendiary, revolvers are to R–C

87.27   foreordination] fore-ordination 50–70, R–C

88.1   tomorrow] to-morrow 50–C

88.10   I knew a] I know a 70–76

88.20   onesidedness] one-sidedness 50–C

88.23   selfdevotion] self-devotion 50–C

88.26   piglead] pig-lead 50–C

89.23   elusive] illusive 70–76

90.25   chimæras] chimeras 50–C

90.34   selfcontaining] self-containing 50–C

91.4   cannot] can not 50

Although the 1850 edition prints "cannot" consistently as one word in the earlier part of the volume, from this point on it usually prints "can not" as two. The 1870 and 1876 editions always print it as one word; the Riverside and Centenary editions are inconsistent.

91.22   dwellinghouse] dwelling-house 50–C

91.25   sea. [¶] The wise] sea. [no ¶] The wise 50–C

*91.28   Every thing] Everything 70–76

This is one of the few cases in the MS where "every thing" is clearly two words, and was probably intended as two, since the original sentence follows it with "every form ... every arm ... every mouth ... every brain."

92.6   Paris and London] Paris or London 50–C

92.9   speculation. [no ¶] These] speculation. [¶] These 50–C

"These" begins a new page in the MS (following a blank page) and was set by a different compositor; this may account for the unnecessary paragraphing in 50.

92.33   the (London) Westminster] the Westminster 50–C (Chap as in 50)

Emerson sometimes used parentheses as a sign for deletion, but in this MS he usually also lined through the material to be deleted. In three places, including this one, words in parentheses but not lined through do not appear in the printed text of either the Boston or Chapman's edition. Emerson may have made the changes in correcting proof for the one and in checking the WT for the other; or they may have been made independently by the compositor and the transcriber, not understanding what he intended. The correct title was *The London and Westminster Review;* but in the absence of certainty, copy-text is followed.

92.33   Review, Hazlitt] Review, Mr. Hazlitt 50–C
92.35   newly discovered] newly-discovered 50, R–C
93.4   flyleaf] fly-leaf 50–C
93.16   plaindealing] plain-dealing 50, R–C; plain dealing 70–76
94.6   and I am afraid that Plato, in his purest virtue, (I, who am as sincere and perfect a lover of virtue of that stamp as any other whatever,) if he had listened] and I, who am as sincere and perfect a lover of virtue of that stamp as any other whatever, am afraid that Plato, in his purest virtue, if he had listened R–C

Copy-text here is 1850 (see the Emendation note for 94.4). The Riverside version is smoother, but is presumably by Cabot. 1850 follows the source passages (see PP).

94.12   fastidiousness about colour] fastidiousness at color 50–C
94.16   gipsies] gypsies 70–76
94.16   streetballads] street ballads 50–C
94.16   in doors] in-doors 50–C

The phrase is divided at the end of a line in the MS without a hyphen, which may mean that Emerson would have written it solid within the line. However, it is printed as two separate words in the 1856 edition of *English Traits* at 111.9 (*W,* V, 107).

94.27   title page] title-page 50–C
94.36   crowquill] crow-quill 50–C
95.4   cannot] can not 50
95.10   anything] any thing 50, R
95.13   everything] every thing 50, R–C
95.19   anywhere] any where 50

This was marked by Emerson in his correction copy.

95.22   that we have in] that he feels in R–C

95.27   half sentence] half-sentence 70–76
96.1   selfrespecting] self-respecting 50–C
96.13   endorsed] indorsed 70–76
96.17   generosity. [¶, no white line] Shall] generosity. [¶ and white line] Shall 50–C

The MS has a wide empty space before the next paragraph (96.18–20), which begins on the next page; but there is no direction for a "white line" at this point.

96.21   connection of cause] connection between cause 50–C

The source passage (*JMN*, IX, 220) also has "of cause."

97.4   non-conformist] nonconformist 50–C
97.10   crowbar] crow-bar 76
*97.28 conservative; he] conservative, he R–C

The revised punctuation makes a smoother and perhaps a better sentence; but the semicolon in the MS is quite clear and is supported by the original wording before revision.

98.3   schoolbooks] school-books 50–C
98.21   cannot] can not 50, R–C
98.30   this detection] this defection *conj.* ed.

In the context, "defection" would seem to be the more appropriate word; but the MS clearly reads "detection," which makes sense and must therefore stand.

99.4   babyhouses] baby-houses 50–C
99.5   crockery shops] crockery-shops 50–C
99.13   nought] naught 70–76
99.26   commonsense] common sense 50–70, R–C; common-sense 76
100.4   selfinterest] self-interest 50–C
100.16 everything] every thing 50, R–C

Probably one word in the MS, but may be two.

100.23 children, with customs, with sciences] children, with // sciences 50–C

The MS has seven successive phrases beginning with the word "with"; the compositor omitted, probably through haplography, or eyeskip, the one that should have comprised the last word on one page and the first word on the next.

101.10 react] re-act 76
101.19 cooperation] coöperation 50; co-operation 70–C
101.22 He had been] He has been 50–C
101.22 balked] baulked 50, R–C

Usually spelled "baulked" in the MS, but not here.

102.15 or parasitic faith] or parasite faith 50–C
102.25 souls come with] souls comes with 70
102.25 cooperation] coöperation 50; co-operation 70–C
102.28 not sneering and] not freezing and 50–C (Chap as in MS)

In Emerson's handwriting, the initial "s" looks much like an "f," so the word might easily have been misread by the compositor.

102.36	good nature] good-nature 70–76
103.1	cannot] can not 50, R–C
103.2	so, that] so that 50–C

With the comma, "so" means "in such a manner"; without it, "with the purpose" or "with the result."

103.9	farsighted] far-sighted 50–C
103.9	goodwill] good-will 50–C
104.8	morningstar] morning star 50–C
104.13	sung] sang 50–C
104.33	world spirit] world-spirit 50–C
104.33	cannot] can not 50
104.35	means. (The needles are nothing; the magnetism is all.) Through] means. Through 50–C (Chap as in 1850)

Emerson may have intended to delete this sentence and have done so in correcting proof; the fact that it is not in Chapman's edition gives some support to this possibility. But it seems more likely that both the Boston compositor and Weir mistook the parentheses for a mark of deletion (cf. the RSS note to 92.33), and that Emerson in reading proof did not notice that the sentence had been dropped. The same compositor set this passage and the one at 138.31, where a similar variant occurs (see the discussion in the penultimate paragraph of Annex A, Appendix 1). For other uses of this sentence, see PP.

V. SHAKSPEARE

Emendations in Copy-Text

110.11	brought] 50; bro't
110.20	through] 50; thro'
110.24	religious within the] RWE, ed.; religious among the
110.32	Punch] RWE, 70; punch
110.36	considerable because] R; considerable, because

The comma obscures (and perhaps even contradicts) what is probably the intended meaning of the sentence.

*111.12	of, every] RWE, 57; of every
*111.23	copyright in this] RWE, 57; copyright on this
112.21	Henry VI, in] ed.; Henry VI., in

See Emendations note to 93.23.

112.36	Shakspeare's] 50; Shakspeares
*113.17	he; only] 50; he. only
113.23	world, — /"Presenting] 50; world. / "Presenting
113.34	Boccaccio] 50; Boccacio

114.25	friends, lovers] 50; friends / lovers
*115.6	Liturgy, admired] 50; Liturgy admired
115.8	these selected, too] RWE, ed.; these collected, too
116.19	was the poet] 50; was the // the poet
116.29	Shakespeare's] 50; Shakspeares
*116.30	Wotton was] 50; Wotton, was
116.31	twenty-three] 50; twenty / three
116.36	Cotton, John] 50; Cotton / John
117.30	Blackfriars] ed.; Blackfriar's MS; Blackfriars' 50–C
117.37	thirty-five] 50; thirty five [*possibly* thirtyfive]
118.19	their oil. The] 50; their life. The

No doubt an authorial change made in proof. The source passage (*JMN*, IX, 315) has "life," as does Chapman.

118.21	Betterton, Garrick] 50; Betterton Garrick
118.23	crown, elucidate, obey, and] 50; crown elucidate obey and
118.27	Hamlet of a] 50; Hamlet of / of a
118.33	moon?" / [no ¶] That] 50; moon." / [¶] That
119.16	new, which sees the . . . and asks in] RWE, 57; new, who see the . . . and ask in
119.17	Shakspeare, and] ed.; Shakspeare and

Emerson used a comma here in a deleted version of the same sentence, and he probably intended one here. The 1850 and later editions use a semicolon.

119.21	analyzed] 50; analysed
*120.7	men? What] 50; men? what
120.17	man's] 50; mans
120.29	good a dramatist] 50; good dramatist

Probably a slip of the pen.

120.30	say is of] 50; say is // is of
*121.12	the eye. [no ¶] And the] 50; the eye. [¶] And the

The last two sentences of the paragraph appear to be a later insertion at the bottom of the MS page, and (although indented) were probably not intended as a separate paragraph.

121.35	peculiarity, no] 50; peculiarity / no
*122.8	or of transferring] 50; or of / of transferring
122.16	point; finishes] 50; point. finishes
*123.6	Cultivated men] 50; Cultivated Men
123.20	hilarity, he] 50; hilarity / he
123.21	Epicurus says that] RWE, ed.; Epicurus relates that

Emerson's first marginal correction in the text of his copy is "notes," deleted and replaced by "said"; but this becomes "says" in the list pasted in the front of the book.

124.19	*very superior pyrotechny this evening?*] RWE, ed.; "very superior pyrotechny this evening?"

1850 and later editions vary in final punctuation, but all retain quotation marks rather than italics.

125.17 trifle, with ... graves, with] R; trifle with ... graves with

The lack of a comma after "trifle" gives the sentence an unintended meaning. The comma after "graves" is not equally necessary, but provides a better balance.

Rejected Substantives and Spellings

109.9 rattlebrain] rattle-brain 70–76
109.10 everything] every thing 50, R–C
109.20 today] to-day 50–C
110.26 Innyards] Inn-yards 50–C
110.26 roofs, or extemporaneous] roofs, and extemporaneous 50–C

The 1876 edition has a typographical error in the third word, "extemporaneaus," but otherwise follows 1850.

110.37 baker's shop] baker's-shop 50, R–C
111.9 stage plays] stage-plays 50–C
111.31 street ballads] street-ballads 50–C

Compare 94.16, where this is one solid word in the MS but two words without hyphen in the 1850 edition.

112.6 arranged] arrayed 50 (*corr.* RWE, 57)
112.21 the second and third parts] the First, Second, and Third parts 50–C

Since Emerson was copying the figures from Malone, who referred only to the second and third parts (see *JMN*, XI, 174), and would have known from Malone's account that there is no earlier version of Part One than the 1623 Folio, he would not have been likely to introduce such an error into the text while correcting proof. He even checked Malone's addition and subtration in the margin of the MS. See also the Informational note to 112.19.

112.36 unmistakeable] unmistakable 50–C
113.9 anywhere] any where 50, R–C
113.19 finds it. [¶] Such] finds it. [no ¶] Such 50–C

"Such" is the first word on a new MS page (following a blank page) and is indented. A new paragraph seems desirable here, though perhaps not necessary.

114.1 Meun] Meung R–C
114.4 brickkiln or stonequarry] brick-kiln or stone-quarry 50–C
114.12 aukwardness] awkwardness 50–C

The *OED* lists the MS form as a variant spelling, sixteenth to nineteenth century.

114.29 at last in] at least in 70–76

115.16   sharpsighted strongminded] sharp-sighted, strong-minded 50–C

The first word is divided (with a hyphen) at the end of a line in the MS, but is printed solid in this edition for consistency with the second word.

116.3   bookstall] book-stall 50, 76, C; book-/stall 70, R

116.8   second best] second-best 50–C

116.34   Sidney, Earl] Sidney, the Earl R–C

116.35   Isaak] Isaac 50–C

Emerson spelled the name "Isaac" two lines above.

117.2   Massinger, two Herberts] Massinger, the two Herberts R–C

117.11   was on the] was with the R–C

An "improvement" of Emerson's grammar by Cabot.

117.27   I adverted] I have adverted 50–C

117.37   tenpence] ten pence 50–C

118.2   goodnatured] good-natured 50–C

In the MS the word is divided with a hyphen at the end of a line, both here and at 144.13. But at 34.14 "goodnaturedly" is written solid as one word, and so are some other compounds of "good" (e.g., "goodwill" at 16.27, 103.9, and 164.9).

118.11   birthplace ... schoolmates] birth-place ... school-mates 50, R–C

119.2   green room] green-room 50–C

In the MS the phrase is divided without a hyphen at the end of a line.

119.10   transcendant] transcendent 50–C

119.16   new, which] new age, which 70–C (new one, which Chap)

Since Emerson had changed other words in this passage for the 1857 printing (see the Emendations note), and did not mark any further changes in his correction copy, it is likely that the 1870 variant was an editorial refinement. It is not needed for clarity—though Chapman's version shows that he felt something was needed there—and spoils the sentence rhythm.

119.22   skiey] skyey 70–C

121.20   farthest] furthest 70–76

121.29   coordinates] coördinates 50; co-ordinates 70–C

121.36   cowpainter ... birdfancier] cow-painter ... bird-fancier 50–C

122.5   lovesongs] love-songs 50–C

122.18   microscope. [no ¶] In short] microscope. [¶] In short 50–C

122.33   poem. [no ¶] Though] poem. [¶] Though 50–C

The word "poem" is the last word on a MS page, and the sentence ends in the middle of the line. But "Though" on the next page is not indented, and a new paragraph does not seem to be needed.

123.2	irreconcileable] irreconcilable 50–C
123.9	with parties] with the parties R–C
123.20	light which sparkles] light that sparkles 50–C
124.19	fireworks] fire-/works 70, R; fire-works 76
124.22	trumpet text] trumpet-text 50–C
124.28	Midsummer's night's dream] Midsummer-Night's Dream 50, R–C; Midsummer Night's Dream 70–76

Apparently Emerson was deliberately varying from the standard forms of the titles of all three plays mentioned in this sentence; but his printers or editors were trying to set him right in capitalization and other details. They did, however, leave "Evening's" in "Winter evening's tale."

124.29	or a Winter] or Winter R–C
124.31	cannot] can not 50, R–C
125.15	sunk] sank 50–C
125.16	halfviews . . . halfmen] half-views . . . half-men 50–C

VI. NAPOLEON

Emendations in Copy-Text

*130.23	indulge all] 50; indulge, all
*131.33	means. All] 50; means: All
132.13	magic. He] 50; magic. // he
133.7	which no] 50; which, no

The comma obscures the syntax.

134.1	talkers and] R; talkers, and

The comma makes "confused" appear to be a verb (instead of a participial adjective) and gives an unintended meaning to the sentence.

134.8	Directory: "I] 70; Directory; "I

Emerson was not consistent in punctuation before direct quotations, but a colon is preferable here.

*135.10	artillery, gives] 50; artillery gives
135.12	Austerlitz. "At] ed.; Austerlitz." "At

The 1850 edition also deletes the quotation marks (the result of incomplete revision), but otherwise changes the punctuation.

135.15	masses. They] 50; masses. they
135.31	everything] 70–76; every / thing MS; every thing 50, R–C

Probably another case of neglect to hyphenate at the end of a line. The word is written solid in the source passage (*JMN*, IX, 158).

136.11	enemy's] 50; enemies'

The source passage (*JMN*, V, 508) reads "enemy's"; Emerson probably corrected this in proof.

136.14   could. He] 50; could. / he

136.17   *mêlée*] 70; melée

136.21   achievements] 70; achievments

136.22   conquest must maintain] 50; conquest alone can maintain

The MS agrees with the source passage (*JMN*, IX, 160), but the change is not one likely to have been made by a compositor.

*136.33   Las Cases, he] ed.; Las Cases; he MS; Las Casas, he 50–C

The MS spelling (which is also that of the source passage, *JMN*, V, 474) is the correct one; but Emerson sometimes spelled it "Las Casas" in his journals. The semicolon resulted from incomplete revision.

136.34   two-o'clock-in-the-morning] 50; two o'clock in the morning

Hyphens are used in the same phrase in the MS at 137.2, except after "two," and are adopted here for consistency. In the source passage (*JMN*, V, 474) the hyphens are omitted in both places, but are used in another version at *JMN*, VIII, 41.

137.1   eminently endowed with] 50; eminently gifted with

The source passage (same as preceding) reads "gifted".

137.2   two-o'clock- . . . -morning courage) 50; two o'clock- . . . -morning-courage

Apparently in inserting the hyphens in this phrase, Emerson accidentally omitted one and added one in the wrong place.

137.4   Everything] 70–76; Every thing MS–50, R–C

137.7   eight hundred . . . six thousand] 50; 800 . . . 6000

137.17   Tuileries] 70; Tuilleries

137.19   communicate, with] ed.; communicate, // With

137.26   achievement] 50; achievment

138.22   saying, 'Respect . . . Madam.' " In] 50; saying, "Respect . . . Madam." In

139.4   even when he decimated . . . his conscriptions] 50; even decimated . . . his deadly conscriptions

*139.13   society. Instead] 50; society; Instead

139.14   Tuileries] 70; Tuilleries

*139.28   kindred, took] 50; kindred, — took

The dash is misleading and confuses the syntax. It was left over from the original draft of the sentence, where it was one of a pair.

*140.9   them." This] 50; them." this

140.18   Masséna] ed.; Massena

140.35   baptized] 50; baptised

*141.1   satisfied. The] 50; satisfied. the

142.11   and as] 50; and, as
142.25   which all] 70; which, all
143.2   twenty-five] 50; 25
143.8   difficulty: it] 50; difficulty, it
             The source passage (*JMN*, IX, 139–140) has a semicolon.
*143.10   speculation on ... topics. He] 50; speculation. on ... topics,
             He
             Revisions in this passage account for some of the confusion in
             punctuation; but the period after "speculation" may indicate
             that the sentence originally ended there.
143.36   Antommarchi] ed.; Antonomarchi
             Emerson consistently spelled this name correctly in his jour-
             nals (e.g., *JMN*, IX, 138, 140) and probably misspelled it here
             through a lapse in memory. No authority for the MS spelling
             has been found. It was, however, followed in all previous edi-
             tions.
*144.15   subject. The] 50; subject. the
*144.17   wisdom. In] 50; wisdom, In
144.37   anything] 70–76; any thing MS–50, R–C
146.16   everything] 70–76; every thing MS–50, R–C
147.3   age; yes] 50; age; Yes
147.28   paralyzes] 50; paralyses

Rejected Substantives and Spellings

129.9   &c.] etc. 76, C
129.26   business-men] business men 50–C
130.3   everywhere] every where 50, R–C
130.25   dress, dinners] dress-dinners (*or* dress dinners) *conj.* ed.
             The common man does not have to deny his taste for "dress"
             (i.e., clothing) or "dinners" (i.e., food), but he may be unable to
             afford "dress dinners." For a discussion of this institution, see
             "Manners" in *English Traits* (*W*, V, 113–114). But Emerson
             clearly wrote a comma here, not a hyphen.
131.2   showed to Lord] showed it to Lord 50–C
             Emerson first wrote "showed it to" and then deleted "it."
131.5   tomorrow ... tomorrow] to-morrow ... to-morrow 50–C
131.19   battles] battle 50–C
131.29   satisfaction] satifaction 50
             Emerson marked this in his correction copy; the change was
             first made in the 1870 edition.
132.15   master workman] master-workman 50–C
133.6   common sense] common-sense 76
133.20   baulked] balked 70–76

133.24   ascribed to it his] ascribed it to his 70–76
           The 1870 version says just the opposite of what Emerson
           means and results in nonsense.
133.26   allusions to] allusion to 50–C
133.36   cannot] can not 50, R–C
134.12   everything] every thing 50, R–C
134.18   ministers, not knowing what] ministers, knowing not what
           R–C
           Probably influenced by "they know not what" one line
           above.
134.28   everything] every thing 50, R–C
134.28   everything to his aim, — money] every thing, — money R–C
           Evidently Cabot felt that the repetition of "to his aim" in suc-
           cessive clauses was awkward and unnecessary.
135.3   wo] woe 70–C
           Emerson often used the spelling "wo" in letters and jour-
           nals.
135.6   cannot] can not 50, R–C
135.14   towards] toward 50–C
135.16   engulfed] ingulfed 70–76
135.31   everything . . . every thing] every thing . . . every thing 50, R–C;
           everything . . . everything 70–76
           In the MS the first "everything" is divided without a hyphen
           at the end of a line, but (as pointed out elsewhere) Emerson
           often omitted the hyphen in that position. The second is clearly
           two words (within the line), and a difference of meaning is prob-
           ably intended.
135.32   rattlesnake] rattle-snake 50–70, R–C
135.36   second hand] second-hand 70–76
136.6   grapeshot] grape-shot 50–C
136.9   horse chasseurs] horse-chasseurs 50–C
137.3   this particular] this respect 50–C (Chap as in 50)
           Emerson first wrote "respect," which is also the reading of the
           source passage (*JMN,* V, 474), then lined it out and wrote "par-
           ticular" after it; the compositor apparently set the first instead
           of the second. Or possibly Emerson returned to "respect" in cor-
           recting proof, to avoid repetition with "particulars" two sen-
           tences later, but there is no evidence for this.
137.37   they had learned] they have learned 70–76
138.25   marketplace] market-place 50–C
138.31   troops, (and of the perfect understanding between them,) is]
           troops is 50–C
           See the RSS notes to 92.33 and 104.35 for other passages in
           parentheses that are not in the 1850 edition. This one may have

been intended for deletion, but is not lined through. Chapman omitted even more of the passage (everything between "document" and "is") and thus distorted the meaning; perhaps Weir was told to delete something here but misunderstood the instruction.

139.4   controuled] controlled 50–C

The *OED* shows "controul" as still a current spelling in the nineteenth century, but Webster does not list it.

139.10   of all its] of its 50–C

Emerson deleted "all" (and similar words) a number of times in his 1847 revision of *Essays: First Series,* as well as in this MS, and he may also have done so here in correcting proofs; but it could have been a compositor's error.

139.14   vampire] vampyre 50, 76–C

Cf. 73.34, where the MS spelling is "vampyre" and the 1870 and 1876 editions print "vampire."

139.21   ironbound] iron-bound 50–C
139.26   anything] any thing 50, R–C
140.8   gold lace] gold-lace 76–C
140.15   towards] toward 50–C
140.30   depth or draught] depth and draught 50–C
140.34   connexion] connection 70–76
140.37   every body] everybody 70–76

In this MS Emerson always writes "every body" as two words (but "anybody" is usually one word).

141.2   horseboy ... powder monkey] horse-boy ... powder-monkey 50–C
141.5   enlists an universal] enlists a universal 70–76
141.12   steamengine] steam-engine 50–C
141.15   and sovereignly disposing trains] and disposing sovereignly trains 50–C

Emerson wrote the words in the same order as in 1850, but put the figure "2" under "disposing" and "1" under "sovereignly" to direct reversal of order. The compositor either overlooked or didn't understand this marking.

141.22   Gulf by the] gulf of the 50–C
141.23   Ptolemais] Plotemais 50
141.31   cannot] can not C
142.3   commonsense] common sense 50–70; common-sense 76–C

This may be either one word or two in the MS.

142.9   today] to-day 50–C
142.15   baubles] bawbles 70–76
142.18   every body's] everybody's 70–C
142.24   commonsense] common sense 50–70; common-sense 76–C

142.30 on those high] on these high C

143.1 Arcole] Arcola 50–C

    Emerson spelled the name "Arcola" at 136.16 in the MS and in the source for that passage (*JMN*, IX, 144), but "Arcole" here and in the source for this (*JMN*, IX, 139). The MS spelling is retained because it is a direct quotation.

143.27 philosophes] philosophers 50–C (Chap as in 1850)

    Apparently both Weir (or the London compositor) and the Boston compositor either misread the word or thought it was an error.

144.1 anything] any thing 50, R–C

144.7 pharmacopeia] pharmacopœia 76–C

144.11 good nature] good-nature 50–C

144.13 goodnatured] good-natured 50–C

    In the MS this is divided with a hyphen at the end of a line; but see the note on a similar case at 118.2.

144.22 stratagem or a] stratagem in a 50–C

    The source passage (*JMN*, IX, 156) has "or"; Chapman omits the rest of the sentence after "stratagem."

144.23 dim lighted] dim-lighted 50–C

    In the MS this may be either one word or two.

145.3 everywhere] every where 50, R–C

145.4 make this history] make his history 50–C

145.14 highest placed] highest-placed 50–C

145.21 "Moniteurs,"] *Moniteurs,* 70–76; "Moniteur," R–C

145.25 éclat] eclat 50; éclat 70–C

145.26 stage-effect] stage effect 50–C

146.7 and in purpose] and purpose 50–C

146.20 good humour] good humor 50, R–C; good-humor 70–76

146.22 horseplay] horse-play 50–C

146.26 fully deserved the] fully deserves the 50–C

147.5 counterparty] counter-party 50–C

    Emerson's inconsistency is shown by "counter-revolution" in the preceding phrase: one hyphenated, the other solid.

147.22 downbeds] down-beds 50–C

147.22 chateaux] châteaux 76

147.26 cannot] can not 50, R–C

147.34 of man] of the man 70–76

    The 1870 variant is certainly incorrect and is a good illustration of the fact that not all changes in that edition can be by Emerson, although many are.

147.34 baulked] balked 70–76

147.37 will be] would be 70–76

Emendations in Copy-Text

151.6	engaged in writing] 50; engaged in // in writing
*152.1	experiences. The] 50; experiences, The
*152.6	peachstone: his] ed.; peachstone, his
	The 1850 edition also uses a colon, but hyphenates "peach-stone."
152.13	write. In his eyes, a] 50; write. (In his eyes,) a
	The parentheses are not appropriate and may be a sign that Emerson intended to delete the phrase; but he did not line it out, and apparently decided to let it stand.
152.16	materials; as] 50; materials, as
*152.38	office; for] 50; office. for
153.2	in ideal order] RWE, 70–76; in order MS–50, R–C
153.21	railroad] 50; Railroad
153.21	mesmerism, or California; and] 50; mesmerism, or phrenology, and
	Chapman (besides omitting "Texas" in line 21) reads "mesmerism, phrenology, or California"; this must represent a state of the text later than the Buffalo MS but earlier than Emerson's final proof corrections for the Boston edition. Whether it was made in the WT or by separate correspondence cannot be determined.
153.38	Bonaparte's] 50; Buonapartes [no apostrophe]
	Since the name is spelled "Bonaparte" throughout the essay on him (and later in this essay at 156.4), the 1850 spelling is adopted here for consistency.
155.5	class share] ed.; class, share
	The comma (found in all editions, as well as in the MS) is typical of Emerson's punctuation of relative clauses, but confuses the syntax and meaning.
155.11	*anybody*] RWE, 70–76, C; *any body* MS–50, R
*155.16	craftsman, or captain] ed.; craftsman, or / or captain
	See the RSS note for this line, and Appendix 2.
*155.22	person: he] 50; person, he
155.36	inspiration? [¶] Some] 50; inspiration. [¶] Some
	When a rhetorical question ends in one or more subordinate clauses in declarative form, Emerson sometimes uses a period at the end, as here in the MS; but a question mark improves clarity, and he may have changed it in proof.
156.11	traits; when] 50; traits. when
156.17	saint, but] 50; saint; but

Textual Apparatus

The original semicolon obscures the balance of contrasted pairs in the sentence.

*156.27   ease; a] 50; ease. a

157.3   philosophies, sciences, and] 50; philosophies sciences and

157.15   a prouder laurel] 50; a loftier laurel (Chap as in 50)

Not likely to be a compositor's error; probably Emerson's proof correction to avoid alliteration with "laurel," and perhaps also to avoid possible ambiguity, since "loftier laurel" might suggest a tall laurel tree.

157.26   speculation. The] 50; speculation. the

158.34   So the tapeworm] 50; So the the tapeworm

160.31   rank, they] ed.; rank [?] they

The last two letters of "rank," together with any punctuation that may follow, are hidden in the binding of the MS. The 1850 edition has a semicolon here, but a canceled version of the sentence in the MS has a comma.

161.18   characterized] 50; characterised

161.18   book as "thoroughly] 50; book as // as "thoroughly

161.21   poeticized] 50; poeticised

162.19   is? [¶] It] 50; is? tis a bonfire, or boy's squib, though France and England mistake it for a star. [¶] It

Since it is unlikely that a compositor would have inadvertently omitted two and a half lines in the middle of a MS page, and since the sentence is not in Chapman's text, it is assumed that Emerson deleted it in proof as well as from the WT.

*163.1   talent. [no ¶] Hence] 50; talent, // [¶?] Hence

As in numerous other cases, it is hard to tell whether a sentence that begins a new page also marks a new paragraph. The close connection of ideas here suggests that it does not.

163.31   culture, the] 50; culture. the

163.32   spiritualist. There] 50; spiritualist, / There

164.3   form. "Piety ... culture." And] 50; form. Piety ... culture. And

For a variant in the part of the text indicated by ellipses, see the next entry.

164.3   itself," he says, "is] RWE, ed.; itself is

Not adopted in any previous American edition; curiously, Chapman makes a similar insertion, but after "aim" in the same line — another indication that Emerson made changes in the WT (or by letter) that are not in the Buffalo MS. Chapman also has the quotation marks around the whole sentence (see the preceding note), which are in the 1850 edition but not in the MS.

164.16   my Life] 50; my life

The word is capitalized in a canceled draft of this passage on an earlier page of the MS.

164.35   importance. He] ed.; importance. / he
165.11   to that of Iphigenia] 50; to Iphigenia

The "improvement" in grammar might be the work of an editor or compositor; but since the change is also found in Chapman, it is more likely that of the author. One of the two source passages (*L*, II, 164) agrees with the MS and the other (*JMN*, VII, 92) with 1850. The journal passage is part of a draft of the letter.

165.14   whole? He] 50; whole? / he

Emerson often follows a question mark by a lower-case letter when the next unit is another question or a part-sentence, but not usually when (as here) it is a complete declarative sentence.

165.23   *Xenien*] R–C; Xenien MS; *xenien* 50–76
165.30   Staël] 50; Stael
165.30   side; (namely, of Paris.) It] 50; side. It

Since a similar change (but without "namely") appears in Chapman, Emerson probably added this in proof.

165.33   anybody] 70; any body

Compare the change directed by Emerson at 155.11.

*166.7   Goethe, coming ... claims, taught] 50; Goethe coming ... claims taught
164.12   *morgue*] 50; morgue
166.30   call to us affectionately] 50; call affectionately

The added words are also in Chapman.

*166.30   affectionately. We] 50; affectionately we

Rejected Substantives and Spellings

151.3   everywhere] every where 50
151.10   leaf its modest] leaf, their modest 50–C

The 1850 edition is perhaps more logical in treating "fern and leaf" as a plural antecedent, but Emerson may have wished all four pronouns in the sentence to be the same (as well as the one in the next sentence).

151.15   the ground is] the round is C

The space between "the" and "round" in the C edition is larger than those between words in the rest of the line, but not enough for the letter "g" plus a normal space.

151.23   lookingglass] looking-glass 50–C
151.25   facts which transpired do] facts do R–C
152.1   cooperates] coöperates 50, C; co-operates 70–76; co-/operates R

152.6	peachstone] peach-stone 50–C
152.10	undescribable] ineffable [written in MS above "undescribable," neither word being deleted; not used in any edition]
	Evidently Emerson was undecided between the two words and failed to delete one of them.
152.32	cannot] can not C
152.35	everywhere] every where 50, R–C
153.1	writers, namely, who] writers, who 50–C
153.1	connexion] connection 50–C
153.7	agent in nature, one] agent, one 50–C
	The phrase may have been deleted in proof by Emerson, but there is no firm evidence for this. The line in 1850 has rather wide spacing between words, suggesting the possibility of proof alteration, but not quite wide enough to accommodate the missing words.
153.13	the mind, in] the mine, in C
	Probably influenced by "the mine" in the line above.
153.14	whimsy] whimsey 76
153.20	mumbojumbo] mumbo-jumbo 50–C
154.4	agoing] a-going 50–C
154.4	negociations] negotiations 50–C
154.24	today] to-day 50–C
155.9	wellmeaning] well-meaning 50–C
155.12	Statestreet] State-street 50, R–C; State Street 70–76
155.13	commonsense] common sense 50–70; common-sense 76–C
*155.16	or captain. [¶] Society] or king. [¶] Society 50–C
	In the MS "king" was written first, then deleted and replaced by "captain." Possibly Emerson restored the first word in correcting proof, but more likely he failed to notice the compositor's error. Chapman also printed "king," probably because the WT was made before Emerson revised the MS to "captain."
155.17	wellbeing] well-being 50–C
155.30	in the crowd] in a crowd C
156.12	cooperation] coöperation 50, C; co-operation 70–R
156.14	post captains] post-captains 50–C
	The phrase is divided at the end of a line in both the MS and 1850, but it is not hyphenated in the MS.
156.18	readingrooms ... bookclubs] reading-rooms ... book-clubs 50–C
156.24	hundredhanded] hundred-handed 50–C
156.28	encrusted] incrusted 70–76
156.33	bosom] bosoms 70–76
157.4	encyclopædical] encyclopedical 76
157.6	Cyclopean] Cyclopæan 50–70

157.32	hitherto existing] hitherto-existing 50–C
158.31	considered the] considered as the R–C
158.32	vertebra] vertebræ R–C
158.34	tapeworm] tape-worm 50–C
159.12	paper money] paper-money 76–C
159.16	to realize or verify] to verify 50–C (Chap as in MS)

The omission, though it may be either an author's change or a compositor's error, is considered more probably the latter.

159.26	bluefire] blue-fire 50–C

This may be two words in the MS, but is not hyphenated.

159.30	everything . . . everything] every thing . . . every thing 50, R–C
160.3	specify the Wilhelm] specify Wilhelm 70–76
160.30	chess table] chess-table 50–C
160.30	conventions] convention 50–C
*161.19	thoroughly prosaic and modern] thoroughly modern and prosaic 50–C
161.27	nation, a habitual] nation, an habitual 70–76
161.36	spriteliness] sprightliness 50–C
162.5	cannot] can not 50, R–C
162.9	cannot] can not 50, C
162.9	today . . . tomorrow] to-day . . . to-morrow 50–C
162.29	writings] writing 50 (*corr.* RWE, 57)
162.35	cannot] can not 50, R–C
163.20	selfsurrender] self-surrender 50–C
163.27	selfcommand . . . selfdenial] self-command . . . self-denial 50–C
164.9	goodwill] good-will 50–C
164.9	cannot . . . cannot] can not . . . can not 50, C
164.11	anybody] any body 50, R
164.16	of this idea] of the idea 50–C
164.34	love-affairs] love affairs C
165.4	&c. And] &c.; and 50–70, R; etc.; and 76, C

Since the word after "&c." in the MS is written as an ampersand, it is capitalized in this edition on the basis of editorial judgment.

165.23	&c.] etc. 76, C
165.25	self culture] self-culture 50–C
165.32	ill assorted] ill-assorted 50–C

This may be one word in the MS.

166.7	overcivilized] over-civilized 50–C

This may be two words in the MS, but most of Emerson's compounds of "over" are written solid as one word.

166.27	fainthearted] faint-hearted 50–C
166.31	the heavenly and] the heavens and 50–C (Chap as in MS)

This may be an author's revision in proof, but "heavenly" matches "earthly" in the next phrase.

THE MANUSCRIPT

Emerson's holograph manuscript — whose history, present location, and textual significance are discussed in the Textual Introduction — is bound in brown cloth and three-quarter brown leather, with brown endpapers. In binding, the inner edges of the leaves were sewn or pasted together in such a way that some letters (and probably some punctuation marks) at the ends of lines on verso pages — less frequently, at the beginnings of lines on recto pages — have disappeared and cannot be recovered without taking the binding apart. This is discussed under Emendations in Copy-Text in the Textual Apparatus.

The manuscript consists of 411 leaves, 822 pages, of which 770 are written on and 52 are blank (although many of the latter are numbered). Some of the pages that are written on are not numbered, and others are numbered incorrectly or renumbered. In addition, some pages are numbered in a separate sequence, which suggests that they are the first pages of 4-page units (possibly sheets folded to form double-leaf folios) or of 2-page leaves inserted inside or between some of the 4-page units. Six pages (three leaves) in "Uses of Great Men" are bound in incorrect order, apparently because a single leaf was placed inside a double-leaf sheet instead of between two such sheets; and one 4-page group in "Swedenborg" is bound upside down. A single leaf in "Montaigne" seems to have been lost (see the Emendation note to 94.4). A table and lists summarizing the arrangement and numbering of pages appear at the end of this annex. Although they may seem to show that the last four essays were less extensively renumbered and thus presumably less revised than the earlier ones, the evidence presented in Appendix 2 proves that this is only relatively true; in "Shakspeare," for instance, which has no renumbered pages, there is about as much reshuffling of pages as in "Plato" and "Swedenborg," which show much renumbering. Probably Emerson grew tired of renumbering in the first four essays and decided not to number the pages of the rest until he had finished revising them.

Most of the leaves are white, faintly ruled in blue (usually on both sides of the leaf, sometimes on only one), with 29 lines to a page; these are almost all 242 x 190 mm. There are some white unruled leaves of slightly heavier paper, 249 x 197 mm, and a few light blue ruled leaves, 250 x 195 mm. One leaf is made from a light blue envelope, 236 x 195 mm, the inside being used as a MS page and the outside blank except for the address ("Mr R. Waldo Emerson / Concord / Ms") and postmark ("B[ost]on / 7 Mar / [year not legible]"). A few leaves have been slightly damaged by tearing or staining, but have been patched where necessary; and in only one place (124.8) are any letters lost as a result, and only two letters there.

The MS itself is written almost entirely in dark brown ink (which may have been black originally); only five words of the text as printed, "He has that opulence which" (33.36, MS page 60 of "Plato"), are in pencil. Several words in deleted passages are also in pencil: "I am in search of" (page 3 of "Uses of Great Men"), "men" (page 103 of "Swedenborg"), and "to be" (page 53 of "Napoleon"). Some punctuation marks and deletion marks are also in pencil (occasionally traced over in ink) as well as instructions to the printer such as "Broad white line," a few page numbers, and the page headings (perhaps left over from the lecture MSS) "Excess" on MS page 43 of "Uses" and "Theology" (deleted) on MS page 91 of "Swedenborg." Compositors' names (see Appendix 1) are generally in pencil, but their stint-marks and page numbers are in ink. Except for those names and marks, and possibly some paragraph symbols, the writing appears to be entirely in Emerson's hand. It is for the most part clear and legible, though some letters are doubtful and some deleted matter has not yet been deciphered. On some pages the writing is quite regular and almost (or completely) without alterations, giving the appearance of a "fair copy" from an earlier draft; the first page of the text is a good example of this, and there are others throughout — most numerous in "Napoleon." Most of the handwriting is fairly large, averaging about fifteen lines to a page on most pages (skipping every other line on the ruled pages); but sometimes Emerson crowded several lines into a small space, and at other times he wrote only a few lines on a page. Occasionally large gaps are left between paragraphs. In many cases a sentence ends within the line but the next sentence begins (without indentation) on the next line or the next page; Emerson often changed this by deleting the first few words of the new sentence and reinserting them in the empty space on the line above (or the last line of the preceding page) to show that a new paragraph was not intended. The text is extensively corrected and revised in other ways, which are discussed (and, with certain exceptions, fully recorded) in Appendix 2 of this Annex.

Used and blank pages in the manuscript

Essay	Written on	Blank	In 1850 ed.
Front matter	2	2	3[a]
Uses of Great Men	89	3	31
Plato	116[b]	4	38
Plato: New Readings	28	2	10
Swedenborg	162[b]	20	51
Montaigne	101	13	36
Shakspeare	94	4	29
Napoleon	99	1	34
Goethe	79	3	28
Total	770	52	260[c]

a. Title page, copyright page, and table of contents

b. Includes half-title pages

c. Does not include half-title pages and blank pages

Numbering of pages in the manuscript

(Page numbers in square brackets indicate pages in normal sequence but not numbered; most of these, but not all, are written on.)

Front matter. No pages numbered.
Uses of Great Men. 1–2, 2½ (verso not numbered), 3–41, 38–41 (second series so numbered), 42–86.
Plato. Half-title and verso (not numbered), 1–103, [104–105], 106–107, [108–109], 110–111, [112–113], 114–115, [116–117], 118.
Plato: New Readings. 1–30.
Swedenborg. Half-title and verso (not numbered), 1–126, (1 page numbered "127, 128, 129"), 130–138, (1 page numbered "139, 140, 141"), 142–182, (2 blank pages, not numbered).
Montaigne. 1, [2–4], 5, [6–8], 9, [10–12], 13, [14–16], 17, [18–20], 21, [22–24], 25, [26–28], 29, [30–32], 33, [34–36], 37, [38–40], 41, [42–44],

45, [46], *47, [48], 49, [50–52], 53, [54–56], 57, [58–60], 61, [62–64], 65, [66], 66 (recto, incorrectly so numbered), (3 unnumbered pages), 69, [70–72], 73, [74–76], 77, [78–80], 81, [82], 82½, (3 unnumbered pages), 83, (1 unnumbered page), 84, (3 unnumbered pages), 85, [86–88], 89, [90–92], 93, [94–96], 97, [98], (2 blank pages, not numbered).

Shakspeare. 1–97, (1 blank page, not numbered).

Napoleon. 1–5, [6–8], 9, [10–11], 12–13, [14], 15, [16], 17, [18–20], 21, [22–23], 24–25, [26–27], 28–29, [30–31], 32–33, [34–35], 36–37, [38–39], 40–41, [42–43], 44–45, [46], 47–49, [50], 51, [52], 53, [54–55], 56–57, [58–60 (p. 60 numbered but number deleted)], 61, [62], 63–66, [67], 68–69, [70–71], 72–73, [74–76], 77, [78–79], 80–82, [83], 84–85, [86–88], 89, [90–92], 93, [94–95], 96–97, [98–99], (1 blank page, not numbered).

Goethe. 1–5, [6], 7, [8], 9, [10], 11–13, [14], 15, [16], 17, [18], 19–21, [22], 23–25, [26], 27–29, [30], 31, [32], 33, [34], 35, [36], 37, [38], 39, [40], 41, [42], 43, [44], 45, [46], 47, [48], 49, [50], 51, [52] 53, [54], 55, [56], 57, [58], 59, [60], 61–63, [64], 65–79, 98 (incorrectly so numbered), (2 blank pages, not numbered).

* One leaf of two pages seems to be missing between pages 46 and 47 of "Montaigne" (see the Emendation note to 94.4); if numbered, the pages would probably have been something like 46½ and 46⅔.

Renumbering of pages in the manuscript

(After the final number of each renumbered page, the earlier number or numbers are shown in parentheses. [?] indicates an illegible or doubtful number.)

Uses of Great Men. 11 (9), 17 (15), 20 (18), 29 (19, 25, 27½), 30 (26, 27¾), 31 (27⅘), 33 (23, 29), 34 (24, 30), 35 (25, 31, 33), 36 (26, 34 [?]), 37 (35), 38 (34), 39 (35) 40 (36), 41 (37) (the last four listed are the first of two sequences numbered 38–41; see the preceding list), 43, (35, 37), 44, (38), 47 (35).

Plato. 61 (60¼), 63 (60½), 64 (60⅔), 67 (60¾), 69 (63), 70 (64), 71 (65), 72 (66), 73 (65, 67), 76 (68), 77 (68½), 79, (69), 80 (70[?]), 81 (71), 82 (72), 83 (73), 84 (74), 85 (75[?]), 86 (76), 87 (77), 90 (80), 91 (81) 94 (84), 95 (85), 98 (88), 99 (89), 102 (92), 103 (93), 106 (96), 107 (97), 110 (100), 111 (101), 115 (105).

Plato: New Readings. 13 (12½), 14 (12⅔), 15 (13), 16 (14), 17 (15), 18 (16), 19 (17), 20 (18), 21 (19), 22 (20[?]), 24 (22), 25 (23), 26 (24), 27 (25), 28 (26[?]), 29 (27[?]).

Swedenborg. 15 ([?]), 18 (16), 27 (19), 31 (22), 35 (27), 61 (29), 63 (30), 65 (32), 71 (35), 73 (36), 75 (37), 77 (39), 79 (41), 80 (42), 81 (43), 85 (47), 89 (51), 97 (55), 101 (59), 103 (61), 104 (62, 63, & 64), 105 (65, 66), 106 (65), 107 (67), 121 (69), 122 ([?]), 127–128–129 (75), 135

(77), 139–140–141 (85), 143 (87), 144 ([?]), 145 (89), 147 (89), 149 (91), 151 (93), 153 (97), 173 (171), 175 (173), 181 (103).
Montaigne. 82½ (83), 91 (89½).
Shakspeare. No renumbered pages.
Napoleon. 81 (77).
Goethe. No renumbered pages.

Supplemental numbering and titling of pages

Many recto pages carry (usually in the upper left-hand corner) a supplemental number, a short title, or both. This indicates the first page of either a four-page group or a two-page group. Some of the numbers are deleted; of these, some are replaced by other numbers. In this list the final page number is given first, followed in parentheses by the supplemental number, the replacement number or numbers (if any), and/or the short title (if any).

Uses of Great Men. No supplemental numbers; but pages 5, 11, 29, 43, 47, 57, 61, 67, 71, and 75 have the short title "Uses."
Plato. No supplemental numbers; but pages 45, 49, and 111 have the short title "Plato."
Plato: New Readings. No supplemental numbers or titles.
Swedenborg. 5 (2 Swed), 9 (3 Swed), 13 (4 Swed), 17 (5), 19 (5½), 21 (6 Swed), 25 (7), 27 (8), 111 (6 Swed), 113 (9), 121 (7), 123 (8).
Montaigne. 1 (Skeptic), 5 (Skeptic), 9 (Skeptic), 21 (Skeptic 6), 25 (Skeptic 7), 29 (Skeptic 8), 33 (Skeptic 9), 49 (13), 53 (14), 85 (22), 89 (23).
Shakspeare. 5 (2 Shakspeare), 9 (3 Shakspeare), 13 (4), 17 (5), 19 (12½, 5½), 23 (5¾), 25 (6), 29 (7 Shaksp), 33 (8 Shaksp), 37 (9 Shaksp), 41 (10 Shaksp), 45 (11 Shaksp), 49 (12 Shaksp), 51 (12¼), 53 (12¾), 55 (13 Shaksp), 57 (14, 13½), 59 (13¾), 61 (14), 63 (14½), 65 (15), 67 (15¼), 71 (15¾), 73 (15¾), 75 (15¼), 77 (15¾, 16), 79 (16½ Shaksp), 83 (17 Shaksp), 87 (18 Shaksp), 89 (19), 93 (20), 95 ([?], 21).
Napoleon. 1 (1), 5 (2 Nap), 9 (3 Nap), 13 (4 Nap), 17 (5 Nap), 21 (6 Nap), 25 (7 Nap), 29 (8 Nap), 33 (9), 37 (10 Nap), 41 (11 Nap), 45 (12 Nap), 49 (13 Nap), 53 (14), 57 (15 Nap), 61 (16 Nap), 65 (17 Nap), 69 (18 Nap), 73 (19 Nap), 77 (20 Nap), 81 (21), 85 (22 Nap), 89 (23 Napoleon), 93 (24 Nap), 97 (25 Nap).
Goethe. 1 (1), 5 (2 Goethe), 9 (3 Goethe), 13 (4 Goethe), 17 (5 Goethe), 21 (Goethe 6), 25 (7 Goethe), 29 (8 Goethe), 33 (Goethe 9), 37 (10 Goethe), 41 (11 Goethe), 45 (12 Goethe), 49 (13 Goethe), 53 (14 Goethe), 57 (15 Goethe), 61 (16), 63 (17, 16½), 67 (16¾), 69 (17), 73 (17, 18), 77 (18, 19).

APPENDIX 1 TO ANNEX A

The 1850 Compositors and the Manuscript

The copyright page of the 1850 Boston edition of *Representative Men* states that it was "Stereotyped by Charles W. Colton, No. 2 Water Street." The type evidently was set in the same shop, for the name "Colton" appears among those of the compositors who signed various parts of the manuscript. The others were Badger, Manning, Magee, Cox[?], and someone designated as "Office," which may be either a man's name or an indication that the office-boy or a clerk took his turn at setting type. ("Office" is written in a hand that resembles that of "Magee," and at 94.25 the two words appear together; so Magee may have been the office-boy). The name "Cox" is queried because it is not clearly written and may be "Con" or "Cn" — possibly an abbreviation for "Colton."

Most of the places where compositors' names appear are at the beginnings of paragraphs, often where these coincide with the beginnings of manuscript pages. However, not all parts of the manuscript are so signed; no name appears, for instance, at the beginning of any essay except "Montaigne," "Shakspeare," and "Napoleon." The distance between signatures varies from a few lines to several pages, but averages about three pages of the 1850 edition. Besides the signatures, which are in pencil, there are also stint-marks (usually a heavy and elongated bracket in ink between two words of the text, or sometimes in the middle of a word, together with a page number in the margin) at the points where the compositors' stints actually joined, which would be as close as possible to a break between pages of the printed text. (One compositor would, if necessary, set type for that part of the page from the first line to the paragraph break where he had signed on, although that section had originally been assigned as the end of his predecessor's stint. This made it easier to compute each compositor's pay, which was based on the number of lines he set, though figured in terms of ens rather than lines.) In several cases the same compositor's name is signed to two or more successive stints. Some of the page numbers in the margin beside stint-marks agree with the final pagination and lineation of the printed book, but others are anywhere from one or two lines to several pages off; evidently there were some miscalculations in estimating copy, and adjustments were made.

The following table includes signatures and stint-marks, the latter indicated by the abbreviation SM. Cases where a compositor's name appears (with or without a bracket, but without a page number) not at the beginning of a paragraph but at or near the beginning of a printed page are considered stint-marks and so labeled. Each entry gives, in order, the page and line number in the present edition, the first two or three words after the signature or stint-mark, the name or page number appearing in the manuscript, and (for stint-marks with or without page numbers) the actual page and line number in the 1850 edition. At 39.14, 71.5, 90.25, and 120.26, in each case the bracket does not coincide with the beginning of a printed line. Although one 1850 compositor (Badger) signed and set a new paragraph at both 27.24 and 92.9, a new paragraph is not indicated in the manuscript at either point or set in the present edition.

Compositors' signatures and stint-marks

Page/Line (this ed.)	First words	Signature or page number	Page/Line (1850 ed.)
5.32	[¶] Our common	Badger	
9.9	of Falkland	Colton (SM)	20.1
9.16	[¶] This is the	Badger	
12.6	[¶] I must not	Colton	
12.21	know, they know	SM - 26	26.1
15.6	[¶] Great men	Office	
16.1	His attractions	SM - 32	32.1
16.14	[¶] There is	Office	
19.23	[¶] The genius	Badger	
20.16	(after end of essay)	SM - p. 41	end of p. 40
25.19	[¶] Great geniuses	Cox [?]	
27.24	[¶] Before Pericles	Badger	
29.9	flute, is	SM - 54	53.27
30.17	[¶] European civility	Cox	
32.23	-//empt from envy	SM - 60	60.1
34.13	[¶] What moderation	Cox	
37.25	of faith	SM - 69	68.27
37.29	[¶] A happier	Badger	
39.14	than beauty, as	SM - 72	71.27
42.14	[¶] The rare	Colton	
44.14	style; or the	SM - 81	80.26
45.6	[¶] Modern science	Badger	
49.10	-/peared often	SM (no page number)	89.6
56.9	[¶]In modern	Badger	
57.37	[¶] The genius	Badger	

59.8	[¶] Swedenborg was	Cox	
59.15	trained a race	SM - 108 (deleted)	105.27
59.16	shown the	SM - 108	106.1
60.20	[¶] The thoughts	Manning	
62.6	[¶] Gravitation, as	Badger	
63.31	[¶] He knows	Cox	
64.11	be known	Badger (SM)	114.20
65.24	[¶] Was it strange	Office	
67.31	in another life	SM - 123 [122?]	120.21
68.34	[¶] Swedenborg styles	Cox	
69.21	[¶] There is no	Badger	
71.5	done work	SM - 124	126.19
71.12	heaven:" "What	SM - 127	127.1
71.24	[¶] In the "Conjugal	Badger	
74.27	these books	SM - 133	132.28
75.7	into each mind	Cx [Cn?] (SM)	133.22
78.5	has the advantage	SM - 139	139.1
79.1	[¶] The secret	Cox	
79.27	should not	[C]ox [-on?] (SM)	141.24
80.21	[¶] It is remarkable	Badger·	
85.1	[¶] Every fact	Cox [Cn?]	
89.4	[¶] But I see	Badger	
89.28	[¶] Who shall forbid	(pencil line, but no name visible)	
90.25	go abroad	SM - 159	159.1
91.1	philosophy. He	Cox (SM)	159.19
92.9	[¶] These qualities	Badger	
92.13	-//sentative of	SM - 162	162.1
93.25	[¶] Montaigne is	C[ox?]	
94.1	six as ridiculous	SM - 165	165.1
94.25	position of	Office / Magee (SM)	166.7
95.12	[¶] The Essays	Magee	
96.4	[¶] Montaigne did	Manning	
98.7	[¶] I mean to	Badger	
99.13	[¶] There is the	C[ox?]	
101.1	[¶] Or, shall I	Office	
101.28	[¶] There are these	Badger	
103.15	[¶] The final	Cox	
104.24	Things seem to	Manning (SM)	183.27
109.1	[¶] Great men	Badger	
111.5	[¶] The secure	Cox	
112.18	[¶] In point of	Manning	
113.3	[¶] Shakspeare knew	Colton	
114.15	[¶] Thus all	Manning	
114.37	[¶] It is easy	Badger	

Appendix 1 to Annex A

Page/Line (this ed.)	First words	Signature or page number	Page/Line (1850 ed.)
117.24	[¶] The Shakspeare	Magee	
119.8	idle," of Othello's	SM - 205	205.1
120.22	[¶] Some able and	Magee	
120.26	exhaling thoughts	SM - 207	207.20
121.15	[¶] Shakspeare is as	[Ba]dger	
123.16	[¶] One more royal	Colton	
125.6	[¶] Well, other men	Manning	
129.1	[¶] Among the eminent	Magee	
129.15	fortunes, and the	SM - 220	220.2
130.32	[¶] It is true	Colton	
132.11	[¶] Napoleon renounced	Manning	
133.13	[¶] Nature must	Badger	
134.15	[¶] History is full	Cox [?]	
134.26	As he is	SM - 229	229.2
135.33	[¶] We like to	Magee	
137.4	[¶] Everything depended	Badger	
137.36	the Bourbons. He	SM - 235	235.1
138.12	[¶] His grand weapon	Manning	
139.23	as the necessary	Magee (SM)	237.27
139.33	[¶] Napoleon met	Colton	
141.31	[¶] We cannot, in	Badger	
143.9	[¶] This deputy of	Magee	
144.8	[¶] His memoirs	Manning	
144.26	I call Napoleon	SM - 247	247.3
145.13	[¶] Bonaparte was	Badger [?]	
146.28	[¶] In describing the	Badger	
152.35	[¶] This striving	Manning	
154.8	[¶] If I were	Colton	
155.1	proceeds. The greatest	SM - 264	264.1
155.17	[¶] Society has	Badger	
156.24	[¶] Goethe was the	Colton	
157.19	[¶] The wonder of	Magee	
157.34	all. He had	Manning (SM)	269.5
159.15	[¶] Take the most	Magee	
160.5	[¶] Wilhelm Meister	Colton	
	[Some doodling (by Colton?) in left margin of manuscript page.]		
161.26	[¶] What distinguishes	Badger	
163.17	to any other	SM - 279	278.27
163.31	[¶] He is the	Colton	
165.12	[¶] This lawgiver	Manning	
166.20	[¶] It is the last	Magee	

Appendix 1 to Annex A

Compositor analysis. An analysis of compositors' errors as a guide to decisions on emendations and rejection of variants in this volume is not as helpful as we would wish, for various reasons: (1) about 6 percent of the substantive variations between manuscript and book occur in passages not signed by a compositor; (2) it is not always possible to be sure where one compositor's stint ends and the next one begins; and (3) it is not certain whether Colton and Cox(?) are the same person, or whether Magee is the same as "Office." Within these limits, however, some generalizations are possible from a study of the substantive variants. (Variations in accidentals are very numerous, but since most of them probably reflect house styling rather than individual preferences (or errors) of compositors, they have not been analyzed. It is amusing that of the three clear cases of misspelling resulting from typographical error — "inportation" at 76.9, "satifaction" at 131.29, and "Plotemais" at 141.23 — two can be charged against the boss printer, Colton, and the third against "Cox," who may be the same man.)

Substantive variants from the manuscript in the 1850 edition.

Compositor	Pages set/ Percentage	Number of variants/ Percentage	Variants per page
Badger	97.7 (38.5)	37 (30.8)	0.37
Colton	29.0 (11.4)	16 (13.3)	0.55
Cox[?]	51.8 (20.4)	28 (23.3)	0.54
Magee/"Office"	34.5 (13.6)	14 (11.8)	0.41
Manning	24.0 (9.5)	18 (15.0)	0.75
Passages not signed	16.6 (6.6)	7 (5.8)	0.42
Total or average	253.6 (100)	120 (100)	0.47

Badger, who set almost two-fifths of the volume, had the lowest rate of variants per page, and Magee (and/or "Office") the next lowest. Manning had the highest rate of variation, but set the smallest number of pages, less than one-tenth of the volume. Colton and Cox between them set over three-tenths of the volume and had slightly higher variation rates than the general average (rates so nearly the same that they strengthen the possibility that they were the same person). The rate in

315

the unsigned passages is slightly below the general average. None of these rates can be taken as safe evidence of relative compositorial accuracy or inaccuracy; to assume that all the variants are errors would be unwarrantable. Few of them in fact can be categorically established as errors; some are almost certainly changes made by Emerson in correcting proofs — the kind no compositor would have made — such as the change from "book on mines" to "Dædalus Hyperboreus" at 57.1. Others are corrections of obvious slips of the author's pen, which a compositor would consider a normal part of his job. If such variants are subtracted from the figures in the preceding table, Badger's and Magee's rates of variation are even lower than they are in the first tabulation; so is Manning's, though his is still about as high as Colton's and Cox's, which remain about the same as before.

A few compositorial idiosyncrasies are identifiable. Badger is more likely than the others to change nouns from singular to plural (or vice versa), and to change the preterit forms of certain verbs: for example, from Emerson's "sung" and "begun" to "sang" and "began." The unsigned passages include three singular–plural variants of the type characteristic of Badger, but this is not firm enough ground on which to assign those pages to him. Badger and Cox have more variants of the type apparently caused by misreading Emerson's handwriting: "expression" for "expansion," "freezing" for "sneering," "manifestation" for "manipulation," and "arrayed" for "arranged" (the last is certainly an error, for Emerson marked it in his correction copy). The largest class of variants comprises the omission, insertion, or substitution of unimportant words (articles, prepositions, conjunctions, and so on) in contexts where the change does not affect meaning and one version is about as suitable as the other. These occur in pages set by all the compositors, but most frequently in the work of Colton and Cox. There are also a few changes in word order: two by Badger, one each by Colton and Manning. In almost all of these, unless a strong reason for emendation exists, this edition has retained the manuscript form.

In one type of variant, a consideration of the compositor has helped in deciding how it should be treated. In three cases words within parentheses in the manuscript, not marked with any signs for deletion, do not appear in the printed book (one word at 92.33, a phrase at 138.31, and a sentence at 104.35). The last two occur in passages set by Manning; and in all the material he set only one pair of parentheses appears — around three words at 165.30, which must have been added in proof. It is true that parentheses are not much used in this book, but there are some in the pages set by each of the other compositors. Emerson sometimes put parentheses around words he wished deleted, but he also crossed them out with horizontal, vertical, or diagonal lines. Manning probably assumed that parentheses alone indicated deletion and acted accordingly. It is of course possible that Emerson did want these passages omitted, but no evidence exists; and Manning's record does not inspire confidence. Accordingly, this edition retains both passages. The other word in parentheses is also retained, even though it is in a passage set by Badger, whose record is considerably better.

With this exception, few if any variants offer problems that can be solved on the basis of compositor analysis alone, or even primarily. Each decision has been made on a case-by-case basis, with all available evidence, including the identity of the compositor, considered.

APPENDIX 2 TO ANNEX A

Revisions in the Manuscript

The manuscript of *Representative Men* is rather extensively revised. In proportion to the lengths of the several chapters, those most altered are "Plato" (including "Plato: New Readings"), "Swedenborg," and "Shakspeare"; those least altered, "Montaigne" and "Goethe." Colton and his compositors deserve a good deal of credit for setting the book so accurately.

The more significant revisions include deletions, insertions, substitutions, and transpositions, sometimes of single words (or parts of words), sometimes of phrases, sentences, or whole paragraphs. Passages are moved forward or backward, often within the same sentence, occasionally between points several pages apart. Some pages are not changed at all, but these may be fair copies made from earlier, much-revised versions. In passages where there are two or three layers of revision, it can be difficult to be sure of the exact order of changes; when it can be determined, an attempt has been made in this appendix to show that order as clearly as possible, either by the order of words in the transcript or by an explanatory note. Inserted words are printed after the words they replace, even when the inserts appear in the manuscript before the deletions. However, when words are deleted on one line and reinserted on the line above (or on the last line of the preceding page) to eliminate a break between paragraphs, the insertion is printed before the deletion, and the lineation (or pagination) is shown.

To allow the reader to concentrate on the more important revisions, the following types of revision are not recorded (unless they occur within a passage included because it contains a significant revision):

(1) Simple corrections made only to delete false starts (where there are too few letters to give any idea of what word Emerson may have had in mind) and obvious slips of the pen, or to correct misspellings caused presumably by haste (for example, "multutude").

(2) Cases where a word written illegibly (or smeared or blotted) has been replaced or duplicated by the same word written (in script or printing) more legibly over, above, or beside the original word, whether or not the latter is deleted. This is frequently done with foreign words and proper names, probably to assist the printer.

(3) Words deleted on one line and reinserted on another simply to fill blank space, not to indicate a change in paragraphing or in the order of words or larger elements.

(4) Cases where an initial capital letter is changed to lower case or vice versa, unless this involves either an abstract noun such as "Justice" or changing from one sentence to two or from two to one.

(5) The simple deletion of a punctuation mark without any resulting change in meaning, emphasis, or sentence structure.

(6) The rewriting of arabic numerals as words.

Other features of the manuscript not included in this appendix unless they occur in a passage recorded because of significant changes are: Emerson's failure to use a hyphen when dividing a word at the end of a line; his use of the ampersand, which is always silently emended to "and"; his use of other abbreviations (such as "y^t" for "that"), which are shown as emendations in the Textual Apparatus; possible changes of punctuation marks (period to colon or comma to semi-colon) that are not certain; and the loss of letters and/or punctuation marks through the binding of the manuscript. Some deleted letters and words cannot be deciphered with certainty (or at all), especially when they are smeared or blotted and something else has been written over them. These are recorded by symbols, in the hope that eventually they may be recovered.

Emerson, when deleting words, often did not clearly indicate deletion of the punctuation marks preceding or following them. The text is thus left with unnecessary, misleading, or incorrect punctuation: for example, at 27.37 there are uncanceled periods both before and after the deleted "of things," only one of which is needed. Elsewhere a line used to delete words extends through a punctuation mark needed in the revised sentence: for example, at 35.7 the period after the deleted passage ending "eternal" is actually crossed out, but is needed after the new ending of the sentence at "facts," rather than the uncanceled semicolon. Such cases are recorded in the form which represents what Emerson probably intended; this usually (though not always) agrees with the punctuation adopted by the 1850 Boston printers.

Symbols used in transcription. These are in general the same as those used in *JMN* and *EL,* except that where the two editions differ, we have chosen the symbol that seems most useful.

↑	↓	inserted matter
⟨	⟩	deleted matter (see Note below)
⟨ ‖ ... ‖ ⟩		deleted matter not decipherable
⟨this [?]⟩		deleted matter not clear, but transcription is considered probable
[	]	editorial notes and comment
[[	]]	letters or punctuation marks lost in the binding of the manuscript and supplied from the 1850 edition or by editorial conjecture
{	}	Emerson's square brackets
(	)	Emerson's curved brackets or parentheses
[45]		page numbers in the manuscript
/		new line in the manuscript
//		new page in the manuscript
// [blank] //		blank page in the manuscript between pages written on
¶		paragraph symbol in the manuscript
[¶]		indentation in the manuscript, but without paragraph symbol
[¶?]		paragraph indentation not certain
[no ¶]		no paragraph indentation or symbol in the manuscript, but new paragraph in the 1850 edition, or vice versa

Note. Words (or parts of words) written to replace deleted matter appear in the manuscript in three different ways. (1) If the replacement matter is written directly over the deleted matter (in the same space), the transcription shows the replacement matter immediately to the right of the second angle bracket, without any space between: for example, "th⟨e⟩ose" or "of ⟨these⟩those things." In many such cases the original matter has been blotted out or smeared by finger-wiping, but is often decipherable. (2) If the replacement matter is written after the deleted matter (in the space to the right of it on the same line, or on the next line or page if the deletion runs to the end of a line or page), the transcription shows the replacement matter to the right of the second angle bracket with a normal space between; for example, "of ⟨these⟩ those things." In most such cases the original matter has been deleted by lining through it horizontally, vertically, or diagonally, but sometimes by blotting or smearing. (3) If the replacement matter is written above or below the deleted matter (in a separate space between the lines) or in the margin, the transcription shows a vertical arrow to the right of the second angle bracket: example, "of ⟨these⟩ ↑those↓ things" or "th⟨e⟩↑o↓se." In almost all such cases the original matter has been deleted by lining through. The manner of deletion and replacement often shows whether the correction was one that Emerson made immediately or at some later time.

I. USES OF GREAT MEN

3.11   superiors. ↑[Insert A]↓ / [¶] The search
        [Insert A, on a separate page [2½] with blank verso, runs from 3.11 "We call" through 3.14 "of them."]
3.13   verbs ⟨and nouns of our⟩ ↑of↓ language
3.18   English are ⟨ ‖ . . . ‖ ⟩ ↑practical↓, the Germans
3.21   find ↑comfortable,↓ rich, ⟨or⟩and hospitable
3.24   persons ⟨↑I am in search of↓⟩ who
        ["I am in search of" is written in pencil.]
4.2   they be ⟨⟨paddy⟩ ↑animal↓ populations⟩ ↑beggars↓, are disgusting
4.8   Mahometism ⟨and they⟩ are the
4.10   carpets: ⟨The new buyer⟩ ↑he↓ fancies
4.14   paint or ⟨think⟩make or think
4.17   distributed. / [Broad white line] [written in pencil] / [¶] ⟨Let us see how others serve us.⟩ ↑If now we . . . low enough. We↓ / ⟨We⟩ must
        [The inserted passage, in very small writing, occupies three lines above the deleted sentence, which it replaces and expands.]
4.20   the ⟨relative⟩ ↑substantial↓ existence
4.26   minds. / ↑Each↓ ⟨[¶] Each⟩ man
        [This change, like many similar ones, was made to cancel the beginning of a new paragraph.]
4.26   of quality different from
        [Emerson wrote the figure "2" below "quality" and "1" below "different" to indicate that the words should be transposed.]
4.29   more ⟨stringent the⟩ ↑it is↓ reacti⟨on⟩ve. Let
4.30   alone. ⟨The⟩ ↑A↓ main
4.34   and ⟨as⟩ in sport
5.1   hand. ⟨It costs a beautiful person⟩ // [9] ⟨and⟩ I count ↑him↓ a great

[The new page [9] is inserted after [8] on a separate leaf, with verso blank but numbered [10], and the original page [9] is renumbered [11]. "It costs a beautiful person" is repeated on the last line of the new page [9].]

5.3 difficulty: ⟨so that when he⟩ ↑he has but to↓ open⟨s⟩ his eyes ⟨he⟩ ↑to↓ see⟨s⟩ things

5.5 make ⟨many⟩ painful

5.7 paint ⟨the⟩ ↑her↓ image ⟨of herself that lies⟩ on our

5.15 answer ⟨the questions⟩questions which

5.20 some ⟨great⟩ instinct

5.23 makes ↑for itself↓ room, . . . allies↑.↓ ⟨for itself.⟩ A sound
[Presumably the period after "allies" was inserted after the other changes were made.]

5.27 own ⟨means⟩ ↑channels↓ and welcome

5.29 true ⟨man⟩ ↑artist↓ has the . . . adventurer ↑after years of strife↓ has nothing

5.35 senses, ↑arts of healing,↓ magical

6.1 endogenous, ⟨The⟩ ↑and↓ ⟨E⟩↑e↓ducation is ↑this↓ unfolding.
[The comma after "endogenous" probably was a period originally.]

6.3 is ⟨so⟩ ↑thus↓ learned . . . and ⟨permanent in effect⟩ ↑the effect remains↓. Right

6.7 the Spirit⟨!⟩: — 'Coxcomb⟨: — ⟩! would

6.12 ideas. // [17] ⟨and of things.⟩ [¶] As plants
[The new page has been renumbered from [15] to [17]; probably two or more preceding pages have been rewritten, for the last few lines on [16] are crowded, and seem to replace an earlier version that ended with the deleted first line on [17].

6.16 cotton; the ⟨inventors⟩makers of tools; the inventor

6.18 all ⟨into⟩ ↑through↓ unknown

6.20 bees; ⟨Euclid, of lines; // Newton of fluxions; Dalton of atomic forms; Van Mons of pears.⟩ Fries of lichens; Van Mons . . . fluxions.
[The first version was deleted and rewritten in slightly different form just below, apparently because it was ink-smeared and somewhat illegible. "Fries" and "Van Mons" are printed just above the same words in the revision, probably to make sure the compositor spelled the names correctly.]

6.27 brain. ⟨or reason.⟩ It waits

6.30 corn, ⟨to⟩and cotton

6.31 are ⟨yet⟩ ↑still↓ hid

6.34 shape. ↑In the history of discovery the ripe and↓ ⟨[¶] The possibility of interpretation lies in the⟩ // [20] ⟨identity of the observer with the observed. The genius that has done what the world desired, say, to find his way between azote and oxygen, to detect the new rock-superposition, to find the law of the curves, can do it, because he has just come out of nature, or, from being a part of that thing. He knows the way of azote, because he is azote. Man is a piece of the universe made alive. He can⟩ // [21] ⟨[¶] In the history of discovery, the ripe and⟩ latent

[The deleted page, originally numbered [18] and renumbered [20], continues from "He can" in the last line to "do what just now he suffered" at the top of page [29] (previously numbered, successively, 19, 25, and 27½); see entry for 8.3. It has been revised into what is in the printed text from 7.21 "The possibility" to 7.35 "compose him."]

6.37   Swedenborg, ↑or Oersted,↓ before ... entertain ⟨the importance of the quality.⟩ ↑its powers. [New paragraph]↓ If we

7.8   day the ⟨divine⟩ ↑first↓ eulogy

7.13   botany, ⟨in⟩ music, ⟨in⟩ optics, ⟨in⟩and ⟨astronomy⟩ ↑architecture↓, another. ⟨Everything is enhanced by mixture, and man must adopt every property in nature to raise it to its highest power. There are⟩ ↑There are↓ advancements

7.17   conversation, ↑character and politics.↓ // [24] ⟨character, and politics.[¶] But this comes later. We speak now only of our acquaintance with them in their own sphere, and the way in which they seem to fascinate and draw to them so[[me]] genius who occupies himself with one thing all his life long. ⟨The possibility of interpretation lies in the identity of the observer with the observed.⟩ ↑The possibility of interpretation↓ lies in the identity of the observer with the observed.⟩ // [25] [¶] But this ... the observed. Each

[The first three words on page [24] were inserted at the bottom of [23], and the rest of it was copied on [25]; page [24] was then deleted. The reason for this is not clear, since no change in wording was made.]

7.20   to fas⟨ten⟩cinate and
[Possibly a slip of the pen in copying.]

7.22   Each ⟨thing⟩ material thing

7.32   them: ⟨H⟩he has

8.3   and Davy[[s?]] // [29] ⟨do what just now he suffered. ⟨We see them as⟩ ↑Men are↓ incarnations of the laws of nature.⟩ [¶] Thus we
[See note on 6.34.]

8.9   beauty ⟨&⟩in many

8.11   labours↑!↓⟨, and verify their results!⟩ Every ship

8.14   inventor. ⟨The physician, the jurist, the man skilful in the conduct of affairs, the⟩ ↑Life is girt all round with a zodiack of sciences the contribution of men who have perished to add their point of light to our sky. Engineer, broker, jurist, physician,↓ moralist, ⟨the⟩ theologian

8.21   gainers by ⟨new⟩ finding a new ... planet. // [blank] // ↑[¶] We are too passive in the reception of↓ ⟨[¶]⟩ These ⟨we have named are⟩ material or semi-material aids↑.↓⟨, in which we are ↑too↓ passive ↑in the reception↓. But⟩ we must not be ⟨mere⟩ sacks

8.30   mind, ⟨and new eyes bud in your brow; you⟩ ↑and we↓ acquire

8.36 but all ⟨your⟩ mental . . . is a ⟨direct and contagious⟩ ↑positive↓ good.

9.3 fresh resolu↑tion.↓ / ⟨tion.⟩ ↑We are ⟨piqued to⟩ emul⟨ation⟩ous of all that man can do.↓ Cecil's

9.14 manners of ⟨Pih E⟩ ↑Loo↓ are heard

[The last four lines on page [36], from 9.12 "and I accept" to the end of the paragraph, may have been inserted later, as they are written in a smaller hand than the rest.]

9.25 railroad ⟨shall⟩will not again

10.3 Yet these ⟨unchoked channels⟩ ⟨floodgates of expression and⟩ unchoked channel[[s]] ↑and floodgates of expression↓ are only

10.5 benefits↑.↓ ⟨we owe to genius.⟩ [¶] Senates . . . swords, ⟨or⟩and armorial

10.11 in a ⟨lifetime⟩century, the

10.17 is the ⟨reflection.⟩ ↑show.↓ [¶] ⟨There is a salutary⟩ ⟨As w⟩We go to . . . see the ↑power and↓ beauty of the body↑:↓ ⟨, so⟩ there is ⟨a salutary influence⟩ ↑the like pleasure and a higher benefit↓ from witnessing

10.22 abstraction, the ⟨act⟩ ⟨miracle⟩ ↑transmutings↓ of the

10.25 For we ⟨are⟩ thus ⟨inst⟩ ⟨introduced into⟩ ↑enter↓ a new gymnasium and ⟨taught⟩ ↑learn↓ to choose

10.28 and to ⟨b⟩Being." ⟨Especially in⟩ ↑Foremost among↓ the↑se↓ activit⟨y⟩ies ⟨of the imagination the joy is at its height. To⟩ ↑are the summersaults, spells, and resurrections wrought by ⟨the⟩↓ the ⟨excited⟩ imagination↑.↓ ⟨nothing is incredible or impossible.⟩ ↑When this wakes,↓ a man seems to ⟨acquire ⟨the⟩⟩ ↑multiply↓ ten times or a ⟨hundred⟩ ↑thousand↓ times his ⟨energy⟩ ↑force↓. It opens ⟨a⟩ ↑the↓ delicious

10.33 gunpowder, ⟨and small and tame as we walk here with folded arms, a⟨n imaginative⟩⟩ ↑and a sentence in a↓ book ↑, or a word dropped in conversation,↓ sets free our fancy, and ⟨in a moment⟩ ↑instantly↓ our heads

10.36 the Pit. ⟨And ⟨The Imagination has⟩ ↑Poetry is↓ a flute that sets the atoms of our frame in a dance like planets and ⟨once so flagellated,⟩ the whole man reeling drunk to the music, they never quite subside to their old marble.⟩ And this

[Compare *JMN*, XI, 117; "Books," *W*, VII, 213; and "Poetry and Imagination," *W*, VIII, 18.]

11.2 minds: ⟨but not always ⟨in⟩ or often in mathematicians But beside the poets usually⟩ ↑⟨except⟩ even in arithmeticians of the first class, but especially↓ in ↑meditative↓ men of ⟨insight and⟩ ↑an↓ intuiti⟨on⟩ve ↑habit of thought[[.]]↓ This class ⟨are sure benefactors⟩ ↑serve us,↓ ⟨if⟩ so that they

[The order of changes is not certain; "except" may have been a replacement for either "but not" or "always," rather than the first word of a new insertion.]

11.7 laws ⟨indicates the calibre of⟩ ↑is a kind of metre of↓ the mind. ⟨The 1⟩Little ↑minds↓ are little

11.10 [The passage from 11.10 "Even these" through 11.13 "dominion" appears to be inserted as the last five lines on page [42]. Page [43] begins as follows:] ⟨[¶] There are some famous examples of intellectual oppression. The long dominion⟩ of Aristotle

[At the top of [43] is the word "Excess," in pencil, not deleted.]

11.28 is her ⟨law of⟩ remedy. The soul ⟨as it opens⟩ is impatient

11.32 go, and ⟨rather catch⟩ ↑sip↓ the ⟨genius of life,⟩ ↑foam of many lives.↓ ⟨than drink the dregs.⟩ Rotation

12.6 [At the top of [47] is the deleted phrase "Debt to the Ethical Class"; below it begins the paragraph of the text which starts "I must not forget."]

12.11 lawgivers. The↑se↓ ⟨highest class⟩ teach us

12.12 swim ↑, day by day,↓ on a river . . . which ⟨men⟩the men about

12.16 worn the ⟨foolscap⟩ ↑fool's cap↓ too long

12.23 born. ↑These men↓ ⟨[¶] These ⟨highest⟩ men⟩ correct

12.25 selects these ⟨men⟩ for the

13.9 philanthropists↑.↓ ⟨, of abolitionists.⟩ Do what I can, I ⟨k⟩cannot keep

13.12 law that ⟨ranges⟩ ↑disposes↓ these particulars, ⟨in their natural order,⟩ and so certifies . . . player, ⟨and⟩ bankrupts

13.25 system: ⟨A⟩↑a↓nd a man . . . regrets, ⟨and⟩ envies, and

13.27 room; ↑here are↓ no selfesteems

13.37 power. ⟨These fellows with s⟩↑S↓word and staff, or ⟨with⟩ talent↑s↓ sword-like

14.5 nothing. ↑Then↓ He is

14.9 empire↑.↓ ⟨;⟨himself⟩ a witting hermit, ↑gladly forgotten↓ hiding not like the cuttlefish in his ⟨own⟩ ink, but like the angels in deluges of light.⟩ / Broad white line [in pencil between horizontal lines] / [¶] But

[Three very faint vertical pencil lines may originally have been intended to cancel everything following "servants" (14.7) down through "Broad white line"; but ink lines were used for the actual deletions.]

14.11 service. ↑Nature↓ // ⟨But to specify in three particulars. / 1. Nature⟩ never spares

["But to . . . particulars" is written at the top of the page, with a space between it and the next line.]

14.25 uses what ⟨grain⟩spark of perception

14.31 by, which ⟨booby⟩ ↑⟨Caliban⟩ Thersites↓ too can

15.1 persons, ⟨finding that⟩ ↑since↓ our receptivity is unlimited, ⟨that⟩ ↑and,↓ with the

15.3 energy. ⟨On this account,⟩ there needs . . . contagion. // ⟨2⟩ [¶] Great

15.10 or in ⟨other⟩ persons

15.15 assimilation, ⟨all unsuspected,⟩ goes on between men of ⟨the same⟩ ↑one↓ town, of ⟨the same⟩ ↑one↓ sect, of ⟨the same⟩ ↑one↓ political

15.18 point ⟨of view⟩, this city of New York, ↑yonder city↓ of London, ⟨this⟩ ↑the↓ western

15.21   stingings ⟨and alar⟨ms⟩ums⟩ of conscience
15.32   cabalism. / ⟨3⟩. [¶] Thus we
15.34   conversation with ⟨ourselves and⟩ our mates
16.2   attractions ⟨ ‖ . . . ‖ ⟩warp us from
16.6   last. ↑Perhaps↓ Voltaire
16.12   health of ⟨all⟩ ↑the state↓ depends
16.14   use of ⟨great men⟩ ↑heroes↓. Every genius
16.17   we are ⟨attracted⟩ ↑drawn↓, the more
16.21   substantiated it ⟨by experiment⟩. It seems . . . dressed each ⟨wandering⟩ soul
16.32   individual ⟨by selfpreserving instinct,⟩ strives to . . . protect each ⟨individual⟩ against
16.35   is more ⟨wonderful⟩ ↑marked↓ than the power by which ⟨each⟩individuals are
17.3   interfering. ↑We↓ / ⟨We may well talk⟩ ↑rightly speak↓ of the
17.8   of such ⟨foolish⟩poor educators
17.12   permitted. ⟨Grudge no office thou canst render. Be the⟩ ↑Serve the great. Stick at no humiliation.↓ Grudge no

       [The whole inserted passage ("Serve . . . humiliation") is written over the deleted passage ("Grudge . . . Be the"), which is smeared out but still legible, in the same space.]

17.19   In vain. ⟨and in vain.⟩ The wheels
17.23   water. ⟨After a time,⟩ ↑Presently,↓ a dot
17.26   Children ⟨cannot⟩think they cannot
17.31   Virtue? ⟨One thinks of Bonaparte's phrase, "neither is my blood ditchwater."⟩ The thoughtful ⟨man⟩ ↑youth↓ laments

       [The deleted sentence is used in "Napoleon" at 139.9.]

17.32   'Generous ⟨he⟩and handsome,' he
18.4   man is ⟨the⟩ ↑every day's↓ tragedy↑.↓ ⟨of the world.⟩ It is
18.7   Is it ⟨an answer to this doubt,⟩ ↑a reply to these suggestions,↓ to say
18.8   served ⟨by our seniors and by our juniors,⟩ by receiving
18.13   benefit ⟨and pleasure⟩ it is to ⟨the⟩ ↑each↓ speaker . . . himself. ↑We pass very fast↓ / ⟨[¶] We pass very fast⟩ in our
18.15   dependence, ⟨from the chair of power to the apprentice's stool.⟩ And if . . . assume the ⟨seat⟩ ↑chair↓, but always
18.18   about. ↑As to what↓ / ⟨[¶] As to what⟩ we call
18.19   men are ↑at last↓ of a . . . talent has ⟨also⟩ its apotheosis
18.21   play ↑and an open field↓! ↑and freshest laurels to all who have won them!↓ ⟨We are willing that antiquity should have its glories, and saints theirs, and ⟨Greece, and India, and England,⟩ ↑Greek and Roman and Englishman↓ but we are persuaded that⟩ ↑but↓ heaven
18.24   produced his ⟨strict [?]⟩ private ray

       [The deleted word may be "short"; compare *JMN*, IX, 453.]

18.25   [There is a space between the line ending with "exaltation" and the one beginning with "The heroes"; but square brackets are drawn in the left and right margins to close up this space; "The heroes" is not indented. However, the 1850 edition starts a new paragraph here.]

18.28 qualities. ↑Some rays escape↓ / ⟨[¶] There are rays which escape⟩ the common

18.34 soul. [¶] ⟨The o⟩One gracious fact ⟨appears,⟩ ↑emerges⟨,⟩ from these studies,↓ that there

19.8 lost, ↑or wherein ⟨or⟩all touch by their summits.↓ Thought

19.11 power of ↑the↓ greatest men, ↑ — ↓ their spirit

20.7 appears ↑as↓ an exponent

II. PLATO

23.1 [¶]⟨The work of Plato is that writing, which, in the history of civilization, is entitled to Omar's ⟨account of⟩ ⟨↑praise of↓⟩ ↑fanatical compliment to↓⟩ ↑Among books, Plato only is entitled to Omar's fanatical compliment to↓ the Koran ... libraries; for ⟨, if they contain any / thing good, it is ⟨contained⟩ ↑inscribed↓ in⟩ ↑their value is in↓ this book

23.5 literatures. ⟨⟨Nothing but⟩ ↑only↓ God can give invention: Everything else, one would say, the study of Plato ⟨can⟩would give.⟩ A discipline

23.7 speculation. ⟨Buonaparte was nicknamed *Cent-mille:* Plato, by his breadth, deserves the name, and much more.⟩ Out of ⟨him⟩ ↑Plato↓ come all

23.13 generation, — ↑Boethius,↓ Rabelais, Erasmus, ↑Bruno,↓ Locke

23.19 after him. ⟨The broadest⟩ ↑For it is fair to credit the broadest↓ generalizer ⟨anticipates⟩ ↑with↓ all the particulars ⟨in⟩ ↑deducible from↓ his thesis

23.22 philosophy Plato⟨.⟩, ⟨Plato is⟩ ↑at once↓ the glory ... mankind; ⟨Vain are the laurels of Rome, vain the pride of England, in her Newton, Milton, and Shakspeare, whilst⟩ ↑since↓ neither Saxon ... idea to ⟨the⟩ ↑his↓ categories↑.↓ ⟨of Plato. What a posterity is his!⟩ No wife

23.25 are his ⟨children⟩ ↑posterity↓, and are

24.7 in its ⟨famed book⟩ ↑hand-book↓ of morals ... from him. ⟨It is very easy to feel in him that the culture of modern Europe and America is his.⟩ ↑Mysticism finds in Plato all its texts.↓ This citizen

24.13 genius. ⟨He⟩ ↑His broad humanity↓ transcends all sectional lines↑.↓ ⟨, — the great, humane Plato.⟩ [¶?] This range
[There is a space between lines after "humane Plato," but no paragraph indentation.]

24.17 a man ⟨of extraordinary power,⟩ higher by

24.20 Shakspeare. ⟨I explain it thus. that⟩ ↑For↓ these men ... contemporaries, ⟨⟨draw them to them⟩,⟩ so that ... for them ⟨, or in their atmosphere,⟩ what they

24.25   school. [¶] ⟨It is certain, too, that⟩ Plato, ↑too,↓ like

24.28   all arts, ⟨al⟩sciences, all . . . food? ⟨He⟩ ↑he↓ can spare

24.31   borrow: ⟨he turns lead to gold;⟩ and society . . . for him. ⟨Quoted — did he? Who does not?⟩ ↑When we are praising Plato it seems we are praising quotations from Solon, and Sophron, and Philolaus. Be it so.↓ Every book

24.36   of all ⟨mines⟩forests, and mines

25.1   And this ⟨monstrous⟩ ↑grasping↓ inventor

25.2   absorbed ⟨into himself all⟩ the learning . . . else: then ↑his master↓ Socrates↑;↓ ⟨himself:⟩ and, finding

25.8   mind. This ⟨great⟩ breadth ⟨it is, that⟩ entitles

25.9   Republic, ⟨(Book VI),⟩ "⟨that⟩Such a genius as ⟨they ( ) philosophers ( )⟩ must of . . . seldom ⟨to⟩in all its

25.12   persons." ⟨I should even add to his remark, this other, — that⟩ ⟨e⟩Every man . . . ground; ⟨and⟩ a philosopher must be ⟨much⟩ more than

25.14   Plato ⟨is⟩ ↑is clothed with the powers of↓ a poet . . . poet; and, ↑⟨though I doubt he wanted the decisive gift of lyric expression,⟩↓ ⟨only⟩ ↑mainly↓ is not

25.18   purpose. [¶] ⟨I have called these lectures biographical. But⟩ great

25.23   readers ⟨can tell you most, for he⟩ most resembles

25.25   burns ⟨up all⟩ its ⟨own⟩ smoke, so a ⟨good⟩ philosopher con⟨sumes⟩↑verts the value of↓ all his ⟨own events,⟩ ↑fortunes↓ in↑to↓ his ⟨extraordinary⟩ intellectual

25.30   war: but ⟨meeting⟩in his twentieth year meeting with

25.33   invitations of Dion⟨ys⟩, and of Dionysiu↑s↓, to the court of S⟨yracuse⟩icily; and ⟨, it seems,⟩ went

25.35   treated↑.↓ ⟨by the tyrant.⟩ He travelled . . . then ⟨went⟩ ↑in↓to Egypt

26.4   interior. ⟨The fact before us is⟩ ↑We are to account for↓ the ⟨singular⟩ ↑supreme↓ elevation of this man ⟨Plato above all other men⟩ in the intellectual history of ⟨mankind;⟩ ↑our race;↓ how it

26.11   poet, ⟨so that it is⟩ ↑making it↓ impossible

26.17   arms: here ⟨it is already ripe in⟩ ↑are↓ all its ⟨characteristics⟩ ↑traits already discernible↓ in the

26.20   every ⟨work considered as a⟩ work of

26.22   traits. How ⟨the man⟩ Plato . . . solve. [¶] ⟨Men are not moved without cause any more than stones fall without something that draws them to fall⟩ This could not ⟨be⟩ ↑have happened↓ without a

26.26   honour ↑at the same time↓ the ideal . . . mind, and ⟨, at the same time,⟩ Fate . . . nature. ⟨It needed a broader and a clearer mind than ⟨any⟩had yet appeared.⟩ // ⟨[¶] This leads us to the point so familiar in universal history, the tendency to perfect expression.⟩ The first period ⟨from which history descends, is, with nations as with men,⟩ ↑of a nation as of an individual, is↓ the period of unconscious ⟨ef⟩strength. Children

26.31   gentle. ⟨It is the same with adults.⟩ ↑In adult life,↓ ⟨W⟩↑w↓hilst the perceptions . . . quarrel: ⟨T⟩↑t↓heir manners

26.34   soon as ⟨, by ripeness of faculty, and experience of the world,⟩ ↑with culture↓ things have

26.36   distributed, ⟨⟨as they are in nature⟩,⟩ they desist . . . meaning ⟨also⟩ in detail

27.2   occurs ↑daily↓ in the ⟨history⟩ ↑education↓ of ⟨all⟩ ardent

27.4   one who ⟨understands⟩ ↑comprehends↓ me:" and they ⟨sob and⟩ sigh⟨,⟩ ↑⟨and start,⟩ and weep,↓ write

27.17   moment of ⟨perfect⟩ ↑adult↓ health

27.21   with them ⟨, for philosophy,⟩ the dreams

27.25   partialists, — ⟨one⟩ ⟨fro⟩deducing the origin of ⟨all⟩things from flux or water; ⟨one⟩ ↑or↓ from air; ⟨one⟩ ↑or↓ from fire; ⟨one⟩ ↑or↓ from mind. All mix with the⟨ir⟩se causes

27.28   Plato, the ⟨articulate speaker⟩ ↑distributor↓, who needs

27.30   superlative // ⟨the simple suffices him.⟩ he is

27.32   define." ⟨said Plato.⟩ [¶] This defining

27.35   base; ⟨there is⟩ ↑the↓ ⟨o⟩One; and ⟨there are⟩ ↑the↓ two. 1. Unity⟨;⟩ or Identity; and, 2. Variety. ⟨There is one.⟩ We unite all things ⟨in our minds⟩ by perceiving

27.37   perceiving ⟨how slight are the⟩ ↑the superficial↓ differences, ⟨how⟩ ↑and the↓ profound ⟨the⟩ resemblances↑.↓ ⟨of things.⟩ But every ↑mental↓ act ⟨of the mind⟩, — this very

28.4   speak, ⟨it is impossible⟩ ↑or↓ to think without embracing both↑.↓ ⟨these facts.⟩ [¶] The mind . . . ask for ⟨a cause,⟩ one cause of . . . effects; then ⟨again⟩ for the

28.7   that ⟨, at last,⟩ it shall ⟨rest in⟩ ↑arrive at↓ an absolute . . . shall be ⟨a⟩All. "In the

28.9   midst of ⟨the⟩ truth . . . being," say⟨s⟩ the Veda⟨nta⟩↑s↓. [¶] All

28.11   centripetence. ⟨As surely does the mind⟩ ⟨u⟩Urged by an opposite necessity, ↑the mind↓ return↑s↓ from . . . effect; and affirm↑s↓ the necessary

     [In the part of the passage marked by ellipsis, the words "one," "not one," "other," and "many" were originally underlined, but the underlining was crossed out.]

28.15   These ⟨two⟩ ↑strictly-blended↓ elements ⟨blended in every thing and thought,⟩ it is . . . reconcile⟨,⟩. ⟨⟨to see how each is so universal, and how the existence of each is compatible with the other.⟩⟩ ↑Their existence is mutually↓ // ⟨[¶] The extreme difficulty of the problem lies herein, that their existence is mutually⟩ contradictory

28.23   of the ↑fundamental↓ Unity↑.↓ ⟨, the Identity, at the foundation of things.⟩ The raptures . . . devotion ⟨fly to this thought, — the loss of⟩ ↑lose↓ all beings

28.24   tendency ⟨has nowhere found such⟩ ↑finds its ⟨most⟩↓ ⟨memorable⟩ ↑highest↓ expression ⟨as⟩ in the . . . the East, ⟨particularly⟩ ↑and chiefly↓ in the

28.28 they rise ⟨sometimes⟩ to ⟨sublime⟩pure and sublime . . . celebrating it.
      [¶] ⟨Identity, identity⟩ ↑The Same, the Same↓: friend

29.1 shall now ⟨briefly⟩ learn

29.3 decay, omni⟨pot⟩present, made up

29.7 is the ⟨great end or true⟩ wisdom . . . unity ⟨and the true principles⟩ of
     things

29.10 nature of ⟨a⟩the great

29.13 distinction." — ↑"The↓ / ⟨[¶] "The⟩ whole

29.14 and is ⟨therefore⟩ to be regarded

29.23 nature. [¶] If ⟨all⟩ speculation . . . absorbed, —⟨all⟩ action

29.26 gravitation of ⟨Mind⟩mind; the second

30.10 delighting in ⟨the highest⟩abstractions, of men

30.16 boundaries. // ⟨[no ¶] European civility is⟩ ↑¶ European civility is↓ the
      triumph

30.20 had been ⟨doing these works, and⟩ ↑working in this element↓ with the
      joy ⟨and stimulus⟩ of genius . . . of the ⟨ill consequence⟩ ↑detriment↓ of

30.23 Malthus, no ⟨city⟩ Paris or London ⟨City⟩, no pitiless

30.27 understanding was ⟨yet⟩ in its

30.31 ship at ↑the↓ Medford ↑yards,↓ or ⟨a⟩ new mill↑s↓ at Lowell

30.32 granted; — ⟨T⟩the Roman legion, ⟨the Roman⟩ ↑Byzantine↓ legislation

30.37 pilgrimages, ⟨had been⟩ imbib⟨ing⟩↑ed↓ the idea

31.1 absorbed. ⟨This⟩ ↑The↓ unity of Asia and ⟨this⟩ ↑the↓ detail

31.4 join, and, by ⟨joining⟩ ↑contact, to↓ enhance the energy of each↑.↓ ⟨in
     contact.⟩ ↑The excellence↓ ⟨[¶] More excellent in defining than the
     acutest of the Eleatics, he stands yet on the ⟨vast⟩ ↑steppes↓ of Asia by
     taste and extent. The excellence⟩ of Europe

31.6 philosophy ⟨seemed⟩ ↑expressed↓ the genius of Europe. / he ⟨added⟩
     ↑substructs↓ the religion . . . base. [¶] ⟨I tell the whole when I say⟩ ↑In
     short,↓ a balanced

31.9 elements⟨,⟩. ↑It is as↓ // ⟨yet balanced. It is⟩ as easy . . . small. The
     ⟨only⟩ reason

31.11 is, because ⟨it is against⟩ ↑they are not in↓ our experience

31.12 life, ⟨we know⟩ they are

31.15 But ⟨so it was,⟩ whether voices

31.16 that the ⟨newborn⟩ ↑infant↓ manchild . . . or not; ⟨this is certain, that⟩
      a man . . . was born. ⟨That⟩ ↑The↓ wonderful . . . Jove, ⟨that⟩ ↑the↓
      union

31.22 a man↑.↓ ⟨, so that it could be interpreted.⟩ [¶] The balanced soul
      came. ⟨Precisely as high as he soared, so deep he dived.⟩ If he

31.26 distinctions ⟨above the vision of ordinary men⟩, he fortified

31.29 horsedoctors↑,↓ ⟨and⟩ butchers⟨.⟩, and fishmongers. ⟨Herein following
      nature, jealous of partiality, if he plants his foot here, and ⟨says one
      thing,⟩ ↑maintains a side,↓ he is sure to plant his foot there, and make
      the counterweight,⟩ ↑He cannot forgive in himself a partiality, but is↓

resolved that the two poles ↑of thought↓ shall appear ↑in his state-ment↓. ⟨The two poles never fail to appear;⟩ ⟨h⟩His argument and his sentence ⟨is⟩ ↑are↓ selfpoised and spherical↑.↓ ⟨as the world.⟩ The two

31.34   own. [¶] ⟨Synthesis is all.⟩ Every great artist has been ⟨that⟩ ↑such↓ by synthesis

32.7   by the ⟨D⟩↑d↓ifferent⟨;⟩. ⟨t⟩Thought seeks . . . unity; ⟨P⟩↑p↓oetry to . . . variety, ⟨i.e.⟩ ↑that is↓ always

32.10   pigment, ⟨always⟩ at his

32.12   are ⟨mere⟩ inventories. Things // [blank] // ⟨inventories or lists. Things⟩ used as

     [Probably the page preceding the blank one was a revised version, written later than the one that follows.]

32.14   Plato ⟨is ⟨a⟩ master of the game, and⟩ turns

32.15   Jove. [¶] To ⟨illustrate this by an important⟩ ↑take an↓ example: . . . philosophers ⟨who preceded him,⟩ had sketched

32.18   mathematics, ⟨delighting in geometry,⟩ studious . . . causes, ⟨yet⟩ feels

32.28   dogma ⟨is not once asserted, and then forgotten, but it is never out of mind, and it⟩ animates and impersonates ⟨the whole⟩ ↑his↓ philosophy

32.30   in all ⟨the⟩ ↑his↓ talents ↑.↓ ⟨of the man. As soon as we come to⟩ ↑Where there is↓ great

32.35   power. ⟨Thus⟩ ⟨i⟩In him ⟨is⟩ the freest abandonment⟨,⟩ ↑is↓ united

33.2   elegance, ⟨pointed⟩ ↑⟨qualified⟩ edged↓ by an . . . paralyses, ⟨arms⟩ ↑adorn↓ the soundest . . . frame. ⟨⟨He is cast in Olympian proportions, and, according to the sentence which⟩ ↑According to the sentence which↓ antiquity loved to repeat,⟩ ↑According to the old sentence,↓ "if Jove

33.6   With this ⟨hard-finished air of the man of the world, and⟩ ↑palatial↓ air↑,↓ ⟨of courts,⟩ there is

33.12   assembly ↑to Plato↓ is preserved; ⟨— "Of those that come down!" ↑by Diogenes Laertius.↓ But also⟩ ↑⟨And⟩ and↓ the indignation

33.16   people↑.↓ ⟨, so ready is he to bow the knee to any shadow of religion⟩ Add to this, ⟨that⟩ he believes ⟨in preternatural faculties, as to have al-most reduced them to a science;⟩ that poetry

33.18   master; ⟨that is strictly divine:⟩ that the . . . by a ⟨truly⟩ celestial

33.21   regions, ⟨and⟩ ↑visits↓ worlds

33.23   with the ⟨spindle⟩ ↑rock↓ and shears; and hears the ⟨hum of⟩ intoxicat-ing hum of their spindle. ⟨ — ⟩ Poetry has ↑never↓ attempted heights beyond the Timaeus // [59] [¶] ⟨At the same time he is uniformly cir-cumspect⟩ ↑But his ⟨discretion⟩ ↑circumspection↓ never forsook him↓. One would

     [For the last sentence on page [58], which does not appear in the 1850 edition, see Emendations in Copy-Text.]

33.26   inscription on the ⟨famous⟩ gates . . . Bold;" and ⟨then again⟩ on the second

33.29 bold." ⟨The whirlwind of⟩ his strength ⟨resembles⟩ ↑is like↓ the momentum . . . discretion ⟨is⟩ the return

33.31 reading ⟨an almanac, or a book of⟩ logarithms

33.34 playing ⟨abroad⟩ ↑in the sky↓. He has

33.37 needs. ⟨For Plato is a very rich man⟩ ⟨What pleases us most in the rich is the just selection.⟩ ⟨⟨H⟩The⟩ ↑↑As the↓ rich man↓ wears
["He wears"→"The rich man wears"→"As the rich man wears."]

34.2 poor⟨;⟩, ⟨B⟩but he has . . . need; ⟨And⟩ ↑so↓ Plato in his plenty ⟨has⟩is never

34.5 use, epic, analytic ⟨musical, and intuitive⟩ ↑mania, intuition, music, satire and irony↓, down to

34.7 polite. ⟨How much wit in finding that word 'cookery' and 'adulatory art' for *rhetoric*, in Gorgias. No orator can measure in effect with him who can give good nicknames. His⟩ ↑His↓ illustrations are ⟨standing texts⟩ ↑poetry,↓ and his . . . Socrates' ⟨ob⟩ profession of obstetric . . . good nicknames.

34.15 against ⟨philosophy⟩ ↑⟨the⟩ ↑⟨our[?]⟩⟩the↓ schools.↓ "For philosophy ⟨, O Socrates,⟩ is an

34.18 the man⟨,⟩." ⟨said Callicles. / T.P. IV. 400⟩ // ⟨[¶] Ah he⟩ ↑He↓ could well . . . generous, he ⟨whose faith was without a cloud⟩ ↑who↓ from the ⟨elemental⟩ sunlike . . . vision ↑had a faith without cloud↓. Such as

34.21 doubt and ⟨exaggerates it⟩ ↑makes the most of it:↓ he paints

34.30 too, I ↑in turn↓ invite . . . contests here." ⟨and⟩ ⟨⟨Cary p 231⟩⟩ // [blank] // [¶] He a
[The word "is" (supplied from the 1850 edition) presumably was omitted inadvertently between the last two.]

35.3 cities to the ⟨New⟩ Atlantis. He omits

35.6 raptures. / Broad white line [written between horizontal lines] // [no ¶] Plato ⟨,then,⟩ apprehended the cardinal facts ⟨; knew there was an origin; knew there was something which could not be known, causal, eternal⟩. He could ⟨bow his head,⟩ prostrate

35.16 race, ⟨cried aloud⟩ ↑affirmed↓, —And yet

35.17 was first ⟨amply and⟩ heartily

35.19 and now, ⟨and now⟩ refreshed . . . Culture, ⟨comes to him,⟩ ↑returns,↓ and he cries↑,↓ ⟨out, *And*⟩ ⟨y⟩*Yet things are knowable!* ⟨Nay,⟩ they are knowable, ⟨because there is one, and not two, or, if two, yet a two of one; they are knowable,⟩ because, being

35.29 to unite ↑to↓ an object

35.32 of it. ⟨It is⟩ dialectic ⟨which⟩ must teach

35.33 that no ⟨truly⟩ intellectual ⟨mind⟩ ↑man↓ will enter on any ⟨particular investigation, whether of more or less importance,⟩ ↑study↓ for its . . . view to ⟨strengthen and⟩ advance ⟨it⟩↑him↓self in that . . . embraces all↑.↓ ⟨, namely, Dialectic.⟩" [¶?] "The essence

36.4 form." ⟨Things are knowable. Joy to the human race!⟩ I announce

36.8 lawreceiver. ⟨Joy to you⟩ ↑I give you joy↓, O sons of men! ⟨for see,⟩ that, truth

36.11 of the ⟨view⟩ ↑sight↓ of essence . . . be ⟨fed⟩ ↑stuffed↓ ⟨on⟩with conjectures: ⟨↑But see↓ that⟩ ↑but↓ the supreme good is reality, ⟨that⟩ the supreme beauty is ⟨also⟩ reality; ⟨that⟩ ↑and↓ all virtue and all felicity depend⟨s⟩ on this . . . real: for, ⟨that⟩ courage . . . knowledge; ⟨that⟩ the fairest

36.16 his own. ⟨And t⟩↑T↓his also . . . nay, ⟨that⟩ the notion

36.28 education. ⟨How⟩ he delighted ˙. . . performance ⟨, from the lowest to the highest⟩; above all

36.31 achievment ↑"The whole of life,↓ / ⟨"The whole of life,⟩ O Socrates,⟨"⟩ said Glauco ⟨"⟩is with
  [Emerson restored the deleted quotation marks in his correction copy; see Emendations in Copy-Text.]

37.1 celebrates! // ↑In the Timaeus ↑Timaeus↓ he indicates the highest employment of the eyes.↓ "By us it is asserted, that ⟨the Deity bestowed sight on us⟩ God invented and bestowed sight on us for

37.10 our own ⟨silly⟩ wanderings

37.12 purified and ⟨exsuscitated⟩ ↑reanimated,↓ which

37.15 he first ⟨fully⟩ admitted its basis⟨.⟩, ⟨He first said, *Nature*. With the instinct of every superior man, he⟩ ↑and↓ gave . . . nature. ⟨Still more by⟩ his patrician

37.18 caste ⟨, a doctrine much insisted on by Plato⟩. "Such as ⟨are⟩were fit to

37.23 silver, // [85] ⟨and artificers." The East confirms itself in all ages in this faith. [¶] The Mahometan Ethics (in Akhlak-y-Jalaly) distributes men into five classes. "1. Those who are by nature good, and whose goodness has an influence on others. This class is the aim of ⟨c⟩Creation. In fact, the other classes are admitted to the feast of being, only as following in the train of these." [¶] The Koran ⟨, too,⟩ is always explicit on this point⟨.⟩ ↑of caste↓. "Men have their metal as of gold and silver;⟩ // [86] those of
  [All material on page [85] has been deleted and rewritten in a shorter form on the preceding page [84], which runs from 37.20 "for husbandmen" through 37.23 "silver."]

37.25 not less ⟨rigorous and exclusive.⟩ ↑firm.↓ "Of the five . . . of men."⟨*⟩ In the Republic
  [Deleted footnote at bottom of page [86]:
  ⟨* 1. Name; 2. Definition; 3 Example; 4. Science; 5. The Comprehensible.⟩]

37.27 on the ⟨nature and dispositions⟩ ↑temperaments↓ of the

37.32 with him, ⟨tis⟩ no thanks ↑are due↓ to him

37.34 not to ⟨understand⟩know the way

38.1 with me.⟨"⟩ ↑Such O Theages,↓ / ⟨[¶]"Such, O Theages,⟩ is the association

[The inserted "Such O Theages" is underlined, but the underlining has been crossed out by a series of small "x"s.]

38.15 and he ⟨forbore⟩ ↑failed↓ not to ⟨avail himself of ⟨that⟩ ↑a↓ profound religion, of which he was born capable, now in his maturity, and to take a third step, ⟨and say⟩ ↑and to say↓ ↑add↓ *There is . . . Divine.* ↑There is no thought in↓ / ⟨⟨Wonderful is the fact, I submit it to your deepest wisdom, that⟩ ⟨t⟩There is no thought in⟩ any mind

38.17 organizes a ⟨whole⟩ ↑huge↓ instru⟨e⟩mentality of

38.20 attempted ⟨as an intellectual man⟩, as if . . . homage fit ↑for↓ the Immense

38.23 said, then, ⟨'Behold⟩ ⟨o⟩'Our faculties . . . infinity, and ⟨all⟩ return

38.24 little way: ⟨But⟩ ↑but↓ here is

38.27 results ⟨, I see to be⟩ ↑are↓ beginnings. // [¶] A ⟨sort of⟩ key to ⟨the mind of Plato, to its⟩ ↑the↓ method and ⟨its⟩ completeness ⟨↑of Pla↓⟩ ↑of Plato↓ is his twice

38.30 illustrated ⟨, in Book VI of the Republic,⟩ the relation between ⟨A⟩the absolute . . . he says ⟨"That which Good is, in the intelligible sphere, in relation to intelligence and its objects, that the sun is in the visible sphere, in relation to sight and its objects." [¶] When the eyes are turned on things not enlightened by the sun, they have difficulty in dis⟨covering⟩cerning them, and are, as it were, blind, but when turned on what the sun illumines, they see. The same thing befals the soul. When it looks on that which is enlightened by truth and by Being, it comprehends and knows; it shows itself endowed with intelligence; but when on that which is mixed with darkness, which is born and dies, its sight is troubled; it has only opinions, and passes from one to the other. You would say, it was without intelligence. Hold it, then, for certain that what gives the soul the faculty of knowing, is, the idea of the Good." [¶] After this, comes the scale — ⟩ "Let there

39.4 correspond:
⟨εικασια ⟨science of forms, imitative arts⟩ ↑conjecture↓
πιστις faith
διανοια ⟨acquaintance with good and evil in the sensible reality.⟩ ↑understanding↓
νοησις ⟨reflection reasoning intelligence⟩ or Reason⟩
// ↑conjecture, faith, understanding, Reason.↓ As every

39.8 perforated ⟨with⟩by a ⟨chann⟩million channels

39.11 lovely ⟨and most apparent⟩ of all

39.13 degree into ⟨all⟩ / all things: ⟨B⟩↑b↓ut that

39.18 of art. ↑"When ⟨therefore⟩↓ / ⟨When therefore⟩ an artificer

39.21 work, it ⟨is then necessary⟩ ↑must follow↓ that ⟨the whole of⟩ his production

39.23 beautiful." / ⟨Timaeus / Cousin XII 116⟩ / [space but no ¶] Thus ever

39.26　initial ⟨merely⟩, and symbolizes at a distance the ⟨upward⟩ passion

39.29　God only. ⟨[¶] "There is not, never was, and never will be, a moral education which can avail against that of which the people disposes. I mean, my friend, a human education, and of course except that which is divine. Be assured, that if in such governments, there be found any soul which escapes the common shipwreck, it is a divine protection which has saved it." / Repub. Cousin X. 20.⟩ / In the same

39.33　leads me ⟨to what cannot be omitted,⟩ to that central figure which ⟨Plato⟩ ↑he↓ has established

39.35　and whose ⟨life and history⟩ ↑biography↓ he has . . . laboured ⟨, with his genius,⟩ that the

40.2　is the ⟨very⟩ best example

40.8　potters ⟨frequently⟩ copied

40.11　defeat in ↑any↓ debate

40.14　feasts, ⟨where⟩ ↑whither↓ he goes

40.17　was what ⟨we Yankees⟩ ↑our country people↓ call

40.25　[The word "sycamorespoons" is written solid, but "sycamore-" is inserted ⟨in somewhat clearer handwriting⟩ above the first part of it. For this reason, and because of "soup-pans" in the same line, it is printed with a hyphen in this text.]

40.28　to go ↑on foot↓ to Olympia

40.35　opposing ⟨alone⟩ ↑singly↓ the popular

40.37　[Five lines, from 40.37 "usually" through 41.5 "barefooted," are written in very small handwriting and were apparently inserted later between "olives" and "and it."]

40.37　olives: ⟨often⟩ ↑usually↓, in the . . . friends. ⟨h⟩His necessary

41.23　draw them ↑in the pleasantest manner,↓ into horrible doubts and confusion↑.↓ ⟨, in the pleasantest manner.⟩ But he

41.28　realist⟨,⟩↑!↓ — ⟨Meno⟩ ↑Meno↓ has . . . times⟨,⟩ at length . . . to him: ⟨B⟩↑b↓ut, at this

41.34　bonhommie ⟨, delighted⟩ ↑diverted↓ the young

42.2　affirms the ⟨sublime doctrines of⟩ the immortality

42.6　prison, whil⟨e⟩st he was

42.10　you say." ↑The fame of this↓ / ⟨[¶] The fame of this⟩ prison

42.13　world↑.↓ ⟨, and too well known than that I should go into that tragedy now.⟩ [¶] ⟨But it seems, as if this⟩ ↑The↓ rare

42.15　with the ⟨most precious⟩ ↑sweetest↓ saint

42.19　fittest ⟨vehicle⟩ ↑dispenser↓ of ⟨all⟩ the intellectual treasures he had ↑to↓ communicate⟨d⟩. It was . . . that this ⟨wise⟩ Aesop
　　　　["Æsop" is written more legibly above "Aesop."]

42.22　faculty↑.↓ ⟨and usefulness.⟩ The strange

42.24　means, ⟨Plato⟩ ↑he↓ was able . . . of the ⟨wonderful⟩ wit and

42.29　quality. ⟨He is ever himself, and refuses to be another.⟩ He is

42.30　Mounting into ⟨the⟩ heaven

42.33　otherwise. x x x It is ⟨the chief deduction,⟩ almost

[The significance of the three "x"s is not clear; they were not repro-
duced in 1850, and are not in this edition.]

42.34 have not ↑what is no doubt incident to the regnancy of intellect in his
work,↓ the vital

42.38 necessary. ⟨I kn⟩ / [¶] I know

43.8 place, and ⟨another⟩the reverse

43.13 thought; ⟨but the⟩ ⟨the⟩but the theory of

43.14 patches. ⟨T⟩ ⟨[¶] The greatest man // underlies the human nature.⟩ [¶]
The longest ... the sea. ⟨No individualism can make head against
⟨this⟩the swallowing universality.⟩ Plato

43.22 overran, ⟨the⟩with men

43.24 of men, ⟨thoughts, truths, all actual and possible things,⟩ have passed

43.27 the world. [¶?] ⟨Well, t⟩This is the

43.31 Nature ⟨goes⟩lives on

43.32 Plato. ⟨Alas!⟩ ⟨i⟩In view of

44.1 dispose of ⟨n⟩↑N↓ature, — ⟨Nature⟩ ↑which↓ will not

44.3 smallest ⟨effect⟩ ↑success↓ in explaining

44.7 him is ⟨not⟩to compare him, not

44.10 remains, it ⟨is as broad as man, and⟩ requires all the ⟨variety⟩
↑breadth↓ of human

44.13 respect. ⟨The ⟨profoundness⟩ ↑depth↓ of⟩ his sense ↑deepens,↓ ⟨, the
multitude of⟩ his merits ⟨grows on us⟩ ↑multiply↓ with study

44.14 we say, ⟨it⟩ ↑there↓ is a fine

44.19 should ⟨be⟩ ↑have↓ 1760 yards↑.↓ ⟨long.⟩ The greateyed

PLATO: NEW READINGS

45.1 Bohn's ↑serial↓ "Library,"... benefits ⟨it⟩ the cheap press

45.5 to add⟨∧⟩ a bulletin ↑like the journals↓ of Plato
[The phrase "like the journals" was first intended to follow "add,"
as is shown by the deleted caret there, replaced by a caret after "bulletin."]

45.12 glorious ↑when prospectively beheld↓ from the

45.13 Nature, in ⟨contemplating⟩ ↑regarding↓ the ⟨long⟩ geologic ... men,
↑as Homer, Phidias, Menū, and Columbus,↓ was nowise
["Menu" (without the macron) is repeated in clearer handwriting
below the line.]

46.6 Socratic ⟨argumentation⟩ ↑reasoning↓ or on

46.8 geometer ↑or the prophet of ⟨of⟩a peculiar message↓. He represents

46.9 of the ⟨human mind⟩ ↑intellect↓ the power ↑, namely,↓ of carrying up
every ⟨subject⟩ ↑fact↓ to ⟨new⟩ ↑successive↓ platforms, and so disclosing
in every ⟨subject⟩ ↑fact↓ a germ

46.12 of thought↑:↓ ⟨; they are essentially magnificent.⟩ ↑The naturalist↓ /
⟨The naturalist⟩ would

46.20 say, ⟨Here⟩ ↑there↓ was a ↑more↓ complete man ⟨who reported nature.
Nature stands before the enchanted eyes of the multitude, like a picture, which they see, but cannot touch, or at all break into parts. In
Plato's description, things reappear as they stood in ⟨the⟩ common
daylight, hardly shorn of a ray, yet now divided, detachable, paint-
able, portable, and tangible. He has broken the spell, and touched
them one by one. Henceforth anybody may.⟩ ↑who could apply ⟨the
whole⟩to nature the whole scale of the senses, the understanding, and
the reason.↓ / ⟨[no ¶?] These⟩ ↑[¶?] These↓ expansions or extensions
⟨ ‖ ... ‖ ⟩consist in continuing
  [There is a space between the line beginning "These expansions"
and the line above it; and the inserted "These" is indented slightly to
the right of the deleted one below it, probably to indicate a new paragraph (not adopted in the 1850 edition, but adopted in this edition).]

46.25 secondsight ⟨he sees⟩ ↑⟨following⟩ ⟨he⟩ discover⟨s⟩ing↓ the long lines of
law ↑↑which↓ shoot⟨ing⟩↓ in every direction. ↑Everywhere[[e]]↓ /
⟨⟨Wherever he stands,⟩ ↑Everywhere↓⟩ he stands on

46.28 becomes ⟨at once⟩ an exponent

46.31 death, —that ⟨wonderful⟩ law by which ↑in↓ ⟨n⟩Nature, ⟨in⟩ ↑decom-
position is recomposition and↓ putrefaction and cholera ⟨is⟩are only

46.34 studying ↑⟨y^e⟩ the↓ state in the ⟨man⟩ ↑citizen,↓ and the ⟨man⟩ ↑citizen↓
in the

46.36 allegory on ↑the↓ ⟨E⟩↑e↓ducation of the

46.37 the lin[[e,]] ⟨and⟩ sometimes ... defining of ⟨justice⟩Virtue, courage,
justice

47.3 the chariot↑eer↓ and tw[[o]] horses

47.6 which have ⟨implanted⟩ ↑imprinted↓ themselves in the human ⟨mind⟩
↑memory↓ like the ⟨constellations⟩ ↑signs of the zodiac; his soliform
eye and his boniform soul[[;]]↓ his doctrine of assimilation, ⟨that all
knowledge is approach to the object of knowledge[[;]]⟩ his doctrine of
reminiscence; ⟨But especial[[ly]]⟩ his clear
  [The last twelve lines on this page, from 47.6 "fables which"
through 47.13 "laws above," are written in a smaller hand than the
rest, and may be inserted. It is more likely, however, that the whole
page was an expanded revision of an earlier draft, and that Emerson
wrote smaller to get it all on one page. The line from 47.7 "signs of"
through 47.8 "boniform soul" is probably an insertion.]

47.11 specially in the ⟨saying⟩ ⟨sentence⟩ ↑doctrine↓, "What

47.13 laws above [[.]] // ↑[¶] More striking examples are↓ / ⟨His⟩ ↑this↓
moral conclusions↑.↓ ⟨are examples.⟩ Plato

47.16 knows ↑both↓ itself and

47.19 justice ⟨and lose the credit of it⟩ ↑from gods and men↓; that it

47.23 homicide; ↑that the soul is unwillingly deprived of true opinions, and
that ↑no↓ man sins willingly;↓ that the

47.26 a sound ⟨mind⟩body cannot ⟨me⟩ restore a↑n↓ unsound mind, yet a ⟨sound mind can⟩ good soul can by its ⟨own⟩ virtue . . . possible. ↑⟨that t⟩↑T↓he intelligent↓ / ⟨that the soul is unwillingly deprived of true opinions / that ⟨m⟩ letters are to be repudiated as ruinous to the memory / the intelligent⟩ have a right over the ⟨unin⟩ ignorant

[Several of the sentences on this manuscript page end in the middle of a line, some without end punctuation, as if they were ideas jotted down to be filled in later. The last five and a half lines (from 47.29 "The right" through 47.33 "which will") are written smaller than the rest.]

47.31 man[[;]] that ⟨the⟩ ↑this↓ guards

47.33 which will ⟨make men willing to give them everything which they need.⟩ // [11] ↑make men willing to give them everything which they need.↓ ¶ This secondsight

[The deleted words are written from bottom to top of the left margin of page [10]; the same words are inserted across the top edge of page [11].]

47.36 that the ⟨world⟩ ↑globe of earth↓ was not

48.3 water, ⟨and clay,⟩ and slate, and ⟨iron⟩ ↑magnesia↓; not less

48.7 everywhere; ↑hating insulation;↓ and appears . . . cabins of ⟨barbarians⟩vagabonds

48.10 vacant, ⟨to⟩ when Plato . . . arguments are left // [13] ⟨[¶] This represents itself in another way, as the doctrine of ⟨r⟩Reality, or the Nature of things, on which, in every age, Philosophy endeavours to found the religion of mankind; but, ↑is↓ always resisted by the affectionateness of men, who impute impiety to bare science. The world might well appear new and vacant to the lawgiver who could write ↑is forced to say↓; — "Of all whose arguments are⟩ left to

[Possibly the last sentence on page [12], beginning with 48.10 "Ethical science," which seems to be a revision of part of the deleted matter on [13], is an insertion; or the whole page may be.]

48.20 [At the top of page [15], above the new paragraph beginning "His definition," the date "24th Oct" has been deleted.]

48.22 world. ⟨I conceive Plato⟩ ↑He↓ was born . . . ends, ⟨and inviting contemplation, — which⟩ a power which . . . evanescence ↑of things.↓ Plato

48.26 to him the / the ⟨whole⟩ ↑⟨stupendous⟩ fact of↓ eternity

48.29 connection ↑between our knowledge and the abyss of Being↓ is still

48.34 tablet. ⟨One would say, that his fore-runners had mapped out each a farm, or district, or island, in intellectual geography, but that Plato first drew the sphere.⟩ He put

[The deleted words are used in the text, almost without change ("forerunners" without hyphen), in lines 36–38 below.]

49.3 casual in ⟨a⟩the action

49.6   sense. ⟨to the wise⟩ The gods

49.7   contemplative; ⟨and⟩ Jove

49.13   nature. ⟨He describes his⟩ ↑⟨First of⟩ ↑Before↓ all men, he saw the intel-
        lectual values of the moral sentiment. He describes his↓ own ideal

49.16   order. ⟨So averaged, so modulated.⟩ He kindled . . . a theory so
        averaged, ⟨and⟩so modulated, that

49.22   happened ⟨so⟩ that a very wellmarked class ↑of souls↓, ⟨⟨as well-marked
        as the four temperaments,⟩⟩ namely
        [Note "wellmarked" and well-marked" in successive lines.]

49.25   it, are ⟨called⟩ ↑said to↓ Platonis⟨ts⟩↑e↓. ⟨said to Platonise.⟩ Thus Michel
        . . . Platonist in ⟨all⟩ his sonnets

49.32   [There is a large canceled ⟩ in the left margin between the last line of
        the quotation and the next line.]

49.33   Hamlet is ↑a pure↓ Platonist, and tis only ↑the magnitude of↓ Shak-
        speare's ⟨transcendant profusion⟩ ↑proper genius↓ that hinders

50.1   school // ⟨and⟩ Swedenborg ⟨again⟩ throughout . . . is Plato↑nist.↓ /
        ⟨"Truth needs no colour with his colour fixed / Beauty no pencil
        beauty's truth to lay, / But best is best, if never intermixed"⟩ [¶] His
        subtlety ⟨secured him⟩ commended him
        [Shakespeare, *Sonnet* 101, 6–8.]

50.5   earth" ⟨and⟩↑, but,↓ in Plato, intellect is always ⟨paramount, but it is⟩
        moral

50.7   For the↑ir↓ argument↑,↓ ⟨of⟩ most of them

50.9   he is ⟨exclusively⟩ ↑only↓ contemplati[[ve.]] He . . . Pythagoras,
        ⟨bur[[n]] his fingers⟩ ↑break himself↓ with an

50.13   charlatan. [¶] ↑It was a ⟨noble idea — ⟩ ↑high↓ scheme, his absolute
        privilege for the best, ⟨which to make emphatic, he expre[[s]]sed by
        community of women,⟩ as the premium↓ // ⟨⟨I think it⟩ ↑It was a↓
        noble ⟨the⟩ idea, ⟨of⟩ his community for the best, ⟨to⟩ ⟨which to make ⟨it⟩
        emphatic he expressed by community of women,⟩ as the premium⟩
        which he

50.18   first, ⟨outlaws⟩ those who . . . protection, outlaws; and

50.20   desert, are ⟨above all⟩ ↑out of the reach of your↓ rewards; let ⟨them⟩
        ↑such↓ be free . . . law. ⟨Th⟩ We confide

50.22   Let ⟨no gossips⟩ ↑none↓ presume

50.24   scales. // [28] ⟨[¶] There is something fatal and beautif[[ul]] in the
        succession of men Nature is an artist with whom time and space are
        cheap and we must wait ⟨for the hour⟩ ↑the↓ stupendous periods of pa-
        leontology for the hour to ⟨arrive⟩ be struck when man shall arrive
        then periods must pass before the motion of the earth can be suspected
        then before the map of the instincts and of the cultivable power↑s↓
        can be draw[[n]] But Plato has the fortune in the history of mankind
        to express that crisis⟩ // [29] [¶] In his
        [There is no punctuation at all on page [28], though some punc-

tuation marks may be lost in the binding (for example, after "arrive," "suspected," "drawn," and "crisis"). It appears to be an earlier draft of the passage in the printed text at 45.19–46.4.]

50.25   little mathematic↑al↓ dust

50.27   governors. ⟨He plays Providence a little, as people allow themselves with their dogs and cats, so⟩ Plato plays . . . sort, ⟨in his ⟨r⟩Republic⟩ as people . . . dogs and cats.

III. SWEDENBORG

53.3   have not ⟨invented the art of⟩ cultivat⟨ing⟩ed corn, ⟨and making⟩ ↑nor made↓ bread: they have not ⟨taught the use of fire, nor discovered some continent for colonization; no, nor a new⟩ ↑led out a colony nor invented a↓ loom↑.↓ ⟨nor a safety-lamp.⟩ A higher

53.12   faculties↑.↓ ⟨, and acquaint him with the light of a new sphere.⟩ ↑Others may build cities; he is to understand them, and keep them in awe.↓ [¶] But there

53.17   precedence of ⟨all things and beings.⟩ ↑everything else.↓ For other

53.26   Essence ⟨is⟩must take precedence

54.2   poem is ⟨only⟩ a proximate . . . problem. ⟨That⟩ ↑The↓ atmosphere . . . reduces all ⟨things⟩ ↑material magnificence↓ to toys, yet ⟨makes every⟩ ↑opens to ⟨the⟩ every↓ wretch that has reason, ⟨no wretch but a native of it.⟩ ↑the doors of the universe.↓ Almost

54.12   universe into ⟨one⟩ ↑a↓ person

54.14   all are ⟨t⟩↑T↓hou." [¶] ⟨There is somewhat commanding to⟩ ⟨a⟩All men ⟨in⟩ ↑are commanded by↓ the saint. ↑The Koran makes a distinct class↓ Of those who . . . on others, ⟨the Koran makes a distinct class, and declares, ⟨"⟩This class is the⟩ ↑and pronounces this class to be the↓ aim of creation: ⟨in fact,⟩ ⟨↑and↓⟩ the other

54.19   train of ⟨these⟩ ↑this↓.⟨"⟩ And the ⟨p⟩Persian Poet ⟨, addressing such a soul,⟩ exclaims⟨,⟩ ↑to a soul of this kind,↓ / "Go boldly

54.24   method than ⟨ex⟩by experience

54.31   property ⟨of the soul,⟩ which Plato . . . by the ⟨Hindoo⟩ Bramins

54.33   having been ↑often↓ born

55.3   heaven, and ⟨all⟩ those which are beneath, ⟨and all things⟩ there is . . . wonder ⟨, then,⟩ that she

55.6   linked ⟨together in relationship⟩ ↑and related↓, and the . . . known all↑,↓ ⟨things,⟩ nothing

55.10   the rest↑,↓ ⟨of things,⟩ if he . . . faint⟨s⟩ ⟨not[?]⟩not in the

55.13   by being ⟨brought near and⟩ assimilated to the ⟨First Cause, or⟩ original Soul . . . subsist, ⟨easily and naturally⟩ the soul of man does then ↑easily↓ flow

55.17   law. [¶] This ⟨secret⟩ path

55.19 think. ⟨The⟩ ↑All↓ religious history ⟨of all nations⟩ contains

55.23 eyes, ↑whence our word↓ ⟨m⟩Mystic. ↑The trances of Socrates, Plo-
       tinus,↓ / [space] ⟨[¶] The trances of Socrates, Plotinus,⟩ Porphyry

55.26 to mind ⟨, in this connection,⟩ is the

55.27 comes ⟨not only⟩ in terror, ⟨but⟩ ↑and↓ with shocks

55.28 mad, or ⟨, oftener,⟩ gives . . . bias↑,↓ ⟨to his mind⟩ which . . . judgment.
       ⟨It is singular, that,⟩ ⟨i⟩In the

55.31 spite of the ⟨bent[?]⟩unquestionable increase
       [The deleted word may be "bait."]

56.4   Therefore ⟨all⟩ the men

56.8   mud. [¶] ↑In modern times,↓ ⟨N⟩no such . . . this ⟨introversion⟩ intro-
       verted mind has occurred ⟨in modern times⟩ as in Emanuel Sweden-
       borg, ⟨born in Stockholm in 1688, and son of the bishop of Skara.⟩↑
       born in Stockholm, in 1688.↓ This man

56.13 now when ↑the↓ ⟨the⟩royal and ducal
       [Apparently Emerson first wrote "now when the and ducal," next
       wrote "royal" over "the" (in the same space,) and then inserted "the"
       above "when."]

56.19 blossoms. His ⟨system⟩ ↑frame↓ is ⟨of⟩ ↑on↓ a larger ⟨stature⟩ ↑scale↓,
       and possess⟨ing⟩es ↑the↓ advantages

56.23 calibre ⟨stil[?]⟩though with . . . Newton, ⟨still⟩ help

56.27 mountains, ↑prying↓ into chemistry

56.29 of his ⟨Briarean talent and⟩ ↑versatile and capacious↓ brain

56.36 sloop, ⟨two and a half⟩ ↑some fourteen English↓ miles

57.1   [Hyperboreus,] and ⟨toiled⟩ ↑from this time↓ for . . . years ↑was em-
       ployed↓ in the ⟨incessant⟩ composition
       [For "Hyperboreus," see Emendations in Copy-Text.]

57.4   theology. ⟨And is it because it was not pure ⟨force⟩ ↑mind,↓ but only
       this composite force of many in one, ⟨⟨since when you have many, you
       have the vices of many⟩⟩ that brought into so ⟨distinguished⟩ ↑excel-
       lent↓ a genius so large infusion of / of mere people's theology?⟩ ↑In
       1743, when he↓ / ⟨[¶] In 1743, when he⟩ was 54 ↑fiftyfour↓ years
       [The figure "54" is not deleted.]

57.7   scientific ⟨works⟩ ↑books↓, withdrew . . . to the ⟨composition⟩ ↑writ-
       ing↓ and publication

57.11 Amsterdam. / ⟨The Arcana 12 vols / Heaven and Hell / True Chris-
       tian Religion / Apocalypse Revealed / Conjugial Love⟩ // ⟨In 1747⟩
       ↑Later,↓ he resigned
       [The deleted lines are centered at the bottom of the page and prob-
       ably were never intended as part of the text. For the spelling "Conju-
       gial," see the Informational note to 71.24.]

57.12 salary ⟨of this⟩attached to this . . . life. His ⟨labours⟩ ↑duties↓ had
       brought

57.15 was much ⟨ ‖ . . . ‖ ⟩consulted and honoured
       [The deleted words may be "honoured & con."]

57.17 memorials ⟨i⟩on Finance

57.18 regard. ↑His rare↓ // ⟨His ⟨credit for⟩ rare⟩ science and practical skill ⟨had procured him reputation, and ⟨the⟩ ↑some ↓ fame⟩ ↑and ⟨some⟩ ↑the↓ added fame↓ of ⟨his⟩ secondsight . . . gifts ⟨added to his reverence in that religious Lutheran country, ⟨Queens,⟩ ↑brought queens,↓ nobles,⟩ ↑drew to him queens, nobles,↓ clergy . . . voyages⟨,⟩↑.↓ ⟨surrounded and consulted him.⟩ The clergy

[Two sentences seem to have been revised into one; the comma after "country" was probably changed from a period.]

57.23 importation ⟨or⟩ ↑and↓ publication

57.26 bread, ⟨and⟩ milk, and

57.27 situated in ⟨an extensive⟩ ↑a large↓ garden

57.32 habit, ⟨kind to the children, fond of coffee⟩ ↑not averse to tea and coffee,↓ and kind to children. He ⟨never laughed⟩ wore . . . full ↑velvet↓ dress, and whenever he walked ↑⟨abroad⟩ out,↓ carried . . . cane. ⟨His face in the⟩ ↑There is a↓ common portrait ↑of him↓ ⟨is ⟨lifeless⟩ absent⟩ in . . . wig, ↑but the face↓ has a

57.37 penetrate ↑the↓ science

58.5 man is ⟨able⟩perhaps able to

58.7 those who ⟨know⟩ ↑understand↓ th⟨o⟩ese matters

58.9 of the ↑seventh↓ planet, ⟨Herschel,⟩ but . . . of the ⟨planet Neptune;⟩ ↑eighth:↓ anticipated

58.12 sun: ⟨anticipated⟩ in magnetism

58.16 on his ⟨inventions⟩ ↑discoveries↓, since he

58.21 suggests, as ⟨Selden, Bacon,⟩ Aristotle, ↑Bacon, Selden,↓ Humboldt

58.25 picture ⟨of⟩, in the "Principia," of the

58.28 exhibit ⟨the sto[?]⟩a storm. There

58.34 university. ⟨Books⟩ ↑Our books↓ are false . . . fragmentary: ⟨But Swedenborg is systematic and respective of the world in every sentence.⟩ ⟨T⟩their sentences

[See the insert in the entry for 59.4.]

58.36 parts of ⟨a⟩natural discourse

59.2 nature, and ⟨so⟩ ↑purposely↓ framed ⟨as⟩ to excite surprise, ⟨and attention⟩ as jugglers

59.4 means. ⟨In Swedenborg,⟩ ↑But Swedenborg is systematic and respective of the world in every sentence:↓ all the

59.8 ideas⟨,⟩↑.↓ ⟨and he found such in the world.⟩ Tis hard . . . life was ⟨magnificent with⟩ ↑dignified by↓ noblest

59.10 method with ⟨all⟩ its . . . adequateness↑,↓ ⟨to nature,⟩ shaming . . . logic ⟨with⟩ ↑by↓ its genial . . . series and ⟨degrees,⟩ ↑degree,↓ with effects . . . discriminate ⟨life from nature,⟩ power

59.15 race of ⟨military⟩ ↑athletic↓ philosophers

59.17 Descartes, ⟨from⟩ ↑taught by↓ Gilbert's magnet ⟨and⟩⟨with⟩ ↑with↓ its vortex, ⟨spila⟩ spiral, and

59.21 established ⟨Un⟩the Universal

59.23   to the ⟨doctrine⟩ ↑dogma↓, that Nature ... minimis exist⟨a⟩it na-
tura⟨:⟩." ⟨⟨The⟩ unrivalled anatomists,⟩ ↑⟨T⟩Unrivalled dissectors,↓
Swammerdam

59.32   Grotius had ⟨urged⟩ ↑drawn↓ the moral

59.35   problems. // ⟨[¶] He⟩ [no ¶] ↑He↓ had a

60.8   who can. ⟨When I read them, I think these are alone valuable, and the⟩
↑His↓ theologic works ⟨only⟩ ↑⟨would be⟩ are↓ valuable to ⟨explain⟩ illustrate

60.10   athletic ⟨reader⟩ ↑student↓, and the

60.15   sparkles with ⟨i⟩crystals. The
    [Perhaps a false start at "ice" or "icy."]

60.16   style. He ⟨had a natural aptitude⟩ ↑was apt ⟨for⟩↓ for cosmology, because ⟨he had such an insight of quality ⟨that he had⟩ ↑as to induce↓ a
habitual insensibility to mere magnitude.⟩ ↑of that native perception
of identity which made mere size of no account to him.↓ In the

60.19   saw the ⟨p⟨o⟩roperty⟩ ↑quality↓ which would

60.22   degrees↑;↓ ⟨in nature;⟩ the version

60.24   and the ⟨o̅mnipresent⟩ connection ... throughout ⟨the universe;⟩ ↑all
things.↓
    [At this point a line is drawn around the following passage, which
runs from 60.27 "so that" through 60.29 "the Deity" (divided at "the
// skeptics" between pages [43] and [44]), and the figure "2" is
placed just outside this line at the beginning of the passage. A similar
line is drawn around the next passage, which runs from 60.25 "He
saw" through 60.27 "of matter"; and though the figure "1" is not visible, it is presumably hidden by the binding. The 1850 edition reverses
the order of the passages, as does this edition.]

60.25   He saw ⟨with clearness⟩ that the

60.27   by the ⟨whole ↑of↓ mat↑t↓er⟨ial system⟩⟩ whole of matter [[:]] [¶?] In
short
    [The second passage referred to in the note to 60.24 is written
smaller than the rest of the page, and was probably inserted in what
was originally intended as a space between paragraphs.]

60.32   years of ⟨varied and incessant⟩ labor with the ⟨bone and marrow⟩
↑heart and strength↓ of the ⟨hairiest Berserkir⟩ ↑rudest viking↓ that his

61.4   on leaf ⟨to the⟩ ↑without↓ end↑,↓ ⟨of the world,⟩ the more ... light,
⟨and⟩ moisture

61.9   end of the ⟨universe⟩ world. ⟨[¶] The mystical⟩ ↑A poetic↓ anatomist
↑in our own day↓ teaches

61.13   type ⟨of⟩or prediction of

61.34   taken up into ⟨a higher,⟩ ↑the next,↓ each

61.35   adapted to ⟨it⟩ ↑infinity↓. We are

61.37   use, is ⟨taken up⟩ ↑lifted↓ into a ... daemonic and ⟨angelic⟩ ↑celestial↓
natures

62.5   fills ⟨heaven⟩earth and heaven

62.15   shoes ⟨and⟩ ↑or↓ marries

62.23   generation, ↑metamorphosis,↓ vortical

62.24   These ↑grand↓ rhymes ... nature, — ⟨startling us every where with⟩ the dear best-known face ↑startling us at every turn↓ under a

62.28   he ⟨made the ↑most↓ resolute ⟨steps⟩ ↑attempts↓ to reduce them to a science. these elusive and untameable⟩ ↑must be reckoned a leader in that revolution, which, by giving to science an idea, has given to an aimless accumulation of experiments, guidance and form and a beating heart.↓ [¶] I own

62.36   have just ↑now been↓ translated ... edition [¶] ⟨It is a curious circumstance[[e]] in literary history that⟩ Swedenborg

63.4   critic with ⟨a brain like Lord Bacon's, and⟩ a coequal ... only to ↑Lord↓ Bacon's

63.9   tongue. This ↑startling↓ reappearance ... pupil is ⟨a more⟩ ↑not the least↓ remarkable ⟨psychological⟩ fact ⟨than any in his Revelations.⟩ ↑in his history.↓ ⟨↑Aided↓ ⟨B⟩by⟩ ↑Aided, it is said, by↓ the munificence ⟨↑mainly↓⟩ of Mr ... literary ⟨aid⟩ ↑help↓, this piece

63.13   with which ⟨his editor⟩ ↑Mr Wilkinson↓ has enriched these volumes, ⟨leave⟩ ↑throw↓ all the cotemporary philosophy of Engla↑n↓d in↑to↓ ⟨total⟩ shade ⟨and forbid me any entering⟩ ↑and leave me nothing to say↓ on their ⟨higher⟩proper ground↑s↓. [¶] The "Animal

63.18   to put ⟨the⟩ science ... estranged ⟨at⟩from each

63.22   repulsive. He saw nature // [60] [blank] // [61] ⟨[¶] It was a picture of nature so wide and free ⟨of all pedantic narrowness⟩ as the most impatient poet could not have surpassed He saw nature⟩ "wreathing

       [The material at the bottom of [59], though it repeats the last three words of the deleted passage on [61], does not appear to have been inserted; probably the whole page [59] was a revision, written after [61].]

63.24   sometimes ↑sought↓ "to uncover

63.30   experience. ⟨"It behoves us," he said, "to follow and unwind the thread of experience, that thread which is the true guidance of Pallas and the Muses, lest we lose ourselves, and fall an easy prey in these labyrinths of nature."⟩ [¶] He knows

63.34   manners, ⟨as he,⟩ or expressed ... goings. ↑He thought as large a demand is made on our faith by nature as by miracles.↓ ⟨"It seems as if when proceeding⟩ ↑He noted that in her proceeding↓ from first

63.37   subordinations, there ⟨were⟩ ↑was↓ no state ... not pass, ⟨or,⟩ as if

64.6   steps." ⟨[¶?] "As large a demand is made on our faith by nature as by miracles themselves."⟩ // [no ¶] The pursuing

       [Note the insertion in the entry for 63.34.]

64.11   mass, or, ⟨of⟩in Plato

64.27   exists ⟨in⟩entire in leasts

64.33   universe." The unities . . . the stomach⟨s⟩, little stomachs, // [68] those
of . . . by the little // [69] ⟨The unities of each organ in the body are so
many little organs homogeneous with their compound. The unities of
the tongue are little tongues, those of the stomach are little stomachs,
those of the heart are little hearts. [¶?] This fruitful idea furnishes a
key to every secret. What was too ⟨large⟩small for the eye to detect, was
read by the aggregates; what was too large, by the units. There is no
end to his application of the thought. "Hunger is an aggregate of very
many little hungers, or losses of blood by the little⟩ // [70] veins

[With no change except the omission of "in the body," all the material on the deleted page [69] was copied on the preceding page and a
half, perhaps for greater clarity or to fill in empty space for the guidance of the compositor.]

65.13   hardihood ↑and thoroughness↓ of his
65.16   and next highe⟨st⟩r form
65.23   or spiritual." // [blank] // ⌊Begin a new page⌋ / [¶] Was it

[Whether Emerson wanted a new page to begin here or only a new
paragraph, the compositor evidently understood the direction in the
latter sense, for that is what he set.]

65.24   so bold ⟨and great⟩ should take
66.1   mortal ⟨c⟩would have predicted
66.9   body." ⟨A.K. Vol I p 451⟩ // [¶] ⟨This explicit statement is not ⟨quite⟩
new, for the heavens are not; it is as new, and as old as they. It⟩ ↑The
fact thus explicitly stated↓ is implied . . . use of ⟨badges and⟩ emblems
66.11   evident from ↑this twice bisected line in↓ the sixth
66.14   translation into ↑a↓ moral
66.15   law in ⟨all⟩ their dark
66.16   use it, ⟨or play with it,⟩ but it
66.20   not seen. ↑⌊Insert A⌋↑ It required

[Insert A, at the bottom of the same manuscript page, surrounded
by a line and headed by the letter "A," runs from 66.20 "It was"
through 66.22 "material series."]

66.23   or rather, ↑it required↓ such rightness
66.25   world: ⟨for, on one side, things are porous to the light, and on the other
sides, they are opaque.⟩ [Insert A follows; see 66.20.] // [¶?] The earth
. . . millenniums, ⟨shown them its forms and colours;⟩ and they
66.29   which the symbol⟨ical force⟩↑ism↓ of things
66.32   space ⟨and⟩or time, subsists ⟨here⟩ not for
66.36   what they mean⟨?⟩: Why does
67.4   rare and ⟨composite⟩ ↑opulent↓ a soul . . . fossil, fis[[h,]] ↑quadruped,↓
spider
67.10   mind ⟨seems to have ⟨run⟩ passed that ⟨fatal⟩ ↑dangerous↓ bourne, so⟩
↑admitted the perilous opinion, too↓ frequent in religious history, ⟨the
belief⟩ that he

[Possibly "dangerous" was the original modifier of "opinion" (replaced by "perilous"), rather than replacing "fatal" as modifier of "bourne."]

67.12   spirits; and ⟨it connected⟩ this ecstasy connected

67.34   Testaments were ↑exact allegories, or↓ written in th⟨is⟩e ⟨symbolical⟩ ↑angelic and ecstatic↓ mode, he ⟨⟨devoted⟩ ↑gave↓ his later⟩ ↑employed his remaining↓ years ⟨to the⟩ ↑in↓ extricating

68.4   signified. ⟨And⟩ ⟨t⟩The correspondence

68.9   in the heavens and ⟨the⟩on earth

68.16   each ↑natural↓ object ⟨of nature⟩ to a theologic notion; ⟨as,⟩ a horse . . . faith; ⟨a field, doctrine[[;]] a city, heresy:⟩ a cat

68.22   parts, as ⟨every⟩each particle

68.26   speedily ⟨of⟩ ↑on↓ the hard . . . waves⟨,⟩↑.↓ ⟨and leaves the pedant to perish in his forms.⟩ She is

68.28   and we ⟨ought to⟩ ↑⟨should⟩ must↓ be at

68.33   so near ↑to↓ the ⟨true problems.⟩ ⟨right points of inquiry.⟩ ↑true problem.↓ // Broad white line [written between horizontal lines] / ⟨Theology⟩ [written in pencil] / [¶] Swedenborg ⟨writes⟩ ↑styles↓ himself

68.35   intellect, and ↑in↓ effect . . . Church, and ⟨will not probably ⟨be⟩⟩ ↑is not likely to ⟨have⟩↓ have a successor. ⟨When⟩ ↑No wonder that↓ his ⟨ethical⟩ depth of ethical . . . teacher. To the withered // [92] [blank] // [93] ⟨[¶] No wonder that Swedenborg has exerted, especially in this country, where our people are by nature contemplative and metaphysical, a powerful influence as a religious teacher. To the withered⟩ traditional church

[The last three and a half lines on page [91], beginning with "⟨When⟩ ↑No wonder that↓ his," are a condensed revision of the deleted material on the first half of [93]; but (except for "No wonder that") they do not appear to be an insertion.]

69.5   escaping from ⟨his⟩ ↑the↓ vestry

69.9   visited him ⟨as it were⟩ diplomatically⟨,⟩ three or four times↑,↓ ⟨in his life,⟩ when he

69.17   and what ↑are↓ hurtful

69.20   books. // [96] ⟨[¶] Yet ⟨I think⟩ these books should be used with ⟨some⟩ caution. ⟨Swedenborg gave a veracious picture of what he saw in flowing moments; but⟩ it is dangerous to sculpture these evanesc⟨ent⟩↑ing↓ images of thought. True in transition, they become false if fixed. It requires for his just apprehension almost a genius equal to his own[[;]] but when his visions become the stereotyped language of mult⟨u⟩itudes of persons of all degrees of age and capacity, they are perverted. The wise people of the Greek⟩ // [97] [¶] There is

[Most of the material on deleted page [96], with minor changes, is used on page [131], and appears from 74.16 to 74.21 of the printed text.]

69.26   exaggerated. ⟨He makes his cartridges too small⟩ Men . . . very fast.
↑Yet,↓ // ⟨He⟩ ↑⟨Yet⟩ he↓ abounds

70.5   errors, the ⟨noble⟩ announcement of ethical laws, ⟨place⟩ ↑take↓ him

70.7   mankind ⟨This merit accounts for⟩ that slow . . . acquired, ⟨⟨and deserved; an influence,⟩ ↑and↓ which,⟩ like that of other ⟨geniuses, and
especially⟩ religious geniuses

70.10   course, ⟨that which⟩ ↑what↓ is real and universal ⟨in this mind,⟩ cannot

70.12   but will ⟨rapidly⟩ pass ↑forth↓ into the . . . thinking↑.↓ ⟨in the world.⟩
↑The world has↓ / ⟨The world has⟩ a sure chemistry ⟨of its own,⟩ by
which it ⟨will⟩ extract↑s↓ ⟨without fail⟩ what . . . children, and ⟨will⟩
let↑s↓ fall . . . grandest ⟨as readily as of the humblest mind.⟩ ↑mind.↓
¶ ⟨I conceive him to be of all modern men, the strict and faithful idealist. In his mind,⟩ ⟨t⟩That metempsychosis

       [In the phrase "all modern men" the word "men" is in pencil.]

70.17   Greeks, ⟨say⟩ ↑collected↓ in Ovid⟨'s⟩↑,↓ ⟨Metamorphoses,⟩ and in . . .
place in ⟨the form,⟩ ↑bodies by ⟨arbitrary⟩ ↑alien↓ will,↓ —in Swedenborg's

70.24   sees. The ⟨exterior⟩ marriages

70.26   looked upon ⟨with eyes,⟩ was to

70.29   to like: ⟨What we⟩ ↑what we↓ ca[[ll]] poetic

       [Probably a change from period to colon. In the line above, the
semicolon after "states" is followed by a capital "E" in "Everything"
and may also have been changed from a period, three (or four) sentences being made into one.]

70.33   present. ↑Every one makes↓ // ⟨Every ⟨body⟩ ↑one↓ makes⟩ his own . . .
state. The ⟨evil spirits⟩ ↑ghosts↓ are . . . death, and ⟨do not know they⟩
cannot remember that they

70.37   flee: ⟨and whatever⟩ ↑the↓ societies ↑which↓ they approach

71.4   [The two sentences from "I asked" through "merit heaven" are deleted and reinserted (the only substantive change being that from
"reply" to "replied") in the space just above the original. The reason
for this is not clear.]

71.6   heaven. ⟨It appears to them as if somewhat of the Lord was underneath the wood, so that the wood is merit. // "I heard two Presidents
of ye Eng. Royal Society, Sir Hans Sloane and Martin Tolkes, Esq[[.,]]
conversing with each other in ye spiritu[[al]] world concerning ye existence of seeds and eggs. — one ascribed y^m to nature, asserting y^t nature had ye power of producing such things by means of ye sun's heat.
The other said, y^t power is continually from God ye Creator [¶?] Then
there was exhibited to Sir H.S. a beautiful bird, and he was told to examine it, whethe[[r]] in any ye least thing it differed from a similar
bird on earth: he held it in his hand, examined it, said there was no
difference; — and it presently vanished, and he perceived that it was
no other than an affection of a certain angel without him, represented

as a bird, and it would vanish or cease, with his affection. — ") // ¶ He delivers

[The name transcribed as "Tolkes" was probably meant to be "Folkes," for Martin Folkes was President of the Royal Society (1741–1753) and was named by Swedenborg in the passage (*Divine Love and Divine Wisdom* [Boston, 1847], pp. 179–180) which Emerson refers to here; cf. *JMN*, X, 27, and note 86. But the first letter seems to be a capital "T," and the "l" and "k" are written in the same space, one over the other. Sir Hans Sloane (see 75.13) was President of the Royal Society from 1727 to 1741.]

71.12 use:" ↑"Man in his↓ // ("Man in his) greatest and most / perfect
[The 1850 edition omits "greatest and most"; see the RSS note.]

71.12 heaven:" ↑("Ends) / "What is from Him is Him:" Ends↓ / ("Ends) always ascend as nature descends:" (↑"What is↓ / (What is) from Him is Him.") ↑(A)and the truly poetic account↓ // (and the truly poetic account) of the writing
[Many of these changes were made to fill up space, since each quotation originally started on a new line. The net result was to reverse the order of two quotations.]

71.15 which, as it (is) consists

71.17 claim to (new organs) ↑preternatural vision↓ by (occasional) strange . . . mind. ↑"It is never↓ // [blank] // (He had strange insights of the structure of the human body and mind (which he betrays in his writing and) which suggest a source not open to any other / "It is never) permitted

71.24 he has (attempted) ↑unfolded↓ the science

71.26 be the (song of love) ↑Hymn of Love,↓ which . . . "Banquet;" ↑(the Hymn of Love) the Love↓ which

71.29 rightly (sung) ↑celebrated,↓ in its . . . effect, (is the history (w)of worlds and) might well . . . it would (go through and through all our) ↑lay open the genesis of all↓ institutions, customs, and (arts and explain them) ↑manners.↓ / ↑The book had been grand↓ / (Swedenborg too literally pinned to) // (after his mode to the (human) form) (and it is tedious prose) (The book had been) grand if the

71.32 stated (as) without Gothicism as ethics, (Science of) ↑and with that scope for ascension of state which the (flux) nature of [[things requires.]]↓↓ It is
[The last few words of the inserted passage run down the right margin and are lost in the binding.]

71.35 marriage; ↑teaching↓ that sex . . . virility in ↑the↓ male

72.1 momentary, (as with men) but incessant

72.5 he saw ↑, in heaven,↓ were beautiful . . . went on (advancing) ↑increasing↓ in beauty

72.8 Yet (one would say that) Swedenborg . . . theory (too strictly) to a

72.10   fancies a ⟨better⟩wiser choice

72.14   divorced, and ⟨all the⟩ ↑no↓ tension in nature can⟨not⟩ hold

72.17   child's ⟨adherence⟩ ↑clinging↓ to his

72.21   desolate, ⟨to you⟩ whilst you . . . again, ⟨you will⟩ ↑we↓ pity

72.23   cards. ⟨I suggest that⟩ ↑Perhaps,↓ ⟨t⟩⟨T⟩the true subject of ↑the↓ "Conjugal . . . laws are ⟨truly⟩ ↑profoundly↓ eliminated

72.26   soul⟨:⟩↑.↓ ⟨⟨or, each soul is entitled to nothing less than all things.⟩ ↑and other marriage if eternal were death.↓ Heaven is the marriage⟩ ↑Heaven is not the pairing ↑of two,↓ but the communi[[on]]↓ of all

72.30   there being any↑thing↓ divine ⟨meaning⟩ in the

72.32   yourself on a ⟨noble⟩ sentiment

72.34   and demand ⟨my⟩ love

72.35   world, we ⟨seem to⟩ change

72.37   that fixes ↑the↓ love . . . that is be⟨gin[?]⟩yond me

73.5   thought are ⟨subject⟩liable, he has

73.8   good "from ⟨sensuals and⟩ scientifics

73.11   sensibility is ⟨variously and⟩ incessantly

73.11   are therefore ⟨an odious class to him.⟩ Vipers . . . serpents↑;↓ ⟨are his kindest words, and⟩ literary

73.14   topic ⟨inevitably⟩ suggests a ⟨deeper consideration⟩ ↑sad afterthought,↓ that here

73.16   or a ⟨happy⟩ ↑fortunate↓ genius seems to depend ↑on↓ a happy . . . proportio[[n]] ↑hard to hit↓ // [123] ⟨[¶] Perhaps Swedenborg paid the penalty of introverted faculties / Success seems to depend on happy adjustment of heart and brain on a due proportion⟩ hard to hit of moral

     [The deleted material at the top of page [123] is revised on the lower part of [122].]

73.20   combine in ⟨proportions of 6 and 4   12 and 8⟩ ↑certain fixed rates↓ but not ⟨in indifferent mixture⟩ at any ⟨other⟩ rate. ⟨Happy they who know nothing of their anatomy mental and materia[[l]] but⟩ ⟨i⟩It is hard

73.22   man, ⟨wonderfully⟩ ↑profusely↓ endowed . . . discord ⟨and civil war⟩ with himself[[.]] ⟨H⟩ In his

73.24   that he ⟨went for⟩ ↑loved↓ analysis ↑and↓ not ⟨for⟩ synthesis

73.25   falls to ⟨suspicion and⟩ ↑into↓ jealousy . . . and, though ⟨theoretical[[y]]⟩ aware

73.27   both must ↑ever↓ mix and marry, ⟨eternally,⟩ he ⟨declares war against⟩ ↑makes war on↓ his mind . . . against it, and ⟨bu[?]⟩ on all occasions traduces ⟨, defames,⟩ and blasphemes it↑.↓ ⟨; and, by this means a divorce between these powers follows, with all the jangle and misery which attend such quarrels. The violence⟩ ↑The violence↓ is . . . Beauty is ⟨unbeautified⟩ ↑disgraced,↓ ⟨and love⟩ ↑love↓ is unlovely, ⟨and the soul undone⟩ when truth

[The deletion transcribed as "bu" may be a start at "by."]

73.31 much as ⟨when by⟩ ↑[[w]]hen a bitterness in↓ men . . . satire↑,↓ ⟨and heartlessness⟩ and destroys

74.1 pain. ↑Indeed, [[a]]↓ // ⟨[¶] ⟨Yet h⟩↑H↓is Memorable Relations exhibit a wealth of imagery with much force of painting / But Swedenborg has turned with a certain gloomy appetite to the images of pain. Indeed a⟩ bird

74.4 round ⟨some⟩ ↑every↓ new crew

74.13 Except ↑Rabelais and↓ Dean Swift . . . science of ⟨the ⟨foul side⟩ ↑filth backside filth back↓ of natur[[e,]] of the jakes, putridity, stench, salacity, the secrets of the sexton the hangman and⟩ ↑filth and↓ and corruption. ⟨His books are so painful that I should never open them but for the true science which is / he is continually exhibiting.⟩ // [¶] ⟨Yet ⟨I think⟩⟩ ⟨t⟩These books

74.29 hells and ⟨hea⟩the heavens are opened to ⟨him⟩ ↑it↓. But these

74.32 good: then ⟨it⟩ ↑this↓ is safely seen. // ⟨[¶] After poring over these lurid phantoms, impatient and perplexed between the indisputable truth and the ugliness, we cry, Begone nightmare.⟩ [Broad white line.] [¶] Swedenborg's . . . it is ⟨essentially⟩ dynamic ↑not ⟨for⟩ vital,↓ and lacks power to generate ⟨real individuals.⟩ ↑life.↓ There is

75.1 and lamina↑e↓ lie . . . unity, ⟨but there is no life.⟩ ↑but cold and still.↓ What

75.5 univers[[e]] ⟨under⟩in his poem

75.9 same ⟨thin⟩few things↑.↓ ⟨: horses, ships, trees, garments, mountains, islands, bowl and spoon, all mean goods or truths.⟩ All his

75.12 all over ⟨, cheek by jowl,⟩ in his boat

75.14 and all ⟨acquire⟩ ↑gather↓ one ⟨Stygian croaking⟩ ↑grimness of hue and style↓. Only when

75.18 his mouth, ⟨all⟩ Rome and eloquence have ⟨long since⟩ ebbed

75.19 the rest. ⟨I find his ⟨universe⟩ ↑hell is↓ uninteresting[[,]]⟩ ↑His heavens and hells are dull,↓ fault of

[The precise order of substitution in this passage is uncertain.]

75.21 relation of men / ⟨of each man,⟩ is not

[It is not certain whether "of men" preceded "of each man" (there may be a comma after "men" lost in the binding), or whether it was inserted to replace it.]

75.26 [The last four and a half lines on page [138], running from 75.26 "This want" through 75.30 "of beings," are in smaller handwriting than the rest of the page and may have been a later insertion.]

75.30 of beings[[.]] // ⟨[no ¶] The vice of Swedenborg's mind⟩ ↑[¶] The vice of Swedenborg's mind↓ is its

75.36 sacred. ⟨Judaea⟩ ↑Palestine↓ is ever

76.7 carries ⟨ten thousand⟩ ↑innumerable↓ christianities, ↑humanities, diviniti[[es]]↓ in its bosom. // [143] ⟨and Europe, by binding himself

hand and foot and flinging himself at his feet by way of first saluta-
tion.⟩ [¶] The excess of influence ⟨becomes ridiculously obvious⟩ ↑shows
itself↓ in the ↑incongruous↓ importation . . . rhetoric↑.↓ ⟨to the exclusion of that which is native to each speaker.⟩ 'What . . . to do ↑' asks the
impatient reader '↓ with jasper and sardonyx, ⟨with⟩beryl⟨,⟩ and chalcedony; what with ⟨tabernacles,⟩ arks, and passovers, ⟨shekels,⟩ ephahs,
and ephods; what with lepers, and emero⟨i⟩ds, what

[The deleted passage beginning "and Europe" at the top of page
[143] is continued from "fascinated Asia" at the bottom of [144];
originally these pages must have been written in reverse order.]

76.15　unicorn? // [144] ⟨to reanimate and conserve what had already arrived at its natural term, and, in the great secular Providence, was retiring from its prominence before western modes of thought and
expression. Swedenborg and Behmen both failed by attac[[h]]ing
themselves to the Christian symbol, instead of to the moral sentiment.
[space, no ¶] Swedenborg showed his inc[[a]]pacity for attempting the
portra[[it]] of that wonderful youth who has so long fascinated Asia⟩
// [145] Good for

[The first part of the deleted material on page [144] is revised on
[142], and appears at 76.2–7 of the printed text. The second part, as
mentioned in the preceding note, is continued at the top of [143]. See
JMN, XI, 160–161.]

76.20　in the ⟨study⟩ delight and study of
76.25　needless. ⟨One would think that God made figtrees and dates, pome-
granates and // and olives, but the Enemy made pippins and pound-
pears, cherries and cranberries, Canad[[a]] crooknecks and sweet-
potatoes[[.']]⟩ // [¶?] Locke said
76.27　history ⟨confirms and⟩ points the
76.27　parish ⟨questions⟩ ↑disputes in↓ of the Swedish church ⟨the disputes⟩
between . . . Melancthon, ⟨between⟩ ↑concerning↓ "faith
76.34　in his ⟨endless⟩ books ↑as under a heavenly mandate↓ the indisputable
. . . nature ⟨remains⟩ with all these grandeurs ⟨↑remains↓⟩ resting upon
him, ⟨through it all and after all a⟩ ↑remains the↓ Lutheran bishop's
son; ⟨His⟩ ↑this↓ judgments
76.37　enlargements ⟨seem⟩ purchased . . . limitations. ⟨Swedenborg⟩ ↑He↓
carries . . . with him in⟨to the⟩ his visits
77.3　who, ⟨put⟩in his frescoes, put the
77.8　got the ⟨pip; so he with his pains[?]⟩↑pip. Swedenborg confounds us
not less, with the pains of↓ Melancthon
77.10　own ⟨↑bag of↓⟩ books which
77.20　better. ⟨The possibilities of⟩ ↑No↓ man ⟨are too large than that he⟩ can
afford
77.27　making. ⟨But⟩ ⟨t⟩That pure malignity ⟨should⟩ ↑can↓ exist
77.32　none." // [no ¶] ⟨It is⟩ ↑To what↓ a painful perversion ⟨of⟩ ↑had↓
Gothic theology ↑arrived↓ that Swedenborg

77.34 spirits. ⟨↑(See Arcana Vol I p 408 note)↓⟩ But the

78.1 and man, ⟨wheresoever thou seest him⟩ though in . . . his way ⟨upward⟩
to all that is good and ⟨fine⟩true. ⟨The wild poet⟩ Burns ⟨with⟩ ↑with the
wild humour of↓ his apostrophe

78.15 entitle ↑it↓ to any

78.28 Light, ⟨as⟩not as somewhat

79.7 soul. ↑But it is certain↓ // ⟨But tis certain⟩ that it

79.8 works of ⟨that⟩ ↑the↓ artist

79.11 mountains, ⟨radiant as summer mornings,⟩ agreeing with ⟨lilies and
violets with harvests⟩ ↑flowers,↓ with tides . . . stars. ⟨Poet Milton poet
Homer⟩ ↑Melodious poets↓ shall

79.14 sounded, — ↑the↓ earth-beat, . . . heart-beat, ⟨which shall make / the
deaf ear musical, for it is⟩ the tune

  [The line crossing out "which shall" runs part of the way into
"make"; Emerson may not have intended to delete the latter word.
See the Emendations note.]

79.16 trees. [¶] ⟨With these thoughts⟩ ↑In this mood,↓ we hear

79.18 beauty, ⟨no truth⟩ no heaven: ⟨F⟩↑f↓or angels

79.22 cognisant, as ↑a man's↓ bad dreams ⟨do to each man's⟩ ↑bear to his↓
ideal

79.25 gentleman ⟨of⟩ benevolent ⟨life and upward aims⟩ ↑but dyspeptic,↓
into . . . like a ⟨whipped⟩ dog . . . yards and ⟨leavings⟩ ↑kennels↓ of
creation. ⟨In like manner,⟩ ⟨w⟩When he mounts

79.27 A man ⟨shall⟩ ↑should↓ not tell

79.29 me one. ⟨But one cannot accept this ⟨musty⟩ ↑sexton's↓ paradiso.⟩ Shall
the . . . majestic ↑and sweet↓ than the . . . earth? ↑⟨t⟩These angels that↓
/ ⟨If these angels that⟩ Swedenborg paints ⟨have been long in that
world, they⟩ give us

79.34 peasants. ↑Strange, scholastic,↓ // ⟨Broad white line⟩ / ⟨[¶] Strange,
scholastic,⟩ didactic

79.36 botanist ⟨would⟩ ↑⟨picks up⟩ disposes of↓ a carex, ⟨and geologizes new⟩
↑and visits doleful↓ hells

79.38 men, a ⟨sort of⟩ ↑modern↓ Rhadamanthus

80.3 to him ⟨only⟩ a grammar . . . procession. ↑How different is↓ Jacob
Behmen⟨,⟩↑!↓ ⟨how different!⟩ ⟨↑the earlier seer!↓⟩ he is

80.7 asserts that ↑, "in some sort,↓ love . . . God,↑"↓ his . . . high th⟨e⟩at the
thumping

80.11 wise, and ⟨for all his worlds we would not be he⟩ and with . . . repels. //
[blank] // [¶] ⟨I find Swedenborg to have no future.⟩ It is . . . opens
⟨heavens,⟩ ↑a foreground,↓ and like

80.15 divest ⟨this great sexton⟩ ↑him↓ of his

80.20 genius. ⟨He will not be read longer. His great // [172] name will turn
a sentence. His books have become a monument. His laurel so largely
mixed with cypress, a charnel breath ↑so↓ mingles with temple-incense, that boys and maids will avoid the spot. ⟨The inevitable effect is

to paralyse and imprison.⟩ // [173] How cd. it be otherwise than that he who possessed the key to nature in his habitual sight of her proceeding from affection and will into plant and animal shd. also have the secret of poetic ⟨production⟩construction?⟩ [¶] It is remarkable

[The deleted matter on pages [171–172] is revised on [175–176] and appears at 81.2–5 of the printed text.]

80.24 creates↑.↓ ⟨for itself.⟩ He knew ... of the ⟨Ursprache⟩ ↑Mother-Tongue↓[[, —]] how could

80.26 Saadi, who ↑in his vision,↓ designed ... lap with ↑the celestial↓ flowers ↑as presents↓ for his friends, but ⟨when he came⟩ the fragrance

80.29 or is ⟨it⟩ ↑reporting↓ a breach

80.35 We ⟨walk⟩ ↑wander↓ forlorn in ⟨this⟩ ↑a↓ lacklustre

80.36 in all ⟨that vast architecture Tis a kind of Petra a city of the dead a palace of catacombs.⟩ ↑these gardens of the dead.↓ The entire ... transcendant a ⟨genius⟩ ↑mind↓ betokens

81.1 person is ⟨added as⟩ a kind of warning⟨,⟩↑.↓ ⟨or like the rattle to the snake.⟩ ↑I think sometimes, he↓ // [176] ⟨[¶]⟨He⟩ ↑I think sometimes, he↓⟩ will not

81.5 spot. [¶] ⟨And y⟩↑Y↓et, in this ... at the ⟨ ‖ ... ‖ ⟩shrine

81.7 lived ⟨for something⟩ ↑to purp[[ose]]↓, he gave a verdict. ⟨I respect Swedenborg as having⟩ ↑He↓ elected goodnes[[s]]↑as↓ the ⟨golden⟩ clue

81.9 opinions ⟨prevail⟩ ↑conflict↓ as to

81.17 but ⟨R⟩↑r↓ectitude only, ⟨R⟩↑r↓ectitude forever

81.24 mankind, ⟨which is as yet far from being exhausted,⟩ which

81.26 steps; he ⟨apprehended⟩ ↑observed↓ and published ... degrees, ⟨to⟩from ⟨gross phenomena⟩ ↑events↓ to ... fired with ⟨a⟩ piety ⟨and love⟩ at the harmonies he ⟨saw and shared,⟩ ↑felt,↓ and abandoned ... worship↑.↓ ⟨in view of them.⟩ This was

81.31 excellent ⟨then⟩ is the spectacle

IV. MONTAIGNE

85.7 tire of th⟨is⟩e game

85.9 flushed with ⟨some⟩ success, ↑and↓ bethinks

85.18 predisposition to ⟨the⟩ one or ... devoted to ⟨the⟩ one or

85.21 surfaces; ⟨with⟩ cities and persons; ⟨with⟩ ↑and the↓ bringing

85.25 drives ↑too↓ fast. ⟨Thus⟩ Plotinus

86.10 object. In ⟨certain⟩ powerful

86.15 mistake, or ⟨imperfection⟩friction, which

86.21 realizations? ↑&, like↓ / ⟨D⟩dreaming beggars

[At the end of the manuscript line, "&, like" is probably but not certainly an insertion. The "&" could be transcribed as either "and" or "And."]

86.28 the rest, weigh⟨s⟩ heavily

86.36 reason⟨,⟩↑.↓ ⟨moonstruck, hair-brained.⟩ They alone

87.4 denies more: ⟨V⟩↑v↓erities have

87.23 Are you ⟨squeamish⟩ ↑tender↓ and scrupulous, ↑you must↓ eat more mince-pie. ⟨"Salvo grata puella viro."⟩ They hold
[The deleted Latin passage (from Propertius, IV. iii. 72) is quoted in *JMN*, XI, 116.]

87.28 drunk. ↑"The nerves," says Cabanis, "they are the man."↓ My neighbor ... money is ⟨to⟩ sure ... of it." ⟨—"The nerves," says Cabanis, they are the man."⟩ [¶] The inconvenience

88.17 party ⟨which⟩ ↑to↓ occup⟨ies⟩y the middle

88.33 their heads are hot, the⟨ir⟩ night

89.7 have not⟨,⟩↑?↓ ⟨respecting⟩What is the ... not, respecting

89.19 objections ⟨insurmountable⟩lie in the way insurmountable

89.21 to my ⟨chair⟩seat by arguments

89.26 and unlike. ⟨There is mud, and music, and roses, and the parts of speech, and the nine solids, and snakes, and many other things.⟩ Why fancy

89.28 practical ⟨suggestion⟩question ↑on↓ which

90.2 Church? ⟨ ‖ ... ‖ ⟩Or to put

90.4 at a ⟨success in the old forms, as of a⟩ leading

90.7 cutting ⟨all these⟩ ↑the↓ stays

90.9 question ⟨now agitated⟩ between the

90.13 is from ⟨huts, from⟩ the poor man's hut

90.15 labourers cry ⟨with⟩unanimously, 'We

90.18 beauty of ⟨ins⟩spontaneousness. Excellent ... no longer ⟨n⟩able not to

90.24 clutching after ↑the↓ airy and

90.36 stable, and ⟨all that is⟩ good

91.10 rule is, ⟨Not too high nor⟩to set it not too high nor

91.17 inhabit. An⟨y⟩ angular

91.20 sea. The ⟨form of man, the⟩ soul of man

91.23 nature⟨,⟩↑.↓ ⟨a fluctuating movement, a circumlation through all the limits of imperfection, a shifting with the revolution of all things, so as to master the whole mass of reality in all its ramifications"⟩ ↑We are↓ Golden averages, ... the sea⟨,⟩↑.↓ ⟨are we.⟩ // [¶] The wise skeptic wish⟨ing⟩↑es↓ ⟨not to be fooled, but⟩ to have a near view ⟨of the game, and⟩ of the ... players, ⟨what is best in his times,⟩ what ... planet, ⟨*that* he will see;⟩ art, and

91.28 excellent in ⟨that kind, in⟩ mankind, ⟨every⟩ ↑a↓ form of grace, ⟨every⟩ ↑an↓ arm of iron, ⟨every mouth⟩ ↑lips↓ of persuasion, ⟨every⟩ ↑a↓ brain

91.35 he ha⟨ve⟩s played with ... the temper, ⟨the⟩ stoutness, and the

92.2 boys, ⟨nor⟩or coxcombs

92.10 And yet, ⟨lest⟩ ↑since↓ ⟨(I may have been deceived by)⟩ the personal ... ↑for ⟨him⟩ ↑Montaigne↓ may be unduly great↓, I will

92.13 electing ⟨Montaigne⟩ ↑him↓ as the

92.36 library. And ⟨the⟩ ↑oddly enough, the↓ duplicate ... autograph,

⟨turned out to have⟩ ↑⟨as I was informed ⟨by Mr Watts (?)⟩ in the Museum,⟩ turned out to have the autograph↓ // the autograph of Ben

[The query after "Watts" is Emerson's, not the editor's.]

93.6 satisfaction. Oth⟨er[?]⟩er coincidences ⟨, not less affecting to me, but⟩ not . . . here, ⟨have served⟩ ↑concurred↓ to make

[Possibly "Other" was originally "these."]

93.10 retired from ↑the practice of law at↓ Bordeaux

93.23 Gibbon ⟨thinks that,⟩ ↑reckons↓ in these bigoted times ⟨, there were⟩ but two

93.27 confessions. ⟨It is to be pleaded in further extenuation, that,⟩ ⟨i⟩In his times, ⟨↑too,↓⟩ books

94.1 six ⟨ri⟩as ridiculous . . . living." ↑But, with all this really superfluous frankness, the opinion of an invincible probity grows into every reader's mind.↓ // [47] ⟨But with all this really superfluous frankness, the opinion of an invincible probity grows into every reader's mind⟩ // [48] [¶] Here is

[The transfer of the sentence on page [47] to the bottom of [46], together with the fact that the next paragraph in the 1850 edition is not in the manuscript, suggests that a separate leaf containing the missing paragraph was inserted between pages [46] and [47] and was later lost. See the Emendations note on this passage, and the Textual Introduction.]

94.16 sailors and gip⟨seys⟩↑sies↓, use flash and streetballads⟨,⟩: he has

94.20 is. He ⟨is solid and sincere.⟩ ↑likes his saddle.↓ You

94.27 under it. ⟨You may⟩ / ↑As I look at his effigy opposite the title page, I seem to hear him say, You may↓ / play ⟨o⟩Old ⟨poz⟩Poz, if you will; you may ⟨lash yourself to fury, and⟩ rail and

94.31 overstate the ⟨poor⟩ dry fact . . . know; ⟨about⟩ my . . . barns; ⟨about⟩ my father, ↑my wife↓ and my tenants; ⟨about⟩ my . . . pate; ⟨about⟩ ↑my↓ knives

95.5 and his ⟨composition⟩fortune an hour

95.6 vapour ⟨and swell ⟨either by⟩ ↑and↓ play⟨ing⟩ the⟩ // ↑and play the↓ philosopher, ⟨or the swine[?]⟩ instead of

95.10 life, ⟨at least⟩ the blame is not mine: ⟨L⟩let it lie at ⟨ ‖ . . . ‖ ⟩Fate's and nature's

["Fate's" is written over a blot, but there may be no other word under it.]

95.13 head. ⟨allowing nothing to pass for settled,⟩ treating . . . yet with ⟨the most⟩ masculine

95.17 cares for. [¶] ⟨The charm of this inimitable book is in its style also.⟩ The sincerity . . . sentences. ⟨They are he, he is they.⟩ I know

95.20 book ⟨, and sounds, page after page, ⟨still⟩ like strong talking⟩. Cut . . . alive⟨:⟩↑.↓ ⟨they walk and run.⟩ One has ⟨precisely⟩ the ↑same↓ pleasure . . . to the ⟨strong⟩ necessary

95.25 bullets; ⟨whilst⟩ ↑It is↓ Cambridge men ⟨are apt to⟩ ↑who↓ correct

95.33 solid ⟨, and speaks so⟩; tastes

95.35 plain; he ⟨never or⟩ rarely ... underneath⟨,⟩↑.↓ ⟨incessantly;⟩ His writing has no enthusiasm↑s↓, no

96.1 of the ⟨wa⟩road. There ... exception, — in ⟨his ⟨love of⟩⟩ ↑⟨affection⟩
↑his love↓ for↓ Socrates. ⟨He ⟨seems to have⟩ ↑had↓ conceived a love for
that heroic lover of virtue, and⟩ ↑In ⟨writing⟩ ↑speaking↓ of him,↓ for
once
[Apparently Emerson first wrote "his love of Socrates," changed it
to "his affection for Socrates," and finally "his love for Socrates," deleting the first "his" and inserting another. The order of changes is not
certain.]

96.18 given the ⟨last⟩ ↑right↓ and permanent

96.27 calamity ⟨that came⟩ out of ... of it, ⟨a fool born of a hero,⟩ a hero
⟨born⟩ ↑born↓ from a fool,⟨ — ⟩↑ a fool from a hero, — ↓ dispirits
[The first dash is canceled by the "a" written over it as the first word
of the inserted phrase.]

96.33 preserves, ⟨constructs,⟩ and dislike

97.6 state of ⟨his⟩their own

97.13 reason, ⟨and value,⟩ and every

97.17 bigots and ⟨pedants.⟩ ↑blockheads.↓ [¶] Skepticism

97.19 society ⟨reverences,⟩ ↑adores,↓ but which

97.21 is the ⟨first stair⟩ vestibule

97.26 itself ↑equally↓ at odds ... society, and ⟨also⟩ with the

97.28 conservative; ⟨for⟩ he sees

97.29 But ↑neither↓ he is fit

97.33 Kreeshna, in ↑the↓ Bhagavat. ⟨"I neither love not hate,"⟩ ↑"There is
none who is worthy of my love or hatred;"↓ whilst
["Kreeshna" (in a clearer handwriting) is inserted above the same
word (not deleted). Emerson's usual spelling was "Krishna," which
appears here in the 1850 edition.]

98.1 stands thus ↑in his mind↓: Our life

98.3 say. ⟨He finds that these cannot help him.⟩ He does ... against these
benevolen⟨t⟩ces ⟨men⟩, to play

98.6 doubts. ⟨[¶] I mean to use the occasion, ⟨as if it were⟩ ↑and celebrate↓
the ⟨birth-⟩↑calender-↓day of our Saint Michel de Montaigne, ⟨to an
appropriate purpose, ↑namely,↓ to⟩ ↑by↓ count↑ing↓ and de-
scrib⟨e⟩↑ing↓ these doubts or negations. I wish to ferret them out of
their holes, and sun them a little. Tis high time that these old rogues
should be shown to the Police at the⟩ // [¶] I mean to use ... at the
Marshal's office

98.23 subtle and ⟨elevated⟩ ↑admirable↓ friend, ... most ⟨clearsighted⟩ ↑pen-
etrating↓ of men

98.28 saw ↑and would not tell,↓ // [blank] // [69] and would not tell; and
tried to choke off ⟨men,⟩ ↑their approaching followers,↓ by saying

98.32 In the ⟨moment[?]⟩mount of vision

98.36 Understanding, ⟨nicknamed⟩ ↑the↓ Mephistopheles

98.37 This is ⟨the first⟩ Hobgoblin the first, and though it ⟨is heralded from high quarters and⟩ has been . . . much ⟨art and ⟨song⟩⟩ ↑elegy↓ in our
      [It looks as if Emerson first wrote "much art and song," then replaced "song" by "elegy," and finally deleted "art and."]

99.1   Goethe, and ⟨Brow⟩ ⟨Paracelsus⟩ ⟨Browning⟩ ↑other poe⟨m⟩ts of less fame↓, not to . . . private ⟨talkers,⟩ ↑observers,↓ I confess
      [The first deleted word is probably "Brov," but in the context this looks like a false start at "Browning."]

99.4   seems to ⟨respect⟩ ↑concern↓ the ⟨disturbance⟩ ↑shattering↓ of baby-houses . . . shops↑.↓ ⟨rather than of temples.⟩ What

99.7   faith. I ⟨am of opinion⟩ ↑think↓ that the . . . extirpates ⟨Muggletonians, ↑and↓ Mormons⟩ ↑bugbears↓, yet it . . . check↑s↓ of vice and ⟨the true⟩ polarity to the soul. I ⟨am of Swedenborg's opinion⟩ ↑think↓ that the

99.11 absolute ⟨and sublime⟩ reliance

99.13 moods ⟨in our experience⟩, each setting . . . all but ↑its↓ / ⟨our⟩own tissue
      [Probably "its own" replaces "our"; "own" is written over "our," and "its" is inserted at the end of the preceding line. Or the word under "own" that looks like "our" may be "own" badly written and corrected.]

99.15 the disposition↑s↓ and sentiment↑s.↓ ⟨of each.⟩ The beliefs . . . structural↑,↓ ⟨in each man,⟩ and, as soon as each ↑man↓ attains

99.18 need ⟨to find these opinions in⟩ extreme . . . alternate ⟨them⟩ all ↑opinions↓ in his

99.22 bust, or ↑only↓ the sound . . . and we ↑suddenly↓ believe in will; ⟨this⟩ ↑my↓ finger-ring . . . Solomon; ↑Fate is for imbeciles.↓ All is possible to ⟨those whose [?]⟩ the resolved mind. ⟨Fate, we say, is for imbeciles.⟩ ↑Presently,↓ A new

99.29 the best ⟨citizen⟩ commerce, and the best citizen

99.31 causation, ⟨, to be⟩ at the mercy . . . indigestion? ⟨If he believes⟩ ↑Is his belief↓ in God and Duty, ⟨it is⟩ no deeper

99.34 French ⟨rapidity of Revolution; a new government and⟩ ↑celerity, a new↓ church and state

100.1 all the states; ⟨What is⟩ ↑Does↓ the general

100.5 I can. [¶] ⟨3. The laws of the world do not always befriend us, but often hurt us; as the experience of mankind attests in⟩ / ⟨↑3.↓⟩ ⟨t⟩The ⟨use of the⟩ word Fate or Destiny ⟨as a dangerous and often crushing activity.⟩ expresses . . . crush us

100.9 scythe; ⟨and⟩ Love . . . deaf↑.↓ ⟨and ⟨omnipotent⟩ ↑decisive↓.⟩ We have . . . us up. ⟨Behold⟩ ↑What front can we make against↓ these

100.13 against the ⟨power⟩ ⟨determination⟩ influence . . . against ⟨scrofula⟩ hereditary . . . against scrofula, ... against ↑climate, against↓ barbarism, in my country? ⟨What against⟩ I can

100.17   perpetual ⟨b⟩Belly. ⟨Feed⟩ feed he ... respectable. // [two blank
         pages] // [Broad white line] [¶] ⟨4. The last⟩ ↑But the main↓ resis-
         tance

100.19   finds ↑and one including all others↓ is in ... Illusionists. ↑There is a
         painful rumour in circulation that↓ We have been ⟨sopped and
         drugged⟩ ↑practi⟨c⟩sed upon↓ in⟨to⟩ all the ... name. We have been
         sopped and drugged with

100.25   leave ⟨us where they find us⟩ the mind where they find it

100.28   sciences the ⟨Baby⟩ ↑churl↓ he was

100.31   come to ⟨say⟩ ↑accept it as the fixed rule and theory of our state of
         educati[[on]] that↓ God is

101.8   dozen ⟨such happy and noble⟩ ↑reasonable↓ hours

101.11   converge. Experience↑s↓, fortunes, ↑governings,↓ readings

101.14   so much ⟨azote and carbon⟩ ↑bone and fibre↓ as he

101.20   impossible. The ⟨heaven which the⟩ young spirit pants to enter ⟨is⟩ so-
         ciety. But ⟨the condition of selfdevelopment is⟩ ↑all the ways of cul-
         ture and greatness lead to↓ solitary imprisonment. ⟨He is chilled by
         the discovery⟩ He had been ⟨ba⟩often balked. He

101.26   misapplied ⟨each to other.⟩ and the

101.35   catechism, and ⟨that he⟩ want⟨s⟩ a rougher instruction, want⟨s⟩ men,
         ⟨wants⟩ labour

102.1   and has ↑he not↓ a right

102.7   common ⟨language⟩ ↑discourse↓ of their

102.9   return. ⟨They have no valves of interruption; the blood of the Uni-
         verse rolls at all times through their veins in unbroken streams.⟩
         ↑Once admitted to the heaven of thought, they see no relapse into
         night, but infinite invitation on the other side⟨,⟩. Heaven is within
         heaven, and sky over sky, and they are encompassed with divinities.↓
         Others

102.13   question of ↑temperament, or of↓ more or

102.15   have a ⟨secondary⟩ ↑reflex↓ or parasitic faith. ⟨a faith⟩ not ⟨in things
         themselves⟩ ↑a sight of realities↓, but ⟨of⟩ ↑an↓ instinctive reliance on
         the ⟨bel⟩ seers and believers

102.19   themselves. But ⟨with⟩ their ↑sensual↓ habit ⟨it is⟩ would ⟨fain hold⟩
         ↑fix↓ the believer to his ⟨former assertion⟩ ↑last position↓, whilst ...
         advances: ⟨This quarrel arises and⟩ ↑and presently↓ the unbeliever

102.21   believer. ↑[¶] Great believers are always reckoned infidels, impracti-
         cable, fantastic, atheistic, and really men of no account.↓ // ⟨[¶] I
         said, that the devout man astonishes by his coldness to the phi-
         lanthropies of the day. Great believers are always reckoned infidels,
         impracticable, fantastic, atheistic, and really men of no account.⟩
         ⟨And⟩The spiritualist

102.26   hesitate? ⟨It is the instinct of man to take on each turn the part of
         hope.⟩ It is

102.28   But he ⟨denies them. He⟩ is forced

102.30   griefs ⟨and oppressions⟩ and crimes are the ⟨⟨inevitable⟩⟩ foliage

102.34   for him↑.↓ ⟨to work in.⟩ The people's . . . not // ↑this;↓ their methods are not his; ⟨that,⟩ ↑and↓ against

102.37   of man, ⟨the doctrine⟩ of the divine

103.3   rather ⟨be⟩stand charged ⟨in your eyes⟩ with the ⟨melancholy and weakness⟩ ↑imbecility↓ of skepticism, than with ⟨the meanness of an⟩ untruth

103.6   weal of ⟨all⟩ souls . . . seem ⟨paltry⟩ ↑to me↓ caricatures↑.↓ ⟨of the truth.⟩ Why

103.9   goodwill, that ⟨his heart sees that it⟩ can ⟨afford to grant to the adversary all that ground⟩ ↑abandon to the adv[[ersary]] all the ground of tradition and common belief↓, without ⟨abating the omnipotence of good.⟩ ↑losing a jot of strength.↓ It sees

103.17   safely ⟨contemplated,⟩ ↑tried, and↓ the↑ir↓ ⟨greatest⟩ weight ⟨given⟩ ↑allowed↓ to ↑all↓ objections

103.19   sea. ⟨The student⟩ ↑I↓ play⟨s⟩ with the

103.24   and flow. ⟨that⟩ [¶] This faith

103.32   announced ⟨as the basis of his doctrine the cheering sentiment⟩ that "the attractions

103.34   satisfaction. Yet ⟨see everywhere in⟩ ↑all↓ experience ↑exhibits↓ the reverse of this; the incompe⟨nt⟩tency of power ⟨, to the idea, which⟩ is the universal

103.37   parsimony↑.↓ ⟨in the distribution of power.⟩ It has

104.4   administered ⟨a drop,⟩ a single drop

104.9   he could ⟨wrestle with Orion, or⟩ try conclusions . . . motion to ⟨try⟩ ↑prove↓ his strength

104.15   this chasm is found, — ⟨this chasm⟩ between ⟨a monstrous⟩ ↑the largest↓ promise

104.18   elastic, ⟨⟨invincible,⟩⟩ not to be

104.19   generalizations, ⟨⟨and exults in the new immensities of his horizon.⟩⟩ The lesson . . . generalize, ⟨⟨to hold ⟨all⟩ particulars lightly in ⟨a view⟩view of the whole;⟩⟩ to believe

104.22   penetrate to the↑ir↓ catholic sense↑.↓ ⟨, which is really expressed, though occultly, by every particular.⟩ Things . . . thing, and ⟨do⟩ say

104.24   moral↑.↓ ⟨and immutable. All⟩ ⟨t⟩Things seem

104.26   Although ⟨history teaches that⟩ knaves

104.30   civilization is a⟨n endless⟩ train . . . answered↑.↓ ⟨, — no thanks to the felons.⟩ We see now, ⟨as heretofore,⟩ events

105.4   is here ⟨⟨in the world⟩ a pupil, here⟩ not to work

V. SHAKSPEARE

109.5   men. The ⟨great man⟩ ↑hero↓ is in the press of ⟨men⟩ ↑knights↓, and

109.8   needful ⟨strength⟩length of sight

358

109.9   is no ⟨giddypated⟩ rattlebrain . . . good; but a ⟨man⟩ ↑heart↓ in unison
        with ⟨↑the heart of↓⟩ his time
109.25 their hands ↑all↓ point
109.26 him amidst ⟨her⟩ rites
110.6   consumption, and ↑he↓ hits on a railroad. ⟨Every great genius⟩
        ↑Every master↓ has found
110.8   people, ↑and↓ ⟨and⟩in his love
            [Emerson first wrote "people, and his"; then wrote "in" over
        "and," and inserted another "and" to the left; in both cases he used
        ampersands.]
110.9   power ⟨, is this⟩! and ↑what↓ a compensation for the shortness of
        ⟨human⟩ life!
            [It is uncertain whether the comma or the exclamation point was
        meant to be deleted; so the 1850 edition is followed.]
110.13 the rivers↑.↓ ⟨for his road.⟩ Men
110.17 Great geni⟨us⟩al power, one would ↑almost↓ say, . . . in being ⟨to the
        greatest possible degree receptive, mediate, vehicular;⟩ ↑altogether
        receptive;↓ in letting
110.20 thro' the ⟨channels of the poet's⟩ mind
110.22 entertainments↑.↓ ⟨of some kind.⟩ The court . . . suppress them⟨;⟩.
        ⟨t⟩The Puritans, . . . among the ⟨Established⟩ ↑Anglican↓ Church ⟨saw
        seduction and sin in stage plays and⟩ would suppress . . . people
        ⟨would not be denied.⟩ ↑wanted them.↓ Innyards
110.28 players. ⟨The play was ballad, epic, picture newspaper⟩ The people
        . . . neither ↑then,↓ could king . . . united, ⟨then⟩ suppress an organ,
        which was ↑ballad, epic, newspaper,↓ caucus
110.35 great ⟨historian of the times⟩ ↑scholar↓ would
110.37 shop. The ⟨m⟩ best ⟨attestation⟩proof of its . . . writers ⟨"a wild insur-
        rection of genius,"⟩ which suddenly broke ⟨out in England into⟩ ↑in-
        to↓ this field
111.4   Fletcher. ¶ Th⟨is⟩e secure
111.6   no time ⟨, and makes no⟩ ↑in↓ idle
111.9   Stratford, and ⟨came⟩ ↑went↓ up to London . . . and were ⟨occasion-
        ally⟩ ↑in turn↓ produced on the boards↑.↓ ⟨, (which the audience are
        extravagantly fond of.) There was⟩ ↑Here is↓ the Tale of Troy, which
        the⟨y⟩ ↑audience↓ will bear . . . part of ⟨in some shape⟩ every
111.15 which men ↑hear↓ eagerly
111.19 tattered ⟨copies⟩manuscripts. It is
111.22 scene, or ⟨only⟩ adding . . . copyright ⟨i⟩on this work
            [Emerson first wrote "in," changed it to "on" (which was printed
        in the 1850 edition), and changed it back to "in" in his correction
        copy.]
111.35 for his ⟨airy⟩ edifice
112.2   temple. ⟨What is the secret of the admirable expression of Greek

359

sculpture in the best age? Whence that perfect composure, that calms and invigorates the beholder?⟩ Sculpture

112.9 architecture still ⟨gave an admirable⟩ ↑enforced a certain↓ calmness and ⟨solemnity.⟩ ↑continence ⟨to⟩in the statue.↓ As soon

[The word "still" is smeared over and may have been intended for deletion; it was retained in 1850.]

112.17 create. // [18] ⟨Shakspeare knew that tradition supplies a better fable than any invention can. If he lost any credit of design, he augmented his resources, and, at that day, our petulant demand for originality was not so much pressed. There was no literature for the million. The universal reading, the cheap press,⟩ // [19] [¶] In point

[In the right margin of page [18] these figures appear:

$$
\begin{array}{ll}
1771 & 6043 \\
\underline{2373} & \underline{4144} \\
4144 & 1899
\end{array}
$$

This is obviously Emerson's checking of the figures quoted from Malone on the next page (112.22–24 of the printed text). The rest of page [18] is repeated without change on [22] (113.3–7 of the printed text).]

112.18 appears that ⟨this sole creator among all writers⟩ ↑Shakspeare↓ did owe . . . found; and ⟨in Malone's laborious computations⟩ the amount . . . inferred from ⟨a⟩Malone's laborious computations in regard to the ⟨historical plays,⟩ ↑second and third parts of Henry VI.,↓ in which

112.24 and 18⟨4⟩99 ↑1899↓ were entirely his own." And ⟨as the process of⟩ ↑the proceeding↓ investigation ⟨proceeds, it is now affirmed that⟩ hardly ↑leaves↓ a single drama ⟨can be deemed⟩ ↑of↓ his ⟨own original⟩ ↑absolute↓ invention[[.]] Malone's sentence is ⟨the most⟩ ↑an↓ important ↑piece of↓ external history ⟨of his mind, and is his panegyric⟩. In Henry

112.29 thoughtful man, ⟨but⟩ with a vicious ear. ⟨The⟩ I can . . . cadence. See ⟨the double endings of the lines in⟩ Wolseys ↑Wolsey's↓ soliloquy . . . Cromwell, ⟨where the eloquence is vicious⟩ ⟨where the ⟨declamation⟩ ↑verse↓ has a touch of pulpit eloquence⟩ where, instead of the ⟨inimitable⟩ metre

[The deleted clause about "pulpit eloquence" is used, slightly revised, at the end of the sentence (112.35 in the printed text).]

112.33 the tune↑,↓ ⟨of the lines⟩ so that reading ↑for↓ the sense . . . rhythm, ⟨th⟩ here the . . . on a ⟨plan⟩ given tune

112.35 But the ⟨piece is⟩ ↑play↓ contains . . . and some ⟨scenes⟩ ↑passages↓, as the . . . Coronation, are ⟨in his most vigorous style.⟩ ↑like autographs.↓ What is . . . the bad ⟨style⟩ ⟨hand⟩ ↑rhythm↓[[.]] [¶] Shakspeare

113.14 inspiration⟨,⟩: ↑from whatever source,↓ they are . . . audience↑.↓ ⟨, from whatever source.⟩ Nay, he . . . home. ⟨Every man⟩ ↑Other men↓ say⟨s⟩ wise . . . as he. ⟨The difference is, that others⟩ ↑only they↓ say a

113.19 puts it ⟨with its fellows⟩ ↑in high place,↓ wherever

113.21 Saadi. ⟨As representatives of thought and learning to their countrymen,⟩ ⟨t⟩They felt

113.21 librarians ↑and historiographers↓ as well as poets. ⟨ ‖ . . . ‖ ⟩Each romancer ↑Each romancer↓ was heir

[The first "Each romancer" is written over something not yet deciphered and is itself almost illegible.]

113.26 Chaucer is ⟨very⟩ conspicuous . . . have been ⟨indebted⟩ ↑beholden↓ to him, but ↑in the whole society of English writers↓ a large

113.29 with the ⟨redundancy of materials which ⟨furnishes⟩ ↑feeds↓ so many borrowers⟩ ↑opulence which feeds so many pensioners↓. But Chaucer ⟨, like so many geniuses,⟩ is a huge

113.31 through Lydgate⟨'s translation,⟩ and Caxton, . . . Colonna↑,↓⟨s⟩ ⟨grand prose⟩ ↑whose↓ Latin ⟨R⟩romance of the Trojan War ⟨, which⟩ was ⟨itself⟩ ↑in turn↓ a compilation from Dares Phrygius, ⟨and⟩ Ovid, and

[The comma after "Colonna" is inserted before the canceled "s."]

113.35 the ⟨"⟩Romaunt of the ↑Rose↓ / ⟨Rose"⟩ is only

114.3 Marie: ⟨A French harmless[?]⟩The House of Fame, from . . . Italian: ⟨And⟩ ↑and↓ poor Gower

114.7 leaves it. ⟨Indeed,⟩ ⟨i⟩It has . . . a sort of ⟨ ‖ . . . ‖ ⟩rule in literature

[Although the material under "rule" may be only a blotted smear, it seems to contain some writing.]

114.11 entertain it; ⟨Thought is the property⟩ ↑and↓ of him

114.13 our own. ¶ ⟨To come a little nearer to this fact, one would say, that all⟩ ↑Thus all↓ originality

114.16 legislature at ⟨London⟩ ↑Westminster↓ or at

114.17 Show ⟨me⟩ ↑us↓ the constituency . . . wishes, ⟨all⟩ the crowd

114.22 something of ⟨its⟩ ↑their↓ impressiveness. ⟨Well,⟩ ⟨a⟩As ⟨Sir⟩ ↑Sir↓ Robert . . . so there ⟨are⟩ ↑were↓ fountains

114.25 which they dr⟨a⟩ew; friends . . . which ↑, if seen,↓ would go

114.27 speak with ⟨might?⟩ ↑authority?↓ ⟨Did he feel original? was he matched, was he⟩ ↑did he feel himself↓ overmatched

114.29 last in ⟨the man⟩ ↑this breast↓ a ⟨power⟩ ↑Delphi whereof↓ to ask . . . thing, ⟨in the recess of his own bosom,⟩ whether

114.32 on that↑?↓ ⟨infinitely? Then,⟩ all the

114.34 minds ⟨, to which he is most indebted,⟩ are ⟨but⟩ a whiff . . . conversed. // [new paragraph] ⟨Shakspeare preferred a divided fame to a small originality. And⟩ ⟨i⟩It is easy

114.38 came by ⟨great⟩ ↑wide↓ social ⟨united⟩ labour, . . . impulse. ⟨⟨Thus see how⟩ a catholic genius ⟨ever⟩ inherits more than he earns. He finds the stones collected, and the workmen waiting. What is already done instructs him in what is desired, he does the one thing waited for, he lays the topstone, and all the rest are forgotten in his memorable name.⟩ Our English

[The passage from "a catholic genius" through "memorable name" is enclosed in large square brackets as well as being deleted by double diagonal lines.]

115.3 it was ↑not↓ made ⟨not⟩ by one . . . time; ⟨but long periods and generations of men⟩ ↑but centuries and churches↓ brought

115.6 existing. ⟨So with⟩ The Liturgy ⟨so much⟩ admired for . . . pathos, ⟨it⟩ is an

115.10 makes the ⟨same⟩ ↑like↓ remark

115.13 forms↑.↓ ⟨of prayer⟩ He picked

115.15 truth of ⟨our [?]⟩the legal

115.18 gets its ⟨wonderful⟩ excellence

115.20 and national⟨ly generic⟩ phrases are kept, and all ⟨the⟩ others

115.24 ["RobinHood" was first written as one word, but copied as two words in the space above the line.]

115.26 such ⟨bo⟩works, the time thinks↑,↓ ⟨for us,⟩ the market thinks↑,↓ ⟨for us,⟩ the mason

115.29 of the ⟨times⟩ ↑day↓; and the generic

115.31 as the ⟨true⟩ recorder

115.35 from the ⟨m⟩Mysteries celebrated

116.1 his own↑.↓ ⟨⟨and immortal⟩.⟩ ↑Elated↓ / ⟨Elated⟩ with ⟨this⟩ success, . . . garret ⟨in⟩ unopened

116.7 school, ⟨or not,⟩ and why . . . wife. [¶] ⟨And truly⟩ ⟨t⟩There is somewhat

116.11 turned; the ⟨painful⟩ care with which ↑it registers↓ every⟨thing⟩ ↑trifle↓ ⟨relative to⟩ ↑touching↓ Queen . . . Buckinghams↑,↓ ⟨are recorded and illustrated // people whom we could forget, or not have heard of, without any loss,⟩ and lets pass ⟨without a glance,⟩ without a single valuable ⟨record,⟩ ↑note↓ the founder

116.17 thoughts ⟨; they,⟩ the foremost . . . world⟨,⟩ are now

116.23 times, ⟨both of what was done and what was deficient in science and in letters,⟩ never mentioned ⟨the⟩ ↑his↓ name↑.↓ ⟨of one greater than all his illustrious correspondents.⟩ Ben Jonson

116.29 proverb, ⟨one would say that⟩ Shakspeares time ⟨was⟩ ↑should be↓ capable of recognizing it. ⟨I take, for example,⟩ Sir Henry Wotton, ⟨who⟩ was born . . . and ⟨who⟩ died . . . among his ⟨contemporaries⟩correspondents and

117.1 enumerating ⟨all those⟩ ↑many others↓ whom

117.4 appeared ↑in Greece,↓ in the time of Pericles, ⟨in Greece,⟩ there was

117.6 impenetrable↑.↓ ⟨, his incognito complete.⟩ You cannot

117.17 readers. Now, ⟨all⟩ literature, ⟨all⟩ philosophy, ⟨all⟩ ↑and↓ thought

117.20 are the ↑only↓ critics who

117.22 of his ⟨transcendent⟩ ↑superlative↓ power and beauty, which↑,↓ ⟨is

more important fact to history than⟩ like Christianity, ⟨colours⟩ qualifies

117.24 Society have ⟨set on foot⟩ inquir⟨y⟩ed in all

117.26 result? ⟨With that which I have mentioned; namely,⟩ ↑Beside↓ some
important ... stage ⟨. But, further, with⟩ ↑to which I adverted, they
have gleaned↓ a few

117.30 share ⟨of⟩in the Blackfriar's ... bought a↑n↓ ⟨valuable⟩ estate ... with
⟨the proceeds of his profession⟩ ↑his earnings↓ as writer and shareholder ⟨in the theatre⟩; that he

117.35 was a ⟨bonafide⟩ ↑veritable↓ farmer

118.2 excess. ↑He was a good-natured sort of man, an actor and share-
holde[[r]] in the theatre, not in any ↑striking↓ manner distinguish[[ed]] from other actors and managers.↓ ⟨[¶] But whatever
↑scraps of↓ information ⟨history may have rescued⟩ concerning
⟨the⟩ ↑his↓ condition ⟨of this poet history⟩ ↑these researches↓ may
have rescued, ⟨it⟩ ↑they↓ can shed no light upon that witchcraft of
invention which is the con-⟩ // [51] ⟨The result of the biographies is
that this creator was a common man enough, shareholder in his theatre, and not in any manner distinguished from other actors and
managers.⟩ I ⟨do not affect to disguise⟩ ↑admit↓ the importance ...
worth ⟨all⟩ the pains ... procure it. // [52] [¶] But whatever ... that
infinite invention which is the con- // [53] cealed magnet of

[The manuscript pages appear to have been written originally in
the following order: [50] (except for insert, "He was a good-natured
... actors and managers."), [53], [51], [50] (insert), [52]. The canceled sentence on [51] was inserted, with some revisions, near the
middle of [50]; the material from that point to the bottom of [50]
connected with the top of [53] but (to make room for the two remaining sentences on [51]) was transferred, with one further change,
to the bottom of [52] (the upper two-thirds of which is blank). The
leaf containing pages [51–52] is almost certainly an insert.]

118.11 schoolmates, ⟨acquisition of property,⟩ ↑earning of / ⟨of⟩ money,↓
marriage ... of this ⟨external history⟩ ↑gossip↓, no ray ... appears
between ⟨all this lumber⟩ ↑it↓ and the

118.19 Malone, ⟨and⟩ Warburton, ⟨and⟩Dyce, and Coll⟨y⟩↑i↓er have

118.22 dedicate the⟨m⟩ir lives ... crown ⟨adorn⟩ elucidate

118.25 all this ⟨wretched mortality,⟩ ↑painted pedantry,↓ and sweetly ... inaccessible home↑s↓. I remember

118.29 simply ⟨an expression of⟩ Hamlet↑'s question↓ to the

118.32 That thou, d⟨r⟩ead corse ... moon." / ⟨That dissolving power of
Shakspeare's imagination which at pleasure ⟨swells⟩ ↑swells the
chamber he writes in to↓⟩ ↑[¶] That imagination which ⟨expands⟩
↓dilates↓ the closet he writes in to↓ the world↑'s↓ ⟨to huge rotundity,⟩
↑⟨immensity⟩dimension,↓ crowds it

[The order of changes is not certain. The original version of the passage apparently was, "That dissolving power of Shakspeare's imagination which at pleasure swells the world to huge rotundity, crowds it"; the second version, "That dissolving power of Shakspeare's imagination which at pleasure swells the chamber he writes in to the world's immensity, crowds it"; and the third was the final, except that "expands" became "dilates." A new paragraph may have been intended with "That imagination" at 118.34, or the indentation may have been accidental; the 1850 edition does not have a new paragraph here, and none seems needed.]

118.35 order, ⟨will in a moment⟩ ↑as quickly↓ reduce↑s↓ the big

119.2   green room. ⟨and⟩ Can any . . . on the ⟨wonderful⟩ localities

119.10 of th⟨e⟩ose transcendant secrets? ↑In fine,↓ ⟨[¶] Shakspeare is the only biographer of Shakspeare, and even⟩ // [57] ⟨In fine,⟩ in this drama

        [The deleted sentence fragment at the bottom of page [56] is repeated on [58] (the rest of which is blank) and continues on [59]. The material on [57], which appears at 119.11–16 in the printed text, is copied with slight revisions from the deleted material on [61]. The leaf containing pages [57–58] is evidently an insert.]

119.12 of Egypt ↑and India↓; in the

119.18 can tell ⟨us⟩nothing except

119.21 extricated, ⟨copied,⟩ analysed, . . . and Coll⟨y⟩↑i↓er; and

119.27 the man. // [61] ⟨In fine, in this drama, as in all ⟨the⟩great works of art, — in the Cyclopean architecture of Egypt; in the Phidian sculpture, the Gothic Minsters; the Italian painting; the Ballads of Spain and Scotland; — the Genius draws up the ladder after him, when the creative age goes up to heaven, and gives way to a new, who see the works, and ask in vain for a history.⟩ [¶] Hence, though

        [See the note on 119.10 above.]

119.32 with him, ⟨to be the companions of his sphere,⟩ would most

119.33 answer at ⟨the⟩ ↑every↓ heart↑,↓ ⟨of every thoughtful man,⟩ on life

120.1   which yet ⟨seem to⟩ interweave

120.7   of men? ⟨Or,⟩ what trait

120.9   him; his ⟨own⟩ delight

120.12 is the ↑one↓ person . . . to us↑.↓⟨most intimately.⟩ What point . . . of taste, of ↑the conduct of↓ life

120.23 purely on the⟨ir⟩ dramatic

120.25 critics of ↑this↓ / ⟨his⟩dramatic ↑merit,↓ but still

120.27 hand. Had ⟨Shakspeare⟩ ↑he↓ been less

120.31 as to ⟨degrade⟩ ↑withdraw some attention from↓ the vehicle↑;↓ ⟨to a mere accident⟩ and he is like ⟨the⟩ ↑some↓ saint

120.36 application. ↑So ⟨had Shakespeare⟩ it fares with the wise Shakspeare and his book of life. He wrote the air[[s]]↓ // ⟨His capital merit is his wisdom of life He wrote the airs⟩ for all

121.3 man, and ⟨drew⟩ ↑described↓ the day . . . in it: he ⟨knew⟩ ↑read↓ the hearts

121.7 he could ⟨split a ray of light, or⟩ divide . . . face of ⟨a⟩the child, . . . fine ⟨boundaries⟩ ↑demarcation[[s]]↓ of freedom and of fate⟨,⟩: he knew

121.10 police of natur⟨al⟩e ⟨law⟩: ⟨⟨leave a blank⟩⟩and all the sweets ↑and all the terrors of human lot lay in his mind as truly but as softly as the landscape lies on the eye.↓ [¶] And the importance

[The words "and all the sweets" are written over "⟨leave a blank⟩" (which is in pencil and is probably a direction to the printer). The last five lines on the page, from "And the importance" through "message is written" (121.12–14 in the printed text), may also have been a later insertion.]

121.13 notice. Tis ↑like making↓ a question . . . written. //↑¶ Shakspeare is as much out of the category of eminent authors, as he is out of the crowd.↓ ⟨[¶] Shakspeare⟩ ↑He↓ is inconceivably . . . conceivably. A ↑[[g]]ood↓ reader . . . brain, and ⟨look⟩ ↑think↓ from thence

121.20 farthest ⟨bound⟩ ↑reach↓ of subtlety

121.22 authorship. ↑With↓ / ⟨⟨Next to⟩ ↑With↓⟩ this wisdom of life, is the ↑equal↓ endowment

121.26 characters ↑as these fictions↓. And they

121.29 string[[.]] ↑An omnipresent humanity↓ // ⟨⟨[¶] His⟩ ↑An↓ omnipresent humanity⟩ coordinates

121.35 has no pecularit⟨ies⟩y ⟨nothing urgent to⟩ ↑no↓ importunate

122.5 farce, ⟨and in⟩ tragedy, ⟨in⟩ narrative, and ⟨in⟩ lovesong[[s;]] . . . perception of ⟨the⟩ other readers. // ¶ ⟨It is this ⟨power⟩ ↑lyric skill↓ of expression or ↑power↓⟩ ↑This power of expression, or of↓ / of transferring . . . verse, ⟨that⟩ makes

122.10 metaphysics. ↑This↓ / ⟨⟨Here⟩ ↑This↓⟩ is that

122.18 like nature's, . . . solar microscope. // [77] ⟨nature's ⟨works⟩ will bear the scrutiny of the solar microscope⟩ [no ¶] In short, he ⟨seems⟩ ↑is↓ the chief

[The last lines on page [76] are copied from the deleted material at the top of [77], but do not appear to be a separate insertion; probably the whole leaf containing pages [75–76] was written later than its neighbors.]

122.22 flower ⟨paint itself⟩ ↑etch its image↑ on his plate of iodine; ⟨he can now⟩ ↑and then↓ proceed↑s↓ at leisure to ⟨paint⟩ ↑etch↓ a million

122.25 now let ⟨it too⟩ the world⟨.⟩ of figures

122.26 possibility of ⟨p⟩ the translation of things into song, is ⟨settled⟩ demonstrated [[.]] ⟨for ever⟩ // [79] ⟨[¶]There is nothing comparable in literature to Shakspeares expression, for strength, ↑and↓ for delicacy. Men have existed who affirmed that they heard the language of celestial angels and talked with them, but, that, when they returned into the natural world, though they preserved the memory of these conversations, they ⟨found it impossible to⟩ ↑could not↓ translate the things that had been said into human thoughts and words. But Shakspeare is ⟨like⟩ one who ⟨had⟩ ↑having↓ been rapt into some purer state of sensation and existence, had learned the // [80] secret of a finer diction, and, when he returned to this world, retained the fine organ which had been opened above.⟩ ¶ His ↑lyric↓ power ⟨of expression has this virtue, that it lies (not in particulars, but)⟩ ↑lies↓ in the genius

122.32 beings, and ⟨the smallest⟩ ↑any↓ clause

122.33 speeches ↑in the plays,↓ and single

122.37 satisfied. ⟨All⟩ ⟨h⟩His means are . . . ends; ⟨every fetch, ⟨every expedient,⟩⟩ every subordinate

123.2 He is ⟨never⟩ ↑not↓ reduced

123.4 rides. ⟨Poets, like vaulters in the circus round, / ⟨Can⟩May step from horse to horse, but never touch the ground. / His means are never mechanical, but purely poetic.⟩ [¶] The finest . . . experience: but ⟨, in all true poets,⟩ the thought

    [For the canceled verse couplet, see "Fragments on the Poet and the Poetic Gift" in *W*, IX, 331.]

123.6 experience. ↑Cultivated↓ Men ⟨of talents⟩ often attain . . . verses, but ⟨with this imperfection, that⟩ it is easy to ⟨see⟩ ↑read↓ through

123.9 figure: ⟨T⟩this is Andrew, and that is ⟨Phebe⟩ ↑Rachel↓. The sense

123.11 butterfly. ⟨Not so with the poet.⟩ In ⟨his⟩ ↑the poet's↓ mind, . . . thought, ↑and↓ has lost all that is ⟨sordid and⟩ exuvial↑.↓⟨, lost all personality, and emerges pure and immortal.⟩ This generosity

123.14 closeness of ⟨the⟩his pictures

123.15 trace of ⟨intrusive⟩ egotism. ⟨All is purified to clear and sunny tone.⟩ [¶] One more royal trait ⟨I may stop to specify, even in so general a sketch, because it⟩ properly

123.19 woman, ⟨not for necessity, but⟩ for the

123.23 bards have ⟨always drunk that wine, and poured it out for the nations.⟩ ↑been noted for their firm and cheerful temper. Homer lies in sunshine,↓ Chaucer

123.30 would not ⟨walk⟩march in his

123.32 with this ⟨great⟩ bard . . . solitude ⟨and in silence⟩, shutting

123.34 Solitude has ⟨grave instructions; it is almost frightful to see how many things, how dear persons we can do without. Its⟩ austere lessons↑, ⟨and⟩↑it can↓↓ teach⟨↑es↓⟩ us to

124.2 imperfection of ⟨all⟩ humanity. ⟨Shakspeare as the chief poet may well draw our attention to that wonderful problem that ranges the poets and the mystics on one and on the other side.⟩ [¶] Shakspeare, Homer, ⟨Chaucer⟩ Dante, Chaucer, saw

    [In the space below "imperfection" is what may be either a deleted word or only a blot.]

·24.7 the mind, ⟨of⟩ ↑being emblems of its thoughts, and conveying in all
thei[[r]] natural [[hi]]story a certain mute commentary on human
life[[.]]↓ // [89]⟨[¶] Shakspeare had the keys to the cipher: he knew
that the rock was there for more than building-stones, the sea for
more than fish, the tree for more than timber, the cow for more than
milk, the horse for more than to carry burdens. He⟩ ↑Shakspeare↓
employed

[The last two lines on page [88], starting with "being emblems,"
are written smaller than the rest. It is possible that the whole paragraph beginning with "Shakspeare, Homer" (124.3 in the printed
text) on that page is an insertion, for it seems to be a revision of the
deleted matter on the first part of page [89]. The first two letters of
"history" (124.8) are missing because a corner of the leaf was torn
and patched.]

124.10 beauty; ⟨he held this cipher, and used it for the amusement of na-
tions⟩ and never . . . explore the ⟨deity⟩ ↑virtue↓ which resides

124.18 orbits to ⟨embellish⟩ ↑⟨outblaze⟩ glare with↓ the municipal

124.24 Think ye we ↑have↓ created

124.25 question is of ⟨comparative⟩ talent

124.29 or less? ⟨[¶] Well, other men, priest and prophet, Israelite,⟩ ↑The
Egyptian verdict of the Shakspeare Societi[[es]] ⟨comes to mind, that
he was a⟩↓ // [93] ↑comes to mind,↓ that he was a jovial

[The deleted passage "Well, . . . Israelite" near the bottom of page
[92] is repeated at the bottom of [94] and appears at 125.6 of the
printed text. The leaf containing pages [93–94] may be an insert.]

124.35 authors, ⟨as⟩of Bacon, . . . Cervantes, ⟨I should⟩we might leave

125.7 objects: ⟨Their eyes were opened also, and things were transparent,
and⟩ they ↑also↓ saw

125.13 purgatorial ↑and penal↓ fires before us; and the ⟨spirit⟩ ↑heart↓ of the
seer and the ⟨spirit⟩ ↑heart↓ of the listener ⟨was blighted, and the
fountains of life poisoned.⟩ ↑sunk in them.↓ [¶] ⟨These⟩ ↑It must be
conceded that these↓ are halfviews

[For the addition of "penal," cf. *Paradise Lost*, I, 48.]

125.17 wants its ⟨poet and its priest in one⟩ ↑poet-priest,↓ a reconciler . . .
Shakspeare⟨,⟩ ↑the player,↓ nor shall grope in grave↑s↓⟨yards⟩ with
Swedenborg

VI. NAPOLEON

129.1 [¶]⟨Among the ⟨principal figures⟩ ↑eminent ⟨men⟩ persons↓ of modern
history, Bonaparte best expresses the average character and aims⟩
↑Among the eminent persons↓ of the nineteenth century, ⟨He is⟩
↑Bonaparte ⟨though⟩↓⟨not the best, nor the worst,⟩ ⟨but⟩ is far . . .
powerful↑,↓ ⟨individual, who has lived within the period,⟩ and owes

[The comma after "century" was probably changed from a period, as "He is" began a new sentence.]

129.4 cultivated men. ⟨⟨And we cannot better arrive at the popular mode of thinking and action, than by seeing them enlarged and invigorated in this colossal individual.⟩ [¶] It is a theory of natural history⟩ ↑[no ¶] ⟨It is a⟩ ↑It is Swedenborg's↓ theory ⟨of natural⟩↓that every

[The canceled passage "And we cannot . . . natural history" runs from the bottom of page [1] to the top of [2]; but the inserted material replacing it, transcribed here as following it, actually precedes it on [1].]

129.9 analogy, ⟨it may be safely affirmed, that,⟩ if any

129.15 fortunes, ⟨⟨and wish to keep them,⟩⟩ and the young

129.24 births. It ⟨claims to be the workingmen's party, and⟩ desires

130.1 skill. ⟨I do no injustice to this class in calling⟩ Napoleon ↑is↓ its representative. The instinct ⟨of this class, the instinct⟩ of ⟨free,⟩ active, . . . everywhere, has ⟨always⟩ pointed

130.4 He had the↑ir↓ virtues and ↑their↓ vices↑;↓ ⟨of this class;⟩ above all, he had ⟨its⟩ ↑their↓ spirit

130.6 material, ⟨aiming⟩ ↑pointing↓ at a ⟨material or⟩ sensual . . . richest ⟨means⟩and most various means . . . conversant with ⟨vast⟩ mechanical

130.9 skilful, but ⟨sternly⟩ subordinating

130.14 and sent. [¶] ⟨I cannot but think that⟩ ⟨e⟩Every one

130.17 Napoleon ⟨attracts the humblest reader, because he⟩ is thoroughly

130.20 sense. The ⟨common man⟩ ↑man in the stree[[t]]↓ finds . . . powers of ⟨common men⟩ ↑other men in the street↓. He finds

130.23 could indulge, ⟨and did indulge⟩ all those

130.29 honours, ↑ — ↓precisely

130.34 minds ⟨; as in the wellknown example of Mirabeau⟩. Thus Mirabeau . . . France ↑.↓ ⟨and made it his own.⟩ Dumont

130.37 speech. ⟨Immediately⟩ ↑It struck↓ Dumont ⟨wrote in pencil a⟩ ↑that he could ⟨write a⟩ ↑fit it with a↓↓ peroration↑,↓ ⟨for the discourse,⟩ which he wrote in pencil immediately, and showed ⟨it⟩ to Lord . . . Elgin ⟨warmly⟩ approved

131.4 read it↑,↓ ⟨with eagerness,⟩ pronounced

131.9 it with ⟨grand⟩ ↑much↓ effect

131.10 personality, ⟨had come to feel⟩ ↑felt↓ that these

131.14 was the ⟨great⟩ successor

131.17 to be ⟨an office⟩ ↑a bureau↓ for all

131.20 Alps; he ⟨makes the ‖ . . . ‖ ⟩builds the road. All . . . kind: he ⟨seizes not only⟩ ↑adopts↓ the best measures, ⟨adopts them,⟩ sets his stamp on them, — ⟨but also,⟩ ↑and not these alone, but on↓ every happy

131.26 of France⟨,⟩. ⟨and not of one Frenchman.⟩ [¶] ⟨Let us look, then, a little nearer at the qualities and powers he exerted. He⟩ ↑Bonaparte↓ was

131.30   for we ⟨, at least,⟩ get rid . . . hypocrisy. ⟨The position and pretensions of⟩ Bonaparte ⟨are very intelligible. He⟩ wrought . . . represented, ⟨for an external success, for⟩ ↑for↓ power and wealth, ↑ — but Bonaparte specially↓ without . . . means: ⟨not honest power and wealth, but power and wealth, by right or by wrong.⟩ All the sentiments which ⟨commonly⟩ embarrass

132.1   "ideologists;" — ⟨This was⟩ a word
      [The semicolon was probably changed from a period, and the dash inserted.]

132.4   proverb, ⟨sufficiently familiar⟩ ↑too well known↓, declares

132.8   bar to ⟨ourselves,⟩ ↑us,↓ and still

132.10   smoothest of ⟨all⟩ roads

132.16   precision of ⟨stone and water and frost and fire.⟩ ↑natural agents.↓ He has

132.18   events. ⟨It is true,⟩ ↑To be sure,↓ there are

132.22   grammarians: ⟨B⟩↑b↓ut these men ordinarily ⟨have only that power of manual skill, and no⟩ ↑lack the↓ power ⟨of thought to generalize and arrange. So that they⟩ ↑of arrangement, and↓ are like

132.29   working with, ⟨and does not deceive himself as to⟩ ↑and what is↓ the ⟨result⟩product. He knew . . . iron, ⟨of earth and water,⟩ of wheels . . . diplomatists, and ⟨expected⟩ ↑required↓ that each . . . kind. ⟨He does not guess, but ⟨sees⟩feels and foresees his way.⟩ [¶] The art of war was the ⟨perpetual⟩ game ⟨which he studied, and⟩ in which

132.36   talent is ⟨exerted⟩ ↑strained↓ by endless

133.4   constitution, and ⟨the⟩ ↑this early↓ circumstances ⟨of his youth and education⟩ combined to develop this ↑pattern↓ democrat↑.↓ ⟨to the highest degree.⟩ He had the virtues of ⟨this⟩ ↑his↓ class

133.10   all was ⟨guarded⟩ ↑seen↓, and the energy

133.18   scruples;" ⟨but⟩ compact

133.23   head." He ⟨knew ⟨very well⟩ how to⟩ respect↑ed↓ the power of nature and ⟨F⟩fortune, and ⟨to⟩ ascribe↑d↓ to it . . . inferior men, ⟨only⟩ on his

133.26   and he ⟨, no doubt,⟩ pleased himself as ⟨mankind⟩ ↑well as the peo-ple↓, when he

133.29   crimes: ↑ — ↓ Men of

133.37   circumstances." [¶] He ⟨was born strong, and⟩ had a . . . so much comprehensi⟨veness⟩↑on↓. He is ⟨ever⟩ a realist

134.3   hinges, ⟨what is the precise difficulty to be overcome,⟩ throws himself on ⟨that⟩ ↑the precise point of resistance↓, and slights

134.4   right ⟨and perfect⟩ manner

134.9   consulting any⟨body⟩one. I should

134.16   persons ⟨very⟩ much to

134.24   abroad. ⟨Had⟩ Napoleon⟨'s ends been public, ⟨as they were⟩ ↑and not↓ egotistic, ⟨he⟩ ↑Na↓⟩ had been the first man of the world⟨.⟩, ↑if his ends had been ↑purely↓ public↑.↓ ⟨and not egotistic.⟩↓ As he . . . vigor ⟨in the beholder⟩ by the

135.29 [The second "to his aim" was underlined, but the underlining was then canceled by short vertical lines.]

135.2 [The comma after "cruel" looks as if it may originally have been a semicolon.]

135.10 forward!" [¶] ⟨"Senurier one of his staff officers⟩ ↑Seruzier, a colonel of artillery↓ gives in

135.23 batteries, ⟨and in less than no time we buried ⟨⟨3⟩5000?⟩ Russians and Austrians under the waters of the lake."⟩ and in less than no time we buried" some* "thousands ⟨*"⟩ of Russians . . . the lake."

[A circle is drawn around the "3" of "35000," and another circle around the whole figure. A horizontal line is drawn below "the lake"; the footnote follows.]

135.28 Paris as ⟨eve⟩any town

135.29 Having ⟨settled in his mind⟩ ↑decided↓ what was . . . that, with ⟨the utmost thoroughness.⟩ ↑might and main.↓ He put

135.35 national diff⟨iculties⟩↑erences↓, ⟨as large

136.5 position ⟨he⟩ rained a torrent of iron, — ⟨bomb⟩shell↑s↓, balls

136.7 concentrated ⟨his troops, and poured⟩ squadron . . . existence. ⟨When reviewing⟩ ↑To↓ a regiment . . . Napoleon ⟨, turning to the regiment,⟩ said, "My

136.12 fury of ⟨the⟩ assault

136.13 to the ⟨very⟩ edge of his possibility ⟨,⟩. ⟨so heartily bent was he on his objects.⟩ It is

136.14 came ↑several times↓ within an inch of ruin↑,↓ ⟨several times,⟩ and his

136.19 enough. ⟨Victory⟩ ↑Each victory↓ was ⟨only⟩ a new

136.23 as much ⟨power⟩life is needed

136.32 nature." ⟨There is a remarkable passage⟩ ⟨i⟩In one of his conversations with Las Cases; ↑he remarked,↓ "As to

136.37 decision:" ⟨He⟩ ↑and he↓ did not

137.3 in this ⟨respect."⟩ particular."

137.12 battle." ⟨⟨Antonomarchi⟩⟩ "Before he . . . little about what ⟨she⟩ ↑he↓ should do

[An obvious slip of the pen, anticipating "should."]

137.15 fortune." ⟨⟨Bourrienne⟩⟩ The same

137.21 be lost." / ⟨Bourrienne⟩ / It was

137.28 have been ⟨so[?]⟩many working kings, ↑from↓ Ulysses ⟨, Alfred, Justinian, Czar Peter,⟩ ↑to↓ William of Orange, ↑but none who↓ / ⟨but none who⟩ accomplished

[It is not certain whether "William of Orange" was inserted along with the preceding and following words, but probably not; all five names (without "from" and "to") are in Chapman's edition.]

137.33 to his ⟨numerous⟩ crowns and badges the ⟨grace and⟩ prescription . . .

but he ⟨was too sagacious not to be aware of⟩ ↑knew↓ his debt to his
austere education,⟨ — ⟩ and ⟨he⟩ made no

138.3 citizenship. ⟨He is not a baby, like a hereditary monarch, but all
h⟩↑H↓is remarks . . . class. ⟨Every one⟩ ↑Those↓ who had to deal with
him, ⟨felt,⟩ ↑found↓ that ⟨this man⟩he was not to

138.7 Helena. ⟨"The Grandmaster of Malta's Palace was the house of a
gentleman with 100 000 livres a year" — "The Patriarch of Alexandria lives in a convent at old Cairo in the style of a head of a religious
order ↑in France↓ with 30 000 francs per annum."⟩ When the expenses ↑of the Empress,↓ of his household, ⟨of the Empress,⟩ of his
palaces

[For the deleted quotations, see *JMN*, IX, 141.]

138.10 and errors↑,↓ ⟨in amounts,⟩ and reduced the claims ⟨often⟩ by ⟨very⟩
considerable sums. ¶ ⟨Napoleon had ⟨thus⟩ a strength by nature and a
strength by circumstance: ⟨still then⟩⟩ ⟨h⟩His grand . . . millions
⟨which⟩ ↑whom↓ he directed

138.13 interests us ⟨only as far⟩ as he . . . exists as ↑captain and↓ king, ⟨legisla-
tor, and captain,⟩ only as far as the Revolution, ↑or↓ ⟨⟨⟩ the interest of
the industrious ⟨and ambitious⟩ masses, ⟨⟩⟩ found

138.16 in him. ⟨⟨This man,⟩ ⟨t⟩Though a soldier,⟩ ↑In the social interests,↓
↑he↓ ⟨was not disqualified from knowing⟩ ↑knew↓ the meaning and
value of ⟨work. He⟩ ↑labour, and↓ threw himself naturally on th⟨e⟩at
side↑.↓ ⟨of labour.⟩ I like ⟨the⟩an incident

[In the first revision "he" was inserted between "soldier" and "was
not"; after those words were deleted, "he" remained in place, but is
now between "interests" and "knew."]

138.23 directed ⟨particular⟩ attention

138.26 him, are ⟨the⟩ ↑his↓ magnificent roads ⟨he built for the comfort of the
French and Italian nations⟩ He filled

138.31 could do. ↑The↓ / ⟨"The French do not march, but run," said the
humbled and astonished Italians. The ⟨very⟩⟩ best

138.36 explains the ⟨confidence and⟩ devotion

139.2 lay in ⟨this, that the people ⟨knew and⟩ felt him ⟨as⟩ ↑to be↓⟩ ↑⟨the
people's⟩ ↑their↓ conviction that he was↓ their representative

[The words "to be" are in pencil.]

139.4 controuled and ↑even↓ decimated

139.11 secluded ⟨as by an iron wall⟩ from all . . . soil, and ⟨they⟩ holding . . .
long-forgotten ⟨period and⟩ state of society; ⟨but⟩ ↑Instead of↓ that
vampire↑,↓ ⟨was hurled from their breast, and⟩ a man of themselves
⟨was placed⟩ ↑held↓ in the ⟨seat, with⟩ ↑Tuilleries↓ knowledge and
ideas like their own, ⟨and, of course,⟩ opening, ↑of course,↓ to them
and their children all ⟨the⟩ places

139.17 selfish ⟨, narrow⟩ policy, ever narrowing . . . day of ⟨invitation⟩ expansion . . . come. A ⟨boundless⟩ market

139.21 France, was ⟨suddenly⟩ changed

139.27 master, — ⟨still,⟩ the whole talent of the country, ⟨ — (the talent — which springs up, by the favor of Heaven, with equal readiness in cottages and in castles,)⟩ in every rank and kindred, — ⟨embraced every / where his cause,⟩ ↑took his part,↓ and defended him ⟨, each in its own family and caste,⟩ as its natural patron↑.↓ ⟨and chieftain.⟩ In 1814

[The last three lines on this manuscript page, from "Napoleon said" through "the Faubourgs" (139.30–32), are in a smaller handwriting than the rest, and the whole sentence may be an insertion.]

139.34 required a ⟨great⟩ hospitality ... feeling went ⟨heartily⟩ along with this policy. Like every ⟨strong spirit⟩ ↑superior person↓, he undoubtedly felt a ⟨keen curiosity and appetite⟩ ↑desire↓ for men

140.4 years, ⟨after his⟩ ↑with larger↓ experience ⟨of men was much enlarged,⟩ his respect for ⟨society around him⟩ ↑mankind↓ was not

140.6 bitterness, he ⟨exclaimed⟩ ↑said↓ to one

140.8 coat of ⟨one of⟩ my virtuous ... wish them." ⟨But⟩ this impatience at levity was ⟨only⟩ ↑however↓ an oblique

140.12 his will. ↑He could not confound↓ Fox and ... Bernadotte, ⟨he could not confound⟩ with the ... spite of ⟨all⟩ the detraction

140.16 for him, ⟨the most generous⟩ ↑ample↓ acknowledgments are ⟨explicitly⟩ made

140.28 And, in ⟨actual⟩ fact, every

140.31 court. ⟨and s[?]⟩Seventeen men

140.36 my eyes." [¶] ↑When a natural king becomes a titular king, every body is pleased and satisfied.↓ ⟨Although the history of⟩ the Revolution ⟨and the steps of Bonaparte's career⟩ entitled

141.3 to look ⟨up with pride to⟩ ↑on↓ Napoleon ... *his* party↑;↓⟨. But⟩ ↑but↓ there is ⟨yet⟩ something

[It is possible that when the sentence began with "Although" (see preceding entry), the latter part of this passage read "*his* party there is" and that "But" (with the period preceding it) was inserted later and finally changed to "but" preceded by a semicolon.]

141.5 enlists ⟨a far wider, and even⟩ an universal sympathy. ⟨When a natural king becomes a titular king, every body is pleased and satisfied.⟩ For, in

[Compare the second deletion here with the insertion at 140.36.]

141.14 revolving and disposing ⟨⟨of⟩so⟩ sovereignly ⟨of vast⟩ trains

[Emerson wrote "2" below "disposing" and "1" below "sovereignly" to direct that the words be transposed.]

141.19 Sicilian sea; ⟨or,⟩ drawing ... Pyramids, and ⟨exclaiming⟩ ↑saying↓ to his troops, ... on you:" ⟨or,⟩ fording the ⟨r⟩Red ⟨s⟩Sea; ⟨or,⟩ wading

141.27 little ⟨too obvious⟩ ↑puerile↓, the pleasure ... glaring; ⟨He⟩ ↑as when he↓ pleased ... Tilsit, ⟨and⟩ at Paris, and at Erfurt↑.↓⟨; and, as the no-

tary Raguideau had dissuaded Josephine from marrying the poor
general of artillery, by saying, "he has nothing but his cloak and his
sword," Napoleon took pains to send for Raguideau, on his corona-
tion-day, and said to him, — "Well, have I nothing but my cloak and
sword now?"⟩ ¶ We cannot
      [See *JMN*, IX, 156–157.]

141.33 us how ↑much↓ may be
141.37 I should ⟨almost⟩ cite him⟨, until ambition drove him mad,⟩ ↑in his
        earlier years↓ as a model
142.2   force, ⟨unattainable to common men;⟩ in any ... exercise of ⟨plain⟩
        commonsense
142.8   military men, ⟨⟨in Europe,⟩⟩ that there
142.11 it is, ⟨in⟩at all times
142.14 we so ⟨lyingly⟩ ↑volubly↓ commend ... presentiments. ⟨But⟩ Bona-
        parte
142.17 world ⟨, to be sure,⟩ treated ... all the ⟨old⟩ impediments
142.20 difficulty↑," ⟨he says,⟩ ↑the remar[[ks,]]↓ "↓in the profession
142.24 commonsense ⟨, acting with his sharp observation,⟩ is what
142.32 the air." ⟨Another example is⟩ ↑Read↓ his account ↑, too,↓ of the way
        ... battles,⟨" he says, "⟩a moment
143.3   handful. ↑You see that↓ ⟨[¶] You see that⟩ two armies
        [A space of several lines was originally left between "handful" and
        the following words.]
143.8   addition." ¶ ⟨We have not sufficiently characterised⟩ ⟨t⟩This deputy
        ... century ⟨, until we have noticed his⟩ ↑added to his gifts a↓ capac-
        ity ... topics, ⟨quite removed from ↑this↓ ordinary themes of war and
        government. He was highly intellectual, and⟩ ↑He↓ delighted in ⟨dis-
        cussing⟩ ↑running through↓ the range
143.13 Egypt, ⟨one of his pleasures was⟩ ↑he liked↓ after dinner
143.14 He gave ⟨out the subjects,⟩ ↑a subject,↓ and the discussions ⟨most fre-
        quently⟩ turned
143.21 talking o⟨n⟩f religion
143.26 inexorable. ⟨He⟩ ↑To the philosophes he↓ readily yielded ⟨, in ⟨some⟩
        his discourse ⟨ ‖ ... ‖ ⟩with infidels, all⟩ ↑all↓ that was proved
143.29 on deck, ⟨with some persons arguing in favour⟩ ↑amid a clatter↓ of
        materialism, Bonaparte ⟨raised his hand to heaven, and⟩ point⟨ing⟩ed
        to the stars, ↑and↓ said, "You
143.33 slighted; ⟨he said,⟩ "they were
144.4   filthy ⟨preparations and⟩ mixtures
144.6   taken ⟨together⟩collectively, are more
144.15 subject. ⟨Far⟩ the most agreeable ... Egypt. [¶] ⟨The most grateful
        part of the picture of his life are these hours⟩ ↑⟨There are⟩ He had
        hours↓ of thought and wisdom, ⟨when, out of sight of blood and
        power and money,⟩ ⟨in⟩In intervals

373

144.19 genius, ⟨with a taste for all excellence, — and,⟩ directing ... truth, and ↑the↓ impatience ... in war. ⟨He was then a fine example of the universality of genius.⟩ He ⟨delighted in⟩ ↑could enjoy↓ every play of invention, ⟨in⟩ a romance, ⟨in⟩ a bon⟨-⟩mot, as well as ⟨in⟩ a stratagem

144.22 fascinate ⟨and affright⟩ Josephine

144.26 [¶] I ⟨have described⟩ ↑call↓ Napoleon ⟨as⟩ the agent ... society; ⟨that is,⟩ of the throng

144.28 world, ⟨pursuing a material success,⟩ aiming to be rich. ⟨These powers and gifts were the claims by which he held his agency, and drew the aspiring to his party.⟩ He was ... destroyer of ⟨old⟩ prescription, the

144.29 [The words "internal," "improver," "liberal," "radical," and "inventor" originally were capitalized.]

144.33 Rome ⟨the centre of⟩and Austria, ⟨the⟩ centres of

144.37 iron, ⟨and⟩ the vain

145.4 history ⟨so⟩ bright ... constituents: ⟨We must not be surprised, if⟩ he had

145.6 sorry that ↑the↓ brilliant

145.8 it is ⟨deeply⟩ treacherous ... breaking or ⟨the⟩ weakening

145.10 of this ⟨unscrupulous⟩ champion ... simply ⟨the highest external success⟩ ↑a brilliant career↓, without

145.16 unjust to ⟨all⟩ his generals

145.21 paper, ⟨the⟩ his "Moniteurs," ... believed; and, ⟨⟨what is ⟨most extraordinary⟩ ↑worse↓,⟩⟩ ↑worse,↓ he sat ... falsifying ⟨the⟩ facts and dates and characters↑,↓ ⟨of his history, studying to impose on men⟩ ↑and giving to history↓ a theatrical

145.26 breathes ⟨at all⟩ of generosity

145.35 theory of ⟨moving men⟩ ↑influence↓ is not ... are two ⟨ways of⟩levers for moving men

146.9 steal, ⟨and⟩ slander, ⟨and⟩ assassinate, ⟨and⟩ drown, and

146.12 [The colons that follow "perfidious" and "cards" were inserted to replace deleted semicolons.]

146.15 intelligence ⟨respecting⟩concerning the men

146.19 women ⟨without respect and⟩ with ⟨disgusting⟩ ↑low↓ familiarity

146.24 through all ⟨this immense⟩ ↑the circles of↓ power

146.26 rogue: ⟨And⟩ ↑and↓ he fully

146.35 seed; ⟨for⟩because both parties
[The word under "because" may be "by," but "for" seems more probable.]

147.2 Bonaparte ⟨rightly⟩ may be

147.4 The counter⟨party⟩-revolution, the counterparty ... aims. [¶] ⟨This instructive history has its perfect moral.⟩ Here was ... intellect ⟨unsupported, and, if you will, untrammelled by⟩ ↑without↓ conscience

147.16 attempt ⟨itself⟩ was in principle

147.18 with him: ⟨But⟩ ↑but↓ when men
147.22 Men ⟨soon⟩ found that ... other men. ⟨I can compare that egotism to nothing but⟩ ↑It resembled↓ the torpedo ⟨or electric eel⟩, which ⟨is said to⟩ inflict↑s↓ a succession
147.28 victim. So ⟨the perpetual tendency of⟩ this exorbitant egotist ⟨was to⟩ narrow↑ed↓, ⟨and⟩ impoverish↑ed↓, and absorb↑ed↓ the ⟨whole⟩ power
147.31 1814, was, ↑"Enough of him;"↓ "assez de Bonaparte." ⟨Enough of Bo⟩ [¶] It was ... fault. ⟨h⟩He did all

VII. GOETHE

151.2   secretary, ⟨of nature and of men,⟩ who is ... works. ⟨This⟩ ↑His↓ office
151.7   pebble, ⟨the hair,⟩ goes attended
151.8   rolling ⟨sto⟩rock ⟨has left⟩ ↑leaves↓ its scratches
151.14 face. ⟨[¶] Nature reports to the intelligent.⟩ The air
        [A line is drawn from "face" to "The air" to show that a new paragraph should not begin here.]
151.16 hints, which ⟨, in proportion to the skill of the observer, declare innumerable secrets.⟩ ↑speak to the intelligent.↓ ¶ In nature
151.22 which it record⟨s⟩ed is alive
151.25 a new ⟨manner⟩order. The facts
152.1   the eminent // ⟨↑eminent↓⟩ experiences, ⟨⟨and which is a compendium or digest of history⟩. ⟨And these things, like plants, all turn their heads toward the light, and await their second appearing in the world of art⟩. [¶]⟩ The man
        [A line is drawn from "experiences" to "The man" to show that a new paragraph should not begin here.]
152.3   lies ⟨like⟩as a load
152.6   seed ⟨, picks up every⟩ ↑and↓ peachstone, ⟨and puts it in his pocket to plant. That is⟩ his vocation ⟨in the world,⟩ ↑is↓ to be
152.8   model, ⟨which is to⟩ ↑and↓ sit↑s↓ for its
152.10 things ⟨⟨rebuke literature, and⟩⟩ are undescribable ↑ineffable↓. He believes
        [Although "ineffable" is written just above "undescribable," the latter is not deleted and appears in the 1850 and all later editions.]
152.12 Ghost↑,↓ ⟨itself⟩ or attempt it. Nothing so broad, ⟨nothing⟩ so subtle, ⟨nothing⟩ ↑or↓ so dear
152.15 reported. In ⟨every⟩ conversation, in ⟨every⟩ calamity
152.20 angry, ⟨then⟩ I can pray ... fine ⟨pieces⟩ ↑strokes↓ of eloquence, ⟨and fiction, it⟩ ↑they↓ might recall
152.25 victories. ⟨Each emancipating thought, each agitating passion reveals

to⟩ ↑A new thought or a crisis of passion apprises↓ him that

[The two deleted phrases have the numbers "2" and "1" written below them to indicate transposition of order and are underlined lightly.]

152.28 pen? no; ⟨⟨true to his art,⟩⟩ he ⟨instantly⟩ begins ↑again↓ to describe ... save some ⟨one⟩ ↑true↓ word↑.↓ ⟨of the heavenly language.⟩ Nature

152.36 significant ⟨enough⟩ of the aim of nature, but ⟨this⟩ is ⟨low;⟩ ↑mere↓ stenography

152.38 office. ⟨I find a provision in the constitution of the world⟩ for the class of scholars or writers, ⟨⟨for the theorist,⟩ for men who share the powers of the philosopher and of the poet or painter,⟩ ↑namely,↓ who see

[For the first deleted passage, compare the first sentence of this essay.]

153.4 turns. ⟨⟨In all the tasks and endeavours of men in reference to all that is permanent and causal, we are made to feel that⟩⟩ Nature has

153.6 things. ⟨The scholar⟩ ↑He↓ is no permissive

153.10 cheer him ⟨on to his work⟩. There is

153.16 incitements, ⟨he has⟩ ↑there is↓, on the ... gift↑.↓ ⟨⟨in society.⟩ He is the publisher of beauty and order, and diffuser of cheerfulness among men. ⟨[¶]⟩ Scholars are the sane men in our Bedlam.⟩ Society

[A line is drawn from "men" to "Scholars" to show that a new paragraph should not begin here.]

153.25 insanity ⟨only⟩by an equal ... man have ⟨so⟩ ↑the↓ comprehensive ⟨an⟩ eye that ⟨he⟩ can replace this isolated prodigy in its right ⟨place⟩ neighborhood and bearings, ⟨it loses instantly all⟩ ↑the↓ illusion ↑vanishes,↓ and the

153.33 people, ⟨at the present time,⟩ thrown on ... heed it. ⟨⟨He should be apprised of it beforehand, and look it in the face.⟩⟩ In this country, the ⟨whole⟩ emphasis of ... man, and ⟨every scholar is sure to hear⟩ the solid portion of the community ↑is↓ named with

154.5 caucus, ⟨or⟩and the practising

154.8 strain ⟨than this I speak of⟩ with a life

154.10 former. ⟨All⟩ ⟨m⟩Mankind have ... said by ↑the↓ hermit ⟨and⟩ ↑or↓ monk

154.13 certain partiality, a ⟨certain⟩ headiness, and

154.18 was to be ⟨only⟩ an experiment

154.20 friends ⟨hold on⟩ ↑cleave↓ to the form

154.22 although ⟨he⟩ ↑each↓ prates of spirit, there is ⟨spirit⟩no spirit, but

154.30 negation. ⟨[¶]⟩ The ⟨wise⟩ Hindoos

[A line is drawn from "negation" to "The" to show that a new paragraph should not begin here.]

154.36 great ⟨and high⟩ action must draw ⟨deeply⟩ on the spiritual

155.2   circumstance. [¶] ⟨I ought to say that ⟨it is not⟩⟩ ↑(t)This disparagement ⟨does⟩ ↑will↓ not come↓ from the leaders↑,↓⟨of the so-called
practical class, that this disparagement comes,⟩ but from
    [The first version probably was, "I ought to say that it is not from
the leaders of the so-called practical class, that this disparagement
comes, but from"; the second version, "I ought to say that this disparagement does not come from the leaders of the so-called practical
class, but from"; and the third as in the 1850 and later editions. It is
not certain whether "so-called" is hyphenated or written solid.]

155.6   sympathy with ↑the↓ speculative

155.9   faculty? ⟨but⟩is he of the movement ⟨is⟩? is he of

155.12   That is ⟨all men ask⟩ all that Talleyrand

155.16   whether it be ⟨an⟩ ↑orator,↓ artist, ⟨a mechanic,⟩ ↑craftsman,↓ or ⟨a
king.⟩ ↑or captain.↓ ¶ Society

155.19   accomplishments. ⟨[¶]⟩ Still the
    [A line is drawn between the words to cancel the beginning of a
new paragraph.]

155.21   A pound ⟨always⟩ passes for

155.22   person, ⟨through his joy in truth, and his impatience to make it
known. Then⟩ he wrote

155.25   nations ⟨in⟩to new life

155.29   necessity↑.↓ ⟨than his own. [¶]⟩ But how
    [A line is drawn from "necessity" to "But" to show that a new
paragraph should not begin here.]

155.30   himself in the ⟨anonymous⟩ ⟨↑selfindulgent↓⟩ crowd . . . opinion of a
↑reckless↓ public↑;↓ ⟨as reckless, as he; a jumping jack; a penny a
liner;⟩ when he must ⟨ ‖ . . . ‖ ⟩sustain with shameless advocacy ⟨a
bad⟩some bad government, or must bark ⟨like a dog⟩ all the

156.5   half, ⟨⟨its genius,⟩⟩ its poet is Goethe, a man ⟨entirely⟩ ↑quite↓ domesticated

156.10   spread itself↑,↓ ⟨over the world,⟩ and has smoothed

156.13   poet, but ⟨a hundred⟩ ↑scores of↓ poetic writers: no Columbus, but ⟨a
thousand⟩ ↑hundreds of↓ post captains

156.16   number ↑of↓ ⟨of⟩clever parliamentary

156.18   learned m⟨e⟩an, but learned

156.27   dispose ↑of them↓ with ease↑.↓ ⟨of these materials.⟩ a ⟨great⟩ manly
mind . . . encrusted, ⟨very⟩ easily . . . these, and ⟨by⟩to draw . . . in full
⟨habitual⟩ communion

156.33   part in ↑the↓ world↑'s↓ affairs . . . cheered ⟨in⟩a French

157.2   work of ⟨a man⟩ ↑one↓ who ⟨showed⟩found himself the

157.9   but if ⟨he⟩ ↑one↓ should chance

157.12   elaborate ⟨designs⟩ ↑forms↓, to which . . . observation. ⟨But⟩ ⟨t⟩This reflective and critical wisdom ⟨only⟩ makes

157.16   under this ⟨genius⟩ ↑plague↓ of microscopes

157.20 wit, the ⟨ages⟩ past and the present ⟨century,⟩ ↑ages↓ and their . . .
thinking ⟨lie⟩ ↑are↓ ⟨there⟩ dissolved

157.22 head! ⟨They⟩ ↑The Greeks↓ said, that

157.27 journeys with ⟨him⟩us lends its

157.30 population, ⟨wide culture,⟩ compact

157.33 this man's ⟨wit⟩mind had ample
[Emerson had written "this man's wit" two manuscript pages earlier (157.20).]

157.34 He had ⟨, which is the material fact,⟩ a power

157.35 clothed ⟨life⟩ ↑our modern existence↓ with poetry. . . . Genius of ⟨our⟩
life

158.5 rich in ⟨New York or⟩ Liverpool, ⟨Frankfort⟩ or the Hague, than once
in ↑Rome or↓ Antioch↑.↓ ⟨or Rome.⟩ He sought

158.15 omitting ⟨, ⟨one would say,⟩⟩ a great

158.16 explained the ⟨true⟩ distinction

158.29 organ, and ⟨ma⟩any other ↑organ↓ into a

158.33 the flower and ↑the↓ seed

159.1 head." ↑In optics,↓ // ⟨[¶] In optics,⟩ again, he

159.13 whatever else, ⟨⟨has this convincing reality, and⟩⟩ refuses

159.20 committed." — ⟨so⟩ ↑So↓ he flies . . . of this ⟨Imp.⟩ ↑imp.↓ He shall

159.28 that in ⟨throngs⟩ ↑crowds,↓ or in solitude . . . found th⟨e⟩at the portrait

159.31 found ⟨, shall I say,⟩ that the essence

159.33 applied↑,↓ ⟨to the senses⟩as always there is a tendency, to the service
of the senses: ⟨And⟩ ↑and↓ he flung

160.1 of translations, ⟨of⟩ criticism, ⟨of⟩ dramas, ⟨of⟩ lyric and ⟨o⟩every other
description of poems, ⟨of⟩ literary

160.13 into life and manners ⟨, into⟩ ↑and↓ characters

160.18 Lovers of ⟨r⟩light reading

160.20 with ⟨a⟩ ↑the↓ higher hope ⟨, expecting⟩ to read

160.22 complain. ⟨In ⟨the last⟩ ↑a noted↓⟩ ↑We had an↓ English romance
↑there not long ago↓, ⟨I suppose, most readers felt a sad surprise, that,
in a book⟩ professing . . . England,' ↑in which↓ the only reward of
virtue ⟨that genius can devise,⟩ is a seat

160.29 story, ⟨and⟩ the ⟨rise⟩ ↑characters↓ of the hero and heroine ⟨, they lose
rank and title,⟩ ↑expand at a rate that shivers the porcelain chess
table of aristocratic conventions; they quit the society and habits of
their ra[[nk,]] they↓ lose their
[The comma after "heroine" was changed to a caret.]

160.35 no longer ⟨heeds⟩ ↑answers to↓ his own

161.11 argument ⟨externally considered⟩ is the passage

161.17 courage. ⟨The ardent and holy⟩ [¶] The ardent and holy Novalis . . .
"thoroughly modern and prosaic, the
[The numbers "2" and "1," written below "modern" and "pro-

saic" respectively to indicate transposition, are clear but quite small
and could easily be overlooked, as they presumably were in 1850.]

161.23 dreaming:" — ⟨And⟩ ↑and↓ yet, — what is also characteristic, No-
        valis ↑soon↓ returned

161.26 Goethe ⟨among the crowd of writers is a property⟩ for French and
        English readers is a property which

161.31 there is ⟨perhaps⟩ ↑even↓ a greater

161.32 talent ⟨try to⟩ write from talent. ↑It↓ ⟨T⟩is enough

161.35 filled in a ↑lively and↓ creditable way. ⟨⟨But⟩ ⟨t⟩The⟩ ↑The↓ German

162.8   holding th⟨ese⟩ings because they

162.11 burden on his mind, — ↑the↓ burden

162.14 known↑.↓ ⟨as honestly as he can.⟩ What signifies ... stammers, ⟨in his
        ⟨speech⟩words,⟩ that his voice

162.17 it would ⟨come forth⟩ ↑speak↓. If not

162.26 men: his ⟨voice⟩force and terror

162.30 poet, ⟨may have devoted much time to the study of his verses,⟩ with-
        out any

162.31 Plato and ⟨Epictetus⟩ ↑Proclus↓, does not afford ⟨the smallest⟩ ↑a↓
        presumption

162.34 subjects; ⟨and⟩ the student

162.36 application to ⟨Germany↑.↓ ⟨also.⟩⟩ ↑Berlin and Munich.↓ This ear-
        nestness ... talent, ⟨⟨by the mere circumstance of being in the right.⟩⟩
        // [¶?] Hence almost

163.6   character ⟨⟨or constitution⟩⟩ to the topic

163.10 better ⟨behind it⟩ ↑in view.↓ It awakens ⟨instead⟩my curiosity He has
        ⟨somewhat better⟩⟨this⟩ ↑the↓ formidable independence which con-
        verse with truth gives; ⟨that,⟩ — hear you, or forbear,⟨ — ⟩ his fact
        [The words "this formidable" were written over "somewhat bet-
        ter"; then "this" was crossed out and "the" written above it.]

163.17 not say ⟨of Goethe⟩ that ⟨he⟩ ↑Goethe↓ ascended ... spoken↑.↓↓⟨to
        men.⟩ He has ... unity; he ⟨seems⟩ ↑is↓ incapable of a ⟨total⟩ selfsur-
        render

163.21 There are ⟨nob[?]⟩writers

163.27 selfdenial, ⟨yielding to nothing but truth,⟩ and having ⟨that⟩ one
        test

163.29 by him ⟨only⟩ for that ↑only↓; ⟨all⟩ rank, ⟨all⟩ privileges, ... being it-
        self. [¶] ⟨In this mind, he wrote his autobiography, under the title of
        "Poetry and Truth out of my Life." The genius of the book is the
        idea ⟨now⟩ familiar to the world, through the German mind, but a
        novelty to England ↑Old and New↓ when that book appeared,⟩ //
        [63] He is the type
        [The deleted material at the bottom of page [62] is repeated (with
        slight changes) on [66], and appears at 164.15–18 of the printed text.
        Probably pages [63–66] were inserted between [62] and [67]. In the

left margin on [62], between the line ending "being itself" and the
next (deleted) line, there is a large angle bracket ⟩ about half an inch
high.]

163.34   but with ⟨the⟩ peremptory . . . moment ⟨thu[?]⟩ ⟨affected⟩ ↑prejudiced↓
by his

164.7   worm out ⟨a⟩ ↑the↓ secret

164.9   goodwill cannot,↑ — ↓were it

164.26   selection of ⟨all⟩ the incidents

164.30   with us a "⟨l⟩Life of Goethe

165.2   ["Theory of" is underlined, but the underlining is deleted.]

165.14   fragmentary; ↑a writer of occasional poems, and of↓ an encyclopae-
dia of sentences. ⟨a writer of occasional poems.⟩ When he

165.19   parties, ⟨or⟩ leaves from

165.21   cohesion to: and ⟨so,⟩ ↑hence↓ notwithstanding . . . we have ⟨whole⟩
volumes . . . Xenien, &c. [¶] ⟨The⟩ I suppose the

165.28   did not ⟨sufficiently⟩ ↑quite↓ trust

165.33   afraid ⟨or ashamed⟩ to live

166.2   by it, is ⟨certainly⟩ higher

166.4   this is ↑very↓ truth↑,↓ ⟨itself,⟩ and has

166.6   dignity. [¶] ⟨I find then the genius of⟩ Goethe ⟨instructive as one who⟩
coming into ⟨⟨what was called⟩⟩ an overcivilized . . . talent ⟨seemed⟩
↑was↓ oppressed

166.11   subservient↑.↓ ⟨⟨by no other arts than reliance on truth.⟩⟩ I join

166.15   time. This ⟨great⟩ cheerful . . . provocation, ⟨but⟩ drawing

166.25   ages. ⟨His courage should⟩ ↑Goethe↓ teach↑es↓ courage, ⟨It behooves
us to know⟩ ↑and↓ the equivalence of ↑all↓ times; that the ⟨differences
and⟩ disadvantages

166.27   Genius ⟨is never far off,⟩ hovers with

166.30   affectionately ⟨Tis time the chosen experiences of this very hour, what
is grave↑st↓, wise↑st↓, hol⟨y⟩iest, glad↑dest↓, were collected that⟩ we
⟨should⟩ ↑too must↓ write
    [It is not certain whether or not the final "st" of "gravest" and
"wisest" were later insertions.]

166.31   world⟨,⟩. ⟨such as ⟨should⟩ ↑shall↓ be no provincial record, but ⟨should⟩
↑shall↓ open the history of the planet, bind all tendencies, and dwarf
the old epics, and philosophies, by a truth more ample and divine.⟩
The secret

PARALLEL PASSAGES

Even Emerson's earliest editors recognized the value of the journals and notebooks he called his "savings bank" (*JMN,* IV, 250), in which he deposited thoughts, outlines, quotations, and so forth for further use in lectures, essays, or other forms of literary production. A given passage or reference might appear several times in the journals of subsequent years, in manuscripts of lectures prepared for oral delivery, and in the more formal addresses and essays. Sometimes the passage used appeared in the new context almost verbatim, but more often it would be altered in varying degrees for thought-content or style, and often only the general idea was carried over. A prose work by Emerson must therefore be regarded as a composition — in the sense that one speaks of musical composition or the composition of a painting — rather than as a piece of exposition or argument developed according to a set plan or logical outline. The process of assembling the elements of a composition and then organizing and revising them to produce the effect that he desired was an art which he developed slowly. In the 1820s, when he began to keep notebooks and journals, they served mainly as a place to record thoughts and impressions which he did not wish to forget; but in the 1830s and 1840s, when he was gradually developing as a professional lecturer, orator, and essayist, they became more nearly the instruments of the art of composition itself. He reminded himself to observe the transformations of his words from journal to essay, as when he noted after an anecdote used in "The Poet": "See how this passage has been used in *Essays II series* p. 26" (*JMN,* VIII, 316). He early formed the habit of drawing a diagonal or vertical line through any sentence or paragraph when he carried it over in whole or in part into either oral lecture or written prose, but this reminder did not necessarily prevent him from using it again if a new context required it.

By the 1840s Emerson had also developed the habit of indexing the volumes of his journals and notebooks, even preparing an "Index Major," an "Index Minor," and special topical indexes covering several journals in order to have his accumulated resources more easily available for current work. These indexes are part of the Houghton Library's collection of Emerson material, which includes, listed here by Houghton catalogue numbers, the following volumes: (104) "Index Minor 1843"; (104a) "Index Summary"; (106) "Index Major 1847"; (107) "Index II"; (107a) "Index Platoniana"; (110) "Index Psi"; and (131) "Index Minor [A]." Emerson's outlines and working notes in these index volumes show how he sifted through previous journals for valuable material and how he used that process of review and revision as a spur to writing. We have appended to the Parallel Passages a list of the outlines for chapters of *Representative Men* that appear in *JMN*, XII, a volume containing several index and lecture notebooks.

Most of Emerson's previous editors accepted each finished work as Emerson released it for print without inquiring consistently into the process of its composition, even though the sources for such an inquiry had been carefully preserved (and cross-referenced) by Emerson himself; by James E. Cabot, his first editor; and by his son Edward. Edward Waldo Emerson was probably the first editor to become aware of the importance of identifying earlier versions of the more finished work, and he marked on the manuscripts of the journals, notebooks, and lectures such later uses of any given passage as he could recall from his well-stocked memory of his father's thought and writing. The significance of Emerson's method can now be more fully appreciated as a result of the restudy, undertaken by professionally trained editors, of all his surviving manuscripts. This study has resulted in new editions of the journals and miscellaneous notebooks, the letters, and the lectures. The sermons are now in the process of being edited, but they are too early to be much involved in the process of composing the essays.

In the following list of used or parallel passages, the findings of recent scholarship have been brought together and collated. Manuscript lectures not yet published are identified by their titles. Even though it is obvious that many more parallel passages will be subsequently identified, we now have enough material for deeper and fuller examinations of Emerson's art and thought than were formerly possible.

I. USES OF GREAT MEN

10.31 It opens the delicious ... mental habit. *JMN*, XI, 181; *W*, VIII, 18.

10.32 We are as elastic ... floor of the Pit. *JMN*, V, 370; VIII, 102; XI, 181; *CW*, III, 161; *W*, VIII, 231–232.

11.4 This class serve ... to see them. *JMN*, XI, 170.

11.20 If a wise man ... their resources. *JMN*, IX, 258–259.

11.28 But nature brings ... law of nature. *JMN*, IX, 400; X, 77; XII, 520, 599.

11.33 When nature removes ... western general. *JMN*, XI, 23.

12.7 Life is a scale ... wide intervals. Cf. *JMN*, IX, 161; XII, 526.

12.12 We swim, ... fool's cap too long.' Cf. *JMN*, XII, 570.

12.29 "Ever their phantoms ... words of good." *JMN*, IX, 24; X, 373.

13.7 the *peau d'âne*, ... for every wish. *JMN*, VIII, 284; XII, 537, 574; *L*, III, 221.

13.8 I go to a convention ... forget the clock. *JMN*, IX, 163; XII, 549, 569.

13.24 Every child of the Saxon ... be first. *JMN*, IX, 218, 350; X, 90; XII, 528; XIV, 419.

13.31 "Darlings of the human race." *JMN*, VI, 209.

14.11 Nature never spares ... every day. Cf. *JMN*, VIII, 200–201.

14.21 Is it not a rare ... fastest of cements? *JMN*, IX, 265–266.

14.32 This is he ... way we were going. *JMN*, IX, 340.

15.3 We are all wise ... the contagion. *JMN*, XII, 528, 549, 568.

15.8 Men resemble ... their progenitors. *JMN*, IX, 286.

15.9 It is observed ... know them apart. *JMN*, IX, 310.

15.23 We learn of our contemporaries ... her husband. *JMN*, IX, 323.

16.6 Perhaps Voltaire ... man's name again." *JMN*, VIII, 337; cf. *CEC*, 371 (Carlyle).

16.11 The centripetence augments the centrifugence. *JMN*, IX, 276; XI, 94; *W*, VII, 146; VIII, 223.

16.14 Every genius is defended ... unavailableness. *JMN*, IX, 310.

16.21 It seems ... garments of the soul. *JMN*, IX, 282.

16.30 you are you, and I am I. *JMN*, X, 471; XI, 370; *Conduct of Life* (1860 ed. only), 238.3.

16.35 Nothing is more ... social and interfering. *JMN*, IX, 224; XII, 577.

17.4 We rightly speak ... second thought! *JMN*, IX, 51.

17.7 Therefore they are not ... elsewhere. *JMN*, IX, 73.

17.21 The microscope ... their independence. *JMN*, IX, 300.

17.33 yonder poor Paddy ... wheelbarrow; *JMN*, IV, 351; V, 228; IX, 65; XII, 328.

17.34 Why are the masses, ... hire and kill? *JMN*, IX, 199; XII, 534.

18.9 Men who know ... thought to himself. *JMN*, IX, 379; X, 78; cf. *W*, VIII, 320.

18.18 As to what we call ... no common men. *JMN,* IX, 346; XII, 529, 569.

18.19 All men are ... nobility and exaltation. *JMN,* IX, 453.

18.21 Fair play, and ... have won them! *W,* V, 78.

18.25 The heroes ... relatively great; Cf. *JMN,* XII, 529.

18.32 Nature never sends ... another soul. *JMN,* X, 105, 370.

19.2 The history of the universe ... is mnemonical. *JMN,* IX, 243; XII, 578.

19.5 Could we one day ... compose! *JMN,* XI, 134.

19.26 Once you saw phœnixes; ... delegated quality. *JMN,* IX, 171–172; XII, 527, 553.

20.5 In the moment ... as an effect. *JMN,* IX, 334.

II. PLATO

23.5 A discipline ... men of thought. *JMN,* IX, 245.

23.9 Great havoc ... twenty-two hundred years. *JMN,* IX, 216; X, 478.

23.12 every brisk young man ... good things. *JMN,* IX, 215; X, 478.

23.18 St Augustine, ... from his thesis. *JMN,* IX, 216; X, 478.

23.22 Plato is philosophy, ... his categories. *JMN,* IX, 179.

24.8 This citizen ... sectional lines. *JMN,* IX, 248.

24.11 As they say that Helen ... related to her. *JMN,* IV, 389; VI, 199; *EL,* I, 101.

24.17 It is singular ... Raffaele, Shakspeare. *JMN,* IX, 184, 252; XII, 562; XIV, 64(?), 134(?).

24.35 Every book is a quotation; *JMN,* IX, 112; X, 386.

25.12 Every man who ... powers of a poet. *JMN,* IX, 304.

25.19 Great geniuses ... intellectual performances. *JMN,* VII, 248–249; IX, 266.

25.25 He ground them all into paint. *CW,* III, 141.

26.2 and died ... at eighty-one years. *JMN,* X, 479.

26.16 Here is the germ ... abiding traits. *JMN,* IX, 215–216; X, 478; *W,* VII, 198.

26.29 Children cry, ... such in philosophy. *JMN,* IX, 324–325.

27.25 Then the partialists, ... or water, *JMN,* III, 363.

27.28 At last, comes Plato, ... and intelligence. *JMN,* IX, 325, 332.

27.31 "He shall be ... divide and define." *JMN,* V, 79; VI, 209; X, 483; *EL,* I, 378.

27.35 Two cardinal facts ... and, 2. Variety. *JMN,* IX, 303.

28.8 "In the midst ... unperishable being," *JMN,* IX, 292.

28.19 The Proteus is as nimble ... of matter. *JMN,* IX, 267–268.

28.30 The Same, the Same; ... unimportant. *JMN,* VII, 428; IX, 224, 232, 322; *CW,* III, 105.

28.33 "You are fit," . . . nor am I, I." *JMN*, IX, 319–321.

29.18 As if he had said, . . . nature. *JMN*, IX, 322.

29.24 If speculation . . . executive deity. *JMN*, IX, 307, 332–333; cf. XII, 572.

30.8 The country of unity, . . . delighted in boundaries. *JMN*, IX, 287, 329; cf. X, 90.

30.17 European civility is the triumph of talent. *JMN*, IX, 189, 333; XII, 528.

30.19 Pericles, Athens, . . . of an excess. *JMN*, IX, 333.

31.4 Plato came to join . . . in his brain. *JMN*, IX, 333.

31.9 In short, a balanced . . . be small. *JMN*, IX, 328.

31.18 The wonderful synthesis . . . medal of Jove; *EL*, III, 195.

31.23 The balanced soul . . . fishmongers. *JMN*, IX, 328; cf. 40.24 below.

31.30 He cannot forgive . . . their own. *JMN*, IX, 331.

31.37 The seashore, . . . his philosophy. *JMN*, IX, 279–280, 296, 330; *W*, VIII, 289.

32.27 "All things . . . everything beautiful." *JMN*, VIII, 219, 364; IX, 280; X, 487; *W*, X, 271; "Discourse at Middlebury College."

33.4 According to the old sentence, . . . style of Plato." *JMN*, II, 246; IX, 185, 329.

In *JMN*, II, 246, Emerson was copying a passage by his aunt, Mary Moody Emerson.

33.25 he had read . . . "Be not too bold." *JMN*, IX, 294–295, 329.

33.34 He has finished . . . literary master. *JMN*, IX, 185, 329.

33.37 As the rich man . . . the fit word. *JMN*, VIII, 528.

34.8 Socrates' profession . . . good nicknames. *JMN*, IX, 233; X, 113; XI, 135.

34.15 "For philosophy . . . corrupts the man." *JMN*, XI, 128.

34.21 he paints and quibbles . . . sea and land. *JMN*, IX, 29; X, 165.

34.22 The admirable earnest . . . contests here." *JMN*, XI, 136.

34.32 He is a great . . . poetic raptures. *JMN*, VII, 334–335.

36.31 "The whole of life, . . . discourses as these." *JMN*, X, 476; XIII, 419; *W*, VII, 179.

37.17 In the doctrine . . . artificers." *JMN*, IX, 287; X, 481.

37.22 The Koran is explicit . . . embrace it." *JMN*, IX, 285; XII, 569.

37.29 A happier example . . . it may happen." *L*, VI, 27–28.

38.29 A key to the method . . . bisected line. *JMN*, IX, 337, 346.

39.18 "When an artificer, . . . beautiful." *JMN*, X, 481.

39.29 Body cannot teach wisdom, God only. *JMN*, X, 477.

39.37 Socrates and Plato . . . entirely separate. *JMN*, IX, 215.

40.7 The players personated . . . stone jugs. *JMN*, X, 482.

40.17 In short, he was . . . *an old one. JMN*, X, 482.

40.24 illustrations from cocks . . . unnameable offices; — *JMN*, IV, 38; VIII, 108; X, 472; cf. 31.25 above.

40.26 He had a Franklin-like . . . easily reach. *JMN*, X, 482.

40.36   He is very poor; . . . went barefooted; *JMN*, X, 87.
42.5   Socrates entered . . . everything you say." *JMN*, III, 107; X, 483.
42.22   The strange synthesis . . . contact is necessary. *JMN*, IX, 293; X, 485–486; cf. VIII, 369.
43.3   The qualities of sugar . . . with salt. *JMN*, IX, 380.
43.9   He is charged . . . ideas to matter. *JMN*, IX, 331.
43.15   The longest wave . . . question from him. *JMN*, IX, 279, 329.
44.9   A chief structure . . . our life. *JMN*, IX, 248.
44.18   a mile . . . and sixty yards. *JMN*, X, 478 (n. 45).

PLATO: NEW READINGS

45.1   The publication . . . press has yielded. *JMN*, XI, 137.
45.10   The human being . . . tedious preparation. *JMN*, XI, 166–167.
45.20   She waited . . . can be suspected; *JMN*, V, 72; IX, 124; *CW*, III, 104–105.
46.5   Plato's fame does not . . . the reason. *JMN*, XI, 148.
46.31   decomposition is recomposition, . . . new creation; *JMN*, XI, 173; XIII, 291; XV, 353, 428; *W*, VIII, 204; X, 248.
47.3   the ring of Gyges; *JMN*, II, 281–282; V, 147.
47.7   his soliform eye *JMN*, III, 211; IX, 215; X, 474.
47.12   Socrates's belief . . . laws above. *JMN*, VI, 32; XV, 323; XVI, 66; *W*, VIII, 223.
47.20   that the sinner ought to covet punishment; *JMN*, XI, 135.
47.21   that the lie . . . than homicide; *JMN*, IX, 215.
47.23   that the soul . . . true opinions; *JMN*, VI, 95, 191; *EL*, I, 128; *CW*, III, 159.
47.30   the fine which the good . . . a worse man. *JMN*, IX, 184, 266; X, 475; *W*, VII, 62.
47.31   that his guards . . . which they need. *JMN*, IX, 184; X, 475.
47.35   This secondsight . . . the moral elements. *JMN*, XI, 92, 149.
48.32   He wrote on the scale . . . in nature. *JMN*, XI, 149.
49.5   All the gods . . . intellectual illustration. *JMN*, X, 480, 488; XI, 46.
49.19   the winds of ages . . . shortlived scribe. *JMN*, XI, 163.
49.26   Shakspeare is . . . makes that mean," *JMN*, VI, 83; X, 164; *EL*, I, 44; II, 35.
50.26   I am sorry . . . lie to governors. *JMN*, IX, 331.

III. SWEDENBORG

53.12   Others may build . . . keep them in awe. *JMN*, IX, 226; XI, 106; XII, 571.

53.17   For other things, . . . poetry of me. *JMN*, IX, 130, 223; XII, 526, 549, 558.

53.19   I have sometimes . . . this problem. *JMN*, VIII, 229–230; XII, 342, 554; lecture, "Recent Literary and Spiritual Influences."

54.7   In the language . . . return to us?" *JMN*, IX, 263, 284; 124.22 below.

54.13   "The realms of being . . . all are Thou." *JMN*, XII, 558.

54.15   The Koran . . . admitted with thee." *JMN*, IX, 286.

54.27   The Arabians . . . he knows, I see." *JMN*, IX, 284.

55.1   "travelling the path . . . thousands of births," *JMN*, IX, 264, 290, 317.

55.18   The ancients called it *ecstasy* . . . to think. *JMN*, XII, 558; W, VI, 116.

55.20   All religious history . . . the alone." *JMN*, VII, 254, 430; XII, 573; *EL*, III, 283, 299; *L*, II, 328, 342.

55.22   Μύεσις, the closing . . . word Mystic. *JMN*, VI, 222.

55.23   The trances . . . come to mind. *EL*, II, 90–92; *CW*, II, 167.

55.34   "Indeed it takes . . . our attribute." *JMN*, VII, 136; X, 173.

56.7   instead of porcelain, . . . or mud. *JMN*, IX, 409.

56.16   As happens in great men, . . . capacious brain. *JMN*, IX, 409; XI, 91.

56.25   Such a boy could not whistle Cf. *JMN*, II, 377.

57.3   With the like force . . . theology. *JMN*, IX, 409.

57.34   a common portrait . . . coat and wig, *JMN*, XI, 131; cf. 79.38 below.

58.8   It seems that . . . seventh planet, — *JMN*, VIII, 162.

58.19   A colossal soul, . . . is possible. *JMN*, VII, 116.

58.26   Over and above . . . a hero. *JMN*, VIII, 168; XII, 558.

58.32   One of the missouriums . . . ordinary scholars. *JMN*, IX, 310.

58.34   Our books are false . . . or egotism. *JMN*, IX, 178.

59.10   The robust Aristotelian . . . athletic philosophers. *JMN*, XI, 157.

59.22   Malpighi, following . . . minimis existit natura." *JMN*, VI, 312; IX, 410; XI, 17, 390, 393; XIII, 21; XV, 7, 280; *W*, VII, 176.

59.22   Malpighi, . . . Wolff, in Cosmology; *JMN*, IX, 410; XI, 144.

59.26   left little for . . . microscope to reveal *JMN*, VII, 112; *EL*, III, 9.

59.27   Linnæus, . . . always like herself:" *JMN*, XI, 157; XII, 555, 566.

60.13   His varied and solid . . . sun and planet. *JMN*, XI, 119–120, 180–181.

61.1   In the old . . . *always self-similar.* Cf. 59.27 above, 158.25 below.

61.9   A poetic anatomist . . . shoulders of the last. *JMN*, V, 67; X, 32; XI, 153, 154, 157.

61.31   In the brain . . . here is fruit. *JMN*, XI, 157.

61.36   We are hard . . . dæmonic and celestial natures. *JMN*, XI, 159; *W*, VIII, 335.

62.12　If one man . . . marries his grandmother. *JMN*, XI, 91.

62.17　Astronomy is excellent; . . . globes and spaces. *JMN*, XI, 154.

63.3　he has at last . . . his history. *JMN*, XI, 116–117, 180.

63.31　He knows, . . . rivers that flow in." *JMN*, XI, 91; XIV, 233.

63.35　as large a demand . . . all things. *JMN*, X, 27; XI, 117; *W*, X, 12.

64.21　"The principle . . . entire in leasts;" *JMN*, XI, 17–18; and see references for 59.22 above (first entry).

64.36　The unities of each . . . little hearts. *JMN*, VIII, 360; IX, 7, 223; cf. 129.5 below.

66.9　The fact . . . frame of things. *JMN*, IX, 346–347.

66.13　truth and nature . . . riddle writing. *JMN*, VIII, 161; cf. VI, 301.

66.17　it is known . . . as a toy. *JMN*, VII, 215.

67.33　Having adopted . . . ecstatic mode, *JMN*, XI, 180.

68.11　This design . . . real being. *EL*, III, 513–514; *L*, I, 450–451.

68.25　In the transmission . . . hose fits every hydrant. *JMN*, IX, 221, 347; XI, 18; *W*, XII, 20.

69.3　To the withered . . . every circumstance. *JMN*, IX, 345–346.

69.9　Instead of a religion . . . same laws. *JMN*, VIII, 131.

69.19　His disciples allege . . . his books. *JMN*, VII, 36; IX, 346.

69.28　His thought dwells . . . built it. *JMN*, IX, 260.

69.35　a theoretic . . . Lycurgus himself would bow. *JMN*, IX, 314.

70.25　Interiors . . . the spiritual world. *JMN*, V, 116; VI, 312.

70.27　Each Satan . . . heap of carrion. *JMN*, V, 116; VI, 311.

70.34　The ghosts . . . to cut wood. *JMN*, VI, 311.

71.7　He delivers golden . . . the youngest." *JMN*, V, 115; XIV, 277.

71.10　"The more angels, the more room:" *JMN*, VIII, 320, 337; X, 380; "Address to the Temperance Society at Harvard, Massachusetts."

71.11　"The perfection . . . love of use:" *JMN*, XI, 171.

71.14　and the truly . . . without instruction. *JMN*, VI, 315.

71.18　"It is never . . . Lord is disturbed." *JMN*, VI, 315; IX, 114; XII, 533.

71.20　The angels, . . . his science. *JMN*, VI, 314.

71.27　the Love which, . . . in Paradise; *JMN*, VII, 86.

72.8　Yet Swedenborg . . . that influence. *JMN*, VII, 532–533.

72.27　We meet . . . we parted not, *JMN*, VII, 215; *CW*, II, 126.

74.16　These books . . . images of thought. *JMN*, VIII, 224.

74.18　It requires . . . equal to his own. *JMN*, X, 162.

75.5　The universe . . . like the rest. *JMN*, VIII, 225; XII, 342; lecture, "Recent Literary and Spiritual Influences."

75.31　The vice . . . always in a church. *JMN*, IX, 121–122.

75.33　That Hebrew muse . . . in its bosom. *JMN*, IX, 418; XV, 126.

76.10　'What have I . . . the most needless.' *JMN*, VIII, 233; XII, 551.

76.17　The more coherent . . . to the purpose?" *JMN*, IX, 302.

76.21　Of all absurdities, . . . shittim-wood, *JMN*, XII, 342.

76.26   Locke said, ... adamantine limitations. *JMN*, VI, 52; IX, 337, 339.

77.12   His cardinal position ... lives with God. *JMN*, IX, 313, 314; XI, 176-177.

77.20   The less we have ... compunctions. *JMN*, VII, 518.

77.21   "That is active ... unto weariness." *JMN*, IX, 319.

77.25   Another dogma, ... makes them none." *JMN*, VIII, 62, 182-183; *CW*, III, 163.

77.29   Euripedes rightly ... makes them none." *W*, X, 313.

78.2   Burns ... and mend!" *JMN*, III, 304; IX, 79; *W*, X, 299.

78.20   and the English, ... by themselves; *W*, V, 129.

78.22   The teachings ... particulars, negative. *JMN*, VIII, 382; XII, 559.

78.24   Socrates's Genius ... dissuaded him. *JMN*, III, 106-107.

78.26   "What God is," ... Internal Check." *JMN*, IX, 291-292.

78.32   Swedenborg's revelation ... dislocation and chaos. *JMN*, XI, 119.

79.19   His Inferno ... kennels of creation. *JMN*, XI, 176.

79.32   they are all country-parsons: *JMN*, XI, 160.

79.34   Strange, scholastic ... paralyzes and repels. *JMN*, VIII, 224; XI, 179.

79.38   in gold-headed cane and peruke, Cf. 57.34 above.

80.13   It is the best ... pure genius. *JMN*, X, 114-115, 132.

80.24   He knew the grammar ... pervades his books? *JMN*, VIII, 446-447; XII, 559-560.

80.32   his books have ... gardens of the dead. *JMN*, X, 160.

80.33   In his profuse ... no beauty. Cf. *JMN*, X, 357.

81.8   He elected goodness ... and to God. *JMN*, XI, 176-177 (n. 345).

IV. MONTAIGNE

85.1   Every fact is related ... fine names beside. *JMN*, VII, 363; VIII, 82, 412; XII, 521, 572; Journal S [Salvage], page [61].

85.20   One class has ... men of genius. *JMN*, IX, 72; XII, 535.

85.25   Plotinus believes ... materialism, *JMN*, XII, 535.

86.19   Having at some time ... superfluous realizations? *JMN*, IX, 242; XII, 534.

86.28   The trade in our streets ... have reason. *EL*, II, 362-363; III, 48.

86.37   Things always bring ... in any other. *JMN*, IX, 312.

87.2   In England, ... in any other. *W*, V, 153.

87.8   Spence relates, ... man by the pound. *JMN*, XII, 61, 530.

87.19   They believe ... suspenders hold up pantaloons; *JMN*, VII, 220; XI, 47; XII, 455.

87.21   that there is ... chest of tea; *JMN*, VII, 419; *W*, VIII, 281.

87.24   that Luther . . . get well drunk. *JMN*, X, 107.

87.25   Wer nicht liebt . . . Leben lang, *JMN*, XI, 116.

87.28   "The nerves," . . . are the man." *JMN*, VI, 367; XII, 534.

87.29   My neighbor, . . . the good of it." *JMN*, XI, 46.

87.34   Life is eating us up. *JMN*, IX, 449; XV, 116.

87.34   We shall be fables presently. *JMN*, VI, 19.

88.1   [Life's well enough . . . glad to have us.] [For parallels to this passage, which is in earlier versions but not in this (*CW*) text, see the Emendation note to 88.1.]

88.3   "Ah," said my languid . . . and no matter." *JMN*, X, 246.

88.5   Our life is like . . . bundle of hay. *JMN*, IX, 201; XII, 534.

88.7   "There is so much . . . here at all." *JMN*, VI, 328; XII, 534.

88.10   I knew a philosopher . . . damned rascal." *JMN*, IX, 9, 30.

88.12   the natural corollary . . . so will I.' *JMN*, IX, 75.

88.19   He labours to plant . . . beyond his card. *JMN*, XII, 535.

88.26   You believe yourselves . . . delusions. *JMN*, IX, 295.

88.31   Neither will he . . . heads are hot, *JMN*, VIII, 249; XII, 369, 540.

89.18   Of what use . . . arguments I cannot refute? *JMN*, IX, 173; XII, 533.

89.33   And the reply . . . would repent it." *JMN*, XII, 535.

90.8   There is much to say on both sides. *JMN*, X, 84.

90.14   it is alleged . . . spirit of man, *JMN*, VIII, 406; IX, 226; XII, 533.

90.15   and the labourers . . . no thoughts." *JMN*, VIII, 38.

90.19   Excellent is culture . . . Plutarch's heroes. *JMN*, IX, 272.

91.1   He is the Considerer, *JMN*, IX, 350.

91.2   believing that a man . . . his own; *JMN*, IX, 150, 165; XII, 525, 577.

91.10   when we build . . . out of the dirt. *JMN*, VI, 50; XII, 205.

91.12   The philosophy we want . . . dwellinghouse is built. *JMN*, IX, 222–223; XII, 528, 536.

91.17   An angular, dogmatic house . . . founded on the sea. *JMN*, IX, 268.

91.20   The soul of man . . . dwellinghouse is built. *JMN*, IV, 367–368; VI, 334; VII, 376–377; *CW*, III, 18.

92.15   A single odd volume . . . written there. *JMN*, VIII, 373–374, 376.

92.21   It happened, . . . Essays of Montaigne." *JMN*, IV, 200–201, 408–409.

92.34   I heard with pleasure . . . the flyleaf. *JMN*, X, 295.

93.35   He pretends . . . by stealth. *JMN*, V, 285; XII, 533.

94.1   "Five or six . . . any man living." *JMN*, VI, 148.

94.5   "When I the most . . . by himself." *JMN*, III, 315; VI, 319.

94.12   Here is an impatience . . . that matter. *JMN*, X, 9; XII, 533.

94.20   He likes his saddle. *JMN*, VIII, 322.

94.23   He makes no hesitation . . . that matter. *JMN*, IX, 28.

94.26 Over his name, ... *Que sçais je?* under it. *JMN*, VI, 208; cf. 96.11 below.

94.31 I will rather mumble ... a fine romance. Cf. *JMN*, VII, 68.

94.37 I am gray and autumnal myself. Cf. *JMN*, VIII, 43.

95.8 I live ... with decency. *JMN*, VI, 26.

95.20 Cut these words, ... every half sentence. *JMN*, VII, 374; XII, 532; *EL*, II, 231.

95.31 [Montaigne] does not wish to jump out of his skin. Cf. *JMN*, VIII, 252; XII, 533.

96.11 *Que sçais je?* What do I know? Cf. 94.26 above.

96.21 We are natural believers ... real ones. *JMN*, IX, 220, 350.

96.34 One man appears ... axe and crowbar. *JMN*, IX, 113–114; XII, 533.

98.19 The first dangerous symptom ... intellect kills it. *JMN*, IX, 434.

98.31 there was still ... gymnastics of talent. *JMN*, IX, 338.

99.19 Our life is March weather, ... best citizen.' *JMN*, X, 84.

100.8 Fate in ... *Kinde* or Nature, *JMN*, XI, 118; *W*, VII, 172.

100.13 What can I do ... respectable. *JMN*, IX, 365, 394.

100.26 The mathematics, ... events and actions. *JMN*, VIII, 162; IX, 448; X, 99; XIII, 412; *EL*, III, 378; *W*, VI, 284.

100.32 God is a substance, ... illusion. *JMN*, X, 355; XI, 95.

100.33 The eastern sages ... world is beguiled. *JMN*, IX, 322.

101.1 The astonishment of life ... we say. *JMN*, IX, 65–66; XII, 533.

101.31 — and lie for the right? *JMN*, X, 20; cf. IX, 198, 363.

102.5 Some minds are incapable ... company. *JMN*, XI, 163.

102.7 They may well ... secure of a return. *JMN*, XI, 167.

102.9 Once admitted ... encompassed with divinities. *JMN*, XI, 181.

102.12 Others there are, ... the earth. *JMN*, XI, 163.

102.22 Great believers ... irresistibly streams. "Discourse at Middlebury College."

102.23 The spiritualist ... will not say so. *JMN*, IX, 229.

103.3 He had rather ... than with untruth. *JMN*, IX, 198.

103.12 George Fox saw ... of darkness." *EL*, I, 171.

103.15 The final solution ... as any one. *JMN*, XII, 526; cf. *EL*, III, 145.

103.19 I play with ... undulate and flow. *JMN*, IX, 431.

103.32 Charles Fourier ... proportioned to his destinies;" *JMN*, IX, 116; XI, 246; XIII, 51, 265; *W*, VIII, 41–42; cf. 104.13 below.

103.37 It has shown ... emperors, all whistling: *JMN*, VII, 475.

104.3 Then for the satisfaction ... life in it. *JMN*, VIII, 397.

104.13 and still the sirens ... destinies." Cf. 103.32 above.

104.26 Although knaves win ... answered. *JMN*, IX, 218.

104.31 We see, now, ... finger at laws. *JMN*, IX, 180; XII, 560.

104.35 heaven seems . . . magnetism is all.) *JMN*, IX, 224, 229; "Discourse at Middlebury College."
105.4 he is here . . . to be worked upon, *W*, VI, 213.

V. SHAKSPEARE

109.16 The genius . . . unobstructed through the mind. Cf. *EL*, II, 99.
109.18 A great man . . . hits on a railroad. *JMN*, IX, 344.
109.26 The Church has reared . . . chants and processions. *JMN*, V, 402; *EL*, II, 268; *CW*, II, 7–8.
110.4 and he betters the instruction. *JMN*, XV, 407.
110.6 Every master . . . first preparations. *JMN*, IX, 344.
110.17 Great genial power, . . . through the mind. *EL*, II, 49; III, 139.
110.22 The court took offense . . . same time. *JMN*, IX, 344.
111.20 They have been . . . Theatre so long, *JMN*, IX, 337.
111.27 Shakspeare, in common . . . to the temple. *JMN*, IX, 253; XII, 551.
111.35 It holds him . . . his imagination. *JMN*, IX, 345.
112.19 the amount . . . entirely his own." *JMN*, XI, 174 (n. 335); XII, 551.
112.24 And the proceeding . . . absolute invention. *JMN*, IX, 253.
112.27 In Henry VIII, . . . the bad rhythm. *JMN*, XI, 147 (n. 240); *EL*, I, 308–309.
112.31 instead of the metre . . . pulpit eloquence. *JMN*, VIII, 96–97; *EL*, III, 359; *W*, VIII, 54.
113.3 Shakspeare knew . . . so much pressed. *JMN*, V, 94, 99, 226; XII, 551; *EL*, I, 316; II, 47; *Dial*, I (1841), 372; *W*, VII, 46.
113.11 he comes to value . . . his invention. *JMN*, IX, 38.
113.16 Other men say . . . have spoken wisely. *JMN*, IX, 79.
113.20 Such is the happy . . . as well as poets. *JMN*, IX, 38; XII, 562.
113.26 The influence of Chaucer . . . *Lais* of Marie: *EL*, I, 283–284.
113.35 the Romaunt . . . John of Meun; *JMN*, IX, 51.
114.4 and poor Gower . . . build his house. *JMN*, IX, 345.
114.7 It has come . . . at discretion. *JMN*, IV, 376; IX, 113; X, 386.
114.10 Thought is the property . . . thoughts; *JMN*, X, 155.
114.15 Thus all originality . . . conversed. *JMN*, VIII, 67, 70.
114.37 It is easy to see . . . same impulse. *JMN*, IV, 312.
115.2 Our English Bible . . . of his own. *JMN*, IX, 253–254, 345; XII, 562.
115.6 The Liturgy, admired . . . over the world. *JMN*, X, 35.
115.10 Grotius makes . . . rabbinical forms. *JMN*, III, 328; X, 10.
116.22 Bacon, who took . . . mentioned his name. *JMN*, IV, 376; *EL*, I, 306.

116.23   Ben Jonson, ... poet of the two. *EL*, I, 300; cf. *JMN*, IV, 376.
116.30   Sir Henry Wotton ... in the universe. *JMN*, IV, 89; *EL*, I, 305–306, 353–354.
117.8   and not until ... begin to appear. *JMN*, VII, 147.
117.10   It was not possible ... intimately connected. *JMN*, VII, 116; *EL*, III, 8, 208; *W*, XII, 312.
118.7   But whatever scraps ... attraction for us. *JMN*, VII, 17; *EL*, III, 80.
118.10   We are very clumsy ... history. *JMN*, IX, 314–316.
119.11   In fine, ... vain for a history. *JMN*, VIII, 354–355; X, 389–390.
119.17   Shakspeare is the only ... the man. *JMN*, VII, 248–249; XVI, 143.
120.2   Who ever read ... of men? *JMN*, IV, 286.
120.17   What king ... Talma taught Napoleon? *W*, VI, 170.
120.22   Some able and appreciating ... its application. *JMN*, XI, 150 (including n. 252).
121.15   Shakspeare is as much ... into Shakspeare's. *JMN*, VII, 17–18; *EL*, III, 80.
121.20   He was the farthest ... authorship. *JMN*, XI, 172.
121.34   But Shakspeare has ... small, subordinately. *JMN*, IX, 345; cf. VIII, 358 and X, 393 (on Daniel Webster).
122.1   He is wise ... as the other. *JMN*, VIII, 220.
122.8   This power of expression, ... style. Cf. *JMN*, XII, 552.
122.28   The sonnets, ... splendour of the dramas. *EL*, I, 293.
122.37   His means ... he always rides. *JMN*, IX, 345.
123.16   One more royal ... erect; *JMN*, VIII, 188–189; XII, 349.
123.21   Epicurus says ... of them. *JMN*, VI, 341; XII, 551.
123.24   and Saadi says, ... repentance?" *JMN*, IX, 37–38.
123.26   Not less sovereign ... tone of Shakspeare. *JMN*, VIII, 188; XII, 552; "Discourse at Middlebury College."
123.32   And now how stands ... imperfection of humanity. Cf. *JMN*, VII, 309; *EL*, III, 205.
124.22   One remembers again ... in jest?" Cf. 54.7 above.
125.3   the best poet ... public amusement. *EL*, I, 161.

VI. NAPOLEON

129.5   It is Swedenborg's theory ... little kidneys, &c. (See references for 64.36 above.)
129.10   if Napoleon is France, *JMN*, IX, 140; XII, 531.
129.16   between the interests ... capitalists, — *JMN*, VIII, 411; IX, 193.
130.2   The instinct ... incarnate Democrat. *JMN*, XII, 531.
130.10   "God has granted," ... own tongue." *JMN*, VI, 292; *CEC*, p. 165.

130.15 Every one . . . powerful man possessed. *JMN,* III, 277; IX, 152; XII, 531.

130.35 Thus Mirabeau . . . in France. *JMN,* VI, 113; XIII, 252.

131.15 Indeed a man . . . sense of France. *JMN,* IX, 140–141.

131.27 Bonaparte was the idol . . . of common men. *JMN,* IX, 158; XII, 531.

131.29 There is a certain . . . hypocrisy. *JMN,* IX, 131.

131.35 Fontanes, in 1804, . . . human mind." *JMN,* V, 242; XII, 523; *EL,* III, 13.

132.1 The advocates . . . Lafayette is an ideologist." *JMN,* V, 253; VIII, 88, 105; IX, 204; *EL;* II, 37; "Discourse at Middlebury College"; cf. 153.37 below.

132.4 An Italian proverb, . . . too good." *JMN,* II, 130; cf. *CEC,* 107.

132.13 He is a worker . . . intellectual power. *JMN,* IX, 177–178.

132.28 This ciphering operative . . . after its kind. *JMN,* IX, 158; XII, 531.

132.33 The art of war . . . forces in detail. *JMN,* VI, 33, 229; IX, 122–123, 155; *W,* V, 56; VII, 84.

133.13 Nature must have . . . and so in his. *EL,* III, 37; cf. *JMN,* IX, 65.

133.14 a man of stone . . . by snatches, *JMN,* VIII, 528; IX, 275.

133.21 "My hand of iron," . . . my head." *JMN, V,* 508.

133.28 "They charge . . . crimes be to me?" *JMN,* V, 472, 474; XII, 407, 531.

133.35 Again he said, . . . creature of circumstances." *JMN,* V, 94, 226; IX, 65; XII, 407; XIII, 364.

134.5 He never blundered . . . won them on the field. *JMN,* V, 486; VIII, 68, 139; IX, 159, 168; XII, 525; *EL,* III, 370; cf. *JMN,* III, 168 (for the same idea applied to Wellington's victory over Bonaparte).

134.7 In 1796, he writes . . . my thoughts." *JMN,* IX, 143; cf. XII, 531.

134.15 History is full, . . . to do next. *JMN,* IX, 133, 135; cf. XII, 531; XV, 146.

134.19 Here was a man . . . impulse from abroad. *JMN,* IX, 145.

134.25 Napoleon had been . . . system at all." *JMN,* IX, 116, 142.

134.36 He would shorten . . . his object. *JMN,* IX, 145.

135.8 "Let him carry the battery." *JMN,* III, 169.

135.26 "There shall be no Alps," *JMN,* IX, 145, 154.

135.31 He risked everything, and spared nothing, *JMN,* IX, 158.

136.2 "The grand principle . . . capable of making." *JMN,* IX, 142; cf. XII, 531.

136.4 He never economized . . . annihilate all defense. *JMN,* IX, 158; cf. XII, 531.

136.8 To a regiment . . . the enemy's ranks." *JMN,* V, 508.

136.12 He went to the edge . . . prisoner. *JMN,* IX, 144.

136.19 He fought sixty battles. *JMN,* V, 475; VIII, 238; XII, 532.

136.20 "My power would fall . . . courage. *JMN,* IX, 160.

136.30 His idea of the best ... party. *JMN*, IX, 155.

136.31 "My ambition," ... this particular." *JMN*, V, 474; VIII, 41.

137.6 "At Montebello, ... fate of a battle." *JMN*, IX, 153.

137.12 "Before he fought ... of fortune." *JMN*, IX, 158.

137.17 "During the night, ... moment to be lost." *JMN*, IX, 154.

137.21 It was a whimsical ... an answer. *JMN*, IX, 145.

137.26 His achievement ... powers of man. *JMN*, IX, 87; *EL*, I, 107; *W*, XII, 228 (all applied to Michelangelo).

137.28 There have been ... this man's performance. *JMN*, VIII, 370; IX, 53; XII, 532; cf. *CW*, I, 238.

137.34 but he knew ... styled the Bourbons. *JMN*, V, 472; *EL*, III, 352.

137.37 He said, that, "in ... forgot nothing." *JMN*, V, 473.

138.2 also was citizen ... middle class. *JMN*, IX, 141; XII, 531.

138.19 "When walking ... 'Respect the burden, Madam.' " *JMN*, V, 485; VII, 416; XV, 473.

138.23 In the time ... common people." *JMN*, V, 474.

138.31 The best document ... to their leader. *JMN*, IX, 158; XII, 531.

139.7 when allusion ... blood ditch-water." *JMN*, V, 503.

139.29 In 1814, ... rabble of the Faubourgs." *JMN*, IX, 157.

140.1 In Italy, ... Dandolo and Melzi." *JMN*, IX, 145.

140.6 "Men deserve ... what I wish them." *JMN*, IX, 245.

140.19 "I made my generals out of mud," *JMN*, V, 473; *EL*, III, 352.

140.22 In the Russian ... give them all for Ney." *JMN*, V, 508; VII, 11; XII, 522; XIV, 155; *EL*, III, 13.

140.29 "I know," ... one of my generals." *JMN*, V, 475.

140.35 "When soldiers ... rank in my eyes." *JMN*, V, 486.

141.9 As soon as we ... steamengine does our work. *JMN*, IX, 159.

141.17 what events, ... face of the world." *JMN*, IX, 140, 152.

141.36 "The Austrians," ... value of time." *JMN*, IX, 142.

141.37 I should cite ... model of prudence. *JMN*, XII, 531.

142.5 The lesson he teaches ... world is used up. *JMN*, IX, 165, 192, 198; XII, 553.

142.22 If he allows ... expeditions will fail." *JMN*, IX, 180, 192.

142.26 "The winter," ... calmness in the air." *JMN*, IX, 144; XII, 531.

142.33 Read his account, ... casting up an addition." *JMN*, IX, 139–140; *EL*, III, 239.

143.12 On the voyage ... made all that?" *JMN*, IX, 154–155; XII, 531.

143.34 Of medicine, ... my pharmacopeia." *JMN*, IX, 138–139; XII, 531.

144.21 He could enjoy ... lent every addition. *JMN*, IX, 156.

145.2 the instinct ... bright and commanding. *JMN*, IX, 133; XII, 531.

145.13 Bonaparte was singularly ... to be believed. *JMN*, IX, 160; XII, 531.

145.36 Love is a silly infatuation, depend upon it. *JMN*, IX, 153.

146.25 you were not dealing with a gentleman *JMN*, IX, 160.

146.28 In describing the two . . . universal aims. *JMN,* IX, 113, 192, 193; *EL,* III, 187–188; *W,* X, 325–326.

146.35 The democrat is . . . other to keep. *CW,* III, 144.

147.10 And what was . . . to be begun again. *EL,* II, 156.

147.21 they could not . . . their chateaux, *JMN,* IX, 153.

147.23 It resembled the torpedo, . . . kills his victim. *EL,* I, 141 (said of Martin Luther, not Napoleon).

147.31 *"assez de Bonaparte."* *JMN,* IX, 159.

148.5 Only that good . . . serves all men. *JMN,* VII, 128–129; *EL,* III, 109.

VII. GOETHE

151.1 I find a provision . . . and works. *EL,* I, 317.

152.1 composed of the eminent experiences. *JMN,* VIII, 438; IX, 231; "Discourse at Middlebury College"; *W,* VIII, 10.

152.5 The gardener saves . . . possibility of being reported. *JMN,* VIII, 438; IX, 121, 163; XII, 540, 548; cf. *EL,* III, 348–349.

152.15 In conversation, . . . what I suffer." *EL,* III, 357.

152.18 By acting rashly, . . . talking wisely. *JMN,* IX, 82; XII, 540.

152.22 the complaisance . . . of the neck. *JMN,* VI, 14 (applied to other persons); VII, 311.

152.25 A new thought . . . some true word. *JMN,* IX, 121.

153.10 There is a certain heat . . . is a power. *JMN,* IX, 196, 268; "Discourse at Middlebury College."

153.17 Society has, . . . reason of the monitor. *JMN,* IX, 186, 197; "Discourse at Middlebury College."

153.37 Our people . . . opinion concerning ideologists. (See references for 132.1 above.)

154.8 If I were to compare . . . circumstance. *JMN,* XII, 540; "Discourse at Middlebury College."

154.30 The Hindoos write . . . doctrines are one." *JMN,* IX, 231, 254; X, 114; "Discourse at Middlebury College."

155.8 With such, Talleyrand's question . . . mankind asks. *JMN,* IX, 117, 177; XII, 574; cf. VIII, 492.

155.14 Able men do not . . . craftsman, or captain. *JMN,* IX, 88–89; XII, 532, 573.

156.24 Goethe was the philosopher . . . controlling genius. *EL,* III, 219; *W,* XII, 322.

157.1 The Helena, . . . brought himself safe back. *JMN,* IX, 43–44.

158.3 "His very flight . . . disguise." *JMN,* IX, 286, 317, 386.

158.14 He writes . . . a thing for a word. *JMN,* V, 133; IX, 223; cf. 159.17 below.

158.19   He treats nature . . . or microscopes. *JMN,* IX, 394.
158.25   Thus Goethe suggested . . . new proportions. *JMN,* IV, 285; V, 137, 220; XV, 97, 321; *EL,* II, 23–24; III, 27–28; *W,* X, 338.
159.1   In optics, . . . new proportions. *JMN,* V, 191.
159.17   Goethe would have . . . cover a thing. *JMN,* IV, 301; V, 133, 315, 401; *EL,* III, 219; *CW,* II, 19; cf. 158.16 above.
159.31   He found that . . . Prometheus. *JMN,* IX, 58–59, 77.
160.22   We had an English . . . and a peerage. *JMN,* IX, 241.
162.20   It makes a great . . . far and live long. *JMN,* VI, 92, 168; VII, 501; XII, 573.
163.23   His is not even . . . being itself. *JMN,* IV, 301.
163.36   He lays a ray . . . dearest property. *JMN,* VIII, 189; XII, 540.
164.21   An intellectual man . . . low success. *JMN,* IX, 415.
165.3   In the last, . . . of Iphigenia and Faust. *JMN,* VII, 85, 92; *L,* II, 164.
166.11   I join Napoleon . . . two stern realists, *JMN,* IX, 146; XII, 553.
166.20   It is the last lesson . . . extreme. *JMN,* IX, 299.

Outlines for chapters in *JMN,* XII

Representative Men	p. 580
"Swedenborg"	pp. 558–560
"Montaigne"	pp. 532–536
"Shakspeare"	pp. 549–552
"Napoleon"	pp. 531–532
"Goethe"	pp. 539–540

INDEX

Abu Ali Seena (Avicenna), 54
Abul Khair, 54
Academy, the (Plato's), 26, 39
Acre, siege of, 141
Action, 133–134, 154
Aeschylus, 220 (n113.22)
Aesop, 42; *Fables,*115
Akhlak-i-Jalaly, xxxvi, 24, 174 (n15.8),
 183–184 (n31.17), 189 (n54.8), 190
 (nn54.13, 54.15, 54.27), 254
 (n158.3)
Alcott, Amos Bronson, xxxix, liv
Alexander the Great, 43, 157
Alexander I, Czar of Russia, 234
 (n135.10), 243 (n141.28)
Alexandria, 176 (n23.1), 177 (n24.1)
Alfieri, Vittorio, 23
Allston, Washington, 179 (n25.25)
Alps, 131, 135, 141–142
Amasis, 63
America, 161
Ammonius Saccas, 177 (n24.1)
Amurath (Murad) III, Sultan, 152
Angel(s), 17, 70–71, 79
Anglican Church, 110
Antommarchi, Francesco, xxi, 143, 230
 (n131.20), 236 (n137.6), 244
 (n142.33)
Arabian Nights' Entertainment, 115
Archangels. *See* Angel(s)
Architecture, 112
Arcola (Arcole), battle of, 136, 143
Argus, 254 (n156.25)
Aristocracy, 161

Aristophanes, *The Clouds,* 184, (n40.7)
Aristotle, 11, 58, 199 (n64.9)
Arminius, Jacobus, 116
Art(s), artist, 5, 18, 30, 119, 158,
 163–165
Asia, 30–31, 35
Athenaeum, The (London), lix
Athens, 30, 165
Aubrey, John, 119
Augereau, Pierre F. C., Marshal of
 France, Duc de Castiglione, 140
Augustine, Saint, 23
Austerlitz, battle of, 135, 138, 141
Avicenna. *See* Abu Ali Seena

Bacon, Sir Francis, 11, 24, 58, 63, 66,
 116, 124, 180 (n27.31)
Bacon, Roger, 165
Balcombe, Jane (Mrs. William), 138
Balzac, Honoré de, *La Peau de Chagrin,*
 174 (n13.7)
Bangs, Edward, xliv, liv, 234 (n135.10)
Barchou de Penhoën, Baron Auguste
 T. H., 200 (n66.11)
Bartol, Cyrus, lxi–lxii
Bausset, Louis F. J., Baron de, xxi, 244
 (n143.12)
Beaumont, Elie de, 8
Beaumont, Francis, 111, 117
Beauty, the beautiful, 39, 73, 85–86,
 122–123, 125
Behmen, Jacob, 23, 55, 66, 76, 80
Belief, believers, 96, 99, 102
Bellarmine, Robert, 116

399

Index